The Individual, Work and Organization

The Individual, Work and Organization

Behavioural Studies for Business and Management

Second Edition

Robin Fincham and Peter S. Rhodes

OXFORD UNIVERSITY PRESS

Oxford University Press, Walton Street, Oxford OX2 6DP

Oxford New York

Athens Auckland Bangkok Bombay
Calcutta Cape Town Dar es Salaam Delhi
Florence Hong Kong Istanbul Karachi
Kuala Lumpur Madras Madrid Melbourne
Mexico City Nairobi Paris Singapore
Taipei Tokyo Toronto
and associated companies in
Berlin Ibadan

Oxford is a trade mark of Oxford University Press

Published in the United States
by Oxford University Press Inc., New York

© by Robert Fincham and Peter S. Rhodes 1992
First published by George Weidenfeld & Nicolson Ltd, 1988

Reprinted 1989
Second edition 1992
First OUP impression 1994

British Library Cataloguing in Publication Data
Data available

Library of Congress Cataloging in Publication Data
Data available
ISBN 0–19–877426–5
ISBN 0–19–877427–3 (Pbk)

3 5 7 9 10 8 6 4 2

Printed in Great Britain
on acid-free paper by
Biddles Ltd., Guildford & Kings Lynn

Contents

Tables

Figures

Introduction

The nature of behavioural studies

Our reasons for wanting to write this book arose initially from a quite common experience of academics, that of teaching in an area for which there seemed to be no adequate textbook. Indeed, in our case, there appeared to be no text at all. This impression has to be put into context immediately, for there is certainly a well-developed literature covering a variety of 'behavioural' disciplines. However, we would argue that very little of this really covers the scope of the subject we take to be behavioural studies. The most significant of these related subjects, organizational behaviour, is squarely based on occupational psychology, with the addition of an account of organization theory usually from a psychological perspective. There are also other versions of behavioural studies (e.g. Cowling et al., 1988) drawing in the main from sociological studies of work and organizations.

In contrast, our approach has been to develop behavioural studies by drawing *equally* on the two major disciplines of psychology and sociology – or, to be more precise, on a number of specific areas of these disciplines. The way in which these are selected and integrated will, we hope, become clearer as we go along.

The development of behavioural studies has been an integral part of the development of business and management studies as a whole. On vocationally oriented degrees, for example, a discipline-based approach is regarded as too narrow to encompass the many-faceted nature of business problems. Instead, an interdisciplinary approach is favoured where practical problems are tackled by bringing together the relevant parts of various disciplines. Early formulations of business studies degrees in the polytechnics saw economics and accounting as major building blocks, with the central business topics of corporate policy and decision-making taking precedence in later years. Psychology and sociology, bought together with equal weight to form behavioural studies, formed a third major part of the foundation.

Nowadays business and management is taught on a greatly expanded range of courses, at different levels and to many different audiences. These subjects are particularly important for university under-graduate degrees and fast developing post-graduate business education – the ubiquitous MBAs.

Not surprisingly, what is thought to constitute 'business education' has become very fluid, and along with that the social and behavioural sciences are also treated in a variety of ways. Related subjects, like organization theory and management theory, can be integrated with a behavioural or sociological perspective in many different, but still perfectly valid combinations. Nevertheless, a broad foundation in industrial psychology and sociology remains important for any business education. This includes an understanding of the methodology of the social and behavioural sciences as well as the 'human' problems of work. It also forms the basis of more advanced study in areas like organizations, strategy and human resources.

INTEGRATION AND APPLICATION

It is important at the outset to have a clear idea of the basis on which the subjects of psychology and sociology are being brought together. Attempts to integrate different academic disciplines have sometimes been confused because of the terms themselves being defined rather loosely. Part of the problem is that a fully integrated, or interdisciplinary, approach involves a true synthesis between disciplines. And this would mean, in effect, a new discipline being created with its own distinctive methodology and theory. The great demands that such an approach would make on the teacher mean that in practice something more modest is usually attempted, and different disciplines are brought together in a co-ordinated fashion while retaining their distinctive identities. In this way, the developed theories and subject matter of the separate disciplines can still be drawn upon.

The model of integration that we have employed to some extent reflects both the above options. On the one hand, the individualist perspective of psychology and the structural perspective of sociology are quite distinctive, so it is appropriate that they should be developed as complementary but separate frameworks. In addition, though, something much closer to a true integration of the two subjects occurs in the subdiscipline of social psychology. The study of groups, with which social psychology is concerned, is an area of common ground on which the individual and social perspectives overlap.

This kind of subject integration follows direct from a clear commitment to an applied emphasis. The belief in the promotion of managerial effectiveness, and the study of business as an entity in its own right, have meant a shift from a strictly 'academic' approach. In this context, the topics covered in this book reflect an abiding concern with the practical problems of the workplace. Topics of central relevance to managerial efficiency and effectiveness – such as the development of occupational skills, the control of effort and motivation, and organizational goals – are all treated prominently. At the same time, there are other issues not reflecting quite so directly on human performance which are still of great practical interest. The basic processes of human behaviour, such as learning and group interaction, fall into this category, as do the more critical sociological topics, like the impact of technology on work and the role of women in employment.

Of course, these issues also constitute intellectual problems, the study of which supports broader education aims. In this book we have tried to do justice to the theoretical developments of behavioural science, for we believe strongly that there is a place for a critical behavioural science within a business and management context, and that career-oriented students are not averse to such an approach so long as its relevance to real-world problems is clear. Nor are they averse to an analytical framework being developed if this can broadly be seen to support the understanding of practical issues.

These practical and education concerns affect each other in several ways. At one level, we have attempted to provide a rigorous and thorough introduction to a range of central topics in behavioural science. However, for the students for whom the book is intended, a fully developed introduction to psychology and sociology would hardly be appropriate. These subjects are being studied not primarily for their own sake, but for their wider relevance. This does not mean that we have abandoned all concern with theory and method. Rather, the emphasis will be on treating them in the context of discussions about concrete issues and problems.

SELECTION OF TOPICS

The original idea of behavioural studies as a combination of two established disciplines does give rise to constraints of space, and the upshot of this has been the adoption of a *selective* approach in formulating its contents. Not everything within the disciplines concerned can be covered, even in an introductory fashion; and there are good reasons for taking fewer topics in order to treat the ones selected in some depth. It is important to show how debates have taken shape, and how empirical evidence has been used to support or refute particular arguments, especially if knowledge is ever to be put to practical use.

Our own selection of materials inevitably contains some personal bias, and others no doubt would have chosen differently to some extent. The reasoning behind our choice of topics reflects a range of concerns. The desire to provide a foundation in the behavioural disciplines, and to pick out areas which have an applied emphasis, were obviously prime criteria. But the problem of translating a practical criterion into actual teaching materials is not always straightforward. We have tended to stick closely to the work setting, and to emphasize 'objective' areas of study – so that, for example, topics relating more broadly to industrial society or to subjective processes of interaction have been played down, although certainly not omitted entirely. We have also tried to give a flavour of some of the modern debates and key contemporary issues in occupation psychology and the sociology of work and organizations.

LEVEL OF TOPICS

The selective emphasis and limitations of space can also give rise to problems to do with the *level* of materials in what is after all an introductory subject. Of course, a core of introductory materials remains the basis of the book. But there is certainly much less of an emphasis on building this up than there would be on a standard, discipline-based course. Because students frequently have a limited exposure to behavioural studies, the staff teaching the subject will want to progress as far as possible in the time available. This tendency is reinforced from within the areas of business and management studies, where naturally there is a demand for the most up-to-date arguments that behavioural science has to offer. Certainly the trend of continually bringing forward topics from later years seems widespread in business and management degree courses. These courses often develop over time by way of the gradual elimination of introductory materials and 'standard' topics in favour of more relevant advanced-level topics (which have themselves probably been displaced from later years of degree courses by the expansion of key business topics like strategy and information systems).

All this can mean that quite early on students who are not studying a single discipline may be required to assimilate materials that many of their counterparts on single-discipline degrees would not come to until the later years of their courses, after a solid foundation in the subject.

These difficulties, which are very common in business education, can be tackled in several ways. In some cases the topics being considered are not necessarily complex in themselves; rather, they relate to a particular context in some vocational area, and once their relevance has been established then no further problems arise. But for other topics which are perhaps rather difficult to grasp – the managerial uses of power, for example, can present these sorts of problem – then *presentation* becomes vitally important. The emphasis on making issues as clear and understandable as possible, avoiding the use of unnecessary jargon, is a prime responsibility, and one which relates directly to the broader relevance of behavioural science. The critical test of relevance is whether the most important findings and arguments of behavioural science can be made intelligible to the non-specialist, and their connection with real-world problems spelled out.

The behavioural science disciplines

Like all systems of rational enquiry, the behavioural sciences provide a set of conceptual tools which help in classifying and explaining the phenomena in their area of study. Unlike most other disciplines, however, the subject matter of behavioural science – the structures and processes shaping the social world and human behaviour within it – makes up the everyday experience of the general population. This means there is a pre-existing 'baseline' of common-sense understanding of the social world with which the explanations of behavioural science have to compete.

The claim of being able to advance from common-sense understandings of human behaviour and society rests on the developed theoretical frameworks and research methods. Firstly, it can be argued that much common-sense knowledge is flawed by the limitations of everyday experience. People's knowledge of the social world necessarily reflects the set of experiences that have occurred during their lives. Thus, for example, it would be difficult for an individual to form abstract prepositions about the functioning of the labour market – such as the level of job choice available – when his or her experience has been restricted to one occupational group, and knowledge of other parts of the market is based only on anecdotal group, and knowledge of other parts of the market is based only on anecdotal evidence. There are also biases present in people's thinking which produce a great deal of selectivity in what is noticed, understood and remembered. People tend to think in the form of attitudes and stereotypes which oversimplify complex patterns of social interaction. In contrast to this, the analytical frameworks and theories that behavioural scientists develop provide a much sounder basis for understanding human social behaviour.

Secondly, behavioural scientists claim that they can improve on the baseline of common-sense understandings by using research techniques to collect data more systematically than the layperson could. Research methods include laboratory experimentation, questionnaire and interview surveys, and participant observation. The value of the first of these three can be greatly enhanced by using statistical techniques that enable prepositions about the social world to be tested. For example, if we are interested in the effects of certain *variables*, such as social class, intelligence and the type of school attended, on the qualifications that individuals leave school with, we can, by using statistics, isolate both the specific effect of each of these variables and their interaction – thus, being intelligent in one kind of school might have more effect on the level of examinations passed than it does in another institution.

Laboratory experimentation involves careful manipulation of aspects of the experimental setting, known as the *independent variables*, and seeing what effect these have on the *dependent variable*. Occupational psychologists have for some time been interested in the effect of the environment on people's work rate. Thus, independent variables have included levels of heat, lighting, noise and humidity; and these have been related to dependent variables like workers' output per hour, their level of fatigue and their job satisfaction. Laboratories have also been used to study complex social phenomena. For example, the emergence of a leader in a small group can be observed and perhaps related to the amount that the individual contributes to the group's discussion. Although critics claim that laboratories are an artificial situation which necessarily generates artificial knowledge, a lot of evidence suggests that individuals can quickly forget the setting and participate in the activity, virtually unaware of being observed. In fact, in one notable study in which subjects were given the tasks of playing the parts of prisoners and prison warders, the researchers had to stop the experiment because subjects were playing their parts too realistically – prison warders had become aggressive and prisoners had become withdrawn (Zimbardo *et al.*, 1973).

Questionnaire and interview surveys are also powerful techniques for the collection of data on a range of biographical and attitudinal variables. Questionnaire design and interviewing both require a high degree of skill and experience. A well-constructed questionnaire uses no ambiguous words and phrases, and is lengthy enough to obtain the information needed but not so long that it taxes the stamina and goodwill of the respondent. Surveys of this kind can be used extensively, covering hundreds or even thousands of respondents, and where the data collected is necessarily standardized and fairly superficial; or they can be used intensively to obtain much more detailed information, though usually from fewer respondents.

While laboratory experimentation and survey techniques mainly collect *quantitative* data, participant observation is especially useful for collecting *qualitative* data. Here, the experimenter actually becomes involved with the individuals who are being studied, often engaging in the same activities. The assumption is that whatever is lost in terms of not being able to control the experimental environment is made up by gains in the realism of the observations. The insights gained by attempting to experience the world in the same way as the people being studied, and to establish the 'rules' which structure their behaviour, can be particularly valuable. Some of the most notable studies of real-life organizations, such as factories, schools and mental hospitals, have been carried out using this method.

All this is not to say, however, that behavioural scientists are necessarily dispassionate or detached observers of the social world. They possess, as much as anyone else, values, beliefs and principles; and they often pursue particular social or political ends. But the important point is that such values should not be allowed to compromise the objectivity of research. Research groups within the behavioural sciences manage, on the one hand, to make their values explicit, while on the other demonstrating integrity in their research. To do otherwise would be counterproductive. If researchers were to cut short proper research procedures they would reduce the chances of their conclusions standing up to critical scrutiny, and therefore ultimately damage their cause.

If behavioural scientists' claims about being able to improve on the everyday understanding of the social world are correct, then their skills will be especially useful in the workplace – an area where competing interests and perceptions often generate misunderstandings and prejudice. This means, however, that the behavioural sciences can be challenging for business and management students, because research often opposes existing interpretations, or theories may make totally different assumptions about events from those the students are used to. But while the behavioural sciences can and do produce critiques of existing workplace practices, this relationship between academics and practitioners is not the only one available. Very often the insights provided by behavioural scientists can join with managerial thinking and practice. And behavioural scientists themselves may become involved in the workplace as *change agents* – using diagnostic skills to enhance organizational effectiveness and employee well-being. A strong claim can therefore be advanced for the practical contributions that each of the behavioural science disciplines has made to positive change in the workplace. Occupational psychology has had a significant impact on selection, training and job design. Social psychology, with its group dynamics emphasis, has formed the basis of management development. And industrial and organizational sociology have helped in the wider policy study of issues such as the impact of technology on work and the role of women in employment. It is to brief accounts of the separate disciplines that we now turn.

THE PSYCHOLOGICAL PERSPECTIVE

Psychology is a highly diversified field of study which bridges the gap between biology and sociology, and has as its chief focus the individual and the individual's interaction with the environment. All psychologists try to respond to one key question: why did this person behave in this way? An adequate answer involves not only explaining why the particular behaviour occurred in the particular situation, but also, more importantly, producing a theory of the psychological processes which caused the behaviour, and cause it in similar situations. By developing such theories future behaviour can be predicted. This means that psychological theory can be of great value in the workplace, where effective decision-making requires accurate information about human psychological functioning.

The list of the basic processes investigated by psychologists includes perception (the functioning of the senses), human information-processing, memory and learning. All of these have considerable practical implications. Human information-processing, for example, is concerned with the way people detect and respond to signals in the environment. The simplest question here is, how long does it take to perceive a signal, say a light or tone, and respond to it? More complex questions might ask, what are the boundaries to human information-processing capacity for a given unit of time, and how do we cope with these limits? Psychologists have demonstrated that there are indeed limits to the amount of information that can be processed (about one bit of information per second) and that we are unable to perform other actions while the nervous system is occupied with this task. To compensate we develop various 'search strategies', so that what information-processing capacity we have is used economically. It has also been shown that our attention is highly selective – in general we cope by processing only a small fraction of the incoming signals.

Much of the research into information-processing has been funded by military sponsors who needed guidelines for the design of man-machine environments, such as aircraft cockpits and air-traffic control systems. However, information-processing is an example of a universal psychological process, and increasingly industrial jobs make considerable demands on human information-processing capacity. The limits of that capacity, and the search strategies we develop to cope, are psychological properties that all individuals bring to the workplace, and some of their implications for an understanding of workplace behaviour are described below, in Section One, when we consider skill acquisition and stress.

Some psychologists, however, are more concerned with the ways in which people differ, and the study of these differences represents a key area in the modern discipline of psychology. Much research effort has gone into discovering the fundamental dimensions along which people's personalities and intellects vary. Closely associated with this research is a branch of psychology known as psychometrics, the measurement of the various attributes that have been identified within the broader field of psychology.

Like the study of processes within individuals, research into individual differences also has important applications in the workplace. If psychologists have discovered the fundamental ways in which people's personalities and intellects differ from one another, to what extent do these differences predict variations in job performance between individuals? In Chapter 3 we will look at psychologists' success in answering this question.

In sum, then, psychology clearly has an important role to play in understanding workplace behaviour, and as we will see it has made a major contribution to the design of, for example, training programmes, employee selection procedures and physical working environments – and thus ultimately to the whole of the quality of working life.

THE SOCIAL-PSYCHOLOGICAL PERSPECTIVE

Social psychology has as its basic unit of analysis the social group. Social psychologists assume that an individual's behaviour can be better understood if reference is made to the groups which he or she identifies with or is a member of. In this sense, social psychology represents the interface between psychology and sociology, since it describes and explains how social structures can become *internalized* by individuals and thus affect their psychological make-up – their attitudes, perceptions and beliefs – which in turn affect behaviour. These structural forces, generated on the wider social stage or in specific groups, form the chief part of the subject matter of social psychology.

Within groups there emerge customary ways of behaving among members, the observance of special rituals, or even a shared style of dress. Similarly, specific patterns of behaviour will be enacted by individual members – the roles of leader and follower are two very common ones – and each member will enjoy a particular standing or status within the group. The point to bear in mind is that although we usually think of concepts like role and status as qualities which inhere in individuals – we frequently think of roles in terms of the behaviour of the people filling them, while the possession of status also seems to be an individual characteristic – in reality these are social factors generated in the process of interaction. The truth of this can readily be demonstrated if roles are regarded as rather like 'scripts' written for us by society; we may interpret them in individual and personal ways, but we are still expected to 'act out' the basic role according to the images that other people hold. Similarly, the example of changes in status – of enjoying high status in one social group but low status in another – is a common experience, and again it shows the social character of this process. In both cases the distinctive feature of group structure is evident, namely the existence of forces outside the individual and present in the social group as a whole.

What is also evident is that the behaviour and attitudes of individuals are being modified by their membership of groups – they are having to conform with ways of behaving already established. Much of this process does not take an oppressive or coercive form at all. It will seem natural to individuals, on entering new situations, to learn the accepted manner of interaction with other people. What social psychologists have observed, however, is the massive potential that groups seem to have for enforcing conformity, whether unconsciously or through more coercive means.

Over and over again it has been shown that groups have quite astonishing powers to induce members who might otherwise want to express some non-conformist behaviour – an independent opinion, or resistance to some group norm – to fall into line. Even where group members do manage to resist having to conform, the very pressures they have to withstand in order to retain their independence demonstrate the forces of control that groups are bringing to bear. For instance in a famous series of experiments conducted by the American social psychologist Asch, subjects were persuaded to change their identification of various images and pictures presented to them – literally to deny the evidence of their own eyes – merely because the other group members had already given their answers and established a group consensus.

This is all the more remarkable when one is reminded that the controls in question may be purely social in nature. In real-life situations people's careers or other major rewards may depend upon their conforming, but these pressure can also be reproduced without any 'material' controls acting on the individual. Group conformity can be obtained simply via social rewards, like acceptance in the group, or through the threat of negative sanctions, such as ostracism or ridicule. These effects can readily be reproduced in the laboratory, and newly set-up experimental groups quickly generate such normative patterns of behaviour. Yet the dynamics of group interaction are often so subtle that it can be difficult for the outsider to detect what is taking place.

The practical uses of such research findings – which form the main topic of the chapters in Section Two – become apparent when we recognize that virtually all interaction in organizations can be tied down to groups of one form or another. In the work setting, for example, it is common nowadays to find group techniques being used to improve the environment for workers (see Chapter 9). Also, the recognition of the power of informal groups and friendship cliques to influence workers' behaviour has served, and still serves, as the impetus for an enormous research effort.

In addition, there is now increasing interest in decision-making situations. It can readily be seen that many, perhaps most, important decisions are taken not by individuals acting alone but by small groups of influential or technically qualified people. Think of the specific contexts where decisions are taken, like the flight deck of an aircraft or a hospital operating theatre, or large organizations where the corporate group which holds real power will number, say, five or six senior managers. In all these sorts of situations, processes of conformity and integration within groups may compete with technical expertise, and group pressures may even have the power to override the habits of training. It is all the more important, then, that the dynamics of groups are understood so that optimal use may be made of the skills possessed by decision-makers.

THE SOCIOLOGICAL PERSPECTIVE

In the past the role of sociology in the teaching of business and management has been more problematic than that of psychology. The reason has been the prominence of radical or Marxist accounts, while consensus-based theories like functionalism and systems theory have seen their influence wane. This has caused some to worry about how sociology could be fitted into business programmes. It was never suggested that radical sociology should somehow be gagged. But Marxist accounts might be restricted to explanations of social conflict in organizations, while more 'conventional' sociological theories could be applied to the broader range of topics. Problems of this sort led to the concern that sociologists would either have to compromise their discipline or risk antagonizing students (Brown and Harrison, 1980; Deem, 1981). As a result, the views of sociology's role have tended to polarize – one camp in effect saying that the discipline should not be taught as part of business and management, and the other stressing that sociology should select only theories from the body of the discipline that are sympathetic with a business ethic.

The view we have taken is neither of these – and indeed most of the above problems are ancient history. By now it is widely accepted that an approach drawn from sociology's full range can very usefully

11

engage with management interests. Advances in the teaching of business and management studies, and in behavioural science, have outflanked other views. The degree courses involved have 'come of age' and are fully able to benefit from a variety of alternative perspectives. And radical theories, for their part, are now inseparable from broader sociological analysis. Indeed the 'radicalization' of sociology was always something of a myth; the middle ground of the discipline has long been held by interpretive sociology, and this has hardly changed much. Other strands of sociology that reflect conflict (and consensus still, for that matter) only add to and enrich our thinking. As Thompson (1989, p. 36) has asserted, we now have a 'new sociology of work' in which radical theories and an existing tradition are joined in an exciting and fruitful debate.

Explanations that sociology provides are based on the idea of social action as a *duality* comprising the structures of behaviour to which people conform, and the more creative and active role played by the human agent. As before, structure refers to the patterns of expectations and forms of behaviour which have become ordered and which persist over time. It suggests that society consists of a 'world out there' existing independently of any one of us. This is only part of the picture, though. Even at the social level, behaviour obviously originates in the interaction between people – and the intervention of these interests and motives introduces the possibility of changes and developments. Together, structure and agency account for the opposing forces of stability and change present in all human affairs.

Social structure
As noted above, structural forces overlap at the group level. However, an aspect of structure which is wholly a product of the societal level is *social class*. Although the class structure has long been one of the chief interests of social scientists, our focus on the work context meant that we shall not be concerned with these broad patterns of inequality. In keeping with the aims of the book, we have attempted to treat class not as an issue in its own right but as something which can throw light on the nature of work and occupations. But as an issue class does arise in at least two ways in Section Three.

Class may firstly be thought of as a *relationship*. In the work context this translates into the relation between the employer and employees. Analysis of the employment relationship in class terms has been vital in understanding one of the major issues of industrial sociology, namely the problems of conflict in the workplace. Secondly, class may be thought of in *occupational* terms. Nowadays an individual's class position is based on his or her occupation, and changes that effect occupations also affect the class structure. The power of occupations to attract material rewards and status represents a dynamic and changing aspect of social class.

Human agency and meaning

Aside from structure, sociology's emphasis on the creative aspects of social action shares with psychology a concern with the individual. But unlike psychology this is not here a question of individual processes or differences. Rather, the concern is with the subjective responses shared within particular groups of people – how a workforce experiences its employment, for example, or the manner in which a community perceives some event that impinges upon it. In other words, the concern is not simply with opinions or attitudes, but with the social character of the *meanings* that people assign to situations they find themselves in. Social situations turn out to be complex, many-sided events, giving ample scope for different groups affected to perceive them in quite different ways.

The meanings that people assign – how *they* understand and define situations – take on a concrete reality. Meanings become self-fulfilling 'social facts' because they form the basis on which people act. This viewpoint provides an answer to another criticism often levelled at sociology, that it is concerned only with subjective factors and not with objective events in the real world. The answer we can give is to point out that subjective meanings have an objective reality, because people's understanding is the basis of the response they make. In the discussion in Sections Three and Four we will encounter several cases where knowledge of how particular groups define their work situation is the key to understanding behaviour.

Social conflict

Another difference of emphasis between the psychological and sociological perspectives hinges on the question of conflict. On the whole, the individualist approach is not concerned with issues of conflict – unless the resolution of personality conflicts is considered, or perhaps the conflict between external demands and human needs that causes stress. But as we move to the social level, structural conflict comes much more clearly into focus.

Concern with the conflictual aspects of social relationships lies behind another criticism of sociology, namely the complaint that the discipline is not 'scientific' and cannot provide 'solutions' to real-world problems. The response we might give is that social life itself involves conflicting interests, and that solutions to complex problems are rarely unambiguous technical answers, but options and choices which emerge from the interplay of more than one set of interests.

The mobilization of power in pursuit of interests is part of day-to-day reality – and nowhere is this more evident than in the work context and in organizations. Sociological analysis recognizes this, stressing that conflict is not irrational or always the result of mis-understandings; it must be explained and explored in its own right.

This readiness to take issues of conflict seriously reveals the critical nature of sociological analysis, for academic disciplines cannot divorce themselves from their own subject matter. Virtually all of the topics we cover in Section Three, and many in Section Four, attract some very different views and opinions, and part of our aim will be to explore these alternative perspectives and debates.

The structure of the book

LEVELS OF ANALYSIS

The psychological, social-psychological and sociological approaches discussed above broadly correspond with the structure of this book, which divides into three distinct levels of analysis: individual, group, and work/organizational.

In Section One we look at the ways in which various *individual differences* affect behaviour. As we have suggested, the psychologist wishes to know how processes *within* individuals such as learning and motivation, are manifest in behaviour – and also how differences *between* individuals, in terms of their aptitudes, abilities and per-sonalities, can be studied. Further, the occupational psychologist is concerned with applying these explanations to the work setting.

In Section Two the processes that occur in the context of the work group are explored. The emphasis here is on *social interaction* and the ways in which behaviour in organizations is generated and adapted in face-to-face situations. The main forms of group dynamics, includ-ing the emergence of basic rules of human interaction, the processes of group formation, and the leader–follower relationship, are all of special interest here.

Sections Three and Four adopt a wider *social* level of analysis applied to the work and organizational contexts respectively. As we have noted, the sociologist is concerned not as much with the properties of individuals, or with the nature of group-based inter-action, but with relatively enduring social structures. Industrial sociologists apply these broader categories, looking at the relationship between employers and workers considered as classes, for example, or the role of gender in employment, while organization theorists have developed accounts of the functioning of modern, large-scale organizations. There is also concern with wider social and economic structures, such as the labour market, within which organizations operate.

Using these distinctive levels of analysis should help provide a holistic view of the human problems of work. Complex, multi-dimensional problems depend for their resolution on a variety of different approaches and perspectives being applied – one approach rarely has all the answers. Indeed, as Gowler and Legge (1982) have observed, 'problems although surfacing at one level in the organization are likely to have antecedents and effects at different levels'.

The central task of behavioural science, according to Landy (1982), is to describe the functional relationship that exists between these levels and estimate their relative importance in understanding behaviour. Behavioural scientists have shown an increasing willingness to consider the interaction between different levels of analysis, their underlying assumption being that one level provides the context or environment for the next. This is the real basis of an integrated approach to understanding the human problems of the workplace.

Section One

The Individual and Work

By the beginning of the First World War many psychologists in Europe and the United States had recognized that there were problems within the workplace which could be both analysed and remedied using the concepts and methods developed more broadly within their own discipline. As with many other areas of research with military or industrial applications, wartime conditions provided the impetus for a rapid development of industrial psychology. Firstly, the armed forces began to realize the value of a systematic psychological assessment of recruits as an aid to decisions about a soldier's rank and suitability for technical training. Secondly, the increased demand for output and the reduction in available manpower produced by wartime conditions prompted many managers to seek the assistance of psychologists to improve the productivity of the residual workforce.

After the First World War, interest in industrial psychology was consolidated by groups of psychologists who wanted to offer their skills to employers forming research and consultancy companies such as the National Institute of Industrial Psychology in Britain and the Psychological Corporation in the United States.

Industrial psychology in these formative years, therefore, was attempting to answer two broadly inter-related questions. Firstly, what factors increase a worker's productivity? And secondly, how can the match between the employee and the job be improved?

Early attempts to answer the first question involved the careful measurement and manipulation of environmental factors such as temperature, lighting, noise levels, humidity and aspects of work like the length and number of rest breaks, and establishing their effect on a worker's productivity. This approach produced some remarkable early successes. For example, a wartime study demonstrated that a drop in daily hours from twelve to ten actually increased productivity and brought about a large decrease (50 per cent) in the accident rate. At the time, industrialists had believed that output could be improved by increasing working hours.

It was gradually realized, however, that the relationships between

17

objective work conditions and productivity were moderated by subjective phenomena, such as the employees's attitude to work and job satisfaction. Thus, seemingly straightforward concepts like fatigue were found to involve physiological processes such as the build-up of lactic acid in muscle tissue, as well as the psychological willingness of the individual to work.

The second question – how to improve the employee-job match – produced a variety of answers. Some psychologists believed the answer lay in more careful selection of employees. This involvement preparing an inventory of the relevant skills, aptitudes and temperaments required for high job performance, and constructing psychological tests which identified individuals who possessed these qualities. Other psychologists developed the 'training solution', allowing individual deficiencies to be compensated for by training employees up to required standard. Finally, a solution which emerged during the Second World War – the 'equipment solution' – proposed a radically different approach to the problem. It suggested that a better match could be achieved by applying psychological knowledge of human capabilities and particularly their limits to the design of man-machine systems. The body of knowledge these psychologists produced became known as ergonomics.

What answers to both questions – improving productivity and the employee-job match – had in common was the assumption that solutions could be sought based on the individual employee as the fundamental unit of analysis. In this first section, we will examine the main research findings based on this assumption and which underpinned the solutions to the initial questions psychologists were asked to provide answers for.

In Chapter 1 we look at the research on the training solution which seeks to explain how people acquire complex occupational skills. Humans, as we will see, have a remarkable capacity to learn; in fact virtually all of our behaviour is acquired through learning. The practical implications of this in the workplace are considerable, and an understanding of how learning occurs obviously enables better training programmes to be designed.

While Chapter 1 describes the remarkable adaptive capacities of humans, Chapter 2 explores one consequence of the limits of this capacity, stress. Trying to adapt to certain types of environment involves severe mental and physical health risks, but the problem of stress at work has been recognized only recently by psychologists and employers. We will examine some of the types of stress that have been identified in the workplace and discuss methods of reducing their damaging effects.

In Chapter 3 we look at the research on which the selection

solution was based. We focus on personality and intelligence, perhaps the most important ways in which individuals differ from each other. We will also examine some of the implications differences in personality and intelligence have in the workplace.

In Chapter 4 we explore how assessments of individual differences occur in the workplace. We will examine a number of assessment techniques and discuss the relative merits of each.

Finally, in Chapter 5 we examine the two most significant contributions psychologists have made to the understanding of employees' productivity: the concept of motivation and job satisfaction. As we suggested above, although early successes were achieved by manipulating objective aspects of the workplace, it was soon realized that subjective factors, particularly the needs workers brought with them to the workplace and the way employees felt about their jobs, also affected their productivity. This realization, combined with the rising expectations of employees after the Second World War and relatively full employment, prompted an enormous amount of research and discussion on how employees' needs could be met and thus how a motivated and reasonably satisfied workforce could be created.

1

Learning

Perhaps most fundamental of the questions psychologists ask – a question that applies in the work context as well as in the wider social one – concerns how people acquire the various abilities needed to survive in a social world and to interact with others. It is in this context that *theories of learning* form the basis of our understanding of human behaviour. The development, via evolution, of a relatively large brain has provided us with an enormous mental capacity which has meant that learning has displaced instinct. Instinctual behaviours seen in other animals appear only briefly in the first year of human life and then recede.

Learning is also central to the explanation of behaviour in the workplace, where individuals need to acquire very specific responses and skills to carry out the tasks that make up their jobs. In fact, much of the interest in the psychological processes of learning stems from the practical implications of research findings.

The design of effective training programmes is increasingly linked with models of the learning process, particularly where workforces are needed that can adapt quickly to technological change. Training designed with an awareness of the learning process is more likely both to help learners acquire new skills and, perhaps more crucially, increase confidence in their own learning abilities. The importance of this has been emphasized by a number of politicians. Neil Kinnock, for example, stated in 1989: 'Now and for all time in the future human skills and human talents will be the major determinants of success or failure – not just for individuals but for a whole society in all its social, cultural and commercial life.' It is in the context of training for the future that learning theories which identify key features of the learning process are increasingly valuable.

Learning theories have other practical applications. If they can explain how people acquire competence they may also be able to tell us what differentiates excellent from merely competent individuals. In many jobs this difference can be accounted for by motivation, personality, intelligence or aptitudes. However, there are often key differences between the way excellent and competent individuals perceive and comprehend their environments. If identified, these can become the basis of training programmes aimed at bringing about the changes in perception and comprehension necessary for improved performance (e.g. Harri-Augstein and Thomas, 1991).

Learning theories can also help when considering how occupational activity is best described. Trainers need valid methods of describing what people at work do in order to identify what skills individuals need to do a job and what opportunities a job provides for the development of skills in individuals. Traditionally the main concern has been to develop ways of describing the tasks that people actually perform. Learning theories also suggest that it is often as important to describe skills, how people accomplish the tasks involved in their jobs and the learning processes involved in acquiring these skills.

In this chapter we will examine the two main types of learning theory: stimulus–response and skill theories. The former focuses on conditions *external* to individuals. A stimulus is something perceived by an organism in the environment. A doorbell, a supervisor's request and the smell of food are all examples of stimuli. A response is a unit of behaviour (usually observable) emitted by an organism. Answering the door, anxiety and salivating are all responses which might be found to be associated with the respective stimuli. Stimulus–response theorists explain how responses are acquired by examining what precedes the response and what happens in the environment after the response has occurred. Many researchers, however, have preferred to stress the part that *internal* cognitive processes play in learning, and use larger units of learning such as skill; they relate changes in the way people make sense of their environments to improvements in the performance. As we will see, both approaches have contributed a great deal to our understanding of how learning, perhaps the most important of human capacities, occurs.

Learning theories

STIMULUS–RESPONSE THEORIES I:
CLASSICAL CONDITIONING

The initial concern of the Russian physiologist Pavlov (1849–1936) was the innate reflex responses of animals. While studying one of these reflex responses, salivation, he noticed some dogs would sometimes salivate when the lights in the laboratory were switched on in the morning or when they were removed from their pens. At first he found these 'psychic secretions' a nuisance since they disrupted his experiments. He soon realized, however, that these responses were far more important than the simple physiological reflexes he had intended to study. He began a series of experiments to investigate them in more detail. In a typical experiment Pavlov would present a dog with a neutral stimulus such as a tone or a bell. This would be quickly followed by meat powder to which the dog would automatically salivate. If the pairing of a neutral stimulus with the meat powder occurred enough times, Pavlov found the salivation response could be elicited by the tone bell alone. The dog had been *conditioned* to respond to the neutral stimulus.

Pavlov's contribution to the explanation of learning has proved to be of immense significance. It explains how a wide range of human responses are acquired. It has also helped in the treatment of a number of behavioural problems, from phobias to sexual difficulties such as impotence.

In order to generalize Pavlov's research methods to other situations, a specific vocabulary describing the components of conditioning has been devised. The original reflex is composed of an unconditioned stimulus (UCS) and an unconditioned response (UCR). In Pavlov's experiment the meat powder was the UCS and the dog's salivation the UCR. The neutral stimulus, the bell, buzzer or tone, is known as the conditioned stimulus (CS). When salivation occurs after the presentation of the CS on its own it is termed the conditioned response (CR) (Figure 1.1). The CR is never quite as strong as the original UCR. In Pavlov's experiments the dogs salivated less for the CS than for the UCS. If the CS is presented on a number of occasions without the UCS, the CR will decline further in strength. This decline in the CR is known as *extinction*. Zero extinction is said to occur when the CS does not elicit a CR at all. However, even at zero extinction the association between CS and CR does not disappear altogether as relearning the CR requires fewer pairings than were necessary for the original conditioning.

Two important features of the conditioning process have been identified: *generalization* and *discrimination*. Generalization refers to the organism's capacity to respond in a similar way to stimuli that are similar in certain respect to the original CS. For example, young children sometimes refer to all adult males as 'daddy'. Generalization in evolutionary terms is highly useful; it reduces the complexity of the stimulus environment since the organism can apply the same response to a range of stimuli. However, as we shall see later, generalization can also be maladaptive if the learned response is generalized to situations in which it is inappropriate. Discrimination is the opposite tendency, allowing organisms to respond differently to similar stimuli. The young child eventually learns to apply the word 'daddy' to one adult male only.

Reflex behaviour

Learning trial

Learned behaviour

Figure 1.1   *The classical conditioning sequence.*

Classical conditioning has been observed in a number of human and animal subjects and there seems little doubt that it is a basic learning process. However, when it came to more complex behaviours Pavlov believed that these could be acquired through *secondary conditioning*. This occurs when the CS–CR connection is so well established that a CS acts as a UCS in subsequent conditioning. For example, if a child automatically responds to an unpleasant stimulus (UCS) such as a smack from a parent by experiencing anxiety (UCR), words which precede the blow, such as 'no' or 'stop that', can become conditioned stimuli. Through conditioning, then, these words may be enough to control a child's behaviour without resorting to physical punishment. Through secondary conditioning the child may even learn that particular facial expressions precede these words so that they, in turn, become the conditioned stimuli which elicit the anxiety response. In this way the child learns to recognize increasingly subtle indications of parental disapproval.

Classical conditioning is particularly useful in explaining behaviour mediated by the autonomic nervous system. This is the part of the nervous system which controls reflex action and emotional states such as pleasure and anxiety. Extreme emotional reactions, phobias, like the fear of heights, crowds or small spaces, can be acquired through classical conditioning. If phobias are acquired through classical conditioning they can also be cured by helping individuals to 'unlearn' the phobia by replacing the conditioned anxiety with a more neutral emotional response. In fact, treatment based on conditioning principles is now commonplace and has very high success rates. Weaker emotional responses, such as the emotions that inanimate objects like buildings, rooms and food can elicit, are also often the result of classical conditioning. An aversion to a particular food, for example, can be the result of a single pairing of the food (CS) with a powerful aversive stimulus (UCS) such as food poisoning. The single pairing may be sufficient for the food to elicit anxiety or nausea (CR) on subsequent occasions and the food is therefore avoided.

Conditioning can provide us with what are termed *patterns*, that is 'conditioned feelings, thoughts or behaviours which are unresponsive to what is new and changing in situations' (Evison and Horobin, 1983). These patterns are formed during experiences which have caused an individual distress. In childhood, distress is particularly significant because it tends to be associated with situations which occur frequently. Being simpler than adults, children are also less likely to understand what the causes of distress are. Distress is then generalized so that it can be elicited by a range of situations.

Once patterned, we can only pay attention to the characteristics of the situation which elicit distress. This means we are unlikely to acquire improved methods of dealing with these situations, so that, for example, it can be difficult to shed the patterns we acquire in childhood to cope with authority figures. Hence we will continue to experience distress in the presence of authority figures and perceive them as threatening even though in reality they no longer are. Our conditioned distress will prompt the same rapid and unthinking response that it did in childhood. For example, we may find we automatically acquiesce to requests from our supervisors since this quickly reduces the unpleasant feelings restimulated by these situations.

Management training programmes often attempt to make trainees aware of their own patterned feelings, thoughts and behaviours. Trainees can then begin to explore more effective methods of dealing with the situations which elicit their maladaptive patterned responses.

Classical conditioning also has implications for task performance and training in organizations. We have a fixed capacity to attend to a given task. The capacity available for any task depends on the number of other demands on our attention. Thus, pleasant or unpleasant feelings evoked at work demand part of an individual's attention and will interfere with his or her ability to attend to a task. This impairs an individual's performance and can increase the likelihood of accidents. Coercive or punitive supervisors can become the conditioned stimuli which elicit negative feelings. The conditioning may be generalized so that these feelings are evoked by all managers.

In training programmes some trainees may already have conditioned negative feelings about instructional situations and instructors. Trainers on government training schemes for young people who have recently left school are often faced with the problem of having to deal with individuals who have conditioned negative feelings elicited by learning environments. Individuals who experience these feelings are both unlikely to learn much and likely to prove disruptive to other trainees. A good deal of research has been undertaken recently to devise training programmes in which the anxiety that learning situations have normally evoked is 'unlearned' and replaced with more positive feelings.

STIMULUS–RESPONSE THEORIES II: OPERANT CONDITIONING

Learning of stimulus–response associations also occurs through operant conditioning. An operant is a unit of behaviour emitted by an organism; eating a meal, placing a bet and smoking a cigarette are all examples of operants. The most noted operant theorist, B.F. Skinner, believed that the environment *shapes* an individual's behaviour by maintaining certain responses and suppressing others.

Skinner's major contribution has been to outline how the shaping of an individual's responses by the environment occurs. He believes the most powerful shaping mechanism is *reinforcement*. If we return to the hypothetical example of the patterned behaviour elicited by authority figures, classical conditioning, as we saw, explained why anxiety was experienced. Situations in which authority figures make demands are perceived as threatening. This perception elicits the classically conditioned anxiety response, which in turn is followed by an operant: acquiescence. In operant conditioning the key question is, what occurs after a response? In this example the response caused an immediate reduction in anxiety. In operant terms the response was reinforced. The reinforcement has been powerful enough to stamp the response into an individual's behaviour pattern.

Reinforcement operates either negatively or positively. *Positive reinforcement* occurs when a pleasant stimulus follows a response. Money, status, recognition and praise can all act as positive reinforcers since they all increase the likelihood of the preceding response being emitted again.

Any response which reduces the intensity or removes an unpleasant stimulus is said to be *negatively reinforced*. Like positive reinforcement, negative reinforcement increases the probability that the response will reoccur. Negative reinforcement produces two types of learning: *escape* and *avoidance*. Acquiescing to the demands of authority figures in the example above falls into the first category since it allows individuals to escape from their conditioned distress. An individual could also learn to avoid supervisors and thereby reduce the threat of anxiety-loaded encounters.

Skinner believed escape and avoidance behaviours were very common in human society. Aversive conditions are, wittingly or unwittingly, frequently created by other people. Unwittingly, other people can be boring, annoying or unpleasant, and we quickly develop avoidance relationships with them. Aversive conditions are created intentionally as a method of social control. A supervisor, for example, may become more autocratic, coercive and punitive to increase output. To escape these aversive conditions, workers may increase their work rate, which in turn reinforces the supervisor's belief in the effectiveness of an autocratic style of supervision. However, other escape behaviours can be learned: striking, sabotage or displacing the aggression their aversive environment has caused on to people outside the workplace are all possible consequences. Alternatively, workers may acquire avoidance behaviours which put them out of the aversive stimuli's range, for example, by staying at home or changing job. Proponents of operant conditioning believe a number of social phenomena are explained by avoidance or escape learning. Conformity, for example, may be the result not so much of the positive reinforcement of behaviour by others but of learning to perform in a way that avoids their contempt.

While positive and negative reinforcement serve to increase the strength of responses, *punishment* and *omission* have the opposite effect. Punishment involves an aversive stimulus following a response. Contact with aversive stimuli very quickly reduces the probability of a response reoccurring. A child who puts his or her hand on a hot oven ring is unlikely to do it again. In adult life we learn to withhold the responses that have attracted contempt, ridicule or criticism. The term 'ommission' is used to describe the removal of pleasant stimuli after a response. Parents make use of this contingency when sending a child who misbehaves to bed. This removes pleasant stimuli such as television or the company of siblings. Table 1.1 provides a summary of these four response categories.

Operant theorists believe that reward is a more powerful method of shaping behaviour than punishment. Reward has the virtue of indicating what behaviour is required, while punishment only indicates what response an individual should withhold. Punishment can also cause anxiety, hostility and resentment in an individual. Aversive stimuli, as we have already seen, can also lead to avoidance learning. The individual can learn to avoid the parent, teacher or supervisor or to perform the undesired response out of their range. Skinner (1971) believed that society in general has gradually shifted from systems of control based on the use of aversive stimuli to ones which

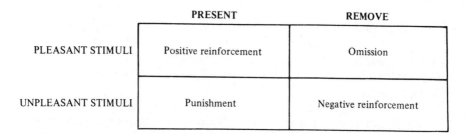

	PRESENT	REMOVE
PLEASANT STIMULI	Positive reinforcement	Omission
UNPLEASANT STIMULI	Punishment	Negative reinforcement

Table 1.1   *The four types of reinforcement proposed by Skinner.*

use reward. Teachers now try and make children want to learn through reward rather than through punishment. Parents increasingly offer rewards to their children in the form of approval rather than using punishment to shape their children's behaviour. And some organizations have replaced aversive autocratic managerial practices with the potentially more rewarding democratic supervisory styles.

Skinner was also interested in the effect of what he termed *schedules of reinforcement* on behaviour. The simplest schedule is one in which every response is followed by a reward. However, in everyday life, this schedule, known as *continuous reinforcement* is highly unlikely: teachers, parents, colleagues or supervisors cannot reinforce every desired response. You are more likely to experience *intermittent reinforcement schedules* in which your behaviour is not always reinforced. For example, you were not rewarded as a child each time you performed a desired response such as sharing a toy, but you may have been rewarded intermittently. Experiments have found that intermittent schedules of reinforcement exert a more powerful influence on behaviour than a continuous schedule since we seem to learn not to expect reinforcement each time we make a particular response. This means behaviour persists in the absence of reinforcement whereas responses learned with a continuous schedule, where an organism expects reinforcement after every correct response, rapidly disappear when not reinforced. In fact, intermittent schedules can often have a major influence on behaviour in return for very little reward. For instance, a gambler does not need to win very often to sustain the habit.

Reinforcement schedules have been used to explain a number of workplace phenomena: motivation, absenteeism and the effects of different payment systems. Ferster and Skinner (1957) argued that

27

there are two basic types of intermittent schedule. Firstly, there are those schedules in which reinforcement occurs after a fixed number of the desired responses have been made or after a fixed period of time has elapsed. Secondly, there are those in which reinforcement occurs regularly or irregularly. By combining these two criteria, four intermittent schedules are created, which they believed had different effects on behaviour.

1. A *fixed-ratio schedule* is one in which reinforcement occurs after a given number of responses. This schedule can produce a great deal of the desired behaviour for very little in return. Piecework, where an employee is paid for producing a fixed number of units, is an example of a fixed-ratio schedule. In theory, piece-rate working ought to produce the response pattern normally associated with the fixed-ratio schedule: a high and constant response rate. In practice, however, many employers have found a pay structure which attempts to link specific response rates with pay too cumbersome and have opted for a 'flat ' weekly wage. In a car plant, for example, the rate of pay for each of the thousands of assembly tasks has to be negotiated and renegotiated every year. Employees also tend to learn a work rate which is not high enough to cause management to increase the response–earnings ratio and not so low as to reduce earnings below a desired level.

2. A *variable-ratio schedule* can be even more effective in terms of the effort–reward ratio in producing the desired behaviour than a fixed-ratio schedule. A gambling machine, for example, pays out on average once in fifteen bets. Since a variable ratio makes it difficult to know when a payment is likely, gamblers are prepared to place bets at a constant (often high) rate. Some payment systems are variable-ratio schedules. One of the present authors has carried out research in a firm which sold pension plans. Sales staff were paid according to the number of plans they sold. To sell a plan it was necessary on average to make about thirty calls. Some weeks the ratio for a member of staff would stretch to well above this level. Like the gambling machine, it was impossible to know whether a response would be rewarded and work rates were therefore high and constant.

3. In *fixed-interval schedules*, reinforcement occurs at regular intervals, regardless of what response precedes it. Monthly or weekly payment systems are examples of this schedule. Fixed-interval reinforcement produces a distinctive pattern of responding. As the reward time approaches, the response rate increases, dropping immediately after reinforcement. This drop in response rate indicates that the organism has learned there is no relationship between response and reward in the period closely following reinforcement. The absence of any relationship between response and reward

immediately following reinforcement in this schedule may help to explain higher rates of absenteeism found in organizations after a pay day.

4. The length of time between reinforcement in a *variable-interval schedule* varies around some average value. This schedule elicits moderate and constant response rates. For example, if the time between assessments of suitability for promotion varies in an organization, employees learn their performance needs to be consistently good to ensure a favourable rating.

STIMULUS–RESPONSE THEORIES:
A TECHNOLOGY OF BEHAVIOUR?

Skinner has argued that operant theory provides the framework for a 'technology of behaviour' – enabling environments to be designed so that desired responses are systematically strengthened while less desirable responses are weakened.

An important instance of the application of operant principles is known as *behaviour modification*. This is often found in clinical settings, although behaviour modification can be applied equally well in an organizational context. For example, Nord (1969) argued that organizations tend to be designed in ways which largely ignore the recommendations of operant theory. Firstly, staff may be unaware of what they have to do to gain rewards such as a rise in pay or status Secondly, hard work is sometimes punished, rather than reinforced, by loading more work on to conscientious staff. Thirdly, group or departmental productivity bonuses weaken the link between individual performance and reward. Finally, managers tend to think reinforcement can best be achieved via monetary reward. But while this may well be the case generally, for some staff recognition and praise can be more potent reinforcers.

Luthans and Kreitner (1975) were the first to outline clearly how operant principles could be applied to organizational behaviour. Their programme begins with the identification of *critical behaviours*. These are the responses thought to be necessary for effective performance in a job. For example, the initial approach of a customer may be a critical behaviour for effective selling. The second phase establishes the *base rates* for target behaviours. These are the rates at which these critical behaviours normally occur. Identifying base rates enables the impact of the programme to be assessed at a later stage. The third stage, termed *functional analysis*, involves careful observation of what normally precedes and follows various types of work behaviour. For example, a functional analysis may reveal that customers are normally greeted only if they approach a member of the sales staff. After the functional analysis has been completed an *intervention strategy* is devised. This makes reward contingent on critical behaviours. Finally, there is a *systematic evaluation* of the intervention strategy. The rate at which target behaviours are now displayed is compared with the base rate.

Luthans and Kreitner argued that this procedure offered significant benefits in training programmes, and collected a good deal of evidence to support their claim. One study of sales staff in a large department store attempted to change staff performance on a number of critical behaviours (Luthans, *et al.*, 1981). The base rates for attendance, stock-keeping and various aspects of interaction with customers were identified. The functional analysis revealed what responses were linked to successful selling. They found, for instance, that sales staff needed to stay close to their goods, greet customers as soon as they appeared, and keep display shelves at least 70 per cent full. The researchers divided sales staff into two groups. For one group they devised an intervention strategy which for a period of time made such rewards as time off with pay and free package holidays contingent on critical behaviours. These rewards were not made available to the second group. The behaviour of both groups was observed for the twenty days incentives were available and for a further twenty days. The performance of the intervention strategy group was significantly better relative to the second group in both observation periods. On the basis of this and other studies, Luthans believes operant principles can be applied in the workplace in such a way that significant benefits occur for both staff and management.

As yet, organizational behaviour modification has not been widely employed by British managements. Nonetheless, some insights provided by operant conditioning are clearly pertinent: motivation and performance can be low because contingencies are unclear, rewards insufficient or inappropriate, and desirable performance punished rather than rewarded.

A second example of Skinner's 'technology of behaviour' is *programmed instruction*. For example, if you were to enroll on a mathematics course which used this method, you would interact not with a tutor but with a teaching machine. The machine would take you through the course by presenting you with a series of *frames*. These would contain a small amount of information, for instance, a worked example of multiplying fractions, followed by a question. If your response to a question is correct, the machine moves you on to the next frame. Two views have developed about the place of *incorrect responses* in programmed instruction. Skinner (1954) believed programmes should be designed to make the chances of a learner making a mistake as close to zero as possible. This means material has to be broken up into a large number of frames, each containing a small amount of information. With a mathematics programme a number of examples of the same procedure would be used, each frame presenting a question only slightly more difficult than the previous frame. The increase in complexity in the material between each frame is therefore kept to a minimum. The disadvantage of these *linear programmes* is that learners are all presented with the same order of frames whatever their previous knowledge may be. *Branching programmes* (Crowder, 1960) attempted to create more flexible instruction by using errors diagnostically. If your response is incorrect you are 'shunted' into a series of remedial frames until a response indicates you are able to rejoin the main programme. Since larger increases in the complexity of material between frames are possible with branching programmes, learners familiar with some of the programme's content can progress rapidly through mainstream frames until they reach a point where their responses indicate remedial frames are necessary.

The availability of relatively cheap and increasingly powerful small computers has meant that very sophisticated branching programmes can now be written and made widely available. The arrival of interactive videodiscs has added further realism to this form of training. Programmed instruction, however, need not involve investing in personal computers or laser video technology. A series of cards, each of which is a frame, and a piece of cardboard to mask answers can constitute a linear programme.

Programmed instruction has been utilized in commercial, industrial, military and educational settings and a number of advantages have been claimed for it.

Firstly, it enables organizations to specify what is called *terminal performance*, what trainees will need to do to pass the *criterion test* at the end of the programme, and *pre-entry behaviour*, the level of competence required before training commences.

Secondly, it enables employees to use free time available for training as and when it occurs. In many occupational settings, training may be possible only at irregular times of the day.

Thirdly, it allows the slow learner to learn at his or her own pace, thus experiencing less anxiety and embarrassment than when learning with a teacher and peers.

Finally, it is thought to be highly cost-effective, with savings in training time more than offsetting the capital cost of any equipment involved.

However, programmed instruction does have some disadvantages. Firstly, producing a good course based on programmed instruction is very difficult. Programme writing is a highly skilled task requiring a knowledge of both the subject and operant principles. In addition, there may not be a simple correspondence between a learner's responses and his or her comprehension of material. Learners do not always fully understand why their responses are correct or incorrect. There are also some studies indicating that learning achieved with programmed instruction is not necessarily superior, in terms of retention of material over time, to what is possible with conventional methods (Nash *et al.*, 1971). However, programmed instruction, particularly when combined with computers and videodiscs, is still in its infancy compared to traditional methods. The potential of the technique is only just beginning to be realized.

Both these applications of operant theory produce changes in behaviour by establishing a link between certain responses and the environmental outcomes an individual experiences. In organizations the principles of operant conditioning suggest that work settings should encourage employees to perceive some relationship between their effort and some valued reward. And, in contrast, the condition that should be avoided in organizations is *learned helplessness*, where employees believe there is no link between the events they experience and their behaviour (Seligman, 1975). Organizations that create environments which foster a sense of helplessness in employees face the immense problem of managing staff whose motivation has been drastically lowered. Organizations, therefore, should always create conditions in which it is difficult for employees to learn helplessness.

Perhaps the major residue of operant conditioning and Skinner's Technology of Behaviour in the UK is the current concern with the specification of clear outcomes in vocational training (Jessup, 1991). Under the guidance of the National Council for Vocational Qualifications, standards of competence and performance criteria for assessing competence have been identified for a number of occupational areas.

Many researchers have argued that stimulus–response theories are overly mechanistic and reductive. Mechanistic because by using only observable phenomena such as stimuli and reinforcement schedules and treating humans as passive recipients of them, they take no account of the mental activity which may occur in individuals during learning. Reductive because the theories have to break down complex behaviour into small stimulus–response units in order to explain how they are acquired. Critics of stimulus–response theories have claimed we need to develop more holistic units of analysis and accept that internal mental processes, though difficult to monitor, do play an important part in the learning process.

There is some empirical support for the claim that these mental or *cognitive* processes do need to be included in explanations of learning. For example, studies during the Second World War of air-gunners tracking simulated enemy aircraft found they often displayed negative response times. They were able to respond before the stimuli appeared. This indicated that gunners had developed mental models of the flight paths of enemy aircraft which enabled them to predict positions of aircraft and respond before they appeared. Similarly, in a classic experimental study of behaviour analogous to that of refinery process workers, Crossman and Cooke (1962) found the behaviour of their subjects could not be explained adequately within a stimulus–response framework. Their subjects were simply asked to control the temperature of boiling water by using a thermometer and adjusting a thermostat dial. If a subject's performance was shaped simply by feedback of response outcomes, the size of the adjustments should have correlated with the size of temperature error at its rate of change. These correlations appeared in inexperienced subjects only. Experienced subjects were able to predict the effect of adjustments on temperature, and this indicated that they had developed a mental *model* of the process. Experienced subjects' actions were therefore not simply controlled by information provided by the thermometer.

The acquisition of skill

There is some evidence, then, that complex human activity does not fit easily into a stimulus–response framework. What seems to happen is that people actively develop models of the systems they are interacting with. In other words, individuals do not respond directly to the environment, as stimulus–response theories assume, but to the models they construct of it. A number of researchers have claimed that a concept which can accommodate these less observable aspects of learning is *skill*. The definition of 'skill' is complicated by its wide use in ordinary language. In industry it is used to mean 'time served', or a qualification to carry out a craft or trade. Work is often classified into skilled, semi-skilled and unskilled. But in behavioural science the term is used in a much wider sense to refer to all the factors which go to make up a competent, expert, rapid and accurate performance. Skills in this sense are seen as natural units of activity which cut across task boundaries. This means that although two jobs involve different tasks, they can require similar skills for the effective performance.

Skill theorists believe that improvements in performance can be related to changes in the models people possess of the systems they are interacting with. Gibson (1968) has provided an influential description of the changes that human perceptual systems progress through. He proposed a sequence of developmental stages, each representing an increase in the ability to process, store and cross-reference information from different perceptual systems. Gibson suggested that at first we learn the range of stimulus inputs. We can understand a specific input better if we are able to relate it to the entire range of inputs. A learner driver, for example, will learn to discriminate between engine noises by learning the range of possible engine noises. This is the basis of what Gibson termed *learning affordances*, understanding what meaning or value an input has and what its implications for action are. This involves individuals developing *categories* for processing information. A learner driver, for example, develops categories for processing ranges of engine noise which indicate whether he or she should accelerate, decelerate, change gear or take no action.

The concept of categorization has important practical implications. Techniques have been developed which enable differences in the categories used by the skilled individuals and beginners to be identified, thus providing important insights into the nature of the skill and a firm basis for the design of training programmes.

Gibson suggested individuals will then establish the covariation between inputs from different perceptual systems. We can make more sense of an input if we can associate it with inputs or cues from other senses. In many skilled activities it is essential to learn the auditory, tactile and balance inputs associated with a visual input. This also enables the skilled individual to make more use of sensory information derived from receptors in muscles and joints. These *kinaesthetic* cues are more immediate than visual cues and so make possible increases in the rapidity and accuracy of movement. Knowing what efficient performance 'feels like', gear-changing for example, is an important guide to skilled activity.

We also acquire what are termed *constancies*. These allow us to perceive certain characteristics of the visual world, shape, size, colour and brightness, as constant. Without constancies the visual world would be extremely confusing; objects would appear to change shape if viewed from different angles, they would very rapidly diminish in size as they moved away from us, and would vary in colour and brightness according to the specific lighting conditions in which they were viewed. A dinner plate, for example, appears circular if viewed directly from above; if seen at an angle the shape formed by the parcel of light rays reflected from it on to the retina is an ellipse. The plate does not, however, change its shape as we change our angle of view. Constancies appear to be learned early on in life but can break down and need to be reacquired. Colour constancy, for example, disappears with unfamiliar objects, and size constancy can fail in specific visual environments such as when travelling at very high speeds.

Next our perceptual system incorporates what Gibson termed the *invariants in events*; these are the unchanging characteristics of the systems we interact with. We first learn the laws which determine how objects fall, roll, collide, break and pour. We then move on to learn more abstract invariants such as inertia.

These developments in the perceptual systems of individuals increase the *selectivity* of attention, enabling more efficient monitoring of both performance and the environment: 'only the information required to identify a thing economically tends to be picked up from a complex of stimulus information' (Gibson, 1968, p. 286). This means skilled individuals need less information to select a response. The skilled driver, for example, requires less visual information than the learner driver to be able to perceive a shape in the distance as a child emerging from behind a parked car. Similarly, skilled process workers in refineries can assess the state of the system with quick and infrequent inspections of display panels (Bainbridge, 1978).

Constructing models of the environment which categorize and store inputs also reduces the demand on memory. Descriptions of human memory usually assume two stores, termed *primary or short-term memory* and *secondary or long-term memory*. This division implies that two processes are involved in the storage of information. Primary memory appears to be the conscious or working store in which information can be stored for a few seconds. If important, information is transferred to a secondary, long-term store. Primary memory is thought to be located in circuits in the frontal lobes of the brain, whereas secondary memory appears to involve irreversible changes in the molecular structure of the brain cells. Primary memory is a fragile store and is easily disrupted. For example, if you have to attend to another input while trying to memorize a telephone number, you are unlikely to be able to remember what the number is. Fatigue and stress also disrupt the primary memory.

As well as being a fragile store, primary memory also appears to have a limited capacity. Whereas secondary memory has an almost infinite storage capacity, primary memory seems to be able to hold a small amount of information. In fact its capacity seems to be between five and nine 'chunks' of information (Miller, 1956). These chunks need not represent individual items such as numbers. By subjectively grouping items more information can be contained in the primary store. A nine-figure number, for example, can be remembered as three chunks each containing three digits. Skilled workers seem to be able to deal with many more items of information by chunking them according to the action-relevant categories they have developed. By reducing the load on short-term memory, skilled

35

individuals considerably increase their resistance to the effects of stress and fatigue.

Skill theorists believe that it is useful to think of skill in terms of two dimensions: *horizontal* and *vertical*.

The horizontal dimension refers to the organization of activity over time. Unskilled performances are marked by a confused response order and imprecise timing. Learner drivers, for example, usually stall at the points where they are required to make a number of responses in a particular order with reasonably precise timing.

In the training context this implies that 'micro'-behavioural training, in which trainees acquire a specific response routine – for example, sales trainees being drilled with 'scripts' – may be inadequate. The correct sequencing and timing of responses may very in specific contexts, and a trainee's ability to vary the order and timing of responses will depend on more macro-cognitive learning – for example, understanding how to provide information at a rate which corresponds to the client's ability to understand it.

The vertical dimension reflects the hierarchical organization of skills. It is believed that skilled activity differs in the extent to which it involves conscious awareness. Some behaviours, termed *subroutines*, are so well learned that they can be retrieved from secondary memory and employed without passing through our conscious or primary memory. For highly skilled individuals so much of their activity consists of automatized subroutines that their conscious memory has little to do. This can give rise to the strange feeling they often report, of being able to 'step outside of themselves' during an activity which appears to observers to involve a great deal of conscious effort. Further up the hierarchy are *operating programmes* (Randall, 1981). These convert the contents of our models into behavioural outputs by triggering patterns of subroutines. The model is then updated to include outcomes of the action. Operating programmes can themselves be relegated to subroutine status if they are so well learned that they can be elicited without conscious awareness. At the apex of the hierarchy is the *executive programme*, which selects the skill most appropriate to a situation.

Improvements in performance occur when either the model or the operating programme develop. The model contains more powerful representations of this situation, the operating programme acquires new sequences of subroutines. These improvements need not happen in parallel; the operating programme and model can move out of phase with each other, one leapfrogging over the other. For example, when an individual's modelling of a new system, whether mechanical, human or administrative, improves, the model is able to include enhanced states of that system. However, for this new state to be achieved, the operating programme must acquire new responses. This process continues until the operating programme is unable to produce a sequence of subroutines which would result in outcomes not already contained in the model. Similarly, the model reaches a point where it both deals economically with all relevant inputs and cannot produce improvements in the state of the system that are not already included in it. What sets the upper limit on the refinement of model and operating programmes is the individual's level of *motivation*. Highly motivated individuals will always struggle to improve their modelling of a situation and the ways they are able to respond to their models. A racing car driver, for example, requires a more highly developed model and operating programme for driving than an ordinary driver. A highly motivated student will try to comprehend how academic performance can be improved upon and attempt to acquire the information-gathering, analytical and writing skills that enable the improvements to be realized. In general, the development of models and operating programmes slows down once we feel we have mastered the system we are interacting with.

SKILLS AT WORK

Skill theory has considerably improved our understanding of the way in which people acquire complex behaviours. It is now possible to appreciate the crucial role that people's construction of the environment plays in their level of skills. We can see that skilled activity is in a sense an extension of their understanding of the systems they are interacting with into the external environment. These insights are important since they provide clues about the practical analysis and development of skills in training programmes.

Developing a satisfactory *skills appraisal* is the starting point for satisfactory selection or training procedures. With complex jobs it is often necessary to construct both a task description to indicate what the skilled individual does and a skills appraisal to explain how the tasks are accomplished. Singleton (1978) suggested the transition from the tasks to the skills domain could be accomplished by:

1. Discussing the skill at length with the skilled individual; supplementing this information by talking to his or her supervisors and subordinates.
2. Making the verbal communication from the skilled person more explicit by focusing on the categories he or she uses to distinguish inputs and the way he or she copes with specific events or problems which occur in his or her work.
3. Observing the development of skill in trainees.
4. Structuring the activity by identifying the dimensions skilled individuals use to perceive their environments and make decisions, and where possible developing measures for each dimension.

37

5. Checking the conclusions of this analysis by direct observation, performance measurement and experiment.

This form of skills analysis has provided useful insights into the nature of a number of complex occupational skills. Bainbridge (1978), for example, found that process controllers developed two internal representations of the environment, a working memory which contained information about the current state of the process and a more abstract model which housed their knowledge of the dynamics of the refining process. From time to time controllers updated their working memories on the basis of what was in the primary memories. This revealed what categories skilled controllers used to reduce raw display panel data to quantities that could be managed by their primary memories.

This approach to skills appraisal has also been helpful in the analysis of managerial skills. Moorhouse (1981), for example, clearly identified differences between the key skills necessary for departmental managers within a factory and the overall production manager.

Skills appraisals of various complex occupations have found that the ability to refer between different domains of information is a crucial component of skilled performance. Managers, particularly, are often required to weight and synthesize limited information from different sources when making decisions.

The concern with skills has prompted the development of packaged skills appraisal systems to describe the skills needed for less complex jobs. Most of the research that has underpinned these systems has been sponsored by the government's Employment Training Divisions. Their ultimate goal was to provide a common language to describe the world of work in order to relate what people are capable of to what jobs require. This objective has not, however, been realized. People involved in activities like training, careers guidance and wage-setting all seem to require different forms of description, and within each of these specialisms different levels of analysis are possible. So research has been geared to developing appraisal systems that meet specific training or labour market needs.

Basic skills analysis (Freshwater, 1982), for instance, was designed to analyse the skills required by young people entering the labour market. It consists of nearly 400 descriptive statements grouped under six skill headings: basic calculations; measurement and drawing; listening and talking; reading and writing; planning and problem-solving; and practical skills. The item-checklist enables the trainers to identify quickly the training needs of the individuals and the opportunities for skill development provided by these jobs. The trainers do this by indicating whether a basic skill item is a prerequisite for a particular job – that is, trainees should possess it before training begins – or whether the skill can be taught.

The skills involved in a broader range of occupations can be identified using an appraisal system known as the *job components inventory* or JCI (Banks *et al.*, 1982). Items in this system are grouped into five skill areas:

1. Use of tools and equipment.
2. Perceptual and physical skills.
3. Mathematical skills.
4. Communication skills.
5. Decision-making and responsibility in the job.

Three kinds of question are asked when completing this inventory: whether the skill is used or not, if it is used then how often, and what the skill is used for. The frequency with which a skill is used in a job can therefore be indicated in the inventory (Figure 1.2).

The potential of data gathered using these appraisal systems is increasingly being realized. Data can be used to produce:

1. Skills matrices which compare skill requirements of different job categories (e.g. between clerical and selling jobs).
2. Skill wheels, which assess the relative skill requirements of closely related jobs (e.g. different clerical jobs). This information is important in deciding on regrading or wage-setting.
3. Job profiles, which convert checklist data into narrative form. Job profiles are more easily understood by the general public and so can be used when preparing job specifications in management–union negotiations on wage-setting and regrading issues.

Skill matrices and wheels enable trainers to create more broadly based training programmes by identifying what are termed *portable* or *transferable* skills: that is, skills which can be used in a variety of occupations. Identifying these skills and designing training programmes around them is a central theme of current government training policy. This is because it is thought that nowadays young people starting work will have to be able to adapt to rapid technological and job changes, so training ought to concentrate on the skills that can be used in different work settings (NCVQ, 1990).

Skills which are the most transferable are learning skills. One objection to the current emphasis on learning *content* seen in the formulation of outcome-based core skills and competencies is that this may be achieved at the expense of learners not acquiring an understanding of their learning processes (Harri-Augustein and Thomas, 1991). These authors offer MAR(4)S, a framework designed to enable individuals to become more aware of their learning

COMMUNICATION AND INTERPERSONAL SKILLS	Professional Technical	Professional Managerial	Clerical with figures	Secretarial/Typing	Active Clerical	Clerical without figures	Receptionist	Clerical public contact	General Clerical	Selling
Receive written information	●	●	●	●	●	●	●	●	●	●
Advise or help colleagues or workmates	•	●	○	○	•	○		○		○
Complete standard forms or letters	●	●	●	•	●	●	●	●	•	•
Use codes	•	●	●	●	●	●	●	●		●
Write notes, letters, memos, short reports	●	●	●	●	•	●	●	●	●	•
File or sort things	●	●		●	●	•	●	●	•	•
Fill in a record book or manual	●	•	○	•	•	●	●	•	●	
Look up written information	○	●	●	●	○	●	●	●	●	•
Advise or help customers or clients	•	●	○	○	○	○	○	●	•	●
Receive complaints	○	•	•		○	○	○	●		•
Negotiate with colleagues or workmates		•		○	○			•		○
Use a manual or follow written instructions	•	○	○	○					○	
Instruct or train other people						○				○
Use or react to signals		○								
Persuade colleagues or workmates		○								
Negotiate with customers or clients		•					○	○	○	○
Persuade customers or clients		•								•
Interview people — simple information										
Interview people — queries								○		
Interview people — formal										
Give talks										

Figure 1.2 *Extract from a skills matrix using the job components inventory. Large black dots indicate very frequent usage of the skill, small black dots frequent usage of the skill, large white dots occasional usage of the skill and a blank cell that use of the skill is extremely rare or never occurs.* From M. Banks, P. Jackson and E. Stafford (1982) *A Skills Compendium.* Sheffield: Manpower Services Commission.

processes. MAR(4)S stands for monitor, analyse, record, reconstruct, reflect, review, spiral. This encourages the learner to articulate his or her experiences, check the validity of his or her model of the domain (e.g. playing tennis, selling, flying jet fighters) and develop insights into how the model can be spiralled upward to support a higher level of skill.

The MAR(4)S framework is designed to enable learners to get closely in touch with their own personal learning processes. Downs and Perry's (1984) taxonomy specifies a general list of learning skills which include: observing; questioning; memorizing; recording; assessing own performance; following instructions and diagrams; error identification; listening; comparing and contrasting. These learning skills are involved in acquiring skill as different as balancing a cash till and deciding how a company should respond to changes in exchange rates (Downs and Perry, 1986). The practical implication of learning skills research is that people can become more skillful in learning. Thus, training can be designed in such a way as to encourage the acquisition of learning strategies in general and the ability to choose the correct strategy for a particular task.

Learning difficulties from these perspectives occur when people either choose an inappropriate strategy or are not encouraged to recognize and gain control of their own learning processes. Harri-Augustein and Thomas (1991), for example, argue individuals build up disabling 'personal myths' about themselves as learners, such as 'I am no good at figures'. These researchers outline methods which enable learners to challenge and overcome the myths individuals possess about their own learning capacity.

Training must now be designed to improve the fundamental skills of learning if the objective of current training policy, the creation of active, confident and versatile young people capable of dealing with changes in their jobs by learning quickly and effectively, is to be achieved. Designing training programmes that concentrate on *how* people learn requires a radical revision of approach on the part of trainers and teachers who are more used to thinking *what* people learn. However, those seeking to bring about these changes now have a sound basis of theory and research to guide their attempts to produce more effective training programmes and policies.

Further reading

Harri-Augustein, S. and Thomas, L. (1991) *Learning Conversations*. London: Routledge.

Howe, M.J.A. (ed.) (1990) *Encouraging the Development of Exceptional Skills and Talents*. Leicester: The British Psychological Society.

Jessup, G. (1991) *Outcomes: NVQs and the Emerging Model of Education and Training*. London: Falmer Press.

Lieberman, D.A. (1990) *Learning Behaviour and Cognition*. London: Wadsworth.

Merrlam, S.B. and Gaffarella, R.S. (1991) *Learning in Adulthood: A Comprehensive Guide*. New York: Jossey-Bass.

Singleton, W.T. (ed.) (1978) *The Analysis of Practical Skills*. Lancaster: MTP Press.

Sternberg, R.J. (1990) *Wisdom: Its Nature, Origins and Development*. Cambridge: Cambridge University Press.

Sternberg, R.J. and Kollogan, J. (1992) *Competence Considered*. Yale University Press.

Weil, S.W. and McGill (1989) *Making Sense of Experiential Learning*. Milton Keynes: Open University Press.

2

Stress

In Chapter 1, the processes were examined which enable people to adapt to and integrate with their environments. These adaptive capacities, however, have limits and risks attached to them. For example, the person who constantly struggles to master a turbulent environment or a demanding task faces an increased risk of peptic ulcers, mental illness, hypertension and coronary heart disease. Less dangerous but still serious symptoms, like headache, eyestrain, dizziness, loss of appetite, depression and nervousness, may also occur. And these can result in responses, like the increased consumption of tranquilizers or alcohol, which only compound the problem.

These are all stress-related symptoms, and their prevalence in occupational and wider contexts has given rise to much interest in the causes and alleviation of stress. There is probably no doubt that this has sometimes had rather 'elitist' overtones, as stress has traditionally been associated with executive and managerial occupations. But, in point of fact, stress never has been a 'middle-class disease'; incidents of stress-related symptoms are just as frequently caused by factors like shift-working or excessive fatigue, which are typical of manual jobs. Also, nowadays the new technologies are making stress increasingly a problem in manual and low-grade white-collar work. There is growing concern, for instance, over the impact of word-processing on secretarial work, and the incidence of stress-related symptoms among typists.

In this chapter we will examine some of the major theories of stress and some of the recent attempts to reduce the impact of stress on individuals.

What is stress?

The earliest and most influential conceptualization of stress came from Selye (1936). He observed an identical series of biochemical changes in a number of organisms adapting to a variety of environmental conditions. He termed this series of changes the *general adaptation syndrome.* During the initial phase, termed the *stage of alarm*, the organism orients to the demand the environment is making on it and begins to experience it as threatening. This state cannot be maintained for very long. If the stimulus which has elicited the alarm response is too powerful (for example, a poison) the organism dies; if survival is possible the organism enters the *stage of resistance* in which the organism musters the resources to cope with the demand. If the demand continues for too long these adaptive resources are worn out and the organism reaches the *stage of exhaustion* in which serious damage can occur. Selye was not sure what it was that an organism lost in the stage of resistance that caused it to pass into the stage of exhaustion, although he was convinced it was more than simple calorific energy (Selye, 1983). The general adaptation syndrome can operate at different levels, from a subsystem to an entire organism. Certain kinds of athletes (footballers, for example) make severe demands on specific ligaments and joints in their training and performance. The general adaptation syndrome and the conse-quences of the stage of exhaustion will therefore tend to be localized.

Selye's discovery of the biochemical and physiological pathways of the stress response has been of immense significance. A number of researchers, however, have not followed Selye in seeing stress as simply a response. One major group of writers has argued that stress has to be seen as a function of an individual's *appraisal* of a situation. As we saw in our earlier discussion of skills, people do not respond directly to a stimulus but to the meaning a stimulus may have in relation to their model of the environment. This implies that events in the environment are not of themselves stressful; they must be perceived by the individual as a threat before the stress concept can be applied (Lazarus *et al.*, 1980). The stress experience, according to this view, is therefore determined by the *appraisal of what is at stake* and the analysis of the resources available to meet the demand.

The notion of appraisal broadens the concept of stress to include psychological factors, particularly personality variables such as 'the need for power' and 'locus of control' (see Chapter 3). In other words, what one person sees as a threat, another may see as a challenge. These different appraisals seem to produce specific physiological changes which, in turn, have different implications for the health of the individual. Some evidence has supported the view that appraisal plays a crucial role in determining the impact of a stressor on an individual's health. Jemmot *et al.*, (1983), for example, found the secretion rate of the immune systems of a group of students under academic pressure was not uniform. The relationship between exam pressure and the activity of the immune system was moderated by certain personality variables. Similarly, Arsenault and Dolan (1983) found the relationship between job stress and work outcomes, such as absenteeism and performance, varied according to the subject's personality type.

The concept of stress which dominates current research is an extension of the appraisal hypothesis that stress represents a relationship between a stressor and an individual's reaction to it (Dewe, 1991). Current research is based on the assumption that stress, inferred from physiological, behavioural, psychological and somatic signs and symptoms, is the result of *a lack of fit between a person (in terms of their personality, aptitudes and abilities) and the environment*, and a consequent inability to cope effectively with the various demands it makes of him or her. One study which tested this view found that, while neither a worker's report of the actual complexity of a job nor the level of complexity a worker wanted was related to a measure of depression, there was a strong relationship between measures of the person–environment fit and depression. The relationship the researcher found was curvilinear; when the person–environment fit was exact, depression was minimal, but when there was either too much or too little complexity present in the work, the depression score was increased (Harrison, 1976).

Types of stress at work

ROLE INTERACTION

Though individuals' perceptions of the environment play an important part in determining the experience and consequences of stress, it is nonetheless possible to identify objective features of work which are likely to be perceived as threatening. An individual's activities within an organization are a function of what *role(s)* he or she occupies in it. A role can be defined as the set of expectations that others have of a role incumbent's behaviour. Research has identified the ways in which roles become stressful. Firstly, in what is termed *single role conflict*, the various components of a given role become difficult to reconcile. For example, the expectations of a supervisor's staff may include defending their interests, taking an interest in them and affording them a significant degree of freedom in their work. The supervisor's managers, however, might have very different expectations. They may expect the supervisor to represent the interests of senior and middle management and to employ a much tougher style of supervision. Secondly, *multiple role conflict* stems from the fact that people invariably fill many different roles; and here the demands of one role clash with those of another an individual occupies. For example, a manager who is also the factory's safety officer might find

45

the demands of each role difficult to reconcile, which may mean taking certain short cuts such as removing safety guards. In a wider context, women, particularly when married with children, can experience conflict and stress when attempting to combine familial and work roles (Lewis and Cooper, 1983).

Some roles, such as negotiator or salesperson, because they involve relating the activities of the organization to the outside world, seem to carry a higher than average level of stress. Miles (1980) developed a typology of these *boundary-spanning roles* which he claimed discriminated between high- and low-stress jobs of this type. The most stressful boundary-spanning job, according to his typology, would be one which involved performing complex tasks in a changing environment with a variety of outside parties to whom there is a long-term commitment, and where there are clear performance criteria and independent sources of information on achievement available to the parent organization. Thus the role incumbent is exposed to numerous novel and unanticipated problems, as he or she attempts to develop relationships with different types of client, while the availability of hard performance data means that employers can press the individual for results and ignore the delicate processes involved in a boundary-spanning role.

Another common source of role stress, termed *role ambiguity*, occurs when an individual is uncertain what tasks, responsibility and authority have been assigned to the role he or she occupies. Complex, flexible, non-bureaucratic organizational structures can cause role ambiguity since roles include responsibilities within a project team in addition to the individual's regular functional (personnel, marketing, finance or production) duties.

Work role transitions have also been identified as potentially stressful experiences (e.g. West *et al.*, 1987; West and Rushton, 1989). These occur when an individual enters a new work situation and is faced with a novel, uncertain environment which creates a threat to his or her need for control and predictability. This is a fairly common form of role stress since about 33 per cent of individuals involved in work role transitions are moving into newly created jobs where they are without predecessors (West *et al*, 1987). Therefore, individuals entering these jobs have less help available, for example through feedback. And socialization into the role requirements tends to be achieved informally and somewhat randomly. While some individuals find these conditions provide an opportunity for personal growth and role innovation, others find them traumatic and stressful.

An increasingly common source of stress occurs when individuals feel *locked into roles*. Such stress is particularly common in large bureaucratic organizations where employees may believe they are unable to change their job, because very few job opportunities are available or they are not sufficiently able or qualified to move into another post. This can be caused by distortion in the promotion patterns in organizations. If an organization has recently been reorganized or created, new senior posts may be filled by relatively young people. Once these posts are filled there is little opportunity for promotion within the organization. The stagnation experienced when career paths are blocked leads to frustration, apathy and eventually to what Freudenberger (1974) termed *burnout*, where the initial enthusiasm for the job is replaced with negative attitudes. Burnout was originally identified in the caring professions such as social work and nursing but is identifiable outside of these occupations (Garden, 1989). The defining feature of burnout is 'energy depletion' or exhaustion. This then leads to the 'symptoms' of burnout such as a lack of concern for others and a reduced concern with achievement and progression.

Personnel departments and senior management in large organizations are increasingly recognizing the problems in terms of reduced physical and mental well-being of staff feeling locked into roles. Strategies for reducing burnout attempt to reduce the concern an individual has with the limitations of his or her current position within a hierarchy by negotiating career plans which may involve sideways as well as upward moves, or by setting up project teams which create new networks of responsibility and authority in addition to the existing ones. It may also be possible to provide realistic career changes for people by a general restructuring of career scales within an organization.

DECISION-MAKING STRESS

One of the most potent types of stress in organizations occurs as a result of having to make difficult decisions. Janis (1982) suggested two reasons why this may be so: people's awareness of their limited knowledge and problem-solving capacities, and their awareness of the various losses which may result from choosing any of the options available. Janis argued that *decisional stress* significantly reduces the quality of an individual's decision. At its most extreme, this can cause people simply to withdraw from a situation and make a decision without seeking out or considering relevant information. More usually, however, individuals' attempts to deal with decisional stress fall into one of five categories:

1. Unconflicted adherence, where behaviour is unchanged and information about the risks of continuing in the same way is ignored.
2. Unconflicted change, which involves uncritically adopting whichever course of action is most salient or most strongly recommended without

making contingency plans and without psychologically preparing for setbacks.

3. Defensive avoidance, where the individual procrastinates but eventually chooses the least difficult alternative, ignoring any information that suggests this decision may be wrong.
4. Hypervigilance, which involves searching frantically for a way out of the conflict and seizing upon any plan which seems to offer an immediate solution.
5. Vigilance, which consists of a careful search for relevant information followed by a thorough appraisal of the alternatives.

Of these five strategies, Janis suggested vigilance was the only one which involves enough cognitive work to meet the criteria of true decision-making. Hypervigilance, where attention shifts on to a variety of sometimes quite trivial cues, introduces the most error into a decision. The individual's thinking in this condition tends to be based on simple stereotypes and can involve obsessional dwelling on the worst possible outcomes. Janis saw 'time pressure' as the main cause of hypervigilance. When individuals are constantly overloaded with urgent business, they are more likely to commit themselves impulsively to courses of action which soon after appear to have been inappropriate.

One approach to reducing the stress experienced by individuals when making important decisions, known as *stress inoculation*, seeks to provide individuals with resistance to decisional stress by improving both their understanding of what causes it and their ability to cope with it. Cameron and Meichenbaum (1982), for example, developed a programme based on the appraisal concept of stress, that stress is a function of an individual's perception of a situation and his or her resources to cope with it. The programme consists of three stages:

1. Conceptualization, in which the individuals' understanding of decision-making situations and their own experiences in them are improved by explaining the appraisal model of stress. Meichenbaum suggested that this model provided individuals with a highly effective conceptual framework within which they could organize their own experience of stress. To achieve accurate appraisal, they are encouraged to recognize that appraisals of situations are often inaccurate or incomplete and that allowances have to be made for the biases which creep into their perceptions. Individuals then consider the skills which enable pertinent evidence to be examined and reasonable propositions to be formulated.
2. Skill acquisition and activation. This part of the programme examines whether an individual lacks a particular skill for accurate diagnosis of a situation, or possesses it but does not apply it. A relevant skill might

be efficient gathering of information about the likely outcomes of a decision.

3. Rehearsal and application. In this final phase of the course, the individual practises and applies the newly acquired coping skills using role-play techniques. It is hoped that these skills can then be transferred to help deal with real problems.

The attitudinal, personality and cognitive variables that provide the psychological context for coping with decisional stress are relatively stable characteristics of individuals. Complex changes, particularly in an individual's sense of self-efficacy (how competent individuals feel), are necessary before improvement in coping with decisional stress can occur. While short interventions like Meichenbaum's can only serve to improve a decision-maker's awareness of the dysfunctional biases caused by decisional stress, it is unclear to what extent changes in the underlying psychological dimensions of coping occur.

OVER- AND UNDERSTIMULATION

Welford (1973) suggested that humans and many other organisms appear to have evolved to function under conditions of moderate stimulation. Such aspects of the environment as noise, temperature, light, humidity and barometric pressure are tolerable at moderate levels but cause stress if they are too high or too low.

In the work context, the level of stimulation a job provides is likewise associated with the amount of stress it can cause employees to experience. Understimulation can occur in jobs which involve repetitive work and underutilization of skills. The emotional responses to these jobs are apathy, boredom and reduced levels of motivation (Caplan *et al.*, 1975). Behavioural responses are likely to be less well organized than they would have been at higher levels of stimulation. Many studies have shown that people who do repetitive work also face increased risks of stress-related illnesses (e.g. Ferguson, 1973). Cox (1980) has suggested that the effect of repetitive understimulating work on health occurs through what he termed an *emergency stress response*. This occurs when someone performing a repetitive task has to readjust his or her attention suddenly because it had drifted away from the task. He argued that because of the increased physiological 'wear and tear' these adjustments involve, the higher frequency of attentional shifts inherent in repetitive work was detrimental to health. His explanation, however, is tentative at present and it remains unclear why repetitive work carries health risks.

Many people at work face the opposite problem of having to cope with too much stimulation. Overstimulation can be as stressful, if not more so, than understimulation. Perhaps the classic example of a job in which large amounts of variable information have to be coped with is air-traffic control. The health costs in terms of ulcers, skin disorders, hypertension and respiratory complaints have been well documented (Martindale, 1977; Rose *et al.*, 1978). In fact it was noteworthy that American air-traffic controllers were involved in a particularly bitterly fought strike in 1981 largely in an attempt to improve their working conditions. And several of the issues at stake involved reducing the variety and quantity of stimulation they were having to cope with.

Numerous studies have demonstrated the damaging effects of overload on managers. Working long hours is actually a coping strategy used by many managers. Quick *et al.* (1990) cite the comments of a fairly typical manager who would 'read every night or work every night and bring home a briefcase full and really feel guilty if I didn't'. But long hours and excessive workloads inevitably lead to stress-related problems such as increased alcohol and cigarette consumption, depression, low self-esteem and coronary heart disease (e.g. Cooper and Melhuish, 1980).

While managers can exert some control over their workload – for example, by delegating or rescheduling – jobs which combine overload with low control are experienced as particularly stressful. Carrère *et al.* (1991) studied urban bus driving, an example of an occupation which combines overload with low control. They measured the hormones associated with blood pressure and coronary heart disease (adrenaline and noradrenaline) and found drivers had about twice the amount found in other blue-collar and office workers. While not enough is known about the effects of this heightened hormonal activity, this may account for the much higher risk of coronary problems among bus drivers. Other studies have also found the combination of overload and low control a particularly stressful one (e.g. Mackay and Cooper, 1987).

TYPE As AND TYPE Bs

Even though occupations vary in the stress-related health risks they carry, it is now accepted that individuals similarly differ in their proneness to stress-related health risks. As early as 1868 a German doctor, Von Dusch, noted that people who developed coronary heart disease (CHD) were often excessively involved in their work. In 1943 another doctor, Dunbar, noted that his CHD patients could frequently be characterized by compulsive striving, self-discipline and an urge to get to the top through hard work. In the late 1950s, Friedman and Rosenman began a series of studies on managers in a range of companies. In an early study, fifty accountants were monitored for six months. Blood samples were taken every fortnight to gauge their cholesterol levels, which were then compared with their diaries where they reported the amount of stress present in their work and homes. With other factors such as diet and exercise held constant, they found cholesterol levels went up and blood coagulation times went down during periods of stress. In 1959 Friedman and Rosenman made their most controversial contribution to the understanding of the relationship between stress and heart disease. They operationalized a behaviour pattern, termed type A, which they believed encapsulated what Von Dusch, Dunbar and others had observed in their CHD patients. This behaviour pattern, they argued, carried a risk of CHD independent of all other known risks. Individuals who fall into the type A category display:

1. A strong and sustained drive to achieve poorly defined goals they have set for themselves.
2. An intense desire to compete.
3. A desire for recognition and promotion.
4. Involvement in numerous and varied activities which have deadlines.
5. Habitually fast completion of physical and mental functions.
6. High levels of mental and physical alertness.

In extreme instances type A behaviour involves tense facial and body muscle tone, rapid body movements, hand- or teeth-clenching, excessive gesturing and explosive speech characteristics. Conversely, the type B individual displays less striving, aggression, hostility and competitiveness, and is in general more relaxed. While these are extremes, most people do in fact fall into only one of the categories, 40 per cent being type A and 60 per cent type B (Glass, 1977).

A large body of evidence has been accumulated which has confirmed the association between type A behaviour and CHD. One series of studies observed a sample of over 3,500 men over a fifteen-year period. Of the twenty-five deaths caused by CHD, twenty-two had been classified as type As. This yielded a risk factor in the type A group for CHD some six times larger than that for type Bs (Rosenman et al., 1975). Why does type A behaviour carry such an increased risk of CHD? Chesney and Rosenman (1980) argued that some behaviours in the type A constellation are more predictive of CHD than others. They saw four facets of type A behaviour as particularly predictive of CHD:

1. *Time urgency:* type As feel time passes too quickly.
2. *Their competitive and hard-driving style* makes type As work harder and faster than type Bs, even when no deadline is present. Type As seem to impose deadlines on themselves. This enables type As to maintain and even enhance their performance on multiple tasks compared to a fall in performance by type Bs (Fazio *et al.*, 1981).

51

3. *Suppression of symptoms:* though type As work harder and faster than type Bs, they report less fatigue and complain less. In fact, hard work and self-imposed deadlines seem to reinforce their suppression of symptoms since it is only at times when the pressure has eased that symptoms are experienced.
4. *Hostility and aggressiveness* are thought to be the facets of type A behaviour which best predict CHD. Type As are more impatient, aggressive and irritable with others. When provoked, type As are much more hostile than type Bs in similar circumstances (Carver and Glass, 1978).

The motivational basis for type A behaviour is thought to be their 'need for control'. Type A behaviours are elicited by situations in which type As feel challenged, under pressure or threatened. It is at these times that differences in blood pressure, heart rate and adrenaline level are observed between type As and Bs. Carruthers (1980) tentatively suggested that adrenaline accelerates the ageing of the cardiovascular system and so increases the CHD risk.

In a work-oriented society, type A behaviour is not seen as a clinical problem. If anything it tends to be rewarded. Measures of type A behaviour are positively correlated with occupational status, though, interestingly, type Bs are most prevalent at the top of organizations (Friedman and Rosenman, 1974). Byrne and Reinhart (1989) provide data which suggest it is the willingness of type As to devote their own time to the organization rather than their competitiveness or speed and impatience which is the key to their success.

Healthy type As are obviously a great asset to organizations, given that their hard-driving style may be necessary to cope with the work environment. For example, Rose *et al.* (1978) found type A air-traffic controllers had higher rates of stress but the largest single chronic illness in the sample, hypertension, was suffered by type Bs. This finding is consistent with the view that stress results from a mismatch between an individual and the work environment. Air-traffic control, a type A job, produced more stress-related illness in type B controllers.

Type As' increased risk of CHD, however, often confronts them with the choice of either curtailing their ambitions and accepting positions of lower status with less responsibility, or learning to face challenges without eliciting the health-damaging physiological responses. We will now examine some of the recent developments in occupational stress management which provide type As and others suffering stress-related problems with the second option.

Occupational stress management

The costs of stress-related problems to the economy are substantial. Absence, illness, accidents and staff turnover can, as we have seen, be the direct or indirect result of stress. Interest in stress counselling and management programmes has therefore burgeoned in recent years. One important line of research has been into the coping strategies individuals employ at work.

Moos and Billings (1982) have provided a comprehensive classification of coping strategies, which proposes three broad categories:

1. *Appraisal-focused coping.* This includes *logical analysis*, where individuals try to identify the causes of their current difficulties, considering one aspect of their work situation at a time and using their past experience to predict the possible outcomes of their actions. Individuals may attempt some *cognitive redefinition* of their work problems – accepting their situation but trying to find something favourable in it which makes it possible to perceive it as less stressful. Some individuals use *cognitive avoidance* – attempting to cope with the situation by denying the fear or anxiety they are experiencing, or by trying to forget that the problem exists.

2. *Problem-focused coping.* In these strategies individuals actively tackle the problems that are causing their stress. Firstly, by utilizing the social support system available at work individuals can *obtain guidance* on how best to deal with a situation. Secondly, by *taking direct action* an attempt can be made to modify or eliminate the source of stress. For example, an individual could, by renegotiating a work role, remove ambiguities in his or her present position. Finally, some individuals *develop alternative rewards* by substituting rewards which had been difficult to obtain with rewards that are more easily obtainable.

3. *Emotion-focused coping.* These strategies provide ways of dealing with the emotional consequences of stress. Firstly, by *affective regulation* individuals try to avoid paying attention to their feelings – perhaps best summed up as showing a 'stiff upper lip'. Secondly, by *resigned acceptance* individuals can passively accept the situation and expect that the worst is likely to occur. Finally, individuals can attempt to cope with their emotions by *emotional discharge* – 'letting off steam'. This form of coping, however, can involve behaviours such as spreading rumours, stealing, damaging property and violence, which will actually increase the problems an individual faces.

More recently Dewe (1991), using coping data derived from a checklist, statistically identified seven coping strategies:

1. Working on the problem, for example by getting advice or taking immediate action.

2. Trying to not let it get to you, perhaps by not thinking about it.
3. Emotional release, possibly by losing one's temper or taking feelings out on staff.
4. Taking preventative measures, for example by getting plenty of rest or setting priorities.
5. Recovery and preparation, achieved by ignoring the problem for a while until the individual feels ready to cope with it.
6. Obtaining support from the family, by talking the problem through at home.
7. Passive attempts to tolerate the problem, found in people who take a day off, daydream, smoke or drink more.

These two classifications, like others available (e.g. Folkman and Lazarus, 1980), emphasize the distinction between the active appraisal or problem-focused strategies and more passive emotion-focused strategies. Investigations of the relationship between coping strategies and stress outcomes have demonstrated that individuals using the active appraisal or problem-focused strategies experience fewer harmful physical and psychological outcomes than those using the passive avoidance methods (e.g. Quick *et al*, 1990; Moos and Billings, 1982).

These and other classifications provide people involved in stress counselling with the means to explore an individual's method of coping with stress and to facilitate effective coping. The availability of instruments which enable rapid and objective identification of coping styles will further assist counsellors (Dewe and Guest, 1990).

Alternatively, in the work situation, where there is often less time for individual counselling, 'off the peg' programmes can be usefully introduced.

Table 2.1   *Stress management techniques.*

INDIVIDUAL FOCUS	ORGANIZATIONAL FOCUS
Biofeedback	Improved communications
Progressive muscle relaxation (PMR)	Improving selection
Imagery training	Investment in training
Positive self-talk	Increasing autonomy
Assertiveness training	Increasing participation
Exercise	Clear role definition
Nutrition and weight control	Manageable workloads

Table 2.1 summarizes the range of stress management programmes and techniques available to organizations. Physical exercise, fitness and nutritional advice are usually offered by organizations in the context of general health promotion programmes. But evaluation of these programmes also found them to be useful for individuals coping with stress (e.g. Durbeck *et al.*, 1972; Heinzelman, 1975). For example, Durbeck's study of NASA employees found that, after a year of regularly using exercise facilities provided on the site, the subjects reported less stress and indicated that they felt able to handle stress more effectively. Subsequent research has confirmed the beneficial effects of exercise (e.g. Bruning and Frew, 1987).

Selye (1975) suggested the reduction in stress produced by exercise stems from what he termed the *cross resistance effect*, whereby the increased strength of one bodily system or process has an impact on another bodily system or process, and thus affords organisms some physical protection from environmental stressors.

Biofeedback, progressive muscle relaxation and imagery training are methods of controlling anxiety and inducing relaxation. Biofeedback involves measuring pulse, blood pressure or the activity of sweat glands and providing immediate feedback. With practice, individuals can gain some degree of control over these. Relaxation techniques such as PMR or imagery training are methods designed to help individuals gain control over their internal stress response. PMR involves the systematic tensing and relaxing of muscle groups. Tense muscles can be relaxed more effectively by further tensing them for a few seconds and then relaxing. In imagery training people try and quieten their minds down by imagining being in a restful place.

Techniques of positive self-talk, assertiveness training and time management aim to enhance an individual's appraisal of a situation and analysis of the resources he or she has available to meet the demand (Charlesworth and Nathan, 1986).

One key question concerns the extent to which any of these techniques transfer to the workplace. For example, the control an individual acquires over his or her physiological arousal in an off-site setting seems to be easily disrupted by stressors present at work (Holroyd and Lazarus, 1983). Additionally, considerable commitment is required to acquire relaxation techniques like PMR and then to continue practising them both inside and outside of the workplace.

Even when worksite programmes appear to be able to produce reductions in reported and measured levels of stress, it is often difficult to establish why the improvements have occurred. The fact that many programmes use more than one of the methods in Table 2.1 makes it difficult to disentangle the effects of any one of them.

Research on worksite programmes also indicates that control

groups often show as many changes on physiological and self-report psychological measures of stress as the experimental groups (Drazen *et al.*, 1982; Murphy, 1984). This implies that a number of effects, over and above the specific factors being tested for, are operating to reduce stress levels. As Murphy (1984) pointed out, 'non-specific factors inherent in all training strategies like sitting in a comfortable position, the intention to relax, a credible training strategy, and motivation due to self-selection into the study, are responsible for some of the observed self-report changes and physiological changes.' At present, however, we know that many of the multi-method programmes currently being used on worksites do help to bring about improvement on both objective and subjective indices of stress. There is also some evidence to suggest that reduced absenteeism, and other benefits quite unrelated to stress, more than repay the costs of such programmes to organizations. One study suggested that the cost–benefit ratio was as high as 1:5 – each £1 spent was £5 saved (National Institute for Occupational Safety and Health, 1987).

The major criticism these programmes face comes from writers who argue that organizations can use these methods to adapt employees to poorly designed work environments and so avoid the need for reorganization (Newman and Boehr, 1979). Instead, they suggest, attention ought to be given to reducing the prevalence of objective stressors in organizations by increasing communication, participation, autonomy and training.

Although this represents a valid criticism, there are at least two reasons why the need for occupational stress management programmes remains. Firstly, as Ganster *et al.* (1982) point out, many stressors cannot be designed out of organizations: for example, deadlines like the end of a financial year. And secondly, many organizations are unwilling to change their structure and practices, which means stress management programmes are the only way of reducing occupational stress and thus improving employee well-being.

Further reading

Beech, H.R., Burns, L.E. and Sheffield, B.F. (1982) *A Behavioural Approach to the Management of Stress.* Chichester: Wiley.

Campbell, Quick, J., Nelson, D.L. and Quick, J.D. (1990) *Stress and Challenge at the Top: The Paradox of the Successful Executive.*

Cooper, C.L. and Payne, R. (eds.) (1988) *Causing, Coping and Consequences of Stress at Work.* Chichester: Wiley.

Cooper, C.L. and Smith, M. (eds.) (1985) *Job Stress and Blue Collar Work.* Chichester: Wiley.

Ivancevich, J.M. and Ganster, D.C. (1987) *Job Stress: From Theory to Suggestions*. New York: Haworth Press.

Lovelace, R.T. (1990) *Stress Master*. Chichester; Wiley.

Murphy, P.M. and Kupshik (1992) *Loneliness, Stress and Well-being: A Helper's Guide*. London: Tavistock.

3

Individual Differences

While many psychologists attempt to identify processes which are common to all individuals – the way information is processed and stored, for example – others are preoccupied by the differences they observe between people. In general, because of their practical applications in clinical, educational and work settings, the study of individual differences has concentrated on two areas: personality and intelligence.

Common to the study of both are a number of key assumptions. The first is that although individuals are *unique* they are also *consistent*; character and intelligence are developed early and remain much the same throughout adult life. Thus, a bright, sociable child becomes a bright, sociable adult. Secondly, although differences between individuals' intellectual abilities and personalities seem bewilderingly complex, there are, in fact, just a few *underlying dimensions* along which these attributes vary. And finally, reducing the complexity of observed differences between individuals is usually achieved by making the assumption that individual differences are *normally distributed* (Figure 3.1).

The idea that the normal distribution – which had been shown to apply to physical characteristics such as height and weight – could also be applied to psychological attributes was first suggested by Francis Galton (1822–1911). By assuming a normal distribution, psychologists can use sophisticated statistical techniques which both identify connections between aspects of personality or intelligence and describe an underlying set of personality or intelligence factors which explain the observed associations.

In the workplace the study of individual differences is useful in at lease two ways. Firstly, a sounder basis for the prediction and understanding of behaviour can help those whose jobs involve dealing with other people. Secondly, it is important to have the best possible match between people's personalities and intellectual abilities and their jobs since a bad match leads to poor performance and stress. Thus the ability to identify and measure the individual differences

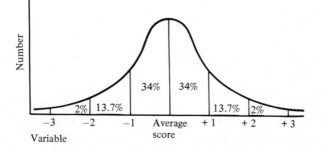

Figure 3.1 *Normally distributed variables produce this characteristic bell-shaped curve. With a measure of dispersion – the standard deviation – it is possible to calculate the proportion of a population falling above or below a particular point on the scale. It can be seen that 68 per cent of the population fall within + 1 and – 1 standard deviation of the average score for the population.*

associated with high job performance enables organizations to select and recruit individuals with these attributes.

In this chapter we will examine the extent to which psychologists have managed to identify the key dimensions of personality and intelligence and what relationships these dimensions have with job performance. Finally, we will discuss the relative merits of two common methods of assessing individual differences in the workplace: interviews and psychometric tests.

Personality

We all at times need to develop accounts of other human beings in order to make sense of their current behaviour or to be able to predict future behaviour. To do this, often without realizing is, we develop and use concepts that describe their personality. Normally our judgments about other people's personalities are based on their behaviour. For instance we might say, 'she behaved *conscientiously*'. If she often behaves like this we might be prepared not only use the adverb to describe her behaviour but also to employ the adjective *conscientious* to describe her as a person. Eventually, we may find ourselves – by using the noun *conscientiousness* – inferring the existence in her of something called a *trait*. The important point to bear in mind is that, although traits are nouns, seemingly representing mental structures, they are, in fact, *dispositional concepts* which reflect a person's characteristic behaviour.

59

Behavioural scientists define personality as the relatively enduring combination of traits which makes an individual unique and at the same time produces consistencies in his or her thought and behaviour.

Normally, if asked to produce character descriptions we would be unlikely to apply the same traits to each person, since some would appear highly relevant to some people but not to others. Each individual would probably elicit a unique set of traits. This is termed an *idiographic* description. This type of description also occurs in certain professional contexts, psychiatry for example, where each patient's character is explored in considerable depth. Many behavioural scientists, however, use what are termed *nomothetic* descriptions where a trait is applied universally. The advantage of this approach is that it enables standardized assessments of groups of individuals, such as job applicants, to be made.

In this section we will examine three perspectives that have made significant contributions to our understanding of personality.

Firstly, from the nomothetic perspective, we will describe some dimensions of personality produced by a statistical technique known as factor analysis. Secondly, we will outline the model of personality developed within the idiographic tradition by Sigmund Freud. His view of the developmental processes which shape people's personalities from childhood has been both controversial and influential since its appearance eighty years ago. And finally, returning to the nomothetic perspective, we will examine some personality dimensions proposed by psychologists who believe that *social learning* – the learning that occurs through interaction with others – has effects that are permanent enough to be considered part of a person's personality.

PERSONALITY FACTORS

A factor analysis of personality begins by collection data from a large sample of individuals using a variety of rating scales and behavioural measures. On the former, subjects would rate themselves along scales measuring very specific traits such as patient–impatient or conscientious–expedient. On the latter, subjects would provide information about fairly specific behaviour patterns: for example, how many hobbies they had or how often they went to parties.

The next step is to identify what associations exist between the various measures. This is achieved by calculating the correlation between two sets of scores. A correlation coefficient indicates the strength of any linear relationship between two measures. It varies from + 1.00, a perfect positive relationship in which the subject's position on one scale corresponds exactly with his or her position on the other, through 0.00 where there is no relationship between subjects' scores on the two measures, to − 1.00, a perfect negative relationship in which the subject's position on one scale is the opposite of his or her position on the other (Figure 3.2). Thus, for example, there may well be a positive correlation between the behavioural measure of party-going and the trait scale patient–impatient, subjects who attend numerous parties also tending to rate themselves as impatient.

The third stage of a factor analysis is the construction of a *correlation matrix* in which the correlation between each of the behavioural measures or rating scales is plotted against all the others used in the survey (Figure 3.3).

A factor analysis then attempts, by using some sophisticated mathematics, to identify the smallest number of *factors* that need to be postulated to explain the pattern of associations found in the correlation matrix. Factors are given names by examining which of the original behavioural measures or rating scales correlate best with the factor – although some researchers prefer to invent names for their factors to remind us that we are dealing with statistical abstractions that may not necessarily correspond exactly to the psychological make-up of individuals.

The best known advocate of factor-analytic techniques in Britain is Hans Eysenck. Since the late 1950s, Eysenck has used the technique to derive, test and modify his personality theory. He has proposed that most of the differences we observe between people's personalities can be accounted for by just three factors, expressed as bipolar dimensions.

1. *Introversion-extraversion.* Individuals at the extravert end of the dimension are characterized as 'stimulus hungry', requiring a variety of stimulus inputs. Extraverts meet their need for stimulation by engaging in a variety of social and physical activities. Extraverts also tend to be aggressive and unable to keep their feelings under control. At the other end of the dimension, introverts are quieter, have fewer friends, are less active, have fewer interests, are serious-minded, conscientious and manage to keep their feelings under control.
2. *Neuroticism-stability.* High-scoring individuals report anxiety, moodiness, worry, depression and sleep loss, are easily upset and if upset take a considerable time to return to an even keel. Conversely, stable individuals experience less emotional upset, embarrassment and worry. When upset, stable individuals quickly return to their emotional baseline.
3. *Psychoticism.* Introduced some time after the first two factors, psychoticism is unlike them in that most individuals have low scores. Moderate scores are obtained by displaying lack of empathy, sensitivity

Figure 3.2   *Correlation representing the association between two variables. In A and C, subjects' scores on variables X and Y are perfectly correlated (directly in the former and inversely in the latter). In B, however, there is no relationship between individuals' scores on the two scales.*

and regard for others. The high scorer is hostile even to relatives and friends, enjoys making fools of others and enjoys indulging in dangerous or bizarre activities.

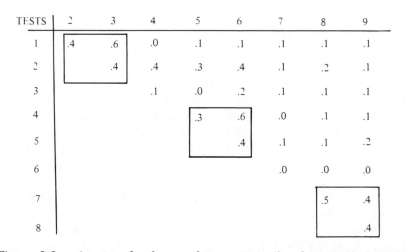

Figure 3.3   *An example of a correlation matrix (based on Guilford, 1967). The outlined figures represent significant correlations between scores on tests. The three groups of correlations indicate the presence of three underlying factors.*

By combining the first two dimensions, four broad characterizations of personality are created: stable–introvert, stable–extravert, neurotic–introvert, neurotic–extravert. Interestingly, this modern statistically derived typology corresponds to that developed by Hippocrates in ancient Greece: phlegmatic, sanguine, melancholic and choleric. Hippocrates attributed these four temperaments to the relative level of four essential body fluids or 'humours': blood, yellow bile, black bile and phlegm.

Eysenck also gave his typology a biological basis, linking it not with body fluids but with the central nervous system (neuroticism–stability). He proposed that individual differences on the first dimension – introversion–extraversion – are explained by inherited differences in the *excitatory potential* of the central nervous system (CNS). Individuals whose excitatory potential is low are predisposed towards extraversion since the bias in their CNS is towards cells being inactive (inhibition) rather than active (excitation). This means extraverts require more going on around them for their brains to function adequately, and thus to maintain a reasonable level of alertness, than introverts do. Extraverts not only have a CNS which switches off more readily, they also take longer to dissipate the inhibition that has built up in their CNS while attending to a stimulus. Conversely, introverts, through their higher excitatory potential, are already reasonably alert and thus less prone to switching their attention to other sources of stimuli: in other words, they are less easily distracted.

They will also be less likely to have what are termed 'micro-sleeps' (switching off for a few seconds) since they dissipate any inhibition much more rapidly than extraverts.

Even before Eysenck's theory was available, large individual differences had been observed in the ease with which individuals in some occupational settings doing jobs like radar and sonar operating could cope with the low levels of stimulation the jobs involved. In such jobs, some operators missed critical signals on their screens or reported signals when none were present, while the performance of others seemed relatively unaffected by the low level of stimulation. Eysenck's theory seemed to offer an explanation of this and other similar differences in behaviour. Extraverts, because of the low level of activation in their central nervous systems, find it difficult to cope with environments which provide low levels of unvarying stimulation. Introverts, on the other hand, with central nervous systems already reasonably activated, find these environments ideal. Conversely, they would be 'swamped' by high levels of stimulation, which would cause a considerable reduction in their task performance.

Much of the impact of this *physiological* difference on *psychological* differences between individuals was presumed to arise from its effect on an individual's 'conditionability'. Introverts, since they build up inhibition slowly, are easier to condition than extraverts. This implies that introverts are constitutionally more likely to assimilate, through conditioning, the rules, obligations and attitudes of their social environment. Conversely, the impact of socialization on extraverts is attenuated by their weaker conditionability. Extraverts are therefore less likely to acquire conforming and conscientious behaviour patterns than introverts.

Though Eysenck for the most part has concentrated on exploring the biological substrate of the introversion–extraversion dimension, he has suggested that an individual's position on the second dimension – neuroticism–stability – reflects the stability of his or her autonomic nervous system (ANS). The ANS is the part of the nervous system not directly under conscious control that carries a number of reflex activities; it is also involved in certain emotional responses. Some individuals inherit a *labile* ANS which responds vigorously to stress and also takes some time to return to baseline. In addition, they will experience more spontaneous activity: that is, shifts in activation which are not clearly attributable to external events. Conversely, some individuals are born with a *stabile* ANS characterized by weaker responses to stress, a more rapid return to baseline and less spontaneous activity. This means individuals with a labile ANS are constitutionally more prone to worry, anxiety, embarrassment and stress than those with a stabile ANS. Thus individuals towards the neuroticism end of the dimension have a greater amount of 'free-floating' anxiety which, through conditioning, can become attached to events or people. This may mean, for example, that social interaction can for some individuals become 'loaded' with a considerable amount of anxiety. However, an important implication of Eysenck's theory is that neuroticism is normally distributed along a continuum. In other words, there is not a discontinuity between 'normal' people and neurotics. Thus, the difficulties experienced by people with conditions such as agraphobia (fear of open spaces) are simply the result of somewhat higher levels of anxiety being paired with certain stimuli. If follows that such symptoms can be easily treated with behaviour modification programmes in which the individual 'unlearns' the existing anxiety response and learns a more neutral response, so enabling him or her to resume a normal life.

The third factor, psychoticism, is again presumed to reflect physiological differences between individuals. The relationship here has only been tentatively sketched by Eysenck and Eysenck (1976). They pointed out that, since the behaviours that load on to the psychoticism factor are essentially 'male', variation in the levels of androgen, a male hormone, in a population could be responsible for this factor. This claim still awaits empirical support.

Eysenck's theory attempts, then, to provide both a fundamental *description* of personality and an *explanation* of personality. Not surprisingly, a theory which suggests firstly that personality can be described using only three dimensions and secondly that it is ultimately reducible to physiological differences has attracted a great deal of attention. Much of the research using the factors has demonstrated differences between introverts and extraverts on other measures. For example, from about age 14 onwards, introverts tend to do better at school and college (Entwistle and Wilson, 1977; Rhodes, 1983). But the connections between physiology and personality suggested by the theory have not all been confirmed. Claridge (1970), for example, found that tolerance to sedatives which, because introverts are presumed to have a higher level of central nervous system activation and hence greater tolerance to sedatives, should be predicted by the introversion–extraversion factor alone, was best predicted by a combination of introversion–extraversion and neuroticism–stability scores. The assumption of a general conditionability trait by Eysenck has also not been clearly supported. Conditioning appears to occur at different rates for particular types of response within the same individual. For example, conditioning an individual's eye blink to occur after a click might be achieved relatively rapidly, but conditioning another autonomic response in the same individual may occur relatively slowly. While the precise nature of the links between

65

Eysenck's dimensions and physiology are unclear, most factorists would agree that the three factors account for a considerable proportion of the differences we observe between personalities.

Eysenck's dimensions were produced by a type of factor analysis which extracts what are termed *orthogonal* factors. These are large factors, each accounting for a considerable proportion of the observed differences in personality. They are also independent of one another, which means that an individual's score on one of the dimensions is unrelated to his or her score on any of the others. Extracting orthogonal factors from personality data produces what is termed a *type* description.

Some factorists feel that Eysenck's approach to factor analysis loses a good deal of more specific information about human personality. In some contexts, like personnel selection and clinical assessment, the use of only three broad personality factors mean that a number of important aspects of a candidate's or patient's personality may be concealed. For example, introversion–extraversion can be divided into a number of factors such as assertiveness, self-control, sociability, conscientiousness and conformity which may be of great value in personnel selection or patient assessment. Deriving a number of somewhat intercorrelated *oblique* factors produces what is termed a *trait description*. The most widely used trait profile was produced by Cattell (1967). He found sixteen trait factors in his data. His traits have been used to show the average profiles of individuals, from successful students and salespersons to sufferers from anxiety, neurosis and psychopathy (Figure 3.4). We should stress that Cattell and others who used trait profiles do not deny the existence of Eysenck's factors – indeed data from Cattell's profile, if factor-analysed, produce Eysenck's factors – they simply prefer to use a more detailed description of an individual's personality.

One disadvantage of oblique factors, however, is that they are not as robust mathematically at the larger orthogonal ones. This means that they do not always appear with the same clarity as the larger dimensions when factor-analysing data. The most robust factors seem to be the big five (Norman, 1963; McCrae and Costa, 1987; Rust et al; 1992. The big five which can be measured with John Rust's personality questionnaire, are as shown in Table 3.1.

Ultimately, the choice between the big orthogonal and smaller oblique personality factors depends on subjective judgements about the nature of personality and the context in which the personality description is used. Factor-analytic techniques currently provide the most systematic method of investigating the basis of differences between individuals' personalities. The fact that many dimensions produced by this method are able to improve predictions about

FACTOR	LOW SCORE DESCRIPTION	TRAIT										HIGH SCORE DESCRIPTION
		1	2	3	4	5	6	7	8	9	10	
A	Reserved	.	.	.	.	.	.	.	.	●	.	Outgoing
B	Less intelligent	.	.	.	.	.	.	.	●	.	.	More intelligent
C	Affected by feelings	.	.	.	.	.	●	.	.	.	.	Emotionally stable
E	Humble	.	.	.	.	.	.	●	.	.	.	Assertive
F	Sober	.	.	.	.	.	●	.	.	.	.	Happy go lucky
G	Expedient	.	.	.	.	.	●	.	.	.	.	Conscientious
H	Shy	.	.	.	.	.	.	●	.	.	.	Venturesome
I	Tough minded	.	.	.	.	.	.	●	.	.	.	Tender minded
L	Trusting	.	.	.	.	●	.	.	.	.	.	Suspicious
M	Practical	.	.	.	.	.	.	.	●	.	.	Imaginative
N	Forthright	.	.	.	.	●	.	.	.	.	.	Shrewd
O	Self assured	●	.	.	.	.	.	.	.	.	.	Apprehensive
Q1	Conservative	.	.	.	.	.	.	.	●	.	.	Experimenting
Q2	Group-dependent	.	.	.	.	.	●	.	.	.	.	Self-sufficient
Q3	Undisciplined self-conflict	.	.	.	.	.	●	.	.	.	.	Controlled
Q4	Relaxed	.	.	.	.	●	.	.	.	.	.	Tense

Percent of population obtaining score	1	2	3	4	5	6	7	8	9	10
	2.3	4.4	9.2	15.0	19.1	19.1	15.0	9.2	4.4	2.3

Figure 3.4   Cattell's sixteen personality factors. Each individual is profiled on the basis of his or her answers to a questionaire which takes about thirty-five minutes to complete. Scores for each factor are assumed to be normally distributed, here divided into ten, thus 38.2 per cent of the population fall within the middle band. Since a large amount of data on various occupational groups are available, Cattell's personality factors are used widely in selection and vocational guidance. As well as being predictive of job performance, the profile has also been used to build effective staff and managerial teams. The profile shown here belongs to one of the authors.

Table 3.1 *The big five personality factors*

1. *Extroversion*	e.g. Talkative	Silent
	Open	Secretive
	Bold	Shy
2. *Agreeableness*	e.g. Good natured	Irritable
	Not jealous	Jealous
	Mild	Headstrong
	Co-operative	Negative
3. *Conscientiousness*	e.g. Fussy	Careless
	Reliable	Undependable
	Scrupulous	Unscrupulous
	Persevering	Quitting
4. *Emotional stability*	e.g. Poised	Nervous
	Calm	Anxious
	Composed	Excitable
	Not hypochondriacal	Hypochondraical
5. *Culture*	e.g. Artistically sensitive	Artistically non-sensitive
	Intellectual	Unreflective
	Polished	Crude
	Imaginative	Direct

various aspects of behaviour lends weight to the view that they represent fundamental attributes of human personality and not merely statistical artefacts.

FREUD AND THE DYNAMICS OF PERSONALITY

Many researchers believe personality is the outcome of processes too dynamic to be captured by any statistical technique. The best known of these dynamic theorists is Freud. his theory of personality represents one of the major intellectual achievements of this century, and we can only hope to provide a glimpse of its complexity, scope and applications.

One of Freud's basic propositions was that most of the material in our minds was housed in what he termed the *subconscious*, a vast repository which for most of the time was inaccessible to us. What was available to individuals in the conscious mind represented just the tip of the iceberg (Figure 3.5). Between the conscious and subconscious mind lies the *preconscious*, similar to what we would usually term the 'back of our minds'. Here information is more readily available than if it were in the subconscious. Appointment times or the chores for a day are examples of the sort of items which might be stored in the preconscious.

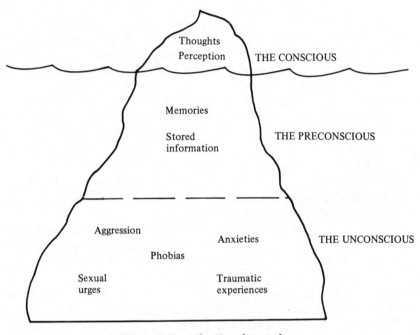

Figure 3.5   *The Freudian iceberg.*

Freud also proposed a tripartite structure for personality, consisting of *id*, *ego* and *superego*. The id is driven by a fixed source of instinctual 'psychic energy' which fuels two innate *drives*: sex and aggression. (It should be noted that what Freud meant when he employed the term 'sex' was very different from its current meaning. Freud meant the term to include all forms of sensual experience and certain 'sublimated' substitutes such as friendship.) The id operates on what Freud termed the *pleasure principle*: it seeks immediate gratification of impulses produced by its two drives.

The social world, however, is not organized in a way that makes this possible; its demands are housed in the ego. Using the *reality principle*, the ego strives to relocate the id's impulses to times or activities in which their gratification is possible. Freud saw the ego as existing only partly in the conscious mind, much of it, like the id, being housed in the subconscious and preconscious.

The superego is also concerned with control of the id and further restricts the range of situations in which the id can be gratified. It differs from the ego in that it incorporates values and morals. Whereas the ego may restrict gratification of the id to a range of feasible situations – for example, the release of aggression in contact sports only – the superego further restricts the range to situations which are morally acceptable as well. This, for example, may mean that boxing is dropped from the set of contact sports in which aggressive impulses are gratified because it is found morally unacceptable, whereas fencing is continued. The superego, also, is not wholly conscious since it is acquired through a long process of internalizing parental and societal values.

Freud's theory of personality set the scene for a struggle between the id and the superego for control of the ego. The superego will contain various negative prescriptions forbidding behaviour of certain sorts, often leaving little room for the gratification of basic desires sought by the id. This conflict, besides absorbing a large proportion of the fixed amount of 'psychic energy' available to the individual, was assumed, if severe, to result in abnormal behaviours such as are found in obsessional and neurotic disorders.

Freud proposed a number of ways in which the subconscious mind develops mechanisms which enable individuals to live with these conflicts. They have the general label of *defence mechanisms*. The principal defence mechanism is *repression* or motivated forgetting. Extreme instances involving a total loss of memory (amnesia) are often traceable to a single traumatic event. Freud believed the memory of the event was not lost but buried with other details of the individual's identity in the subconscious. The material can become available again through associations, dreams and psychotherapy. In less extreme cases of repression, memories of painful past experiences are kept out of consciousness or can lead to forgetting to do things loaded with anxiety, like visiting the dentist.

Another way in which individuals can be protected from their anxieties and conflicts is through *projection*. The defence mechanism achieves its defensive function by projecting the problem on to other people. For example, feelings of inferiority can be projected on to other people assumed to be of lower status. Other defence mechanisms include *reaction formation*, in which the individual develops a trait which is the opposite of the original predisposition (for example, sexual preoccupations are transformed into exaggerated prudishness); *denial*, where an individual struggles not to notice potentially ego-threatening events; *regression*, during which an individual retreats into the behaviour patterns of an earlier stage of development; and *displacement*, where an individual redirects unacceptable impulses.

One of the major determinants of people's personalities, in Freud's view, is what happens in early childhood when the conflicts between the id and the outside world first occur and when methods for dealing with them are first acquired. Freud believed childhood could be divided into *stages* corresponding to the principle sources of physical pleasure for children. The adult personality, he believed, contains residues of the conflicts experienced at each one. If, however, conflicts were experienced which were not satisfactorily resolved at the time, the individual becomes *fixated*, progresses no further and displays the cluster of traits associated with that stage.

Since the mouth is the primary source of satisfaction of the very young infant's bodily needs, the infant begins life in the *oral* stage. The infant is also assumed to derive pleasant physical stimulation from sucking. Freud suggested that oral fixation stems from too much or too little oral gratification. Too much gratification produces the oral-optimistic character, characterized by dependent and trusting attitudes. Too little gratification creates the oral-pessimistic personality in which the individual is sarcastic, caustic or even sadistic.

Freud suggested that at about 2 years old, as control of the muscles employed in elimination is acquired, the focus of pleasure shift to the anus, since pleasant sensations can now be derived from the expulsion or retention of faeces. He therefore termed this the *anal* stage. It is at this point that the outside world begins to oppose the id. The conflict for the child is between parental authority, in the form of toilet training, and gratification of the desire to retain or eliminate the faeces. Fixation here occurs through strict or too weak toilet training. Toilet training that is too severe produces the anal or obsessional personality in which the individual is excessively neat, pedantic, orderly and controlled. There is some statistical research supporting the notion of the obsessional personality (Kline, 1983), though these researchers would not necessarily agree with Freudians about the way it develops. Conversely, where toilet training has been too weak the child may become untidy and sloppy in adult life.

At about the age of 4, children enter what Freud termed the *phallic stage*, as he believed the child's sensual experiences were essentially penetrative and thus masculine in character. Freud suggested that in this stage, to avoid the guilt associated with the experience of attraction towards the parent of the opposite sex, the child begins to identify with the parent of the same sex. During the *latency* period, which begins at about the age of 5 and ends at puberty, the id appears to be relatively quiescent. Finally at puberty we enter the *genital stage* where we leave behind the self-centredness of childhood and begin to seek pleasure through satisfactory sexual relationships.

Freud's analysis of personality and behaviour has attracted a great deal of criticism. People in Freud's time, during the culturally restrictive Victorian era, found the explanation of behaviour in terms of sexuality, particularly infant sexuality, very difficult to accept. More recently, the theory has been dismissed as unscientific. One view is that for a theory to be considered scientific it must generate testable propositions so that is can be in principle be disproved. The number of non-observable concepts in Freudian theory and the difficulty of generating specific testable predictions for it has meant that many psychologists, especially those who advocate factor-analysis methods, consider the theory worthless (e.g. Eysenck, 1985). Despite these problems, many people have continued to use and develop the Freudian theoretical framework, believing it to be a powerful tool for the exploration of human personality.

PERSONALITY DIMENSION AND SOCIAL LEARNING

Locus of control

One problem with Freud's analysis of personality development which many of those who are currently developing the theory have sought to rectify is his neglect of the effects of interacting with the social world. Many personality theorists believe that the social learning that occurs when interacting with siblings, peers, parents and teacher produces cognitive changes in individuals which are sufficiently enduring to be considered as stable personality traits. Two traits identified by social learning theorists have been found to be particularly useful in predicting behaviour in a variety of contexts.

Firstly, *internal vs external locus of control* represents the extent to which people have built up the generalized expectation that they can exercise control over their environments. If our experience of the world teaches us that we can influence events, we tend to acquire an internal locus of control. If, however, the environment seems to be largely beyond our control we develop an external locus of control (Rotter, 1966). An extreme example of this type of learning would be if a child experiences the death of a parent at an age when he or she cannot understand why this should happen. The child may therefore come to believe that he or she has very little control over events. A great deal of research suggests that the locus of control we develop has important implications for behaviour in later life. For example, Brown and Harris (1978) found that depressives were far more likely to have lost a parent before the age of 5 than non-depressives. In occupational settings, research has found that internals tend to achieve higher status and incomes than externals, who in turn are more likely to feel that their workload is high and their working conditions are poor. Because internals tend to believe that they have control over the outcomes they experience, they believe that there is a connection between their performance at work and their reward level, and thus they are more easily motivated than internals, who feel there is less connection between effort and outcome.

Because locus of control is produced by people's experience of the world, it is not a completely unchanging aspect of personality. Significant changes in the control people can exercise over their environment may produce changes in their locus of control. At work, for example, experiencing participative decision-making procedures may cause a shift towards an internal locus of control in employees (Frese, 1982).

McClelland and need for achievement
Secondly, differences in social learning were also seen as the explanation of variation in David McClelland's dimension, the *need for achievement* (N-ach). A considerable amount of research carried out by McClelland suggests that the learning that fixes an individual's portion on this dimension occurs early on in life and so can be considered as a relatively stable feature of personality. Child-rearing practices and the father's occupation were seen as combining to influence the child's level of achievement motivation. Families producing high N-ach children tended to stress self-control, high standards, and individual initiative and independence, whereas low N-ach children came from families which emphasizes compliance, dependence, a collective orientation and getting on with others.

One of the most interesting aspects of McClelland's work was his attempt to show that the general level of achievement in individuals was linked with economic and technological growth in society as a whole. Children who have grown up in cultures and families that stressed achievement are more likely to engage in entrepreneurial activity in adult life. In *The Achieving Society* (1961), McClelland put forward his well-known hypothesis that increases in achievement motivation spread throughout a society precede periods of economic and technological innovation. One notable form of evidence for this was to derive measures of achievement imagery in children's books in different cultures at different times. He found that the amount of achievement imagery predicted economic activity in the society a generation later.

Cassidy and Lynn (1989) have identified seven factors which go to make up McClelland achievement motivation. Table 3.2 indicates the factors and items used by Cassidy and Lynn to assess them.

Many researchers have found McClelland's concepts useful in exploring other achievement-related issues such as women's achievement. This research typically uses a projective test known as the

Table 3.2 *An example of an N-ach scale adapted from Cassidy and Lynn (1989).*

FACTOR	EXAMPLE ITEM	YES	NO
Work ethic	I like to work hard	Y	N
	I get bored if I don't have something to do	Y	N
Acquisitiveness	It is important for me to make lots of money	Y	N
	The most important thing about a job is the pay	Y	N
Dominance	I think I would enjoy having authority over other people	Y	N
	I think I am usually a leader in my group	Y	N
Excellence	I hate to see bad workmanship	Y	N
	There is satisfaction in a job well done	Y	N
Competitiveness	It annoys me when other people perform better than I do	Y	N
	It is important for me to perform better than others on a job	Y	N
Status aspiration	I like to be admired for my achievements	Y	N
	I like to have people come to me for advice	Y	N
Mastery	I prefer to work in situations that require a high level of skill	Y	N
	If I'm not good at something I would rather keep struggling to master it than move on to something I may be good at	Y	N

Award yourself two marks each time you circled a yes, then total your score. People on average will score about sixteen. If you have scored more than twenty, your N-ach is high. If you have a score of less than twelve, your N-ach appear to be low. However, because of the small number of items on this scale results should be treated with considerable caution.

Thematic Apperception Test, which requires subjects to write a story about an ambiguous figure, thus prompting them to project their own personalities on to the image in order to provide it with meaning. The story is then analysed and scored for the degree to which achievement imagery is present. For men, early research found that this measure of achievement motivation predicted achievement behaviour reasonably well. For women, however, the results were more complex, inconsistent and puzzling. There was often no correlation between the achievement imagery a woman used on the test and her achievement behaviour. One intriguing explanation was that women who do want to achieve also acquire through social learning a fear of success (Horner, 1972). This conflict between need for achievement and fear of success creates tension, anxiety and stress in women whose need for achievement is high. This stress will only be reduced by radical changes in the social learning that occurs in females during childhood and adolescence.

PERSONOLOGY

Much recent interest has centered on the work of Theodore Millon, an American clinical psychologist. Millon (1990), like Eysenck, believes there is much to be gained from building bridges with the physical and biological sciences. Unlike Eysenck, he casts his net much wider to include not only psychology but also evolutionary theory, chemistry, population biology, ecology and ethology. Additionally, from the psychological sciences he borrows from psychoanalysis and social learning theory. His theory is thus an impressive synthesis of existing sources. The evolution of our species – basic adaptive and survival mechanisms which have developed personality at the most fundamental level – can be considered across three broad dimensions:

> Active vs. Passive
> Pleasure vs. Pain
> Self vs. Others

These relate to whether an individual takes the initiative as opposed to reacting to events, whether he or she is motivated towards pleasure or pain, and whether the self or others are seen as the main source of social reward. An individual's position on each of these dimensions is seen as a function of his or her biology and coping strategies acquired thorough social learning. Combinations of these dimensions produce the nine different personality types outlined in Table 3.3.

Table 3.3 *Millon's nine personality types*

1. Detached Personalities (Schizoid or Avoidant)
The hallmark of detached personalities is lack of warmth. They appear to others as cold, aloof, humourless and lacking in empathy. They have few friends and are distant even with relations. The roots of this may be early childhood experiences such as loss, rejection or critical parenting. The extremes of this personality style are termed schizoid or avoidant.

2. Dependent Personalities
Lacking in self-confidence, dependent types see themselves as weak and inadequate. At work their passivity means they want others to assume responsibility for them. They need others around them to make things happen and will thus absorb a good deal of a supervisor's time. The psychological roots of this style are either overprotection or frustrated dependency needs during childhood.

3. Histrionic Personalities
This personality style is characterized by a desperate need to attract attention. Thus histrionics can be flirtatious, seductive, approval-seeking and self-dramatizing. For these reasons they tend to change their 'fronts' to maintain others' interest. Histrionics pay little attention to detail and so tend to lack organization and judgement. The origins of this appear to be an inability to capture the attention of parents as a child.

4. Narcissistic Personalities
Superficially, narcissists can appear extremely charming or even charismatic. However, a longer acquaintance changes this perception to one of arrogance, egotism and lack of consideration for others. Narcissists are capable of ruthlessly exploiting others for their own ends while managing somehow to justify their behaviour to themselves. They are preoccupied with their own success or brilliance but also envious of others. When criticized they react with rage or humiliation. Above all, narcissists feel they are exceptions. The psychological roots are parents who have not created a secure sense of self-worth in the child. This may occur, for example, if the child has been 'loved' because he or she possesses a particular talent or quality.

5. Aggressive (Sadistic) Personalities
Aggressive personalities take pleasure in dominating, humiliating and possibly even brutalizing others. They believe themselves to be unsentimental, competitive and tough-minded. They may be able to mask their personality at work, but may give themselves away through vindictively persecuting another employee. Their dominance makes them quite rebellious employees. However, their competitiveness and brutality may well be rewarded through promotion. The psychological basis of this style is the aggressive belief that attack is the best form of defence.

6. Passive-Aggressive Personalities
The hallmark of these personalities both occupationally and socially is resistance to demands for performance. They seem to be unable to decide

between responding actively or passively towards others. Thus, they passively accept a request, for example, from a spouse or manager and then express their resistances by not accomplishing the task. In personal relationships this means passive-aggressives are seen as unpredictable. At work, when their defiance is manifested in forgetfulness, inefficiency, lack of attention to detail or the occasional outburst, they underachieve and may well be seen as a problem. The psychological basis for this behaviour is thought to be conflicting and confusing parental behaviour. Passive-aggressives never really learn as children what behaviour works, and in adult life they end up with a pessimistic negative feeling that nothing ever really works for them as adults either.

7. Controlling Personalities (Obsessive-Compulsive)

The basis of this personality is the need for control. Controlling types are happiest operating systems where the performance requirements are clear and the method of achieving these requirements is known. They want their world to be orderly and predictable and thus tend to be rigid and inflexible. They place a very high value on authority and will be highly deferential in the presence of a superior but contemptuous and hostile towards subordinates. Controlling types tend to be hard-working perfectionists often to the point where they afford themselves very little opportunity for recreation. Their conformity and conscientiousness are thought to be the result of reaction formation against oppositional, rebellious and self-orientated feelings. They resolve the conflict between their basic hostility towards others and the fear of punishment by developing the opposite traits of conformity and passivity.

8. Paranoid Personalities

A high sensitivity to pain is thought to be the psychological basis for the paranoid personality. Paranoids are overly concerned with potential threats to their self-esteem. This often means they misread other people's behaviour, construing it as critical or rejecting. Their favourite defence is projection, blaming others for their own faults, which makes them overly hostile and contemptuous towards others. They are difficult to live or work with. Their great sensitivity puts them constantly on the defensive and makes it difficult for them to relax. The origin of this degree of sensitivity may lie in having had extremely intrusive parents, making it difficult for the child to establish any degree of autonomy.

9. Masochistic Personalities (self-defeating)

In common usage masochism has a sexual connotation. In Millon's typology the term has a much broader meaning. The masochistic individual prefers pain to pleasure. This leads to self-denial, self-blaming and self-sacrificing behaviour. By demonstrating their worst characteristics, masochists encourage others to take advantage of them. When others do take advantage, masochists respond with anger followed by guilt. There has been considerable speculation about the origins of this personality. Social learning theory suggests masochists have internalized the 'badness' they used as a child to get a reaction from their parents. Another possibility is some anomaly in the wiring of the cortex.

The nine types described in Table 3.3 can be considered to be on a continuum and are found in varying degrees throughout the population. It is also possible for an individual to be a 'hybrid', demonstrating aspects of more than one personality style: for example, narcissism with control creates a mixture which, organizationally, can be very successful. Millon has developed a test designed to assess these characteristics in the 'normal' population (Psychological Corporation, 1993). The implication of each type for managerial effectiveness are described later in the chapter.

Intelligence

CONCEPTIONS OF INTELLIGENCE

The concept of intelligence has probably attracted more public attention and aroused more controversy than any other in the field of individual differences. This is partly because it has affected more people's lives than any other psychological construct. The old tripartite educational system of grammar, secondary and technical schools formed the basis of public education in the period between 1944 and 1971; and this was founded on the assumption that the ability of a child to benefit from a grammar school education could be predicted at the age of 11 from his or her score in an intelligence test. Similarly, many large organizations believe an individual's ability to perform in professional or administrative roles can to an extent be predicted from an intelligence test score. Controversy has particularly surrounded the use of test scores to support arguments about the heritability of intelligence and its distribution in different racial groups.

While the use and abuse of intelligence tests and test data aroused a level of concern that spread to the general public, another important debate was taking place between academics about what the term itself actually meant. Sternberg (1985) has provided a useful classification of conceptions of intelligence. He suggested the major distinction is between *explicit* and *implicit* theories. The former are 'based on data collected from people performing tasks presumed to measure intelligent functioning'; whereas implicit theories are based on intuitive assumptions about the nature of intelligence.

Explicit theories can be based either on dimensions of intellectual abilities that have emerged from factor analysis, such as verbal comprehension or spatial reasoning, or on assumptions about the cognitive processes that contribute to intelligent functioning. The former differ in the number of factors they propose, ranging from one (Spearman, 1927) to one hundred and fifty (Guildford, 1982). The latter differs in the level of cognitive processing that they use to explain intelligence. Cognitive processes assumed to represent the basis of intelligent functioning have included:

1. The *pure speed* of an individual's information-processing measured by simple reaction time experiments.
2. *Choice speed*, an individual's ability to make a quick choice between two simple stimuli measured by choice reaction time experiments.
3. *Speed of lexical access*, the time taken by an individual to retrieve information from long-term memory.
4. *Speed of reasoning processes*, an individual's speed at higher-order information-processing, such as completing a series of numbers.

Thus, both types of explicit theory develop tests which are assumed to isolate and provide measures of the important aspects of intelligence. Implicit theories have included:

1. The power to generate accurate responses.
2. The ability to use abstract thinking.
3. The ability to adjust to the environment.
4. The ability to adapt to new situations.
5. The capacity for knowledge and knowledge possessed.
6. The capacity to learn or to profit by experience.

Because psychologists are mainly interested in measuring intelligence, they have preferred to use the more quantifiable explicit theories. Thus, although in this section we will describe only explicit theories, we should stress that implicit theories dominate the assessment of intelligence in everyday life – during the conversations and interviews we have at work, at college or in informal social situations it is implicit theories that we use to make inferences about other people's intelligence.

MEASUREMENT OF EXPLICIT INTELLIGENCE FACTORS

Of the explicit theories, those based on factor-analytic techniques have been highly influential in the field of intelligence research. Unlike personality which, as we have seen, can be broken down into a number of factors, there is a considerable amount of agreement that a large proportion of the variance in intelligence scores can be accounted by a a single, large factor: G. This general factor permeates all our intellectual activity, determining to a large extent how well we do on spatial, verbal, numerical, memory and other types of test. G seems to account for just over half the observed differences in test scores in a group (Vernon, 1971).

The belief in a general intelligence factor can be traced back to the work of Spearman (1904). He used a technique of factor analysis similar to that used by Eysenck in personality research, which extracts factors independent of each other. G was produced by the correlations of scores on all ability tests. Individual who did well on one type of test tended to do well on all the others. There was, however, a certain amount of variance specific to each test. So, for example, an individual's score on a vocabulary test was determined firstly by his or her level of G and secondly by his or her standing on a factor specific to that test.

As we have already seen, it is possible to use factor analysis to provide a larger number of less independent factors. Some researchers have therefore preferred to break G up into a number of more specific abilities. Thurstone (1938), for example, described what he termed seven *primary abilities*:

1. Spatial ability.
2. Verbal reasoning.
3. Perceptual speed.
4. Numerical ability.
5. Memory.
6. Verbal fluency.
7. Inductive reasoning.

Though tests devised to measure individuals on each of these factors will provide more specific information about their abilities, test scores on each will tend to be inter-correlated. Vernon (1971) proposed that by deriving different types of factorial solution from test data, a hierarchical model of intellect can be constructed which identified four levels of ability: G; major group factors (verbal–educational ability and practical–mechanical ability); minor group factors; and specific factors (Figure 3.6).

In a sense, then, as far as explicit theories are concerned, the question of how best to describe the structure of intellect is a technical question: what is the most compelling factorial solution to a set of data? With the availability of cheap computational facilities it has become easier to explore the various methods of factor analysis and so some agreement has recently developed about what requirements a factorial solution to test data should meet (Barret and Kline, 1980). Applying these criteria had produced a refinement in the notion of G: fluid ability, Gf, and crystallized ability, Gc. Essentially, the distinction represents the difference between an individual's reasoning *processes* (Gf) and the outcomes or *products* of these processes (Gc). Thus, tests which measure an individual's ability to solve problems or respond

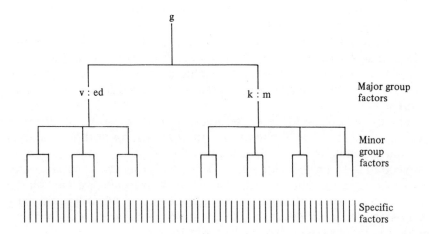

Figure 3.6 *Vernon's model of the structure of human abilities.* From Vernon (1971).

to novelty, tests of spatial reasoning for example, provide measures of Gf, whereas tests which measure knowledge acquisition, tests of vocabulary for example, provide measures of Gc. Logically, then, Gf is the precursor to Gc, and since performance on tests of Gc will also have some reasoning component, measures of Gc and Gf tend to be somewhat inter-correlated.

The Gf and Gc constructs have become the factors which many contemporary psychometricians believe account for a large proportion of the variance in scores on any aptitude or attainment test (Kline, 1986).

Personality and intelligence in the workplace

If we turn now to look at the application of the above concepts of intelligence and personality in the work setting, an understanding beyond the 'common-sense' one of the nature and causes of individual differences is important in the workplace in at least two ways. First, the management of people is likely to be more skilful if managers are better equipped to comprehend and predict the behaviour of others. Secondly, it can be used to make better decisions about people's suitability for posts.

PERSONALITY

Freudian concepts, for example, can help managers and employees to consider what may be occurring beneath the surface of their own and others' behaviour. Organizations are designed and managed on

81

the assumption that people act rationally. Freud's view, as we have seen, suggested that people's behaviour often falls short of this ideal. One of the ways this can occur is through the operation of defence mechanisms, which protect individuals from threats to their self-esteem. This means that defensive behaviour can be triggered by an event or by other people who threaten an individual's sense of self-worth.

The increased threat to our self-esteem at work caused by pressure for performance, fear of failure and the presence of authority figures means we may utilize the most powerful of defence mechanisms – projection – to protect our egos. This enables us to externalize any difficulties we may be having at work. For example, we can blame poor supervision or unhelpful colleagues rather than accept the part personal inadequacies have played. By projection we can off load unacceptable feelings of inferiority and inadequacy.

Two features of projection increase the difficulties of individuals using this defence mechanism. First, if we project difficulties onto other staff we will not only blame them for our problems but also tend to treat them with contempt or even hostility. This obviously may cause a deterioration in relationships. Secondly, projection makes it very difficult for individuals to perceive that their own inadequacies have contributed to their current problems. This means people may resent and ignore advice or counselling from colleagues or superiors.

Ego strength is important in determining an individual's ability to cope with the daily wear and tear of working life. Individuals with high ego strength are able to cope with the frustrations and obstacles which confront them at work without losing their tempers or giving up. Karson and O'Dell (1976) liken individuals with low ego strength to tyres with little tread – a 'blow out' at some stage is inevitable, for example when small problems assume a significance out of all proportion to the threat they actually pose.

The workplace is also where we are likely to meet higher levels of formal authority than were experienced at school or college. Any conflicts people have had with previous authority figures, such as teachers or parents, are likely to be transferred to the workplace if they were not resolved at the time. So according to Freud we can unknowingly transfer our feelings towards earlier authority figures to our current managers and supervisors. Additionally, Freud believed that people are largely unaware of the intensity and ambivalence that may be locked up in their feelings towards authority figures. When transference occurs, individuals may cope with these feelings by 'acting out'. This means that a relatively minor event in adult life can cause a quite disproportionate amount of either hostility or affection to be displayed or experienced in the presence of an authority figure. Doctors and psychiatrists are regularly faced with patients experiencing inappropriate feelings towards them through transference. Managers ought similarly to be aware of this possibility.

Both of the social learning variables we described earlier offer interesting insights into behaviour in the workplace. David McClelland claimed that by adding two further personality dimensions, the need for power (N-power) and the need for affiliation (N-aff), he would be able to identify the relative importance for each variable to high job performance in particular types of management (McClelland and Burnham, 1976). People who are high in N-ach, for example, set themselves very high standards of personal performance. A surprising consequence of this is that although they make very good entrepreneurs, they do not make particularly good managers. This is because they feel they are the most competent person to do a job and tend not to delegate as often as they should. In addition, McClelland demonstrated that effective managers are higher in N-power than N-aff (McClelland and Boyatzis, 1982). In short, they enjoy the exercise of power more than they enjoy being liked by colleagues and subordinates. However, he found that managers had also to possess a considerable amount of self-control to be effective. Without self-control a high need for power channels energy into attaining personal rather than organizational goals. For example, a manager may suppress information which indicates the line of action he or she has chosen is incorrect (Fodor and Smith, 1982).

There is a good deal of evidence to suggest that locus of control is related to a wide range of organizational variables: occupational level; income; perception of job characteristics; perceived autonomy; perception of working conditions; job satisfaction; occupational advancement; and performance (Mitchell et al., 1975; Kimmons and Greenhaus, 1976; Evans, 1973). In terms of these variables this research indicated that organizations are best staffed by internals. They tend to perceive their workload as manageable and so tend to experience less stress. Furthermore, they perceive a connection between their effort and their performance, and so are more easily motivated and more satisfied with their jobs. This appears to be particularly important in sales occupations. The belief that rewards are contingent on one's own performance in internals motivates prospecting and insulates the salesperson from rejection.

As we saw, an individual's locus of control, though believed to be stable enough to be considered as an aspect of personality, is not completely fixed. This means that if organizations allow people more control over their work, job satisfaction and motivation are likely to be increased and stress reduced. As we shall see later, one theory of leadership (path goal theory) and a theory of motivation (VIE) focus on increasing an individual's perceptions of control. Similarly, an important approach in designing work to increase motivation and job satisfaction involves using groups, which are afforded a greater degree of autonomy over the way work is performed.

The relationship between Millon's typology and managerial effectiveness has been extensively researched by Kets de Vries (1989). He has found many of the self-destructive tendencies in each of Millon's personality styles can ultimately undermine a manager's ability to cope with the psychological forces present in the leader–follower relationship. These forces will be discussed more fully in Chapter 8. Table 3.4 summarizes the managerial or leadership potential of each personality style.

Table 3.4 *Relationship between Millon's personality typology and leadership potential.*

STYLE	LEADERSHIP POTENTIAL	FOLLOWERSHIP POTENTIAL
Narcissistic	very high	low
Aggressive	high	low
Paranoid	high	medium
Histrionic	medium	high
Detached	medium	medium
Controlling	high	high
Passive-aggressive	low	high
Dependent	very low	high
Masochistic	very low	high

Eysenck, as we have seen, suggested an individual's standing on the introversion–extraversion dimension reflected how 'stimulus-hungry' he or she is. The significance of this for workplace behaviour is that individuals differ in the sort of work environment they are constitutionally best equipped for. Introverts appear to be able to cope with jobs which provide low levels of stimulation. On vigilance tasks, where attention has to be focused for long periods of time on a single stimulus source, a radar screen for example, most people are subject to a *performance decrement*. As we pointed out earlier, signals are missed and signals which did not occur are reported. Introverts, however, display far less deterioration over time in performance on vigilance tasks. Conversely, extroverts tend to prefer and be better at jobs where the work is complex and varied (Sterns *et al.*, 1983). Knowing an individual's position on this dimension can therefore help predict what kind of task he or she will prefer and perform well.

The neuroticism-instability dimension essentially indicates an individual's emotional stability. Therefore jobs like selling, which routinely involve a good deal of rejection, may not be suitable for people scoring high on the N scale. Rejection would reinforce the low opinion that high scorers tend to have of themselves and could ultimately lead to depression.

INTELLIGENCE

Because occupational status is a fundamental form of achievement in any industrial society, and the basis of most other aspects of consumption, we might assume that such status is determined by an individual's intellectual capacity. But access to professional and managerial occupations largely occurs through achievements in higher education. This means we first need to consider the relative importance of intelligence in gaining access to higher education. In fact, social class and the type of school an individual attends are better predictors of his or her chances of going on to higher education than intelligence (Halsey *et al.*, 1980). The relationship between intelligence and occupational status, therefore, is not a simple or direct one.

What intelligence does seem to do is set a threshold for entry into occupations which makes access to higher-status jobs difficult for people with low scores. Large-scale research on army recruits in the Second World War found that the median IQ scores increased and the range of scores decreased with increasing occupational status. Thus, the median score for accountants was 128 with a range from 94 to 154 while the median score for labourers was 88 with a range of scores from 46 to 145 (Harrell and Harrell, 1945). Some researchers have argued than even this relationship can be questioned. They argue that this simply reflects the way the concept of intelligence has been operationalized. Psychologists, they argue, have wittingly or unwittingly developed intelligence tests to measure an individual's ability to function in high-status jobs. In other words, part of what has come to be meant by intelligence is the likelihood that an individual can function at certain levels in the occupational structure.

If there does not seem to be a simple association between measures of occupational intelligence and status, what relationship does IQ have with actual performance in a job? The average correlation between test scores and some measure of job performance appears to be about .5 (Smith *et al.*, 1990). However, the relationship between the two seems to vary according to whether the job is professional, intermediate (e.g. clerical) or routine. Performance in professional jobs appears to have little to do with intelligence test scores. As we suggested earlier, intelligence seems merely to set a minimum level below which entry into an occupation is difficult. Above this level, however, performance in a job is unrelated to intelligence. Fielder and Leister (1977a) have argued that effectiveness is determined not only by a manager's intellectual capacity but by a number of other personal attributes and aspects of the work environment. They suggested that poor relationships between manager and staff, a manager's lack of experience and motivation, and his or her inability to cope with uncertainty all reduced the strength of the relationship between intelligence and effectiveness. This implies, for example, that the knowledge which comes with experience has to be present before the intellectual ability to manipulate information can be used to predict a manager's effectiveness. Fielder and Leister (1977b) have supported this by demonstrating that the relationship between IQ and managerial effectiveness dropped from .36 with experienced managers to .15 with inexperienced ones.

In intermediate occupations, where there is a wider range of intelligence than in professional and managerial jobs, a fairly strong relationship between test scores and measures of job performance has been observed. In routine jobs, however, there again appears to be little relationship between the two, presumably because the reduced variety and autonomy and increased automation of routine work leaves little opportunity for intelligence to affect the level of performance. However, despite a good deal of research to suggest that IQ is not a powerful predictor of job performance, there remains a widespread belief among managers that intelligence is directly related to high and low achievement in the workplace, which ensures that IQ tests continue to be included in selection procedures for a wide range of occupations.

Further reading

Anderson L. (1991) *A Personality Theory: An Inquiry into Realities and Fiction of the Human Psyche.* London: Vantage Press.

Burkitt, I. (1991) *Social Selves: Theories of the Social Formation of Personality.* London: Sage.

Child, D. (1990) *The Essentials of Factor Analysis.* London: Cassell.

Kets de Vries, M.F.R. (1988) *Unstable at the Top.* Chichester: Wiley.

Kline, P. (1990) *Intelligence: The Psychometric View.* London: Routledge.

Millon, T. (1990) *Toward a New Personology: an Evolutionary Model.* Chichester: Wiley.

Pervin, L.A. (1989) *Personality: Theory and Research.* (5th edn). Chichester: Wiley.

Richardson, K. (1991) *Understanding Intelligence.* Milton Keynes: Open University Press.

Sternberg R.J. (1990) *Metaphors of Mind: Conceptions of the Nature of Intelligence.* Cambridge: Cambridge University Press.

Storr, A. (1992) *The Integrity of the Personality.*

4

Assessing Individual Differences

The assumption that an individual's job performance is underpinned by his or her traits and abilities has long been the cornerstone of personnel selection (Sparrow, 1989). And as the staffing requirements of modern organizations become increasingly complex, the need for more careful consideration of differences between individuals becomes more pressing. The penalties for failing to take proper account of individual differences are high. For the individual, the experience of being unable to cope with a set of job demands will be a bruising one and can lead to a massive loss of self-confidence. For the organization, the immediate costs will be poor performance and staff wastage. In the longer run, failure to identify and utilize human potential is ultimately a competitor's gain.

Taking decisions about the suitability of applicants for a post represents the end point in a *selection process*. The stages in this process are outlined in Figure 4.1.

Job profiling instruments such as the PAQ, Position analysis Questionnaire (McCormick *et al.*, 1969), or the CMQ, Common Metric Questionnaire (Harvey, 1991), provide objective, systematic methods of analysing the performance requirements of jobs. The PAQ, for example, examines job demands across five broad areas.

1. *Information input*. Where and how does the employee get the information used in performing the job?
2. *Mental processes*. What reasoning and information-processing is necessary?
3. *Work output*. What physical actions occur during task performance?
4. *Relationship with others*. What is the nature of any social interaction with other people?
5. *Job context*. What physical and social contexts are present (noise, danger, dirt, etc.)?

In the United States the concern with rigorous job profiling techniques has been driven by the *Uniform Guidelines on Employee Selection Procedures* (EEOCC, 1978). Subjective judgements about job demands

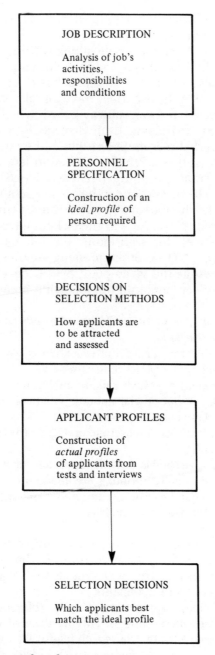

Figure 4.1 *Stages in the selection process.*

and the abilities and traits required for task performance can become the basis for litigation.

'Defensible' job and person specifications will increasingly become a requirement in the UK. Already some major employers have found themselves defending selection decisions based on dubious person specifications. In 1991 British Rail, for example, faced a claim for compensation from seven Asian railway guards who had been rejected when they applied to become train drivers. Part of the selection procedure was a verbal reasoning test which the guards claimed had discriminated against them. British Rail had in fact used the PAQ to profile the job. Verbal reasoning had been identified as the least important ability. The decision nonetheless to use a verbal reasoning test when it was clearly unrelated to job demands enabled the guards to establish discrimination and win their claim for compensation.

A classic framework for translating the job descriptions which emerge from PAQ, CMQ or other profiling methods into a person description is known as the seven-point plan (Rodger, 1952), which divides individual differences into the following areas:

1. *Physical make-up.* Are there are defects of health or physique that are occupationally relevant?
2. *Attainments.* What type or level of education is required? What occupational training and experience is necessary?
3. *General intelligence.* How much general intelligence is required?
4. *Specific aptitudes.* What special aptitudes such as mechanical, mathematical or verbal ability are necessary?
5. *Interests.* What interests, intellectual, practical, artistic, social or physical, are required?
6. *Disposition.* How acceptable does the applicant for a job need to be to others? What personality attributes are important to job performance?
7. *Circumstances.* What domestic circumstances are relevant: for example, does the applicant need to be mobile?

By using the seven-point plan, or other similar frameworks, it is possible to construct a fairly clear picture of what sort of person is required to fill a given job. The next stage is to decide what methods are to be used in assessing applicants.

These include using application forms, references, interviews, biodata, tests or assessment centres. Having decided what method or mix of methods is appropriate, the search begins for individuals whose *actual profiles* match or come nearest to the ideal profiles. Here we will examine the power of each of these major assessment techniques to predict job performance.

Interviews

Though the most widely used method in the selection process, the interview is considered by many to be of little use in predicting actual performance in a job (e.g. Smith *et al.*, 1989). Critics of its use claim it is subject to the same problems which reduce our capacity to perceive and judge others accurately in all situations, namely:

1. *Impression formation.* We tend to make judgements about others very quickly and tend to ignore information which later contradicts our first impression.
2. *Halo effect.* If we perceive certain key traits, we tend to judge all other aspects of the individual according to whether we have judged the person favourably or unfavourably on these traits.
3. *Stereotypes.* Ready-made generalizations about members of social categories can distort judgements about individuals.
4. *Limited capacity.* The number of evaluative categories we use when judging others tends to be very limited.
5. *Idiosyncrasy.* The categories we use may reflect our own interests and attitudes.

Ross and Nisbett (1991) suggest the general effect of these person perception problems is to reduce our 'conservatism' and 'charity'. In other words, we seem to be willing to ascribe characteristics to individuals (conscientious, sociable, intelligent, etc.) on the basis of very little evidence. We rarely withhold judgement. Moreover, the judgements are often quite negative. They offer some interesting insights into why we are prone to such errors. They argue that our forebears spent their working and domestic lives with intimates: siblings, parents and spouses. Ascribing qualities to intimates was reasonable since there were massive behaviour samples to infer traits from. By comparison an interview provides us with a relatively minute behaviour sample. But we are stuck with a trait language which, they claim, is more appropriate for use among intimates.

In addition to these general problems of person perception, the interview faces a number of specific problems which further undermine its usefulness.

First, judgements about a candidate can be affected by the quality of previous candidates. This is termed the *contrast effect*. Thus, for example, a very poor candidate A can mean the assessment of candidate B is artificially inflated.

Secondly, with a large pool of candidates interviewers can wittingly or unwittingly come to view the task as primarily a *rejection procedure*. This means the interviewer searches for reasons to reject a candidate. Negative information about candidates therefore becomes disproportionately weighted. One negative piece of information, such as failing an exam, can wipe out the positive effects of work experience, for example.

Thirdly, the nature of human memory means the first and last candidates will be remembered more vividly. The first candidate benefits from what is termed the *primacy effect*, the last from the *recency effect*.

Fourthly, there is a tendency to avoid probing – asking awkward and sensitive questions. There seems to be a moral obligation to accept an individual's 'front', their definition of themselves (see Chapter 6). To do otherwise seems to break a fundamental 'rule' of social life. This, in practice, means candidates can make claims about themselves during an interview which will not be subject to much critical scrutiny. One of the authors was providing consultancy to a large organization which had recently employed an individual who had claimed at interview he worked two days a week at a local university. When it became clear the individual was not as competent as he had claimed, his curriculum vitae was checked. The local university had never heard of him.

Fifthly, there seem to be two interwoven strands in an interview: information-gathering and rapport building. Many interviews tend to concentrate on the rapport-building at the expense of the information-gathering element. In other words, the social encounter has been warm and friendly but at the end of it very little concrete information is now available that was not already known from the references and application form.

Finally, interviewers tend to delude themselves about their interviewing skills and their ability to assess individuals, and so rarely take into account the above defects.

In reply to these criticisms, advocates of interviewing have defended the method on a number of counts. They point out that it often serves more than just an assessment function. The task of an interviewer can include a public relations function, representing an organization to applicants and in a way helping to attract them. If talented candidates are scarce, this function may even become more important than assessment itself. Supporters of interviewing suggest that it is an effective method of gathering certain types of personal information that would be difficult to acquire from application forms. Also they claim that interviews can be improved by increasing interviewing skills (Taylor and Sniezek, 1984).

Like other social skills, effective interviewing depends on the ability to progress smoothly through the encounter, on sensitivity to cues and on developing a rapport with another person. These in turn are assisted by having an agenda of items that enables the ideal profile to be systematically related to the applicant's written evidence. For instance, one frequently used agenda employs this sequence: technical aspects of current job; human aspects of current job; selected items of previous jobs; education and training; personal and domestic topics; and dealing with applicant's questions about the job.

Progression smoothly through an interview is also assisted by the behaviours outlined in Table 4.1. Behaviours such as summarizing or reflective listening do not occur in ordinary conversation. They are unlikely to appear in an interview unless an individual has realized they are crucial or has been trained to use them. Training programmes are available which enable interviewers to practise these behaviours. Feedback, through audio or audio-visual tapes of practice interviews, is combined with the comments of instructors and other trainees to produce changes in an individual's performance.

More radically, researchers such as Latham *et al.* (1980) and Wright *et al.* (1989) have argued for a completely different style of interview. They claim *structured* or *situational* interviews provide more robust predictors of future job performance. Based on on a thorough job analysis, these interviews use the same job-related questions with all candidates. Responses to questions are evaluated using predetermined standards. Some structured interviews ask questions which require applicants either to think about how they would respond to problematic work situations or to say how they have responded in the past. An applicant could, for example, be asked how he or she would respond to a customer complaint. This type of interview considerably increases the agreement between interviewers about the acceptability of candidates.

Finally, proponents of the traditional interview argue that decisions about the suitability of the interviewee can be improved by taking them in a more systematic manner. One way this can be done is by using a *rating scale* to quantify the degree to which applicants match the ideal profile on each of the areas of the seven-point plan, an example of which is given in Table 4.2. Producing tables like this one considerably clarifies the relative advantages of each candidate. Applicants can be either accepted or rejected on the basis of calculations of a total score or on a selective basis where some attribute is considered or has emerged in studies as more important than others. Decisions made in this way also make the risks of a decision more explicit and can indicate where training for a new recruit is necessary.

Biodata

An abbreviation of biographical data, this technique involves identifying what biological characteristics predict outcomes such as length

Table 4.1 *Key interview behaviours*

BEHAVIOUR	EXAMPLE	COMMENT
Open question	Why did you leave your first job?	Used for opening up an area for discussion
Closed question	You need to give a month's notice in your present job?	Used to clarify details or give an anxious candidate an easy question to reduce his or her nervousness
Advisement	Let's move on to your time at university	Used to guide the thoughts and feelings of the candidate
Reflective listening	So you're saying that you've achieved everything you can in your present company	Used when attempting to capture the thoughts and feelings behind what the candidate has said. Also a powerful method of conveying acceptance. Is possibly the most difficult interviewing skill
Interpretation	You seem to enjoy having to respond quickly to difficulties	Used to communicate the interviewer's perspective on what the candidate has been saying
Process disclosure	I feel you are not being as open as you perhaps could be	Used occasionally by the interviewer to reveal how he or she is reacting to the candidate at that moment, thus giving the candidate a chance to comment on the interviewer's reaction
Biographical disclosure	Yes, that happened to me when I moved down from the North	Used to reduce the asymmetry and formality of the interviewer–candidate relationship
Summarizing	So for the last five minutes you have been telling me . . .	Allows the interviewer to check his or her understanding of what has been said and provides the interviewee with opportunity to alter the interviewer's opinion
Probing	Could we go back to your time with . . .	Enables the interviewer to pursue claims made by the interviewee

of stay in a job and training performance. Biodata questions are then used as part of the application form or as a separate questionnaire. Biodata information ranges from concrete variables, such as length of stay in previous jobs and marital status, through to softer attitudinal areas, such as opinions about education.

Biodata can be as powerful a predictor of behaviour as pencil and paper tests. For example, Drakely *et al.*, (1988) found biodata was as successful as psychometric tests at predicting training performance and better than tests as predicting voluntary withdrawal from training.

Biodata involves a high initial investment by the organization as a study has to be commissioned to identify what, if any, biographical predictors exist. To be sufficiently robust a reasonable sample has to be available. One of the authors has, for example, recently completed a biodata study involving over a thousand employees' application forms. However, once the critical characteristics and their weightings have been identified, the ongoing cost is minimal.

The predictive power of biodata is assumed to arise from past experiences and behaviour shaping future experience and thus behaviour. It is undoubtedly a powerful technique. For example, in the study referred to earlier the biodata formula was able to predict correctly eighty-five times out of a hundred whether an applicant would stay in the company more than two years. Intriguingly, in this study one of the usual predictors of tenure, average length of stay in previous jobs, operated in the opposite direction to what was expected. Usually an individual with short previous tenure repeats this in future posts. Similarly, long previous tenure predicts subsequent lengthy tenure. In our study this did not appear. Long tenure elsewhere predicted a brief spell with this organization. This confirmed the 'gut feeling' of some senior managers that they were losing individuals with a wealth of experience and background.

This example actually indicates one of the problems with biodata. The circumstances which caused those with long track records with other companies to leave (essentially, in this instance, lack of support) would be changed as a result of the biodata study. Thus, the prediction that long previous tenure indicates an unacceptably short stay would probably not hold in a year's time. Generally, biodata cannot be expected to last more than three years.

As well as being volatile it can be seen from this example that biodata tends to be very job and organization specific. What characteristics predict performance or tenure in one job grade probably could not be used to predict these outcomes in others. In practice this means if organizations decide to invest in biodata, each job grade requires a separate study.

However, despite these drawbacks Biodata is one of the most cost-effective selection techniques. With some exceptions, notably the life insurance industry, Biodata is at present underutilized in the U.K.

Table 4.2 *Example of a rating scale using the seven-point plan. Candidates are ranked on a five-point scale where (5) = fully matches the specification, (4) matches very well, (3) matches fairly well, (2) matches in some respects but with important omissions and (1) does not match specification. The candidates were interviewed for the job of home help organizer in a Social Services Department.*

| | CANDIDATES | | |
	A	B	C
Physical make-up			
Essential: Fit, active, 25–40, work well under stress	4	5	3
Desirable: 28–35, fluent speech	Health needs examining		Poor appearance
Attainments			
Essential: Good level of general education	5	5	5
Desirable: Home Help Organizer Diploma/Certificate in Social Services			
General intelligence			
Essential: Think quickly and clearly	5	5	3
Desirable: Ability to relate to and communicate effectively orally and in writing with a wide range of people			Poor communication skills
Special aptitudes			
Essential: Ability to plan and deliver instructional sessions	5	4	2
Respond sensitively to people and situations			Doubt about ability to plan
Desirable: Quickly establish rapport and relationship with clients			
Ability to distinguish fact from opinion and fantasy			
Interests			
Essential: Social welfare and the needs of the elderly, handicapped and mentally ill	5	3 Little empathy for handicapped	1 Too concerned about salary

| | | CANDIDATES | | |
		A	B	C
Contra-indication	Instrumental attitude			
Disposition				
Essential:	Sympathetic, ability to form good relationships with manual staff and clients	5	3 Little ability to lead	5
Desirable:	Ability to cope with crises			
Circumstances				
Essential:	Driving licence and car owner	5	3	1
Desirable:	Reside locally		Lives 25 miles from district	No car
TOTAL		34	28	20

Tests

Critics of the interview are also usually advocates of the psychometric test. The British Psychological Society (1981) defined a psychometric test as 'an instrument for the quantitative assessment of some psychological attribute or attributes of an individual'. The key words here are 'quantitative' and 'attribute'. The type of number provided by tests is somewhat different to the numbers seen, for example, in Table 4.2.

Not all numbers have the same information value. The most basic form of number is the *nominal* number, where values allocate individuals to categories: for example, 1=Full driving licence; 2=Provisional licence. At the next level up we have *ordinal* numbers. Here, as in Table 4.2, the numbers indicate a ranking. Interviewers would normally have access only to nominal or ordinal data on candidates: for example, an interviewer could intuitively rank Camilla as a brighter applicant than Rebecca. But it is only at the next level up, the *interval* level, that we could say by *how much* Camilla differs from Rebecca. Good psychometric tests provide interval-level data. Thus the primary value of a psychometric test is to *raise the status of the information available to an interviewer*.

Psychometric tests also have to provide information about psychological attributes. Thus, for example, an applicant's performance in a mechanical reasoning test should not be affected by how much physics teaching he or she has been exposed to. If the test is contaminated by educational experience it measures physics knowledge rather than the more pervasive and fundamental psychological attribute, mechanical reasoning.

Tests commonly used in selection include the following:

1. *Dexterity tests.* For employees whose work involves manual skills such as soldering, wiring or fitting, tests of fine or gross eye–hand co-ordination such as the Crawford Small Parts Dexterity Test and the Bennet Hand Tool Dexterity Test (The Psychological Corporation) provide interval-level data about the relative level of an applicant's dexterity.

2. *Aptitude tests.* Verbal, numerical, spatial and mechanical tests provide an indication of how well applicants will cope with jobs or training which involve these aptitudes. A typical aptitude test profile is presented in Figure 4.2.

3. *General ability tests.* Historically, as was discussed in Chapter 3, a great deal of emphasis has been placed on tests of general ability. The assumption that intelligence is one 'thing' has meant that very often one score has sufficed as an indication of an individual's ability. More appropriately nowadays, general ability tests are used to indicate how well applicants will 'learn the ropes', 'grasp essentials' and 'think on their feet'.

4. *Critical thinking tests.* Tests such as the GMA-V (NFER-Nelson, 1985) and the VA3 (Saville and Holdsworth, 1980) have their origins in the Watson Glaser Critical Thinking Appraisal (Psychological corporation, 1990), originally published in 1937.

The critical thinking construct includes an amalgam of attitudes, knowledge and skill:

- Attitudes of enquiry – an acceptance of the general need for evidence in support of what is claimed to be true.
- Knowledge – of the nature of valid inferences, abstractions and generalizations.
- Skills – in employing the attitudes and knowledge outlined above.

Critical thinking tests simulate situations where managers are presented with persuasively or emotively argued reports prepared by people who know more about the subject matter than they do. When this occurs, to be effective the manager must be able to suspend emotions and prejudices and deal with the report on its own logical merits.

Critical thinking, unlike verbal reasoning, can be improved. In assessing numerous managers one of the authors has frequently come across bright managers who do well on traditional verbal

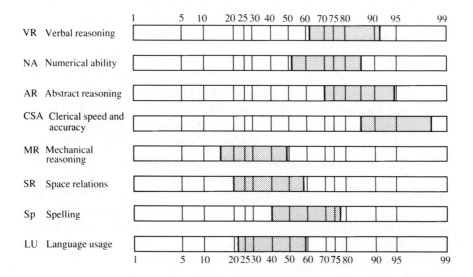

Figure 4.2   *Aptitude profile*

This Figure displays an individual's results on the Psychological Corporation's Differential Aptitude Test (DAT). With approximately ten million administrations in educational, clinical and occupational settings, the DAT is the world's most widely used aptitude battery.

Scores for each test are translated into percentiles – the proportion of the population performing as well as or worse than this particular individual. Since tests are not perfect, each score is effectively only a sample of the individuals' ability. Like all samples it contains error – for example, because the individual misunderstood some of the questions. As a sample each score is therefore only an estimate of an individual's true ability. The band on each of the percentile bars represents the 95 percent confidence limits. In other words, there is only a 5 per cent chance we have wrongly estimated the individuals's ability.

The tests measure abilities which are important components of a wide range of occupations. The eight tests measure:

Verbal reasoning – the ability to grasp and use concepts expressed verbally.

Numerical ability – the ability to reason with numbers.

Abstract reasoning – a measure of non-verbal intelligence.

Clerical speed and Accuracy – an information comparison task measuring two of Thurstone's primary abilities: perceptual speed and memory.

Mechanical reasoning – the ability to apply physical principles to practical problems.

Space relations – the ability to visualize the three-dimensional object from a two-dimensional representation.

Spelling and language usage – attainment tests measuring spelling and whether the individual can recognize good formal English.

Data are available for each of the DAT tests for a number of occupational areas. An individual's profile can be matched against these data to assess whether he or she could cope with the cognitive demands of a job and the training associated with it.

reasoning tests but very poorly on critical thinking tests. This indicates they absorb verbal concepts quickly but on occasion have their intellect clouded by their emotional response to material.

5. *Personality tests.* Where interpersonal skills such as selling, influencing, motivating or team working are important to job performance, responses to personality questionnaires can provide clues about how applicants will cope with these demands. Personality questionnaires will also provide data on more general personality issues such as coping with stress, rigidity, attitudes to authority and creativity.

A good test will provide a table of results which enable an individual's score to be compared with the scores of the general population. For occupational assessment, test often provide norms for particular occupational groups, so that individuals can be compared to the relevant sub-population. For example, the score on a mechanical aptitude test of an applicant for an apprentice's job can be compared with the range of scores for apprentices who successfully completed their training.

Tests have two technical criteria to meet before they are useful in occupational assessment: *reliability* and *validity*. The concept of reliability addresses two questions. First, is the measure self-consistent? In other words, to what extent does each test item measure the same variable? This is sometimes termed *internal reliability*. Secondly, does the test yield the same score for an individual on retesting (assuming the trait or ability is itself stable)? This is often called *test–retest reliability*. Internal reliability can be calculated by correlating scores for each question with those for each other question. The average correlation indicates the extent to which questions are measuring the same thing. Alternatively, scores on one half of the test can be correlated with scores on the other half. Test–retest reliability is measured by establishing the extent to which scores obtained on two administrations of a test are similar. To reduce the chances of subjects remembering their answers from the first sitting, the interval between testing seasons should be a least a month.

Normally we would expect test scores to possess test–retest reliability and not be subject to fluctuations. Reliability coefficients (in other words, the correlation between test scores at time 1 with test scores for the same group of subjects at time 2) of about .7 or better are usually expected in tests used in occupational assessment.

The validity of test scores is equally important. A test is said to be valid when it measures what it purports to measure. This means that differences between individuals' scores actually reflect differences on the variable being measured. First, if a test looks like it measures what it claims to measure, it is said to have *face validity*. This is important because if applicants can see that a test seems to be measuring relevant attributes, they are more likely to co-operate with the tester. Face validity therefore increase the acceptability of tests in the selection procedure. Secondly, when scores on a test correlate well with scores on other tests of the same attribute, the test is said to possess *concurrent validity*. For example, if scores for a group on a new IQ test correlate well with their scores on other IQ tests, we can be reasonably confident that the new test is measuring intelligence. Concurrent validity does not, however, imply *predictive validity*, the ability of a test to predict real-life performance. The predictive validity of an aptitude test used in employee selection would be its ability to predict some aspect of job performance.

Validity is usually expressed as a correlation coefficient. For example, one of the authors was employed to conduct a study of the relationship between a test and sales performance. Figure 4.3 indicates the scatter of results obtained. The diagonal line represents the line of 'best fit' for the data. The scatter represents a correlation of about .5. If the organization decides that in future it wants to employ people who are likely to sell more than 45 units per month, 'cut-off' scores on the test can be established by extrapolating across to the line of best fit and dropping down.

If these fifty individuals were now to apply for their jobs, what use would the test be?

In the top right-hand corner we have our *true positives*. These are people whose performance we would correctly predict. They have 'passed' the test and have turned out to be successful in the job.

In the bottom left-hand corner we have the *true negatives*. these are individuals who 'failed' the test and whom we have predicted currently would not perform adequately.

In the bottom right-hand corner are the *false positives*. These are individuals who have 'passed' the test and who would therefore be recommended. However, they do not succeed in achieving the sales targets.

In the top left-hand corner we have our *false negatives*. This group would be the most hard done by. Their score on the test suggests they would be unsuccessful, but if given the chance they would succeed.

Out of the fifty individuals in the study we have made eleven errors using this cut-off point. This represents an error rate of 22 per cent. This is much better than could be expected by chance and would have significant financial implications.

Incremental validity is the extent to which test 2 increases the overall predictive value over and above test 1. For example the DAT

Figure 4.3   *Deriving a cut-off score from a validity study.*

mechanical reasoning test has been fund to correlate .69 with City and Guilds Motor Vehicle Craft Studies exam grades. For mathematical reasons, we square the correlation to indicate how much of the differences in City and Guilds performance is explained or determined by differences in mechanical reasoning.

The square of .69 is .47, thus 47 per cent of the difference in students' exam performance is attributable to differences in mechanical reasoning. If spatial reasoning were to correlate .4 with performance (assuming the two abilities were independent), this would explain another 16 per cent of the differences and mean the two tests explained 63 per cent of performance in the City and Guilds exam.

Finally, it is sometimes difficult to find a measure against which a test's predictive value can be assessed. In these situations the test's *construct* validity is measured instead. This involves generating a number of hypotheses about the test variable as a construct or concept and then finding evidence to support or reject these hypotheses. For instance, to demonstrate the construct validity of a measure of job satisfaction we might hypothesize that high scorers would have less absenteeism, be less inclined to leave the organization and show higher levels of job performance. Low scorers should be absent more often, should be more likely to leave and should demonstrate poorer work performance than high scorers.

Test usage in the UK has grown enormously in recent years. Inevitably a great deal of controversy has accompanied this explosion of interest. Like any other assessment technique the status of the information provided by tests varies wildly. High-status information comes from ability and aptitude tests where there are clear right and wrong answers.

More problematic are personality tests, whose reliability and validities are much lower. Blinkhorn and Johnson (1990) have gone as far as claiming that much of the validity of personality tests reported in test manuals is illusory. They point out that validity correlations are close to what would be expected by chance given the sample sizes involved and the number of scales the tests possess.

One reason why the validity of personality tests may be lower is the nature of correlation. Correlation indicates the presence of a linear relationship. With personality we might expect some relationships to be curvilinear. For example, a low level of dominance produces a poor ability to close sales. But customers might find very high scorers too 'pushy' and 'overbearing.' The middle-range scorers will therefore be associated with higher sales. While there clearly is a relationship, it would not show up in a correlation coefficient and thus personality would not seem to be a 'valid' predictor of performance.

More worrying is the use of what are called'quick and dirties' – five-minute personality tests usually requiring the applicant to indicate which adjective is most and least like him or her. These tests yield scores which are mathematically interdependent – so, for example, as you go up a sociability scale you go down the other scales. Johnson et al. (1988) conclude that these 'forced choice' or ipsative tests should not be used in personnel selection. Despite arguments to the contrary (Saville and Wilson, 1991) this is currently the view of the British Psychological Society (1989).

The appeal and market penetration of the 'quick and dirties' have been the cause of a great deal of concern among the UK psychological community. The British Psychological Society (1989) has attempted to curb their usage by credentialling test users. The British Psychological society Level I certificate is obtained by demonstrating competence in test usage to a chartered psychologist. This ensures a minimum level of understanding of the importance of reliability, validity and proper standardization among test users. The Level I certificate provides access to ability and aptitude tests. This credentialling system will be extended to personality tests in due course.

While tests are more objective than interviewing, testing does involve considerable problems of procedure and interpretation. The reliability and validity of a test can be seriously undermined by the practical realities of test administration in the workplace. One of the authors has come across one organization testing applicants in corridors, another in the lobby. When standardized administration procedures are not followed the utility of test scores is reduced. Similarly, as with interviewing, if insufficient rapport with the candidate is established, his or her willingness to participate fully in the procedure is greatly reduced.

While the poor administration of tests may produce scores lacking reliability and validity, inability to interpret scores properly is even more of a problem. Statistics rarely speak for themselves, and test scores, like interview data, can only be a starting point when assessing individuals. They have to be interpreted not only with information provided by the authors of the test, but also with other sources of evidence concerning the applicant's education, attitudes and interests. Blind acceptance of test scores without adequate consideration of these other aspects of the applicants' abilities can result in serious injustices.

Assessment centres

The term 'assessment centre' refers to a method rather than a place. The objective of an assessment centre is no different from other techniques already described: 'to obtain the best possible indication of a candidate's actual or potential competence to perform at the target job or job level' (Woodruffe, 1990). The assessment centre approach, however, is to combine a range of assessment techniques to give the fullest picture possible. While assessment centres will utilize interviews and tests, the critical and perhaps defining feature of the method is the use of work simulation (Feltham, 1988).

Work simulations can be written or interactive. An example of a written simulation is the 'in-tray' exercise. Typically, the applicant is told he or she has just returned from holiday or is going on holiday this evening. A tray full of faxes, memos, letters and reports have to be read and acted on. The way the applicant prioritizes and demonstrates incisiveness, sensitivity, market awareness, customer orientation or other dimensions identified as important to effective job performance can be rated.

An interactive exercise might involve role-playing a negotiation exercise where each applicant has a somewhat different brief. How the applicants deal with the conflict this may cause and arrive at an outcome to which they can all subscribe is observed and rated. The use of work simulations has the additional benefit of giving applicants a 'feel' for the job and helps some applicants to realize they would not be suited to the job.

Assessment centres typically last two days. They are grueling, intense experiences which normally provide both the applicant and the assessors with valuable insights into suitability.

Assessment centres represent the Rolls-Royce of selection techniques. They are expensive to build, usually involving consultants developing custom-made exercises. They are also expensive to run. The assessors observing and rating candidates' performance on interactive exercises are usually senior managers who will therefore be away from their own jobs for the duration of the centre.

While having the drawbacks of the Rolls-Royce they also have its advantages. Assessment centres have repeatedly demonstrated they are the most powerful and robust of selection techniques (Feltham, 1988). Increasingly used as a development event, assessment centres can also identify what an individual needs to develop in order to move up to the next job grade.

Most organizations using assessment and development centres try to make them as collaborative as is feasible: in other words, something being done *with* rather than *to* applicants. Most of the data on candidates' reactions to assessment centres has indeed shown favourable reactions to them. Applicants typically rate them as fair and valid. Fletcher (1991) has, however, identified some long-term effects in unsuccessful candidates, most notably a drop in self-esteem, competitiveness and work ethic. This underlines the crucial importance of sensitive, supportive feedback of assessment centre performance and the need for counseling to be available after the assessment centre.

Better than chance?

The overall aim of the assessment process is to obtain the fullest and clearest picture of each candidate, and as we have seen there are many processes which can contribute to this. The key question when using one or more of these approaches is to keep in mind the relative status of the information each provides. The key concepts are reliability and validity. High-status information will have both these qualities.

Recent work by Smith (1991) indicates the relative status of each

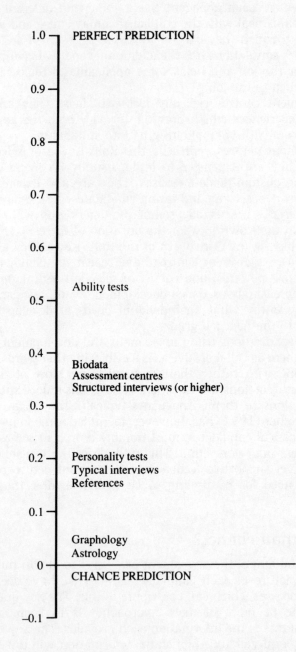

Figure 4.4 *Validity of selection methods.* Adapted from Smith (1991).

of the techniques we have discussed. Using a technique called *meta analysis* which enables the results of numerous studies to be combined, they indicate the relative value of each method. The results of his analysis can be seen in Figure 4.4.

When interpreting this figure, remember we normally square the correlation coefficient to indicate how much of the difference in performance is 'explained'. Thus ability tests seem to do best, explaining about 25 per cent of job performance. Personality tests explain only about 8 per cent.

Assessment centres often achieve validities as high as .65, well above ability tests. The figure illustrated reflects the effect of poorly constructed and run assessment centres. It also suggests many assessment centre decisions are affected by the subjective impression developed at interview. Subsequent performance on objective exercises is often overlooked (Smith, 1991).

In this chapter we have discussed the importance of individual differences in the context of point of entry assessment. Of course, organizations utilize assessment techniques for a variety of other reason. High-status information about abilities and personality is useful in establishing development goals, a career plan, redeployment options and effective management teams (see Chapter 7). Assessment has an increasingly vital role to play in helping individuals and organizations to maximize the talents available to each.

Further reading

Cook, M. (1988) *Personnel Selection and Productivity*. Chichester: Willey.

Courtis, J. (1988) *Interviewing Skills and Strategy*. London: I.P.M.

Fletcher, J. (1988) *Effective Interviewing* (3rd edn). London: Kogan Page.

Goldsmith, T.H. (1992) *The Biological Roots of Human Nature: Forging Links between Evolution and Behaviour*. Oxford: Oxford University Press.

Rust, J. (1989) *Modern Psychometrics*. London: Routledge.

Smith, M. and Robertson. (ed.) (1989) *Advances in Selection and Assessment*. Chichester: Wiley.

5

Motivation and Job Satisfaction

In the years following the Second World War, western industrialized societies experienced increasing prosperity and relatively full employment. Developments in housing, welfare and education policies both reflected and fostered the rising expectations of people in post-war society. In this context employers were faced with a workforce which could, if dissatisfied, change jobs relatively easily. This led to an interest in what creates a stable and well-motivated workforce, and in particular to an interest in the concepts of *motivation* and *job satisfaction*. Nowadays, though relatively full employment is no longer a feature of the labour market, because of its practical implications (particularly productivity and labour turnover) interest in motivation and job satisfaction has persisted. Indeed, there are still a great many occupations where employers experience difficulties in obtaining skilled staff, where the demand for such types of labour is high and the problems of attracting and maintaining a stable workforce continue.

In this chapter we will examine research which has sought to identify the conditions which creates a motivated and satisfied workforce.

Needs at work

Motivational theories can be divided into two categories, termed *content* and *process*. Content theories assume that all individuals possess the same set of *needs*. These theories tend to be heavily prescriptive in nature, since by assuming people have similar needs they are also recommending the characteristics that ought to be present in jobs. Process theories, on the other hand, stress the differences in people's needs and focus on the cognitive processes that create these differences.

CONTENT THEORIES

Although content theories are based on the assumption that we can attribute a similar set of needs to all individuals, theories within this category differ in their accounts of what these needs are. Maslow (1954) outlined what is perhaps the most influential of the content theories. He suggested there is a *hierarchy of needs* up which people progress. Once individuals satisfy a need at one level in the hierarchy, it ceases to motivate their behaviour; instead they are motivated by the need at the next level up the hierarchy. Thus, at first individuals are motivated by physiological needs such as hunger and thirst. If conditions are such that these needs can be satisfied, security needs such as the need for shelter and protection become the major influence on an individual's behaviour. A favourable environment allows an individual to progress from behaviour activated by these *deficiency needs* to behaviour which reflects what Maslow termed *higher-order needs*.

As can be seen from Figure 5.1, this progression ultimately leads to behaviour motivated principally by the need to realize one's full potential, which Maslow termed the need for *self-actualization*. Maslow, however, believed that because of the uneven distribution of satisfying work only a small proportion of the population reached this level. Thus, self-actualization is for most of us a need which will motivate our behaviour throughout our lives.

Although not originally intended as an explanation of motivation in the workplace, Maslow's idea of a hierarchy of needs has, nonetheless, been enthusiastically adopted by many management theorists. It was seen as offering a number of predictions about what motivates people in societies offering relatively full employment. When jobs are scarce, employees are motivated solely by deficiency needs. When jobs are readily available, and deficiency needs are easily satisfied, social needs become important motivators in the workplace. This means organizations will have to provide opportunities for employees to satisfy their social needs, for example by providing company sports and social facilities. Once social needs are met, intrinsic aspects of work, the amount of challenge, responsibility and autonomy it offers, become increasingly salient to employee motivation. Thus, the theory suggests that employees will always tend to want more from their employers. Having satisfied their subsistence needs, they strive to fulfil security needs. When jobs are secure they will seek ways of satisfying social needs and if successful will seek the means (increased autonomy, participation, responsibility) to the ultimate end of self-actualization.

Though many found the idea of a hierarchy of needs appealing,

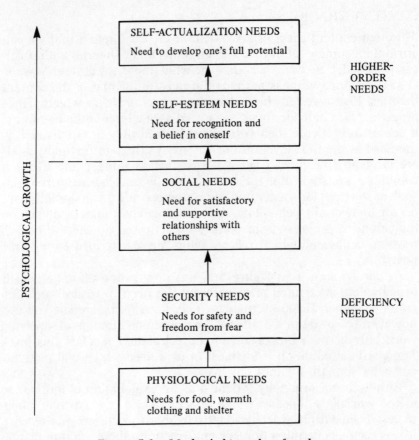

Figure 5.1 *Maslow's hierarchy of needs.*

we should stress that the motion has not much empirical support (Wahba and Bridwell, 1976). In fact, Maslow had not intended his ideas, based on his observations of patients, to be used as a theory in the traditional sense of the term. Consequently he provided no operational definitions of the variables he described, which has made measurement of their relative strengths difficult.

What Maslow's ideas have done is to make one basic, important point: in prosperous societies the need for self-actualization becomes a key motivator.

One content theory which does provide reasonably reliable measures for the needs it proposes is known as ERG theory (Alderfer, 1972). This suggests that individual needs can be divided into three groups:

1. *Existence needs*, which include nutritional and material requirements. At work, working conditions and pay would fall into this group.
2. *Relatedness needs*, which are met through relationships with family and friends and at work with colleagues and supervisors.
3. *Growth needs*, which reflect a desire for personal psychological developments.

Alderfer's theory differs in a number of important respects from Maslow's. While Maslow proposed a progression up a hierarchy, Alderfer argued it was better to think in terms of a continuum, from concrete (existence needs) to least concrete (growth needs); and he believed it is possible to move along it in either direction. This means that if, for example, fulfilment of growth needs is difficult, *frustration regression* occurs, causing individuals to concentrate on fulfilling their relatedness needs. Unsatisfied needs therefore become less rather than more important, whereas Maslow assumed the opposite.

The two theories also differ as regards the importance to individuals of satisfied needs. Whereas Maslow argued that when satisfied a need becomes less important to an individual, research based on Alderfer's ideas has found that relatedness or growth needs actually become more important when satisfied (Wanous and Zwany, 1977). This means, for example, that team working arrangements which satisfy relatedness needs can continue to motivate employees and are not necessarily superseded by growth needs. Employers, according to Alderfer, are in this sense more easily able to satisfy the needs of their employees. In general, tests of the two theories have tended to favour Alderfer's predictions.

By breaking Maslow's and Alderfer's broad variables up, a number of more specific needs can be identified which can offer clearer insights into the nature of motivation in the workplace. Mumford (1976) suggested that workers have:

1. *Knowledge needs* – work that utilizes their knowledges and skills.
2. *Control needs*, which are satisfied by the provision of information, good working conditions and high-quality supervision.
3. *Psychological needs*, such as the needs for recognition, responsibility, status and advancement.
4. *Task needs*, which include the need for meaningful work and some degree of autonomy.
5. *Moral needs* – to be treated in the way that employers would themselves wish to be treated.

Mumford's assumption, therefore, was that employees did not simply see their job as a means to an end but had needs which related to the nature of their work.

A second theory which makes the same basic point is known as

111

Herzberg's *two-factor theory* (Herzberg *et al.*, 1959). The original research for this was based on interviews with 200 accountants and engineers using what is known as the critical incidents technique. This involves asking interviewees to talk about occasions when they felt either particularly satisfied or particularly dissatisfied with their jobs. Two sets of incidents seemed to emerge from these interviews. One involved achievement, advancement, recognition, autonomy and other intrinsic aspects of work. Because these represented sources of satisfaction they were called *motivators*. The second set of incidents concerned working conditions, salary, job security, company policy, supervisors and interpersonal relations. This set, termed *hygiene factors*, were described as sources of dissatisfaction by the sample. Job satisfaction and dissatisfaction therefore appeared to be caused by different sets of factors. The presence of motivators in the workplace caused enduring states of motivation in employees. Their absence, however, did not lead to job dissatisfaction. Hygiene factors, on the other hand, produced an acceptable work environment though not increased satisfaction or involvement with a job; their absence (e.g.

Table 5.1   *Herzberg's two-factor theory of motivation.*

MOTIVATORS	HYGIENES
Responsibility	Supervision
Recognition	Salary
Promotion	
Achievement	Company policies
Intrinsic aspects of the job	Relationship with colleagues

low pay), however, caused job dissatisfaction. Thus motivators reflected people's need for self-actualization, while hygienes represented the need to avoid pain (Table 5.1).

As well as describing employees' needs, the theory goes a stage further and indicates how people's jobs can be redesigned to incorporate more motivators (Table 5.2). And not surprisingly, a theory which describes both what motivates employees and how jobs can be changed to achieve a well-motivated workforce has attracted a great deal of interest both from managers seeking ways of motivating staff and from academics testing Herzberg's propositions.

Support for the two-factor theory has been mixed, however. The independent effect of motivators and hygienes has been questioned,

Table 5.2 *Herzberg's principles of vertical job loading.*

PRINCIPLES	MOTIVATORS INVOLVED
Increasing employees' autonomy while retaining accountability	Responsibility and achievement
Increasing the accountability of employees for their own work	Responsibility and recognition
Providing employees with a complete natural unit of work	Responsibility, achievement and recognition
Making performance feedback available to employees	Recognition
Introducing new and more difficult tasks to employees' work	Growth and learning
Assigning employees specific or specialized tasks at which they can become expert	Responsibility, growth and advancement

and at least one study has demonstrated that both can be related to job satisfaction and dissatisfaction (Schneider and Locke, 1971). By using accountants and engineers, who have fairly lucrative occupations, Herzberg might have introduced a middle-class bias into his research. A wider sample of the working population might have produced a somewhat different list. The validity of the critical incidents technique has also been question. First, it has been argued that people tend to externalize explanations of failure and internalize explanations of success. In other words, interviewees would tend to relate their successes to the exercise of their personal initiative, but see their problems at work as a reflection of other people's or organizational inadequacies. Thus the two distinct sets of factors could simply reflect this tendency rather than a genuine division in the motivational properties of the incidents interviewees talked about. Secondly, there may well be a gap between what people are prepared to admit motivates them and what actually motivates them. This could account, for example, for pay appearing as a hygiene factor.

Despite criticisms of the ideas of Maslow, Alderfer and Herzberg, their notion of a self-actualizing or growth need has had considerable influence on management theory and to an extent on management practice. Before these content theories were popularized there were two 'models of man' on which management theory and practice could be based. There was the model of *rational economic* man and that of *social* man. The former would expend effort to the extent that it was in his or her economic interests to do so. The latter searched for affiliation and supportive relationships in the workplace, and thus effort was significantly influenced by the collective work rate. (Later we shall see how these different approaches to human motivation have produced very different approaches to the design of work and the style of supervision employed in a workplace.)

One notable attempt to illustrate the connection between different models of motivation and managerial practices was made by Douglas McGregor in *The Human Side of Enterprise* (1960). He pointed out that a consequence of assuming people behave like rational economic beings is the belief that they require either reward or coercion to motivate them. McGregor called this model of motivation *theory X*. Autocratic managerial styles are the logical result of translating theory X into managerial practice. Instead, McGregor advocated managerial strategies based on *theory Y*, which uses the self-actualizing model of motivation proposed by Maslow and Herzberg. Theory Y has at its centre *complex man*, possessing a bundle of social and self-actualizing needs, who, given the appropriate conditions at work, can show high levels of responsibility and self-direction. Complex man does not avoid responsibility, but because of the routinization of work and high levels of external supervision is generally provided with a working environment which offers little opportunity to exercise or develop it. The role of management from this perspective, then, is to create the conditions in which this reservoir of hitherto untapped human resources can be utilized.

PROCESS THEORIES

What all process theories have in common is an emphasis on the role of an individual's cognitive processes in determining his or her level of motivation. One major process theory, *equity theory*, assumes that one important cognitive process involves people looking around and observing what effort other people are putting into their work and what rewards follow for them, and comparing this ratio with their own. Individuals can also compare their effort–reward ratio to one which they experienced at another point in time. Equity theorists assume that this *social comparison process* is driven by our concern with fairness or equity. We perceive effort and reward not in absolute but in relative terms (Adams, 1965). When people perceive others enjoying a similar ratio of inputs (effort, qualification, skill level, seniority) to outcomes (pay, advancement, fringe benefits) to themselves, they experience equity. When people perceive a ratio of inputs to outcomes that either favours other people (underpayment) or themselves (overpayment) they experience inequity, which is assumed to be a sufficiently unpleasant experience to motivate changes in either behaviour or perceptions, or both (Table 5.3).

	MYSELF	YOURSELF
EQUITY	Inputs (100) / Outcomes (100)	Inputs (100) / Outcomes (100)
INEQUITY (Underpayment)	Inputs (100) / Outcomes (100)	Inputs (100) / Outcomes (125)
INEQUITY (Overpayment)	Inputs (100) / Outcomes (125)	Inputs (100) / Outcomes (100)

Table 5.3 *The conditions of equity and inequity described by Adams (1965).*

In one notable experiment, Adams and Jacobsen (1964) tested a number of predictions from this theory. To induce equity and inequity in people they set up a fictitious publishing company and advertised vacancies for students to do proofreading. One group of students was told that they were not qualified to earn the going rate but would still be paid it. Theoretically this should induce feelings of inequity. Another group was told they were not qualified to earn the going rate and would earn a lesser rate, which should be experienced as equitable. Finally, a third group was told they were qualified to earn the proofreading rate and would earn it. This again should be experienced as equitable. Results supported equity theory predictions: not only did the first group produce better quality work, they also worked harder than either of the other groups.

Most subsequent studies, however, have found that predictions from equity theory are supported best in conditions of underpayment, since the threshold for experiencing overpayment is high and feelings of overpayment do not appear to last very long (Carrell and Dittrich, 1978). This is perhaps because we find it easier to rationalize why we should be overpaid than underpaid.

Additionally, if the feeling of underpayment is shared by enough people in a workplace, collective industrial action can occur. Managers involved in wage-setting therefore have to be careful to avoid setting wage rates which cause people to feel underpaid relative to others within the same plant (internal inequity) or to comparison groups outside the organization (external inequity).

Although rates of pay are a common cause of perceived inequity, and thus industrial disputes, conflict can be caused by perceived inequity in what is termed the *effort bargain*. Employers and employees may have quite different ideas about the intensity of labour that constitutes 'a fair days's work'. Employers naturally feel that, having paid the wage, they should decide what is a suitable level of effort from workers. Workers for their part fear that if the employer has control of effort intensity he may be tempted to increase it arbitrarily to an inequitable level, which they will resist if they have the power to do so.

Baldamus's classic study *Efficiency and Effort* (1961) remains the most thorough analysis of what is involved in the effort bargain. He points out that in a stable employment relationship the two sides will in effect have struck a bargain, in which the employee's total effort is exchanged for pay and other returns. He draws attention to the fundamental role of 'custom and practice' in industrial relations in determining an equitable effort–reward ratio. A variety of factors will affect effort, the pace and intensity of work, and the individual worker's experience of fatigue and monotony. Reward is comprised chiefly of pay but convivial working conditions, job security, interesting work and reasonable supervision may be involved as well. With so many factors the effort bargain can only be established over time by custom and practice.

In addition, he suggests the effort bargain is potentially unstable. When established there will be a balance between effort and reward. Should any of the elements change, however, the relationship may begin to be perceived as inequitable by one or both of the parties. Baldamus defined situations in which the wages–effort exchange deviates from previously accepted standards under the notion of 'wage disparity', which he suggests is 'the very centre of industrial conflict'. Of course, workers may fail to notice any change that has taken place, or they may be aware of it but unable to do much about it, or they may accept the change as equitable. During periods of high unemployment, for example, workers' expectations tend to adjust to their reduced labour market power, and they may put up with conditions they would previously have found unacceptable. Nonetheless, if an effort bargain is disrupted it may lead directly to conflict as one side or the other attempts to force a renegotiation. Moreover, Baldamus adds, modern industry is dynamic: managements are continually looking for higher productivity, workers' opinions on a fair return for their effort may change, and there are changes in the wider environment which have an impact within the firm. Inflation, for example, undermines the effort bargain by tipping it in the employer's favour, because it reduces the value of wages while the employee still puts in the same effort.

Recent research (Summers and Hendrix, 1991; Dornstein, 1989) in real rather than laboratory settings supports Adams' original predictions and confirms equity theory as one of the most useful frameworks for understanding work motivation.

The key role of employees' perceptions of their jobs is underlined again in the *valence, instrumentality and expectancy (VIE) theory*. This explanation of employee motivation has been popular since the publication of Vroom's study, *Work and Motivation* (1964). He argued that what was crucial to motivation at work was the perception of a link between effort and reward. Perceiving this link could be thought of as a process in which individuals calculated first whether there was a connection between their effort and their performance (expectancy), then the probability that valued rewards (valences) would follow from high performance (instrumentality). The *motivational force* of a job can be calculated if the expectancy, instrumentality and valence values are known. (Figure 5.2).

The motivational force of a job is attenuated by the individual's abilities, traits, role perceptions and opportunities. This implies, for example, that although a person might be motivated to perform a particular task well, he or she may be restricted from doing so by his or her abilities. In addition, opportunities for the exercise of effort also vary and thus affect the impact of an individual's motivational force on his or her achievement. Recession, for example, makes the task of selling more difficult whatever an individual's motivational force.

In summary, VIE theory stresses the rational–cognitive aspects of an individual's work motivation. The theory predicts that jobs which produce low levels of motivation will be those where aspects of job performance are out of the worker's control. In machine-paced assembly tasks, for example, we would find that expectancy and instrumentalities have low values. In fact, one of the desired outcomes may even be machine breakdown (Beynon, 1984).

VIE theory is supported by studies which attempt to predict the tasks on which an individual will work most and least hard. Prediction coefficients for this type of study are usually between .5 and .6 (Matsui *et al.*, 1977). Attempts to use VIE measures to predict which person will work hardest in a group or on a particular task are less successful, producing coefficients of .3 to .4 (Pritchard and Sanders,

Figure 5.2   The VIE model of motivation. In this example the individual perceives only a 50 per cent change of increased effort leading to increased performance. She has ranked four rewards on a +10 to −10 scale and has estimated the probability on increased performance producing each of these desired rewards. The motivational force of the job − the effort she is willing to expend on it − is calculated by adding the products of the valence × instrumentality calculations and multiplying the total by the expectancy value. Thus (.9×6) + (.5×8) + (.3×5) + (.6×9) = 16.3 and 16.3 × .5 = 8.15. This figure can be used to predict some criterion of job performance − a supervisor's assessment, for example, or if available, more reliable measures, such as sales figures for sales staff.

1973). In one study, however, though the validity coefficients averaged out at .52 for the group, individual coefficients varied from −.08 to −.92. Thus, for some students behaviour could be predicted quite well from the VIE measures, whereas for others they were unable to predict performance (Muchinsky, 1977). This has prompted some researchers to suggest that when VIE measures are not predictive of behaviour, unconscious or irrational processes have motivated individuals (Miner, 1980).

There does not seem to be any reason, however, to suggest behaviour not predicted by VIE measures is irrational. As we saw earlier, social rationality is highly complex; the subjects who performed best in the Adams and Jacobsen experiment did so because they felt they were being overpaid relative to their qualifications. Our perceptions and calculations are therefore not solely concerned with the future, predicting the value of our own efforts; we also look sideways at others and often alter our performance according to internalized norms about what is fair and unfair in terms of effort and reward.

The main contribution of both types of process theory has been to highlight the effects of cognitive and perceptual processes on objective work conditions. It suggests that managers need to pay attention to four main aspects of their subordinates' perceptions:

1. They need to focus on the crucial expectancy values – employees must perceive a link between their effort and their performance. This may mean improving training so that effort is utilized more efficiently, providing guidance and ensuring sufficient support for high performance is available, for example by ensuring adequate machine maintenance.
2. Managers should determine what outcomes an employee values. It may well be that employees value recognition and praise more than they do economic reward.
3. They need to link the reward that subordinates value to their performance, since this reflects the simple psychological truth that people are likely to repeat a response if they have been rewarded for doing so.
4. Managers finally need to ensure that wage rates are not set at a level which employees perceive as inequitable.

KNOWLEDGE OF RESULTS AND GOAL-SETTING

Imagine you are set an essay question by a tutor, you are a highly motivated student, you read around the question and carefully prepare an answer. What happens to that essay after you have handed it to your tutor can determine whether you remain highly motivated. Similarly at work, what happens after a particular response may be important to the maintenance or enhancement of motivation. What is required in both cases is what is termed *knowledge of results*. Management theorists have, for some time, pointed to the motivational properties of this type of feedback to employees, and have explored ways in which information systems in organizations provide it (e.g. Nemeroff and Cosentino, 1979; Luthans and Martinko, 1987; Guzzo *et al.*, 1985).

Despite a wealth of research highlighting the positive motivational benefits of knowledge of results, many organizations still provide employees with little or no information about their performance. Often this is because information systems tend to be designed for management functions (accounting, planning, production) and use data that may be incomprehensible to employees.

In some organizations knowledge of results is provided only where performance has fallen below some optimum level. In such cases of

119

'management by exception' managers exert their authority only when performance is poor, and appear on the shopfloor only when something has gone wrong. This is because many managers are reluctant to feed back positive information since they feel that they would be congratulating staff for doing what they are paid to do. Feedback in these contexts therefore tends only to occur when output is significantly less than satisfactory and management comes under pressure to improve it.

To harness the motivational properties of information, feedback needs to be relatively rapid. Daily or weekly summaries of performance are more useful than quarterly or annual. The system should be capable of providing information that is valid to employees: it must be capable of distinguishing, for example, the effects of faulty machinery and employees' efforts, be capable of allocating output correctly to each shift, and be in units that are understood by employees.

It should be stressed that, although an information system that provides comprehensible, unbiased and frequent summaries of an operator team or department's performance has considerable positive motivational and learning consequences, implementing such a system often involves wider organizational issues. For example, it can affect the relationship between shopfloor employees and supervisors since employees are given wider access to data which the latter may resent.

The positive motivational consequences for employees of accurate information on work performance being available can be further enhanced by a practice known as *goal-setting* (Locke, 1968). Goals direct effort, and provide guidelines for deciding how much effort to put into each activity when there are multiple goals. To be effective the goal or goals need to be made reasonably specific. One study of a group of lumberjacks found a dramatic improvement in performance following a specific goal being set. The lumberjacks were responsible for felling trees, loading them on to lorries and delivering them to the mill. Before the goal-setting experiment lumberjacks were simply asked to do their best and on average lorries were being driven to the mill with only 60 per cent of their maximum capacity. They were then requested to load lorries up to 94 per cent of their maximum legal load. The lumberjacks considered this goal difficult but reasonable, and even though it was made clear that there were neither rewards for meeting the goal nor punishments for failing to reach it, the average loads went up to 94 per cent of maximum capacity and remained at this level. The increased loads produced savings in maintenance, replacement and fuel costs (Latham and Blades, 1975).

Although knowledge of results and goal-setting are not general theories of motivation, they offer the most specific advice to managers dealing with the day-to-day problems of motivating staff. First, managers can harness the motivational properties of knowledge of results by providing clear and frequent feedback to staff, particularly when positive. And secondly, managers are able to increase motivation by setting specific and reasonable goals. This is best achieved by allowing staff to take part in and influence the goal-setting process. Participation in goal-setting can both increase staff's commitment to the goal and makes it less likely that unreasonably high goals, which are counter productive, are set.

Satisfaction at work

Few concepts in the applied behavioural sciences have attracted as much interest as job satisfaction. Many popular and academic writers have become increasingly critical of the work performed by a large proportion of the working population, seeing in the workplace a part of society which had neither kept pace with improvements in living standards nor accommodated the rising expectations of the post-war period. Factories were, they argue, often dirty, noisy, dangerous places which offered little satisfaction for the needs we described in the preceding section. And clerical work too often lacked any intrinsic satisfaction, even though this was due to the routine nature of the work and declining status and pay rather than to poor conditions. Managers found themselves facing the behavioural consequences of this central problem in the experience of work: costly levels of staff turnover, absenteeism and poor industrial relations.

WHAT IS JOB SATISFACTION?

If people claim to be satisfied with their jobs, what do they mean? They are usually expressing something more like a feeling about their job rather than their thoughts about it. Locke (1976) attempted to capture the affective nature of job satisfaction in his definition 'a pleasurable positive emotional state resulting from the appraisal of one's job or job experiences.'

Behavioural scientists have argued that it is useful to distinguish two types of feeling people have about their jobs: *global* and *facet*. Global job satisfaction reflects an individual's overall feeling towards his or her job. But in addition, people may express feelings about particular aspects or facets of their jobs. For example, they may be upset by an overbearing supervisor but be fairly happy with their salary and workmates.

Breaking the global concept up into its constituent facets can be done conceptually or statistically. In the conceptual approach, researchers can either use their own hunches and investigations about what the significant facets in a job are, or adopt a particular theoretical framework which specifies a set of facets in advance. Sometimes the specific nature of the organization or occupation in which the job satisfaction research is being conducted means the former is preferable. For example, in an attempt to identify the causes of low job satisfaction in nursing, Wallis and Cope (1980) found that the relevant facets of job satisfaction for nurses included the feeling of being needed by patients, the way hours of work are organized, the adequacy of the in-service training received, and the pay compared to others working outside the hospital.

The statistical method of deriving facets involves using techniques, such as factor analysis, to reduce large quantities of questionnaire data to a few general dimensions. Many of the 'off-the-peg' questionnaires available to people doing job satisfaction research have been developed in this way (e.g., Cross, 1989). Multifaceted questionnaires measuring dimensions such as satisfaction with the organization, pay, promotion prospects, supervisors and co-workers may provide more detailed information to managers and researchers. But scores on such scales tend to be inter-correlated, indicating the presence of a general underlying job satisfaction factor (e.g., Bell and Weaver, 1987).

Some researchers, while deriving measures of facets of job satisfaction, also like to combine these to produce a global measure. This raises the question of whether the predictive validity of a global job satisfaction measure can be improved by weighting facets which subjects have indicated are important to them. In some cases there appears to be a clear justification for doing this. For example, in the study of nurses' job satisfaction cited above, the feelings nurses experienced on the occasions when they thought they had 'got through to patients' were found to be very important to their overall level of the job satisfaction. However, in practice weighting does not seem to improve the ability of a global job satisfaction measure to predict behavior (Mikes and Hulin, 1968). This seems to be because people are already implicitly weighting the importance of a facet when they give a rating of their satisfaction of that aspect of their job. For example, if people indicate that they are highly satisfied or highly dissatisfied with their rate of pay, the chances are that pay is important to them. On the other hand, if people indicate that they are neither satisfied nor dissatisfied with their supervisors, it is probably the case that supervisory style is not an important component of their job satisfaction. In other words, getting a person to weight the importance of a facet adds little new information and so does not improve the predictive validity of global job satisfaction measures.

THEORIES OF JOB SATISFACTION

In this section we will examine two widely used theories in contemporary job satisfaction research. One theory stresses the individual, subjective nature of job satisfaction. It assumes that individuals can differ in their perceptions and experience of similar jobs. The other proposes that there are important objective features of the jobs people do which give rise to job satisfaction. Both provide important insights into either why some jobs are experienced as satisfying while others are not, or why some individuals find particular types of work dissatisfying while their colleagues doing identical jobs are satisfied with their work.

Variance theory

Variance theory is based on a simple idea: if you want x from your work then you are satisfied to the extent that it provides you with x. The major problem for variance theorists is defining what it is that people want from their jobs. One way of solving this is to borrow concepts from motivation theory so that variance in what is wanted and what is available from a job occurs: for example, in the extent to which self-actualizating needs can be fulfilled (Schaffer, 1953; Porter, 1962). This means that by borrowing from motivation theory some researchers can specify in advance the variations in work satisfaction that employees report in their jobs. Another approach assumes that the relevant variances depend on the nature of the work and thus differ from occupation to occupation. This provides a more flexible framework with which to analyse problems of low job satisfaction within occupations.

Either approach, specifying in advance the relevant facets of job satisfaction or identifying them through investigation, enables researchers to establish whether there are significant individual differences present in reported levels of job satisfaction or whether there is a high degree of consensus among staff about what aspects of work lead to high levels of satisfaction and dissatisfaction. By identifying what aspects of a job give rise to high and low levels of satisfaction, managers are better placed when considering what changes can be made to improve job satisfaction.

Job characteristics

If variance theory suggests the causes of job satisfaction are subjective, the job characteristics model suggests the opposite: the causes of job satisfaction are to be found in the objective characteristics of a job. This view was first outlined by Hackman and Oldham (1975). These researchers argued that jobs differ in the extent to which they involve five core dimensions:

1. *Skill variety.* The extent to which they require the use of a number of different skills and talents.
2. *Task identity.* The extent to which they require the completion of a whole, identifiable piece of work.
3. *Task significance.* The degree of impact they are believed to have on other people inside and outside the organization they are situated in.
4. *Autonomy.* The extent to which they provide freedom, independence and discretion in determining such things as work place, work breaks and allocation of tasks.
5. *Task feedback.* The extent to which they provide clear and direct information about the effectiveness of performance.

They suggested that if jobs are designed in a way that increases the presence of these core dimensions – for example, by combining tasks and opening feedback channels – three critical psychological states can occur in employees.

1. *Experienced meaningfulness of work.* This is determined by the level of skill variety, task identify and task significance.
2. *Experienced responsibility for work outcomes.* This is determined by the amount of autonomy present.
3. *Knowledge of results of work activities.* This is determined by the amount of feedback present.

According to Hackman and Oldham, when these critical psychological states are experienced, work motivation and job satisfaction will be high. Furthermore, behavioural outcomes, such as the quality of work and attendance, may also be improved. Hackman and Oldham did, however, include one personal attribute in their theory termed *growth need strength* (GNS), which they believed moderated the extent to which the critical psychological states could be experienced. If an individual has little need for growth it is unlikely that he or she will experienced the critical psychological states strongly. The relationship between the theory's concepts is illustrated in Figure 5.3.

Hackman and Oldham constructed the *job diagnostic survey* (JDS), a questionnaire completed by employees to provide measures for each of their variables. They believed that it was possible to combine these measures to produce what they termed the motivating potential score (MPS), for a job using the formula:

$$MPS = \frac{\text{Skill variety} + \text{Task identity} + \text{Task significance}}{3} \times \text{Autonomy} \times \text{Feedback}$$

Since the first three core dimensions contribute to the same critical psychological state, they are averaged. As scores on measures of the other two dimensions are multiplied and not added, low scores on

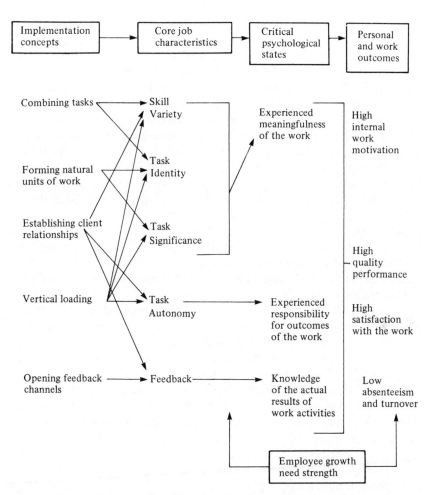

Figure 5.3 *Hackman and Oldham's job characteristics model.* From J.R. Hackman, G.R. Oldham, R. Janson, and K. Purdy (1975) 'A new strategy for job enrichment', *California Management Review*, 17, 57–71.

either produces a low *MPS* value. If no autonomy or feedback is present, the *MPS* value is zero.

Thus, the theory encompasses not only job characteristics and job satisfaction, but also work design principles, psychological states and motivation. The scope of the theory has made it popular with researchers, who find the combination of a clear specification of variables and inter relationships between them and a readily available measuring instrument particularly attractive.

The initial test of the theory by Hackman and Oldham (1976)

125

generally supported it. They found the core job dimensions of skill variety, task identity and task significance did combine to predict the level of experienced meaningfulness of a job, and the three critical psychological states predicted job satisfaction and motivation reasonably well. The one internal variable, growth need strength, did moderate the relationship between the critical psychological states and the personal work outcomes: individuals with a high score reported higher job satisfaction after experiencing the critical psychological states. Hackman and Oldham did not, however, manage to find the expected relationship between autonomy and feedback and their corresponding psychological states. They were also not able to show strong predictive validities of critical psychological states for objective outcomes, absenteeism and work performance.

Since the original test of the theory, further research has also tended to provide it with only partial support. The moderating effect of GNS on the relationship between the critical psychological states and attitudinal and behavioural outcomes has been fairly well supported (Evans et al., 1979).

The relationship between job characteristics and job satisfaction has been particularly well supported. One meta analysis where a number of studies were examined found impressive average correlations with job satisfaction: task identity .32; task significance .38; skill variety .41; autonomy .46; feedback .41; motivating potential score .53 (Loher et al., 1985). Orpen (1978) studied clerical workers in a South African government department and used the model's principles to modify core job dimensions. After six months the clerks in the redesigned jobs displayed lower levels of absenteeism and reported higher levels of job satisfaction and motivation compared to a control group. He was not able to find any increase, however, in the experimental group's performance. Partial support is also found in Kemp et al. (1983). The careful design of this study of four shift groups at two sites within the same company enabled the effects of site, shift and job characteristics to be separated. A clear relationship emerged between job characteristics and job satisfaction, but not between job characteristics and measures of motivation and performance.

In addition to receiving only partial empirical support, the job characteristics model has also been criticized on conceptual grounds. For example, Wall (1980) pointed out that it fails to take account of a range of contextual variables which affect job satisfaction, motivation and work redesign, such as technology, supervisory style and managerial practices. However, despite these criticisms, its clear specification of objective job characteristics and critical psychological states coupled with the availability of measures for them has meant concepts derived from the model have become central to current research in job satisfaction, motivation, work redesign and mental health in the work place (e.g., Kelloway and Barling, 1991).

CORRELATES OF JOB SATISFACTION

As well as the two theories we have just examined, there have also been attempts to establish whether specific variables such as age, sex or occupational status are predictive of differences in job satisfaction. Weaver (1980), for example, found occupational status correlated significantly with job satisfaction. Managerial, technical, professional and self-employed groups all reported higher levels of job satisfaction than blue-collar workers. Status appear to be the only personal variable which does correlate with job satisfaction. We might, for instance, expect age to correlate with job satisfaction (since older workers have an historical basis for comparing their current rewards), but it appears to account for only about 1 per cent of the differences in scores on job satisfaction measures. Similarly, differences in job satisfaction between males and females are negligible once other variables such as education and status are controlled for.

Sociologists have suggested that out-plant factors can be linked with job satisfaction. One classic study of car assembly workers in Luton found that, although they performed repetitive, semi-skilled work at individual work stations, they expressed a general satisfaction with the work (Goldthorpe *et al.*, 1968). During interviews the assembly workers expressed what the researchers described as a calculative, instrumental orientation to work tasks, workmates and the company. The researchers tentatively linked this instrumental attitude to work to a number of out-plant factors. Workers tended to be young and married with high financial commitments. Luton was a new community and so had a population with no familial links there. Generally the assembly workers had experienced downward social mobility relative to their fathers who had been skilled men. These out-plant factors, the researchers concluded, might in turn cause the assembly workers to construe the term 'job satisfaction' not as 'deriving pleasure from a job' but as 'the practicality of a job'. If the wages were relatively high, which they were, the job was seen simply as a means to a high standard of living.

The Luton study is a useful reminder to psychologists that explanations of job satisfaction which focus exclusively on in-plant variables ignore a whole range of important contextual variables which might cause different groups of workers to construct different meanings as to what constitutes a satisfactory job.

BEHAVIOURAL CORRELATES OF JOB SATISFACTION

So far we have discussed the meaning of job satisfaction and the ways in which it has been explained or predicted, but for most researchers the key issue is the practical one: what are the implications of job satisfaction for workplace behaviour? The common-sense assumption is that if people are content with their work, this will be reflected in behaviour favourable for the organization. In short, the behavioural correlates of job satisfaction should be higher work performance, lower absenteeism and lower staff turnover. This highly plausible assumption was what fuelled a good deal of the managerial interest in the concept in the first place. Yet, as we shall see, an enormous amount of research focused on the practical implications of job satisfaction has failed to establish a strong direct link between job satisfaction and workplace behaviour.

One problem which researchers using job satisfaction measures to predict workplace behavior have encountered is common to all attitude–behavior research: an attitudinal measure as general as job satisfaction cannot be expected to predict specific behaviours. More specific attitudinal questions have been found to have a higher predictive validity. This implies that more specific job satisfaction questions, relating, for example to aspects of task performance, would yield stronger correlations between job satisfaction and workplace behaviour.

Another problem facing researchers is the set of 'intervening variables' that stand between job satisfaction and the behaviour they are trying to predict. Correlations between *absenteeism* and job satisfaction, for instance, have been found to be moderate, usually no higher than $-.35$ (Hackett *et al.*, 1989). The relationship seems to be affected by a series of intervening variables. One ingenious demonstration of this fact is seen in a study by Smith (1977). During his research a heavy unexpected snowstorm occurred in an area in which the company he was studying had an office. He was therefore able to compare attendance in this office with another office within the same company. The snowstorm produced an attendance of 70 per cent compared to 96 per cent in the unaffected office. He found that job satisfaction measures were able to discriminate between those who made a special effort to get through the snowstorm to get to work and those who did not. This meant that the job satisfaction–attendance relationship increased dramatically in the snowstorm office compared with the unaffected office: for example, a measure of satisfaction with career prospects correlated as highly as .6 with attendance.

An elaborate model of the job satisfaction–attendance relationship was proposed by Steers and Rhodes (1978). They suggested the relationship is moderated by a string of variables including pressures to attend (economic, normative, organizational) and ability to attend (illness, family, transportation problems). Their model implies that an individual may have a high level of job satisfaction but often be absent through little ability or pressure to attend.

A similarly complex, indirect and weak relationship appears to exist between job satisfaction and *staff turnover*. The relationship between the two in statistical terms is slightly more substantial, around −.40 (Michaels and Spector, 1982). Once again, though, intervening variables appear to reduce the relationship between the two. Mobley (1977), for example, outlined a model of the relationship which suggested that dissatisfied individuals begin by thinking of leaving, then form the intention to search for another job. This leads to the appraisal of alternatives relative to the present job and finally to a decision to leave or stay. In a test of the model, Mobley *et al.*, (1978) found that, for a sample of hospital employees, the strength of the relationship declined in the way the model predicts: job satisfaction correlated −.54 with thinking of leaving, −.21 with actual turnover.

Finally, the relationship between job satisfaction and *productivity* is the one that has been of most interest to management. Research here suggests that for a number of reasons the relationship is far from straightforward. It has been argued that the relationship varies in strength between different types of job. Since a stimulating job allows holders to experience job satisfaction when they perform well, the relationship between the two variables should be higher in more interesting jobs. However, results of studies testing this hypothesis have not been sufficiently consistent to support it in all circumstances.

Some researchers, on the assumption that the most significant source of satisfaction at work is doing a job well, have suggested the relationship is conceptualized better the other way round: high productivity leads to high job satisfaction (e.g., Wanous, 1974). The implications of this for management seeking higher productivity are quite considerable. The common-sense view suggests that management should concern themselves with their employees' job satisfaction to achieve high productivity. The reverse view, that high performance leads to high job satisfaction, if true, means management simply need to reward past levels of high performance to increase productivity.

The strongest implication of much of the research is that the two variables, job satisfaction and output, are virtually independent of each other. There seem to be at least two possible reasons for this. The first is that, in many jobs, variations in satisfaction cannot lead to variations in productivity. In machine-paced assembly work, for instance, the speed of the production line is constant whatever the level of job satisfaction of people working on the line. Secondly, even when correlations do appear, as Porter and Lawler (1968) have suggested, the associated may be spurious, since both may be associated with another factor. In other words, job satisfaction and productivity may well have largely separate casual paths: one set of factors (e.g. investment in technology) determines productivity, another set (e.g. perceived equity of rewards) produces job satisfaction.

Though much of the interest in job satisfaction research stems from a practical concern with increased productivity, managers have not been provided with easy answers to questions about the nature of the satisfaction–performance relationship. Attempts to increase performance have now been set in a more broadly based theoretical and practical context than job satisfaction. This wider context, which includes changing the organization and design of work, will be examined in Chapter 9.

Further reading

Locke, E.A. and Henne, D. (1986) 'Work Motivation Theories', in Cooper, C.L. and Robertson, I. (eds), *International Review of Industrial and Organizational Psychology*. London: Wiley.

Martin, P. and Nicholls, J. (1987) *Creating a Committed Workforce*. Wimbledon: I.P.M.

Robertson, I., Smith, L and Copper, D. (1992) *Motivation: Strategies, Theory and Practice*. Wimbledon: I.P.M.

Sargent, A., (1990) *Turning People On: The Motivation Challenge*. Wimbledon: I.P.M.

Steers, R.M. and Poster, L.W. (1987) *Motivation and Work Behavior*. New York: McGraw-Hill.

Section Two

Groups and Work

In Section I the fundamental unit of analysis was the individual employee. While psychological properties people bring to the workplace are obviously important, by the early 1930s psychologist realized that several important workplace phenomena could not be satisfactorily explained if the individual employee remained the basic unit of analysis. These psychologists suggested that to advance the understanding of workplace behaviour the focus of research would have to shift from individual to group process.

What had prompted this realization was the Hawthorne studies, a series of experiments conducted by a group of psychologists in a large electrical components factory over a fifteen-year period. The studies suggested that work groups were a fundamental unit of social organization which possessed properties that existed independently of their members. Perhaps the most important conclusions of the Hawthorne researchers were that groups were capable of causing profound changes in their member's perceptions, beliefs, attitudes and behaviour.

The results of the studies were popularized by a management writer, Elton Mayo, who believed management had a lot to gain from an increased awareness of the social dynamics of the workplace. He believed there was a fundamental paradox between the technical accomplishments of modern industry on the one hand and the social incompetence he claimed existed among managers on the other. Thus, Elton Mayo and a group of his colleagues began what became known as the *human relations movement*. They believed that their research and writing offered management to opportunity of increasing their behavioural sophistication, and therefore their effectiveness.

Because much of the initial material produced by the human relations movement was based on a rather paternalistic social ideology, in which managers were assumed to act on rational criteria while workers were seen as motivated by unconscious social 'sentiments', much of it is now discredited. Nonetheless, Mayo and his associates did establish the agenda for what social aspects of the

131

workplace merited detailed attention. In this section we have used the agenda the human relations movement provided but have expanded it where recent developments in the behavioural sciences have added items of interest.

In Chapter 6 we examine the nature of social interaction. Since much of a manager's time is spend interacting with other people, an analysis of what occurs during social encounters is particularly useful, especially if it offers insights into why some individuals are better than others at dealing with people. This analysis thus provides for training programmes which develop the social skills required for successful performance in a job.

The social group, as we suggested above, is a fundamental form of social organization and an analysis of its structures and processes is essential to an adequate understanding of workplace behaviour. In Chapter 7, in addition to examining the effects of group membership on individuals we consider in some detail the research and the movement that began the interest in work groups: the Hawthorne studies and the human relations movement.

Leadership in the workplace was another traditional concern of the human relations movement. The view of human relations writers was that supportive leadership leads to high-performing work groups. In Chapter 8 and we summarize and comment on the vast amount of leadership research undertaken by behavioural scientists to test this and other propositions about what constitutes effective leadership. We conclude with a discussion of the various leadership training programmes that have been developed.

In Chapter 9 we close the section by describing and evaluating research of behavioural scientists involved in the humanization of the workplace. Although behavioural scientists began with a narrow focus on motivation and job satisfaction, many have broadened the scope of their research to include all technological and social features of the workplace that affect the quality of working life. Research now includes the effects of changes in job content, provision for group working, style of supervision and the amount of participation and decision-making present. We conclude by considering what progress has been achieved in providing environments at work that fulfil the human needs of the employees.

6

Social Interaction

In Section I we examined attributes of individuals such as personality and intelligence which can be referred to when explaining or predicting behaviour. Though individual differences are undoubtedly important, it is now time to consider other complementary perspectives. In this chapter we will examine the basic processes underlying the activity between people in every day social settings. The concepts of *dramaturgy* and *social skill* will be central considerations here. The former highlights the expressive and symbolic aspects of social interaction. Writers who have explored the dramaturgy of everyday life have argued that the statistical systems of exploration and classification involved in the study of individual differences are static, and so cannot capture the dynamic and creative aspect of our social activity. The concept of skill, you may remember, embraced both cognitive control of actions and automated behaviour. This implies that we may be unaware of the considerable cognitive achievement our automatic social responses represent. The concept also forces us to consider what kinds of modelling and categorization are involved in social interaction and so helps to explain, for example, how changes in social competence occur over time and why some individuals perform better that others at jobs which involve social skills.

Dramaturgy and impression management

A central theme of this perspective involves our ability to engage in *impression management*. The social world is seen as a stage on which 'actors' constantly create and recreate their social selves according to their conceptions of what it is to be a social person (de Waele and Harré, 1976). Interactions between actors are characterized by each monitoring his or he own performance and the performance of others. Personality, from this perspective, is the internal resources an actor can draw upon to construct a 'social face'. Indeed the personality theory of the future may focus on the goals and competencies that go to make up these resources (Cantor and Kihlstrom, 1987). Thus personality is seen as social intelligence.

Harré (1979) use the term *persona* to describe the social face we present to others. He saw persona production as a kind of intellectual puzzle. Actors have somehow to select the correct persona or range of personas for a given situation. Cialdini (1988), for example, found the highest-earning waiter would constantly change his face according to the type of customer he was serving. With families he was warm and homely, with dating teenagers he was haughty and intimidating. And with the older, lone female customers he was solicitous and confidential. Actors have to be able to recognize, create or define the social situation they are in and possess some knowledge of the rules of behaviour within it. Being able to recognize a solution does not guarantee that actors will give good performances, however. They may be able to define a situation correctly, for instance, but not have an adequate supply of personas to draw upon to act appropriately within it.

Goffman (1971) has also attempted to capture the creative and expressive aspects of our social behaviour. He particularly emphasized the symbolic aspects of our self-presentational activity. He saw social encounters as comprising of a manipulation of both *sign activity* (verbal and non-verbal behaviour) and *sign equipment* (props such as clothes). Actors manipulate these symbolic aspects of social inter-action in order to project definitions of themselves on to situations. This self-definition is termed a *personal front*. Social interaction involves a constant monitoring of our own and other people's personal fronts. To do this, we make comparisons between what Goffman called *the given* and *the given off*. The former are the more controllable aspects of sign activity, particularly verbal behaviour; while the principle source of the latter, less controllable, portion of sign activity is an actor's non-verbal behaviour. Of course, other people are not unaware of being monitored and will attempt to control these aspects of their own sign activity. We, in turn, are aware of the possibility of this kind of manipulation. Individuals differ in the extent to which they monitor their behaviour and other people's reaction to it. Some people seem to be consistently conscious of engaging in impression management and their success in doing so. In others, self-monitoring is less marked (Synder, 1979).

When we monitor others we also expect a correspondence between the *appearance* and *manner* of the other's personal front. Our appearance is determined by our choice of sign equipment, such as style of dress. Our manner indicates the part we want to play during an encounter and is the result of our sign activity: for example, the tone of voice we use. Through we constantly monitor the personal fronts of others, it remains true that we rarely, if ever, attempt to discredit the definitions people present of themselves. Goffman suggested this is because there is a moral obligation or social rule that we should accept other actor's self-definitions. Breaking this rule by damaging the integrity of another person's front severely disrupts interaction and is likely to cause considerable embarrassment.

Goffman argued that individuals often project fronts for tactical reasons without really believing in them. For example, at work a front may be adopted in order to gain some reward, such as a coveted appointment or promotion. Assuming the individual does not drop the front, it may be some time before the individual believes it has anything to do with what he or she feels is 'the real me'.

The adoption of particular fronts is often encouraged by organizations (e.g. Neu, 1991). This is because fronts symbolically convey and dramatically highlight information which might otherwise be unapparent. The formal suit of the executive, for example, gives the impression that tasks will be carried out in a similarly reliable and discreet manner. Goffman claimed that there were at least two disadvantages of preferred fronts as far as organizations were concerned. First, some executives will get their jobs because they 'look the part' rather than through genuine managerial talent. Secondly, getting on in an organization may be determined by the extent to which individuals can manipulate their sign of activity and sign equipment to imitate the personal fronts of their organizational superiors. In both cases, impression management can become more important in the struggle for authority, status and power than competence and accomplishment.

According to Thompson (1961), impression management in the workplace involves at least four personal fronts:

1. *Superior*. Impression management here is concerned with the projection of competence, sincerity, poise and activity.
2. *Subordinate*. Employees in subordinate roles have to project loyalty to company and superiors, deference and dependability.
3. *Specialist*. Those engaged in specialist positions have symbolically to convey dedication to their speciality and disinterest in the organizational power game. They therefore appear incorruptible, concerned only with the truths revealed by their speciality.
4. *Lower participants*. Employees with little or no chance of moving up the hierarchy have to display activity even when there is little or no work to do. Though loyalty is not expected, compliance is. By projecting innocence and limited competence they can maintain their aura of compliance when they transgress rules and legitimately reduce their contribution to the organization.

Thus, from the dramaturgical perspective, much of an individual's activity at work or in other social situations involves symbolically conveying through sign activity and sign equipment aspects of the personal front he or she has adopted. However, it has also been pointed out that side by side with the expressive, self-presentational goals of social interaction that Goffman, Harré and others highlight, social situations also usually involve more specific task-related goals such as selling, negotiating or interviewing. Therefore, the likelihood of successfully attaining a goal in a social situation depends upon a dynamic combination of interpersonal skills (chiefly impression management) together with the more straightforward technical skills. This combination we would define as *social skill*.

Social skill

The skills we deploy in social situations appear to involve developing understandings of three aspects of social interaction: the social situations we must interact within, the person(s) with whom we interact and the components of the 'interactional work' which enable us to attain our goals in social encounters.

UNDERSTANDING SOCIAL SITUATIONS

Understanding the nature of a social situation is essential to a competent social performance in it. If we are unable to perceive what behaviour ought to be used in a particular social situation, we are unlikely to achieve whatever goals we may have been pursuing. How, then do individuals develop a comprehension of situations? This has proved difficult to answer. Social scientists have to be careful not to develop inadequate conceptual frameworks to describe social situations, or they risk creating a gap between the characteristics of situations as described by social researchers and as experienced by people themselves. Argyle *et al.* (1981) have suggested that we should characterize situations as discrete entities, each having its own goals, rules, elements, concepts, settings and roles.

Goals
Social situations, as we have already proposed, provide opportunities for the attainment of goals, both expressive and task-related. Individuals often pursue more than one goal and these can interfere with or assist one another. For example, a supervisor may pursue an expressive goal (to be accepted as an approachable person) and a task goal (such as co-ordinating group activity). An important part of social skill is balancing the demands of expressive and task goals.

Rules

Perhaps the most important aspect of any social situation is the rules which guide individual's goal-directed behaviour. Argyle *et al.* (1981) defined rules as the shared beliefs which dictate which behaviour is permitted, not permitted, or required. In social situations our understanding of the rules regulate our conduct, enabling us to respond to cues and predict the likely effect of our actions. Hence social situations seem to contain two clusters of rules (Argyle *et al.*, 1981). One cluster contains universal rules present in all social situations, such as: use a common language or signalling system; make interaction pleasant (e.g., do not embarrass others); and prevent aggression (e.g. be polite). The second cluster applies to specific social situations; for example, do what the doctor says when in the surgery. Poppleton (1981) analysed the rules which appeared to apply to selling. He found both the universal rules and situation-specific rules: show mood control; listen to objections; do not get into lengthy arguments. Another classification of the rules operating in social situations suggests there are the following:

1. *Interpretative rules.* These provide criteria for interpreting and labelling events in the social world. For example, interpretative rules operating on football terraces define what constitutes 'provocation' from a supporter of the other team.
2. *Prescriptive rules.* These indicate what ought to be done in response, once a situation has been interpreted and understood. In this sense, prescriptive rules also reflect the moral concerns and values of participants in the situation.
3. *Non-generalizable rules.* These are 'one-off' rules created on the spot when routines produced by the more stable rules are interrupted. Non-generalizable rules reflect the fact that social situations are often quite complex, and established rules can rarely cover all the variations and possibilities.

Breaches of prescriptive rules often seen as 'mistakes' by other participants and usually call for an 'explanation'. For example, if a football supporter is too violent and breaches rules about acceptable levels of violence, his behaviour might be explained by other supporters by labelling him a 'nutter' (Marsh, 1982). Breaches of rules in occupational contexts, such as selling or negotiating, drastically reduce the chances of successful outcome to an encounter. In the legal and medical professions a breach of a rule by a practitioner may mean the end of his or her career.

Though the action of rules has proved important for the study of social activity, the impact of rules on situations varies. Brenner (1982) provided a useful classification of the extent to which rules govern behaviour in situations. He suggested situations could be *closed, defined* or *open*. Closed situations have a fully rule-guided character. Ceremonial or ritual situations such as weddings or auctions are closed situations. Defined situations are also rule-guided but involve a certain level of ambiguity about how participants' goals are to be realized. Social skills are therefore crucial to success in defined situations. Rules in open situations have less of an impact on activity, since neither fixed goals nor prescribed interactional routes are present. Informal evenings at home with your family or friends are 'open situations'.

Repertoire of elements

The attainment of goals in situations appears to involve a specific repertoire of 'acts' or 'elements'. Each situation defines a specific repertoire of elements as meaningful and others as inappropriate. Elements can be divided into verbal categories, verbal contents, non-verbal communications and bodily actions. For example, in negotiations the verbal categories would include: offer; accept; and reject. Verbal contents would contain information and settlement points. Non-verbal elements would include: looking; frowning; and smiling. Bodily actions would involve various body postures and perhaps walking out. Knowing the repertoire of elements appropriate to a situation is crucial to a skilled or competent social performance in it.

Concepts

We acquire skills be actively abstracting concepts which appear to have some explanatory utility for the system we are attempting to integrate with. Concepts provide us with the categories which enable us to reduce the complexity of incoming stimuli. In Chapter 1, we cited an account of a production manager whose goal of increased efficiency was achieved by conceptualizing the costing and production system and making cross-references between them. Concepts are also the bases of our comprehension of social situations, other people and social interaction. Professional social skills like selling, supervising, interviewing, negotiating and psychotherapy each involve a specialized set of concepts in addition to the general stock of concepts.

Environmental settings

Environmental psychologists have explored for some time the effects of the physical layout of furniture, barriers (e.g. filing cabinets), the amount of privacy, personal space and crowding on psychological variables such as arousal, interaction, self-evaluations and aggression.

For example, props are often used to divide offices up into 'pressure' and 'semi-social' areas. The pressure area, usually around the desk, is where formal interaction 'in role' occurs, with the occupant of the office taking the lead. The 'semi-social' area, perhaps around a coffee table, provides the opportunity for less formal interaction. Skilled managers are able to select the area of there office most appropriate for the type of interaction they expect to have during a meeting (Korda, 1976). Similarly, a skilled selection interviewer uses the semi-social area to obtain biographical information from a candidate and can further reduce the formality of the situation by sitting at right angles to the candidate rather than directly opposite (McHenry, 1981). Props can also symbolically convey information about personal attributes such as status, competence and affluence.

Roles
Social interaction occurs within the context of a social world structured by the relations in which people stand to one another. Such a structure means that we are able to see order in other people's behaviour, and to predict their likely responses. This in turn reflects the fact that much behaviour involves people enacting social *roles*, for we would define a role as the normal way for people to behave in given situations. At home, for example, the relations of marriage and parenthood give rise to the familial roles of wife, husband, father, mother, son and daughter. At work, the division of labour and distribution of authority create roles like supervisor, manager and worker.

The most important aspect of this structure of relations is the *expectations* that others have of appropriate behaviour within a role. In fact, roles are defined by *the set of expectations that others have of the role incumbent's behaviour*. Some expectations are made explicit by legislation: for example, parents must feed their children and protect them from physical and moral danger. Mixed with whatever legal expectations exist are the cultural assumptions about appropriate behaviour within a role. Both legislation and cultural assumptions are subject to modification.

It is often difficult for us to recognize the profound effect that roles have on our behaviour or that they are part of an external social structure, defined by other people's expectations. This is because we experience social roles not as something external to ourselves, but as personal properties. We manage to translate the set of external expectations about our behaviour in a role into a corresponding set of psychological properties such as beliefs, values, attitudes, prescriptions (I ought to) and proscriptions (I ought not to).

This is referred to as *internalization* of expectations, and can result in major changes in an individual's behaviour. Roles are internalized during *role episodes*, which refer to the whole of the process of perceiving others' expectations of us. These involve:

1. The initial expectations of others of what behaviour is appropriate in a role.
2. Communicating these initial expectations to the new occupant of a role. In the workplace this may involve formal procedures such as training or induction courses, or can occur informally by observing others occupying similar roles.
3. Developing a set of initial assumptions about what behaviour is expected.
4. Testing one's own initial assumptions about appropriate role behaviour by performing tasks.
5. Feedback from others on the extent to which performance matches their expectations.

Finally, we must distinguish between the role itself and *role behaviour*. The main point here is that, although the role itself is structured (like the script in a play), behaviour in a role can be modified by the expressive concerns of individuals (like an actor interprets a part). A new manager, for example, may want to be the most popular or the most innovative in the firm. In this way, roles provide an arena for the interplay of the practical requirements we have to meet and our own expressive concerns.

COMPREHENDING OTHER PEOPLE

In our discussion of general skills in Chapter 1, we saw that skilled individuals develop a *model* or inner representation of the dynamics of the system they are interacting with. This enables them to predict the future states of the system and responses of the system to their actions. The models were based on conceptual categories developed to translate 'raw data' from sources into 'action-relevant inputs'. The categories contained in their models mean that skilled workers could quickly 'read the face of the system' by sampling information from time to time, and so update their models of the state of the system. Therefore, in social interaction we need to construct 'models' of others in order to predict their reactions. In some work-related situations, such as selection interviewing and psychotherapy, constructing a model of the candidate or patient is the principal goal of the encounter. In other situations, supervising of selling for example, developing an adequate understanding of the member of staff or customer plays an important part in the effectiveness of an individual's performance.

Though comparison with skilled activity is useful, since it makes us consider what categories or 'sampling strategies' people use, there are some important differences between social and practical skills. First, the uncertainty presented by people can be very considerable, because individuals can change and they differ in terms of their attitudes, beliefs and goals. Secondly, we have to include in our model what model the other person may have of us.

How, then, do we build these models? People we interact with provide us with a continuous flow of data, both verbal and non-verbal. Language is the symbolic system through which a great deal of our practical and expressive activity is achieved. Argyle's work, however, had demonstrated the importance of 'non-verbal channels' as a source of information about the feelings and attitudes of others towards us. Even when contact occurs through speech alone, as when talking on the telephone, we use features of speech such as accent, changes in tone, pauses and variations in tempo to complement our understanding of the speaker and what he or she has said (Singleton, 1983).

Our attention across verbal and non-verbal channels is as selective and organized as perception in other skilled activities. What we attend to is determined by the 'categories' we use to model others. These, in turn, are often related to the purpose of the encounter. The categories you would employ to model someone you have just met at a party are likely to be different from those employed by a supervisor to model a new subordinate. Whatever categories are employed, much of our attention will be directed towards non-verbal aspects of the other's performance since these also provide us with feedback about our own performance.

There are a number of potential sources of non-verbal information provided by others during social interaction. The most important source is the *face*. As Argyle (1983, p. 33) stated, 'the face gives a fast-moving display of reactions to what others have said or done, and a running commentary on what the owner of the face is saying'. We are able to identify with reasonable accuracy eight emotions and cognitive reactions from the faces of others: happiness; surprise; fear; sadness; anger; disgust; contempt; and interest. We should, however, not forget that the face muscles are under voluntary control. This means that, although a rich source of emotional and attitudinal data is available, facial expressions are very often a mix of wanted and unwanted movements: for example, a polite smile in the bottom half of the face and a frown in the top half.

Gaze performs a number of non-verbal communication functions. We gather information from the faces of others with brief gazes aimed mainly around their eyes. The gaze of other people provides an important additional source of information about their attitudes and feelings towards us. High levels of gaze can indicate a range of feelings

141

towards us from love, through interest, to hate. Argyle and Cook (1976) reviewed gaze studies and found high gaze from another person could indicate the other is: interested in you; of low status; attempting to dominate you; extrovert; and not embarrassed. In some contexts, correctly decoding gaze is extremely useful. For example, Goodfellow (1983) described how the skilled teacher could decode the slightest gaze from a pupil to detect whether anything was amiss, and whether the pupil was being mildly mischievous or malicious. Decoding gaze becomes less accurate in encounters between people from different cultures, because the use of gaze varies considerably across cultures (Watson, 1970). This means gaze can become the source of considerable embarrassment and misunderstanding in cross-cultural encounters. Negotiators involved in selling to foreign clients need to be able to decode correctly the level of gaze being received and display the appropriate level of gaze within the context of a particular culture.

Additional sources of non-verbal information include *body posture* and *body movement*. Though these do not usually provide specific information about the attitudes or emotions of others towards us, they can indicate their general emotional state or mood. In some contexts where a person is being judged (such as a selection interview), they may attempt to suppress indicators of mood, and here *non-verbal leakage* can provide an indication of how relaxed, anxious or confident the person is. Skilled interviewers can use leakage, such as excessive lower body movements, to make a guess about the nature of the candidate's feelings on the subject, and if necessary return to the subject later in the interview (McHenry, 1981). Mood is often contagious. An awareness of the role played by body posture and movements in conveying information about mood is important in professional contexts since it reduces the risk of contagion occurring. The sales person, for example, needs to be aware of the mood being signalled by his or her body posture or movements when dealing with customers. If it is not positive it is likely to be 'caught' by customers (Potter, 1983). The selection interviewer similarly needs to be careful he or she does not catch the mood (particularly anxiety) of the candidate.

Appearance often provides us with a rich source of information about others, particularly when little other information is available. Although aspects of the other's personal front are highly controllable, they are nonetheless often assumed to be an important source of information about attitudes, allegiances, status or class. In addition, appearance can be used in an active mode to convey highly specific messages. On the football terraces, for example, minor differences in the way scarves are tied, the precise type of footwear and the length of the trousers people wear all contribute significantly to the models football fans construct of each other (Marsh, 1982).

Personal construct theory
Given all these potential sources of information, how do we make inferences about others? As we suggest earlier, the *filtering and selection* from among these inputs is determined by the categories we employ. This was the basic assumptions of Kelly's (1955) personal construct theory, which has provided behavioural scientist with a novel way of exploring how individuals comprehend situations and others. Constructs are 'bipolar adjectives' with which individuals organize their perception of the world and provide it with meaning. Examples of the type of constructs used in daily interaction are intelligent–dull, rejecting–accepting, autocratic–democratic, stable–unstable and promotable–unpromotable. Marsh's (1982) study provided some more specific examples of the way football supporters examine the appearance of other fans and mold them using constructs such as loyal–disloyal and hard–soft.

Summarizing research on the way individuals construct others, Adams-Webber (1981) found:

1. People exhibit stable idiosyncratic preferences for using particular sets of constructs in characterizing themselves and others.
2. People are consistent over time in the number of different constructs they employ to describe people they know.
3. If they are able to obtain more information about others, people's construct systems develop in terms of a gradual shift of emphasis from a primary concern with appearance, social roles and behaviour to a predominant interest in personality.
4. The personal meaningfulness of any construct used by an individual will depend partly on the context in which the individual typically applies it.
5. The personal meaningfulness of any construct also depends on its implicative potential: the number of specific inferences an individual can make from a particular construct to other related constructs within his or her own system.

According to personal construct theory, the structure and content of an individual's construct system are what determines his or her ability to make a variety of distinctions between people and their personalities. This simplest feature of a construct system which can be considered is how *elaborate* it is. The more constructs an individual can employ in a situation, the more able he or she will be to make inferences above the other's personality and motives. The more elaborate a construct system is, the more an individual is able to construe an interaction from different perspectives and make inferences about the attitudes of others involved (Neimeyer and Hudson, 1985). Professional social skills such as interviewing, selling or negotiating are supported by a stock of valid constructs enabling relevant predictions to be made about other participants. An individual's preference for particular constructs may reduce the validity of the models of others which are constructed. For example, if a selection interviewer's construing of candidates is dominated by very idiosyncratic constructs such as 'plays rugby – does not play rugby', 'will come to the pub at lunchtime – won't come to the pub at lunchtime', the validity of selection decisions will be drastically reduced.

Constructing other people adequately is also facilitated by what Kelly (1955) termed *commonality*, namely the extent to which there is overlap or similarity between the constructs and construing processes of oneself and others. This is because similarity between one's own constructs and those of another person make it easier to understand their psychological processes. Commonality has been found to be a good predictor of friendship formation among groups of individuals (Duck, 1973).

Having an overlap or commonality with other people's construct systems does not always guarantee comprehension. A person may possess very similar constructs and construing processes to others but may still make little or no attempt to understand them. At this more complex level, where we have to take into account people's motives and wishes, comprehending the other involves what Kelly termed *sociality*. This is the deliberate attempt to subsume the construing processes of the other into one's own construct system. Sociality does not necessarily involve commonality. A manager, for example, may be able to subsume a subordinate's construct system without their respective construct systems being similar. Commonality, however, as we have already suggested, does increase the probability of success of attempts to subsume the construct system of others.

Kelly saw sociality as the key to viable social relationships: 'to the extent that one person construes the construction processes of another, he may play a role in a social process involving the other person'. In occupational settings, sociality is essential to skilled social performance. In selling, for example, sociality enables predictions to be made about what aspect of the product or service will be most attractive to the customer (Potter, 1983) and enable the salesperson to anticipate the customer's information-processing capacity (Moorhouse, 1983; Poppleton, 1981). In supervision sociality provides a supervisor with an idea of how subordinates will treat instructions. Sociality is not always one-way or asymmetrical: most social situations, particularly in professional setting, involve some degree of mutual construing. But not everyone is aware that mutual construing occurs in social encounters. Some people model others often quite elaborately but do not comprehend that others are also modelling them. Some people model others but assume others have a fixed and fully established model of them. The hallmark of social skill is when we actively develop models of others while assuming that they are actively modelling us.

Ross and Nisbett (1991) described some of the attributional errors resulting from failing to take another person's construal into account. As they point out:

> the real source of difficulty does not lie in the fact the human beings subjectively define the situations they face, nor even in the fact that they do so in variable and unpredictable ways. Rather the problem lies in their failure to recognize and make adequate inferential *allowance* for this variability and unpredictability. (p. 82)

This failure has important effects on our ability to comprehend others. Because, rather egocentrically, we assume our construal of the situation is 'correct', we believe others' construal will be similar. This leads to what is termed the *false consensus effect*. Assuming others possess similar constructions of events means we explain apparently deviant behaviour in others in terms of unusual and extreme personality traits rather than different construals of the situation.

Thus, in one experiment described by Ross and Nisbett, subjects were asked to help with a study into 'communication techniques'. If they were prepared to help (they could opt to sign up for a later study) they would have to walk around the campus for thirty minutes with a sandwich board with the message 'Eat at Joe's'. Subjects were asked to give their own decisions about whether to participate, and to estimate other people's decisions. The false consensus effect appeared in subjects assuming the majority of their peers would make the same decision as they had. The choice to participate or not depended on the subjects' construal of (a) what the experiment was about (conformity, uptightness, being a 'sport'); (b) the reaction of their peers; and (c) the reaction of the experimenter to a refusal.

These subtle differences in construal of the situation determined the decision to sign up or not. But both 'compliant' and 'non-compliant' subjects confidently attributed extreme personality traits to explain the other group's behaviour. As Ross and Nisbett concluded, not making adequate allowance for differences in construal is ultimately a failure: 'to recognize the degree to which ... interpretations of the situation are just that – constructions and inferences rather than faithful reflections of some objective and invariant reality' (p. 85).

As we have seen, personal construct theory suggests that we actively construct models of one another. It also suggests this process can go wrong. We have already seen the lack of commonality, sociality and adequate constructs reduces the probability of a valid model of the other being constructed.

There are two other ways in which a model's validity can be reduced: *pre-emption* and *circumspection.* Pre-emption, the cutting short of construing processes, is seen when there is lack of time, willingness or capacity to construe others. When construing is pre-empted the model is constructed out of stereotypes and ready-made generalizations. In contrast to this, circumspection involves the excessive construing of others and a consequent failure to commit oneself to a particular view of or lines of action with them. Circumspection is triggered by the uncertainty and ambiguity which other people's behaviour or personalities contain. Attempting to cope with this uncertainty can, as with neurotic thought, cause individuals to become 'preoccupied with' or 'lodged in' construing. Social skills depend on an ability to strike and appropriate balance between the pre-emptive and the circumspective construing of other people.

INTERACTIONAL WORK

The concept of skill is particularly helpful when examining the 'interactional work' which constitutes much of our social life and through which our practical and expressive goals are attained. Like other skilled work, interactional work possesses a hierarchal structure, and therefore offers a number of possible units of analysis. Words form up into sentences, sentences construct social acts (demanding, asserting, complying, rejecting, etc.), social acts build up into episodes (a group of social acts characterized by some internal homogeneity such as an introduction) and episodes form encounters (interviews, sales negotiations, team briefings, etc.). This building up of encounters out of words is termed *concatenation* (Harŕe, 1979). Achieving goals in social situations therefore depends on the ability to build up and progress through social encounters. As we shall see, progress has been made in describing how this is achieved.

Open sequences

If we use Brenner's (1982) topology of situations described earlier, we can consider the skills required for competent interaction in different types of situation. We can begin with those situations he termed 'open', which seemingly involved neither prior goals nor specific interactional routes for participants. For example, simply talking to friends in a chance encounter usually involves no specific objectives or sequences of interaction. In these situations discourse is relatively unplanned, lacking forethought or organization (Ochs, 1983). Sequences of interaction in open situations involve what Jones and Gerard (1967) termed *reactive contingency*: that is, each participant simply responds to what the previous contributor has said.

Even in these seemingly 'open' situations it is possible to discern some rules operating to shape sequences. At the simplest level, participants have to co-ordinate their contributions. *Turn-taking* is achieved using principles acquired at the earliest stages of the development of interactional competence. Young children capable of only one- or two-word utterances take turns to make their contributions, which to the annoyance of many a parent they tend to repeat until the other participant has acknowledged what they have said. Schieffelin (1983), for example, found 30-month-old children attending to each other's contribution and sustaining interactions of over twenty-five turns. In adulthood, the conventions for indicating a desire to retain, obtain or hand over the role of contributor are usually so well learned that we are unaware of them. Analyses of interaction show individuals signal a willingness to hand over the role of contributor by pausing, gazing at each other at the end of a contribution or asking a question. Gaze at the end of a contribution is used not only to signal a willingness to hand over the floor but also to gain feedback on how others have reacted to a contribution. Keeping the floor involves not pausing, not looking at others at the end of sentences, using certain gestures and raising one's voice. To take the floor, a participant needs to listen for what Sacks *et al.* (1974) described as 'transition relevance space'. At these points in the interaction an individual uses particular grammatical constructions as 'place-holders' which give him or her time to construct a well-formed proposition (Duranti and Ochs, 1979).

In addition to turn-taking, participants in conversation also appear to adhere to other rules:

1. Quantity. Contributions should be as informative as possible without providing too much information.
2. Quality. Contributions should be true or have sufficient evidence to support them
3. Relevance. Contributions should be relevant to what has preceded them.
4. Manner. Contributions should be clear, unambiguous and organized (Grice, 1975).

Orderliness also appears at the level of the social acts performed by contributors. Clarke (1983) discovered that subjects could rearrange into the correct order cards containing single contributions taken from informal sequences of interaction. More importantly, they could do the same for a set of cards on which the various social acts constituted by these contributions had been written. The orderliness of subjects detected among social acts was between pairs such as question–answer, offer–accept, request–comply and reject–reason. These sequences are known as *two-step* sequences. The ability of his subjects to recognize orderliness in interaction at the level of both social act and sentences led Clarke to suggest that there was a 'grammar' or 'syntax' of social acts analogous to that of languages. One such rule, which enables people to perceive orderliness, reflects generally held beliefs about sustaining harmony in social interaction. For instance, if an individual is to sustain a pleasant exchange, he or she must provide a reason after refusing an offer because of a general belief that offers should be accepted, even when acceptance involves inconvenience.

Although two-step sequences are observable in many interactions, there do not seem to be regularities in associations between two-step units in most situations. Sequences of more than two acts are generated by the persistence over time of an individual's goals, In the relatively unplanned discourse of open situations, the goal of a participant is often simply to establish and sustain what are termed *discourse topics* (a concern or a set of concerns). If an individual wants to sustain a discourse topic, he or she needs to match a contribution to the preceding utterance of the other person. This produces sequences termed *topic-collaborating sequences.* If, however, an individual wishes to continue the flow of discourse but change the topic, the previous contributor's last utterance can be used to create a new discourse topic. These sequences are termed *topic-incorporating sequences.* New discourse topics can also be introduced by 'breaking and entering': that is, by creating discontinuities in the dialogue. This can be done either by introducing a new discourse topic which has already appeared in the 'discourse history' or negotiating a completely new discourse topic (Ochs and Schieffelin, 1983). The skills required to sustain or negotiate new discourse topics in open situations include: securing the other's attention; articulating utterances clearly; providing sufficient information for the other to identify objects, people or events (referents) included in the discourse topic; providing sufficient information for the other to understand the relationships between referents of the discourse topic; locating and attending to sources of misunderstanding ('repair work'); and shaping utterances taking into account what is termed the other's 'presupposition pool', and estimation of what the other person understands ('recipient design').

Defined sequences
Interaction in defined situations, such as between incumbents of organizational roles, involves more than merely attempting to draw on each other's presupposition pools to sustain discourse topics. At least one participant will invariably have an objective. This may be to provide the other with information, sell the other something or make a selection decision. Utterances are, therefore, preceded by more forethought and planning than in 'open' situations, and discourse is relatively planned. One feature of this is the *four-step* sequence, produced by a goal of one participant persisting after the other's response, as in the following example:

A	Interviewer: (question)	Why do you want to leave your present job?
B	Candidate: (inadequate response)	I would rather not go into that.
C	Interviewer: (accounts for question)	I think we really do need to know why you have decided to leave our major competitor.
D	Candidate: (adequate response)	I felt the company no longer offers me the challenges I'm looking for.

Here, the interviewer's goals of ascertaining the candidate's reason for leaving persists from A through B to C. Sequences structured by the goal of one participant only possess what Jones and Gerard (1967) termed *asymmetrical contingency*, one participant responding according to the objectives of the other.

In encounters between individuals occupying specific roles, it is usually the case that both participants have goals. Encounters in these 'defined' situations, as Benner (1982) point out, may still be relatively under-identified for participants in a number of ways. The precise nature and variability of the other's objectives or initial construction of the situation may not be known. No routine sequences of interaction are built into defined situations so a strategy for dealing with the encounter has to be worked out. This means participants have to establish a *working consensus* of what type of situation they are involved in. This then provides the stable ground on which they can base a strategy for interaction (McCall and Simmons, 1966).

The ambiguity and unstructuredness that still reside in defined situations make social skills an important determinant of effectiveness in them. To establish a working consensus of a situation individuals need to be able to construe the construing processes of others. As

Singleton (1983, p. 291) pointed out, 'in the case of social skills reality is not only physical events, it is also the schemata in other people's minds which control their attempts to communicate'. An individual, therefore, must be able to detect, absorb and recreate the schemata or models which lie behind the initial statements of other participants. As we have seen, the complexity of an individual's construing was related to his or her ability to construe a situation from another's point of view. In selling, for example, the ability to imagine being the customer enables a salesperson to understand the customer's needs

Establishing a working consensus of a situation is also assisted by a degree of commonality between the participants' construct systems. An individual's willingness to share constructs increases the likelihood of this commonality between constructions of a situation being achieved. By sharing constructs, individuals allow others to check to what extent their models of the situation map on to each other. If, for example, a manager's and subordinate's constructions of a situation do not map on to each other reasonably well, interaction is unlikely to get very far and some form of conflict or opposition may ensue. Sharing constructs allows the other to accept, elaborate, modify and return the model until the models map on to each other sufficiently well for a working consensus of the situation to have developed.

Having established a working consensus, participants can develop a strategy for dealing with the encounter and for achieving their objectives. At this stage skilled communication requires the same skills as those required in 'open' situations. To move nearer to our goals our contributions must possess good recipient design. The skilled communicator is sensitive to cues provided by the listener which enable utterances with good recipient design to be constructed. Increasing sensitivity to these cues is now central to training programmes in many areas where professional competence depends on social skills. For example, sales training once consisted of requiring salespeople to rote-learn scripts. In other words, training was based on an implicit model of simple asymmetrical contingency in interaction – a one-way communication from the salesperson to the customer. Nowadays, however, sales training emphasizes the importance in successful selling of sensitivity to cues from customers.

In selling, as in other areas where professional social skills are employed, an accurate estimation of the listener's ability to process information is crucial. The skilled salesperson is able to provide screened and selected information at a pace which matches the customer's ability to assimilate it. One device known as 'checkback', where agreement is sought from a customer (e.g. 'don't you agree?'), enables the salesperson to ensure that he or she is working at the same pace as the customer. If checkback indicates that a customer's pace has been exceeded, the salesperson would need to engage in 'repair work', locating and attending to the points when the customer was lost. Checkback is also thought to increase the commitment of a customer to the salesperson's objectives.

Listeners can also be lost by asking what are known as *closed questions*, which require simple definitive responses. The importance of avoiding these closed questions has been stressed in situations as diverse as selling (Potter, 1983) and psychotherapeutic interviews (Barker, 1983). The closed question often creates a hiatus which allows listeners to disengage from the discourse. A further way listeners are lost is when statements threatening their self-esteem or self-concept are used. This means *tact* is an important component of social skill, since it protects the feelings of listeners and so retains their attention. Argyle (1983, p. 51)) defined tact as 'the production of socially effective utterances in difficult situations'. In selling, for example, a salesperson needs to transform 'do you have the authority to order?' into 'do you normally decide on the ordering or do you leave that up to someone else?'

Tact is also a component of a crucial skill in professional and occupational settings, namely dealing with objections. In modern complex organizations people's objections and grievances often stem from real conflicts of interest, and may not be readily handled even by tactful negotiation. But in many cases objections that result from disappointments or misunderstandings can be resolved. Loveridge (1983) described a sequence for handling grievances in line management: search; probe; handle; and restructure. For example, a subordinate claims she is not able to use her skills fully. By searching and probing on the basis of her statements, her supervisor establishes that the source of the grievance is actually her feeling that she should have been promoted by now. Handling and restructuring involve carefully readjusting her expectations in line with a more realistic time-scale for acquiring the experience necessary for competence in a promoted post. In selling, one commonly used sequence for handling objections is: welcome; restate; overcome; and continue. For example, an objection is welcomed by the salesperson: 'I can understand how you feel, Mr Jones.' It is restated to enable the salesperson to confirm precisely what the objection refers to: 'You're unhappy about using the magazine because you don't believe it is reaching 25,000 potential customers.' The salesperson can then overcome the objection by giving more information: 'As I mentioned earlier our circulation is fully controlled so we can guarantee who is receiving it.' If the

151

customer accepts this response the salesperson returns to the point before the objection occurred.

The ability to progress smoothly through an interactional sequence in pursuit of a goal appears to be crucial at all levels of interaction in social encounters: sentences, social acts and episodes. The generally held beliefs about sustaining harmony in social interaction and presenting pleasant fronts operate at all these levels. Thus, entire social encounters, particularly in defined situations, need to have the practical purpose of the meeting sandwiched between episodes in which a harmonious social relationship is established, for example by recalling the last meeting, and then re-established, perhaps by arranging a future meeting. This gives rise to the common five-episode structure for encounters: greeting; establishing relationship; central task; re-establishing relationship; and parting (Argyle *et al.*, 1981).

All these episodes are themselves built up out of two-step and four-step sequences. the central task, containing the practical purpose of the encounter, may itself by comprised of a number of smaller episodes. For example, the central task in a sales encounter often involves: (1) gaining the interest of the customer; (2) identifying the customer's needs; (3) selling the benefits of a particular item or service to the customer; (4) overcoming the customer's objections; and (5) clinching the sale. Argyle and Lydall (in Argyle, 1983) found that high selling sales staff were those who by developing a good rapport with the customer could move smoothly through the episodes involved in the central task and were thus more likely to clinch the sale.

Like other skilled activity, then, social skills involved a smooth progression towards a goal. This means that responses should be well timed and in the correct order. An appropriate sequencing of responses for socially skilled behaviour ultimately depends on the validity of the models we construct of the people we interact with and of the social situations in which we find ourselves.

Further reading

Argyle, M. (1983) *The Psychology of Interpersonal Behaviour* (4th Edn). Harmondsworth: Penguin.

Argyle, M. (1990) *Bodily Communication* (2nd Edn). International Universities.

Burkitt, I. (1991) *Social Selves: Theories of the Social Formation of Personality*. London: Sage.

Krate, B. (1990) *Situation Cognition and Coherence in Personality:*

An Individual–Centered Approach. Cambridge: Cambridge University Press.

Rakos, R.F. (1990) *Assertive Behaviour: Theory, Research and Training.* London: Routledge.

Ross, L. and R.E. Nisbett (1991) *The Person and The Situation.* New York: McGraw Hill.

Taylor, D. and S. Bishop (1991) *Fifty Activities for Interpersonal Skills Training.* Aldershot: Gower.

7

Group and Intergroup Behaviour

Much of our social interaction takes place in a group context, and we will now go on to discuss the effects of group memberships on social behaviour. Groups can be considered in terms of the *structures* they develop, the *processes* they involve and their *interaction* with other groups. In this chapter we will examine these three aspects of groups, and conclude with a discussion of a series of classic experiments in work groups, the *Hawthrone studies*, which, as we shall see, have had a profound influence on management thinking.

Before considering the effects of groups membership on social behaviour we should first ask the question: how and why do groups form? Although there is no straightforward answer to this, at least two main assumptions about the basis of group formation have been put forward. Some writers stress the *functional* reasons for the existence of groups, such as joint action on a task; face-to-face interaction; or mutually dependent relationships. Others have emphasize the *psychological* processes that cause groups to form; the perception of a shared social identity; and attempting to fulfil needs for affiliation and supportive relationships. In real-life groups we can often see a predominantly functional basis of formation, or a psychological basis; or, as is often the case, a mixture of the two.

Fiedler (1967) has provided a useful typology of work groups based on the nature and intensity of the interaction they involve:

1. *Interacting groups.* Members are interdependent and need to co-operate and co-ordinate their actions to accomplish the group task.
2. *Co-acting groups.* Members work together on a common task but do so relatively independently.
3. *Counteracting groups.* Individuals work together for the purposes of negotiating and reconciling conflicting demands and objectives. Performance is measured by the acceptability of the solution to group members.

This typology reflects the extent to which group members' behaviour is determined by group structure and processes. The impact on members' behaviour, values and attitudes of interacting and counter-acting groups is far greater than in co-acting groups because of the increased intensity of interaction they involve.

Group structure

The structure of a group reflects the basis of group identity – and indeed the very fact that we can speak of a group at all rather than merely a number of individuals. For structure reflects the established patterns of behaviour that are distinctive within a particular group. Structure constitutes a distinctively *social* aspect of group life, and may act as an objective constraint on members' activity. One important aspect of structure consists of the different *categories of membership* that the different individuals making up the group occupy.

1. Early on in a group's history a *group leader* will often emerge because he or she is perceived by other members as the most competent at the functional requirements of the leadership role. The division of status and authority between group leaders and followers that this implies is an important dimension of group structure. Bales and Slater (1955) suggested these functional requirements were related both to the group's task and to the group's socio-emotional requirements. Behaviours associated with the task include co-ord-inating, initiating contributions, evaluating, information-giving, infor-mation-seeking, opinion-giving, opinion-seeking, and motivating individuals. Behaviours associated with the group's socio-emotional requirements include reconciling differences, arbitrating, encouraging participation and increasing interdependence among group members. One individual may be perceived by the group as capable of meeting both the socio-emotional and task requirements of the leadership role. In some groups, however, two leaders may emerge, each with perceived competence in one of these leadership functions.

2. Group *members* can be defined as individuals who have accepted group goals as relevant and recognize an interdependence with other group members in the achievement of these goals. Acceptance of group goals is associated with an individual's needs (subsistence, dependence, affiliation, dominance) and the extent to which his or her social identity is derived from membership of the group. Individuals can also decide whether to accept group goals on the basis of a rational estimation of the utility of group membership.

3. Sometimes, however, an individual's personal goals conflict with the group's goals; and if he or she is not prepared to modify his or her personal goals, dissatisfaction with the group becomes almost inevitable. The individual is then identified as a *deviate*. Group members will usually attempt to increase the deviate's acceptance of

155

group goals. Indeed, persuading a deviate to accept group goals can absorb a considerable proportion of a group's time.

4. If deviates resist group pressure and continue to reject group goals, the group will eventually give up on them and they are left alone by other group members. They become *isolates*. Though they may be tolerated because their output is required, they are unlikely to be included in activities which do not directly involve the task. In extreme cases group members may seek not only the psychological isolation of such individuals but their physical isolation too.

A frequently used typology of membership categories in management teams was developed by Belbin (1981). He argued a manager's personality predisposes him or her towards one or other of his categories.

1. *Chairperson.*This is the person who attempts to establish the goals and agenda of the group. He or she will allocate roles and responsibilities and sum up the feelings and accomplishments of the group. Assertiveness, affiliativeness and conscientiousness drive the behaviours of the chairperson.
2. *Plant.* Essentially the plant is the ideas person. Plants thus tend to be more innovative and to search for possible changes in the group's approach to its problems. They tend to be intelligent, introverted and imaginative.
3. *Company Worker.* This is the team member who converts ideas and objectives into practical operational procedures. Company workers tend to be task-oriented, conscientious and affiliative.
4. *Monitor evaluator.* This team member analyses problems and evaluates the contributions of others. Those around the monitor evaluator may feel he or she pours scorn on their suggestions. Monitor evaluators tend to be sober, introverted and shrewd.
5. *Shaper.* Extroverted, tense and defensive shapers are anxious to prioritize and structure the group's activities.
6. *Teamworker.* Affiliative and not overly dominant, teamworkers focus on the interpersonal behaviour of team members. They encourage participation, arbitrate and harmonize.
7. *Resource investigator.* Extroverted, imaginative and stable, resource investigators identify ideas and resources in the external environment which are available to the group.
8. *Completer.* This team member is keen to complete the tasks to the deadline. Completers identify areas which need more work and possible oversights. Anxiety and conscientiousness are the traits driving this team member.

Belbin argued effective teams require a balance of all these roles. Individuals have a preferred team role or primary role and a back-up role with which there is some affinity. Belbin's work has been extremely useful since it emphasizes the need for a variety of membership categories if teams are going to succeed. It is easy to imagine the consequences of a project team comprised entirely of plants.

More specifically, Belbin suggests for management teams to function effectively there has to be the following:

1. A chairperson – to show patience, command, seek out ability and elicit trust.
2. A strong plant – to produce ideas for the group.
3. A spread in mental ability – the plant needs at least one other member to bounce ideas off.
4. A range of membership categories available to the group.
5. A match between the responsibilities of team members and their preferred membership category.
6. An ability to identify and adjust to imbalances in the group.

Groups have their most significant impact on our behaviour through the operation of *norms*. Indeed, many social psychologists believe that behaviour in groups can be understood only in relation to the norms that are operating within it, since they represent the *expectations* within the group for appropriate behavior of group members. As these expectations are external to each member, norms are thus part of a group's structure. It is often hard for individuals to realize the impact that the expectations of others have on their behaviour (as it was in the similar case of roles, discussed in Chapter 6) because norms become part of their psychological make-up, affecting their attitudes, values, beliefs and behaviour. Guirdham (1990) suggests that there are three norms which are generally present at work.

1. *Fairness*. We have already seen in Chapter 6 how equity operates as a motivator. In the context of group norms we generally expect other group members to behave equitably. If they do not, we either get distressed or attempt to punish them.
2. *Reciprocity*. this implies that if A does something for B, B has a duty to do something for A. This norm helps in initiating contacts since, if A is polite to B, there is a duty on B to be polite to A.
3. *Reasonableness*. Guirdham claims most people in business expect each other to behave reasonably, by for example not exploiting or withholding payment from suppliers and therefore taking excessive credit.

A group's norms do not occur by accident; they represent the interaction of social, historical and psychological processes, and they are thus resistant to change. In Chapter 4, for instance, we discussed an example of the historical development of group norms when

157

considering the effort bargain at work, which we saw emerged from a normative consensus about what constitutes a fair ratio of effort to reward. Although norms are generated out of the practical activity of groups, and are embedded in their experiences and history, when necessary groups can also generate norms very quickly.

If a group suddenly faces very different demands or the novel conditions are such that it is necessary to form a new group, then the ability to generate norms quickly may well be essential to the group's survival. Industrial disputes provide a number of examples of sudden changes in circumstances. For instance, in the 1980 steel strike the unions involved had no previous experience of strikes and thus of strike organization. The norms structuring the activities of the various newly formed groups (local picket cells, picket control groups and the various levels of the strike committee) had to be established quickly in order to carry out the numerous activities (e.g. fund-raising, dealing with the media, striker welfare, support services for pickets) necessary to maintain and enhance the strike.

The principal way in which group norms are absorbed is through observation. At work, for example, a new employee will estimate the norms for attendance, workrate and dress from the group's modal behaviour – that is, how most people in the group behave. Group members also observe the extent to which an individual's behaviour matches the group's norms. Norms usually include a degree of tolerance and specify a range of acceptable behaviour, known as the *zone of acceptance*, so that members will take action only if another member's behaviour falls outside this range. For example, in the Hawthrone studies which we will be discussing in greater detail later in the chapter, the norms included: (1) not 'rate-busting' (turning out too much work); (2) not 'chiselling' (turning out too little work); (3) not 'squealing' (telling the supervisor anything detrimental to the group). Anyone who deviated from these norms was subjected either to sarcasm and ridicule or to a physical penalty – a harsh blow to the upper arm – known in the plant as 'binging'. These sanctions generally ensured conformity to group norms. Groups thus wield an enormous amount of power over their members.

Group processes

We turn now to the *process* of interaction within groups, which refers to the manner in which group action is constructed on a continuing basis. Unlike structure, process emphasizes changes in the flow of activities; indeed group processes indicate how structures become established and how over time they may change. Process also points to the subjective perceptions of group members and their active involvement in group life.

COHESIVENESS

Cohesiveness can be defined as the complex of forces which gives rise to the perceptions by members of a group identity. The cohesiveness of groups has a major impact on their functioning. Its most important effect is on the *potency* of group norms–that is, the extent to which norms determine behaviour within a group. The cohesive work group can develop norms that present management with major problems, for example by enforcing conformity to a workrate far below what is considered acceptable by management. Equally, they can be a great asset to management, for example by having norms which prescribe a willingness to put in additional effort when required. Not surprisingly, then, sources of groups cohesiveness are of considerable interest.

A proportion of any group's time will be spent on what are termed *process issues*, such as getting to know other members and resolving any interpersonal difficulties. And if the problems arising from process issues are successfully dealt with, the group will be a reasonably harmonious and cohesive social unit. The *stability* of group membership plays an important part in a group's capacity to resolve process problems, and if changes in membership are infrequent these problems will be reduced to a minimum and group members can concentrate on task performance. Thus, frequent changes in membership increase the time spent on process issues, and may disrupt the development of group cohesiveness. The stability of groups in the workplace can involve wider issues. Clegg and Fitter (1978), for example, describe how the management of a confectionery company attempted to improve the very low levels of job satisfaction among their workforce by stabilizing membership. Demand for the firm's product was seasonal, and traditional policy had been to lay off staff and employ staff according to demand. But this undermined the cohesiveness of work groups which depended on the stability of membership. Thus management recognized that they had to adopt a policy of evening out production over the year.

The *attractiveness* of group membership is also an important ingredient in the creation of a cohesive group, since the more attractive a group is to its members, the more they will desire its continued existence and work to make it a cohesive social unit. The attractiveness of a group is partly determined by its *composition*. Members of a group have to get along with each other, which may be difficult if they are very different in status, values, attitudes, abilities or interests. At the same time, if group members are too similar, some of the benefits of group cohesion will be lost. For example, if members

159

all have similar views, a range of alternatives is unlikely to be considered. Moderate heterogeneity in a group balances the requirements of cohesion and productivity (Hackman, 1980). Group attractiveness is also influenced by the extent to which its members are *dependent* on it either to satisfy their psychological needs or to achieve their goals (Cartwright and Zander, 1968).

As we will see when discussing intergroup behaviour, a group's relationships with other groups have an important effect on cohesiveness. *Competition* with other groups causes a group member to perceive other members as more similar than they actually are (Turner, 1982). This increases solidarity within the group and the willingness of group members to co-operate with one another.

While the primary importance of cohesiveness, as we stated earlier, lies in determining the impact of a group's norms on its members, membership of such groups has been found to have a number of other important effects on group members and group functioning. Perhaps the most important of these is the beneficial effects a cohesive group has on its members' psychological state. In fact, this aspect is utilized by psychotherapists who treat their patients in groups. Positive identification with a cohesive group enhances an individual's self-concept and self-esteem, while supportive interpersonal relationships reduce anxiety and satisfy a range of ego needs. These benefits do not, however, always occur. Inexperienced psychotherapists may, for example, not be able to prevent one member's self-esteem being damaged if they are victimized by other members of the group. However, most therapists feel the benefits of using cohesive groups outweigh the potential disadvantages.

SYNERGY

If we consider decision-making within groups, or committees in organizations, the common-sense view of committees is that they take a great deal of time to produce poor-quality decisions. Much of the research on groups, however, reveals the opposite, that in most conditions groups outperform even their best member (Hill, 1982). This phenomenon of groups has been termed *synergy*, and is demonstrated by group exercises like 'Lost on the Moon' (Hall, 1971). This begins with each member being asked to imagine being lost on the moon and having to decide on the priority of items he or she would include for the journey back to the mother ship. The members are then asked to achieve a consensus of opinion on the ranking of items. When a consensus has been achieved, individual and group rankings are compared to a ranking produced by NASA experts. The group's ranking is usually superior to any of the individual rankings. This and similar exercises are used widely in management training, since they provide a quick method of demonstrating the synergistic qualities of groups, and thus indicate both the invalidity of the common-sense view of groups and their decision-making potential.

Synergy occurs because discussion within groups generates more alternatives than individuals, tends to eliminate inferior contributions, averages out errors and supports creative thinking. This means groups invariably have the edge over other individuals in situations where accuracy is a priority, errors are expensive and time is relatively cheap.

GROUP INNOVATION

Peters and Waterman in their 1982 bestseller *In Search of Excellence* cite the fostering of innovation as one of the key reasons for the success of the corporations they studied. What norms and processes foster innovativeness in work groups? West and Farr (1990) identify four factors:

1. *Vision* In innovative groups there is more likely to be a shared understanding of the group's goals.
2. *Participative safety.* Participation in group discussion reduces resistance to change. If groups have norms which encourage members to provide ideas, for example by rewarding rather than punishing contributions, then innovation is more likely.
3. *Commitment to excellence in task performance.* This norm creates a culture of 'constructive controversy' where members are constantly reviewing and improving working practices. The Japanese organizations pride themselves on how many millions of suggestions they have received from employee workgroups (Smith and Peterson, 1988).
4. *Support for innovation.* To make change happen there has to be support. This can come from the members' mutual encouragement and co-operation or from the organization providing resources. The success of Japanese quality circles when compared with western attempts to use the technique may come from the presence of a manager in the Japanese quality circle. This increases the upward influence of the group and the likelihood of support for the group's innovations.

GROUPTHINK

One notable disadvantage of groups which are too cohesive is that their decision-making ability can be drastically reduced by what Janis (1972) termed *groupthink*. He defined this as 'a deterioration of mental efficiency, reality testing, and moral judgment that results from in-group pressures'. In other words, the pressures for conformity that can arise in highly cohesive groups may cloud members' judgment and their ability to reach correct decisions.

Interestingly, Janis illustrated this notion with a detailed analysis of the ill-fated attempt by the Kennedy administration to invade Cuba. Janis claimed the decision which instigate the Bay of Pigs fiasco in 1961 was the result of groupthink. He claimed all the symptoms of groupthink were present in the advisory group, comprised of President Kennedy, his cabinet and other senior staff, which took the decision to invade. They became convinced of their *invulnerability* – they assumed that since they were all exceptionally able they could not possibly fail. They believed that the 1,000 Cuban exiles, outnumbered 140 to 1, really could beat Castro's army. Group discussion was characterized by a collective *rationalizing away* of information contrary to the group's beliefs. The group also believed they were *morally correct* in what they were doing, thus giving them a right to interfere with Cuba's sovereignty. This belief stemmed in part from the inaccurate *stereotyping* of the Cubans that occurred within the group – they believed, for example, that the Cuban people would flock to the support of the exiles. Janis argued that *self-censorship* prevented people in the group from expressing dissent, since group members feared being seen as disloyal. This process was reinforced by what he termed *mindguards*, who protected the group from information and individuals that would disrupt the consensus. More recently Reason (1987) has argued decisions by the operators responsible for the catastrophic accident at Chernobyl to experiment with one of the reactors was the product of groupthink.

Janis believed, however, that groupthink was not inevitable even in cohesive groups. Members of such groups can avoid it by actively searching out information, irrespective of whether it is contrary to the group's opinion. The group can also assign the role of 'devil's advocate' to one member to ensure alternative solutions are proposed and discussed. When trust is present in cohesive groups, conflict does not damage relations between members and will ultimately yield more productive solutions.

GROUP POLARIZATION

Another common-sense assumption about groups is that they are inherently more conservative than individuals when it comes to taking decisions that involve risks. Again research evidence appears to undermine this. A substantial number of studies show that groups tend to make more extreme decisions compared to the same decisions made alone by the individual group members (Lamm and Myers, 1978). Since the group seemed to shift towards risk in its decisions it was called *risky shift*. More recently, however, a number of studies have demonstrated that groups could also show the opposite tendency, a *caution shift*. Nowadays it is generally accepted that what is termed *group polarization*, the tendency for group decisions to be more extreme than those of individuals, is responsible of both sets of findings.

Why should groups produce more extreme decisions than individuals? One suggestion is that there is a *diffusion of responsibility*, where individuals, feeling that they will not be held wholly responsible for a decision, are willing to take riskier decisions. Another explanation is that *social comparison processes* are operating (Goethals and Darley, 1977). Here group members, attempting to present themselves in the best light, not only endorse the predominant cultural value but, by comparing their views with others, attempt to endorse it as least as much as everyone else. Thus group decisions become more extreme in the direction of the prevailing social attitudes. This would explain, for example, why groups tend to take riskier business decisions but more cautions decisions about whether an individual should marry. In the former, as entrepreneurial qualities are valued in a wider context, each member will adopt an entrepreneurial stance to ensure the approval of other members; in the latter, caution stems from beliefs about the dangers of broken marriages. Another explanation proposes that *information exchange* and *persuasive arguments* are a major cause of the polarization of views in groups (Burnstein, 1983). In juries, for example, a juror starts off with a fairly moderate view about the defendant's innocence or guilt. After listening to the information and arguments presented by other jurors, he or she becomes convinced of the defendant's guilt or innocence. In other words, group discussion creates a bandwagon which everyone eventually will jump on.

It is no doubt the case that all four processes operate in groups to produce the polarization phenomenon.

GROUP DECISION-MAKING IN ORGANIZATION

As we have mentioned, decisions in occupational and organizational situations are very frequently taken within a group context. Meetings, committees, project teams and so on are important decision arenas. Similarly, at the very highest level, decisions can frequently be traced to a senior corporate group. Even though organizations typically have chief executives who exercise the largest single influence, a plural executive system is still the locus of much of the real power.

This means that the processes discussed above take on a major significance (particularly since a common-sense understanding of groups, as was also mentioned, is not a very reliable guide). The overwhelming advantages of group-based decision-making that were summarized in terms of synergy – the breadth of experience brought to a problem, the benefits of discussion, emergence of new ideas – may be offset in certain circumstances by phenomena like groupthink and polarization. Hence, it is vitally important that people in organizations remain aware of the potential problems, and of the group processes that can cause both excessive conformity or highly extreme decisions to emerge.

Intergroup behaviour

Groups do not exist in isolation; they are usually embedded in a network of relationships with other groups. At work, there are a variety of groups representing different functional, professional, departmental and economic interests. Though not inevitable, it is often the case that when such divisions between groups become salient, conflict follows. An analysis of the reasons for increased competitiveness in intergroup behavior is important, because if we know what processes are involved we are more likely to be able to derive feasible solutions to intergroup conflict. In the wider arena of public policy, where issues such as racial or sexual discrimination occur, this could mean the difference between success and failure in reducing intergroup divisions.

Two main explanations of intergroup conflict have emerged, and they reflect the two different bases of group formation we identified at the beginning of this chapter. The first stems from the assumption that groups form for functional reasons (Sherif and Sherif, 1982). Functional theorists believe that if groups have a functional basis, group conflict must be the result of a group perceiving another group as a threat or a potential threat to its goal attainment. For example, if a firm's management pursues the goals of low unit costs and high volume, while labour seeks high wages and shorter working hours, then according to functional theory intergroup conflict is highly likely.

The second explanation is known as *social identity theory*, which assumes groups form through the perception of a shared social identity (Tajfel, 1978; Turner, 1982; Miller and Brewer,1984). Social identity theorists argue that an individual's self-concept is made up from his or her personal identity, which derives from a unique combination of personality and intelligence traits together with an identity created by membership of various social groups. They argue further that our self-evaluation, and thus our self-esteem, are a function of the *positive distinctiveness* (attributes which are valued by members and are thus used to make comparisons between one's own and other groups) we perceive in the groups to which we belong.

The implications of group membership for an individual's self-evaluation mean that when people perceive positive distinctiveness in other groups they can do one of three things: (1) join the outgroup;

(2) redefine the elements of the status comparison so as to change their own perception of negative distinctiveness into positive distinctiveness (e.g., 'Black is beautiful'); or (3) compete to change the relative position of the outgroup on the significant status dimension(s). The third strategy will lead to conflict between the two groups when the status dimension is a valued resource such as power or money.

The competitiveness involved in intergroup behavior is reinforced by the effects of ingroup membership on the perception, attitudes and ultimately behaviour of ingroup members. The perception among individuals of membership of a common group causes members to stereotype themselves. They see themselves as less differentiated than they actually are on dimensions such as goals, personality traits, status, motives, attitudes and values. This process, termed *depersonalization*, enables ingroup members to perceive themselves as a cohesive social unit. This depersonalization of ingroup members does not occur to the same extent as it does to outgroup members who are seen a completely undifferentiated (Park and Rothbart, 1982). The need for a positive social identity also means that ingroup members are likely to perceive larger differences between themselves and outgroup members than actually exist (Allen and Wilder, 1979). In addition, there is likely to be what is termed *ingroup favouritism*, ingroup members tending to favour each other over outgroup members. This can get to the point where it is unjustified and unreasonable and becomes *ingroup bias*. At this point perception of the outgroup has little basis in truth. Ingroup members tend to remember only negative information about the outgroup. Attributions about the outgroup also tend to be made on the basis of 'illusory correlations' – that is, accidental pairing of events which are perceived as supporting inferences about the outgroup.

How, then, is intergroup conflict resolved? A functional theorist would argue that the solution of intergroup conflict lies in contriving conditions in which shared goals can be perceived. This is based on the assumption that *superordinate goals* will create a *superordinate group*; an example of this would be reducing conflict between managerial groups by drawing attention to outside competition and thus a threat to the shared interest of survival. A modification of functional theory suggests that it is not as much the practical goals which members seek to attain that are the basis of group formation but the social interaction that task-related activity necessarily involves. This modification has produced a solution to intergroup conflict known as the *contact hypothesis*, which predicts that increased social interaction between ingroup and outgroup will break down the intergroup division. An example of this approach is the desegregation of schools in the United States by bussing schoolchildren of one ethnic group to school, where they mix with children of another group. In a famous series of studies testing the functional and contact hypotheses, two groups of boys in a summer camp were made to compete in a number of events, resulting in a considerable amount of inter-group hostility. In the final series of events, groups had to work together to achieve common goals in one event and join forces to compete against a group from outside the camp in another. Both the co-operative task interaction and the threat from out-siders reduced the intergroup hostility that had been established (Sherif *et al.*, 1961).

Though in some instances increased contact and the perception of superordinate goals can successfully reduce intergroup divisions, social identity theorists claim that in many cases this is unlikely to occur, and even where it does, the change in attitudes is not necessarily transferred to other situations. Thus at work, for example, the presence of rewards contingent on management and labour working together for a common goal can provide individuals with precisely the justification they need for their co-operation with the outgroup, so leaving their private attitudes to the outgroup unchanged. For social identity theorists one solution lies in increasing the availability of social identifications that cut across existing div-isions, thus enabling superordinate social groups to emerge. Appeals to identify with the nation or the organization, and the use of slogans and symbols to reinforce this, are examples of attempts to create superordinate social identifications.

In the previous chapter we discussed the effect of differing construal of a situation on decision making. Differences in construal can be a consequence of group membership. For example, studies of pro-Arab and pro-Israeli groups watching news reports demonstrated virtually no overlap in their reaction to the reporting. Both sides were con-vinced the other side had been favoured by the media. More fun-damentally, groups seemed to disagree about what they had actually seen. Judgement of the object and the object of judgement had been affected.

In the context of negotiation, Stillinger *et al.* (1990) and Ross and Stillinger (1991) have shown this produces what they term *reactive devaluation*. The very act of offering a proposal to an outgroup seems to reduce the attractiveness of the proposal to the outgroup and change its meaning. Thus a group offering a compromise will probably be disappointed when its offer is rejected by the outgroup. The outgroup can then be accused of bad faith. Reactive devaluation is a major cause of the mistrust and misunderstanding which often occurs in the negotiation process. What these studies suggest is that both sides fail to recognize the extent to which each side is responding to a subjectively different proposal. Thus what is seen as a fair and reasonable compromise by the ingroup may well be seen as self-serving and trivial by the outgroup.

Unfortunately, individuals' group-based construals seem to remain intact even when new social identifications are contrived that cut across existing boundaries. Social identity theorists believe that a history of conflict at the societal level leads to a general belief that boundaries between groups are immutable. Secondly, the biases in social perception caused by group membership (e.g. self-stereotyping, accentuation of differences between ingroup and outgroup) mean that the chances are that the new social identification will not be perceived (Miller and Brewer, 1984).

For social identity theorists the answer lies in uncovering what factors in situations trigger intergroup behaviour rather than inter-personal behaviour. The salience of group memberships seems to be related, first, to how secure the status differential is between the groups; if it is secure its salience will not, in most situations, be high. Secondly, within a specific setting, the relative proportion of members of each group seems to influence the salience of group behaviour. The most hostility between groups seems to occur between a minority group with a positive self-image and a majority group with a negative self-image (Moscovi and Paicheler, 1978). Finally, Wagner and Schönbach (1984) found that low self-esteem on the part of the individual can enhance the importance of group identification as a means of achieving positive social identity. The greater the importance of a particular group to an individual's self-esteem, the more likely he or she is to respond according to the norms of that group in various social situations.

Schien (1988), summarizing the insights provided by both functional and social identity theorists, proposes four ways to reduce intergroup conflict at work:

1. Emphasizing the superordinate goal of total organizational effectiveness and the role each department has in contributing to it.
2. More social contact and communications between groups. Organizational rewards should be given partly on the basis of how much help a group has provided to others.
3. Reducing the salience of group membership by rotating employees between groups or departments. This would also encourage empathy between groups.
4. Ensuring groups do not have to compete for valued resources. Work groups should never be put in the position of competing for some scarce organizational reward. Emphasis should be on pooling resources and rewards.

167

In many situations, individuals clearly have a choice between intergroup and interpersonal behavior. In negotiations, for example, the relationship between the parties built up over a number of years is often highly valued by each party. At the same time, at an intergroup level, each negotiator is a representative of a group which seeks to achieve distinctive objectives and this usually serves to force groups apart. In one study by Stephenson (1981) it was clear that the necessity of having to treat others as members of a separate group caused considerable embarrassment during negotiations. Indeed, Stephenson suggests that one key skill in negotiation is the ability to enhance interpersonal or intergroup aspects of the situation. He found that by highlighting the interpersonal content of the negotiation, for example by involving the personal relationships and friendships between parties, the negotiation was more likely to result in a compromise solution. Conversely, increasing the importance of the intergroup division, for example by meeting in separate rooms with occasional contact between a nominee from each group, was associated with victory for one side only.

In sum, then, functional theorists can indicate how conflict can be reduced, but only in the range of situations in which intense goal differences are not present. To account for conflict which still occurs, particularly where intergroup behaviour is involved in a wider social context, it is social identity theory which provides the necessary conceptual framework. However, at present, social identity theory provides no solutions to intergroup conflict, a fact which serves to remind us of the salience of our group memberships in society and the enduring effect they have on our perceptions, beliefs, attitudes and behaviour.

Hawthorne and the human relations movement

The emphasis on social interaction and group dynamics that we have been exploring in this and previous chapters reflects very much the modern concerns in the study of behaviour at work. But during the early staged of its development, in the 1920s, occupational psychology relied heavily on a crude 'mechanical' model of human behaviour. Individuals were regarded as acting in isolation and responsive only to 'rational' economic and physical stimuli. A great deal of research was preoccupied with ways of increasing workers' productivity.

There was a consensus among the researchers and managers of the day that an individual's work rate was determined by factors such as temperature, humidity and illumination. Other aspects of the work situation, such as payment systems, patterns of rest breaks and the length of the working day, also played a part in determining a worker's output. The demand for scientific research into the effects of these factors led to the founding of the National Institute of Industrial Psychology in Britain and the Psychological Corporation in America.

However, in the late 1920s this picture was to change radically; and we will conclude by looking at the research which is normally credited with having brought about this transformation, the so-called *Hawthorne experiments.*

In 1927 the Western Electric Company invited a group of researchers from Harvard University to help the management continue their investigation of factors affecting worker productivity at their Hawthorne plant near Chicago. What prompted this invitation was some rather curious findings which had emerged from studies that had taken place in the plant over the preceding three years. The company wanted a definitive answer to a seemingly simple question: what is the relationship between illumination and productivity levels? A group of engineers from the American Academy of Sciences was hired to provide the answer. They ran a series of studies which manipulated illumination levels and recorded output. To their surprise they found that output seemed to increase both in control groups where illumination was constant and in experimental groups when illumination was lowered. In one study illumination was cut to an amount which represented the amount of light available on a moonlit night, but output was maintained and the employees reported no eyestrain and claimed they actually felt less tired than when working under bright lights.

The Harvard researchers assumed the failure to relate illumination and output could be attributed to the fact that the engineers were not systematic enough and took only one variable into account. They believed that if they selected a small group of workers and placed them in a separate room away from the disruptive influences of other employees and departmental routine, they would succeed where the Academy of Sciences' researchers had failed.

The researchers began their first series of experiments, the so-called relay assembly test room experiments, with a group of six female employees. They selected women who reported they would be happy to work together, and who were equivalent in the level of skill they possessed so that differences in performance could not be attributed to a skill difference within the group. They also chose a routine task, assembling telephone relays, which required no machinery, so that an individual's output would be determined by her performance alone. The women were placed in an observation room with one other person, an observer, whose task was to record output data and maintain a friendly atmosphere in the room.

169

The researchers then set about posing the questions that were typical of the day: what is the effect of temperature, humidity, health, number of rest breaks, length of working day, method of production and payment system on output? They manipulated these variables in a long series of experiments, changing the pattern of rest breaks, hours worked, etc. and monitoring the effect on output. What the studies showed were major increases in output achieved by the group under virtually all conditions. Even when original conditions were restored production frequently still went up, and of this course totally contradicted the predictions of the 'rational man' model of behaviour.

Though the relay assembly experiments continued for five years, quite early on the experimenters reached a tentative explanation of their striking results. This is now recognized as a turning point in the development of psychology applied in the workplace and it continues to exert an influence on management theory and practice some sixty years later. What the experimenters gradually realized was that none of the variables which were commonly associated with increases in productivity could explain their findings. What had come into existence in the relay assembly test room was a *social system*. According to Elton Mayo, the person responsible for popularizing the results and developing the implications of the research into a social and managerial philosophy: 'what actually happened was that six individuals became a team and the team gave itself wholeheartedly and spontaneously to cooperation in the experiment' (1943, p. 73).

In other words, the women had become a social group demonstrating the kinds of process which we discussed earlier in this chapter. This does not, however, explain why their output norms were high. To do this the experimenters pointed to what had become known as the *Hawthorne effect*. In fact, nowadays it is more common to distinguish two Hawthorne effects. The first effect is that the mere knowledge of being an experimental subject changes behaviour from what it would otherwise have been. This distortion in behaviour can easily undermine the value of social scientific research. The second is produced by friendly supervision; the observer in the relay assembly experiment had become a trusted friend of the women, allowing the new social organization to develop, which, in turn, had imbued their working lives with new meaning.

The Hawthorne studies continued for twelve years and included a mass interviewing of 21,000 Western Electric employees, observation of a group of men in a bank wiring room (discussed in Chapter 11) and extensive personnel counselling. What was so important about these studies was that although some British industrial psychologists had drawn attention to similar findings (Myers, 1924, Cathcart, 1928), here for the first time was a large body of evidence shaking the settled managerial convictions of the time that workers were wage-pursuing automata (Bendix, 1956). The social organization of the workplace and its implications for effective management were spelled out to a large audience. Thus managers were urged to use the studies to master the nature of the social reality they operated in:

> We have failed to train students in the study of social situations; we have thought that first class technical training was sufficient in a modern and mechanical age. As a consequence we are technically competent as no other age in history has been; and we combined this with utter social incompetence. (Mayo, 1943, p. 120).

The Hawthorne studies marked the beginning of the human relations movement, a tradition in management which stresses the importance of social factors at work. For human relations theorists, the role of management is to provide organizational environments in which employers can fulfill the social needs of their employees, thus providing work with the meaning that routinization has taken out of it, and tap the employees' desire for co-operative activity. This can be done through team-building, supportive supervision, increased communication and opportunity for participation in decision-making and counselling. Thus, human relations theorists assume that, to the extent that managements have insight into the skills to manipulate these social factors, they will be able to harness their employees' social needs to managerial ends.

We will not devote more space here to an account of this vitally important school of thought, because in a sense much of what is discussed in this and certain other chapters reflects human relations interests. The application of group dynamics, the concern with leadership and accounts of work motivation and satisfaction, dealt with elsewhere in this book, are all central issues in human relations research.

However, it is appropriate finally to indicate some of the adverse reaction that this approach has attracted. A number of criticisms have appeared of the Hawthorne studies (Rose, 1975; Rice, 1982) and of the human relations movement in general (Braverman, 1974; Hill, 1981). Carey (1967), for example, argued that the studies were so flawed in terms of the experimental methods employed that their conclusions cannot be regarded as supported from the evidence. In one sense, though, this does not matter. The vitality of the Hawthorne studies now stems not from any academic merits but from their all-round influence on the management process.

For this reason, much of the criticism of the human relations movement has focused on its impact on *management practice*. And

171

here Bendix's noted *Work and Authority in Industry* (1956) has been highly influential. Bendix argues, for example, that Mayo and his colleagues were too preoccupied with group process, often to the exclusion of organizational factors like the impact of managerial power, and wider social factors in the labour market. Sometimes this put the research in rather a dubious ethical position, since the managerial motives for commissioning the research tended to be ignored. Sometimes, too, it led the researchers to adopt paternalistic attitudes towards workers: workers were regarded as being irrationally motivated by social and affectual interests. In contrast, management were seen to act on the basis of rational economic criteria reflecting the drive towards efficiency. Secondly, Bendix and others have pointed out that in reality human relations ideas have found only limited acceptance. In particular, the claim that they have 'superseded' previous mechanical models of man is very much overstated. In fact, the basis of managerial control in industry, as represented by modern methods of production control, remains those very same mechanical models. And thirdly, even where these ideas have been influential, the claim that they represent a new 'humane' approach is likewise largely untrue: they really represent simply another strategy of organizational control. Bendix, for instance, argued that the human relations movement has provided a new 'verbal dress' for mangers who have little sympathy for its message, and who pursue the traditional authority-based relationship between themselves and their employees.

That said, however, the humans relations movement has affected certain specific areas of management, such as personnel practices and management training, even if this is far less true in the central area of managerial responsibility. Moreover, there has been an enduring influence on modern thinking about the managerial role, and about the directions in which that role might be performed and made more progressive. As we will see in following chapters – Chapter 8 on leadership and Chapter 9 on work redesign – the pervasiveness of these ideas has ensured that human relations has had some influence on managerial policies, albeit not as much as the Hawthorne researchers once envisaged.

Further reading

Argyle, M. (1989) *The Social Psychology of Work*. Harmondsworth: Penguin.

Hart, P.T. (1990) *Group Think in Government: A Study of Small Groups and Policy Failure*.

Long, S. (1991) *A Structural Analysis of Small Groups*. London: Routledge.

Schein, E.M. (1988) *Organizational Psychology* (3rd edn.). Englewood Cliffs, N.J: Prentice-Hall.

Tjosvold, D. (1992) *Team Organization: An Enduring Competitive Advantage*. Chichester: Wiley.

West, M.A. (ed). (1990) *Innovation and Creativity at Work*. Chichester: Wiley.

Worchel, S., W. Wood and J.A. Simpson (eds) (1992) *Group Process and Productivity*. London: Sage.

8

Leadership

Why can some mangers and supervisors gain the best efforts of their staff while others are only able to obtain a moderate amount of cooperation, or even attract open hostility? Obviously organizations are keenly interested in the answers to this question. Their hierarchical structure means that organizations continually have to face the problem of selecting and training people to assume positions of authority over others. At every level in organizations and in every department there will be groups of subordinates under the control of superordinates – in other words, there will be leadership situations.

The term 'leadership', however, often conveys a rather more glamorous image than that of the mundane world of work. Leaders like Napoleon, Gandhi and Churchill emerge from a broad political context rather than an occupational setting. Authority is vested in them because of their personal gifts and abilities and the charismatic qualities they posses, or at least so we imagine. The example of such leaders gave rise to the earliest attempts at psychological research on the topic: the so-called *trait* theory of leadership. This assumes that certain people are born with a set of key personality characteristics, or traits, which make them 'natural leaders' – indeed, this view of leadership is sometimes termed an 'implicit' theory, or the 'great man' theory of leadership.

As we shall see, the search for these traits has proved relatively fruitless. Another approach has been to study not what sort of person the effective leader is, but what he or she actually does. In other words, the *behaviour* of leaders becomes the focus of interest. This research has given us a reasonably clear idea of the main dimensions of leadership behaviour. What has been more difficult is the discovery of strong relationships between these dimensions and organizational variables such as productivity, job satisfaction and staff turnover. The recognition that no one pattern of leader behaviour, or leadership 'style', produces high effectiveness has led to the view that certain styles are effective in particular situations but inappropriate in others. We will examine two theories which attempt to predict which styles 'fit' which situation. We will conclude the chapter by examining some of the attempts to translate these insights into what makes a leader effective into leadership training programmes.

Leadership as an attribute of the individual

At first sight the relationship suggested in the heading of this section seems plausible and confirmed by personal experience. The relationship seems further supported by the study of great leaders throughout history. This view of leadership implies that leadership resides in traits or attributes of the individual. In any situation where leadership is appropriate, the person with the largest number of desirable traits emerges as the leader. In organizations this would represent an ideal state of affairs for the selection process. Having located the traits and developed measures for them, personnel selection would become a fairly simple and mechanistic affair.

This traditional view of leadership would also suggest a list of variables we would expect it to be associated with. These could be grouped under such headings as physical (height, weight, age, appearance), personality (dominance, self-esteem, aggressiveness), motivational (need for power, need for achievement), status (socioeconomic, popularity) and abilities (IQ, experience, interpersonal skills). All of these and many more besides have been correlated against leadership variables.

The search for associations between the personal attributes of a leader and measures of his or her effectiveness dominated leadership research for the first half of this century. In a major review of the trait studies, Stogdill (1948) found enough cumulative evidence to conclude that the average leader was higher than subordinates in intelligence, scholarship, dependability in exercising responsibilities, activity, social participation and socioeconomic status. The inconsistency of much of the research results, however, forced Stogdill to a conclusion that proved to be a major turning point in leadership research: 'the evidence suggests that leadership is a relation that exists between persons in a social situation, and that the persons who are leaders in one situation may not necessarily be leaders in other situations'. Stogdill did not rule out the possibility of trait variables explaining some of the differences in the effectiveness of leaders. He regarded their omission from any model of leadership as being as unacceptable as the study of them to the exclusion of all other classes of variable.

More recently, critics of trait research have pointed out that even where correlations do emerge, interpretation of them is far from straightforward. For example, an association between assertiveness and leadership does not tell us whether assertiveness caused the individual to become a leader or the leadership position caused the assertiveness. Even if we had a positive correlation between a trait and leadership variables, where we knew the trait variable was causally prior, we would still be left with a 'partial explanation'. We would not know how or why this particular variable operated to increase leadership effectiveness.

One variable that we would expect to be related to success in leadership is IQ. Organizations consistently prefer to employ bright rather than dull managers. Some studies have found correlations of IQ with leadership effectiveness as low as zero, though the median result of such studies is a small positive correlation of .2 (Fiedler, 1982). The discrepancy between the results of these studies has encouraged some researchers to attempt to explain the absence of a stronger relationship in the data. We have already encountered one such attempt in Chapter 3 when we discussed Fiedler's hypothesis that a series of 'screens' (intervening variables) moderated the effect of a leader's intelligence on his or her effectiveness. Another researcher Ghiselli (1963) suggested that there is a curvilinear relationship between the two variables. Correlations are reduced if relationships between variables are not linear. To test this idea he sorted a sample of managers into high, medium and low IQ groups. He found that managers in the high and low bands were less likely to achieve success in their management positions. This implies that an optimum level of intelligence is where IQ is high enough for managers to be competent but not too high, which itself may carry disadvantages – for example, very high IQ levels may be seen as threatening by superordinates or as intimidating by subordinates.

The plausibility of an 'implicit' theory of leadership has meant that interest in trait research has persisted in spite of Stogdill's evidence and conclusions and subsequent criticisms. Recent trait studies, however, have broadened to include the skills, values and needs that leaders possess. Bass (1981) surveyed factorial studies published since 1945 and found twenty-six factors common to more than three studies. The most frequently occurring factors he found were those which described interpersonal, intellectual and technical skills of leaders. The second most frequent were those concerned with how leaders related to their groups, particularly the methods used to motivate and co-ordinate group activity. The least frequently occurring were factors which related to personal characteristics such as dominance and emotionality. This implies that successful leadership is best understood as resulting from the possession of a set of social skills, rather than personality characteristics.

In the work context, it has often been assumed that attaining a managerial position and being successful in it is not so much a reflection of intellect or personality but more the systematic mapping of the motivational make-up of managers on to organizational life. Research has focused on uncovering what these attitudinal and motivational factors are and to what extent they are related to success in the leadership role. Three large-scale studies provide some tentative answers to these question. Bass *et al.* (1979) surveyed over 3,000 middle managers. Respondents were asked to rank eleven life goals. A clear set of preferences emerged, the most preferred goals reflecting self-actualization needs (self-realization and independence). A middle band related to affection, security and competence. Least preferred were prestige and wealth. Though all managers had emphasized 'higher-order' needs, the goals dealing with assertiveness and accomplishment were more often emphasized by faster-climbing managers, whereas those dealing with comfort were chosen by those with slower rates of promotion. Similarly Hofstede (1978), using factor analysis to identify underlying motivational dimensions in the ranking of life goals by 65,000 IBM employees, found two factors that explained 54 per cent of the variation in rankings. One factor stressed comfort rather than accomplishment, the other stressed assertiveness and leadership as opposed to service.

Two contrasting lifestyles were identified by Bray *et al.* (1974) after studying the progress over eight years of 400 managers in a large American company. These reflected motivational differences in the sample similar to those found in the other studies. They described those who tended to gain in occupational interests and in whom self-actualization needs seemed pre-eminent as 'enlargers'. These individuals were less concerned with friends, parents, family and recreational or social activities than with work. They were more likely to move away from their home towns and stressed the importance of innovation and change in their approach to organizational problems. This contrasted with the 'enfolder', in whom the 'lower-order' security and comfort needs were strongest. They were more likely to stay in their home base and to maintain long-term friendships. They were much less likely to engage in self-improvement activities, but did not lose their interest in recreational and social activities to the same extend as the 'enlarger'. Bray *et al.* found these differences were associated with rates of advancement, 'enlargers' being more successful than 'enfolders'.

What may seem surprising is the lack of evidence suggesting that a need for money and wealth is a key component of the motivational make-up of successful managers. Some managers do in fact express a strong interest in pay. The evidence suggests a manager's position in an organization determines the extent to which wealth is a dominant need. Interest in pay tends to be stronger lower down the managerial hierarchy, whereas intrinsic aspects of work and a spiralling search for challenge seem to motivate successful senior and middle managers.

In earlier chapters we encountered the notions of construal and appraisal which were used to help explain differences in, for example, the stress response or social skills. Jaques (1989) argues these notions are equally important in leadership research. He suggests *cognitive power*, defined as the maximum scale and complexity of the world that an individual is able to pattern, and construe and the complexity of information he or she processes, is central to the understanding of differences in leadership ability. Cognitive power, Jaques argues, is developed over a lifetime and is independent of intelligence, class, education or gender. It is measured by assessing an individual's *time horizon*, the maximum time span of a task an individual is capable of working with (Jacobs and Jaques, 1990). Jaques also argues job levels differ in their *time span of discretion*, the maximum time required to complete a task. For example, at board level a reorganization may take a decade, while at shopfloor level changing an element of working practices may take only a month. Thus a leader's cognitive power determines his or her ability to cope with the critical tasks confronting him or her at each organizational level.

The emergence and maintenance of leadership

Although leadership positions in formal organizations are assigned to individuals on the basis of experience, seniority or expertise, there are many situations at work where leadership emerges without formal sanction. There are many individuals in the workplace who lack formal status but who nonetheless are perceived as leaders. Many researchers have been interested in how these people acquire leadership roles in groups. The examination of group interaction reveals that the people who become leaders tend to participate early on in group discussion (Hollander, 1978; Sorrentino and Boutillier, 1975). Being the strong silent type is not a successful strategy. Initially the person who emerges as leader is the individual who does the most talking. The quantity of a person's contributions seems to indicate to other group members his or her intention to take a leadership role. The quality of contributions, however, dictates whether the individual remains acceptable as leader, since it determines the extent to which an individual is seen by other members as competent and contributing to group goals (Sorrentino and Boutillier, 1975).

Group members seem to look for two types of competence, First, they look for what is termed *socio-emotional* competence. People who are perceived as possessing this are those who appear to be aware of and can influence group relations and cohesion. Secondly, groups identify the level of *task competence* in individuals. People who appear to be able to contribute to the problem-solving capacities and effectiveness of the group (Bales and Slater, 1955). Some researchers have suggested that this broad division can be further broken down into a number of more specific competencies. One study found five types of competence were displayed by naval officers: task achievement; skilful use of leadership; management control; advising and counselling; and coercion. All types of competence other than coercion predicted whether a person would emerge as leader (Winter, 1978).

An interesting distinction has been made between actual and perceived competence. This distinction is similar to that made by Goffman (1971), who argued that the maintenance of the correct 'personal front' enables relatively incompetent individuals to be perceived as competent. Price and Garland (1981) manipulated perceived competence by informing subjects that the leader was either highly competent or relatively incompetent. This had a marked effect both on the willingness of subjects to comply with the requests of the leaders and on the ratings of the leaders' effectiveness, subjects being less willing to comply with leaders perceived as relatively incompetent and rating them as less effective.

Emergence as a leader has also been associated with the extent to which individuals are able to behave with *spontaneity*. People who initiate a wider range of activities within the groups or attempt to develop wider opportunities for individuals to participate are more likely to emerge as group leader. The converse of spontaneity is *contagion*, the extent to which an individual is influenced by others. The skilful leader is able to balance the needs for spontaneity and contagion. Indeed, an individual emerging as group leader is related to the perception by group members of an appropriate balance between the two in his or her behaviour. Unsuccessful initial attempts at leadership may be the result of too much spontaneity and too little contagion – for example, attempting to take the group off in a direction which is not acceptable to group members. On the other hand, the individual who displays no contagion may be seen by group members as simply pursuing the dictates of self-interest.

Having gained the leadership role, a leader may need at some point to initiate activity that does deviate from group norms. This is made possible by earning what are termed *idiosyncrasy credits* (Hollander, 1958; Michener and Lawler, 1975). The leader acquires these by being perceived as displaying competence on the group task and conformity to group norms. Maintaining credits is crucial to survival in the leadership position. It appears that once individuals have acquired the leadership role they may have less latitude to deviate from particular role obligations (Hollander, 1961). This seems to be because leaders have to negotiate with group members a trade-off between being allowed to deviate from general group norms (e.g. hours of work) and conforming closely to other norms such as promoting group cohesion and task performance.

The research on leadership emergence supports the view that what is important is not so much what people are but what they actually do. In the next section we will examine some attempts to identify the key dimensions of leadership behaviour.

Leadership style

CONSIDERATION AND INITIATING STRUCTURE

In 1945 Shartle instigated the Ohio State University Studies to investigate the nature of leadership behaviour and its relationship to various criteria of leadership effectiveness. He and his associates began by collecting a list of 1,800 phrases which described leadership behaviour. These were then placed into nine different behavioural categories. Of the initial items only 150 fell into only one category. These items formed the first questionnaire designed to assess aspects of leadership behaviour (Hemphill, 1950). Two independent factors emerged when data collected by using the questionnaire was subjected to factor analysis (Halpin and Winer, 1957).

The inter-correlations producing the first factor, *consideration*, were among items like 'exhibits concern for welfare of group members', 'appreciates good work', 'is easy to approach', 'responds to suggestions', and 'obtains approval of actions'. The inter-correlations producing the second factor, *initiation of structure*, reflected associations between such leader behaviours as 'maintains standards', 'meets deadlines' and 'defines in detail objectives, methods of work and roles'. Two tests, one for subordinates, the leader behaviour description questionnaire (LBDQ), and another for supervisors, the leader opinion questionnaire (LOQ) were then constructed to provide measure of supervisors along each dimension.

The identification of these two dimensions of leadership behaviour and the development of measures enabling supervisors to be measured on each prompted to great deal of research assessing their reliability and validity. A classic study of the effects of interactions between the scales on two organizational variables, grievance rate and turnover rate, established that quite complex relationships existed between the scales and these organizational variables (Fleishman and Harris, 1962). Some of the results are illustrated in Figure 8.1. As the graph indicates, being low in consideration generates most grievances and is not compensated for by being low in structure. For supervisors medium in consideration, grievance rates were determined by their level of structure. In general a supervisor's level of consideration is positively related to employee satisfaction with the organization and to measures of group and organizational cohesiveness. Initiation of structure, on the other hand, in general negatively correlates with absences, grievance and staff turnover (Science Research Associates, 1989).

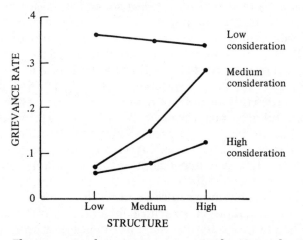

Figure 8.1   *The interaction between structure, consideration and grievance rate.* From E.A. Fleishman and E.F. Harris (1962) 'Patterns of leadership behavior related to employee grievances and turnover', *Personnel Psychology*, 15,43–56.

It rapidly became clear, however, that the effects of consideration and structure on the variables of productivity and job satisfaction were moderated by intervening variables such as the type of size of the work unit. For example, an early study by Fleishman and Harris (1955) found that merit ratings for supervisors by their managers were positively related to their level of structure in manufacturing departments but negatively related for supervisors in service departments. Similarly, Schriesheim and Murphy (1976) found that the supervisor's initiation of structure was positively related to subordinates' job satisfaction in large work groups but negatively related in small groups. A number of other aspects of the workplace – the nature of the task, skill differential between supervisor and subordinates – also appear to alter the relationship between effectiveness and the two types of behaviour. At present we do not have a complete understanding of how the relationship between a leader's behaviour and his or her effectiveness is modified by organizational variables.

Some researchers have pointed out that, although assumed to be conceptually distinct, empirically the scales used to measure initiating structure and consideration do not appear to operate independently. A number of studies have shown that the scales can correlate with each other. In other words, managers who are high on one scale tend to be high on the other (Schriesheim *et al.*, 1976). This has lead to the claim that we can also describe leaders along one general activity factor, termed *motivation to manage vs. laissez-faire management.* Laissez-faire or inactive managers are unwilling to accept responsibility, give directions or provide support. They tend to act not so much on their own initiative but in response to specific requests from their staff. There is some evidence that the level of a leader's activity is an important explanatory variable (Bass *et al.*, 1975). Inactivity in leaders is consistently negatively related to productivity, subordinate satisfaction and group cohesiveness (Stogdill, 1974).

While some people have suggested that the Ohio dimensions can be collapsed into one general activity factor, others have stressed the very opposite, that two dimensions are not enough. Bass (1981) argued that by using only two factors much specific information about a leader's behaviour is thrown away. For example, a moderate score on the initiation of structure dimension may mask certain specific difficulties a leader has, such as maintaining work standards. To counter this, some techniques of factor analysis have produced as many as twelve factors describing leadership behaviour. In practical applications, such as counselling, selection or leadership training, where information about a manager's leadership is required, it may well be important to have available a more detailed description of leadership behaviour.

One of the main problems in interpreting the results of research using the Ohio dimensions is that much of it is of the concurrent correlation type. This means that data on leader behaviour and organizational variables are collected at one point in time. We are not able to tell from the results whether high performance has caused high consideration or vice versa; each is equally plausible. This makes studies of the effects of changes in leadership behaviour and organizational variables over time particularly valuable. Unfortunately, these studies are few and far between. One series of studies, however, has collected data on leader behaviour, subordinate satisfaction and production at different points in time and across a wide variety of industrial settings (Greene, 1975, 1979). The results suggest that considerate leadership was causally antecedent to increased subordinate satisfaction. But it also seems that changes in the productivity of the subordinates resulted in changes in leadership behaviour. An increase in productivity caused an increase in consideration and a decrease in initiation of structure. In other words, there is an *interaction* between leadership behaviour and group output variables. Leaders affect the behaviour of their staff who, in turn, affect the behaviour of their supervisors. Additionally Smith and Peterson (1988) provide evidence suggesting items on the leader opinion questionnaire are culturally specific:

> . . . it could well prove to be the case that leaders in organizations from all parts of the world do indeed need to attend both to the task in hand and also to the maintenance of good relationships within the work team. But *how* this is to be accomplished in each setting will be dependent upon the meanings given to particular leadership acts in that setting. A supervisor who frequently checks up that work is done correctly may be seen as a kind father in one setting, as task centred in another setting, officious and mistrustful in a third. (p. 100)

However, despite methodological problems, there are two reasons why initiation of structure and consideration remain the most widely used concepts in leadership research. First, the availability of a reliable and easily administered measure for them means data on the leadership style of individual or groups of supervisors can be gathered quickly. Secondly, the validity of the measures – their ability to account for some of the variance in organizational variables such as productivity and staff turnover – indicates that the Ohio researchers have identified two key dimensions of supervisory behaviour.

DEMOCRATIC VS AUTOCRATIC LEADERSHIP

An alternative to the Ohio dimensions of leadership behaviour was developed at another American university, the University of Michigan. These 'Michigan studies' now amount to over 500 surveys, involving over 20,000 managers and 200,000 non-supervisory employees. The dimension at the heart of these studies, democratic–autocratic leadership, is perhaps the most complex construct in the leadership literature. It refers to the way in which decisions are taken, whose needs in the organization are met, what characterizes the relations between leader and follower, and how much coercion is present in the relationship between leaders and subordinates.

Many of the studies have used the framework developed by Likert (1961) to capture these aspects of leader–follower relations. Likert proposed four 'systems' of relationships in large organizations which reflected an organizations's position on the democratic vs autocratic dimension:

1. Exploitative autocratic

2. Benevolent autocratic
3. Consultative
4. Democratic

Leadership in systems 1 and 2 emphasizes the *legitimacy* of managerial authority, for example by providing no opportunities for consultation between staff and management. Relationships between leaders and subordinates are formal in system 1. Managers will treat subordinates in an aloof, cold and in extreme instances hostile manner. The chief distinction between systems 1 and 2 involves the nature of control. The benevolent autocrat prefers to control by using rewards; the exploitative autocrat uses more coercive and punitive methods of control. Power in systems 1 and 2 organizations is concentrated at the top with no consultation with subordinates.

The emphasis of leadership in systems 3 and 4 is on the creation of supportive, friendly interpersonal relationships based on trust, participation and two-way communication between follower and leader. The organizational goals of high output and high standards are no different to those in systems 1 and 2, but in systems 3 and 4 the aim is to achieve these objectives by team working and the leader's encouragement of the group members' best efforts, for example by obtaining and making constructive use of subordinates' ideas on improving work methods. Subordinates are also able to influence or determine their performance targets during group goal-setting sessions. In order to study organizations with these different systems of management, Likert developed a measure known as the *profile of organizational characteristics* (POC). This included the range of variables embraced by the democratic vs autocratic dimension – how decisions are taken, whose needs are met, what characterizes the relations between leaders and subordinates, and how much coercion is generally present in the leader – subordinate relationship. Likert was thus able to establish what position an organization occupied along the autocratic vs democratic dimension.

Drawing attention to the autocratic–democratic dimension has, however, led to a critical problem of leadership and management. This is the apparent conflict that exists between the democratic ideals widespread in most western industrialized nations, and the practices of work organizations. It seems paradoxical to many people that most organizations within countries claiming to be democratic are autocratic. As Daniel Bell (1948) put it:

> the problem of leadership is shaped by the fact that while we live in a society of political democracy almost all basic social patterns are authoritarian and tend to instill feelings of helplessness and dependence ... our factories, hierarchical in structure, are, for all the talk of human

184

relations programs, still places where certain men exercise arbitrary authority over others. (p. 375)

Likert was completely in favour of system 4 management. His prescription to organizations to move towards system 4 was not just a political campaign. He claimed that such a shift had a positive impact on organizational effectiveness. These effects could occur in any type of industry and range from improvements in employee motivation and job satisfaction to increased productivity. Research had produced correlations of the POC measure with organizational performances ranging from .3 to .6. Likert found that a period of five years may be required for improvements to appear. One organization in a study of three continuous process plants was able to produce immediate savings of a quarter of a million dollars by autocratically imposing cost-saving measures. However, Likert argued that the stoppages and staff losses this resulted in ultimately cost the firm twice that amount (Likert, 1977a). In eleven commercial organizations that had been encouraged to shift towards system 4, before and after studies showed productivity increases of between 15 and 40 per cent. Where control groups were used no similar improvements were found. These improvements continued if the shifts towards democratic arrangements were maintained (Likert, 1977b).

One problem that the Michigan researchers face is that their ideas were developed and tested before the recession at a time when growth and success were the norm for large organizations in western societies. Currently, change, stress, failure and conflict in organizations have produced conditions that are distinctively different from the period in which the Michigan researchers introduced their arguments. To what extent organizations are willing to experiment by moving towards more democratic styles of leadership in current conditions is, at present, unclear.

PARTICIPATIVE VS DIRECTIVE LEADERSHIP

Although this dimension overlaps with the autocratic vs democratic dimension, it is worth including since it relates specifically to the extent to which supervisors direct or consult. At one end of the dimension supervisors attempt to equalize the distribution of power in decision-making using consultation, participation and delegation. This can range from a supervisor involving subordinates in the decision-making but ultimately taking the decision him- or herself, through consulting and achieving a consensus decision, to delegating the entire responsibility for making a decision to the group. Moving up the other end of the continuum entails an increasing portion of the decision-making being done by the supervisor. This dimension characterizes one key aspect of leader behaviour – decision-making –

185

which may have important effects on group or organizational climate and effectiveness.

Though a useful conceptual contribution, empirically the distinction has proved less useful. Few individual managers have fixed styles of decision-making. Vroom and Yetton (1973) found on asking several thousand managers to indicate their decision-making style in dealing with a variety of situations that only about 10 per cent of managers displayed fixed tendencies to be either directive or participative. Similarly, Bass and Valenzi (1974) found neither extreme reported with any frequency by subordinates. Consultation, the middle ground in the dimension, was the style reported with the most frequency.

If managers do not stick to one style of decision-making, what makes them decide to consult rather than direct? One variable involved is the skill differential they perceive between themselves and their subordinates. If a manager has reservations about the competence of staff to achieve objectives or their commitment to organizational goals, he or she is likely to use more direction (Rosen and Jerdee, 1977). Conversely, where the differential is less because subordinates are highly qualified, highly educated or highly skilled, managers adopt participatory styles of leadership (Maher, 1976; Bass *et al.*, 1975).

One of the major criticisms of the participative approach to leadership is that it can be much slower and more expensive than directive leadership. In some organizations rapid decision-making may be essential because of the very short time perspectives of the business. Market research firms, for example, are often required to turn a client's brief into an interview schedule, and to collect and have data ready by the end of the next day. These organizations therefore may need to use a directive style of leadership. The choice of decision-making style may also be influenced by the nature of the technology utilized in the organization. Woodward (1965), for example, found companies using short time span, batch process as opposed to continuous process production believed directive leadership fitted their technology better than participative leadership.

An interesting approach to the problem of deciding what decision-making style is most appropriate to a particular situation has been developed by Vroom and Yetton (1973). This approach includes both descriptive and prescriptive elements. It enables managers to describe the characteristics of the situation and then derive what style of decision-making he or she ought to adopt. The manager begins by answering seven questions:

1. Is there a quality requirement such that one solution is better than another?
2. Does the leader have sufficient information to make a high-quality decision?
3. Is the problem structured?
4. Is the acceptance of the decision by subordinates critical to effective implementation?
5. If the leader were to make the decision by himself, is it reasonably certain that it would be accepted by subordinates?
6. Do subordinates share the organizational goals to be obtained in solving this problem?
7. Is conflict likely between manager and staff in the preferred solution?

Vroom (1984) increased the scope of the model by adding a further four questions.

8. How much prior information and ability do subordinates have?
9. Is there a time constraint upon problem solution?
10. How important is subordinate development?
11. How valuable is time in this situation?

Vroom (1984) also changed the response to questions from a simple yes/no to a five-point scale indicating the degree to which a condition is present. The response to these questions allows what Vroom and Yetton call the 'feasible set' of leadership styles to be derived:

AI You solve the problem or make the decision yourself using information available to you.

AII You obtain necessary information from subordinates then decide on the solution to the problem yourself. Subordinates are not asked to generate or evaluate alternative solutions.

CI You share the problem with relevant subordinates individually, getting their ideas and suggestions, and make a decision which may or may not reflect your subordinates' influence.

CII You share the problem with your subordinates as a group, collectively obtaining their ideas and suggestions. Again you make the decision yourself.

GII You share the problem with your subordinates and attempt to reach a solution. You do not try to influence the group to adopt your solution and you are willing to accept and implement any solution which has the support of the entire group.

In the revised model a series of complex equations are used to compute the most effective decision-making style for any particular situation. As most of the research has used the original model, the relationship between situational characteristics and decision-making style in the original formulation is presented in Figure 8.2.

Vroom's model has received a good deal of empirical support. In

187

one study (Vroom and Jago, 1978), ninety-six managers were asked to describe their leadership style in a number of situations. They were also asked to describe the quality and acceptance of the solution in each situation. The results indicated that the effectiveness of the solution, particularly subordinates' acceptance of it, declined the more the model's rules were violated. More recently, Paul and Ebadi (1989) used the original formulation with a sample of 216 sales staff and 36 supervisors. They found leaders using the Vroom and Yetton model had staff who were more productive and who reported more satisfaction with the work itself and with their co-workers.

Underlying the Vroom and Yetton model is the assumption that there is a strong relationship between the acceptance of a decision and the level of participation by subordinates in it. Whether quality and acceptance of decisions are important, participation is indicated in the feasible set of leadership styles (Field, 1979).

The assumption that there is a strong positive relationship between the quality and acceptance of a decision and the amount of participation by subordinates in it stems from evidence suggesting participation harnesses positive motivational and group dynamic effects. Decision quality, for instance, is thought to draw on the group dynamic phenomenon, *synergy*, discussed in Chapter 6, which produces group decisions usually of higher quality than the average group member (though sometimes not as good as the best group member). At the individual level, participative leadership is though to increase the 'ego involvement' of subordinates with the organization, and their 'psychological entry' into the organization and its decisions. Most of the available evidence does in fact support the relationship between subordinate acceptance of decisions and participative leadership styles (Bass, 1981). In addition, there is some evidence to suggest that as well as improving decision quality and subordinate acceptance of decisions, participative leadership can also lead to increased satisfaction with the job and supervision.

A major problem for participative leadership is the ease with which group members can perceive it as manipulation. Some research indicates staff in organizations which are attempting to adopt participative methods of decision-making do perceive it in this way and feel they have actually lost some of their power (Richbell, 1976). There are also issues which raise basic questions of power and interests – redundancies, for example – where participation would be difficult if not impossible. Furthermore, the handing over of decision-making power to staff may not be greeted with equal enthusiasm by all supervisors, since it may blur role definitions and reduce the differential in status between staff and supervisor and make many supervisors feel uncomfortable (Clegg and Fitter, 1978). Though

QUESTIONS

1	2	3	4	5	6	7
Is there a quality requirement?	Do I have sufficient information to make a high-quality decision?	Is the problem structured?	Is the acceptance of the decision by subordinates critical to effective implementation?	If I make the decision myself is it reasonably certain that it will be accepted by my subordinates?	Do subordinates share the organizational goals to be obtained in solving this problem?	Is conflict likely in preferred solutions?

NO

YES

NO

YES

YES

NO

YES

NO

YES

NO

YES

NO

YES

NO

YES

NO

YES

NO

YES

NO

YES

NO

YES

NO

YES

NO

YES

NO

YES

NO

AI, AII, CI
CII, GII

GII

AI, AII, CI, CII, GII

GII

AII, CI, CII
GII

CII, GII

GII

CII

CII, GII

CII

CI, CII

Figure 8.2 *Decision tree for identifying appropriate decision-making style.* From Vroom and Yetton (1973); © 1973 by University of Pittsburgh Press.

recent EC legislation now makes it obligatory for companies to give an account in their annual report of the progress made in installing participative decision-making procedures, the types of decision companies are prepared to have taken participatively remain for the most part very limited.

TASK-ORIENTED VS RELATIONSHIP-ORIENTED LEADERSHIP

Stogdill's review of the trait literature encouraged a recognition of the part situational variables played in the explanation of leadership effectiveness. Although much of the subsequent empirical research included situational variables, little theoretical development occurred to assist in the explanation of results of this more broadly based research. However, the publication of Fred Fiedler's *A Theory of Leadership Effectiveness* (1967) ended this atheoretical phase of leadership research. Fielder presented an elaborate theory that attempted to account for the contingent nature of leadership effectiveness.

Fiedler began by distinguishing leadership behaviour from leadership style. Leadership behaviour is the specific response a supervisor makes in a particular situation. Unlike most other researchers Fiedler believed that leadership style – consistencies in the pattern of responses across different situations – was a relatively fixed feature of individuals which reflected a supervisor's motivational make-up.

He proposed that leadership style is fundamentally characterized along a dimension termed *task-oriented leadership vs relationship-oriented leadership*. He developed an instrument, the *least preferred co-worker* (LPC) scale, which provided a measure of an individual's position on the dimension and by implication his or her motivational make-up. The LPC score is derived by a supervisor describing on a number of bipolar adjectival scales the person they have found the most difficult to work with. Thus, a supervisor would rate the least preferred co-worker along eight point scales like friendly-unfriendly, intelligent–unintelligent. A high score is obtained by placing least preferred co-worker towards the positive end of each scale. Fiedler interprets the high-scoring supervisor as an individual who is concerned with establishing good interpersonal relations, more considerate and lower in anxiety. High scorers are also more 'cognitively complex', since they are able to separate out evaluations of the least preferred co-worker's job performance from evaluations of his or her personality and ability. The high scorer acquires self-esteem not through intrinsic satisfaction of a job well done, but through the recognition by others of his or her competence. A low score is acquired by denigrating the least preferred co-worker, describing him or her as unintelligent, lazy and unfriendly. This is thought to reflect

190

a lack of concern with personal relationships and by implication more concern with the task. The low scorer is presumed to be less cognitively complex than the high scorer, being unable to differentiate work performance and personality. Successful task performance is the principal source of satisfaction for the low scorer. Both high and low scorers are concerned with the task and interpersonal relationships. The high-scoring supervisor is concerned with the task in order to achieve successful relationships. The low-scoring leader is concerned with interpersonal relationships in order to achieve successful task performance. Fiedler argued that low-scoring and high-scoring leaders differ in behaviour most when the satisfaction of their needs is threatened.

Fiedler's second task was to construct a satisfactory method of describing and measuring leadership situations. An important feature of leadership positions, he argued, is the extent to which the authority of the leader is legitimized by the organization. Does the leader have the power to hire and fire? Are there large differences in status and rank? This feature of leadership situations he termed the leader's *position power*, and a checklist was devised to provide a measure of it.

The second feature of leadership situations which he sought to describe was the *task structure*. Some tasks are routine and have one route to a single solution, while others are less straightforward. He classified task structure using four dimensions: goal clarity, the degree to which the goal requirements are clearly ascertainable; decision verifiability, the degree to which it is possible to know whether a solution is correct; goal path multiplicity, the number of possible routes to the goal; and solution specificity, the number of possible solutions.

The third feature of the situation that Fiedler built into the model was what he called *leader–group relations*. If leader–group relations were good, the leader was accepted, group members were loyal and communication was easier. Fiedler devised an instrument (the group atmosphere score) which yielded a measure of leader–group relations.

These aspects of the work situation Fiedler presumed captured the essential features of leadership situations. Research on a large number of work groups in a variety of work settings showed that the relationship between a supervisor's style and his or her effectiveness was mediated by the leadership situation. Thus the final task for Fiedler was to describe and explain the interaction between leadership style, the leadership situation and the leader's effectiveness.

In order to identify the pattern of this interaction Fiedler simplified his concept of a leadership situation by combining the three measures of it (position power, task structure and leader–group relations) into one representing the *favourability* of the situation to the leader. To do this Fiedler assumed that the most important determinant of situation favourability was leader–group relations followed by task structure and position power. He then divided each of these three measures into two on the basis of the median point that had been identified for each scale by his research. By combining each of the three, now dichotomized, dimensions in their order of importance he created a dimension comprised of eight (2 × 2 × 2) octants representing situational favourability. Thus, according to Fiedler the most favourable situation was one in which leader–group relations were good and task structure and position power were high. Conversely, the least favourable situation for a supervisor was one in which he or she faced poor leader–group relations, low task structure and low position power.

Fiedler then plotted each of his research studies by placing them on the horizontal dimension according to what octant they fell into and on the vertical axis according to the correlation found between the supervisor's LPC score and his or her team's effectiveness.

To summarize the interaction between leadership style, situational favourability and effectiveness, Fiedler drew a line connecting the median correlations of studies in each octant (Figure 8.3). Fiedler found that low LPC leaders were most effective when the situation was either highly favourable or highly unfavourable. In situations of moderate favourability, high-scoring supervisors performed best. This represented an important correction to the prevailing human relations view that relationship-oriented supervision was always preferable.

Fiedler explained his conclusions by arguing that, since high and low LPC leaders seek to satisfy different needs, situations that threaten the satisfaction of those needs will trigger very different behaviours in each. In situations of low favourability the group is best served by directive and structuring leadership and the needs of low LPC leaders are more likely to produce these behaviours. In jobs where there is a low level of task structure, for example where the goals are not clear or the number of possible routes to a solution is high, directive and structuring leadership may be welcomed by group members in order to reduce their frustration and anxiety.

Conversely, highly favourable situations where jobs are routinized, the position of power is high and leader–group relations are good provide an environment in which the low LPC leaders' needs are not threatened, enabling them to relax and become less structuring. Highly favourable situations produce very different behaviours in a high LPC supervisor. Since there are already good relations, they become more involved and structuring, which, since the

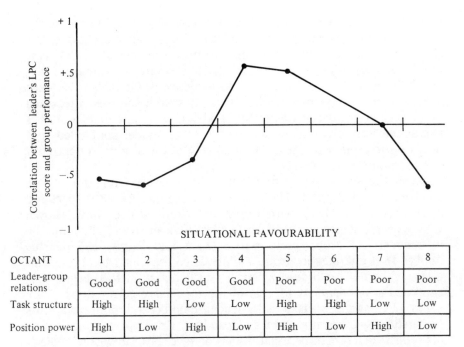

OCTANT	1	2	3	4	5	6	7	8
Leader-group relations	Good	Good	Good	Good	Poor	Poor	Poor	Poor
Task structure	High	High	Low	Low	High	High	Low	Low
Position power	High	Low	High	Low	High	Low	High	Low

Figure 8.3   *The relationship between situational favourability and leaders' LPC score. The bow shape was formed by joining the median correlation for studies in each octant between LPC scores and group performance.* From Fiedler (1967).

task is already highly structured, is likely to be resented by group members.

In situations of moderate favourability where conditions are mixed, the relationship-oriented high LPC scorer performs better, since it is in these positions that interpersonal relations play an important part in determining the work group's productivity.

The hallmark of any good theory is the number of specific and testable predictions it is able to generate. Fiedler's theory produces a large number of predictions, many of which predict results that we would not expect on the basis of common sense. For example, we would expect increased experience to be associated with increased effectiveness in a leader. Correlations between the two do not confirm this (Fiedler, 1970). Fiedler (in Fiedler *et al.*, 1975; Fiedler, 1982) points out that the absence of a relationship can be predicted using his theory. The effect of experience on the effectiveness of a leader would depend on the LPC of the leader and the initial level of situational favourability. The high LPC leader will benefit from experience since it would make this situation more favourable. The effect

193

of increased experience in conditions of low situational favourability for the low LPC leader is to reduce effectiveness, since it changes the situation to one in which their behaviour is least effective. Converse predictions for high and low LPC leaders occur if situational favourability is initially moderate. Some evidence is available to support these predictions (Fiedler *et al.*, 1975). Research has also supported other predictions derived from the model. One review of 178 studies testing various predictions derived from the model concluded that despite numerous exceptions the majority of the studies supported it (Strube and Garcia, 1981).

Given the scope of the model it is hardly surprising that it has received mixed support. There is no doubt, however, that there are some specific problems with the model. Some studies have shown LPC scores are not as fixed as Fiedler envisaged and may not be independent of group performance (Katz and Farris, 1976). This implies that changes in group performance may lead to changes in a leader's style. Additionally, Smith and Peterson (1988) argue that supposedly independent aspects of the model are confounded. They claim LPC scores overlap with leader–member relations and thus leadership style are not at all independent. Group performance may also affect leader–member relations (Vroom, 1976). However, Fiedler's attempt to explain the nature of leadership effectiveness represented a considerable advance in leadership theory, and his basic finding that the effectiveness of a leadership style was contingent on the situation remains a view to which most behavioural scientists still subscribe.

PATH–GOAL THEORY

Path–goal theory is an attempt to integrate theories of leadership, motivation and job satisfaction. It utilizes aspects of the Michigan and Ohio studies, Fiedler's contingency theory and the VIE theory of motivation (see Chapter 5). Path–goal theory began in the late 1950s but did not attract much attention until it was popularized by Evans (1970) and House (1971). Though now considerably modified, the apparent promise of the theory has allowed it to continue exerting considerable influence in leadership research, even in the absence of clear empirical support.

Path–goal theory begins by assuming that leaders must be capable of displaying four types of behaviour:

1. Initiation of structure
2. Consideration
3. Participation
4. Goal-setting

Like Fiedler's theory, path–goal theory is a contingency theory. But while Fiedler specified three factors mediating the effect of leader behaviour on leadership effectiveness, path–goal theory specifies a much broader range of variables. In fact the list of contingency variables suggested by path–goal theory includes any relevant characteristics of subordinates and environment. We have already seen that an important subordinate variable is level of skill or ability; others might reflect motivational and personality characteristics such as the locus of control, need for affiliation and authoritarianism. Environmental variables would include Fiedler's task structure, authority system, type of organization and amount of performance feedback. What integrates the leadership behaviours and the contingency factors is VIE motivational theory. This theory assumes people are motivated if they perceive connections or 'instrumentalities' between their effort and performance and the attainment of valued rewards. This implies that the effective leader is the leader who is able to modify these key perceptions in subordinates. By providing the appropriate leadership behaviour given the nature of the staff and leadership situation, supervisors can influence the clarity of subordinate perceptions of paths to goals, the desirability of goals and the link between effort and goal attainment.

As well as dealing with the perceptions of links between effort and reward, a leader needs to behave in a way that makes subordinates believe he or she is instrumental in goal attainment. Therefore, leaders seen as assisting in attaining valued ends are more likely to be accepted. In practice, this means providing assistance, coaching, guiding and rewarding. It can also mean consulting and standing up for subordinates by defending their interests.

Which of these behaviours is selected is decided by what seems most likely to lead to the attainment of valued rewards by subordinates. For example, considerate leadership is expected to correlate more highly with productivity and job satisfaction in structured situations. Initiation of structure is more appropriate in unstructured situations. Similarly, if subordinates are self-actualizers, they are likely to need participative leadership, whereas authoritarian subordinates would require initiation of structure in order to be satisfied with their job and leader. When the leader is able to display the correct leadership behaviour, path–goal theory predicts rises in motivation, job satisfaction, satisfaction with supervisors and performance.

By combining path–goal variables a large number of predictions can be derived. For example, combining two styles of leadership and three levels of task structure produces six predictions. In view of this, researchers have tended to concentrate on consideration, initiation of structure and levels of task structure. Some predictions of path–goal theory have been supported. Greene (1979), for example, classified the work of a sample of engineers, scientists and technicians according to the amount of structure present in their work. Initiation of structure was positively correlated with subordinate job satisfaction and performance if low task structure was present. If the task was highly structured, initiation of structure was negatively correlated with subordinate job satisfaction and was not predictive of performance.

A wider range of path–goal predictions was tested in two studies by Schriesheim and de Nisi (1981). The first study was based on 110 employees working for a medium-sized bank; the second on 205 employees of a medium-sized manufacturing plant. The task variables used by the researchers included task variety, feedback and whether the job involved dealing with other people. Path–goal theory predicted that initiation of structure would increase job satisfaction when individuals perceived their jobs as varied, low in feedback and involving little contact with other people. Conversely, for routine jobs where feedback was already present and subordinates dealt with other people, initiation of structure would be redundant and would actually reduce job satisfaction. Schriesheim and de Nisi's results confirmed these predictions.

Generally, however, support for path–goal theory has been mixed. Research has provided strongest support for path–goal predictions which have either used consideration as a predictor or job satisfaction as a criterion (the variable being predicted). However, despite mixed support, path–goal theory continues to attract considerable attention from behavioural scientists. It is seen by many researchers as more flexible than Fiedler's theory, since the range of contingency variables it embraces is potentially much larger. In addition, combining contingency variables offers behavioural scientists a large number of specific hypotheses to test. Finally, what makes path–goal theory especially attractive to many researchers is the logic of VIE theory it incorporates, which provides a solid theoretical basis for making predictions about the effect of various leadership styles in specific work situations.

TRANSFORMATIONAL LEADERSHIP

Charles de Gaulle once commented: 'In the designs, the demeanour, and the mental operations of a leader there must be always a "something" which others cannot altogether fathom, which puzzles them, stirs them and diverts their attention.' This mysterious 'something' that some leaders have to inspire their subordinates to do things beyond their capabilities and into sometimes unquestioning compliance seems to have been lost in the theories and research discussed so far. The feeling that the romance, mystery and even the subject matter of leadership have been lost in abstract conceptualizations has caused a resurgence of interest in what is termed *transformational* or *charismatic* leadership.

Burns (1978), for example, makes the distinction between power-holders and leaders. Power-holders have by virtue of their job the capacity to influence others. To be a leader the individual must be able to 'induce followers to act for certain goals that represent the values and the motivations – the wants and needs, the aspirations and expectations of both leaders and followers' (p.19). In what Burns describes as transactional leadership there is simply a mutual exchange for economic or political reasons between leader and follower. In transformational leadership a deeper, more powerful process is present. Here 'one or more persons engage with others in such a way that leaders and followers raise one another to higher levels of motivation and morality'.

The differences between transformational and transactional leaders have been described in more specific terms by a number of researchers (Conger, 1989; Sashkin and Sashkin, 1990; Kotter, 1990). For example, Kotter's distinctions between leaders and managers are described in Table 8.1.

Table 8.1 *Kotter's comparison of leadership and management. Adapted from Kotter (1990).*

	LEADERS	MANAGERS
CREATE AGENDAS	Establishing direction Developing vision of future Developing change strategies	Planning/budgeting Developing plan Developing timetable
BUILDING NETWORKS	Alignment of people Inculcating vision in persons/teams	Organizing/staffing Developing Staffing, delegation and monitoring policies
EXECUTION	Inspiring Energizing others to overcome barriers	Controlling/problem-solving Monitoring and taking corrective action
OUTCOMES	Potentially revolutionary changes Innovation Order out of chaos	Order and predictability Key results expected by significant others

197

As can be seen from the table, Kotter equates leadership with adaptive change, whereas management is about smooth implementation and operation of existing policies. According to Kotter, both processes are important, although some organizations, he argues, lack leadership.

What is central to Burns's notion of transformational leadership is the two-way nature of the leader and follower relationship. There have been a number of attempts to explain the psychological basis of this relationship (e.g. Meindl, 1990. Shamir et al., 1990). The most thoroughly developed explanation is that of Kets de Vries (1989), who has used and expanded Freud's insights into the nature of leadership. For Freud (1939) the appeal of leaders operates at a symbolic, unconscious level. Leaders represent the return of the 'primal father' with whom, like the father of our own early childhood, it is easy to identify. As Freud suggests 'we know that in the mass of mankind there is a powerful need for an authority who can be admired, before whom one bows down, by whom one is ruled and perhaps even ill treated' (1939, p. 109).

Leaders are therefore, according to de Vries, a prime target for the process of *transference*. Thus leaders benefit from a kind of psychological confusion about who they are as they become mixed up in the follower's mind with significant individuals from his or her childhood. And while transference stimulates our dependency needs, another process identified by Freud, projection, enables us to attribute the leader with our own desires and fantasies. The elation experienced by followers of charismatic leaders is partly the result of being able to rid themselves of prohibitions, The leader becomes their conscience.

From this perspective all leadership is potentially charismatic. Some leaders, however, are more aware of these processes and may actively encourage them. By speaking directly to a follower's unconscious through metaphor, simile, simple language and stark contrasts, some leaders can harness the processes of transference and projection. Many organizations have either benefited from or have been rescued by constructive forms of charismatic leadership. However, many spectacular crashes – de Lorean, for example – are the result of the dark side of charismatic leadership. While some leaders can use these processes constructively, others are ultimately destroyed by them.

Leadership training: from theory to practice

SENSITIVITY TRAINING

Leadership research has provided us with a composite picture of effective leaders. They are the individuals who are sensitive to key contingency variables and so can alter their leadership style accordingly. They are able to initiate, maintain and enhance expectations of success within their work groups, Their decisions are accepted because they are perceived as competent by other group members. As we have seen, effective leaders are continuously negotiating their role with their subordinates. In this context, group members exchange their compliance in return for the leader meeting their needs.

In order to meet the group's needs a leader must first be able to perceive them. Therefore, the development of leaders' sensitivity to subordinates' needs has been a key area in leadership training. A number of techniques have been developed to do just this. The best known of these, the *T-group* (T for training), has been the subject of much controversy since it was developed in the late 1940s. A T-group consists of about twelve trainees and one trainer. The usual factors such as agendas and work roles which guide interaction in the workplace are absent. The task of the trainees is to interact and then at points analyse what has occurred in the group – for example, what roles have emerged, who is participating and who is becoming dependent on whom. The trainer throws the burden of keeping the interaction going almost entirely on the group, intervening only occasionally to reflect on what is occurring in the group or to encourage participation. Trainers believe that this sequence of interaction, analysis and feedback promotes:

1. An increased self-awareness.
2. An increased awareness of the needs of subordinates.
3. An increased desire to share information.
4. An increased desire to reach decisions participatively.
5. A shift towards less formal styles of interaction with subordinates.
6. A reduction in assertive and directive leadership behaviour.

A number of studies of the effects of T-groups suggest that the experience does, in general, produce the desired outcomes (Bass, 1981). However, a number of behavioral scientists have doubts about the use of T-groups. Some critics claim the technique is simply *unethical* because it may invade individual privacy, disrupt an individual's defence system and pressure group members to conform. In addition trainees may be required to assume that the trainer's values are superior to their own. While some people undoubtedly find T-groups a powerful psychological experience, the emotional stress involved can produce 'casualties' in the group, trainees sometimes actually requiring psychiatric help afterwards. In reply to these critics trainers claim that the benefits of T-group training make the small amount of stress and damage it may cause acceptable (e.g. Cooper,) 1975).

A second problem for trainers is demonstrating that the learning which occurs in the group is *transferable* to the workplace. Some critics have suggested that trainees can have difficulty perceiving a link between the learning of abstract social-psychological concepts and practical problems in their workplace. In response to this trainers are increasingly complementing the T-group activity with exercises such as role-playing based on trainees' current work problems. Following the failure of trainees to transfer their learning back to their workplace, one trainer went a stage further and decided to move into the company as a consultant. This enabled him to join formal work group meetings within the plant. From this vantage he was able to explore the use of authority, communications, inter-personal relations and role definitions in real day-to-day work problems (Bamforth, 1965).

In an effort to reduce the variability in the effects of T-group caused by differences in the skill of trainers, standardized and self-administered sensitivity training techniques have been developed. These typically involve group problem-solving exercises followed by feedback and discussion. A widely used example of this is 'Lost on the Moon' (Hall, 1971) described in Chapter 7. Though not as powerful an experience as a T-group, the exercise, particularly when combined with audio-visual feedback, similarly gives trainees an indication of the way they respond in groups and of the impact of their behaviour on other people.

LEADER MATCH TRAINING

Fiedler's contribution to leadership theory has been immense and attempts have been made to translate his insights into a leadership programme. You may remember that the distinctive feature of Fiedler's contingency theory was his conceptualization of leadership style. Path–goal theory assumes, in principle, that it is possible for a leader to change the leadership style according to contingency variables. Fiedler, however assumed leadership style was a reflection of relatively permanent personality and motivational variable. If this is correct it would be easier to teach leaders how to change the situation than change themselves. Fiedler and Chemars (1984) developed a training programme called *leader match training* based on this assumption. The first stage of the programme is the assessment of where a trainee is on the task-oriented–relations-oriented dimension. This indicates what sort of situations each leader is likely to be effective in. The trainee is then taught how to assess the favorability of a work situation and how to change the situation to suit his or her leadership style. Support for this approach comes from twelve studies in which performance evaluations of trainees were taken from two to six months after the course (Fiedler and Mahar, 1979). Performance ratings of 423 trained leaders were compared to ratings of 480 leaders in control groups. The results indicated leader match trainees had significantly higher rating than control groups.

The value of leader match training, however, is doubted by a number of researches. We have already seen that the notion of fixed leadership styles has been questioned. In addition the 'match' between leadership style and leadership situation was based on the median correlation of effectiveness and style in the original studies. In some octants along Fiedler's dimension of situational favourability the median result masks a considerable range in the size and direction of correlations between leadership style and effectiveness. Thus, some behavioural scientists claim that Fielder's contingency theory is at present not sufficiently proven for it to form the basis of a specific training programme.

RATIONAL TRAINING

Other contingency theories assume, flexibility in leadership style. Vroom and Yetton's model, as we have seen, provides rules for leaders to assist them in choosing between participative and directive styles of leadership. They have developed a programme known as *rational training*. This, they claim, enables trainees to understand the cause of discrepancies between their own way of approaching leadership problems and that prescribed by their model. Trainees are encouraged to focus on:

1. The situations in which they arc prepared to behave participatively, and those in which they are directive.
2. Whether they are more concerned with the development of their staff or working within time constraints.
3. Whether they are more concerned with decision quality than decision acceptability.
4. Which Vroom and Yetton rules they are adhering to and which they are violating.

Vroom and Yetton's model and the training associated with it operates primarily at the cognitive level; it sensitizes managers to a range of variables and helps them to conceptualize the leadership problem. Support for their approach has, in general, been mixed. One study, for example, found that while managers who had been through their training programme enjoyed greater acceptance of their decisions by subordinates, there was no effect on the quality of their decisions (Vroom and Jago, 1978).

Table 8.2   Yukl's typology of management skills.

BUILDING RELATIONSHIPS
Networking: Socializing informally, developing contacts with people who are a source of information and support and maintaining relationships through periodic inter-action, including visits, telephone calls, and correspondence, and attendance at meet-ings and social events.

Supporting: Acting in a friendly and considerate manner, showing sympathy and support when someone is upset, listening to complaints and problems, looking out for someone's interests, providing helpful career advice, doing things to aid someone's career advancement.

Managing conflict and team-building: Encouraging and facilitation constructive res-olution of conflict, fostering team-work and co-operation, and building identification with the organizational unit or team.

INFLUENCING PEOPLE
Motivating: Using influence techniques that appeal to emotions, values, or logic to generate enthusiasm for the work and commitment to task objectives, or to induce someone to carry out a request for support, co-operation, assistance, resources or authorization; also setting an example of proper behaviour by one's own actions.

Recognizing and rewarding: Providing praise, recognition and tangible rewards for effective performance, significant achievements, and special contributions; expressing respect and appreciation for someone's accomplishments.

MAKING DECISIONS
Planning and organizing: determining long-range objectives and strategies for adapting to environmental change, identifying necessary action steps to carry out a project of activity, allocating resources among activities according to priorities, and determining how to improve efficiency, productivity and co-operation with other parts of the organization.

Problem solving: Identifying work-related problems, analysing problems in a systematic but timely manner to determine causes and find solutions, and acting decisively to implement solutions and deal with crises.

Consulting and delegating: Checking with people, before making changes that affect them, encouraging suggestions for improvement, inviting participation in decision-making, incorporating the ideas and suggestions of others in decisions, and allowing others to have substantial discretion in carrying out work activities and handling problems.

GIVING–SEEKING INFORMATION
Monitoring operations and environment: Gathering information about the progress and quality of work activities, the success or failure of activities or projects, and the performance of individual contributors; also, determining the needs of clients or

users, and scanning the environment top detect threats and opportunities.

Informing: Disseminating relevant information about decisions, plans and activities to people who need it to do their work, providing written materials and documents, answering requests for technical information, and telling people about the organizational unit to promote its reputation.

Clarifying roles and objectives: Assigning tasks, providing direction in how to do the work, and communicating a clear understanding of job responsibilities, task objectives, deadlines, and performance expectations.

SKILL TRAINING

Much leadership training is now based on *skill theory*. Leadership skills such as information-gathering, interviewing, counselling, negotiating, motivating and using feedback are assumed, like other skills, to be organized hierarchically with a cognitive component ultimately governing the behavioural responses. The leadership trainer therefore divides the training programme equally between improving the ability of trainees to develop adequate cognitive models of their staff and work situation and developing the behaviours associated with the skill through practice and feedback. For example, to improve trainees' skill in motivating staff the trainer would spend a day exploring theories of motivation with trainees, using motivational theories to identify the possible 'blocks' in organizations which reduce the inclination to work and 'boosters' which improve motivation.

In the next stage the trainer role-plays a member of the trainee's staff and is interviewed by the trainee, who uses the conceptual material acquired in stage 1 to guide the interview. This is followed by a feedback sessions in which the trainer and other trainees comment on the effectiveness of the interview in terms of how effectively the subordinate's current motivational state was diagnosed and to what extent the interview would have increased his or her motivation. Further practice interviews are arranged for the trainee on the basis of these comments and suggestions, and the procedure is repeated until the trainee's performance is considered satisfactory.

A number of typologies have been developed which specify the nature of management skills. These differ in terms of the broadness of the categories they use. Some typologies, such as the Ohio scales, are extremely broad; others, such as Alban-Metcalfe (1984), describe very specific micro 'skills' which may be more useful in developing very particular areas. Yukl (1989) provides a useful 'middle-range' typology describing skills which are neither too specific nor too broad and which can thus be used in a number of training settings. Yukl uses a questionnaire (Yukl, 1987) to measure the presence of these skills in managers. The typology is set out in Table 8.2.

In conclusion, we have explored a range of attempts to develop training programmes out of the leadership theories available. Human relations theorists have established a tradition which emphasizes an increased awareness of self and of group dynamics. They would argue that the relationship-oriented style of leadership which emerges from an increased sensitivity to group dynamics is preferable and more effective. In contrast, contingency theorists assume that a leader's effectiveness is the result of the interaction of a leader with a situation. They train supervisors to analyse their own behaviour and leadership situation and to change aspects of either to produce a better fit. Skill theorists bring the insights of skill theory to the traditional human relations perspective by developing a leader's ability to comprehend his or her staff and using these macro-cognitive changes to develop the micro-behavioural responses involved in skilled leadership. Each will persist and continue to be developed, and in their different ways will contribute to achieving the broad aims of the human relations movement set out some fifty years ago, to increase social skill and insight into the social dynamics of the workplace among superiors and thus to reduce the level of social incompetence in the management of organizations.

Further reading

Bass, B.M. (1990) *Bass and Stodgill's Handbook of Leadership* (3rd edn). New York: Free Press.

Briner, W., M. Geddes and C. Hastings (1990) *Project Leadership*. Aldershot: Gower.

Carkhuff, R.R. (1989) *Empowering the Creative Leader*. Amherst: H.R.D. Press.

Hunt, J.G. (1991) *Leadership: A New Synthesis*. Aldershot: Sage.

Kets de Vries. (1989) *Prisoners of Leadership*. Chichester. Wiley.

Russell, R. and V. Rus (eds) (1991) *International Handbook of Participation in Organizations: For the study of Organizational Democracy, Co-Operation and Self-Management*. Vol II: *Ownership and Participation*. Oxford: Oxford University Press.

Smith, P.B. and M.F. Peterson (1988) *Leadership, Organizations and Culture*. London: Sage.

Yukl, G.A. (1989) *Leadership in Organizations* (2nd edn). Englewood Cliffs, N.J.: Prentice-Hall.

9

Alternative Work Design

The expectations that we have of employment in a modern industrial society include social rewards as well as purely economic ones. Yet, leaving aside adequate economic returns, the human needs of people in work are very often frustrated by jobs, many of which make little or no allowance for individual commitment or the exercise of skills and initiative. This is widely perceived as constituting a serious problem. The human and social problems of dissatisfaction experienced in work may in turn lean to economic problems for employers. Poor productivity and quality of output, the 'withdrawal' from work manifest as absenteeism and labour turnover, as well as various types of industrial conflict, like strikes and sabotage, have all been linked with low levels of worker motivation. However, there is an equally widely shared conviction that management's goals of performance can be reconciled with workers' interest in more satisfying and fulfilling work.

The attempt to organize work along more humane and democratic lines has long been a concern of social scientists and socially aware employers. And social psychology has made a contribution to these efforts which goes back at least to the Hawthorne experiments in the 1920s. The 'discovery' of socio-psychological factors in work marked the beginning of the Human Relations movement, which developed very fully theories about employee behaviour in work groups. Indeed, in different ways the theories of motivation and group dynamics that were reviewed in the last four chapters have all been concerned with the question of appropriate occupational rewards and appropriate work settings. Recently, however, much of this interest has focused on the problem of changing the actual jobs that people perform, and in this chapter we will be looking at these central issues in the redesign of work.

The objectives of work design reflect the attempt to change the jobs of individuals or groups along one or more of three main dimensions:

1. *Variety*. This refers to the complexity and differentiation of work. An increase in task variety and the multiplicity of skills exercised should improve the content and quality of a job, increasing its interest for the individual and reducing the monotony and routine of work.
2. *Autonomy*. This refers to the degree of control that people have over their jobs. Lack of autonomy is typical of much machine-paced or assembly-line work, and is regarded by workers as a main cause of job dissatisfaction. Conversely, work experience can be greatly enhanced by the introduction of 'higher-level' tasks which involve a degree of discretion and responsibility, and by the group allocation of work and the self-selection of groups.
3. *Completeness of task*. Many routine jobs reflect the imposition of extreme divisions of labour. This creates highly fragmented, meaningless work and means that people are unable to see any sense in what they do. To reverse this trend, effective redesign needs to create 'whole' tasks that are more identifiable and meaningful, and based on integrated work cycles.

The techniques of work redesign

Two basic approaches to the redesign of work involve rotating the jobs that workers do and enlarging individual work tasks. Job rotation does not actually mean changing the work itself, but it permits a greater variety for individuals by moving them between jobs. In practice, managers often use this method without necessarily having a formal system of rotating workers at regular intervals. They may simply ensure that particularly unpleasant or monotonous jobs are shared, and that certain workers are not allocated to them permanently. Secondly, job enlargement involves merging a number of simplified tasks to form a single task with an extended range of work. In mass assembly industries, for instance, this often means that cycle times (i.e. the time taken to complete a single cycle of a repetitive task) are not allowed to fall below some stipulated minimum level, so there is a limit placed on the extent to which jobs can be subdivided.

However, each of these methods is thought to be inadequate as a basis for genuinely humanizing work. Job rotation merely redistributes existing work, and job enlargement involves regrouping unit tasks rather than seeking to improve the work itself. At best, it has been argued, these methods make cosmetic changes. At worst they may bring about an actual deterioration in working conditions. For example, if job rotation is used chiefly to create a more flexible workforce, workers may find themselves being moved from job to job without being consulted. This may disrupt the rhythm of work, and even threaten job security if workers become interchangeable.

Similarly, the enlargement of jobs sometimes merely results in an intensification of work. People often cope with monotonous jobs by mentally 'switching off' to some extent, but work that involves a whole series of repetitive tasks may require much closer attention. The most unpleasant and taxing jobs are often those that are monotonous and also demand high levels of attention.

THE 'ENRICHMENT' OF WORK

There are, however, other methods regarded as more meaningful ways of redesigning work. Two of the most important ones are *job enrichment* and the provision for *group working*. The basic purpose of job enrichment is to introduce responsibilities or additional tasks into a job which genuinely do make it more of a complete occupation. Many routinized production jobs can be enriched by the inclusion of tasks such as machine maintenance, elements of inspection and quality control, or machine-setting. It may also be possible to arrange for workers to obtain their own materials, or to deal with communications with other departments. Changes like these can enhance workers' skills and enable them to deal with complete tasks rather than highly fragmented ones. Thus, instead of similar degraded tasks being combined together, genuine job enrichment means that a certain amount of planning and control is introduced into the work – tasks which otherwise would have been the responsibility of supervisors or specialist groups of workers.

Secondly, group working has many potential advantages. There are manifest social and psychological gains in working co-operatively with others, rather than on isolated tasks; also many of the requirements of job enrichment can be built into the group context. Group tasks by their very nature tend to be based on complete operations and involve greater complexity and variety than fragmented tasks. Groups can be self-regulating, reducing the need for supervision and increasing members' perception of control. Furthermore, it is relatively easy to allow for job rotation and the fair allocation of tasks within a group system of working – indeed it can be beneficial to allow group members to arrange this for themselves.

THE SOCIO-TECHNICAL SYSTEMS APPROACH

The application of group theory to the work situation has been greatly advanced by the researchers of the Tavistock Institute of Human Relations. Their distinctive approach, developed in a series of classic studies in the British coal-mining industry and later in the Indian textiles industry, stressed an active involvement on the part of researchers in diagnosing firms' problems and proposing long-term solutions.

The Tavistock's interest in work groups began in the late 1940s when one of their researchers, Eric Trist, investigated the reasons for the failure of mechanization in coal-mining to bring about improvements in productivity, and for the poor state of industrial relations in the industry. Before mechanization, coal had been extracted manually by small teams of miners. Each shift team worked a section of the coalface, miners shared all the tasks in the coal-getting cycle (cutting, removal and advancing the seam), and teams were paid in a lump sum which would be distributed according to group consensus. These shift teams became highly cohesive social units, with strong emotional bonds developing between members which helped them deal with the dangerous and difficult conditions in which they worked (Trist and Bamforth, 1951).

However, the arrival of new technology (conveyor belts and coal-cutting machinery) transformed the old methods, and also seemed to require a different set of social relationships. With the new method, each shift consisted of a large group of miners under a supervisor, a novel role in coal production. The team was divided into specialists and performed only one phase of the work. An elaborate pay structure led to a status hierarchy developing among miners; and these divisions were compounded by physical separation as miners worked on greatly extended seams. The severe production and industrial relations problems caused by these changes included co-ordination difficulties as shifts were unable or unwilling to clear work left by the previous shift, and problems of control due to miners' resentment of being supervised.

Trist recognized the central problem of the impact of technological advances on traditional group working practices. Any solution would have to involve 'the general character of the method so that a social as well as a technological whole can come into existence' (Trist and Bamforth, 1951). This line of thought led to the concept of work organization as a *socio-technical system*. It implied that the work setting has to be seen in terms of two interrelated systems: a social and a technical system, each with its own independent properties. Further, the optimization of one system could occur at the expense of the other, and of the system as a whole. But while optimizing the overall system does usually mean sub-optimal states for each component, ideally the costs would be balanced out so that no one system carried them all (whereas what had occurred in mining was that optimization of the technology had led to a severely sub-optimal state in the miners' group relationships).

The Tavistock researchers at first carefully observed how particular groups of miners themselves had adapted to the changed conditions. They noted that on certain coalfaces groups emerged naturally that managed to utilize the new technology under modified working arrangements. Interestingly, therefore, in this classic case of job redesign the original impetus came from workers' own design of work, rather than design by 'experts'. Using these observations the Tavistockers developed a 'composite' method in which miners were divided into shift teams. Within each self-contained team, practices were adopted such as the miners acquiring skills in all phases of the work-cycle, and choosing what shift they worked on and the task they wanted within each shift. These modifications reduced the co-ordination and supervisory problems, as well as satisfying miners' socio-psychological needs for more meaningful work and satisfactory relations with other miners.

The first direct application of Trist's socio-technical principle came with research conducted by A. K. Rice in an Indian textile mill (Rice, 1958). As with the mining study, mechanization had disrupted an established work pattern. The introduction of automatic looms had deskilled jobs and turned workers into machine-minders, the effects of which had nullified any expected productivity gains. In this context, Rice helped to introduce a group working system, later extending it to non-automatic weaving. Both systems were based on small groups of workers, self-regulating and self-led, responsible for clusters of looms, and performing all the tasks of weaving. This resulted in steady improvements in output and quality of cloth. Rice also stressed the very high value that workers placed on these co-operative working arrangements. Once they had been given the opportunity to reorganize themselves into secure groups, workers showed great determination in making the new system successful.

The model of production as a socio-technical system provided a framework within which Rice included a broad range of factors. For example, he noted that workers' attachment to the group system was strengthened by elements of Indian culture, particularly the tradition of collective working in family-based cottage industries. In addition, the enhancement of work had meant that jobs became more demanding, and Rice was very clear about the responsibility of management to provide adequate training and technical support for the new groups.

Interestingly, in a follow-up study, conducted some fifteen years after Rice's original research, Miller (1975) confirmed the importance of these aspects of the work context. Miller found that in automatic weaving production had reverted to individual methods, while in the non-automatic sheds the group system had survived remarkably intact. He explained this by the different impact of increased work pressure on the two production systems. Workers' strong attachment to the groups made them resilient over the long term, but under excessive pressure some of the groups had been unable to adjust. Here, a failure of management to continue to provide support and protection for the groups had accounted for the collapse of group working.

Tavistock principles can be applied in their fullest form on new, 'greenfield' sites where the technology is not already established. Innovation is all too frequently obsessed with the technological side, while the human aspects are considered only as an afterthought, or when changes have been resisted. The concept of production as a socio-technical system implies that *both* subsystems are equally important. For example, Klein (1981) has described the design of a new plant for the confectionery company, Trebor. Because of strong company interest in the human side of work, she was able to examine the social consequences of particular layouts and equipment with the design team. This resulted in the building of an impressive factory, with single-status facilities, pleasant surroundings and a group-based production process. As Klein was at pains to emphasize, however, the different groups involved (architects, equipment suppliers, management) were not always in harmony; and the involvement of a social scientist was no automatic guarantee of a humane environment being achieved. Amid the 'welter of activities' a number of potentially important choices as to how work might be organized were lost. Nevertheless, it remains true that the work process is more likely to be optimized where choices can be made which adapt the social as well as technological aspects.

AUTONOMOUS WORK GROUPS

The great virtue of the Tavistock approach, based as it is on an open-systems model of organization, has been in extending the range of variables that are seen to affect workers' attitudes and performance. It has thus greatly increased the *scope* of work design. In classic studies like those of Trist and Rice we see wider factors, such as the culture and the key role of management in managing group boundary conditions, being taken into account. But although the sociotechnical approach has been extremely useful and influential, it has not evolved into a general theoretical framework. The practical concerns of investigators have usually caused them to focus on the particular workplace under investigation, and to adopt 'action' methods in order to intervene at each stage to try to improve different aspects of performance. These factors have made it difficult to define variables and the interrealtions between them, and have proved harmful in setting out more general guidelines for the design of work. In short, the breadth of socio-technical theory has been achieved at the cost of precision.

Recently, however, psychologists have been concerned to develop precise definitions of group variables. They have proposed 'autonomous work groups' as a useful model, both theoretically and for the practical purpose of introducing changes in the workplace. This is seen as a compromise between the very narrow job characteristics model, based on individual motivation, and the much more diffuse sociotechnical systems (Kemp et al., 1983).

The autonomous work group needs to be distinguished from the more ordinary co-acting group, where the main impact of membership on individuals is through higher levels of interaction (see Chapter 6). The crucial difference between the two types of group is the means of *control*. Co-acting groups are controlled externally, whereas autonomous work groups are to a large extent self-regulating, either removing the need for supervisors or greatly reducing it.

For example, Kemp et al. (1983) investigated job design on a greenfield site, where they were able to use several control groups so that plant and shift factors could be eliminated. Groups of eight to twelve operatives had been established, and responsible work roles included job allocation, the resolution of local production problems, organizing work breaks, contacting other departments and training new recruits. When compared with control groups, the researchers were able to show that greater job satisfaction, perceptions of higher job complexity and improved leadership style were successfully established in the experimental groups. However, workers' commitment to the firm and their work motivation remained the same. In other words, this carefully designed experiment showed both that beneficial changes may be brought about, and also that the effects are rarely simple when a broad range of variables is measured.

Case example: Volvo and the Swedish experience of work redesign

Some widely publicized projects have used methods based on job enrichment and autonomy. The Swedish car industry is justly famous for humanized work methods, and Volvo in particular has succeeded in reforming the assembly line, the classic symbol of alienated labour. The company has long had a production philosophy of utilizing group-based methods (Gyllenhammar, 1977). In several of their operations – passenger-car assembly, trucks, engine production – they have introduced autonomous work groups and achieved increases in cycle times and worker responsibility. However, the most dramatic progress has been made at two plants: Kalmar and Uddevalla.

Kalmar and reformed production
The car assembly plant opened at Kalmar in 1974 is probably the best known of all work redesign programmes. Starting from scratch on a greenfield site, Volvo rearranged straight-line assembly into a 'dock'

211

system with workers responsible for clusters of tasks. The car bodies were mounted on self-propelled carriers, which moved in and out of assembly bays where the work groups were located. The plant layout divided assembly into 20 sections connected in series (giving a basic line system of assembly), but the technology allowed groups to call up cars from the main track to be worked on. The design of the carriers, a novel feature of the system, made the tilting of the body possible so that the underside and inside of cars could be worked on easily. Such a technology satisfied a number of requirements of job enrichment. People worked in groups and to a degree controlled their own pace of work; some groups had responsibility for complete tasks and many workers learnt more than one task.

Over the years good economic results have been obtained from Kalmar, and it has been the catalyst for improvements in other plants. However, as Berggren (1989) points out, initial enthusiasm for the project concealed the fact that Kalmar was still only a compromise between line and dock assembly: the basis of centralized control still existed, while the development of full-blown autonomous work groups remained limited. This meant that the Kalmar technology was vulnerable to pressures for productivity. All-important buffer stocks between assembly sections gave the workers discretion over line speeds – workers called up and returned cars into the buffer zones, which meant that sections could run at different speeds. However, the removal of buffer stocks enforced a uniform pace, and in fact by the 1980s this had become the practice in the plant. Thus Kalmar represents an early attempt to reform the assembly line that in the end achieved only a limited success.

Socialized production at Uddevalla
But if Kalmar was production reformed, Volvo's newest plant at Uddevalla, opened in 1989, represents a revolutionary change. The unique layout of the plant consists of a massive automated materials handling centre, surrounded by six independent assembly workshops. Within each of these mini-plants, production teams numbering eight to ten people work on three cars simultaneously. They build complete vehicles on a two-hour cycle. The teams meet the full requirements of autonomous working: they are collectively responsible for job allocation, the scheduling and planning of work, and training; they are supplied with the necessary equipment (including Kalmar-type hydraulic carriers that allow the vehicle to tip at angles for easy assembly). Using computers, the teams call up parts which arrive silently and smoothly on automatic racked carriers. This system therefore eliminates entirely the serial production of the assembly line. 'The plant combines centralization of the materials handling system with the reconstruction of highly skilled labour intensive assembly, all linked by flexible technology and distributed computer processing power' (Clarke, 1990, p. 4). Moreover, the plant was designed on a co-operative basis. The trade union participated fully right from the start to produce the radical new proposals. This fulfilled a basic tenet of socio-technical theory, that

the 'social system of work' should be considered equally with the technical system, not as an afterthought.

As well as technological changes, Volvo also devoted huge resources to what Clarke (1990) calls the 'socialization of production'. Working conditions in the plant – noise levels, cleanliness, safety, facilities – were vastly improved compared with conventional car plants. This had also been true at Kalmar, but the company went to enormous lengths at Uddevalla to create an attractive working environment. Rest lounges with fully equipped kitchens and showers are provided; instead of overalls the workers wear light track suits which they launder daily; the company redeveloped all the hand tools so that female workers could use them comfortably, and so on. As one manager commented, 'Our workers wear designer clothes. They ski in Austria in winter. They go to the Greek islands in the summer. They have a professional life style. They cannot understand, and will not accept being treated differently at work' (quoted in Clarke, 1990, p. 15).

Market context
As the Tavistockers pointed out, however, and as this last quote suggests, the scope of work improvement needs to take in more than just the changes to the production system. It is important to look at social and organizational background. To begin with, the nature of the Swedish labour market has strongly influenced Volvo (and the country's other car maker, Saab-Scania) to adopt humanized work. Volvo has always admitted openly that hard economic motives are behind its job enhancement policies. In Sweden the history of social democratic government, coupled with high living standards and low unemployment, has resulted in strong expectations about work, especially among the young. Attitudes towards repetitive work are very hostile, and traditional methods of car assembly have resulted in constant problems of labour turnover and dissatisfaction. Put simply, you cannot get Swedes to work on assembly lines. These expectations are supported at the institutional level – both the union movement and the Swedish employers' federation are actively interested in job redesign.

This context makes us question how generalizable the Volvo experience might be, given the presence in Sweden of powerful unions willing to bargain over the nature of work and a backcloth of positive social attitudes. Countries not in possession of this unique supportive culture would be less fertile ground for imaginative work solutions. Also, the mere fact that Volvo makes luxury cars, sold on safety and quality features, implies a labour-intensive type of production. These methods would clearly not be as easy to apply in the high-volume, lower end of the market. Even at Volvo reformed production accounts for only a part of output; the bulk of plants are still defined by moderate improvements. Only Uddevalla represents fully socialized production, while at Kalmar the technology has reverted to being machine-paced.

It would also be wrong to think that there are always rational and consistent policies within the company. The different sections of management, industrial engineers and trade unions vary in their opinions, producing a strong debate about the direction of future job design (Berggren, 1989). Plant managers in particular have often been suspicious of giving discretion to workers and have wanted to return to tried and tested systems of control. The 1980s saw rising company sales, which, together with continuing labour market constraints, strongly inclined Volvo to experiment with work improvement. But that climate may change. Deepening recession in the industry and the entry of the Japanese into the luxury car market will mean much sharper competition. At the beginning of the 1990s Volvo was planning for cutbacks and rationalization in its multi-plant operations. There is no suggestion of the traditional assembly line ever reappearing, but the tide of opinion as regards the whole Volvo programme will almost certainly shift (Hammerstrom and Lansbury, 1991).

Clarke (1990) makes the interesting point that the Uddevalla technology (unlike Kalmar's) should be proof against manipulation. The technology cannot be run in any other way than with full worker autonomy, and it is possible to sustain productivity at lower levels of output. But both case studies demonstrate the importance of the *implementation* of job rede-sign. Work systems are not set in concrete but reflect the market and organizational climate in which they are implemented; they alert us to the real-world constraints, even in a company like Volvo famous for its ambitious and imaginative approach to redesign.

The constraints on work redesign

Numerous programmes of work redesign have been initiated. The most widespread and systematic developments have undoubtedly been those in Scandinavian companies, such as Volvo, Saab-Scania and Norsk-Hydro, but other major companies like ICI, Phillips and Fiat have also pursued work redesign as a central element of employee policy. Individual case studies have often shown impressive results. Changes in working conditions and improvements in various criteria of performance and worker satisfaction have all been reported. However, this apparently sound body of research and practical application is now being assessed much more critically.

Part of this criticism has arisen from a re-evaluation of the *evidence*. Although the record is impressive at first sight, under scrutiny the research methodology of many case studies turns out to have been seriously flawed (Kelly, 1982). For example, there have been tend-encies to report only positive findings and to accept managerial assessments of success rather than seek objective measures. There has often been a marked failure to allow for a 'novelty effect' – the possibility that improvements in workers' satisfaction may arise out of the newness of change rather than changes in the working arrangements themselves. Thus, few experiments verify whether improvements are sustained over the long term. Related to this, the problem of 'compensatory rivalry' occurs if other plants within a company, or other departments, get to hear of a particular job redesign project, and their own performance suffers because they feel they have been overlooked. Obviously this may lead to the performance of the experimental group being artificially inflated. Finally, a further drawback is that it may be impossible to isolate the effects of job redesign if, as sometimes happens, a whole package of changes is implemented at one time.

A second general criticism concerns the *influence* of job redesign. Again, the record of research and the support of major companies is superficially impressive. Furthermore, there has been a wide acceptance of work humanization at the level of public policy. Several European governments, Britain's included, as well as international bodies, have supported initiatives in this direction. Nonetheless, the true impact of all this has been far less significant. Many of the programmes have in fact never progressed beyond the experimental stage, and have often been discontinued after a short period. Similarly, many schemes have implemented cosmetic changes, despite claims of far-reaching job enrichment. Child, who on the whole is well disposed towards attempts to humanize work, has conclude rather pessimistically: 'The scale and scope of experiments in job redesign and work restructuring remain extremely limited. There are many minor developments masquerading under the label of job enrichment, but there are possibly no more than 100 or so European schemes that really enrich jobs significantly' (1984, p. 43).

In this context, Guest *et al.* (1980) discovered a yawning gap between workers' and managers' perceptions of job redesign. These researchers found, in a scheme that management regarded as having been very beneficial, that only about half of the workers involved were even aware of any change having taken place, and of these only a small proportion identified the change as being positive and significant. The implications of such a finding for studies that fail to elicit workers' opinions (and many do not) are obviously very damaging.

One of the main reasons why so much research in this area has not conformed to sound methodology is because many case studies have been carried out by paid consultants. Even research conducted by academics is often part of a consultancy exercise and so is far from being independent. Under such circumstances, where management calls the tune, researchers may be under great pressure to short-circuit proper empirical procedures, and to come up with positive findings, to persuade companies that the exercise has been worthwhile. This gap between theory and practice can only be explained by taking seriously into account the *context* in which work restructuring experiments are conducted. In other words, the full range of group variables, as well as wider environmental factors, have to be considered.

THE WORK GROUP CONTEXT

The more detailed experiments that occupational psychologists have developed include a range of factors which can influence work design, and which determine whether any benefits will be sustained (Slocum and Sims, 1980; Wall, 1980; Kemp et al., 1983).

1. *First-level managerial practices.* It is clear that the behaviour of supervisors is critical in determining the value of autonomous work groups to an organization and to group members. Drawing on the leadership behaviour dimensions of 'initiating structure', 'consideration' (see Chapter 8) and 'tolerance of freedom', Wall and Cordery (1982) argued that if autonomous work groups are to be successful – indeed if the groups are to enjoy a measure of true autonomy – then supervisory practice has to change in the direction of more freedom, less initiating structure and more consideration.

2. *Task.* The group task has to be motivationally engaging, otherwise the members as a whole may still exhibit the same pattern of withdrawal from work and low commitment that often characterize performance in routine and repetitive work.

3. *Group composition.* While the group has to possess task-relevant skills, these alone are not usually sufficient for effective performance. To utilize pooled resources, process problems also have to be minimized. We saw in Chapter 6 how cohesiveness within a group can be undermined if members are too dissimilar in status, values and abilities. Hence, effective personal and work outcomes are more likely with moderate heterogeneity in group members.

4. *Norms and performance strategies.* Discussions of how work can be accomplished can cause anxiety in group members and this too can lead to group process problems. Members may avoid discussing appropriate ways of performing group tasks, and develop strategies either as a habitual response or by accident. Autonomous work groups may, therefore, need to be encouraged to develop norms which support the exploration of various performance strategies.

5. *The general work setting.* Good group design, in terms of task, composition and supervisory practices, can be reinforced or undermined by a number of contextual factors. For example, the reward system and the performance targets need to be planned appropriately. Effective task behaviour must be adequately rewarded, and performance targets must be both challenging and realistic, if good work group design is to be enhanced. Management also has a key role in

ensuring that teams are provided with enough information to enable members to distinguish between flexible performance targets and targets which act as real constraints on behaviour. Without such detailed information, the group may develop ways of working based on inaccurate perceptions of an organization's requirements. Finally, the pattern of relationships between a group and other groups may affect the outcome of autonomous working arrangements. A balance has to be achieved between integration and differentiation: too much integration of effort between groups may lead to a loss in group identity; too much differentiation may result in damaging levels of competition.

THE ORGANIZATIONAL CONTEXT

In addition to the immediate context of work groups, the economic demands for profitability in organizations, and established technological practices, impose very powerful constraints on what may be done to improve work. Much of the work humanization literature, it has been suggested, has overlooked or underestimated these realities of organizations.

Job design

An important though often unacknowledged factor constraining work *re*design is the process by which work is designed in the first place. Particularly with complex mass assembly, the production jobs that workers perform have to be seen not as discrete tasks but as the final link in a long chain, beginning in the original design phase and continuing through product and process development. In these early stages little or no consideration will have been given to the human needs of the workers who will eventually carry out production. As Child (1984, pp. 38–9) has pointed out: 'heavily capitalized mass production plant . . . has generally imposed the greatest constraint upon work restructuring'. Inflexible production processes, where individual tasks are highly integrated, can prevent all but the most superficial of changes in the assembly stages. (In car assembly, for example, the design patterns within the vehicle mean that workers' tasks have to be performed in strict sequence.)

Furthermore, while we may assume that programmes of work redesign are based on human criteria, in reality the reverse is often the case: the rationale of job design may continue to constrain attempts to humanize work. Thus, in a survey of work design programmes in Europe, Lupton and Tann (1980) found that production engineers initiated the majority of projects, and efficiency-related goals were uppermost. This was despite the fact that projects were mostly publicized in terms of the benefits for workers.

Organizational power structures
Organizational hierarchies in reality are structures of deeply entrenched power, and this has also proved to be a major constraint on work humanization. The attempt to transfer control to shopfloor jobs may well threaten the status and security of managers and supervisors who presently exercise that control, and in several instances where apparently promising schemes have been abandoned it has been because of the wider repercussions for organizational power. Indeed, to the extent that work redesign really is significant, we should expect it to cut across the existing divisions of power.

One of the commonest causes of failure in programmes is resistance from supervisors. An early experiment carried out in the Norwegian company Norsk-Hydro clearly illustrated this problem. The firm's intention was to enrich workers' jobs by the inclusion of some basic supervisory tasks, which would also allow the foremen to devote more time to forward planning. However, the foremen perceived the changes rather differently. They saw the bread and butter elements of their jobs being taken over by workers, and being compensated by some vague activity, planning, of which they had little experience. Consequently, the foremen resisted the scheme in its early stages and, faced with their disapproval, management called it off. However, by this time the workers had begun to respond positively to the changes and were disappointed when they had to return to the old ways of working. Thus at the end of the day, management were back where they started, but with a suspicious supervisory group and a disgruntled workforce.

The constraint of organizational power is also frequently the explanation behind the common paradox of projects being abandoned because they are 'too successful'. The strict demarcation of power within organizations means that even seemingly small changes may be widely disruptive. Thus Blackler and Brown (1980) described a project involving the dock assembly of trucks (where the stationary vehicle is assembled on a chassis by a team of workers) at Volvo's Arendal plant. The project was initially given a high priority; plant-wide changes were implemented to attempt to make it a success, and in the early stages production and quality levels were comparable with the conventional assembly line. However, when the researchers conducted a follow-up study some three years after, production had reverted to conventional methods. As far as they were able to ascertain, this was simply due to a hardening of opinion against the new methods among senior managers: 'their main objections were more emotional than rational. Dock methods involve a loss of immediate control by management; this factor we felt weighed more strongly with some individuals than did the potential commercial advantages available from the system.'

A similar case involved the introduction of flexitime into an office. The arrangement was started on a trial basis in one section, and quickly became popular as employees began to exercise a degree of control over how work was organized. They would meet informally and arrange timekeeping to cover the work and also to suit their own interests. Management, however, became alarmed as they felt their traditional authority was slipping away; and when there were signs of other employees wanting the same conditions, the scheme was hurriedly cancelled.

Evaluating work redesign

When you stop to think, the whole notion of the 'expert' design of work would hardly be necessary if jobs were skilled and responsible in the first place. Indeed, if we accept the idea of some original stage of development, consisting of traditionally skilled work, we can imagine a kind of three-stage 'cycle' of work design (Fincham, 1989). An initial stage of collaborative production, in which people plan and organize their own work, becomes transformed into routinized machine-paced labour; then at some later stage (perhaps when dissatisfaction or labour turnover sets in) the work is redesigned in order to inject back into it some semblance of skills and discretion (Figure 9.1). Certainly the classic Tavistock cases described above had a strong cyclical element, one of recapturing lost traditions. This reveals the paradox at the heart of the job redesign – the way in which worker autonomy gets designed in and out of work by successive waves of experts

How, then, should we assess the possibility of the meaningful redesign of work? Should these methods be dismissed as ineffective, or perhaps even as a management 'con trick'? Clearly, if the above criticisms are to be treated at all seriously, work redesign cannot be taken at face value. For one thing, despite the claims often made, jobs are rarely if ever redesigned at the expense of *managerial control*. Indeed, restructuring may itself be used as a tactic of control. Schemes may convey the impression that firms are concerned with the welfare of their employees, while management remains only marginally committed to change. Thus several surveys of redesign experiments have found that the reality is often that of increased control and intensification rather than unalloyed benefits for workers (Kelly, 1980; Blacker and Brown, 1978). Similarly, the use of consultants as 'independent experts' may confer legitimacy on schemes, while consultants are still acting on management's initiative. Another way

219

Figure 9.1   *The cycle of work design.*

in which they methods may be used as a means of control is in undermining trade union organization. Job redesign schemes should allow for workers to participate in planned change, yet they may really be intended as a means of diverting workers' grievances away from their trade union representatives.

In this vein, the efforts to humanize work are seen to serve an *ideological* purpose, rather than necessarily being a part of management practice. They represent a body of ideas that may be called upon if management is being held up to public criticism, and that is favoured by certain sections of management (like personnel and public relations) concerned with a firm's outward image, yet with little real impact on the work process. Moreover, as with all systems of ideas, interest in them ebbs and flows with circumstances. Thus, work humanization is essentially seen as a product of the years of full employment when employers had to compete for labour. Recently there has been a sharp decline in the number of projects initiated and in the interest shown by companies. The charitable view of this is that work humanization has been making 'slow progress'. But more critically it has been suggested that employers' concern peaked some time ago. With unsettled economic conditions and higher unemployment, employers no longer need work humanization either as a means of attracting labour or as a justification of their policies (Ramsay, 1985; Hackman, 1978).

However, in spite of all these criticisms there remains a certain amount of guarded optimism concerning work redesign. The gains looked for are more modest and specific, but nonetheless positive. We are now able to define appropriate conditions very clearly. If, in the past, this has been used as a cheap alternative to making real improvements in working conditions – which of course mean capital expenditure and may involve acknowledging trade union demands – it is now accepted that meaningful work redesign itself requires adequate resources. The careful design of projects, the assessment of possible repercussions and the sustained backing of all levels of management are basic requisites. If this kind of commitment is forthcoming, it has been argued, improvements in worker satisfaction and performance can be brought about. Thus, while the evidence is not conclusive, it is at least suggestive of some positive changes.

Work restructuring programmes have left behind a certain residue of change in management practice. Even if this has not been dramatic, there are indications that the designers of jobs and work systems are at least aware of the arguments against fragmented, highly repetitive work; and there are some signs of a move away from strictly Taylorist methods towards an emphasis on overall systems of work organization.

Indeed, the debate has shifted ground in recent years. Awareness of the constraints on alternative design brought its own problems in train because, in the final analysis, redesign is a practical exercise. It cannot rely on ideal circumstances; it has to be carried out in firms that are having to contend with pressures for profit and efficiency. These concerns have been the impetus behind a more pragmatic approach. Kelly (1985), for example, has argued that the shaping of technology always contains choices, and that sufficient 'political space around the issue of work organization' exists for meaningful job design practices to operate. Similarly, Manwaring and Wood (1985) point to the 'tacit skills' that people exercise, even in jobs defined as unskilled. Frequently taken for granted, even by employees themselves, tacit skills reflect the informal knowledge that is the basis of efficiency and co-operation in work.

These sorts of consideration imply that opportunities do exist for workers' own design of work. Trade unionists and workers themselves should begin to make serious attempts to bargain over job design – rather than pondering in some abstract sense whether the techniques of redesign will transform work. It is further suggested that some market trends are on the side of work reforms. With firms having to respond to demands for complex and high-quality products, skills have to be redistributed in ways that encourage workers' commitment to production. Hence managerial motives in redesigning work are likely to reflect the need for more flexibly designed systems just as much as the desire to control and exploit labour.

Job redesign theory has also moved off in other directions. Interest has recently focused on flexible technologies and work systems. This new basis of alternative design partly reflects the fact that wider, comparative considerations have caught up with the debate. The kind of approach that we have been used to, based on the 'expert' design of work, has given way to an interest in the work traditions on which the Japanese and German economies are based. Job redesign itself has tended to take for granted a past 'break' with committed, high-trust forms of work. But the new approaches (particularly those coming out of Germany) stress a continuity with craft traditions. These themes will be picked up in Chapters 14 and 15. There we will see that the qualitative value of human labour, and workers' capacity to find solutions to production problems, are still the points at issue.

Further reading

Bailey, J. (1983) *Job Design and Work Organization*. Englewood Cliffs, N.J.: Prentice-Hall.

Blake, R.R., J.S. Martin and A.A. McCarse (1989) *Change by Design*. New York: Addison Wesley.

Berggren, C. (1989) 'New production concepts in final assembly – the Swedish experience', in S. Wood (ed.) *The Transformation of Work?* London: Unwin Hyman.

Clutterbuck, D. (ed.) (1985) *New Patterns of Work*. Aldershot: Gower.

Cooper, C. and E. Mumford (1979) *The Quality of Working Life in Western and Eastern Europe*. London: Associated Business Press.

Davis, L.E. and A.B. Cherns (1975) *The Quality of Working Life*. London: Collier Macmillan.

Hanna, D.P. (1988) *Designing Organizations for High Performance*. Reading MA: Addison-Wesley.

Kelly, J.E. (1982) *Scientific Management, Job Redesign and Work Performance*. London: Academic Press.

Knights, D., H. Willmott and D. Collinson (1985) *Job Redesign: Critical Perspectives on the Labour Process*. Aldershot: Gower.

Robertson, I.T. and M. Smith (1985) *Motivation and Job Design: Theory and Practice*. Wimbledon: Institute of Personnel Management.

Sauter, S.L., Hurrell Jr and C.L. Cooper (1989) *Job Control and Worker Health*. Chichester: Wiley.

Wall, T.D., C.W. Clegg and N.J. Kemp (eds.) (1987) *The Human Side of Advanced Manufacturing Technology*. Chichester: Wiley.

Weir, M. (1976) *Job Satisfaction*. Harmondsworth: Penguin.

Section Three

The Sociology of Work

The focus in earlier parts of this book has been on the psychological processes acting on individuals and their immediate environment in work groups. Factors in the social and economic environment – the wider context in which work is carried out – were not really considered in their own right. In the chapters in Section Two, where we examined motivation in work, the improvement of work group experiences and job satisfaction, we took for granted the reasons why these alternative forms of work organization were needed in the first place. However, it is now necessary to retrace our steps and consider more thoroughly the nature of work in modern industrial society. We turn to a *sociological* analysis of work, for it is sociology which is concerned with the broader structural and processual factors affecting behaviour.

An important theme helping to set out the different topics discussed below is that of the *division of labour*. This complex process reflects the many ways in which the productive work performed in society has historically become differentiated and apportioned. Within the work situation itself, the strict divisions between different jobs is the basis of control and efficiency in modern organizations, although it has also produced the kind of fragmented, routine jobs that are associated with many of the problems of industry. On another level, the division of labour has produced the occupational structure. The divide between different professions and crafts has always been characteristic, even during pre-industrial times, but in a modern economy we find an enormously complex system of occupations reflecting the vast number of different jobs available. Finally, other aspects of the social division of labour reflect the fact that certain groups of people (differentiated by factors like sex and ethnic origins) are typically found in certain types of work.

Following this general schema, in Chapter 10 we begin by looking at the basic forces that shape work, and the chief characteristics that define it in an industrial economy like our own. This rests on an examination of the classical writings on work of Marx and Weber, which provide the basis of much modern thinking. Other important variables, notably technology and skill, are located within this framework.

Modern forms of administering work, under the approach developed here, are seen essentially as structures of control and authority. Hence the problem of workplace conflict is an integral part of this approach, and an account of conflict follows in Chapter 11. Industrial sociology has usually confined itself to the study of informal conflict based on work groups, leaving trade union action to be the subject matter of industrial relations. To some extent, however, this is an artificial distinction – especially for an applied discipline like behavioural studies – so both types of conflict are explored here.

In Chapter 12 the focus is extended to include occupational variation. A full account of the changing occupational structure is beyond our scope. What we do look at, however, are a number of occupational groups selected for their prominence and social visibility. We examine the labour market situation of manual workers, the nature of white-collar work, and the professions.

The employment situation confronting women is described in Chapter 13. Here, instead of looking at forces that shape and structure jobs, we look at a particular group filling those jobs. Female employment has attracted an enormous amount of interest, and we focus on the broad patterns of discrimination against women at work, as well as some of the more active ways in which women participate in employment.

Finally in this part of the book, Chapters 14 and 15 address recent changes in the character of work. Chapter 14 discusses the 'new technology' of microelectronics. In one sense this follows directly from the sociological account of technology in Chapter 10. However, the impact of computer-based systems represents a new wave of technological change; many think that this has transformed the work process and merits study in its own right. Closely related are the new forms of work organization examined in Chapter 15. The search for 'flexibility' in production that they reflect is a central response to recurring economic crisis. The appearance of these work systems has sparked off key debates about the new era of 'post-Fordism' in the changing industrial society.

10

The Control of Work

Questions about the nature of work in modern society have to begin by asking about the largest concentrations of employment and the types of work that most people do. A cursory examination of the occupational skills structure shows what is perhaps an obvious point, namely that 'lower-level' jobs, in services and industry, constitute the main groupings of employment. Low-grade service jobs comprise about 27 per cent of total employment, and low-grade manual jobs about 22 per cent. These are primarily jobs with a low content of skills and consequently relatively poor pay. The upshot of this is that the experience of work for a great many people is of jobs which are uninteresting and which offer little in terms of a career or hope of advancement.

Of course, this picture needs to be qualified; certainly there is a great deal of *variation* in work. Although the largest single categories of employment are unskilled manual and low-grade service work, many people have satisfying professional or managerial jobs, while others exercise technical or manual skills. There is also an important *subjective* element. People experience work in different ways; and what may be an unrewarding job, done out of pure necessity, to one person, might be perfectly satisfactory to someone else. Also, in a time of high unemployment and deep industrial recession, it can be argued that people's expectations of work change: in such straitened times perhaps many people regard any job as a good job.

Nonetheless, it remains true that as far as objective factors are concerned, a high proportion of work probably affords little in the way of individual fulfilment or hope beyond the immediate present. In order to understand why the typical factory or office job involves routine operations and few skills and is intrinsically unrewarding, we need to develop an analysis of the forces shaping the jobs performed by the bulk of employed people.

Of the various ideas we will need to take into account in a sociological analysis of work, the theory of *alienation* developed by Karl Marx is of central importance. The notion that modern conditions of work produce alienated labour has long been influential, both directly on our understanding of work and in terms of the alternative theories it has evoked. The great resurgence of interest in Marx means that we now have a much more detailed understanding of his analysis of work as a *labour process*.

Another of sociology's founding fathers, Max Weber, also attracts lasting interest. Weber's influence on the whole of the discipline of sociology has been immense, and one of his main contributions was his analysis of bureaucracy. This will be discussed later, in Chapter 14, but behind his theory of bureaucracy lay the conviction that this particular form of organization represented the most rational expression of economic order, and Weber's ideas concerning the *rationalization* of labour are pertinent to our discussion here.

In this chapter, then, we shall first examine the basis which exists in classical sociological theory for an analysis of the work process. We will then briefly turn to historical developments, and to the rise of modern systems of work organization. We go on to single out *technology*, which has often been regarded by industrial sociologists and other commentators as having had a distinctive impact on industrial growth. Here we discuss the classical 'political economy of mechanization' as well as the later sociological study of technology. Finally, as might be expected, these critical perspectives have led to a good deal of debate and disagreement, and we will conclude by examining an important current debate in the sociological analysis of work which concerns the nature of *skills*.

Marx, Weber and the critique of labour

ALIENATED LABOUR

It is important to know how Marx developed his ideas on alienation, as this is a concept which has subsequently been much misunderstood and misused. In particular, it has become commonplace to stress individual experiences, and to equate alienation loosely with feelings of 'dissatisfaction' with work, or indeed any social situation. Marx's usage was very different. For him, alienation was a concrete process of social change, although one which certainly affected people's subjective experiences.

Central to Marx's approach was a 'materialist' view of labour as the basis of human society. The transformation of the natural world through shared labour, initially out of the physical needs for survival, brings the social and cultural world into existence. This is true of all societies, but in advanced ones labour is carried out under definite 'relations of production', and here the institutions of political power shape the forms of useful collective work. Within capitalist class relations, in particular, the creation of a material and social world becomes a distorted and degraded activity. Human labour becomes alienated labour, an idea Marx first put forward among his early writings in the *1844 Manuscripts* (1975, pp. 279–400):

> What constitutes the alienation of labour?
>
> Firstly, the fact that labour is *external* to the worker, i.e. does not belong to his essential being; that he therefore does not confirm himself in his work, but denies himself, feels miserable and not happy, does not develop free mental and physical energy, but mortifies his flesh and ruins his mind. . . . His labour is therefore not voluntary but forced, it is *forced labour*. It is therefore not the satisfaction of a need but a mere *means* to satisfy needs outside itself. Its alien character is clearly demonstrated by the fact that as soon as no physical or other compulsion exists it is shunned like the plague. (1975, p. 326)

Marx set out a number of dimensions of alienation, describing the impact of class relations on work and on the wider human community. Firstly, workers are divorced both from the *product* of their labour and from the *process* of production. In other words, the product and the manner in which work is performed are controlled by the employer by virtue of his ownership of capital. The fact that labour is 'external' to the worker, a mere means to an end, follows from this. These economic factors have social consequences in that *people become alienated from themselves*. The forces that strip work of its creativity in effect remove from it the truly human element, reducing workers virtually to the level of animals which produce only out of instinct or for immediate need. Also, a broader social alienation occurs: *people stand in an instrumental relationship to one another*, defined in terms of the economic power they command rather than their worth as human beings.

Marx contrasted the might of capital – the huge accumulation of private property, the development of a central state, the private ownership of cultural and artistic products – with the impoverishment of the mass of working people. When people lack control over their own labour, the material things people themselves have created confront them as a hostile entity. They become subject to the industrial and technological systems others have designed and built, and they are powerless in the face of market forces. Alienation thus produces the unequal and polarized society in terms of which Marx viewed modern industrial capitalism. He saw in 'this whole system of estrangement' a supreme irony. For at just the point in history where the powers of science and industry conferred a degree of mastery over society's traditional enemies – the natural world

227

(disease, shortage of food) and fear of superstition – so the class divisions in capitalism negated these achievements for the majority of people. Humankind fell victim to itself.

THE LABOUR PROCESS

Until fairly recently, a commonplace criticism of Marx had been that he gradually abandoned his earlier 'humanistic' concern with alienation for the strictly 'economic' analysis found in his later writings, notably in *Capital, Volume 1*. However, it now tends to be acknowledged that he did not reject the idea of alienation. Rather, he focused more narrowly on 'the act of production within labour' and developed an account of alienation within the work process. We shall briefly explore some of the main ideas from this approach (for a more detailed account, see Thompson, 1989, pp. 38–64).

At the heart of Marx's theory of the labour process – and for him the defining feature of capitalist society – was the emergence of the wage relationship and of labour as a *commodity*. When labour itself is bought and sold on a market of exchange, it becomes a cost of production, an object of commercial investment, and this underlines the dehumanization of work. Commodity-status also points to the essential insecurity of much modern employment. Certain things can improve a person's chances of a job (qualifications, trade union protection), but in the end society provides no natural right to work.

However, labour is unique in being an active human commodity. While it contains great potential for productive work, workers may resist their exploitation. In this context, Marx suggested that the exchange between capital and labour is not a simple exchange of wages for work. Rather it has two aspects: the employer first buys the *labour power* of the worker, expressed as an agreement to work for a certain time; and it is then the employer's responsibility to convert this potential into real labour – to set employees to work, in other words. The notion of labour as a 'variable' or 'potential' input to production draws attention to the struggle for control of the labour process, and to the employer's motivation to intensify the use of labour.

Thompson (1990) has identified four key features of labour process theory. First, the employment relationship as the basic producer of wealth occupies a privileged position in analysis. The employer–worker relationship is the basic class relationship, and changes here provide the main 'motor' of change in the rest of the economy and society. Secondly, the employment relationship is highly dynamic. Competing capitalists have to seek ever greater rates of profit, and hence the labour process will continuously be transformed in pursuit of greater productivity. Thirdly, capital is compelled to increase its control over labour. The means of control are often very complex, forms of control exist outside the labour process, and the degree of control over labour is never total – nonetheless, a generalized 'control imperative' within the work process does exist. And fourthly, the employment relationship is a relationship both of production and of exploitation. Hence, although it contains aspects of co-operation, conflict remains an endemic and structural feature.

In sum, Marx's analysis points to the divisive nature of the capitalist labour process. Pre-capitalist work processes, he pointed out, were limited in their productivity and in the extent of the control of any ruling group by the need to rely upon handicraft skills. Effort and efficiency were subjective factors held in check by the worker. In pre-industrial society, where people had control of their working lives to a much greater extent, the historical record shows that a much greater value was placed on creative leisure, and work and leisure were closely integrated (Marx, 1974, p. 381). However, all this began to change under a capitalist economy. The alienation of labour from production then became the root cause of industrial conflict, representing the real basis of broader social conflicts and the massive inequalities of wealth and power that characterize modern industrial societies.

WEBER AND RATIONALIZATION

Modern thinking on work has also been greatly influenced by Max Weber, whose ideas on rationalization have implications that are similar in many ways to the Marxist idea of alienation.

Weber regarded the spread of rational, goal-oriented behaviour as the central dynamic of western capitalist societies. In the transition from pre-industrial society, religious and mystical paradigms for coming to terms with the world declined and gave way to secular forms of explanation based on empirical science; this culminated in the market economy and the rise of industrial capitalism. In particular, the impact of rational criteria on economic action was for Weber the decisive factor which distinguished modern industrial capitalism from more traditional forms of society.

> In the last resort the factor which produced capitalism is the rational permanent enterprise, rational accounting, rational technology and rational law, but again not these alone. Necessary complementary factors were the rational spirit, the rationalisation of the conduct of life in general, and a rational economic ethic. (Quoted in Lee and Newby, 1983, p. 189)

This 'spirit of rationality', which pervaded economic and social life, was especially apparent in the ways in which work was administered and organized. Rationality here refers to the use of formal procedures (capital accounting, systematic management, corporate planning, etc.) in the control of economic enterprises. The point Weber emphasized was that only formal administration provided the basis for operations to be *calculable*. Being able to plan ahead with some degree of certainty is an essential requirement when large amounts of resources have to be committed. Both the massive level of provision in the modern state and the increasing size and complexity of modern industry require that organizations meet forecasts and perform predictably. This would be so, Weber argued, whether in a capitalist market economy or a centrally planned socialist one.

Calculative logic was not, however, the only attribute of a modern society. Here Weber contrasted *formal* with *substantive* rationality. Formal rationality referred to the calculation of economic means, discussed above, while substantive rationality referred to the persistent intervention of human ends and values. The two rationales were 'always in principle in conflict', since human needs are not necessarily met by rational calculation (Weber, 1964, p. 185). This viewpoint was the cause of an undercurrent of profound pessimism in Weber's thought, for although he stressed the effectiveness of rational administration, he believed that this mode of action would inevitably spread to and rule all areas of social life. In this, Weber was author of a fundamental criticism of modern society: the fear of all 'ultimate values' eventually becoming submerged in a society dominated by the cold logic of formal decision-making.

The spread of formal rationality entailed 'the complete appropriation of economic resources by owners' (Weber, 1964, p. 247). The calculability of large-scale enterprise and the autonomy of workers were, Weber stressed, polar opposites. To the extent that formal rationality was enforced, the worker had to be completely excluded from any role in the authority structure of the firm. For Weber, this was the upshot of inevitable technical developments. Technical efficiency depended upon managements having 'extensive control over the selection and modes of use of workers'; any 'rights to participate in management' in practice led to 'irrational obstacles to efficiency' (p. 247).

> From a historical point of view, the expropriation of labour has developed since the sixteenth century in an economy characterized by a progressive development of the market system, both extensively and intensively, by the sheer technical superiority and actual indispensability of a type of autocratic management oriented to the particular market situations, and by the structure of sheer power relationships in society. (1964, p. 247)

For Weber, then, rationalization in the modern world meant the transformation of human relationships into impersonal exchanges under the compulsion of technical rationality. The normal, spontaneous qualities of human society are obliterated as work organizations concentrate on the *means* to achieve economic goals, while the goals themselves may become increasingly meaningless. Rational conduct ultimately produces a society that

> is bound to the technical and economic conditions of machine production, which today determine the lives of all the individuals who are born into this mechanism, not only those directly concerned with economic acquisition, with irresistible force. Perhaps it will so determine them until the last ton of fossilized coal is burnt. (Weber, quoted in Salaman, 1981, p. 59)

CONCLUSION

The notions of alienation and rationalization together point to the problems of productive work being increasingly degraded and overshadowed by the institutions of capital. This is not to say that the theories of Marx and Weber were always in agreement. There remain deep divisions between them. Nonetheless, the similarities in their conclusions were also striking. They both sought the causes of the development of capitalism in the dynamics of production, and distinguished capitalism as a specific way of appropriating labour within distinct institutional forms. Both too gave full credit to capitalism's unleashing of enormous productive powers, but at the same time saw deep-rooted conflict between rational and irrational forces. The trend in recent studies of industrial organization has been to return to these sources. As Hill has remarked, new perspectives owe a great debt to Marx and Weber 'because they have successfully structured the agenda of what is held to be worth discussing' (1981, p. vii).

Emerging forms of work organization

One of the most important concepts to have emerged in recent sociological analyses of work is that of *control*. Here it is suggested that conflicts of interest between employers and employees bring about a fundamental problem of the control of labour. From this it follows that work is often designed for the chief purpose of facilitating control, and that the historical development of forms of work organization is to be understood in terms of employer's strategies to secure control in changing circumstances.

Of course, controls inside the workplace cannot be divorced from wider legitimation of managerial authority that derives from the ownership of capital. The threat of dismissal to workers is the ultimate sanction behind managerial authority. The freedom to dispose of assets (which may involve threats to close a plant, or to transfer production) can also be decisive. Nonetheless, the authority delegated to management by virtue of the legal rights of ownership is not in itself normally sufficient. In addition, there are important structural controls of labour which derive from the basic form of work organization, the modern factory.

THE FACTORY SYSTEM

Throughout the seventeenth and eighteenth centuries in Britain, the system of production of the feudal and mercantile era underwent radical transformation, culminating in the Industrial Revolution of the 1780s. Independent producers in agriculture and in handicraft industries came under the sway of capitalists, and production was being organized on an increasingly large scale. Marx, for example, identified 'two ways' into industrial capitalism. One saw the expansion of small workshops, as master craftsmen began to take on larger labour forces, rather than merely apprentices to renew the ranks of the craft. In the other, merchants began to extend their trading activities into production, particularly in the domestic system where craftspeople working from cottages would be organized and supplied by a merchant-turned-employer (Dobb, 1963, p. 123). Both paths led to the development of the factory as the fundamental form of organizing production.

The emphasis placed on control is not, or course, to deny the purely economic and technical advantages of the factory system. Vastly improved economies of scale were possible, as was the later application of machinery and the new power source, steam. Also, in the developing markets of the nineteenth century, goods of a comparable quality and specification were in demand, a type of output only possible where methods could be standardized. Yet, as Marglin (1974) has pointed out, it was only as this system gradually came to predominate, and technical improvements were diverted exclusively into it, that its economic advantages came to the fore. The prime motive behind the *initial* development of the factory system was enhanced control.

The very fact of work being performed in organizations is itself a control of labour and the basis of other controls. In the preceding domestic system there were limits on the extent to which work could be regulated. With individual tasks dispersed over different households, and even communities, cottage systems were capable of developing only fairly rudimentary forms of control, and employers were often more interested in the profits to be gained from trading off occupational communities (supplying them with materials and selling the finished products) than they were in organizing production itself. But with the advent of the factory all this changed. When workers were gathered under one roof, their activities could be much more tightly controlled: tasks could be assigned, output accurately measured and times of attendance checked.

In this sense the appointment of a special group directly to oversee the labour process – *supervision* in other words – has always been a central element of the factory system. The early labour masters were powerful figures, responsible for recruiting and organizing workers. Later on, as Gospel (1983, p. 98) notes: 'The foreman of the late nineteenth and early twentieth centuries was very much the master in the workplace and was the key figure in labour management.' In more recent times supervisors have lost these powers. The power to hire and fire and to fix wages has been taken over by managerial specialisms, such as industrial relations and personnel. But although their direct control over workers has been eroded, supervisors still play a significant part in the control of labour within modern systems of management. The expanding management structure has absorbed supervision, and the occupation itself has become diversified and developed its own hierarchy.

In terms of the industrial discipline that could be imposed, a *division of labour* was also crucial in forging the link between efficiency and control. The splitting up of work into specialized functions, organized by department and section, raised the productive powers of labour at the same time as it enabled the central control of the labour process. Most observers of the early factory system were surprised by the extreme fragmentation of work, which was qualitatively different from anything that had gone before. Marx spoke of the worker being transformed into a 'detail labourer', with the factory itself becoming the 'collective labourer' where tasks were integrated. Before Marx, Adam Smith had focused specifically on the division of labour as the basis of economic prosperity. Indeed, he begins *The Wealth of Nations* with a detailed account of the productivity gains attendant on 'a proper division and combination' of operations. 'The different operations into which the making of a pin, or of a metal button, is subdivided, are all of them much more simple, and the dexterity of the person, of whose life it has been the sole business to perform them, is usually much greater' (1982, p. 113). However, Smith had mixed feelings about his form of work organization: while he marvelled at its contribution to productivity, he was not blind to the less desirable social consequences. He saw, as did Marx, that the fragmentation of work was the chief cause of labour becoming a degraded activity – a fact no less true of the 'manufactories' of the eighteenth century than of today's assembly lines.

233

MODERN MANAGEMENT AND TAYLORISM

Another aspect of work organization that reflects the class nature of production involves the *intensification* of work. Marx, on this point, distinguished the 'formal' from the 'real' control of labour. Nineteenth-century capitalism inherited a labour process based on artisan production, and in the early factories previously independent craftsmen became wage workers. Marx referred to this as formal subjugation, because at this stage labour still retained its craft nature. Real subjugation arose, Marx suggested, when capital began transforming work itself from its archaic forms.

The Factory Acts of the 1840s and 1850s were an early impetus to labour intensification. Previously there had been very little legal control of employment conditions; but the Acts placed a limit on the length of the working day, and on other abuses like the use of child labour, which encouraged employers to concentrate on raising productivity. Marx notes that employers' interest in *efficiency* greatly increased from that time forward (1974, pp. 442–51).

Still, for most of the nineteenth century the means to increase productive intensity had not progressed much beyond the basic controls of the factory itself. During the last quarter of the century, however, modern methods of the systematic control of labour came into use. These originated in the scientific management movement pioneered by the American, F.W. Taylor. Beginning in the 1890s, Taylor developed a 'science of work', the methods of which involved the detailed study of work processes with a view to increasing efficiency and labour productivity. Tasks were carefully observed and broken down into component actions, which were then measured on the basis of standard times – hence the more popular name of 'time and motion' study.

The far-reaching effects of scientific management, or 'Taylorism', for work in contemporary society have been widely recognized. Weber, for example, spoke of the Taylor system as the pioneer of the application of rationalized methods of work (1964, p. 261). More recently, Braverman in his influential study *Labor and Monopoly Capital* (1974) has been particularly important in drawing attention to the general principles of scientific management that Taylor set out, and to their implications for the 'degradation' of work. (For discussion of Taylorism, see also Clegg and Dunkerley, 1980, pp. 87–98, and Mouzelis, 1975, pp. 79–87.)

First, Taylor recommended the most detailed division of labour that was practically possible: relatively complex tasks should be split up into the maximum number of sub-tasks. More significantly, he insisted that the skills which had built up within a workforce – skills of hand

and eye, knowledge and experience – should be absorbed within the management function and converted into formal procedures. Management should assume 'the burden of gathering together all of the traditional knowledge which in the past has been possessed by the workmen and then of classifying, tabulating, and reducing this knowledge to rules, laws, and formulae' (quoted in Braverman, 1974, p. 112). Taylor also recommended the 'divorce of conception from execution'. All thinking about work – planning, securing of supplies, maintenance of equipment, etc. – should be managed by a specialist staff. The worker should simply have to execute the task in hand, or become an 'operator', to use the modern term. Thus Taylor stressed that 'All possible brainwork should be removed from the shop and centred in the planning or laying out department' (Braverman, 1974, p. 113). Abercrombie and Urry (1983) have usefully summarized the 'Taylorist strategy for capital', and the manner in which it transformed existing labour practices, as follows:

> ... as long as workers knew more than their managers, then management would have to persuade the workers to cooperation. This could clearly be seen in relation to piecework – since management did not know how long in fact it took to do each piece of work; it was rational for workers to ... restrict output. Taylor realised that the only long-term solution to this from the viewpoint of capital was to devise a new system of capitalist control that would overcome the rational tendency for workers to restrict output ... this could only be achieved by transforming the very form of knowledge possessed by workers. (p. 101)

The advantages to employers of adopting such a strategy are overwhelming. Labour is cheapened by reducing its skilled component, the flexibility of labour is increased by simplifying tasks, and there is a great potential for generally streamlining production. Unnecessary tasks can be eliminated, physical layouts improved and work speeded up. Taylor himself conducted thousands of consultancy exercises in his time and often achieved notable increases in output and productivity. Above all, with work designed by staff specialists and integrated within a production plan, management's control of production was intensified in a way which hitherto had not been possible.

Not least important was the *ideological* aspect. Systematic measurement and methods of standardizing tasks, it was claimed, made this a 'scientific' study of work. Standards of effort were argued to have been arrived at by purely rational methods. At bottom this claim was spurious because, as critics have pointed out, work study is always dependent upon agreed notions of what is a fair and reasonable pace of work (Baldamus, 1961; Braverman, 1974, p. 86). Nevertheless, managerial authority has been legitimized to an important degree of the 'neutral' language of scientific management.

Finally, it is important to consider the *historical context* in which scientific management was introduced. Allied to industrialization in the United States, there was a rapid growth in the size of the economy and labour force. America industrialized on the basis of the then new technologies, like steel, chemicals and mass production. Littler (1982) points to the labour crisis created in these new industries as workers entered jobs lacking any traditional standards of pay and effort. In this fluid situation, scientific management represented an employers' initiative to establish a formal system of discipline, one which they very definitely controlled.

Littler has also stressed that Taylorism was chiefly important for extending *direct* managerial control. Up to the 1880s, the most common form of shopfloor organization was based upon the authority of subcontractors and supervisors. Labour masters, gang bosses and foremen were powerful figures in the early factory system recruiting workers and organizing payment and discipline. However, with economic growth, these personal and informal methods of control became a barrier to efficiency. Taylorism helped to eliminate such systems of internal contracting, and provided a form of industrial discipline that enabled owners to employ labour directly.

Like all aspects of industrial development, these methods were adopted unevenly. Their concrete impact varied widely, and other methods that modified Taylor's original system were developed. Yet Taylor's doctrine was taken up enthusiastically in the United States, and by the 1920s and 1930s had spread to continental Europe and Britain. In important respects, this started the process of diversification into specialist functions, such as production control and industrial engineering, which laid the basis of modern management as a rational system of administering work.

Technology and workplace behaviour

So far we have seen how a wide range of developments account for the rise of industrial societies. They include the spread of market relationships and the growth of the money economy, the organization of work in the shape of the factory system, employment as the dominant relationship of production, and generally rational modes of thought and action. Of all such preconditions, however, the one that is linked most directly with industrialism itself is *technology*. This is because advancing technology can be identified with the high rates of *change* that are a defining feature of modern societies. It was essentially the Industrial Revolution, and the first development of machinery which came with it, which brought about the rapid pace of innovation we are now familiar with. Since then the specifically *technical* aspect of change has continued to provide a powerful symbol of conditions that we think of as 'modern'; and sociologists have been particularly interested in this variable as a way of explaining workplace attitudes and behavior.

In the way social scientists use the term nowadays, technology is not simply restricted to the hardware of production systems. (This is in contrast to common-sense usage, where the term usually does conjure up the image of some complex machines or device). Instead, technology is used to refer to entire technical processes. Thus, for example, we might speak of a mass production technology, like car assembly, or a continuous-flow process technology, such as chemicals or oil refining. In these cases the hardware component (machinery, automation equipment, plant) would be included, but the skills and know-how involved are also taken into account, as is the type of work organization within which the hardware is applied. These other considerations are vitally important, since the application of machinery can have very different implications in different circumstances.

A second important point, to be followed up later in the section, concerns the notion of *technological determinism*. This refers to arguments which appear to be saying that technology is the determining cause of particular conditions or behavior in work. Social scientists have rightly criticized such arguments, their main point being that technology itself cannot be the independent cause of anything: it is the manner in which technology is applied, and the motives and actions of groups which control technology, which are decisive. As a result both of the complexity of technological processes and of the active role of social elements, different and often contrasting viewpoints have come to characterize the study of technology.

TECHNOLOGY AND THE LABOUR PROCESS

Commentators on the early industrial scene, like Marx and Adam Smith, perceived the close link between technology and the way in which work is organized. The imposition of the factory system, with its concentration of the labour force and intricate division of labour, actually made possible the development of machinery. Complex and skilled craft work had to be reorganized along rational lines before it could be mechanized. Hence a dynamic relationship exists between work structuring and mechanization, the one progressing under the impetus of the other. Both Marx and Smith had mixed feelings about the factory system, recognizing that the massive increases in the productive powers of labour seemed to go hand in hand with the

237

subjugation of people to work. Marx in particular was preoccupied with mechanization (1974, pp. 351–475); and his critique remains the basis of many more recent attacks on modern technology (e.g. Levidow and Young, 1981; 1985). He believed that the fiercely competitive nature of capitalism compelled employers to force up productivity, and that mechanization was their chief means of doing this.

In its most fundamental form the emergent conflict between technology and labour rested on the so-called 'organic composition' of capital. By this Marx meant that the economy, composed of technical capital (machines, plant, equipment) and human capital (living labour), was constantly changing. He believed, further, that the overall trend favoured an expanding technology. Although many modern economists would disagree with this – recognizing that industrial economies are becoming increasingly capital-intensive, but not accepting that this necessarily occurs at the worker's expense – Marx did believe that over the long term capital intensification diminished the contribution of living labour.

Marx detailed a number of aspects of the 'strife between workman and machine'. Machinery was the great leveler, reducing any special techniques and skills needed in work, so that human labour was rendered interchangeable and easy to substitute. In this is found a central theme of labour process theory, that capitalist work organization has a long-run tendency to produce 'homogeneous' labour. Not only did machinery displace labour, it created actual unemployment. Marx thought that the rate at which labour was displaced by machinery would always outpace the rate at which new work was created via general economic expansion. Hence the tendency of capitalism to generate a 'reserve army' of unemployed people was in large part attributed to technological advances. Marx also stressed the enslavement of workers to machines, particularly in terms of the perpetuation of working hours. This is because machinery, especially complex machinery, runs the risk of becoming obsolete even before it is worn out. Hence employers will be anxious to have it used intensively to extract its full value before obsolescence takes over.

In short, Marx believed that under pressure of existing class relationships machinery played a key role in the alienation of labour. Much of this still rings true, and is especially consistent with the economic problems of recession. Modern ideas about the 'capital-deepening' effects of new technology have led to fears that economies are now so capital-intensive and productive that mass unemployment has become a structural feature. We also find concern being expressed about changing patterns of work. The change to highly intensive forms of shift- and rota-working, such as in complex plant like continuous-process technology and large mainframe computers, seems to pay little heed to the social and physical needs for workers.

Set against these forms of labour displacement, deskilling and work intensification, however, there are some far more positive views of technology. Perhaps the classic version of these was put forward by the American sociologist, Robert Blauner, in his study *Alienation and Freedom* (1964).

BLAUNER AND THE POSITIVIST VIEW OF TECHNOLOGY

Blauner's actual research, which goes back to the early 1960s, now seems outdated in relation to the fast-moving subject matter of technology. Indeed, the purely empirical value of his research was always rather limited, based as it was on secondary analysis of workers' attitudes, and with case study and anecdotal materials included on a highly selective basis. But Blauner's account of technology remains influential for other reasons. What it represents is a theory of a widely popular and prevailing view: the view of technology as a liberating and energizing force. It emphasizes the potential, particularly of the most advanced forms of automation, for 'upgrading' the skills and occupational status of those who work with it.

Blauner contrasted the 'existence of critically different types of work environments in modern industry' with the Marxist notion of diversity within manual labour being eliminated, and working conditions as a whole becoming increasingly degraded. He chose four industries to cover different types of technical system. These were printing, which represented a craft technology; textiles, which typified a machine-minding technology; automobiles as typical of mass assembly; and chemicals to represent continuous-process technology. From his findings worker alienation, firstly, seemed at a minimum in craft technology. Print worker's trade skills and powerful union organization gave them a high degree of job security, as well as control over their jobs. Because they were able to see work through from start to finish they could perceive meaning in their own contribution. In contrast, both machine-minding and mass assembly technologies maximized alienation. Textile workers were powerless in the face of constant work pressure, and lacked any choice over the pace and methods of work. In car plants the nature of work was consistently alienating. The production line dominated all aspects of the work situation. Car workers' jobs were repetitive and meaningless, they were isolated from co-workers, and the work itself gave no feeling of pride or self-esteem.

For the process workers, however, alienation declined once more to a low level. These workers were often technically qualified and their jobs involved the monitoring of entire operations. Whilst routine for much of the time, their work carried freedom and responsibility, so they tended to identify strongly with their jobs and the efficient running of the plant. As Blauner put it: 'the responsibility of auto-mated production confers a new sense of dignity and worth on manual employment – a possibility not foreseen by many students of alienation, who assess manual work by the yardstick of traditional craftsmanship' (1964, p. 165).

The distinctive aspect of Blauner's argument, however, was that the four industries had been chosen to reflect the historical development of technology. The craft occupation (printing) was intended to charac-terize a pre-industrial system of production, while machine-minding and mass assembly technologies (textiles and cars) represented mature industrialism. Most importantly, the automated process technology was held to be representative of future trends in advanced industrial society.

The long-term implications are that unskilled, machine-dominated work will progressively give way to manual work typified by complex technology, and thus alienation will decline from a peak in the traditional industrial society. Hence, Blauner made his well-known assertion that the progress of alienation can be charted as an inverted U-curve.

> . . . with automated industry there is a counter-trend, one that we can fortunately expect to become even more important in the future. The case of the continuous process industries, particularly the chemical industry, shows that automation increases the worker's control over his work process and checks the further division of labour and growth of large factories. The result is meaningful work in a more cohesive, integrated industrial climate. The alienation curve begins to decline from its previous height as employees in automated industries gain a new dignity from responsibility and a sense of individual function – thus the inverted U-curve. (p. 182)

Technological development is therefore seen ultimately as a positive force. The progressive elimination of alienating working conditions, and their replacement by work which is socially integrating, is not only possible within the present industrial economy, it is happening more or less spontaneously under the normal course of industrial evolution. Alienation is regarded as an intermediate and passing phase of industrial society, rather than its culmination as in Marx's theory.

CRITICISMS OF BLAUNER

Blauner's sophisticated argument essentially gave substance to the widely held belief that technological advances are somehow linked with positive progress. He dealt with the Marxist critique of technology extremely effectively – and not by rejecting Marx. Blauner allowed the truth of Marx's argument, but defined it as a special case of his own much broader theory. Nonetheless, Blauner's thesis has been subject to detailed criticism, both on theoretical grounds (Hill, 1981, pp. 90–9; Salaman, 1981, pp. 89–98) and by research which has challenged his findings (Nichols and Beynon, 1977; Gallie, 1978).

Certainly the break with the classical tradition of Marx and Weber is clear enough. As we saw earlier in the chapter, they both conceived of deep processes of change within the capitalist economy. In contrast to this, for Blauner alienation became a function of technology – a factor confined to the circumstance of the work situation, and not implicated in class relationships or in the broader structure of industrial authority. The restricted meaning attributed to alienation stripped the concept of much of its radical force. True, Blauner did clearly define factory work as being alienating. But he has been criticized for concluding on quite limited evidence that work in continuous-process plants was intrinsically rewarding. The findings of several empirical studies since Blauner's have cast doubt on the simple link between technology and alienation which he suggested, particularly for the critical case of the process industries. For example, Nicholas and Beynon's (1977) study of a British chemical plant revealed the existence of much low-grade, unskilled work. They also found that pressure on labour costs caused job insecurity, conflict and the degradation of skills. This was in sharp contrast to Blauner's claim that, because labour is both a small part of total costs and critical for production, workers in high technology industries would be subject to few of these pressures. Similarly, in his major study of British and French oil refinery workers, Gallie (1978) discovered:

> The work of most of the operators was substantially less advantageous than Blauner suggested, and the most common attitude towards work in our refineries was one of indifference. It is extremely doubtful whether automation leads to the overcoming of alienation in work in any profound sense of the word. (p. 296)

Hence the claim that technology has any inbuilt evolutionary trend towards less alienating conditions has been challenged.

SOCIOLOGICAL EXPLANATIONS OF TECHNOLOGY

Blauner was not the only writer to be concerned with the influence of technology on work. Since the 1950s, a growing body of literature has examined the relationships between technology and a range of industrial behaviors: patterns of industrial conflict, workers' integration into firms, and workers' attitudes. It is in this use of technology as an explanatory variable accounting for work-related behaviours that Blauner's argument – quite apart from any of the specific failing noted above – has influenced a much wider debate. Two well-known studies, both of which lend some support to his thesis, were those of Woodward (1965) and Wedderburn and Crompton (1972).

In Woodward's noted 'south-east Essex' study, the climates of industrial relations in different firms were compared with the technical systems used, emphasizing the improved relations in the process industries.

> Industrial relations certainly seemed to be better in process industry than in large batch and mass production, but it is not safe to assume that the good relationships were due to the large number of specialist staff employed . . . there were a number of contributory factors: less tension and pressure, smaller working groups, and smaller spans of control, for instance. (p. 55)

Wedderburn and Crompton studied a large chemicals complex, and their findings also stressed that employees in continuous-process plants had relatively favourable attitudes towards work, got on well with their supervisors and enjoyed some autonomy. However, this was not extended to any broader 'moral' attachment to the firm. Although process technology gave a more convivial work environment, the harsh realities of employment were still present. Process workers 'retained a calculative involvement with the company' and were a group of workers 'directly experiencing conflict of interest between themselves and their employer which had to be bargained about' (Wedderburn and Crompton, 1972, p 151).

These findings lend qualified support to the idea of automated technology providing superior conditions, as Blauner contended, and this being favorably reflected in certain of workers attitudes. But they lend no support to any sweeping notion of a 'new' industrial working class emerging as the product of such conditions. In the plant Wedderburn and Crompton studied, process workers were militant and critical of the company. This conflict was attributed to the traditions in what was a strongly working-class area, and the researchers took the view that technology was only one among many possible factors that explain behaviour.

> . . . there is no simple association to be postulated between expressed attitudes and behaviour . . . The general norms of the community, the nature of the influence and leadership offered by the trade union, as well as the constraints of the immediate work situation, all contributed in the final event to a very complex interplay of forces. (p. 142)

It has also been argued that technology implies too narrow an explanation of attitudes and behaviour. This centres on the socio-logical debate in the late 1960s and early 1970s about the alleged technological determinism of research like that of Woodward and Blauner. Major critics were Goldthorpe *et al.* (1968) in their influential *Affluent Worker* study. These researchers argued that attitudes towards work were not shaped by factors (especially technology) internal to the work situation. The problem of understanding how people assign subjective meaning to work situations is extremely complex, and must be see in the context of adjustments and responses to wider factors than merely those within work. They argued that attitudes were underpinned by 'orientations to work' – stable beliefs and values which originated in workers' past experience, and which they brought into the work situation. Their study of car assembly workers at the Vauxhall plant at Luton showed that, while being dissatisfied with the work itself, workers still wanted to retain their jobs and were uncritical of the company. The researchers explained this by arguing that workers had developed a distinctive *instrumental orientation* towards work. Their attitudes were shaped by their own definition of work as a source of secure and comparatively high income, but of little intrinsic interest or worth. Work had become a means to other ends – the enjoyment of family life, leisure pursuits and so forth. With low expectations of their jobs, and alternatives in their private lives to compensate, these workers were apparently satisfied with jobs that were objectively highly alienating.

Other empirical studies have demonstrated that working conditions, and people's responses to them, can vary independently of technology. For example, Gallie's (1978) study referred to above concluded that 'the nature of technology *per se* has, at most, very little importance' for the social integration of the workforce (p. 295). Industrial relations patterns, particularly the markedly more militant attitudes of French process workers, could be explained only by contextual factors: the structures of power in the industry, managerial and trade union strategies, and wider historical and cultural factors in French and British society.

So, while technology remains important, it is misleading to see it as a prime cause of working conditions. Any narrow focus on technology must be avoided by emphasizing the interest of the groups

243

involved and the social elements in the context of work. There are three main considerations here: (1) technology is developed in the first place to meet specific requirements; (2) managements have the freedom to choose among different technologies; and (3) even when implemented there remains a degree of flexibility over the use of technology. Put simply, it is people who develop, select and implement technical systems, and they do so under the constraints of relations of production.

CONCLUSION

This said, the idea of progress through technological renewal, central to Blauner's thesis, is still highly influential. Technology is readily accepted as a powerful force for change, and the notion of automation eventually placing the worker in control of the work process in both appealing and plausible. This type of explanation from technology remains persuasive because it allows a measure of optimism about the future of work. Based on science, technology is continually developing and thus contains a range of possibilities.

So, any impression of a closed debate about the influence of technology on work and on wider social change should be quite misleading. Interestingly, the recent applications of microelectronics have once again raised the issue of technology and alienation. A number of writers (e.g. Crompton and Reid, 1982) have speculated that the new 'flexible' computer systems could allow the possibility of reversing earlier trends towards routinization. They suggest precisely the same cycle of the early degradation of conditions, followed by improvement, that Blauner postulated with his inverted U-curve. Thus in much the same way as the process industries in the 1960s sparked off debate, a new debate on the relationship between technology and work is being opened up – although an account of this will be deferred until Chapter 14.

The 'deskilling' debate

If technology has been singled out as a key factor in explaining industrial behaviour, we should not forget the broader pattern of workplace experiences. Recently, labour process theory has had a major impact on sociological debates, focusing particularly on the notion of *skill* in work. We referred above to Braverman's account of Taylorism. However, the publication of *Labour and Monopoly Capital* sparked off a major debate concerning the true impact of these forms of work organization. The controversial view Braverman put forward was that the contemporary labour process is characterized by a progressive 'degradation' of work. He focused particularly on craft and trade skill, seeing modern systems of management like Taylorism as methods of degrading and deskilling work. Zimbalist, one of Braverman's main supporters, has summarized this as follows:

> There is a long-run tendency through fragmentation, rationalization and mechanization for workers and their jobs to become deskilled, both in an absolute sense (they lose craft and traditional abilities) and in a relative one (scientific knowledge progressively accumulates in the production process). Even where the individual worker retains certain traditional skills, the degraded job he or she performs does not demand the exercise of these abilities. Thus, the worker, regardless of his or her personal talents, may be more easily and cheaply substituted for in the production process. (1979, p. xv)

Braverman mainly intended his argument as a correction to a view which had become the accepted wisdom in organizational psychology and sociology, namely that Taylor's ideas had been 'superseded' and no longer determined management methods. This orthodox view held that the Human Relations movement (discussed in Chapter 7) heralded a much more sophisticated approach to the design and management of work, one which recognized the human needs of workers and supplanted the coercive Taylorist methods. Braverman's answer was that this was merely wishful thinking, a confusion between what academics were prescribing and what employers were doing. In his view a visit to any modern organization would show that, far from being superseded, Taylorist methods are in fact *institutionalized*. They have been refined over a long period and form the basis of most modern systems of production control.

This interpretation of Taylorism was by no means original. For example, Braverman quotes the noted management writer Peter Drucker, who pointed out that while human relations has had a fairly limited influence, Taylor's methods determine 'the actual management of the worker and work' (1974, p. 88). Bendix (1956, p. 319) also stressed that the main impact of human relations has been a management ideology, while scientific management represents the practice. And Marxist writers before Braverman have reviewed Taylorist methods as an 'employers' offensive' (Cliff, 1970). Braverman's contribution, though, was to make a timely intervention when the shortcomings of certain conventional explanations were becoming obvious.

THE CRITIQUE OF BRAVERMAN

His thesis was not received uncritically, however, and the years following publication of *Labor and Monopoly Capital* saw a growing critique of his work (e.g. Littler, 1982, 1990; Littler and Salaman,

1982; Storey, 1983). This can be briefly summarized as follows.

First, it has been argued that *managerial strategies* towards labour are grossly oversimplified in the Braverman thesis. Braverman insisted that control and deskilling typify the capitalist labour process, whereas, critics argue, Taylorism is only one of the strategies that managements have at their disposal. In particular, alternative strategies of *responsible autonomy* have been identified. These allow workers to act independently, retaining some control over production, but assume that workers will also act responsibly, in line with organization goals. In other words, RA strategies exploit areas of accommodation between management and workers. This concept was originally a Tavistock definition of work reform. In the classic job redesign experiments, the wholeness of the task and multiple skills were deemed to reflect a pattern of responsible autonomy (Trist and Bamforth, 1951; and see Chapter 9). However, Friedman more recently has popularized the concept by contrasting it with strategies of *direct control* like Taylorism. RA and DC strategies, Friedman suggests, encompass all of the specific strategies that management might adopt towards labour. They are two generic types that reflect the fundamental tension between the need to gain cooperation or consent from those who do the work, and the need to force them to do things they do not wish to do (Friedman, 1990, p. 186). He argued that a trend towards responsible forms of control could be detected in practices like job enrichment and declining competitive pressures on workers.

Secondly, the 'universal deskilling' thesis attributed to Braverman was held to be historically inaccurate since *reskilling* also occurs. In effect, Braverman had an idealized romantic image of the craftworker as a survivor from the preindustrial past, implying that skills exist merely as a residue from those times. However, it has been pointed out that technological development is constantly bringing into existence new skills, specialisms and indeed entire occupations. Thus, if capitalism itself can create new skill, there can be no simple process of deskilling.

Thirdly, Braverman offers no analysis of, nor seems to reserve any place for, *workers' resistance*. Hence he has been criticized for having a schematic model of class relations, and for assuming that the employing class is all-powerful and the working class totally passive. What is being emphasized here is the need to reassess the significance of actions like strikes, sabotage and output restriction, which have hitherto been regarded as rather limited defences adopted by workers, or as simply troublesome for efficiency. On the contrary, these are important elements shaping the relationship between workers and employers. Thus, critics have argued that the point of production is an important locus of class struggle, and the employment relationship must be conceived of as an interaction between the two classes.

Fourthly, Braverman has been criticized for a narrow and parochial insistence that employment relations and the workplace are at the centre of things. This crude materialism is typical of some forms of Marxism; it ignores what has been called the full circuit of capital – the influence of capital and labour markets, activities like investment and finance, and the role of the state and political action. There is no reason to suppose that these factors are any less important for change in industrial society than relations of production (MacInnes, 1983; Kelly, 1985).

In sum, his critics have accused Braverman of taking a 'one-dimensional and unilinear' view of changing work organization. They argue that any uniform transition from skilled craftwork to rationalized labour is at variance with the historical record. Rather, industrial capitalism generates technologies which hold out the possibility of skill creation, and workers themselves are an active force in grasping and developing these opportunities.

DESKILLING REASSESSED

While these criticisms are certainly persuasive, they are perhaps somewhat uncharitable to Braverman. The exclusive focus on him has created the impression that deskilling was his idea alone. Yet it is misleading to detach Braverman from the mainstream of Marxist thinking of which he is a part. Other writers have also focused on the concept of skill quite independently. For example, the British Marxist writer V.L. Allen (1975) argued that skills are crucial as they represent the only 'capital' possessed by workers, and the degrading of skills represents a decisive new stage in worker alienation.

In its own right, *Labor and Monopoly Capital* was a deliberately polemical book, and not meant to satisfy the methodological criteria of social science. Braverman wrote within the same tradition of political economy of Marx, and with Marx he shared a selective emphasis on the 'objective' aspects of class relationships. (In the whole of Marx's *Capital*, for example, there is very little mention of workers' resistance or of trade union organization.) It may also be true that Braverman's critics have distorted his argument somewhat. Braverman did allow for more complexity than the 'crude deskilling thesis' (Wood, 1982, p. 18) which is usually laid at his door. Rather ironically, too, empirical research by Braverman's critics has sometimes supported his position. Crompton and Reid (1982), for example, found overwhelming evidence of deskilling among clerical workers, although they themselves supported the argument that Braverman's thesis needed refining.

247

Others have defended the deskilling thesis in more specific terms, notably Zimbalist (1979), Hill (1981) and Thompson (1989). These writers suggest that an even more complex relationship exists between the various types of managerial control than Braverman's critics allowed. Thus, responsible autonomy should not be regarded as an *alternative* to direct control, as Friedman argued it was. Rather, managerial strategies which share control with workers usually operate *within* an overall strategy of direct control. (A similar point was argued in Chapter 9, where it was stressed that a detailed evaluation of job redesign programs have revealed their limited impact) Both Hill (1981, p. 34) and Thompson (1989, p. 136) have argued that the case for 'responsible' strategies being equated in importance with those based on direct control is not sustainable. On the contrary, the long-term trend is clearly that of a shift towards direct control in the central areas of industrial employment.

The criticism that Braverman overestimated the impact of scientific management has also been challenged. While there certainly were barriers to the diffusion of Taylorist methods, and methods other than Taylor's were developed, it would be mistaken to lose sight of the broader pattern of change because of these variations. Thus, Hill (1981, p 31) used the term 'rationalized management' to indicate the growth of formal labour policies and bureaucratic structures. Similarly, Thompson (1989, p 126) refers to 'systematic management' to mean the same general trend towards bureaucratic control. Any slowness in the development of such systems was confined mainly to Britain, and may well have reflected our decline as an industrial power; but in the United States, the world's dominant economy, these principles of work organization spread early and rapidly (Abercrombie and Urry, 1983, p. 102).

The debate probably comes down finally to a difference between the (mainly Marxist) writers who argue for a long-term secular trend towards the degradation of work, and other writers who argue that the changing nature of work is essentially a spontaneous and uneven process. These positions are difficult to reconcile. It is hard to impose a single interpretation on anything so complex as industrial and occupational change. Moreover, the dilemma may be unresolvable in any practical way, since it ultimately rests on more fundamental debates within the social sciences.

What is perhaps more important is to emphasize the deeper understanding of work that the deskilling debate has led to. The clear focus on skills has given a contemporary account of alienation: that of labour being progressively 'disqualified' from the production process, as modern systems of control diminish workers' expertise. The significant amount of research that has come out of the critique of

Braverman also represents a major advance. This has focused attention on the historical development of forms of work organization, as well as on current realities of work.

Still, it remains clear the any comprehensive account of work must cover the areas referred to by Braverman's critics. Consideration of the *active* role that workers play, particularly in terms of resistance to control, and the industrial conflict which arises from this have made a valuable contribution to the emerging sociology of workplace relations. It is to an account of this that we turn in the next chapter.

Further reading

Burawoy, M. (1979) *Manufacturing Consent: Changes in the Labor Process under Monopoly Capitalism.* Chicago University Press.

Edwards, R. (1979) *Contested Terrain: The Transformation of the Workplace in the Twentieth Century.* London: Heinemann.

Friedman, A. (1977) *Industry and Labour: Class Struggles at Work and Monopoly Capitalism.* London: Macmillan.

Knights, D. and H. Willmott (1990) *Labour Process Theory.* Basingstoke: Macmillan.

Littler, C.R. (1982) *The Development of the Labour Process in Capitalist Societies.* London: Heinemann.

Littler, C.R. and G. Salaman (1984) *Class at Work.* London: Batsford.

McKinley, J.B. (ed.) (1976) *Processing People: Cases in Organizational Behaviour.* London: Holt, Rinehart and Winston.

Storey, J. (1985) 'The means of management control', *Sociology*, 19, 193–211.

Thompson, P. (1989) *The Nature of Work.* (2nd edn) London: Macmillan.

Wood, S. (ed.) (1989) *The Transformation of Work?* London: Unwin Hyman.

Zimbalist, A. (1979) *Case Studies on the Labor Process.* London: Monthly Review Press.

11

Conflict and the Employment Relationship

We have seen how, from the workers' point of view, rationalized labour practices can mean a very constrained and potentially unstable working environment. However, the emphasis on structural constraints and formal control provides only a partial view. Relationships between workers and managements are much more complex, involving struggle on the part of the workers, as well as degrees of co-operation and consent. Workers have certain resources even in the most restrictive circumstances: the power to disrupt production, to withhold co-operation, and the practical abilities and skills upon which employers depend. If production is to go ahead at all there has to be some minimum level of co-operation between management and workers, and workers require some autonomy if initiative is to be counted upon.

Still, there can be a sharp discrepancy between the degree of freedom and dignity that workers believe they deserve and the control that employers think is necessary for their authority to be maintained. Therefore, resistance to control on the part of workers, and the conflict which follows from this, remain a constant feature of the labour process.

Dimensions of industrial conflict
Workers' opposition to the constraints of the workplace can vary in a number of different ways. To begin with, the level on which conflict occurs can be based on actions taken by individuals, action taken by work groups, and action at the level of workers' organization, namely the trade union. Secondly, conflict may be formal in the sense of being openly recognized by the parties involved, and perhaps institutionalized as part of an established bargaining procedure; or it can be informal, and confined to a sphere of covert activity outside the organization's authority structure. And thirdly, conflict may be spontaneous or it may be organized.

To an extent, these dimensions occur as patterned forms of conflict. Thus the resistance of individuals would normally be classified as being both informal and spontaneous. Similarly, resistance based on work groups is also usually informal, although it shows a degree of organization in the sense of providing a collective response even if not a pre-planned one. Trade union organization provides a very important basis of opposition, preventing any single group of workers from becoming isolated. Essentially the formal recognition of a union *legitimizes* workers' resistance, and this can immeasurably strengthen their bargaining position.

Having made these distinctions, however, it is important not to oversimplify them. The different dimensions of conflict overlap and interact in a sometimes bewildering variety of ways. For example, types of worker resistance which derive from spontaneous, unofficial initiatives on the part of groups of workers often benefit from a degree of tacit legitimacy, in the sense that those in authority may 'turn a blind eye' to various workshop practices. Conversely, while a trade union provides the basis for claiming legitimacy of action, official industrial disputes may still not actually enjoy widespread legitimacy. The extent to which workers are able openly to contest issues can vary a great deal, depending on factors like prevailing public opinion and the attitude of the particular employer.

Range of industrial conflict
While it is possible to take the view that collective trade union action is of a different kind from initiatives taken by individuals or small groups of workers, most social scientists nowadays would probably accept that these forms of conflict stem from the same root causes in the commodity – status of labour and the constraints of managerial authority. And, indeed, on close inspection there does prove to be an overlap between different levels of conflict.

The great complexity in patterns and forms of industrial conflict that these diverse dimensions point to has often been noted (Hyman, 1989, p. 55). As an individual response, conflict may occur where workers, finding themselves at odds with their work for whatever reasons, respond by taking time off or by leaving the job after a relatively short period. Thus, high rates of absenteeism, lateness or labour turnover usually indicate a 'withdrawal' from the work situation. Industrial sabotage is also seen as a similar reaction to a work situation experienced as disagreeable. As well as conflict individually expressed, there is collective conflict involving the solidarity of the workforce.

The great diversity of industrial conflict means that it often takes the form of a *tactical* response. Interests will be mobilized in pursuit of explicit objectives, and the parties involved will use forms of resistance which seem most appropriate. For instance, if workers and

251

their leaders regard an all-out strike as a measure of last resort, they may wish first to test management's resolve with less drastic action such as an overtime ban, or with subtle forms of non-cooperation which affect output and quality. Similarly, in the case of a plant under threat of closure, a strike would make little sense if the company intended moving the stock and machinery elsewhere. The occupation of the site would be more likely to add to workers' bargaining strength.

Conflict initiated by management can also be a tactical response in changing circumstances. Thus, for example, if the market for a firm's products is buoyant and it can sell all it makes, management would normally be reluctant to provoke action that would disrupt output. Supervisors and personnel officers will be instructed to tread carefully when dealing with workers. However, if demand falls collective action poses less of a threat, and may even be beneficial. A strike of limited duration can improve a firm's financial position by saving on wages. Thus, in times of slack demand it is not uncommon to find management tightening up on industrial discipline.

In this chapter these various aspects of industrial conflict will be explored, essentially by examining the three principal levels of conflict: individual and group conflict (which are here classed under workplace conflict) and broader industrial conflict based on trade union action.

Workplace resistance

The point-of-production resistance of workers has often been interpreted as being a problem of poor communications, of managers and workers unable to understand each others' point of view, or as some other type of human relations difficulty. However, the dialectic between managerial control and workers' resistance is a vital, if often neglected, aspect of class conflict. This suggests that individual and group resistance has a *structural* aspect and stems from a clash of real material interests. Nonetheless, it is a structure which is dynamic and changing. In this sense, for example, the employment relationship was visualized by Goodrich (1975) in his classic study of the British mining industry in terms of a 'frontier of control', the boundaries of which continually shift as one side or the other gains ascendancy. Workers or management may control some aspect of operations, but the struggle may simply shift to another level or another area. As Thompson (1989, p. 127) points out, control reflects 'the degree of power management has to direct work' and this is always relative to the countervailing power possessed by workers.

Edwards (1990) has developed a comprehensive account of workplace conflicts. He suggests that 'structural antagonism' might be a better term than conflict, because conflict can imply that workers and managers are constantly at war. In reality, a perpetual struggle for control in work is not always obvious or observable. The tactics workers adopt are versatile and often covert, so that an intimate knowledge of a particular workplace might be needed in order to be aware of resistance going on. Nor does resistance have to be manifest to be effective. The *threat* of resistance being offered if some change were to be initiated may be enough to maintain the *status quo*. For example, skilled workers may enjoy considerable autonomy by virtue of their employer's reliance on their skills – so the employer may give little thought to attempts to rationalize work or deskill jobs.

Structural antagonism, Edwards argues, lies at the root of the capital–labour relation, and arises from a clash of interests over the distribution of surplus value. It does not determine actual behaviour so much as create the preconditions for action: 'workers and employers respond to these pressures and in so doing develop traditions and understandings that are used to interpret their relations with each other. Their struggles stem from the exploitative character of the capital–labour relation, but they have an autonomy' (Edwards, 1990, p. 126). Thus managers do not have total strategies of control, nor do workers only resist. Day-to-day interaction involves many other behaviours, including forms of co-operation and accommodation. Informal co-operation is not just an optional extra but crucial to economic success; firms need more than a kind of grudging consent from workers, they need active compliance in production. Hence the informal skills that workers develop in so-called unskilled jobs have always been counted on by employers to achieve high output. (This was noted by the earliest observers of the industrial system. As we saw in Chapter 10, Adam Smith (1982) actually attributed the highest economic value to informal skills. He noticed that once you have workers performing simplified tasks, repeated over and over again, they gain enormous speed and dexterity. This Smith believed was the key to productive power and, ultimately, to the 'wealth of nations'.)

Nevertheless, Edwards insists on the primacy of the antagonistic relation and that consent and accommodation are not on par with conflict. Domination by employers and the subordination of labour remain the typical form of production relations. So while the labour process has a relative autonomy, the struggle between capital and labour is still the main dynamic shaping the work process. This can be illustrated if we look again at informal skills and try to interpret what they really mean. Here Manwaring and Wood (1985) have highlighted what they call tacit skills, and are anxious to redress the tendency to devalue or ignore these aspects of subjectivity within the labour process. Workers relate positively to the production process chiefly via tacit skills – the tricks of the trade, the co-ordination of hand and eye, the ability to operate socially. Much of the pride and satisfaction that workers derive from unskilled jobs comes through exercising these forms of discretion. However, others have argued that labour is partly exploited through such tacit skills, as employers derive the extra productivity without paying for it. (If tacit skills were rewarded, they would be explicit skills.) Thus knack, dexterity and speed represent a degraded sense of skill. We can see this in Manwaring and Wood's example of the worker who 'had to pick up twenty-six bolts and washers out of a pallet and place them on the front cover of the engine. After six months he would always automatically pick up the right number' (1985, p. 178). This kind of 'skill' would hardly improve the worker's marketability, and while he many gain some satisfaction surely the real benefits go to the employer in terms of productivity gains. In this sense, Edward concludes that

> conflict in the shape of a structured antagonism is a basic feature of any exploitative mode of production, and consent, tacit skills, the negotiation of order and so forth have to be understood as shaping how this antagonism is developed and not as principles which can totally counteract it. (1990, p. 147)

SPONTANEOUS RESISTANCE AND SABOTAGE

A form of activity which clearly comes under the heading of subtle and covert resistance is industrial sabotage. This is a response from workers who are perhaps seeking a respite from a tedious job, or who wish to defy what they regard as an oppressive management. Sabotage can break the rhythm of work and it can give workers the feeling of having some control over their work situation, however slight. Highly constraining technologies, like assembly lines, can produce in workers a desire to 'beat the system', while other acts of sabotage may simply be a by-product of pressure for output. The removal of safety devices to speed up production, for instance, is often done with the tacit connivance of supervisors.

Industrial sabotage has been a neglected area of research, despite its being one of the commonest forms of worker resistance. However, Taylor and Walton (1971) have provided a sociological framework of analysis. They argued that, although sabotage is usually regarded as irrational or even pathological behaviour, careful investigation shows that 'in many cases the meanings which inform sabotage are explicitly intentional'. A knowledge of the *context* in which acts of sabotage occur – the lack of alternatives available to workers, the frustrations that build up over time – often shows sabotage to have been an understandable response.

Taylor and Walton note that sabotage can be difficult to define: at one end it merges with informal practices which become almost part of normal procedure, 'neither openly demanded nor openly questioned', while in extreme cases sabotage may be identified with explicitly political violence. Indeed, it is possible to argue with Taylor and Walton's own definition: 'rule-breaking which takes the form of conscious action or inaction directed towards mutilation or destruction of the work environment'. Here, they use the common-sense idea of sabotage as a 'spanner in the works', yet several of their own examples do not fit readily into such definitions. Not all acts of sabotage 'mutilate or destroy' the work environment, some merely cause delays and confusion. Nor does sabotage necessarily break rules in any simple sense. Rules themselves may conflict with one another, and sabotage may break one (usually formal) rule while fulfilling some other informal expectation.

WORK GROUPS AND WORK CULTURES

The collective resistance of workers is also a feature of much informal action in the workplace. Given the power of the managerial hierarchy to dispense or withhold rewards, open acts of defiance expose individuals to reprisal. But resistance which is both group–based and informal can be very difficult for management to pin down. The example of sabotage, discussed above, was a case in point. Although covert, sabotage is not necessarily just an individual response. Taylor and Walton noted that 'often the active or passive cooperation of hundreds is observable'.

Work groups may generate distinctive 'cultures of resistance' based on informal relations of friendship, or on some shared occupational identity such as a craft ethic. In any case, work groups often develop common values and a sense of their own history. They may also share distinctive ways of communicating, such as a repertoire of sayings and in-jokes. This culture – frequently the expression of past struggles with management – can form an effective basis of unity and continuing resistance to formal control.

A classic study of work group resistance, which we first discussed in Chapter 7 above, is found in the famous Hawthorne research (Roethlisberger and Dickson, 1943). The management at the Hawthorne plant had been frustrated in their efforts to raise production in a section where electrical assemblies were wired up – the so-called Bank Wiring Room – and the researchers were called in to try to resolve this problem. The researchers discovered the existence of a strong group culture which enforced an output norm. Workers in the

255

section perceived management's standards – arrived at by Taylorist methods – to be outside their control and liable to be raised arbitrarily. Consequently they restricted their output to a level they regarded as reasonable, one that did not undermine their own pay and job security, and one that the slower members could keep up with. The Hawthorne researchers stressed the pressure that groups can bring to bear on members to conform to common norms. In this case positive sanctions involved acceptance in the friendship cliques, while negative sanctions meant ridicule and ostracism for anyone who broke ranks and tried to 'bust' the agreed work rate.

The prevailing view of such work group resistance has often been that it stems from workers' misunderstanding of management's intentions. Indeed such disapproval is implicit in the very notion of workers 'restricting' output. Lupton's noted study *On the Shop Floor* (1963) traced the widespread acceptance of this biased view to the Hawthorne research and the Human Relations movement which followed it. These interpreted output restriction in terms of the *social* requirements of sustaining a group structure. Workers' desire for group membership, and their supposedly effectual motives, were contrasted with management's rational criteria based on technical efficiency. (The focus of the Human Relations school has always centered on the possibility of reconciling these social and technical rationales.) However, as Lupton points out, the conflict of interest may well be genuine, not merely an irrational response by workers. Workers' behaviour, he argues, is really a response to *managerial control*, and is best understood as a counter-attempt to assert workers' own control (1963, p. 6).

Some celebrated empirical studies of work groups have argued that so-called restrictive practices usually reflect the attempt by workers to impose their own definition of a fair day's work. Lupton's own research, in an electrical components firm, showed how an equitable balance between wages and effort can develop on the shopfloor. Not only workers but supervisors too colluded to 'fiddle' earnings and work allocation in a complex piecework system. The 'fiddle' was 'a quite stable adjustment of the discrepant goals of management and workers' (1963, p. 197). Similarly, Donald Roy's well-known studies also showed the conscious manipulation of payment systems. In one case, Roy (1952) observed that output restriction stopped short of the point where management would have retimed jobs and cut the piece rates; in another (1954) study operators, inspectors and supervisors cooperated in informal practices to 'fix' a fair job rate.

Manual workers are not the only occupational group to have to cope with imposed controls. Professionals and white-collar employees nowadays increasingly find their status and conditions under attack.

As a result, it is possible to see in such groups the collective responses normally associated with shopfloor workers. Pettigrew's (1973) study of the implementation of a computer network in a large retailing firm provides a good example of group solidarity among employed professionals. The programmers in the company initially had a good deal of control over the computer installation, which provoked management to cut down their influence. The programmers responded in a variety of ways – by attacking the competence of the 'dilutees' whom management brought in to fragment their work, and by habitually withholding their most important resource: information. They kept details of programs in their heads, and always explained procedures in highly technical jargon. Their varied and imaginative tactics grew out of a strong collective identity developed in the face of the hostility they encountered from management.

Finally, the ways in which employees can adapt systems of managerial control depend to a large extent upon the *work context*, particularly the room for manoeuvre allowed by factors like market pressures, technology and work organization. Patterns like the 'fix' and the 'fiddle' were developed by skilled workers, in piecework systems where considerable discretion was retained on the shopfloor. Similarly, professional groups possessing key skills can often rely on employers' dependence upon them. Where this kind of space exists, informal relationships need not always subvert formal goals. Indeed, workers can adapt in ways which support the organization. Instances in which workers take the initiative to get a job done reflect co-operative elements in the employment relationship. However, in work situations under much tighter constraint, or based on work-placing technology like the assembly line, there is far less scope to manipulate managerial control. In such cases workers' resistance may be defensive and more obviously oppositional.

Industrial Conflict and Industrial Relations

The forms of industrial conflict whereby workers' interests are mobilized on a broader front include strikes and other kinds of industrial action, and here the role of trade unions as workers' official representatives come into play. Of course, in reality there is continuum between these and more informal types of conflict. A great deal of strike activity turns out, on closer inspection, to be spontaneous and based on resistance by specific groups of workers. Likewise, the strength of any union in the final analysis rests on the resolve of workers to oppose managerial control at the point of production. This was well demonstrated, for example, in Huw Beynon's famous study of a Ford car assembly plant, which gave a detailed account of the two-way relationship between official trade union activity and the shopfloor resistance of workers (Beynon, 1984). Still, in focusing on the *collective* character of disputes, we are moving to a level of analysis that includes the wider framework of economic and political changes. Outside the confines of the work organization, factors like public opinion, the state of the economy and government policy on industrial relations cannot be ignored.

Conflict in the employment relationship has had an important influence on theories of industrial relations. The orthodox approach to the subject of the 1950s and 1960s essentially involved a *pluralist* perspective. It viewed management, on the one hand, and workers organized and represented by trade unions, on the other, as both possessing roughly comparable resources of power. Their interests were seen as being conflictual in some degree, but the pluralist model implied that the terms of the relationship were negotiable. As Alan Fox, a major proponent and later criticism of pluralism, has put it: 'The pluralist does not claim anything approaching perfection for this system . . . but the imbalance of strength between employers and union . . . are not seen as so numerous or severe as generally to discredit the system either from the union's point of view or the management's' (1977, p. 136).

However, the weaknesses of this approach have long been recognized. To view workers and employers as equal partners in an agreement lacks any sense of the sharp inequalities of power dividing them. But more importantly, the 'return' of industrial conflict as a major issue in workplace relations created serious difficulties for this analysis. A pluralist perspective sees conflict essentially as a temporary breakdown in job regulation, which means that the emphasis is very much on the resolution of disputes in collective bargaining. So while the model could certainly account for conflict, evidence of a powerful opposition of interests between employers and workers could not be accommodated. The scale of some industrial disputes, together with the manner in which they have been regarded by workers, employers and the state, have made explanations based on pluralism seem less and less plausible.

The failure of conventional pluralist ideas prompted the emergence of what Hill (1976) has called the 'new industrial relations' based on a 'sociological and radical perspective'. The main exponents of this approach – writers like Hyman, Beynon and Fox – all take conflict to be a major structural component of employment; although we should also note that sociology in fact has a longer tradition of exploring the distinctive problems of explanation and understanding associated with industrial conflict (e.g. Eldridge, 1968).

INTERPRETING INDUSTRIAL CONFLICT

At least two main aspects of the sociological approach can be singled out. First, it sees industrial relations as part of a totality of social relations. It is necessary to consider the social context of industrial relations as well as the labour process; and here the new sociology of work, discussed in the previous chapter, is of central relevance. Above all, a sociological view of *power and control* is essential. Thus a unifying theme of the 'new' industrial relations, to quote Hill (1976), is 'the conviction that order and coherence in industry and society rest on relations of dominance and power, and that in modern industrial societies, particularly capitalist ones, power disparities are long-term structured and not susceptible of much modification'.

A second important feature of sociological explanations of industrial conflict is that they assume conflict to be a reasoned response of one form or another. Even where it at first appears to be a rather pointless reaction there is invariably found to be some rational element, which means that conflict must be classed alongside other forms of purposive *social action*. This approach, pioneered by Weber (1964, pp. 88–115), has been widely applied in studies of industrial conflict. Viewing behaviour as social action means that explanations of events must be 'adequate at the level of meaning'. Or, as Eldridge put it, 'adequate description for sociological purposes involves the attempt to delineate the meaning people attribute to their behaviour, and to the situations in which they find themselves' (1968, p. 17). The basic focus of interest here is the different version of events that industrial conflict is likely to produce. What the workers might think is a lively practical joke, management may regard as disruption or sabotage; what workers might see as an intensification of their labour, management may regard as an improvement in flexibility, and so forth. Therefore, as impartial observers, it is important that we take account of all definitions of the situation, and are prepared to understand events as participants themselves experience them.

Implied in this approach is a definitive change of emphasis from pluralist-type accounts. The latter involved a narrow focus on the formal institutions of industrial relations. But the sociological approach argues that this is inherently abstract and artificial, as if decisions taken within the negotiating arena somehow independently shape the course of events. Instead, it is recommended that the motives and actions of the groups involved in workplace relations should be the main focus of attention. It is how they perceive and define events, and how their consciousness forms and changes, that is ultimately decisive.

A SOCIOLOGICAL MODEL OF INDUSTRIAL CONFLICT

In the accounts of industrial action one reads about in newspapers or sees on television, the cause of a dispute will usually be attributed to the issue over which work relations broke down. Most of us therefore tend to think that strikes are brought about by specific disagreements – over pay, for example, or over alleged misconduct by workers or managers. However, a sociological explanation needs to be more holistic than this, and it is not normally sufficient merely

Table 11.1   *Causes of industrial conflict.*

CAUSAL FACTORS	LEVEL AT WHICH APPLIED	TYPES OF EXPLANATIONS PROVIDED
1. Precipitating	Confined to each specific cause of conflict	Necessary to account for the immediate causes of conflict
2. Background	Locally within a particular place of work. 'Custom and practice'	Sufficient to account for the nature of conflict within a particular place of work
3. Contextual	Structure of wider society, particularly socio-economic inequality and power	Sufficient to account for broader relationships between group in conflict

to regard the events leading up to a strike as its cause. Following Eldridge (1968, pp. 19–23), we can distinguish different 'causal levels' on which behaviour is structured. The events that immediately precede a strike are more accurately defined as the factors which serve to *precipitate* the ensuing conflict. But in addition there are issues which form the local *background* to any given dispute, and other factors which constitute the broader societal *context* of conflict.

Thus it is possible to discern three main levels of causality in this model of industrial conflict. Firstly, there is the immediate cause, which is necessary to bring about the specific instance of conflict but which does not provide the sufficient conditions for conflict in general to occur. Secondly, there is the background to the dispute, or the rules of 'custom and practice' which constitute a sort of local social structure within a place of work. Superimposed on them, at the third level, is the wider social structure (Table 11.1).

A classic study which serves as a model analysis of how these levels of explanation may be linked up is provided by Gouldner's *Wildcat Strike* (1955). This traced the course of an unofficial stoppage in a small gypsum mine and a factory in which the mineral was processed into plasterboard. The plant, a major source of employment in a small community, for years had been operated under what Gouldner termed an 'indulgency pattern' of management. Here, the relationships between managers and workers were tolerant and friendly, and involved loyalties and commitments over and above the mere exchange of wages for work. However, the corporation that owned the plant regarded it as being inefficiently run and took steps to introduce a regime of tighter discipline. New machinery was brought in which meant an unpredictable pace of work. All in all, the 'indulgency pattern was subjected to a crippling attack, and workers' hostility rapidly mounted' (p. 28). As events came to a head, there were changes in the supervisory structure, with popular supervisors demoted and unpopular men promoted. Finally, a quarrel broke out between the union steward and a production engineer, who was himself closely associated with the efficiency drive and the focus of much of the tension. It was this which sparked off the strike.

By dwelling on this complex chain of cause and effect, Gouldner indicated that the strike could be understood only against the background of changes in the employment relationship. The employer's intention to retake certain areas of discretion was seen by the workers as the contravention of a rule, the indulgency pattern, which was regarded as fair and legitimate by most people in the plant, including many in supervision and management. Thus the strike came as no surprise to those involved. The researchers, the workers, management and union officials all 'saw it coming' and regarded the strike as a wholly understandable outcome.

While Gouldner described an 'everyday' strike, Lane and Roberts's *Strike at Pilkingtons* (1971) gives an account of a dispute that attained national fame – a seven-week stoppage at the glass-making company in 1970. Their approach was similar to Gouldner's in attempting 'to see the strike through the eyes of its different groups of participants' (p. 18). But the Pilkington dispute could not have been anticipated (although there were issues that precipitated it – pay levels were perceived to be low and the initial walk-out occurred over a wages error). The main point Lane and Roberts stressed was the dynamism of the strike itself. Once under way, sections of the workforce were 'drawn in' and the strike became a liberating experience for many of those involved in organizing it. Crucially, a rift developed between a local strike leadership and the trade union's national officials. The union, notoriously moderate and bureaucratic, repudiated the strike and made several attempts to engineer a return to work (including alleged collaboration with the employer). This produced a deep sense of betrayal among workers; and the 'civil war' between rank-and-file

261

workers and the official union was essentially what turned the strike into a protracted struggle.

Lane and Roberts argued that strikes are not difficult to explain. They are 'normal events', arising almost naturally out of the circumstances of the employment relationship itself: 'A wildcat can break out in perfectly normal conditions, and the structure of the relations between employers, trade unions, governments and workers guarantees that some strikes will grow from small beginnings into mighty struggles' (p. 241).

This brings us to consider the broader *context* of industrial conflict. Factors operating at this level are remote from the event itself, yet they predispose different groups of people towards certain kinds of action and hence define the limits of other causes. The key factor put forward as the underlying cause of conflict is the distribution of wealth and power, reflecting the deep class divisions of our society.

Within the workplace inequality and conflict are inextricably bound up, irrespective of the relationship between particular managements and workforces. Because wages are part of the employers' costs, which they must seek to minimize if they are to survive, workers experience a ceaseless downward pressure on their standards of living. It is only by exerting upward pressure themselves, using whatever means are at their disposal, that workers are able to sustain wage levels and general conditions. Thus the returns going to labour and capital are not simply allocated by the hidden hand of the market, they stabilize only as the outcome of conflict. Work organizations (as we shall see in more detail in Chapter 14) are power hierarchies in which 'lower participants' – manual and white-collar employees who make up the bulk of the employed population – find themselves continuously under the control of others. Sociologists have argued that this sharply divided authority itself provokes conflict (Dahrendorf, 1959). In order to sustain authority structures, managers are obliged continually to assert the power of their position, which inevitably calls forth resistance on the part of workers.

THE SOCIAL RESPONSE TO STRIKES

Although industrial conflict occurs across a wide range of behaviour, there can be little doubt of the massive amount of attention focused on one of its forms: strikes. This partly reflects the fact that strikes are a dramatic form of conflict (or at least they can be portrayed as dramatic events), and partly the fact that public opinion in Britain is firmly fixed upon strikes. Repeated surveys have shown that a large majority of people remains convinced that strikes cause severe economic disruption and that they have been a major contributor to the country's industrial decline (Taylor, 1980, p. 13). This is important because public opinion has a crucial influence on the climate in which industrial relations is conducted. Yet the manner in which strikes are perceived needs some explaining. Indeed, as industrial relations experts have frequently pointed out, albeit with almost no effect, the popular view bears little relation to the known facts.

Table 11.2 *International comparisons of work stoppages 1974–88.* From *Employment Gazette* (London: HMSO), April 1985, p. 150; December 1990, p. 610.

| | Average striker-days per 1,000 employees | | | |
	1974–78	1979–83	1984–88	1988
United Kingdom	380	500	400	170
Australia	690	570	240	260
Canada	990	750	320	310
Irish Republic	700	720	370	180
Italy	1,410	1,210	360	220
Spain	1,030	950	740	1,400
Denmark	90	120	250	40
France	210	120	60	70
Germany (FR)	60	10	50	–
Japan	130	20	10	–
Netherlands	10	30	10	–
Norway	70	50	150	50
Sweden	30	250	100	200

– Fewer than five days lost per thousand.

There has been a strong belief that Britain has been much more 'strike-prone' than other industrial countries, but that during the 1980s this changed. With the action taken on industrial relations legislation, and other measures to curb trade union power, the country's strike record is now believed to be relatively more favourable and internationally competitive.

Table 11.2 compares stoppages in 13 major industrial nations. These data do lend some support to the prevailing public opinion. In the two five-year periods leading up to 1983, the figures for Britain fell within a band of figures for countries (Australia, Canada, Ireland, Italy and Spain) which can be regarded as relatively strike-prone – albeit the number of days lost in Britain was the lowest in the group. Moreover, Britain's striker-days were high compared with countries, particularly Japan, France and Germany, that are our major competitors.

Nevertheless, we can see straightaway that these figures give the lie to any simple notion that Britain used to be excessively strike-ridden. During the 1970s and early 1980s Britain fell just below the middle in this overall ranking of countries. More importantly, while strikes in Britain certainly declined during the 1980s, this was part of an international trend. In several major industrial nations the level of days lost due to strikes had fallen to less than one-third of the average for the 1970s. Britain's own relative position actually worsened. In 1984–8 only one country of those listed had a higher level of working days lost, whereas in the two earlier periods it was five countries. By 1988, again, Britain's ranking had improved, but only to the extent of a return roughly to the position of the 1970s and early 1980s.

In addition, the impact that strikes have on production tends for numerous reasons to be exaggerated. We have already mentioned that strikes need not be damaging to individual firms; and while it is true that the economy as a whole can be damaged by certain groups of workers (e.g. power workers, miners and transport workers), relatively few groups actually have this kind of muscle. Also, strikes are responsible for an almost negligible amount of lost time compared with total hours worked by the employed population. Rarely does this rise above about half a working day a year per employee. Causes of lost production other than strikes, such as sickness, industrial accidents and more recently of course unemployment, affect output much more seriously.

Why, then, the outcry about strikes? In his thorough sociological analysis of industrial conflict, Richard Hyman (1989) has put forward two main reasons. First, the role of the news media in forming public opinion is very important. Certainly recent research has detected an element of straightforward bias in the reporting of strikes. Managers are often subtly portrayed as the more reasonable and responsible party, and greater authority is attributed to their views, while strikes are seen as 'problems' created by workers. However, simple bias is not a complete answer; we need to take into account the way in which news is produced. News cannot just be seen as information about events that is transmitted to the public in some unproblematic way; in a very real sense the news is *manufactured*. The raw material of events is processed – selected, edited, dramatized, presented – by the professionals who run the media; ultimately it is their values which influence the version of events the public receives (Edwards, 1979).

In seeking to present strikes as 'newsworthy', media professionals often convey a quite artificial image of industrial relations. News coverage tends to reduce the complex process of strikes down to a single issue. (In terms of the model developed earlier, only the precipitating causes tend to be brought out.) It is only if a strike remains in the news for a long period that anything of its history or underlying causes will emerge – and then only in the 'quality' press, rarely on television or in the tabloid newspapers where most people obtain their information. Hence, the demand of workers for jobs with reasonable pay and security may command public sympathy, but it does not find widespread legitimacy, and those on strike may simply appear as troublemakers causing dissent unnecessarily. Employers, by contrast, can call upon powerful ideological forces in our culture to legitimize their interests. They need only announce a general aim of improving efficiency or international competitiveness and their case is virtually made for them.

However, this line of argument still leaves unanswered the question why strikes are presented as they are, which brings us to the second of the points Hyman raised. He suggested that the public clamour over strikes reflects their political repercussions rather than any direct economic impact. Strikes, in other words, represent a challenge to *managerial authority.* Even though very few strikes create a real crisis of control in firms, any strike, no matter how short-lived, contains the seeds of a deeper threat to management. As Hyman (1989, p. 157) puts it, it is hardly surprising 'that those who exercise managerial authority typically resent this limitation on their autonomy, and are sometimes haunted by the fear that strikes may escalate into an explicit challenge to the minority control of industry'. Managerial authority, and indeed the whole edifice of organizational power, represent the rights of ownership delegated to management. Thus, when the managerial control of labour is thwarted by industrial action, ultimately the employment relationship itself is being undermined. As we have stressed, this is the basis of a capitalist industrial economy; hence we can see why in the final analysis the disruption of authority in industry should be regarded as being so critical.

CONCLUSION: PATTERNS OF INDUSTRIAL ACTION

Finally, on the issue of strike statistics, the data in Table 11.3 reveal several important aspects of industrial relations. The changing pattern of strikes in the period since 1961 falls roughly into three stages (Durcan, *et al,* 1983). Stoppages in the early 1960s were numerous but tended to be limited in the numbers of workers involved and in duration. This reflected the high level of local organization of the early post-war years: industrial action sprang from the shopfloor, and the preponderance of unofficial or 'wildcat' strikes was a major industrial relations issue. However, during the 1970s this pattern was transformed. The changes were complex, as ever, but there were two important aspects: a shift of union power from plant to national level, and with industry entering the early stages of recession some major struggles occurred. Thus, we can see strikes still frequent, but becoming larger in size and longer in duration.

The pattern changed again in the 1980s. Strikes remained relatively large for a period during the early part of the decade, but the number of stoppages and later the size as well fell sharply; they represent the lowest level of industrial conflict in the post-war years. In 1990 in particular the lowest number of strikes for over 50 years was recorded and the number of days lost was the lowest since 1963. There can be little doubt that this reflects the persistent unemployment that was experienced throughout this period, and the weakened state of the union movement and of labour generally.

The impact of recessions in Britain has compelled employers drastically to reduce labour costs at the same time as it has effectively shifted the balance of market strength in their favour. As a result, a whole range of measures including stricter disciplinary codes and work reorganization have been carried through in large numbers of firms. Nor have the recessions been wholly an 'economic ' matter. The Thatcher administrations of the 1980s broke with the post-war consensus on full employment, and instead became willing to use unemployment as an instrument of economic policy.

The role of government also changed dramatically in other directions. Traditionally, British industrial relations has operated under a system of 'voluntarism'. Employers and unions entered freely into agreements to negotiate pay and conditions without constraint by any third parties, and with minimal legislative guidance. To some extent, free collective bargaining was always a myth; the state often acted to place a ceiling on pay deals even in the 1950s and 1960s. Since the late 1960s the courts and government ministers have been increasingly involved – applying restrictive legislation, regulating collective agreements and encouraging 'social pacts' between business and labour. However, during the 1980s and beyond, Conservative governments greatly extended the interventionist role. Legislation has been passed which restricts many types of strike and supporting activity, and unions are exposed to legal action on many fronts. In this period of 'realism', trade unions are often preoccupied with making sure that any activity they contemplate is lawful, and the immediate concerns of many workers have moved towards job security. As Hyman (1989, p. 226) suggests: 'the political climate of collective organization and action has been radically transformed, at the same time as the economic context has become so hostile. These factors go a long way to explain the rapid change in strike activity.'

Nonetheless, it would be misleading to 'read off' from this situation a total collapse of workers' resolve to take independent action. As the table shows, the level of conflict in the early 1980s fell far below that of the 1970s, but the pattern was certainly not one of uniform decline. In 1979 and again in 1984 enormous numbers of working

Table 11.3 *Stoppages of work in Britain 1961–90.* Compiled from *Employment Gazette* (London: HMSO), various issues.

	NUMBER OF STOPPAGES	WORKERS INVOLVED (000s)	WORKING DAYS LOST (000s)
1961	2,686	771	3,046
1963	2,068	590	1,755
1965	2,354	868	2,925
1967	2,116	731	2,787
1969	3,116	1,654	6,846
1971	2,228	1,171	13,551
1973	2,873	1,513	7,197
1975	2,282	789	6,012
1977	2,703	1,155	10,142
1979	2,080	4,583	29,474
1981	1,338	1,499	4,266
1983	1,352	573	3,754
1984	1,206	1,436	27,135
1985	887	643	6,402
1986	1,053	538	1,920
1987	1,004	884	3,546
1988	770	759	3,702
1989	693	727	4,128
1990	620	285	1,903

days were lost to disputes resulting, first, from the major strikes mounted by engineering and public sector workers, and secondly, from the mines' strike which lasted a bitter fourteen months. In the aftermath of both these outbursts of militancy, stoppages of work declined dramatically. But after 1979 levels of industrial action steadily climbed. Following the miners' strike in 1984, industrial action sank again, to what seems its lowest point in the period under consideration, though it is still too soon to tell if this will be sustained. At any rate, it would be an exaggeration to speak of a collapse of militancy, or to infer that over the long term workers' resistance cannot be maintained. Much depends on the determination of workers to defend jobs and conditions, and factors like this may alter considerably over time. Above all, the changes and uncertainty of the present period mean that the full extent of the current developments in employment patterns remains very much an open issue.

Further reading

Baldamus, W. (1961) *Efficiency and Effort*. London: Tavistock.
Beynon, H. (1984) *Working for Ford* (2nd edn). Harmondsworth: Penguin.
Burowoy, M. (1985) *The Politics of Production*. London: Verso.
Edwards, P.K. (1986) *Conflict at Work: A Materialist Analysis of Workplace Relations*. Oxford: Blackwell.
Edwards, P.K. and H. Scullion (1982). *The Social Organization of Industrial Conflict: Control and Resistance at the Workplace*. Oxford: Blackwell.
Eldridge, J., P. Cressey and J. MacInnes (1991) *Industrial Sociology and Economic Crisis*. Hemel Hempstead: Harvester Wheatsheaf.
Hill, S. (1981) *Competition and Control at Work*. London: Heinemann.
Hyman, R. (1988) *The Political Economy of Industrial Relations*. London: Macmillan.
Hyman, R. (1989) *Strikes* (4th edn). Basingstoke: Macmillan.
MacInnes, J. (1987) *Thatcherism at Work*. Milton Keynes: Open University Press.
Nichols, T. and P. Armstrong (1976) *Workers Divided: A Study in Shop Floor Politics*. London: Fontana.
Nichols, T. and H. Beynon (1977) *Living with Capitalism*. London: Routledge and Kegan Paul.

12

Divisions of Labour

While most people in a modern industry economy have to sell their labour, they certainly do not all do so under the same conditions. Over and above the common factors in the labour process (which were discussed in the previous two chapters), there are also wide variations in the kinds of job available and in the rewards attached to them. Variety in work will be the focus of this chapter; and in order to examine it we need to look essentially at *occupational* themes and at the range of available employment. However, rather than survey the entire occupational structure, or look for wider sources of change in the general distribution of skills, we will take a more selective approach and concentrate on certain of the main occupational areas.

We shall look first at the *labour market* which confronts the manual working class – still the largest section of the employed population in spite of any decline in industrial jobs. The work opportunities open to the bulk of the population and their perceptions of these chances are vitally important for an understanding of modern employment. Secondly, we will examine the nature of *white-collar work*. Here we will be concerned chiefly with 'low-grade' office work, another of the largest job sectors. Interest here will focus on a debate which has exercised the minds of social scientists for more than fifty years: what are the implications for white-collar workers, particularly those in clerical and related occupations, of the declining status of office work? In the third section we look at another occupational group that continues to attract attention, namely *professionals*. The reasons for this interest are not hard to find. The professions are the most rapidly expanding group in the occupational structure, and this itself has created uncertainty and ambiguity as regards their work situation. But the professions also have a highly dynamic impact in that many of the new skills crucial in a modern industrial economy are commanded by these occupations. In examining the professions, however, our emphasis changes, and instead of looking at the structures of available jobs, we consider the strategies adopted by professionals actively to influence their occupational status.

As already indicated, this coverage does not by any means take in all occupations – groups like management, skilled workers and technical staff are omissions that readily spring to mind. But the three above are certainly important occupational groups, and in considering them we will be exploring some of the most important debates in the current sociological analysis of work.

The labour market

In a modern economy the labour market mediates the relationship between employers and employees. A key factor in workers' labour market behaviour is the notion of *choice*. If the market is to distribute labour rationally, the employer must be in a position of maximum possible choice, able to match the requirements of the vacant job with the abilities of applicants. It is also important, from the workers' point of view, to be able to choose the kind of job and the employer they want, since freedom of choice remains vital to the process of obtaining advantageous employment.

Although labour markets are known to depart from conditions of free choice, they have often been assumed to be essentially rational, and to allow a reasonable amount of free movement of labour and efficient allocation. However, some serious doubts have been raised about this. The basic concepts of 'freedom' and 'choice' seem to be notoriously problematic. How much choice constitutes real choice? What apparent choices really represent bowing to the inevitable? The concept of choice can also obscure the conflicting interests and power differences in society – in other words, what exists as choice for a powerful group may well appear as constraint to the less well placed. Thus, any sociological understanding of the labour market must dig deeper than a face-value notion of individual choice. It has to take serious account of the structural forces (class, gender, race, etc.) which influence the opportunities open to people and which shape the images of their own opportunities that they develop.

JOB CHOICE AND WORK ORIENTATIONS

An influential model of the way in which workers choose jobs was developed by Goldthorpe *et al.* (1968) in the 'affluent worker' research. The car assembly workers in the study experienced their work as it really was: routine and dead-end. But they had, as it were, made a rational decision to enter a type of employment that offered little intrinsic interest but high pay, since this reflected their underlying 'orientations' to work – in this case an instrumental orientation. The researchers therefore inferred a causal link between prior orientations to work and job choice: people with particular work orientations would seek out employment which gave the balance of rewards they desired and the deprivations they were willing to put up with.

The Luton study was never meant to be entirely representative of the manual working class. It focused on a certain type of worker – unskilled but in well-paid jobs – of which car assembly was a classic example. Nevertheless, the study can be criticized for implying a higher degree of job choice than exists in practice. Criticism comes on two counts. Firstly, the *origins* of work orientations may need to be questioned. To take their existence for granted, as Goldthorpe *et al.* did, is to ignore the possibility that it may be the labour market experiences of workers that cause them to adopt instrumental orientations in the first place. Thus the *voluntary* nature of the acceptance of unskilled work implied in the affluent worker model tended to play down the extent to which market choice for workers is limited by their educational attainment and by the availability of job opportunities, and so assumed a more rational market than may exist. Wedderburn and Crompton (1972) point out that the Luton sample was chosen to maximize job choice, being in an affluent part of the country (South East England) and based on a mobile, relatively young workforce. Their own study of chemical workers in an area in the North East, with a much higher incidence of unemployment, showed indications of far more restricted job choice.

Secondly, although Goldthorpe *et al.* wanted to avoid any narrow reliance on production technology to explain workers' attitudes (i.e. technologically 'determinist' theories), it has been suggested that they overemphasized factors external to the work situation. Both sets of factors – structural conditions within work, as well as the perceptions people bring to their employment – need to be taken into account. In particular, the happy coincidence between instrumental attitudes and the nature of car assembly work may simply have reflected adjustments and responses to the work situation. Thus, in an earlier American study of car workers, Chinoy (1955) found that attitudes followed a career cycle. Younger people entered the work with a concern for certain intrinsic rewards, particularly prospects and promotion, but with longer service they adjusted to restricted opportunities and their orientations shifted to pay and security. Similarly, Beynon (1984) in his noted study of car assembly workers at Ford's plant in Liverpool, also emphasized workers' limited job choice. In a region of high unemployment and declining industries, Ford offered reasonably well-paid employment. But workers' distaste for their jobs and their powerful sense of alienation were not diminished by positive aspects of the work.

Another account of the job choices open to workers has been provided by Blackburn and Mann (1979) in their intensive study of the labour market in a single town, Peterborough. They found that manual workers who possessed the skills or qualifications to enable them to exercise any real choice over their employment were in a small minority indeed. The jobs open to the vast majority of workers were mostly routine and poorly paid, with few differences between them. Moreover, the market was *hierarchical* rather than *compensatory*, thus removing one of the only areas of choice that is sometimes attributed to manual work. Very few jobs offered any chances of exchanging detrimental features (longer hours, poor conditions) for extra rewards (pay, status). The only chance of gaining additional rewards came with simply getting a better job, and this was both rare and outside workers' control.

> ... the *absolute* level of skill of all but the very highest jobs is – to say the least – minimal. Eighty-seven per cent of our workers exercise less skill at work than they would if they drove to work. Indeed, most of them expend more mental effort and resourcefulness in getting to work than in doing their jobs. From this remarkable result flow two important consequences. In the first place, nobody can choose a challengingly skilled job, no matter how much he is prepared to sacrifice in terms of wages and other work rewards. . . . Secondly, it follows that most workers are objectively capable of acquiring the skills necessary for most jobs; we estimate that 85 per cent of workers can do 95 per cent of jobs. (p. 280)

What workers look for in jobs reflected this highly restricted choice. Blackburn and Mann found little evidence in support of distinctive work orientations. Instead, they found 'weak orientations' in the form of complex patterns of preferences for certain types of work (a leaning towards outdoor work, elements of instrumentalism, a desire for jobs with some autonomy). They concluded that workers retain a sense of the reality in their situation – 'all orientations are confined within the limits of the labour market' (p. 282) – while at the same time making the best of things by valuing very highly the small differences between jobs that did exist. Interestingly, therefore, the labour market can be seen as at least partially rational, but only if workers' subjective perceptions are taken into account.

LABOUR MARKET THEORY AND THE CONSTRAINTS ON JOB CHOICE

The notion of workers competing equally in an open labour market is an ideal far removed from reality. In practice a great many 'substantive' factors – employer's preferences for certain kinds of worker, their desire not to disrupt established workforces, prejudice and discrimination of all kinds – tend to undermine the allocation of labour on a strictly rational basis. Indeed, as Blackburn and Mann

(1979) discovered, in the majority of cases what employers look for in workers is co-operativeness, and this alone would restrict any attempt to select workers rationally on the basis of skills and abilities.

The dual labour market

A major 'imperfection' in the market for labour to which certain economists and sociologists have drawn attention lies in the fact that it is not unified. In reality it is divided into distinct segments, and in particular into a primary and a secondary labour market. Jobs in the primary market are supplied by large firms that are technologically advanced and profitable. Wages and working conditions are relatively good, levels of unionization tend to be high, and employers are concerned with retaining stable workforces. However, this applies only to part of the economy. In addition, there are jobs in the secondary sector provided by small firms, usually in low technology industries and very competitive markets. Such firms normally experience great pressures to exploit their workers to the utmost, so wages tend to be low and conditions poor. In short, work in the primary sector provides what would usually be thought of as 'good jobs', found in the skilled trades and industries like engineering and advanced manufacturing. In the secondary sector are found the 'bad jobs' – or even 'sweated' labour – which tend to be concentrated in the services and in industries such as clothing and food processing.

Internal labour markets

A further aspect of market irrationality is that much allocation of labour in fact occurs *inside* firms as a result of the selection of existing employees. To a large extent the division between internal and external labour markets overlaps that between primary and secondary markets. In other words, it tends to be large-scale organizations in the advanced sector of the economy that restrict opportunities for advancement and training to their own employees. An internal labour market is favoured in the primary sector because it helps firms to stabilize their labour forces. Production here tends to be technically complex, and firms will normally be locked into highly structured product markets, which leads to demands for stable output and quality. Furthermore, primary labour forces contain high proportions of skilled and experienced workers who are not easily replaceable. By restricting such a major reward as promotion to the established labour force, ties of loyalty can be strengthened. In contrast to this, secondary sector firms, which tend to be much less dependent on skilled workers, and are often too small to operate an internal market, rely much more on the wider labour market as a source of labour supply.

The persistence of a secondary labour market has been underestimated in the past, but in general there are no trends to eliminate these low-grade jobs. Primary sector firms often utilize firms in the secondary sector, subcontracting work to them in order to keep wage costs down. The presence of such a relationship maintains the division between jobs, preventing any long-term equalization.

The primary and secondary sectors form a stratified labour market mainly because the workers who fill those jobs are themselves segregated. There is, as Marx originally noted, a 'social' as well as a 'technical' division of labour. The latter simply reflects the divisions between different occupations and branches of industry. However, the social division of labour refers to the manner in which different groups of people are allocated to different work. Probably the most widespread form of segregation (one we pay particular attention to in Chapter 13) is based on discrimination between the sexes. Women workers rarely compete with men for the same jobs; they usually have to accept relatively low-grade work with poor prospects. But almost any kind of labour market disadvantage can drive workers into the secondary sector. As workers become older, for instance, they may have to drop out of well-paid primary sector jobs and accept less advantageous work. Similarly, in areas containing large immigrant populations, sweated industries tend to flourish. Prejudice on the part of those placed to exert influence over selection, like personnel officers and senior management, helps to guarantee that factors like class, sex, race and age are applied in practice.

It may be argued that this merely reflects workers' true value to employers. After all, the primary sector contains a high proportion of workers with marketable qualities, and these have to be rewarded if firms wish to retain such workers. However, this argument is unsatisfactory for at least two reasons. First, even if the purely rational reasons for allocating workers either to the low-wage or to the high-wage sector were removed, much residual prejudice and discrimination would remain. Secondly, the argument ignores the fact that chances to obtain skills are allocated in a discriminatory fashion in the first place. Women and ethnic minorities are often given very limited access to training; also youngsters from middle-class backgrounds have in-built advantages when it comes to obtaining further education and skills.

All these distinctions are to an extent rather limited and static attempts to describe a complex reality. Labour market theory is hotly disputed within the social sciences, with several debates going on. To begin with, there is still disagreement about whether labour markets are truly *segmented* in the sense of particular sectors of jobs being entirely cut off from other sectors. While there are clearly major differences in the work open to different groups of people, this may not amount to fully developed segmentation. The need to refer in such cases to very detailed data on the distribution of rewards and choices between jobs has fuelled both sides of the debate.

Even assuming that labour markets are segmented (as opposed to being merely differentiated), the phenomenon has attracted major differences of interpretation and emphasis. Marxist writers, such as Edwards *et al.* (1975), have stressed that labour market segmentation is the outcome of the control imperative at the heart of the labour process. Employer' need for control inside the firm, they argue, has to be supported by control in the wider labour market, and in particular by a 'divide and rule' strategy towards labour. In this sense, segmentation encourages rivalry between different groups of workers, preventing the labour force as a whole from attaining unity.

Criticism from other radical writers, most notably from feminists, has stressed that the notion of some abstract form of 'capital' which exploits all workers equally is misleading. Pressures from wider society and from within labour itself, such as the forces of sexism, have an independent effect (Rubery, 1980). Primary sector workers frequently seek to exploit the internal promotion market at the expense of other workers. Thus, for example, sexism from men in general – and particularly from inside the trade union movement – may be as important a factor in discrimination against women as that expressed by employers.

In more mainstream social science, the changing organization of work is seen as a more varied process than that envisaged by radical writers. The wide range of labour policies that employers adopt – not all of which can be reduced to a single-minded desire to control workers – challenges the notion of a fixed capitalist logic. This line of argument has strong ties with the critique of labour process theory (see Chapter 10), in which various factors, like 'responsible' patterns of job design, were put forward as alternatives to direct control by employers. The emphasis here is on the Marxist interpretation being a mechanical and one-dimensional view, which implies a far too simplistic relationship of antagonism between capital and labour.

CONCLUSION

What seems to emerge from these debates is that managements are increasingly using *strategic* labour policies. Whereas in previous times firms might have adopted a uniform attitude towards workers, or the presence of some primary jobs may have stabilized the secondary ones, increasingly firms are using employment structures to differentiate groups of workers. One central factor in all this is that of *flexibility* in labour usage, i.e. the combination of internal and external labour markets to enable firms to deploy workers more cost-effectively and efficiently. Competitive pressures and uncertainties have forced firms into seeking labour flexibility, at the same time as unemployment has made workers more willing to adapt to the demands of flexible work patterns.

The ultimate effect of these changes is hard to judge – though the trends may mean a greater proportion of secondary-type jobs if firms use peripheral workers to avoid having to resort to redundancies in skilled labour forces. Factors that permit firms to introduce these diverse work patterns include the new micro-technologies, as well as new systems of work organization that overcome the rigidities of traditional mass production. Recent discussions of the nature of work and industrial society have focused around these themes, which we pick up again in Chapters 14 and 15.

White-collar work

If we now turn from manual work to the other major area of employment, the non-manual or white-collar sector, we at once come up against major problems of definition. Whereas manual jobs tend to be similar as regards the type of work performed and the rewards received – indeed Blackburn and Mann stressed how coherent a category they form – the non-manual sector is extremely diverse and extensive. It ranges across managerial and administrative posts, employment in the professions, in scientific and technical activities, supervision, clerical and secretarial jobs, and jobs in sales and distribution. The differences between these types of work in pay, status and authority are often immense; and as a result, methods of classifying non-manual occupations are beset with ambiguities and inconsistencies.

The reasons for this diversity can be found in the changing occupational structure, itself a product of industrial and commercial development. Economic expansion in the major industrial nations during this century has been heavily concentrated in areas of non-manual employment. The fastest-growing industries have frequently been science-based ones which employ a high proportion of professional and technical staff; and added to this throughout industry managerial functions (e.g. work control, planning and product development) have expanded. The commercial and financial sector (banks, building societies, insurance) has also developed, enlarging the clerical workforce, while the growth of state provision in health and welfare has expanded the numbers of lower professionals. This trend may now be levelling off. Areas like clerical work are expected to remain static or to decline as the effects of new technology and productivity improvements begin to bite. However, as Table 12.1 indicates, the long-term expansion in white-collar work has persisted until very recently, with all groups of non-manual employees showing very strong growth between 1984 and 1990.

The question of the nature of white-collar occupations is bound up with the contemporary sociological analysis of class. Traditionally, the line dividing manual and white-collar jobs has demarcated the working class from the middle class. In the nineteenth century the middle classes shared in the ownership of *property* (small businesses, self-employment and income from investment). Propertyless groups like clerical employees and supervisors were small in size and enjoyed such status and authority as marked them off clearly from manual workers. Hence they were often regarded as being assimilated into the middle class. However, the patterns of economic growth which brought about the expansion of white-collar occupations reversed this situation and the established property-owning middle class declined in numbers. The growing new white-collar groups derived their class position not from property but from their *employment*. This created a problem for analysis since the factors describing occupations (such as pay, status, authority and career expectations) are complex and not always consistent. As Hyman (1983) points out, this adds to the 'structural ambiguity' of extended white-collar hierarchies.

Moreover, there has been no simple transfer from a class position based on economic ownership to one based securely on employment. Certainly there are higher professional and managerial groups which do enjoy superior occupational rewards. Equally clearly, however, groups like clerical and sales workers do not. The expansion in non-manual work has mostly taken place in these lower-ranked kinds of jobs. As Abercrombie and Urry point out: 'the numerical growth in salaried employees is especially traceable to a demand for subordinates rather than fully qualified responsible people' (1983, p. 53). Furthermore, a high proportion of white-collar jobs have been occupied by women, and the sexual divisions in society have been a major influence in reinforcing the downward pressure on employment conditions.

Several writers believe that the diversity and fragmentation of white-collar groups is now such that they no longer constitute a single class. Hyman, for example, stresses: 'The range of internal differentiation in pay and conditions, and the existence of a distinct category of lowly-regarded "women's work", clearly casts doubt on the adequacy of the general category "white-collar employment" as a means of classifying occupations' (1983, p. 13). Thus the lower ranks of white-collar and service workers are to be distinguished from managerial and higher professional employees, who compromise the 'new' middle class. The latter have also been dubbed the 'service class', reflecting their responsibility for discharging functions, critical

277

Table 12.1   *Occupational analysis of persons in employment. From Employment Gazette (London: HMSO), April 1991, p. 183.*

	1984	1989	1990	1984–90
				INCREASE
	(000s)	(000s)	(000s)	%
Managerial, administrative and related professional	3515	4328	4589	30.6
Professional in education, welfare and health	2053	2285	2377	15.8
Professional in science, engineering and technology	1047	1144	1173	12.1
Clerical	3546	4098	4237	19.5
Other non-manual	1779	2011	1949	9.5
Skilled manual	3993	4079	4073	2.0
Other manual	6584	6997	6797	3.2
All non-manual occupations	12193	14241	14703	20.6
All manual occupations	10879	11241	11018	1.3

in a modern economy, of planning, administration and the control of labour.

In sketching out this analysis, however, we have disregarded some major problems. It is difficult imposing *a structure* (of class categories and boundaries) upon what they are essentially dynamic *processes*. Moreover, the notion that some groups, like clerical employees, have actually changed their class membership is still hotly debated. While most writers would agree that their distinctive class position has been eroded, there is a disagreement about how far this has gone, about how these changes are to be interpreted, and about whether in fact 'deskilled white-collar workers' constitute a 'new' element of the working class alongside manual workers.

PROLETARIANIZATION I: THE WORK PROCESS

In the nineteenth and early twentieth centuries, many white-collar employees were clearly differentiated from the manual working class. In the words of Lockwood:

> ... the clerk generally enjoyed a natural status clearly removed from that of the manual worker. His salary, hours of work and holiday were decidedly more favorable; and to be added to these were security of tenure, a greater chance of promotion, and the probability of a pension of some kind ... He was somehow a privileged type of proletarian. (1958, p. 41)

However, the occupational standing and class position of this largest section of the white-collar workforce have subsequently been threatened, in the sense of the gap between them and the working class growing less – a process referred to as the 'proletarianization' of these groups. Abercrombie and Urry (1983), reviewing the contemporary debate about class, stress that proletarianization is the single issue that has 'dominated the literature' on the topic.

Important evidence of proletarianization has come from data on *earning differentials*. What the figures show is a marked narrowing of differentials between clerical workers and unskilled manual workers, virtually closing the gap between them. Broadly speaking, up to the 1930s clerks earned about the same as skilled manual workers, whereas now their pay has fallen to the level of unskilled workers. The gap between them and the managerial/higher professional group (the 'service class') has widened. (For analysis of the earnings issue, see Hyman, 1983, pp. 5–13; Abercrombie and Urry, 1983, p. 114; and Braverman, 1974, pp. 296–8.)

As well as the narrow question of earnings, however, the major sociological studies of white-collar employment have explored the nature of the work and other occupational factors. In particular, it is trends towards deskilling and routinization, identified in Chapter 10 in relation to manual labour, that are also held responsible for alienation in the office.

The American C. Wright Mills was probably the first modern sociologist to write at length about the deterioration of office work. In his classic study *White Collar* (1951) Mills linked two basic processes: the introduction of machinery and the intensification of work.

> As the army of clerks grew, they were divided into departments, specialized in function, and thus, before machines were introduced on any scale, socially rationalized.... It was this social reorganization, under the impetus of work load, higher cost, and the need for files and figures, that made possible the wide application of business machines. (p. 192)

Mill's concerns with the rationalization of office work invited the comparison between office and factory. Changes in work patterns, like open-plan layout and typing pools, led to a workflow that could be centrally planned and closely supervised. The application of 'scientific management' too, he notes, was common in larger American offices by the 1920s. Mills anticipated the full rationalization of office work; certain 'status complications' might delay it, but it was the 'model of the future'.

Another influential account is that of Braverman (1974, Chapter 15 and 16). We noted earlier the stimulus that he gave to the

279

'deskilling' debate, but Braverman was also noted for extending these ideas into his account of white-collar work. He stresses the 'extraordinary enlargement' of these occupations – in the case of clerical workers rising from being less than 1 per cent of the employed population in the mid-nineteenth century, in both Britain and the United States, to developed labour forces respectively composing 3 million and 14 million employees by the 1970s (p. 295). As these groups expanded, office work changes 'from something merely incidental to management into a labor process in its own right' (p. 304). And like Mills, Braverman emphasized the 'merging characteristics of clerical and production labor'. The need to 'systematize and control' white-collar work brought about mechanization (with the typewriter as early as the 1880s, then a range of office equipment, and most importantly the recent introduction of commercial computing), the growth of a separate hierarchy of office management, reorganization of work to give economies of scale, and the erosion of established white-collar skills (e.g. the replacement of shorthand by audio typing). The clerical occupations, Braverman stated emphatically, represented a major section of the working class, and any general white-collar category that included higher-level occupations was 'absolutely meaningless' (p. 295).

PROLETARIANIZATION II: OCCUPATIONAL STATUS

Unlike these accounts, which tend to be confined to the changing labour process, many British sociologists have given prominence to subjective factors concerned with the *status* of white-collar occupations and the *class consciousness* of the incumbents of these jobs. David Lockwood's pioneering early study *The Blackcoated Worker* (1958) set out three separate dimensions of class position. (1) He referred to the basic economic factors related to occupation (pay prospects, conditions) as 'market situation'; (2) 'work situation' stressed the nature of social relationships at work; and (3) 'status situation' was the prestige accorded to occupations in wider society (p. 15). Lockwood argued that, whereas the market situation of clerical employees differed little from that of manual workers, the modern office was still not rationalized to the extent that their respective work situations were identical (e.g. he insisted that office mechanization enhanced clerical work rather than reducing it to mere machine minding). Moreover, considerations of status revealed radical differences, a 'sheer social distance', between clerical and manual workers. Clerks still retained relative advantages in terms of their middle-class origins and level of education. Indeed, the very fact of clerical 'respectability' being insecure, and based on declining occupational advantages, provoked a powerful desire in clerks to remain aloof from the manual working class. Lockwood concluded:

> the traditional superiority of non-manual work has not been entirely eradicated by the changes of the last half-century, even though it has become more frequently questioned. This is best stated by saying that the loss of middle class status by the clerk is not tantamount of the acquisition of working class status, either from the point of view of the clerk or the manual worker. (p. 211)

Two more recent major empirical surveys of clerical employees are those of Stewart et al. (1980) and Crompton and Jones (1984). Stewart argued that if *career expectations* are significant in an occupation, then any approach which focuses on the job itself (whether in terms of its reward, social status or the nature of the work involved) will convey a static and ultimately misleading picture. Furthermore, they discovered significantly high rates of promotion out of clerical work, a finding they used to argue against the proletarianization thesis: 'Clerk is not a well-paid position, or even a highly regarded position, but it is an early stage on relatively lucrative and highly regarded careers ... the image of blocked mobility and non-increasing incomes is far from accurate' (p. 172). However, their study was based on *male* clerks, which limits the relevance of their findings in an occupation three-quarters feminized.

Crompton and Jones's study focused on 'objective' aspects of the labour process and did encompass male and female clerical employees. While these researchers too discovered high rates of mobility for men, the vast majority of women were seen to occupy routine jobs with little control over the work and very limited career chances. They particularly stressed the role of *computers* in deskilled clerical work, and in a sense they here followed Lockwood. His argument against proletarianization was formed in the 1950s before the start of commercial computing, while Crompton and Jones suggest that automated data-processing so radically altered the clerical labour process as to be the decisive factor in creating a (female) proletariat. Also, implicitly, they disagree with writers like Mills and Braverman, who believed that the routinization of the clerical work was well advanced by the first half of the century (although they agree with them that, ultimately, a white-collar working class has come into existence).

CONCLUSION

Any attempt to say the final word on the nature of white-collar work is probably premature. These changes in the occupational structure are still taking place, and in any case they touch upon major differences of theory and interpretation within the social sciences. What does seem clear is that restructuring of the industrial economy has accelerated in recent years, and that the occupational changes at the heart of this process are reflected directly in changes within the white-collar labour force. The complex make-up of this category of employees and the strength of the forces that are reshaping it makes it difficult to arrive at hard and fast conclusions

No matter what disagreement there is between social scientists, however, the key issue remains that of the decline in standing of white-collar groups. Questions of the *improvement* of the class position of large sections of the working population – which were very much discussed during the 'affluent' 1960s – no longer seem to be on the agenda. The high-grade work, created for example by some new technology, cannot in any sense be regarded as compensation for the degradation of clerical work, since these jobs are in a fairly small minority. Nevertheless, this raises as a separate issue the nature of higher-grade white-collar jobs, an important part of which consists of professional work, which we now consider further.

Professions and professionalism

As we have said, the professions form a major section of the white-collar workforce. The term itself tends to be more meaningful than any general category of 'white-collar work' since even low-ranking groups in the professions still seem to enjoy career prospects and conditions of employment which differentiate them from routine white-collar workers. Nevertheless, the differences *among* professional groups remain important. Established professions (such as law, medicine and architecture) command a much superior status and better earnings when compared with lesser professions (like teaching and social work). Moreover, there are pronounced hierarchies *within* professions – the financial controller of a large corporation, for instance, would receive far higher rewards than an auditor, yet both might broadly be described as accountants.

CHARACTERISTICS OF THE PROFESSIONS

This range of variation within the professional groups has meant that defining the essential features of professions has always proved difficult. In an influential early study, Goode (1957) called the professions a 'community within a community', stressing the highly distinctive and integrated nature of their occupational cultures. Professionals have a common sense of identity and values, share a consensus as regards their social role, speak a common language and are lifetime members of their occupation.

What does seem to be of prime importance is the nature of *professional work*. Professions traditionally have enjoyed the high status and material rewards associated with positions of authority, yet they are also involved in the concrete process of work. Sometimes this may in fact be manual work (a surgeon, for example, carries out what is probably quite hard manual work, albeit delicate and skilled); and although most professions are white-collar in nature, there remains a belief that professionals should actually perform the work themselves and not merely delegate it to others. In trying to define professional work the following aspects may be singled out.

1. Professional work typically has a *service* element – either service to the common good, such as in health or education, or service to an individual client, or in an organization the provision of a staff service to line management.
2. The professions are *ethical* occupations. Because they employ a complex technical language, and are often involved with matters of critical importance to society and to individuals, there is a need to regulate professional conduct by some code of ethics. The central relationship of trust between client and professional, upon which the legitimacy of professional advice is based, itself rests on the belief that professionals will act purely in the client's interest, and for no other purpose.
3. The professions tend to be *self-regulating* occupations. Their responsibilities usually involve extensive skills and technical knowledge, for which long periods of training are required; hence professionals themselves prefer to reserve the right to be sole judge of the competence of other colleagues. They determine training requirements, control entry to the profession, and in some cases grant the license to practice.

The skills of professionals, and their concern with services of exceptional importance, have conventionally been used to explain the superior status and rewards that these occupations attract. However, more recently it has been pointed out that to see professional status merely as a reflection of the intrinsic qualities of professional work is to paint a rather static and misleading picture. For example, Johnson (1972) has argued that accounts which focus on the supposed qualities of professions have never been able to agree a list of 'traits' that are typical of all professions in all circumstances. Similarly, the suggestion that professions serve fundamental social needs (for health, law and order, education, etc.) is also rather doubtful. The alleged 'altruism' of professionals has often been the basis of exaggerated claims about their ethical and progressive role. As Johnson indicates, this 'falls into the error of accepting professionals' own definitions of themselves' (1972, p. 25).

Instead of regarding professionalism as an inherent quality of a few select occupations, it is best regarded as an *occupational strategy*, whereby groups attempt to gain recognition as professions in order to reap the rewards of the established professions. This view was pioneered by the American sociologist Everett Hughes, who maintained that he 'passed from the false question "Is this occupation a profession?" to the more fundamental one, "What are the circumstances in which people in an occupation attempt to turn it into a profession and themselves into professional people?"' (quoted in Johnson, p. 31). Here the emphasis shifts to the *dynamic* process of groups attempting collectively to upgrade their occupational standing.

PROFESSIONALISM AS AN OCCUPATIONAL STRATEGY

Although the older-established professions are often taken as the benchmark by which the status of all professional groups is measured, the nature of professional work on the whole has undergone major changes. Indeed, professionalism as a strategy reflects both the opportunities that have risen for groups to move up in status and the threats to the status of existing groups.

C. Wright Mills (1951) pointed out two main aspects of this dynamic situation. First, the established professions themselves have been transformed. The independent practitioner might once have represented the 'model' professional, but nowadays even high-status groups, like architects, accountants and lawyers, are often employees rather than partners in independent practice. Secondly, as we could see from Table 12.1, all the professional/technical categories have grown very rapidly within the occupational structure. Technological changes and industrial development have meant that many entirely new engineering and scientific skills have appeared. Also, the growth of state provision has greatly expanded groups like teachers and social workers. Such a growth in numbers, as much as anything else, poses the problem for these groups of defining and protecting their occupational boundaries.

Several important tactics for securing occupational control can be singled out. One of the chief preconditions of wider occupational control is that the membership itself should be a united force. Thus *professional associations* are vitally important in representing and furthering the interests of the profession. In the more powerful professions, the association will regulate training and educational standards, in order to preserve the status of the occupation by requiring a high level of technical knowledge and practical ability. Strict entry requirements also serve to limit numbers and to keep practitioners in short supply. Indeed, if has often been noted that the main function of professional associations lies in keeping the profession an exclusive club.

The occupational strategy represented here differs from but also shares some common elements with the two other major strategies of advancement: the *trade union* strategy of workers and the *career* strategy of managers. Mindful of this, Parry and Parry (1976) have defined the professional strategy as a form of 'upward collective mobility'. Thus a profession is a coalition of interests and acts collectively, not unlike a trade union. Nor is it unknown for professional associations to resort to industrial action – through they are usually very anxious not to be associated in the public eye with trade unions. To be more precise, professional associations are closer to craft unions than they are to the large general trade unions, which operate on the principle of including as many people as possible in the particular industry. With craft unions the opposing principles of inclusion and exclusion favour the latter more. (Craft unions are very much concerned with preserving the exclusiveness of the craft via control of apprenticeship, for example.) The professions guard their exclusive nature even more jealously. Yet it is a measure of the success of the professions that, while unions are often roundly condemned for using 'restrictive' practices in defense of jobs, the tactics of the profession, which are aimed solely at exclusivity, tend to be readily accepted. In contrast to this, the type of rewards being sought are clearly quite different from those aimed at by workers' associations. The professions provide a setting for members to pursue individualistic career paths and distinctively middle-class rewards, much as do senior organizational members.

Studies have also shown how professional ethics, as well as ostensibly protecting clients, crucially serve the interests of professions. The issue here is the *ideological* character of the professional ethic, rather than the truth or otherwise of professional claims. Indeed, it may well be true that the wider public interest is served by having secure professions, yet it is certainly clear that these forms of control enhance the vested interests of the professions concerned. The professional ethic resembles a sort of occupational ideology uniting the members of the profession. For example, a practitioner threatened with legal action for alleged incompetence can normally expect his colleagues to close ranks behind him, providing he has not broken the code of ethics. Thus, members of the public often find it extremely difficult to bring a case against professionals unless some gross breach of conduct can clearly be proven. Internal discipline within professions tends to be overwhelmingly concerned with cases where the profession itself might have been brought into disrepute (mostly involving illegal or immoral behavior) rather than with investigating cases of incompetence on behalf of clients or the public.

A major basis of professional privilege, as Hughes (1975) points out, lies in the claim to superior knowledge. It is a mark of occupations struggling to gain exclusive rights to practice, to self-regulation and

285

so forth, that they will make great efforts to have their claims on knowledge recognized; and it is characteristic of the established professions that they guard their monopoly of knowledge very closely. In daily contact with clients and the public, professionals seek to 'mystify' their knowledge, to make it appear that, while long training and experience are necessary, there are other indefinable skills that only members of the profession possess or even understand. Doctors, for example, are often extraordinarily reluctant to discuss patients' illnesses with them, the justification being that it would distress patients or that they would not understand anyway. While this may contain some truth, keeping patients in ignorance undeniably helps doctors to manipulate them. Thus the 'manner' that professionals adopt is an important tactic in maintaining their possession of vital knowledge.

The power of certain professions may extend beyond control of their own occupation. Esland (1980) has stressed that the expertise which professions command confers on them a 'mandate to produce and generate certain kinds of knowledge for society as a whole'. While the public as clients may know broadly what service it requires, in important respects this is defined by the relevant profession, and it is this definition that will decide the actual service received.

> Routine definitions of ill-health, social adequacy, school achievement, degrees of criminality, for example, can be seen as grounded in the specific forms of expertness which at any one time are dominant in society.... Many of the dominant categories of thought which permeate our commonsense attitudes – as well as the power to enforce them – are to some extent traceable to the political organization of particular occupations. (Esland, 1980)

CONCLUSION: VARIATIONS IN OCCUPATIONAL CONTROL

In the last analysis, of course there can be no guarantee that occupations will be successful in their demands for professional recognition – or if they have succeeded that they will retain their status over the long term. As a strategy, professionalism is by definition open-ended, and many groups will enjoy only a limited form of autonomy, although the groups themselves would not necessarily see it in this light. Occupations which because of their nature can hardly aspire to the status of the senior professions nevertheless can be very jealous of the trappings of the professional autonomy that they have acquired. Indeed, for groups that are not already fairly influential professionalism may not be the strategy they choose to adopt. Simpson's (1981) study of the regional press has shown that, as the monopoly structure of the newspaper industry has intensified, journalists have suffered reduced status, and control has shifted increasingly to editorial management. These changes have been reflected in the National Union of Journalists adopting the more militant stance of a trade union rather than of a professional association.

The question that remains, however, is how we explain the differences in the progress of different groups along the path of professionalism. Why are doctors, say, capable of sustaining their elite status, while teachers are not? It can be argued that the issue itself is unimportant: certain occupations have simply managed to acquire the totem of professional prestige while other have not. Others, however, seek more distinctive explanations. Any such answer clearly must take historical and institutional factors into account. Thus, for example, it has been pointed out that state intervention into an occupation seems to be a major factor explaining why such groups become only marginally professional (Johnson, 1972; Parry and Parry, 1976). The ethics of occupations that have been shaped by government bureaucracy (e.g. teachers, social workers) reflect rules of the state employing agency, while control over the service being provided resides with the agency – all of which detracts from true professional values.

On a more theoretical level, we can point to two related concepts that help to explain variations in professional autonomy. Carchedi (1977) has drawn attention to the contrasting forces operating on middle-class occupations like professions, some of which degrade and constrain occupational control while others serve to enhance an occupation's market position. The explanation Carchedi gives reflects the extent to which the 'functions of capital' are being served. If the occupation concerned plays an important role in administrative and control functions crucial to the production of surplus value, it will command the market power that will bring prestige and exceptional rewards. (A good example here would be that of accounting, the exclusive authority of which has grown because of its relation with corporate capital.) However if a profession has tenuous links with these fundamental capitalist processes, occupational prestige will be much more marginal.

Secondly, as well as the salience of the function performed, the rewards accruing to a profession are also determined by the nature of the work involved. Jamous and Peloille (1970) have argued that where a high degree of *indeterminacy* exists in the work of a profession – that is, where tasks are variable and non-rationalized – then people who control this uncertainty are likely to enjoy high status. Conversely, where such work has been systematized and subject to laid-down procedures, it becomes possible for forces outside the occupation to intervene and control the work process.

287

To a degree, both these types of explanation still seem to be circular in the way that they distinguish between occupations. One still might want to know why a doctor's job should be indeterminate and salient for capital but a teacher's job not. However, salience and indeterminacy are objective features of the work process in only a partial sense – social and political factors also play a critical role in creating or failing to create these conditions. At crucial points in their development, elite professions are able to capitalize on the objective conditions of their work situation. In other cases, would-be professions have a self-defeating aspect. Their dilemma, as Jamous and Peloille (1970) point out, is that the pursuit of best practice may mean codifying and mechanizing their own work, thereby shifting control to outside managerial elements. Professionals may literally streamline themselves out of a job. In this sense, therefore, concepts of salience and indeterminacy link strategic factors with the structural constraints on strategy. They point to the crucial act of groups seizing or failing to seize on the objective conditions which their work setting provides in their struggles to exert control over an occupational domain.

Further reading

Abercrombie, N. and J. Urry (1983) *Capital, Labour and the Middle Classes*. London: Allen and Unwin.

Blackburn, R.M. and M. Mann (1979) *The Working Class in the Labour Market*. Chapter 1: 'The working class and the labour market'. London: Macmillan.

Child, J. and J. Fulk (1982) 'Maintenance of occupational control: the case of professions', *Work and Occupations*, 9, 155–92.

Crompton, R. and G. Jones (1984) *White Collar Proletariat: Deskilling and Gender in Clerical Work*. London: Macmillan.

Davies, C. (1983) 'Professionals in bureaucracies: the conflict thesis revisited', in R. Dingwall and P. Lewis (eds.) *The Sociology of the Professions*. London: Macmillan.

Elliott, P. (1972) *The Sociology of Professions*. London: Macmillan.

Hyman, R. and R. Price (eds.) (1983) *The New Working Class? White-Collar Workers and their Organizations*. London: Macmillan.

Johnson, T. (1972) *Professions and Power*. London: Macmillan.

Pahl, R.E. (ed.) (1988) *On Work: Historical, Comparative and Theoretical Approaches*. Oxford: Blackwell.

Prandy, K., A. Stewart and R.M. Blackburn (1982) *White-Collar Work*. London: Macmillan.

Smith, C. (1986) *Technical Workers: Class, Labour and Trade Unionism*. London: Macmillan.

13

Women and Employment

So far we have explored some of the ways in which occupational factors and the forms of control inherent in the labour process influence the nature of employment. But the constraints of social structure are evident in another way, in the sense that certain groups of people are typically found to occupy particular jobs or particular roles in organizations. One very important aspect of this social division of labour, central to any discussion of work, involves the divisions between the sexes. It can readily be shown that all societies distinguish traditionally between the work that men do and the work that women do. However, in modern industrial societies, with their enormously complex structure of occupations and authority levels, the sexual division of labour that is superimposed on this is likewise highly complex.

There are many cogent reasons for wanting to understand the special role that women play in employment, and the role of employment in women's lives. This whole subject involves important aspects of recent social change, as well as the fact that women's experiences in the labour force have been ignored or labelled with simple stereotypes until quite recently.

Employment versus work
An important point to make at the outset concerns the use of the terms 'work' and 'employment'. Usually the two are simply equated, so that to ask someone what work they do is the same as asking them what their job is. In the case of men this confusion hardly matters, since the useful work most men perform is confined to their jobs. But in the case of women and work the distinction becomes critical, and we have to bear in mind the crucial differences between paid and unpaid work. In our society, unpaid work in the home and in the form of child-rearing is sharply distinguished from employment, or work done outside the home for a wage or salary.

The sexual division of labour

This division between economic and domestic activities, between paid and unpaid work, marks a major division between the sexes. When the factory system first created economic activity separate from the household, it was women who were consigned to the domestic sphere while men moved into the sphere of employment. The sexual division of labour thus marks a fundamental element of social structure, and one which defines the relations between the sexes in wider society. In the employment sphere it massively influences and ultimately restricts women's choice of jobs.

These structured inequalities originate in and are sustained by a range of factors. First, women's material dependence upon men reflects the low levels of pay they obtain when employed and their reliance on low-grade jobs (two issues we take up later in the chapter). In addition, the state plays an important role in designing taxation and welfare benefits systems which effectively make women dependent upon men as legal heads of households. Secondly, there are the broader processes of socialization and the learning of gender roles. A fact long known, and supported by a mass of research evidence, is that child-rearing practices adopted by parents differ markedly for each sex. They reinforce an active role for boys, while for girls there is an emphasis on passivity, on their own decorativeness and on the importance of emotional rewards.

Thirdly, existing patterns of segregation are greatly reinforced by the education system. In spite of all trends towards equal treatment in modern schools – and what is probably the quite genuine desire of many teachers to liberalize curricula – a high degree of restriction remains. There is always a strong bias towards boys taking the science and girls the arts subjects. Schools are also obviously places where socialization continues. Peer groups and friendship cliques are known to exercise a powerful influence on adolescent children, so that they are internalizing a highly specific image of what they believe is possible and proper for them to aspire to. From around 12 years of age onwards, girls are seriously underachieving in relation to measured IQ. The self-images they acquire in these years cause them to hold back and increasingly to regard academic achievement as irrelevant in the future they anticipate.

The nature of women's work

The division of labour that exists in the workplace is strongly related to these wider divisions between the sexes. When young women first enter the labour market, having been encouraged to take non-technical subjects at school and advised to seek these kinds of job, their occupational placement then reinforces the traditional pattern of female employment. The types of work traditionally open to women frequently reflect their domestic role as wives and mothers. And domestic labour, as Wainright (1984) has pointed out, is seen as something that women perform 'naturally' rather than involving active choice, as in the pursuit of a career or occupation. Moreover, the domination of society by market relationships actually distorts our perceptions of the value of different forms of effort. Effort which commends a price, in terms of wages or a salary, alone enjoys status. But domestic labour, which has no exchange value, is hardly accepted as having any economic function, no matter how socially useful it might be. Thus the identification of women, and women's work, with domestic labour serves massively to undervalue their real contribution.

Each of the above factors – the framework of legislation, the self-images that men and women have, and the exclusion of domestic labour from the rest of the economy – reflect deeply rooted beliefs about women's place in a predominantly male-oriented society. They mean that even where women do work, there exists a sort of 'grand myth' that they are not naturally fitted for employment, or that it is not 'real work' they are doing. Many specific prejudices about women and employment can be understood only against the background of these very powerful beliefs.

Patterns of female employment

LABOUR FORCE PARTICIPATION

The expansion of female employment in the post-war period has been one of the most significant of all recent social and economic trends. In September 1990 in the United Kingdom there were 11.7 million women in employment, comprising 44 per cent of the labour force; and between 1960 and 1980 the workforce increased by about 2 million due almost entirely to the entry into work of the group that traditionally did not work, namely married women. More recently, between March 1983 and September 1990, the number of male employees was almost entirely static at around 12.0 million, the only growth in the male sector being the self-employed, who increased by 0.8 million. But total female employment over this period increased by 1.7 million. This long period of growth has left women very firmly entrenched in the economy.

Over the entire period of industrialization, however, the proportion of women in paid employment has varied considerably. Hakim (1980) has compiled data on rates of female economic activity (i.e. the proportion of women eligible to work that are in employment) from

Table 13.1 *Rates of female economic activity 1851–1981*. From Hakim (1980) and 1981 Census of Population (London: HMSO).

	WOMEN ABOVE MINIMUM WORKING AGE (%)	MARRIED WOMEN AGED 15–59 (%)	WOMEN AGED 15–59 (%)
1851	42		
1861	43		
1871	42		
1881	32		
1891	32		
1901	32	10	38
1911	32	10	38
1921	32	10	38
1931	34	11	38
1941	—	—	—
1951	35	26	43
1961	38	35	47
1971	43	49	55
1981	46	57	61

the national census reports, and some of her data are set out in Table 13.1. The general pattern is one of relatively high activity rates up to 1871, a sharp fall lasting until the period around the Second World War (during which no census was taken), then a steady rise back to the early levels. This, Hakim points out, gives us a longer perspective on the question of the economic role that women are capable of fulfilling. The notion of women entering the labour market in recent years is seen as somewhat misleading; rather, women *returned* to employment after being excluded for the best part of a century.

Explanations of this historical pattern need to take several factors into account. Family labour was frequently used in the early factories, but the rationalization of this system from the 1840s onwards gradually eliminated these forms of organized work, which had survived from the early domestic mode. From the middle of the nineteenth century a combination of factory legislation which banned women from certain types of work, the formation of male-dominated trade unions and the onset of the first great depression in the 1870s did much to exclude women from paid work. The economic expansion that took place later, in the 1890s, came mostly in the new heavy industries – chemicals, steel, engineering – which provided work that women were unable to enter. In contrast to this, the return of full employment after the Second World War drew massive numbers of women into the economy. This period saw expansion in sectors which were labour-intensive and where women were already established: the welfare state, education, consumer manufacturing and, above all, clerical and secretarial work.

Even so, the variation in activity rates that the data show is perhaps not as great as one might have expected. Even at the height of the Victorian era, when there were powerful social pressures against women working, these were mostly confined to 'respectable' (that is to say, married and middle-class) women, But it has always been true that single women and working-class women have had to work. Thus, as the table shows, even at the point of their lowest economic activity about one-third of women were in paid work, while at the peaks of activity about half were and are working.

However, these changes are more sharply defined if we take into account factors which affect women's circumstances, such as marital status and age. As the data show, marital status once made a great difference to activity rates, while the marked tendency in recent years for married women to work has nearly eliminated any differences in activity rates between married women and women in general.

Figure 13.1 gives a detailed breakdown by age, and confirms the traditionally dramatic changes in activity rates between different age groups. However, age and marital status only partially reflect the stage in the life cycle a woman has attained. Marriage by itself has been shown to have no independent effect on activity rates. By far the most significant factor causing women not to work has been the presence of young child to care for. Thus the pronounced 'dip' in activity rates for the 25–34 age group reflects women leaving work during the years when they are likely to be raising a family, and then later returning to work. However, among some groups, particularly young women with no children, the proportion going out to work approaches 90 per cent and differs little from that of men. Interestingly (as we also see later in the chapter), one of the clearest current trends is for women to return to work sooner after the birth of their children. Thus the projection for 2001 is that life-cycle factors will almost entirely disappear. This anticipates women's attachment to work strengthening even further, in response to changing demographic factors and improving childcare provision.

JOB SEGREGATION

The re-establishment of women in the economy has reflected the increased demands of women for economic independence, yet patterns

Figure 13.1 *Female activity rates by age.* From *Employment Gazette* (London: HMSO), May 1991, p. 277. Reproduced with permission.

of discrimination have also continued to be remarkably in evidence. Women are 'crowded' into only a narrow band of occupations. Female employment is concentrated especially in unskilled factory work and low-grade service work – in the minor professions (nursing, school teaching), in the manual services (shop work, cleaning, canteen work, laundry work), and in the secretarial and clerical sector. Conversely, women are very poorly represented in 'higher' occupational sectors, such as skilled manual work, the senior professions and management.

The pattern of female employment is also vertically distorted. Only small proportions of women occupy top jobs in management, administration and the professions. Even in occupations where women are well represented and which offer a career structure, they tend to be confined to the junior levels. Thus, women teachers are concentrated in primary schools, while there are fewer in secondary schools and only a very small proportion in promoted posts like head of department or head of school. In industry, too, it is common to find entire departments of women workers, perhaps with a woman as immediate supervisor, but with all higher levels occupied by men.

International comparisons reveal some different patterns. Women in certain countries (notably Canada and the USA) have gained a markedly high degree of access to management positions, and in Scandinavian countries women are better represented in the professions. However, across the industrialized countries the similarities outweigh the differences (Bradley, 1989, p. 15). Indeed, the variations in patterns which suggest that women have 'done better' in some countries can be misleading. The classic example is Russia, where women are strongly represented in certain professions, particularly medicine – although in that country, because of the historic communist ideology and the priority this gave to heavy industry, the high-status professions are engineering-related, while medicine is actually quite low-status. Thus the different employment cultures and traditions from country to country may affect patterns of occupational segregation, but women still tend to be found in whatever are defined as the low-status, low-reward occupations.

Another clear indication of these distorted employment patterns emerges from the amount of part-time work that is accepted by a great many women. In June 1990, 44 per cent of women's jobs were part-time and women performed 83 per cent of all such work. The effect of recessions has reinforced this trend. In a recession employers experience the need for flexible labour that can be taken on and laid off relatively easily, and part-time workers supply this very effectively. At certain periods part-time female employment has proved to be one of the few dynamic sectors of the jobs market. Thus between 1978 and 1981, 171,000 female jobs were lost as part of the general unemployment associated with the recession; but these were made up of 232,000 losses of full-time jobs and a gain of 71,000 part-time jobs. During the middle 1980s, when unemployment fell and the economy stabilized, the shift towards female part-time jobs slowed down and just outstripped the growth in full-time employment. Between March 1983 and September 1990, total female employment increased by 2.1 million, of which 56 per cent were part-time jobs. However, by about September 1989 the turnaround had begun again; full-time female employment peaked and started to decline, while part-time jobs were still increasing, albeit slowly.

In some ways, therefore, the availability of this type of work has strengthened women's labour market position. Yet what counts as flexibility to employers almost by definition means a second-class job as far as workers are concerned. Part-time workers are in every sense merely 'hired hands'. They have no real contract of employment and very little job security or entitlement to benefits, and their rates of pay often fall well below those of full-time workers. Of course, this is not to say that women necessarily *feel* resentful of being forced into the part-time sector. A great many married women especially are pleased to have a job which enables them to make a significant contribution to family income and where the hours enable them to fulfil their domestic commitments. But the fact remains that the allocation of women to part-time employment represents a major element in discrimination.

PAY INEQUALITIES AND LEGISLATION

Gender segregation is closely tied to the wide differences between male and female earnings. Studies have shown that only about half of the variance in pay levels can be attributed to the lesser amounts of skills and training possessed by women; the remainder reflects discriminatory practices – in other words, the concentration of women in jobs that attract relatively poor pay because they are defined as low-grade (Walby, 1988, p. 2).

This is a gap that legislation has gone some way toward closing. The Equal Pay Act 1970, aimed specifically at the ideal of 'equal pay for equal work', confers the right to the same treatment as an employee of the opposite sex who is doing identical or similar work, or work rated as equivalent under a job evaluation study. The other relevant piece of legislation is the Sex Discrimination Act 1975. This attempts to prevent discrimination on grounds of sex particularly at the stage of recruitment for jobs, and over the distribution of training opportunities and promotion.

Before the legislation was introduced, women received just under half the male wage, then in 1970 the gap closed slightly and gradually improved to around 62 to 66 per cent (Table 13.2). This may have reflected other labour market changes – a decline in men's pay, for instance – although there have been indications that the legislation was in fact responsible for this partial narrowing of the pay gap. The earnings ratio then stabilized for a period, with women receiving about two-thirds of male earnings. This seemed to suggest that the legislation had had an initial impact – probably by eliminating grossly unfair situations where men and women in exactly the same jobs were paid at different rates – but that in the broader sense the effect was more marginal. Perhaps significantly, in the four years leading up to 1991, the improvement in women's relative pay has taken another step forward with the ratio edging up to 70 per cent. This recent change may reflect women's strengths in the labour market and some employers' improving attitudes, rather than being the direct result of legislation.

The most important piece of subsequent legislation was the 1984 amendment to the Equal Pay Act. The original Act had long been

Table 13.2   *Male and female earnings 1969–1991.* From *New Earnings Survey*, (London: HMSO), various issues.

	Average weekly earnings of men aged 21 and over and women aged 18 and over, for all industries and services.		
	FULL-TIME MEN (£)	FULL-TIME WOMEN (£)	FEMALE/MALE EARNINGS RATIO (%)
1969	24.8	12.1	49
1971	32.9	18.3	56
1973	41.9	23.1	55
1975	60.8	37.4	60
1977	78.6	51.0	65
1979	101.4	63.0	62
1981	140.5	91.4	65
1983	167.5	108.8	65
1985	192.4	126.4	66
1986	207.5	137.2	66
1987	224.0	148.1	66
1988	245.8	164.2	67
1989	269.5	182.3	68
1990	295.6	201.5	68
1991	318.9	222.4	70

criticized for having too narrow a definition of 'equal work'. It meant that employers could avoid paying equally so long as women were simply in different jobs. The 1984 amendment required men and women to be paid equally for work of *equal value*. In other words, if it can be demonstrated that in a particular firm or industry a woman's job has similar value to a man's – measured on agreed criteria like skill content, responsibility, etc. – even if the two jobs are quite different they must be grouped in the same grading structure. This allows women crucial forms of comparability on which to base claims. However, the legislation appears to have had little effect. In practice it has been difficult to win equal value claims at industrial tribunals. According to a study by the Equal Opportunities Commission (*Pay and Gender in Britain*. London, EOC, March 1991), despite some successes, employers are fighting the claims tooth and nail, and hearings and appeals are proving very lengthy. The report found that few firms were assessing their jobs on equal value criteria, and even when women were in the same grading structure firms still contrived to pay them less – by marginalizing women in the lower grades, paying bonuses and shift premiums to men, and confining merit awards to senior grades dominated by men.

Women's experience in the workplace

WORKPLACE DISCRIMINATION

It has proved difficult to legislate effectively in the broader area of job opportunities for women precisely because discrimination is so embedded in employment practices. Some of the main forms of pay discrimination occur in ways that legislation is powerless to change. Labour force segregation occurs at the occupational level, but more important is the much more detailed segregation that occurs at the level of firms. In their survey of a range of female occupations, Craig *et al.* (1983) observed that, though complex, segregation was always strictly observed, and invariably the feminization of jobs went with low pay and status. Women's employment was subject to a kind of ghettoized status: once an occupation or a job was defined as 'women's work' many social pressures came into play which then reinforced the distinction.

> There was a time when women were considered unsuitable for jobs handling money, but building society customers are now said to expect attractive young female cashiers. Pharmaceutical dispensing has become so identified as a female job that the chemists had not received any applications from men, despite the general high level of unemployment. (p. 144)

Traditional custom and practice played a major part in sustaining this demarcation: 'women were allocated to particular jobs and excluded from others primarily because this had always been the case, at least as far as the current manager could remember'.

MALE POWER, TECHNOLOGY AND SKILL

Cynthia Cockburn's research (1983; 1985) has been very influential in focusing on the 'gendering process'. How do particular jobs acquire a gendered identity? Cockburn suggests that the active role that men play in differentiating their jobs from those of women is a key factor. (Other writers too have referred to male power as central in helping to structure segregation, e.g. Game and Pringle, 1983; Walby, 1988; West, 1990). Cockburn (1985) examined a number of occupations – clothing, mail order and radiography – where new technologies had disturbed the traditional job segregation. In some cases these had been opened up to women, and unisex situations prevailed for a while, but the long-term tendency was for jobs to re-establish gender identity. Men often left certain types of work if it became feminized and joined new occupations. Men may also move out of women's work through vertical segregation. Radiography was a traditionally feminized occupation which has attracted men in recent years. They bring career advantages, like being geographically mobile and not needing career breaks, and are beginning to fill up promoted posts.

However, the active role of male agents by itself is not enough; broader 'social gendering' acts independently of the workplace. As Cockburn points out, 'the gendering of men and women into "masculine" and "feminine" is a cultural process of immense power' (1985, p. 12). Indeed, gender segregation surrounds some of the strongest taboos and prohibitions in society. Given that our overall culture is gendered, then, it would be surprising if the gendering of work were not equally persistent. Cockburn was particularly interested in the *subjectivity* of job segregation. Her research showed that male workers often felt alienated and resentful if required to do 'women's work'. While some men welcomed women as co-workers, the majority 'scorn and despise women as workers and feel their manliness degraded by the presence of women in "their" jobs' (1985, p. 129).

Perhaps the most important aspect of social gendering concerns technology and skills. These are closely bound up in the sense that new skills evolve in response to emerging technologies. Labour process theory (see Chapter 10) explored some of the values that are implicit in the uses of technology, but other perspectives have shown how the 'maleness' of particular work situations is amplified by technology. Here Cockburn has emphasized the powerful affinity between men and machines, 'the identification of men with technology and of technology itself with masculinity' (1988, p. 38). Again this is partly a cultural process operating outside work. 'Technology enters our social identity: femininity is incompatible with technical competence; to feel technically competent is to feel manly' (1985, p. 12). Thus technology is a 'medium of power', and by colonizing technology men are claiming power for themselves and also power over women. But this process is greatly extended in the workplace where technologies are much more developed and potent. In operating the latest machines, men are working with equipment that massively increases the productive power of the human mind and body. Conversely, women's identities are constructed in non-technical ways. Supposedly lacking any natural mechanical know-how, women get excluded from a whole complex of skills and technologies and the power over work that this represents.

> Women are to be found in greatest numbers operating machinery but ... continue to be rarities in those occupations that involve knowing what goes on in inside the machine.... With few exceptions the design and development of the new systems, the people who market and sell, install, manage and service machinery are men. Women may push the buttons but they may not meddle with the works. (Cockburn, 1985, pp. 11–12)

Several of Cockburn's studies explored the theme of male-dominated occupations being displaced by technological change. For example, her 1983 account of printworkers was an extreme case of an occupation being entirely eliminated. The newspaper compositors were a classic labour aristocracy, contemptuous of other occupations in the industry, and their masculine identity was bound up with membership of an exclusive craft group. When methods of computerized typesetting came in, they were initially able to cling to the new semi-skilled jobs because of the strength of the trade union, but their position was fatally weakened and women began to enter the work. Cockburn reports much stress and ineptness, and resentment of the new jobs as 'glorified typing'. Some men, however, managed to recolonize the technology – they 'found different and better work as the new corps of higher paid, technical and managerial workers who minister to the computerised system' (p. 10).

Clothing was another industry with a powerful division of labour: pattern-making and cutting are a traditional male preserve, while sewing is women's work. But the introduction of computer-driven design and cutting equipment effectively destroyed the male crafts, and semi-skilled female operators moved in. In this transitional period men and women sometimes worked side by side on production teams, but Cockburn suggested that men would not work for long as semi-skilled operators beside women. Already men were moving into technician roles which maintained the sophisticated equipment, and they were acquiring a new status.

Turning specifically to skills, the relatively poor earnings of women mainly reflect their containment in low-skill jobs. However, although skills clearly have a material reality, they should not be seen as purely technical abilities. In important respects, skills too are socially created and depend on legitimation. It is not sufficient merely to possess a skill; practitioners have to be accorded a degree of prestige by society at large, which is determined by their power to protect skills. Thus the discrimination against women's occupational skills can occur at many levels. Where women do possess skills, these are often not recognized or accepted. Examples of women's jobs with as much skill or managerial content as comparable male jobs, yet with far less status and pay, demonstrate how women's tacit skills can be utilized by employers without women ever receiving the rewards commensurate with their efforts. Formalization of training plays a major part in this. Formal training schemes and apprenticeships, with a recognized certificate at the end, are frequently reserved for male workers, while women receive informal on-site training and are not then accepted as possessing equivalent skills.

THE SEX-TYPING OF WORK

The structure of workplace discrimination is sustained in important ways by stereotyped attitudes towards women's abilities – and these are mirrored in the demarcation between male and female jobs to an often remarkable extent. Much of the work performed by women involves the servicing of needs, such as cleaning, the care of children or the sick, and the preparation of food – tasks which directly reflect the nature of women's unpaid domestic labour. Other feminized occupations exploit sexuality and glamour (the model, the air stewardess), while semi-skilled manufacturing jobs rely on women's manual dexterity and supposed ability to cope with monotony. Thus very clear ideas exist about what constitutes men's work and women's work, and in all occupational structures men's work is defined in terms of access to skills, authority and technology, while women's work is low-skilled and service-oriented (Bradley, 1989).

Once a particular job or occupation becomes established as either 'men's work' or 'women's work', the myths and prejudices about the relative abilities of the sexes become powerful justifications for retaining the status quo. Thus the supposed inferiority of women as regards physical strength and mechanical aptitude has long justified their exclusion from skilled manual work. Also, women's supposed lack of 'decisiveness' and willingness to take responsibility are often the justification for excluding them from managerial and supervisory positions. In a similar way, the supposed 'female virtues' such as patience and tenderness have all been given as reasons for allocating women to a whole range of subordinate jobs. The secretary who is supposed to minister to her (male) boss, the canteen assistant who prepares food, the caring professions of nursing and social work, all are heavily feminized and in all of them women supposedly exercise special female skills.

Nevertheless, the sex-typing of jobs perhaps more than anything else reveals that these are socially constructed images. Take the biscuit factory that one of the authors researched, where managers insisted on the production jobs being 'women's work'. Nimble fingers were needed in the main tasks of sorting and packing, the work was repetitive, and it involved food preparation. This last point itself was somewhat far-fetched as the processing of biscuits on a conveyer belt

301

bears little resemblance to domestic food preparation. However, the other surprising thing was that the nightshift consisted entirely of men. Questions about whether the men had any problems coping with women's work – was the nightshift less efficient than the dayshift? – were denied by management and met with the simple answer that women would not work shifts. In the absence of women, the nightshift men were content that their jobs were not women's work. An example like this shows the persistence of sex-typing and how it can be maintained even without any real differences in the work. It shows these categories as artificially and self-consciously defined, rather than reflecting any 'natural' female or male attributes.

WOMEN'S WORK ORIENTATIONS

To emphasize the many ways in which workplace inequalities are imposed and maintained, in other words to focus on the *structure* of discrimination, inevitably paints a rather pessimistic picture of the role of work in women's lives, and some would say a static and one-sided picture. Feminist writers and researchers have tried to overcome this problem by concentrating instead on the actual experiences of women at work. Although this approach still reveals facets of discrimination, a much more positive view has emerged of women's commitment to paid work. Women's attitudes and orientations to work, their ways of coping with the problems of the workplace, and their motives for wanting to work all reveal a stronger attachment to work than earlier preconceptions of female employment would have allowed.

Research of this kind has shown that women do have distinctive experiences of work, which challenge the simple stereotypes of their economic role as being unimportant to themselves and their families. It is now clear, for example, that women's earnings are not, nor do women see them, as a purely optional extra to the male wage ('pin money'); women's reasons for working are firmly based on financial need. It is also clear that work outside the confines of the home, in a collective environment, can be a liberating experience for women just as for men. On the other hand, women's attachment to work differs from that of men in a number of significant ways. Husbands still tend to be regarded as the main wage-earners, so that a strong element of the image of men as the 'breadwinners' still survives – a fact we might expect from women's low pay alone. Neither do most women define work as their central role. Women 'construct' their lives as wives, mothers and employees in complex ways, balancing out domestic and employment responsibilities. The responsibilities for home and children are not left behind when women enter work but stay intimately with them; family matters are much discussed at work, for example, while tasks like shopping will be integrated in the working day.

However, it is important not to overstress the distinctiveness of women's orientations to work. As Dex (1985, p. 43) points out, 'men and women are more similar than was previously supposed' and what we increasingly see are converging attitudes and work experiences. Feldberg and Glenn (1979) suggest that women's work orientations often tend to be explained by an implicit 'gender model' which centres on the importance of domestic responsibilities, while male attitudes are held to reflect a 'job model' that assumes work as the central life interest. Having different explanations of workplace behaviour, however, can be misleading. One example that Feldberg and Glenn refer to is the finding that women often reject promotion opportunities if these arise. Conventionally, this is explained in terms of socialization, or the conflict with a woman's domestic role. However, gender-based accounts overlook the fact that 'promotion' may mean very different things for men and women. For men it is frequently the first rung on the ladder; but for women the first promotion is often the only advancement they can expect, and many will see little attraction in the pressures of, say, a supervisor's job if there are no further career chances.

Martin and Robert's (1983) interview survey of over 5,000 women discovered that most women now 'accept work as their right' and fully expect to work for most of their lives, only stopping when they have young children (or other dependents) to care for. The survey revealed a number of aspects of women's attachment to work. For example, women are returning to work sooner after the birth of their children. They can expect to spend longer total periods of their lives in work, rising from about 60 per cent for the post-war generation to approaching 70 per cent for young women today; and when women are not in employment they anticipate their return to work and retain strong images of themselves as workers.

The issue of redundancy and unemployment has a particular point to make, in the sense that the loss of jobs to women had been thought to cause few problems because they could always return to the home. Indeed the treatment of women as a 'reserve' of flexible labour, to be called into employment or laid off as employers and the economy demand, has always relied upon this notion of women readily giving up work and returning full-time to domestic duties. But recent studies of women's redundancy show that the loss of their jobs can be just as damaging in the lives of women and their families as it is in the case of men, Much the same hardship follows from the reduction of earnings, and women resent the loss of independence that in our

303

society depends utterly on having access to a wage or salary (Martin and Wallace, 1986).

Sexual stereotyping at work can also be re-examined from the point of view of women's active participation in work. Stereotypes are not simply cultural beliefs about women as employees; they serve a crucial *ideological* function in assisting the control and oppression of women by employers and men in general. Ideological beliefs, however, are not simply imposed from the outside; they are partially at least accepted by those under control. Only this element of 'truth' makes them effective and plausible. In this context, Anna Pollert's (1981) study of women's manual work in a cigarette factory – the experience of working-class women selling 'generalised unskilled labour power' – discovered powerful stereotyped attitudes held by managers and supervisors. She defined these as male-generated images of female experience, yet they were real for the women workers who had to 'live out' these stereotypes on a daily basis. Thus the supervisors firmly believed that women had an 'aptitude' for the repetitive, monotonous jobs that were typical in the factory. The women themselves rejected the crudest version of this stereotype, but they did accept their work as 'women's work' in the sense of knowing that no man could be persuaded to do it ('I'd like to see one of them do my job for a week!', p. 87). Although the women refused to believe in the fairness of low-grade jobs, they did accept the reality of themselves as cheap flexible labour, and of the necessity of this as probably the only way they could compete with men's labour. Pollert also analyses 'factory politics', or the relationship between male supervisors and female workers, and the complex ways in which 'sexual banter and pranks' served to bolster authority in the factory.

> Supervision was sexually oppressive, the manner usually cajoling, laced with intimate innuendo, and provocative jokes, hands placed on girls' shoulders as they worked, imposition mixed with flattery. To survive with some pride, without melting into blushes or falling through the floor, the girls had to keep on their toes, have a ready answer, fight back. They were forced into a defensive–aggressive strategy – but always on the men's terms. They had to collude. And in this they also colluded with the language of control. (1981, p. 143)

Thus sexist attitudes were the conventional rules of interaction of the workplace, accepted at a certain level by most of the female workers. But while the women were able to manipulate the rules to their advantage, they had to do this by exploiting their own sex appeal; so these were only 'momentary victories of self-assertion', serving in the long run to confirm their subordinate status.

COLLECTIVE CONSCIOUSNESS

One very pervasive myth is that the 'proper sphere' of women is not in public activity but in private and domestic roles. In industrial relations this is reflected in beliefs about women lacking any real consciousness or militancy, that they are unresisting as employees and that they dilute male collective efforts to win better conditions. Considerable efforts at challenging this widely held view have been made by feminist writers. Purcell (1979), for example, attacks the 'myth of the passive woman worker' and explains women's lower rates of union activity by the *nature* of much women's work. Factors like the high proportion of part-time work done by woman, the breaks in their continuity of employment, and employment locations like offices, make the organization of women workers relatively difficult. However, in an industry or occupation with a tradition of independent action, women are likely to follow these traditions rather than any supposed orientations as female workers (see also Lupton, 1963; Brown, 1984).

Hunt (1980) makes the interesting point that the 'isolation' of women in the domestic sphere may actually make them more militant. Women are less hidebound by tradition and bring to work expectations that serve to widen the struggle and include issues of control and working conditions – rather than just the narrowly conventional trade union objective of pay. And Beynon and Blackburn (1972) have criticized the attitudes of male trade unionists and their job protection strategies. They argue that we should not necessarily accept the popular image of trade union militancy; in fact many (male) unions are fairly docile, and in opposing them it may be women who are taking a radical stance. Thus Beynon and Blackburn found surprisingly positive attitudes towards unionism among women non-members. What the women objected to was the do-nothing attitudes of the male membership, their exclusion from the union and the fact that it was perceived as 'a men's affair'.

WOMEN'S CAREERS

A further factor indicating the dilemmas that women face in employment is the career paths open to them. Undoubtedly the major problem is that of combining the long-term pursuit of a career with care of a family. The fact that the responsibility for child care falls more or less exclusively on women, coupled with the poor provision by public welfare services for the care of young children, means that employment and family responsibilities become very difficult for women to combine. Thus, objectives which are usually wholly compatible for men are often incompatible for women. As Figure 13.1 showed, labour force participation rates fall sharply for women in

Case example: British Airways Cabin Crew

The job of airline stewardess presents a classic case of sex-typing according to sexuality and glamour. The key sector of the airlines' custom is business travellers, and the idea of the weary businessman ministered to by an attractive female retains a strong marketing image. Traditionally, selection and training of stewardesses emphasized appearance and grooming, and the job itself was always one that a 'girl' did for an exciting few years before 'settling down'. Recently, however, some airlines have been making efforts to improve equal opportunities, and this has meant creating real career prospects for stewardesses.

This case example looks at British Airways. In the mid-1970s, when the equal opportunities legislation first came in, BA had no promoted women in its entire cabin crew. Since then the company has managed to enhance overall career changes by creating new grades, and in the case of women by encouraging them to stay on. The figures below compare 1984 and 1991.

		1984		1991	
		Male	Female	Male	Female
Fleet Director	Long haul			45	20
	Short Haul			21	11
	767			11	2
Cabin service director	Long haul	224	13	317	102
	Short haul	75	2	197	104
	767			49	16
Purser	Long haul	409	62	704	725
	Short haul	268	121	224	421
	767			48	99
Steward/ stewardess	Long haul	928	1180	788	2664
	Short haul	250	865	264	1431
	767			75	242
Support cabin crew	All			56	557
Totals		2154	2243	2789	6394

Long haul is international flights and short haul is local/European. 767 is a new fleet operating a mix of long- and short-haul routes. Support cabin crew are employed on a permanent part-time basis.
Source: Reproduced with kind permission of British Airways.

We see that women have made considerable progress and by 1991 occupied almost one-third of the two top-level posts. In the first-line promotion of purser – this used to be the old post of senior steward and represents the bulk of promotion opportunities – women actually have a higher representation then men. Moreover, progress seems to be accelerating. The seven years up to 1991 saw much greater improvement than in the decade between the mid-1970s and 1984.

However, other trends are contained in the figures. The most marked change has been the feminization of cabin crew. Women have moved into the expanding occupation at a much faster rate than men (with the attendant implications for occupational status). Also, the long-haul division has a traditionally higher prestige than European, and women tend to be concentrated in the latter. A high proportion of women on the short-haul flights must work only with other women, and this is also where their promotion chances are best.

---

their mid- to late twenties, when the majority leave work to have children; and the difficulties of coming back to work after a break in employment are a major cause of a great many women having to return to a worse job than the one they left, or of being unable to retain any seniority rights in their jobs. The possession of a qualification can prevent this downward occupational mobility, but far fewer women than men have recognized trade or professional skills. There are some occupations, like teaching and nursing, which do cater more for women returning to work, although even here any upward career mobility is often halted.

Much sociological research has documented the rigid views that employers hold about the unsuitability of women as long-term employees. But there is also an important interrelation between the factors limiting women's careers and women's own aspirations. Rejection of responsibility at work, and the chance of promotion, because these conflict with domestic responsibilities, may come about because they *anticipate* the employer's prejudice. This then 'justifies' their being overlooked for training and promotion. Employers' beliefs that young women will leave work to raise a family may become a self-fulfilling prophecy, since, faced with few prospects of advancement, some women may indeed come to regard work as being of secondary importance (Crompton and Jones, 1984, p. 141).

Informal careers
Because gender divisions are structured in highly complex ways, the career chances of women can often only be understood in the context of specific work settings. Indeed, the very notion of 'career' for women can take on a subtly different meaning. Whereas for men careers simply consist of the climb up a defined hierarchy of positions, within an organization or a profession, the complex work histories that women have can effectively put an end to any hopes of this kind of structured progress. If women are to have careers, it quite often means that they have to create a niches in some alternative work situation. A good example of this comes from Attwood and Hatton's (1983) account of the gender, class and age factors that shape the career patterns of women and men in the hairdressing industry. This is sharply divided into primary and secondary markets, ranging from the fashionable and lucrative end of the business, to the lower-status

'shampoo and set trade'. Attwood and Hatton distinguished two very different career paths. 'Getting on' in the industry meant becoming a salon-owner or manager in the fashionable sector, and this domain was dictated by the male stylists. Female apprentices usually lacked the confidence to advance, but some women did create longer-term careers in the secondary sector and some became salon-owners. The researches stressed the sympathetic relationships that existed between these women and the mainly older working-class women who formed their clientele – a sharp contrast to the extremely competitive and exploitative world of 'fashion'.

Organizational careers

More generally, career paths in large organizations are invariably acutely competitive. Career hierarchies rapidly narrow down, and employers often have great difficulty in offering realistic promotion opportunities. With women competing for promotion alongside men, the chances for men would become significantly reduced. So there is often a strong imperative for employers to exclude female employees from the promotion race, as well as an effective collusion between employers and male employees underlining their common interest in excluding women.

Crompton and Jones (1984), in their study of clerical work, stressed that male clerical workers had good career prospects only because the vase majority of female clerks were denied promotion. They explained the very poor rates of female promotion in the banking, insurance and local government settings they looked at by a combination of factors: (1) women tended to be less well-qualified on entry from school and university; (2) far fewer women obtained post-entry qualifications, due both to 'anticipation of their withdrawal from the workforce' and to being discouraged by management; (3) their actual withdrawal from the workforce to have children was of 'enormous significance' in denying them careers; and (4) lack of geographical mobility, due once again to family constraints, also restricted women's careers. The researchers found that men's and women's attitudes towards work were remarkably similar, with little to suggest that employment was of 'secondary' interest to women (p. 149). There were, however, marked differences in attitudes related to just one factor: promotion. Many more men were interested in and expected promotion, and were oriented towards aspects of their work associated with 'promotability' (e.g. seeking responsibility).

> The picture that emerges . . . is that the majority of young women, especially if they are reasonably well qualified, initially approach employment with at least modest career expectations, comparable in many respects to those of men. (p. 159) . . . The really significant 'break' in the

women's attitudes . . . occurs among the group having made the most emphatic commitment to the domestic role – leaving work to rear a family. Whereas 79 per cent of young, unmarried women express an interest in promotion, this proportion declines massively to 29 per cent, among older women in the second phase of their work cycle. (1984, p. 156)

Within the vast majority of organizations there are powerful pressures towards internalized career paths and traditions of promotion from within. The type of long-term commitment this requires means that careers are rigidly structured, making re-entry after an absence extremely difficult. In another major survey, Fogarty, et al. (1981) looked at the progress women had made in managerial and professional jobs. In the four areas they studied – the civil service, the BBC, manufacturing industry and architecture – the researchers found that there had been a considerable increase in the numbers of women entering promotion paths in junior grades. However, they raised doubts about whether these changes would work through to the top positions because of the mid-career barriers women face.

The key finding of the case studies is that [progress through the middle grades] is in fact unlikely and by far the most important reason for this is the continued neglect by employers, and by other agencies such as public authorities responsible for community care for children, of the difficulties of reconciling a career with a family. (1981, p.9)

Women did not 'easily abandon their careers when they had children'. The failure rather lay with employers who refused to accept wider responsibilities for providing flexible working times and reinstatement after absence, and who simply defined any conflict between career and family as the employee's problem.

CONCLUSION: IMPLICATIONS FOR ACTION

The link between women's abilities and women's work, which seems natural to many, is in fact quite arbitrary, and beliefs about the allegedly inherent capabilities of the sexes can rarely be substantiated. In other countries and at other times women have done the work that nowadays tends to be defined exclusively as male, and vice versa. However, the myths and prejudices about women and employment remain powerful constraints, so that the essential basis of sexual inequality and the allocation of women to inferior work, however, that is defined, has hardly changed in recent years, in spite of the hugely increased economic contribution of women. The very high incidence of part-time and low-paid work, combined with the increased proportion of married women working, shows that the domestic role of women, their responsibility for the home and for child care, has not been changed by their entry into work. In other words, as Wainright (1984) has pointed out, women's participation in the labour force constitutes an *accommodation* to the traditional division of labour rather than any *erosion* of these basic inequalities.

In the Civil Service, women have made little progress. By 1991, although making up 48 per cent of staff, women formed only 13 per cent of Grade 7 (from which senior appointments are made), and there were no women at all in the senior management grades. Other surveys confirm that the male-dominated structures of professions and organizations remain unchanged. The National Economic Development Office in 1991 estimated that, while 27 per cent of managers were women, the proportion fell to only 4 per cent in middle/senior management, and less than 2 per cent in top management. Similarly, a 1991 Institute of Manpower Studies survey of 2,000 firms, with 1.1 million female employees, found that less then 0.02 per cent had children in crèches provided by the employer, and under 0.2 per cent benefited from flexible work practices (job sharing, working from home, working in school term-time). In 1991 women made up a higher proportion of the labour force in Britain than in almost any other European Community country, yet the British male/female earnings gap was the widest in the EC.

One of the key trends favouring women, however, is the changing composition of the labour force. The supply of school-leavers entering work is declining considerably, which means employers having to target groups such as women with children (as well as the long-term unemployed, returners, older workers, etc.). As we just saw, despite all the hype about crèches and job-sharing, very few women benefit from policies that make it easier to combine work with domestic responsibilities. However, some observers project new models of the 'family-friendly firm' as employers adapt their personnel policies to the demographics of 1990s (Berry-Lound, 1990).

Others too have pointed to positive trends. West (1990), for example, stresses that women are playing a crucial role in the restructuring of work. It remains true that many of the new industries offer low-skill and low-pay jobs, like security and contract cleaning; and even some high-profile growth industries, such as electronics and financial services, are often poorly paid. Yet capital requires skilled, responsible workers just as much as it needs to cheapen labour; and not all female work is in marginal occupations. To the extent that change means moving towards 'high-tech' – clean, quiet, physically less demanding – jobs, women's claim on work my be strengthened; at the same time new technology is creating occupations not yet sex-typed.

Cockburn (1985, p. 106) has suggested that 'capitalism' is less to blame than men for the exclusion of women from skilled work. She reports some prejudice among employers, but several who had experienced skills shortages appeared much more ready to take on qualified people of whatever sex. Interestingly, too, Cockburn notes that crossing the boundaries of sex-segregated work is much easier for women than for men. Women may suffer some initial embarrassment, but they usually have strong incentives to enter previously male jobs. What is crucial is initiatives and schemes that help women to acquire professional and technical capabilities, and which enable them to 'come forward' to meet the demand for skilled work. In this sense, Craig *et al.* (1983) were particularly interested in cases where women possessed equal value skills that went unrecognized and unrewarded. Such cases were appropriate for breaking into the vicious circle of workplace discrimination. Craig *et al.* (1983) argued that

> the jobs now normally performed by women should not all be dismissed as low skilled nor should women workers be assumed to be unwilling to become stable and productive employees. . . . An improvement of the position of women in employment requires as a starting point the reassessment of the demands made on employees in 'women's jobs' and recognition of the skills and abilities and of the effort exerted be female employees.

Finally, Ellis (1988) has argued that within trade unions – for long a main institutional agent of male oppression in the workplace – a 'minor revolution has begun'. Change still occurs mostly at the level of getting policies on women's issues into place, but unions are at least adopting increasingly positive attitudes towards improving women's labour market position. These then are areas where some progress may be being made. What is required now to make any meaningful transformation of the prevailing division of labour is change on a broader front, and this must involve the explicit challenges that women themselves are making at all levels in employing organizations, the trade unions and political institutions.

Further reading

Bradley, H. (1989) *Men's Work, Women's Work*. Cambridge: Polity Press.

Carter, S. and T. Cannon (1992) *Women as Entrepreneurs*. London: Academic Press.

Coyle, A. and J. Skinner (eds.) (1988) *Women and Work: Positive Action for Change*. Basingstoke: Macmillan.

Crompton, R. and K. Sanderson (1990) *Gendered Jobs and Social Change*. London: Unwin Hyman.

Davidson, M. and C. Cooper (1992) *Shattering the Glass Ceiling: The Woman Manager.* London: Paul Chapman.

Dex, S. (1985) *The Sexual Division of Work.* Brighton: Wheatsheaf Harvester.

Gamarnikow, E., D. Morgan, J. Purvis and D. Taylorson (eds.) (1983) *Gender, Class and Work.* London: Heinemann.

Hearn, J., D. L. Sheppard, P. Tancred-Sheriff, and G. Burrell (1989) *The Sexuality of Organization.* London: Sage.

Knights, D. and H. Willmott (eds.) (1986) *Gender and the Labour Process.* Aldershot: Gower.

Mallier, A. and M. Rosser (1987) *Women and the Economy.* London: Macmillan.

Spencer, A. and D. Podmore (1987) *In a Man's World: Women in Male Dominated Professions.* London: Tavistock.

Walby, S. (1986) *Patriarchy at Work.* Cambridge: Polity Press.

Walby, S. (ed.) (1988) *Gender Segregation at Work.* Milton Keynes: Open University Press.

Yeandle, S. (1984) *Women's Working Lives: Patterns and Strategies.* London: Tavistock.

14

New Technology

The account of technology given in Chapter 10 was concerned with the ways in which workplace behaviour was influenced by advancing production systems. However, these sociological debates have been overtaken in recent years by developments in the 'new technology' of microelectronics. Many people are convinced of the potential for far-reaching social change contained in these new systems. The so-called microelectronic revolution, based on computerized information networks, programmable industrial equipment, computer-aided design and the like, is expected to transform many areas of social and economic life (Forester, 1987).

New technology contains both threat and promise. The promise of a powerful new industrial economy beckons. Indeed, not to adopt the new technologies is seen as a form of economic suicide, since other countries of course will innovate, and some are already far ahead of us in this race. Potential threats arise if, as many people fear, the technology turns out to be a potent destroyer of jobs. Either way, the implications are clearly of central importance in an industrial society such as ours.

As we saw earlier, the approach taken towards technology has often been flexible and open-ended; it has been argued that a range of possible choices is available, and there need be no fixed or inevitable impact on work. Nevertheless, the new technologies are clearly labour-saving, and they have arrived at a time of unemployment. Thus the new technology debate follows hard on the heels of concern over British industrial decline, and public awareness of these issues is directly bound up with the concern over jobs. (This, incidentally, is in sharp contrast to the 1960s debate on the process industries, which occurred at a time of expansion and optimism for the future.)

In this chapter we shall look at some of the main arguments about the effects of new technology on work, in particular the effect on employment levels and on skills. First, though, it is necessary to look briefly at microelectronic technology itself, together with some current applications.

Developments in microelectronics

Microelectronics is an industry in its own right, the beginnings of which can be traced back to the development of the transistor shortly after the Second World War. This was the first device to use the semiconducting material silicon as a base for electrical circuits, and it replaced the existing vacuum valve. From its inception the electronics industry had needed to miniaturize components, and valve technology and evolved along these lines but always with major limitations. It was the development of semiconductors, however, that proved to be the crucial step towards the miniature components ideally suited to electronics. In the 1950s and 1960s the transistor market expanded enormously based on consumer appliances, like television and radio, and on the early commercial computers and military uses. New companies and the giants of the established electronics industry both exploited the exciting new technology. Then in the late 1950s the 'planar' techniques were developed which enabled very large numbers of electrical circuits to be packed onto a single chip of silicon. Since then the industry has evolved at astonishing speed, producing a stream of increasingly powerful and cheaper devices. The microelectronics industry is now fully independent of the electronics industry, with specialist semiconductor firms dominating the basic devices market (Braun and MacDonald, 1978).

The major users of microprocessors are the armaments, telecommunications and computer industries. Enormous numbers of the devices go into modern military hardware, into telephone systems and into computers and other business machines. But while microelectronics serves these major industries, it is the growing range of possible applications which has led to widespread interest in the technology. There is hardly an aspect of work which does not involve information-processing in one form or another. The decline in the cost of equipment and the remarkable capacity of microprocessors to extend the range of automation mean that it is becoming profitable to replace labour by machinery in many industrial and commercial activities. Among the applications currently in use are the following (Table 14.1).

1. The single most important piece of equipment is the computer. Large 'mainframe' computers are important in administration, for maintaining a basic filing system, but are increasingly used across the whole range of commercial and administrative activities. Visual display terminals provide access to centrally stored information at widely dispersed points throughout the organization. In addition, the new generation of smaller computers, as powerful as the older mainframes and far more adaptable, are coming into use in industry

as central processing units in integrated production systems. Also, the networking of computers, with central file-serving and database facilities, greatly increases their range and power. Local area networks (LANs) link up personal computers and workstations within a location, while wide area networks (WANs) provide long-distance data linkages.

Table 14.1   *User applications of microtechnology.*

COMPUTER-BASED SYSTEMS

Mainframe, mini and micro computers. Visual display units (VDUs). Local and wide area networks (LANs and WANs).

OFFICE INFORMATION SYSTEMS

Word processors, electronic filing, electronic mail. Electronic funds transfer. Tele-conferencing. Management information systems (MIS). Computer-aided design (CAD).

SERVICE SECTOR APPLICATIONS

Electronic point-of-sales (EPOS) systems, computerized stock control. Expert diagnostic systems. Automated laboratory analysis.

INDUSTRIAL MACHINERY AND AUTOMATION

Industrial robots. Computer numerically controlled (CNC) machine tools. Continuous process monitoring and control. Computer-aided manufacturing (CAM). Flexible manufacturing systems (FMS). Computer-aided engineering (CAE). Computer-aided production planning (CAPP).

INDUSTRY-SPECIFIC APPLICATIONS

Telecommunications: computerized exchange equipment, fibre optics. Printing: photo-typesetting, computerized composition. Media: electronic news-gathering.

MISCELLANEOUS

Energy monitoring systems. Plant security systems.

---

2. Within the service sector the new office technology is spreading very rapidly. One of the best-known applications, the word processor, has virtually replaced the typewriter in many offices. Also included is electronic funds transfer in use in banks, communications networks like electronic mail, and electronic conferencing systems. Outside the large office, electronic point-of-sales (EPOS) equipment is used in check-out procedures in retail stores, where the control of stock and shelving is also being computerized. And in laboratory analysis (medical, scientific, commercial) automatic testing is increasingly in evidence.

315

3. The range of applications in industry is just as varied, partly because much existing electro-mechanical machinery can be adapted using microprocessors. In all areas of manufacturing, machines that transform raw materials now employ programmable controls. There are computer numerically controlled (CNC) machine tools, the operation of which is controlled by built-in minicomputers. The CNC lathe is the most familiar example, but again in the engineering industry the range is very wide. These machines are often stand-alones, but they can be integrated into different systems of factory automation. For example, computer-aided engineering (CAE) involves the use of design data (from CAD) to control manufacturing processes; this type of system is also called CAD/CAM. Similarly, design data can be used in production control, or systems of shopfloor data-gathering, as the basis of computer-aided production planning (CAPP). And the application that has most caught the public's imagination is the industrial robot. Microprocessors in the robot's control system enable it to 'learn' the series of movements involved in routine tasks like spot-welding and paint-spraying. In addition, in plants using continuous-process technology, which may include activities as diverse as beer-brewing, flour-milling, chemicals and petrochemicals, micro-electronics can help to monitor and control plant automatically.

4. Lastly, there are industry-specific applications, particularly those in the 'information industries', such as telecommunications, the news media and printing. They are capital-intensive (especially telecommunications), but their product is information, and in these industries are found some of the most highly developed applications of microelectronics. In telecommunications, for instance, computerized telephone exchanges are replacing existing ones that use electro-mechanical switchgear, and optical fibres will eventually replace copper cable. In printing, perhaps the industry most affected, many traditional work practices have been completely transformed by computerized equipment for the direct input of copy.

This classification is not intended to be exhaustive, but merely to give some idea of the kinds of technology currently being deployed. It does, however, help to illustrate the variable nature of technological change. Different technologies have very different implications for production, and are themselves introduced unevenly. Thus there are certain sectors where the effect will be dramatic, others where it will be attenuated, and others still where there are no immediately obvious uses. Thus the likely impact of the technology on work will need to be considered in some detail.

NEW TECHNOLOGY AND MANAGEMENT

Before looking at these special problems, however, it will be useful to outline the managerial objectives and purposes behind the introduction of new technology, as there is a growing acceptance that the new systems also have a major impact on the management task and the structure of organizations. Returning to a theme we explored earlier, in Chapter 12, for a combination of reasons managers nowadays are compelled to act more *strategically* in relation to organizational resources and outputs than they have hitherto. Pressures of competition and receding markets have made it more or less a matter of survival that companies respond positively to these changes – and new technologies have emerged as both cause and effect in this process. On the one hand, they provide improved opportunities for strategic choice across the whole range of management tasks, while on the other companies find themselves having to adopt new technology merely to keep up with competitors who threaten to move ahead in capital investment. The new microtechnologies contribute to key managerial objectives. Fundamental management problems, such as the control and integration of activities, the provision of fast accurate data and the improvement of performance, are potentially enhanced by computerized management information systems.

However, it is possible to become too preoccupied with the potential of these systems, and to ignore the practical aspects of their application. As a counter to this specific problem, Buchanan and Boddy (1983) developed case studies in several different manufacturing industries which highlighted the 'realities' of technological change. They showed, for example, that rather than change always being sweeping, most innovations were introduced on a piecemeal basis and integrated at each stage with existing equipment. Where electronic controls replaced manual or mechanical ones, intervention by operators was still often needed. And the impact of performance objectives (cost, quality, workflow improvements, reduction of scrap, etc.) was often ambiguous – that is, different performance measures varied inconsistently, or management sometimes used new technology to make changes that could not be measured in performance terms, and the technologies themselves sometimes introduced new functions which were not comparable with previous systems. Therefore, in some ways there is nothing 'new' about new technology. The impact on work, as with all forms of technology, is complex and reliant on human judgment and decisions.

Other research has stressed the gap that frequently exists between strategy and its implementation. In the implementation of CAD in

317

design offices, for example, Currie (1989) revealed a wide variation in management strategies, because technology was being initiated and carried through by middle managers and technical groups. Often this was in the absence of any close strategic control by senior levels who originally allocated the investment. Likewise, Senker and Simmonds' (1991) review of CAD applications points to fairly widespread strategic failures. Lack of technical know-how among senior people often resulted in a considerable problem of the management of technology and expertise. This could result in too little spending on training, and on other back-up activities necessary to obtain the full benefits from equipment. Senker and Simmonds also found a hit-or-miss side to technology strategy. Firms in industries like electronics, which have related technical skills, implemented CAD far more effectively than other industries, such as vehicles and engineering: 'failure to adopt appropriate strategies for innovation, lack of appropriate technical skills, reluctance to change work organization and failure to adopt appropriate organisational structures can all inhibit the use of technology' (1991, p. 98).

Perhaps the most familiar question about the effect of computers on managerial patterns has been whether they will cause firms to become more centralized in their power structures, or whether the new systems will encourage a more flexibly organized firm. Of course, these are not the only possibilities. There are also indications of organization structures becoming polarized, with junior managerial and senior clerical grades being eliminated. The work performed at these levels essentially involves the collation and processing of information for forward transmission, rather than actual decision-making which is a middle or senior management task. Flexible modern computing systems are able to produce information of this kind automatically, so the strong expectation is that considerable losses of employment in junior management will result.

In practice, the pattern of decision-making, while not constrained by any fixed technological choices, has favoured the tightening of organizational control. Thus Child (1984, p. 261) has observed that various 'contextual' factors, like a complex market structure or primary task, may force firms to decentralize power to on-the-spot decision-makers. But new technologies sometimes now enable managements to centralize power without losing the flexibility of operations that is vital for effectiveness. Similarly, Robey (1977) detected an interesting pattern in a series of case studies of computerization. Here the majority resulted in less democratic forms of management control. But even in the minority of cases computers were never actually used to decentralize power; the existing level of decentralization was merely maintained. Studies like these indicate how new technology tends to be treated as a 'window of opportunity' to support the managerial instinct for centralized control.

The effects of microelectronics

EMPLOYMENT EFFECTS

A fundamental question about new technology concerns its impact on employment levels. One viewpoint is that new technology will result in a net increase in jobs. Industries like microelectronics, this argument runs, are the industries of the future, and we must embrace them wholeheartedly or face the consequences of national decline. The dynamism of the new industries means that the economy as a whole will be stimulated; and while jobs may be lost in traditional sectors, this is part of the normal process of industrial development and these losses will be more than compensated for by new jobs and additional economic demand created by new technology. Set against this argument is a far more pessimistic view. Even allowing for increased demand, from improved products and equipment using microprocessors, this second view stresses the massive potential of new technology for displacing labour across a range of industries and occupations.

It is no simple matter to prove the truth or falsity of these views. The technological changes to which they refer are far from complete; and in any case, as we have repeatedly stressed, the hardware component of technology is only one element. Just as important are the systems of work organization into which the hardware is introduced. This leaves considerable room for human choice as a determining factor. Nonetheless, some trends are beginning to emerge, and we can at least start to evaluate the initial impact of new technology on employment.

The general outcome of mechanization (and new technology is no exception) is to displace labour. In individual cases this need not apply: new equipment may be introduced to replace worn-out or obsolete plant, to improve production, or for some other reason that has no impact on jobs. But the *aggregate* impact of mechanization in a particular industry or occupation is to reduce the labour force. Taking the argument a step further, reduction of jobs need not then result in unemployment. If the economy is expanding, the labour displaced by capital investment will normally be absorbed. In times of near-full employment, workers may be redeployed within the same firm if their existing jobs are eliminated or they are usually able to find jobs elsewhere. However, at times of economic recession and high unemployment, the chances of finding another job are drastically reduced. It is then that job creation slows down, while technological change is still being channelled into the elimination of jobs.

The case for new-technology-based firms (NTBFs) being responsible for significant employment *generation* has been examined by Shearman and Burrell (1988). They point out that while much research does stress the dynamism of new firms, it confuses industrial regeneration with 'reindustrialization', the development of declining industries. Particularly in Britain, NTBFs have tended to be confined to the latter. True industrial regeneration involves new industries, with innovative products and new markets; but this has been relatively rare. Shearman and Burrell argue that the belief that NTBFs create new jobs is largely a myth – part hype over the new industries, and part 'entrepreneurial rhetoric' about small firms dynamically expanding into large ones. In fact, many entrepreneurs wish to expand only to be bought out, or they simply want to stay small. Thus 'the quantity of employment opportunities generated by NTBFs is not high' and is probably less than 5 per cent of all new jobs.

Similarly, the automatic linking of new technology with job *destruction* is equally problematic. Because new technology has coincided with periods of economic recession, the two developments are often connected in people's minds. However, during the 1980s unemployment caused specifically by technology in fact had a negligible impact. Estimates of technological unemployment suggest that, again, a residual figure of around 5 per cent of total job losses in manufacturing were actually associated with the use of microelectronics (Williams, 1984).

Despite the apparently limited direct employment effects of technical innovation, this is not to deny that the eventual impact may be massive. Many authoritative studies are pessimistic about the long-term threat to jobs. Even the optimistic arguments are very far from convincing; their optimism tends to stem from faith in unpredictable factors like state intervention and prolonged economic upturn, or in standard remedies like increased training and education, while they concede the near certainty of greatly reduced employment in particular sectors and occupations. In the past a dynamic service sector has provided perhaps the greatest grounds for hope (Gershuny and Miles, 1983). However, the level of service sector employment is now declining, and the build-up of service jobs, particularly evident over the last 40 years, seems to have come to a halt. If new technology is about to eliminate jobs on the scale suggested, there are no obvious major sources of new employment that we can look to.

To examine these issues more closely, we need to look at the links between new technology and specific areas of work. Three that have been singled out for attention in previous chapters are also pertinent here: manual work, white-collar work and women's employment.

Industrial employment
As mentioned above, the very high rates of unemployment in manu-facturing, up to the mid-1980s at any rate, were mainly attributable to familiar economic causes in the deepening recession in Britain and the collapse of economic demand, rather than to new technology. But in a number of specific cases there has already been considerable technological displacement of labour.

In many operations like assembly, testing and maintenance, the potential exists for labour forces to be cut back because work can be simplified to the point of merely inserting an electronic component or replacement part. Thus many manufacturing firms have greatly reduced their manual workforces with this type of innovation. Of course, some expansion of employment does take place as jobs move 'upstream' into firms making electronic components and machinery for the firms which fabricate final products. But the fact remains that in such cases a considerable *net* loss of jobs is estimated to have occurred.

In routine assembly operations industrial robots are increasingly being used – the lines of robots assembling car bodies, for example, have become a familiar sight. At present these first-generation machines can do only simple tasks, such as spotwelding, paint-spraying, drilling and some materials-handling. But 'intelligent' second-generation robots, equipped with sensors for vision and touch, will soon perform far more complex assemblies. They will be able to take over a far wider range of jobs, and the huge amount of employment worldwide still concentrated in assembly-type work will come under threat.

Another area of job loss is in some of the traditionally high-skill industries. For example, the information industries, printing and telecommunications, are both on the brink of very rapid change. Printing especially presents the major example of the elimination of skilled manual work to have occurred so far. Since the mid-1960s as many as one-quarter of jobs in the industry have disappeared, due to advances like computerized composition and computer-aided equipment for the direct input of copy. Martin's (1981) study of the newspaper industry in Fleet Street has shown how, by the mid-1970s, a new printing technology was available. The trade unions, while having to accept inevitable job losses, were at first able to retain existing jobs for their members. However, Martin repeatedly stresses the precarious nature of union control over the new tech-nology, because most of these jobs can now be done by workers with no craft training.

Office employment

Two related points bear on the argument here: first the suggestion that office employment is ripe for mechanization; and secondly that the technology to achieve this is now available. The first point relates to the fact that the productivity of office workers has been notoriously low, particularly if factory work is taken as some sort of benchmark. Considered as a *labour process*, most offices are not very efficient. Work study of secretarial and clerical jobs invariably shows quite a small proportion of time spent on directly productive work (typing, filing, etc.) It usually takes longer, for example, to walk to and from a filing cabinet than it does to file a document. When compared with factories, where tasks like materials-handling are usually automated or streamlined, office work is quite loosely organized. Given the continued growth in office employment, therefore, management have had a strong interest in improving productivity as a way of containing the size of office labour forces.

The relative inefficiency of offices in the past has been reflected in the low rate of investment in office machinery, and this has largely been because the technology necessary for office automation has simply not been available. In some ways office machinery has not progressed very far in the past hundred years. The most modern electric typewriter, for instance, is no different in essentials from the first Remington produced in the 1880s – and most other office equipment only enables paper to be handled more efficiently. The computer represents the first really capital-intensive piece of office equipment. But even here the first generation of commercial computers introduced in the 1960s, were invariably confined to basic clerical tasks of payroll and accounts.

New technology is set to change all this. The work done in offices is essentially information-handling, and microelectronics is an information-processing technology; it stores, edits and transmits information in radically new ways. Thus, for example, the word processor, with its storage and text-editing facilities, is fundamentally different from the conventional typewriter, and great claims are made for its ability to improve secretarial productivity. In many large office establishments it is common now for a small group of seven or eight people to be dealing with the typing for an organization of 200 or 300. Particularly where work is highly standardized, very large increases in productivity, of the order of several hundred per cent, have been recorded (Williams, 1984). Similarly, in the main areas of white-collar employment, like financial services (banking, insurance, building societies), the mechanization of the sector is rapidly gathering pace. Systems of branch automation in banks and building societies, management information systems, sophisticated new databases and the like are rapidly automating the bulk of routine clerical work. These powerful and highly integrated computer systems are also increasingly used in 'higher-level' tasks involving decision-making and the interface with customers. Storey (1986) has placed the growth of office automation in a longer perspective. He refers to the period up to the 1980s as a 'phoney war' when the threat of massive reductions in jobs always seemed to be around the corner, but never quite arrived. In fact, during this period productivity was rising, but it was being offset by growth in demand, especially in financial services. However, Storey argues, the real war has now begun: we see both a rapid spread of computer applications and a slow-down in service sector growth. Already by the early 1990s this was leading to some large-scale white-collar job reductions.

Women's employment

A third major concern about the impact of office technology is that women may bear the brunt of change. As we saw in Chapter 13, female employment is heavily concentrated in particular occupations and sectors, and while some of these do not seem directly at risk (particularly in social welfare, education and personal services), much female employment is focused in areas expected to suffer high technological unemployment. Office automation poses perhaps the major threat. About 2 million women in Britain work in clerical/secretarial jobs which are in direct line of fire of the new office technology (West, 1982). In addition, about three-quarters of a million women work in the distributional trades, and much of the work here (like stock control and retail sales) is being rapidly automated.

Despite such indications, the overall effect of new technology on female employment is likely to be quite complex. In clerical jobs, for example, gender issues and technology act on the work situation of women in a number of complicated ways. Clerical work has always been extremely important for women. These highly feminized categories of employment may have suffered a process of decline over the past two or three decades, but (as we saw in Chapter 12) they are still favoured, even 'middle class' occupations. As Liff (1990) points out, clerk represents the highest job status that any significant proportion of women achieve. And while technical change is now widespread, and part and parcel of the transforming status of clerical work, it is not usually seen as gender-specific or targeted on women. Indeed gender has traditionally been a barrier to mechanization, with male managers reluctant to lose the prestige they gain from a secretary or clerical subordinate. In other ways, too, women's jobs may prove rather resilient to the impact of new technology. Female labour is generally cheaper than male labour and so is less likely to be mechanized. Certainly the prime candidates for mechanization – expensive organized labour like car assembly workers, engineers and printers – are rarely female. Given the high proportion of part-time work that women do, they are also more flexible and hence attractive to employers during a time of recession.

The very fact of employers treating women as a flexible labour force, however, means that the *quality* of their jobs may be undermined in other ways. In a wide range of women's occupations, health problems are being linked with new technology. Particularly in clerical and secretarial work, marked increases in stress and related hazards like eyestrain, headaches and tiredness are being reported. Working at visual display units (VDUs) often means an increase in speed, concentration and monotony. Moreover, developments like retail payment systems (Visa, Access, Switch) have brought an expanding volume of data entry, and such work is almost always carried out by women. Some workplaces increasingly resemble the white-collar factory with large female labour forces inputting data under highly intensive conditions. As well as stress-related problems, increasing numbers suffer from repetitive strain injury (RSI), a term which covers a range of injuries to the hands, wrists, arms, shoulders and back. RSI is a symptom common to specific and severely disabling industrial diseases like tendinitis and carpal tunnel syndrome (acute inflammation of the hand).

Much ambiguity surrounds this issue, however, and VDU workers have found it almost impossible to win compensation cases. The incorrect installation of equipment or inadequate training for workers – which results, for example, in screen-glare or poor posture – are often blamed rather than the technology itself. With correctly used equipment and work breaks, experts suggest that there is no danger to health. Nevertheless, the forms of work organization and level of capital investment in many installations create pressures for an intense pace of work. Health workers recommend no more than 8–10,000 keystrokes per hour, yet many employers may be demanding double that. Thus in these sorts of case, even where the numbers of women's jobs are maintained, the quality of work might be adversely affected and might increasingly fall into the category of cheap and degraded or even sweated labour.

SKILLS AND WORK ORGANIZATION

Apart from labour displacement, new technology also has important repercussions on the labour process – on skills and on the ways in which work is organized. In Chapter 10 we reviewed the sociological debate in this area and compared models which stress the *deskilling* effect of technology and work organization with those which take a more positive approach and argue that there is no reason to suppose that the *regeneration* of skills is any less typical than their destruction. The parallel question arises here in relation to new technology: will the new applications on the whole degrade the skills of workers, or will they create new skills and enhanced opportunities for occupational development?

As before, a definitive answer lies beyond our scope, and in any case is probably not possible as the issue comes down to different viewpoints and schools of thought. However, one thing we have learned from the deskilling debate is that there is rarely a simple deskilling versus upskilling choice. Jobs may lose certain types of skill but retain others, or generate new ones; chances of promotion or other job boundaries may open up even if work is losing status, and there are crucial *subjective* factors that make people ambivalent even where a loss of skills seems obvious. The emphasis therefore must be on examining the detailed impact of applications and the choices that technology leaves open, rather than on seeking evidence for any generalized impact.

For example, the computer itself has created wholly new occupations and employment opportunities. Many thousands of jobs, ranging from unskilled assembly work to the highest level of engineering and system skills, have been created in the computer industry which simply were not in existence thirty years ago. Certainly this is skill (and job) creation on a grand scale. However, there are also indications of deskilling. If we take the occupation of programmer, in the early days of commercial computing the programmers controlled most aspects of machine operations. This was reflected in the level of skill required and in their status and pay. Since then, however, the job has been subject to rationalization. Higher-level work is now in the hands of an elite of systems analysts, while programmers mostly write routine specifications and are apt to be tied to specific types of equipment. This has caused a writer like Kraft (1979) to speak of the 'industrialization' of programming. On the other hand, the divisions of labour for producing software are changing fast and expertise is becoming distributed across complex organizational structures.

Friedman (1989) has argued that the deskilling thesis gives only half the picture. He proposes a three-stage model of computer systems development. In the early days of commercial computing, innovative programming was encouraged (or at least tolerated) in order to cope with poorly understood procedures and equipment; later a reaction occurred when much tighter work controls were imposed, which is the period that reflects deskilling. But more recently computing has increased greatly in its strategic importance, and the need now is to link it with wider organizational goals. This has meant more 'responsible' forms of work control and enhancement of the skills and autonomy of programmers.

To take a second example, that of the word processor, Baker and Downing's (1980) research has stressed the deskilling effect of the equipment on secretarial work. The skills of the secretary, they argue, are bound up with the presentation of the typed page – with layout, justification of margins, etc. – tasks which the word processor does automatically. On the other hand, word-processing does not eliminate the basic 'keyboard' skill of touch-typing, and the machine itself possesses more functions than a conventional typewriter, so there are new skills being created as older ones disappear.

Later research has painted a more complex picture. Thus Webster (1990) argues that there is 'no incipient tendency for word-processing to bring about a form of Taylorist control' (p. 117). Her case studies of eight white-collar work locations provide a detailed account of skills and tasks, stressing the *variability* of secretarial work. The context of the typing pool often did bring more repetitive work when converted to word-processing, but this was in contrast to employees with broader administrative control where the machines might enhance status and skills. Many of the women whom Webster interviewed found that word-processing enhanced their jobs, despite the tendency among managers to look down on work like typing. As she points out, it is the complexity of office jobs that gives secretarial workers control; word processors are more complex than typewriters and, other things being equal, are associated with more job discretion.

Crompton and Jones's (1984) study of the impact of computerization on clerical work presents a more straightforward account of deskilling. Traditionally, clerical work resembled a craft in the sense of being based on the clerk's special knowledge of the firm's filing system. However, Crompton and Jones show how computerized batch systems for basic clerical tasks, like payroll and accounts, have eliminated this control of information, and now clerical work mainly consists of preparing information to be fed into the computer.

> ... the value of the clerk to the employer once resided both in a detailed knowledge of clerical work procedures (the clerical 'craft') and also in the fact that, to varying extents, clerical workers have exercised control on behalf of capital.... The clerk now typically performs the function of (deskilled) labour, being increasingly peripheral to the performance of the computer and having little or no responsibility for the coordination and completion of the many separate work tasks in the process as a whole. (1984, p. 76)

Other studies have confirmed this basic picture. For example, Knights and Sturdy's (1990) account of the insurance industry found an entrenched sexual division of labour. These researchers argued that office technology brought about large increases in routine clerical work, and that these jobs became feminized and separated out from managerial and career jobs.

A somewhat more positive view of such changes is apparent in research where workers' own perceptions are taken into account. Thus in Liff's (1990) survey of women office workers, the bulk of respondents reported that interest and skill had increased. On the whole they approved of the changes; they were pleased at being able to perform the work more efficiently and to give a better service to customers, and they found mastering the new equipment a challenge (although stress-related problems had increased and new skills were rarely recognized by regrading). Rolfe (1990) has taken this argument a step further and pointed out that earlier research on technology, by the likes of Woodward and Wedderburn (see Chapter 10), did deal with workers' attitudes. It reflected a broader concern with issues of class consciousness, whereas the recent labour process emphasis has tended to play down the subjective aspect. However, attitudes remain crucial to the experience of technical change. Rolfe's own study of non-manual workers found that, even where deskilling occurred, people's attitudes were never wholly negative – at worst they were ambivalent. Experiences of deskilling were offset by a 'prevailing ideology of progress'. Attitudes towards change were conditioned by the perceived inevitability of technical change, and by the common-sense logic of any situation in which the job could be performed better.

Work restructuring that often accompanies mechanization can itself cause conditions to deteriorate. In the application of word-processing, for example, we have encountered several companies in which a typing pool, where the work was organized to some extent informally by the women concerned, went over to a much more closely supervised operation. With some of the more complex technologies, like computer-aided design and expert systems, forms of rationalization may also affect certain privileged professional occupations. On the other hand, the professions are renowned for their ability to cushion their members against these sorts of pressure; and in this respect new technology may be no different from other forms of rationalization. Thus it remains to be seen what the outcomes will be in the case of specific professional occupations.

Examples such as these indicate the complexity of deskilling and show the importance of the *work context*. A great deal depends upon the situations in which the new technologies are introduced; and the

327

purely technical issue, whether or not it is feasible to mechanize a given work process, is by no means the only consideration.

THE 'IMPACT' OF NEW TECHNOLOGY?

In this connection a number of writers have been critical of what they call the 'impact' approach, in which attempts are made to survey or predict the overall effects of new technology. The particular target of criticism is the type of analysis which proposes a simple relationship between technology and work. Here, new applications are matched with the existing jobs they might affect, often producing a 'hit list' of occupations at risk. The counter-argument the critics put forward is that the *implementation* of technology has to be seen as a much more complex process, involving social interaction. Any final 'impact' on work cannot be pre-defined; it can only be understood by focusing on the particular work context and the role of human agents. As Sorge *et al.* (1982) have argued: 'the constant reference to microelectronics as having "effects" is not often helpful; this glosses over the importance of industry-specific factors which become ever more important as microelectronics is used in an increasing range of industries, services and occupations'. In essence, therefore, this is an argument against technological determinism.

For example, Child *et al.* (1984) studied a range of different work settings in the service sector and argued that there is nothing inevitable about the way new technology is implemented. They found that, in cases of junior-level employees working with new technologies, elements of skill and control were lost and staff expressed dissatisfaction with the way the technologies impinged on their jobs. However, staff who had a developed professional ethic and a relatively strong organizational position remained in control of the new systems. Child *et al.* concluded that the effect of new technology upon work depends on the 'workplace power' of incumbents, and where key areas of organizational uncertainty are being controlled, technology can serve to enhance status and skills.

Case example: Computer numerical control

Computer numerical control (CNC) at first sight appears to be a classic Taylorist/deskilling technology. Machinery is programmed away from the shopfloor by specialist technical staff, and workers are reduced to tasks like machine-minding and loading. The old craft skills of reading engineering drawings and operating machine tools are submerged in the computer program which controls machine operations. Several studies, particularly some early ones, confirmed the loss of skills and showed that workers in complex, CNC-driven systems little resemble the conventional skilled machinist (Noble, 1978; Shaiken *et al.*, 1986). Moreover, the technical logic of CNC's development leads to what is known as direct numerical control (DNC), and this centralizes control even further. Under DNC, machine tools are programmed and scheduled from a central computer (rather than from individual minicomputers in the machines, as happens in CNC). This can make workers very remote from the centre of operations (Fincham, 1982).

However, other research has found that deskilling 'impacts' are crucially mediated by the fact that there is scope for workers themselves to program machines. A number of contextual factors in the strategies and practices of organizations, rather than technology itself, determine job design (Campbell and Warner, 1987; Burnes, 1988). First, managerial objectives and values may stress either the remote control of machinery or the involvement of the workforce. For example, Hendry's (1990) survey of CNC found factories where the strategy was to retain apprenticeship schemes and to retrain workers out of loyalty to existing workforces. Hendry also showed that management strategy can vary on its own, independently of other factors. One operations manager expressed the following very positive view:

> There are two ways you can do it. You can say to the operator, 'you just push the button, to start it and stop it; you don't put a finger on the programme'. And you'll have no development, neither in the person, nor in the component. But by having the man on the machine involved, he's found a better way round, and the company's gained the benefit of that, because he's applied his knowledge in paring down or improving the programme. (Quoted in Hendry, 1990, p. 33)

However, this policy was reversed by a later managing director who favoured the remote control of machine operations.

Secondly, the history of industrial relations and the nature of the trade union can influence skills changes and CNC automation. Shopfloor politics and workers' resistance (as we saw in Chapters 10 and 11) can shape the work situation. The collective resistance of employees has often been important in protecting skills and, in the case of CNC, in claiming involvement in shopfloor programming.

And thirdly, the nature of the engineering operation – whether repetitive light engineering or more skilled small batch engineering – will also have an effect. Our own research provided an extreme example in the case of marine engineering. This is very much at the heavy/high-skill end of the industry, and in these factories the scale of operations is such that deskilled workers would make little economic sense. As one worker we spoke to put it (he was machining a huge shaft for an ocean-going liner): 'You need a PhD just to sit and watch this machine' (Fincham, 1982).

Although sometimes acting independently, the above factors are more often merged into an overall work context. Thus in Hendry's (1990) study, covering seven factories, the impact on skills was 'affected by the existing skill base, the attitudes of employees and management and the strategic importance of particular groups'. He found in one case, where skilled male workers were concerned, CNC had enhanced skills and training and was 'eagerly embraced'; but in a shop containing women workers a major CNC investment had transformed their jobs into mere machine loading and visual inspection, while programming was done centrally by production engineers.

Case example: Computer-aided design

Computer-aided design (CAD) is another technology that has stimulated a large body of research in recent years. Studies have addressed the question of skills and the organizational implications of design automation.

CAD is a range of extremely powerful graphics systems that enable drafting and design operations to be reproduced on the computer. Drawing is done on screen with an electronic stylus, and the design then forms a database which can be stored and retrieved from the computer library. Advantages over manual drafting include the enhancement of drawings – sections, elevations, enlargements and image rotations are produced automatically, and intermediate drawings can be merged on screen. These bring efficiency gains as well as enormous improvements in drawing quality.

Attention was first focused on the potential of CAD for degrading draftsmen's jobs by Mike Cooley's research. The work of production design is increasingly fragmented and intensified by CAD, Cooley argued; manual drafting is marginalized, and only the elite few with design skills are able to use the system as a powerful tool. Also, the imposition of shift-working and bureaucratic hierarchies becomes necessary for this expensive equipment to be cost-effective (e.g. Cooley, 1987). Other research has likewise stressed the 'Taylorization of the drawing office'. CAD removes the craft element of drafting, and it contributes to routinization and managerial control because it enable drawings to be integrated centrally (Kaplinsky, 1982; Baldry and Connolly, 1986).

Nevertheless, as with some other technologies, more recent research has painted a more complex and optimistic picture. Researchers question whether managements actually pursue Taylorist strategies in relation to designers, or whether their objectives in adopting CAD are more varied and concerned with using their expensive labour more efficiently. The point has also been raised that earlier studies reflecting a Taylorist emphasis may have been based on anecdotal evidence, and may not support an overall trend towards deskilling (Jones, 1988). For example, McLoughlin's (1989) study of four drawing offices suggests that on balance the old manual drafting skills were being replaced by newer, conceptual skills. CAD did not diminish the need for engineering knowledge, instead its modelling systems enhanced the creative aspects of design. The survey that Senker and Simmonds (1991) conducted, which covered 32 establishments, also revealed mostly positive attitudes among designers; and they hint that the findings in early research may partly at least reflect a methods problem. Deskilling may in fact be relatively easy to identify, since it concerns the disappearance of familiar skills, whereas reskilling might be more difficult to spot as it involves new (and unfamiliar) skills – and, in the case of CAD, skills that are 'opaque' to the observer. Something of this problem comes through in this quotation from a designer.

My first impressions of CAD were unfavourable: I thought it took away a drafter's skills. But after learning to use CAD, I realised that the CAD 'only draws pictures'. It does not take skills of an engineer away – it enhances them. It does not take drafting skills away – you need drafting skills to produce good work on CAD. Advantages of CAD are that it is quick and you can do more complicated things. . . . CAD makes life easier. It would be a real pain to go back to the old ways of doing things. (Quoted in Senker and Simmonds, 1991, p. 97)

Furthermore, the impact of CAD on the social organization of work may have been overestimated. Senker and Simmonds found that the integration of CAD with manufacturing – to produce systems like CAD/CAM and CAPP – had hardly progressed at all. In most companies up to 1988 managerial objectives were confined to design automation, and electronic links to the shopfloor applied only to simple products. (Indeed, the opposite problem seemed more significant, namely the inadequate use of equipment and lack of any major organizational changes to accompany its implementation.) Moreover, studies in several European countries and North America have also challenged Taylorist predictions (Löwstedt, 1988). They find little evidence of any significant degree of organizational change, and indeed stress the determination of managements to introduce CAD without unduly affecting existing divisions of labour.

It would be misleading, however, to suppose that the earlier research stressing deskilling had been entirely supplanted. Somewhat paradoxically, the international studies lend some support to the view that in Britain at least CAD has had a relatively greater impact. Thus Lee's (1991) comparison of design engineers in Canada and Britain stressed the higher occupational status of the Canadian profession. In Britain CAD was seen more as an opportunity to rationalize the whole design process, and firms were under greater pressure to make productivity gains. A strong trade union presence in many British firms was at least as important in constraining attempts to impose flexible hours as was the goodwill of managers.

Conclusion: the future of work?

Whatever complexities exist in the relationship between technology and work, it would be wrong if we were to detract from the full scope and potential of advanced automation. For when one accumulates the evidence of areas likely to be affected – in office work, middle management, planning and mass production, as well as in specific industries like engineering and telecommunications – it is hard to avoid the conclusion that the medium- to long-term impact might be very dramatic indeed.

When new technology first began to attract attention it was often linked with extreme scenarios of future events. Optimistic scenarios looked to the benefits of a leisure society and an end to the alienating work of the industrial economy. The pessimistic scenario, in stark contrast, prophesied a future of mass unemployment and social decay. Depending on the route society took, each of these stemmed from the same belief that full automation in the long run would eliminate work in the traditional sense. The optimistic route meant expanding those areas which would creatively occupy people, involving a kind of mass programme of social planning and intervention. Or it meant relying on science and technology spontaneously to produce the solutions to society's problems. Both approaches tended to be rather idealistic and utopian. They assumed that an aggressive capitalist system gives rise to the problems of automation (in the sense that competitiveness and the drive for profit makes automation an irreversible process), but they assumed away capitalism when it came to proposing solutions. Equally, the pessimistic predictions rest on a society incapable of any level of planned intervention and impervious to the needs of its members. Many of these visions of the 'future of work' now seem far-fetched. Along the way, too, various mini-scenarios that were fashionable some years ago seem to have dropped out of sight. Who remembers the paperless office or the automatic factory now?

One thing that the experience of high levels of unemployment has amply demonstrated is that we remain a society geared to employment. People identify in a fundamental way with work, just as their material well-being in a market economy depends entirely on access to a wage or salary. This is the basic nature of the industrial society we live in, and whatever changes may bring us closer to the kind of 'post-industrial' or 'leisure' society that some envisage as possible, they will have to start out from these existing realities. Indeed, we have witnessed what seems like the opposite of the 'end of work' scenario. Industrialization is actually extending its logic into areas like the white-collar sector, which were previously regulated by less formal rules and forces.

Recent debate has turned on precisely these realities, which are fast catching up with a country like Britain. This has meant taking a comparative look at work systems in other countries, as well as extending the fairly narrow focus on technology to broader organizational and industrial structures. It is to these aspects of work restructuring that we turn in the final chapter in this section.

Further reading

Baldry, C. (1988) *Computers, Jobs and Skills: The Industrial Relations of Technological Change*. London: Plenum Press.

Braun, E. and S. MacDonald (19878) *Revolution in Miniature*. Cambridge: Cambridge University Press.

Buitelaar, W. (ed.) (1988) *Technology and Work*. London: Gower.

Burnes, B. (1989) *New Technology in Context*. Aldershot: Avebury.

Clark, J., I. McLoughlin, H. Rose and R. King (1988) *The Process of Technological Change*. Cambridge: Cambridge University Press.

Cockburn, C. (1986) *Machinery of Dominance: Women, Men and Technological Know-how*. London: Pluto Press.

Davidson, M.J. and C.L. Cooper (1987) *Women and Information Technology*. Chichester: Wiley.

Forester, T. (ed.) (1989) *Computers in the Human Context*. Oxford: Blackwell.

Huws, U., W.B. Korte and S. Robinson (1990) *Telework: Towards the Elusive Office*. Chichester: Wiley.

Loveridge, R. and M. Pitt (eds.) (1990) *The Strategic Management of Technological Innovation*. Chichester: Wiley.

Lyon, D. (1988) *The Information Society*. Cambridge: Polity Press.

McLoughlin, I. and J. Clark (1988) *Technological Change at Work*. Milton Keynes: Open University Press.

Scarborough, H. and J.M. Corbett (1992) *Technology and Organization*. London: Routledge.

Wall, T., C.W. Clegg and N.J. Kemp (eds.) (1987) *The Human Side of Advanced Manufacturing Technology*. Chichester: Wiley.

Zuboff, S. (1988) *In the Age of the Smart Machine*. Oxford: Heinemann.

15

New Systems of Work Organization

Flexibility and the new manufacturing

In recent years changes have been taking place in the management and organization of production which suggest that industry world-wide is going through a period of transition. Many people believe that the days of the traditional mass industries are numbered. Alternative approaches to manufacturing are taking over. The computerized technologies discussed in the previous chapter are important here, but the wider emphasis is on the market context and work organization in which technology is located. The keyword is *flexibility*: the use of labour and resources in a strategic fashion to enable production systems to be responsive to market changes. Flexibility means the removal of occupational barriers to the rational use of labour, and the creation of new skills that operate across a range of tasks. Such a level of responsiveness is regarded as vital in conditions of tough competition and market uncertainty.

Flexibility is not a totally new concern, of course. Lack of flexibility has been seen as a constant drawback of factory production. In historic terms the highly centralized factory replaced the more loosely organized systems of out-working that dominated in the seventeenth and eighteenth centuries (see Chapter 10). However, this process was protracted, and factory production and out-working existed side by side well into the nineteenth century. Out-working may have put a definite ceiling on efficiency, but it was highly flexible, which made it the perfect form of production for a still-evolving industrial society. As we shall see, forms of out-working hold the key to several of the new manufacturing methods.

The enthusiasm for flexibility reflects a belief that it can resolve the most stubborn contradictions of existing industrial methods. With traditional production systems, for example, huge output could be produced but at some cost to quality; or it was felt that you could have customized goods or cheap goods but not both, or that specialization in skills has been achieved only at a cost to the efficient use of labour. However, the new flexible systems, it is claimed, can provide customized goods at low unit costs; they can produce quality *and* volume, and they are held to be both specialist and efficient. Most of the main quality systems are engineering-based and were pioneered in manufacturing industry. They provide well-established methods of quality assurance and design and development. But there have also been reverberations outside manufacturing. The service industries have been swept by changes that have much in common with the ethos of flexibility: new definitions of quality, customer orientations and new market awareness.

The common interest in flexibility, however, exists alongside some important differences, which we follow through in this chapter. The British model that has achieved prominence in recent years is *the flexible firm*. Emphasis here has been on a set of employment and labour market practices that enable firms to respond quickly and cheaply to changing environments. However, the dominant economies of Japan and Germany are probably most directly linked to the new manufacturing. Some of these methods are well known, like Japanese *just-in-time* production. This involves new systems of inventory and supply, and an emphasis on novel production engineering concepts. JIT has attracted a massive amount of interest in Britain and America, its impact being seen as the 'Japanization' of our industry. Another approach, called *flexible specialization*, has been used generally to describe the most progressive types of new production system, based on full-blown responsible autonomy for workers. This has not had the same impact on Anglo-American management thinking, but has been linked to the successful German economy with its distinctive emphasis on flexible skills.

Like the new technology debate, the flexibility debate has strong tendencies to adopt a positive and enthusiastic line. Many accounts seem to consist merely of a description of some idealized version of flexible automation on the basis of which companies, industries, or indeed nations are urged to adopt the new systems or get left behind. However, there have also been more critical evaluations of the actual implementation of these work systems; evaluations which ask about the implications for labour, and whether the systems really can be seen as dramatic departures or whether they are developments of existing trends.

We will try to take account of both kinds of argument. In doing so we draw extensively on the account of industrial change developed in two books, Charles Sabel's *Politics and Work* (1982), and *The Second Industrial Divide* (1984), which Sabel co-authored with Michael Piore. These studies in many ways have set the terms of the flexibility debate. In them the two authors compare the different paths of industrial development in different countries. They avoid the modernizing tendency of seeing economic systems 'converging' on parallel paths of progress. But at the same time they see flexible specialization as the emerging dominant production form. They develop the broadest kind of framework, including cultural and historic factors, as well as interventions by the state and the strategies of labour and capital. But Piore and Sabel still take a basically 'materialist' view in the sense of seeing the roots of change in the changing nature of production systems. Their basic understanding is that the level of production remains the prime determinant of other levels of social and economic change. It is necessary to begin, however, by looking at the existing forms of manufacture.

Fordism

> *'A method for the efficient production of one thing.'* (Charles Sabel, 1982, p. 210)

In his 1982 book Sabel coined the term 'Fordism' to describe the method of production that has dominated western economies in the recent industrial period. Fordism reflects the rise of mass consumer markers and the standardization of products in the twentieth century. Fordism essentially means mass assembly carried out in the giant factory:

1. Work organization is based on very large, mainly unskilled labour forces.
2. A standardized product is built in massive volumes.
3. Product design is extremely important; products are designed to be easily assembled.
4. Production uses 'dedicated' (i.e. specialized) machinery designed for a given product and production system.
5. Tight control of the labour process is provided by systems of work measurement.

Above all, Fordism is typified by the *assembly line*. This vitally important production technique was invented by Henry Ford in 1913. Ford was the pioneer of mass-produced motor vehicles and the car assembly plant is often taken as the prototype of Fordism – although the principles of line assembly are used in many industries. The first assembly lines were the culmination of that key period, between about 1880 and 1910, when modern markets and production systems were emerging, and Sabel is clear about the breakthrough in industrial methods that this represented.

> ... however they hit on the idea of moving the work to the men rather

than the reverse, Ford's engineers knew at once that they had discovered a new secret of mass production. The first crude moving line cut the time needed for final assembly from just under 12.5 to about 5.8 man hours. It was as though the Ford engineers, putting in place the crucial pieces of a giant jigsaw puzzle, suddenly made intelligible the major themes of a century of industrialization. (Sable, 1982, p. 33)

Fordism has strong connections with Taylor's work system, *scientific management*. Whereas the assembly line is a production technique, scientific management is a control of production: 'Fordism accomplished by technology what Taylor accomplished by administrative means' (Sabel, 1982, p. 236). But the broad attitudes towards work, the persistent downward pressure on labour content and skills, are common to both systems. Taylor's ideas on work study were well established by the time Ford developed the assembly line. Indeed, the assembly line proved to be the perfect means for translating Taylor's ideas into reality. The extreme division of labour and repetitive work cycle on the line can be achieved only by the setting of standard times and work methods. Nevertheless, Sabel identified the age of mass production with Ford, rather than with Taylor as many others had preferred to do.

Case example: The Assembly Line

Line assembly is not a type of machinery or productive process. It is a *transfer technology*; it transports the product on a moving track or conveyer from one work station to another where components are assembled into it. Workers are stationed along the line under a strict division of labour with each job timed according to the line speed.

Like many great inventions, the assembly line is basically simple. If you think of the usual way of assembling anything – think of building a model aircraft – the article remains stationary and the workers move about, obtaining the necessary tools and materials to be assembled into the shell. This is known as 'dock assembly' since production takes place in a dock or bay. Most large scale products, like trucks, ships and aircraft, which tend to be produced in low volumes, are built by dock assembly. Ford's touch of genius was to reverse this natural method. The basic principle of high-volume line assembly is to move the work while the worker remains stationary.

The line has to be 'balanced' which means manning it for a specified range of tasks. Efficiency has to be paid for in terms of a high degree of rigidity in production. In a car plant, for example, the mix of models going down the line can vary only within strict limits – otherwise workers find themselves with either too little or too much time for performing the work cycle. In this environment variation in output creates high pressures of work, and ultimately quality and output deficiencies.

The assembly line is a *work-pacing technology*. It presents tasks to the worker on a regular cycle that allows little variation in the pace of work. For management this means very tight control over production. But for workers it means a major loss of control. Fragmented, deskilled jobs are bad enough, but having to keep up with the line can be extremely oppressive. It is the reason why this form of production has become a byword for monotony and alienation.

Fordism is not, of course, a total system. Around every large factory small supplier firms will grow up where Fordist principles do not apply; and a large proportion of all value added originates from smaller enterprises. A core of large firms with a periphery of smaller suppliers is also basis of *industrial dualism* (see Chapter 12 for discussion of the dual economy). There are strong reasons for relations between core firms and suppliers to persist and no signs that this structure is becoming rationalized. Small supplier companies are better able to keep wage costs low, while the concentration of labour under Fordism tends to push up wages and conditions. But this unevenness and variation, which occurs in all domestic economies, does not mean that an economy cannot be defined in a particular way. The basic industrial pattern can still be deemed Fordist in the sense that giant factories form the hub of the main networks of production and are crucial in the spread of new forms of work rationalization.

FORDISM AND POST-FORDISM

There are signs, however, that the Fordist system is being challenged by new kinds of work organization. Fordist principles – fragmented work, dedicated machinery, serial rather than parallel task-sequencing – create enormous economies of scale but have one crucial weakness, namely *inflexibility*. The presence of a secondary market of small suppliers introduces important flexibilities, but basically line-based operations can cope only with a certain amount of fluctuation in output. Henry Ford's famous phrase. 'You can have any colour you like as long as it's black', goes right to the heart of the assembly line: it works best producing a uniform product. Fordism is thus dependent on stable mass markets that can absorb its huge volumes of standardized output.

And, indeed, the mass markets which stabilized the Fordist system are now breaking up. Sabel argued that this has come about because of a number of global changes, but the chief factor is the changing nature of consumer tastes. The suggestion is that in the latter part of the twentieth century we are witnessing a structural shift in the nature of markets; they are fragmenting and becoming increasingly specialized. This is partly due to the success of Fordism itself. Markets have become saturated with manufactured goods. The enormous impact on social tastes and expectations of placing motor vehicles and other products within the reach of the mass of people has meant that consumers have become much more sophisticated; they are no longer satisfied with standard products. Increasingly, the demand is for customized products that incorporate quality and design features. These social, technological and market changes in the global environment of firms have left Fordism high and dry.

However, the thesis that Sabel (1982) initiated, and which was developed more fully in Piore and Sabel (1984), opposed any 'deterministic' outcome to the crisis. There are no laws of society or economy that automatically pick out the best kind of industrial system to succeed. Piore and Sabel hypothesized two main scenarios out of Fordism: an innovative and a reformist scenario, both of which have considerable uncertainties attached to them (Figure 15.1). Faced with crisis, firms could attempt to meet the demands to innovate, and shift to high-quality specialized products (which we shall explore more fully below). However, this innovative strategy means abandoning the production principles of Fordism, and it is uncertain whether firms could be so adaptive. Instead, firms might hedge their bets and develop types of 'neo-Fordism' which attempt to meet the demand for varied products while maintaining the basic Fordist principles of production. Piore and Sabel's thesis was that world economies are currently at a crossroads or, as they put it, a 'second industrial divide'. The innovative and the reformist paths both represent viable ways out of crisis, and embryonic forms of each can be detected in industrial systems in various countries.

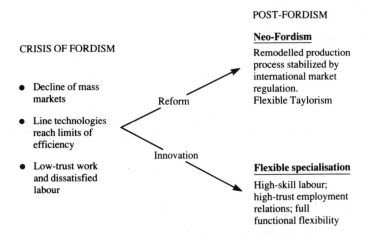

Figure 15.1   *The crisis of Fordism.*

If we consider the path of reform first, the neo-Fordist strategy has to be operated alongside a strategy of stabilizing mass markets. Neo-Fordism (only a variant of Fordism) is still affected by the fragmentation of markets. So the conditions for neo-Fordist solutions – making sure that enough people want to purchase the output of factories – have to be recreated. Piore and Sabel claim that management of demand on a world scale can already be detected. Institutions like the World Bank, the International Monetary Fund, and the European Community have strong policies for stimulating market demand.

On the production front, neo-Fordism involves piecemeal changes to improve efficiency by cutting costs, using labour more strategically, and new technologies which allow more flexibility. Sabel remains clear that these only reproduce Fordist forms of low-trust, intensified work.

> When reorganization involves the introduction of new, computer-based technologies such as numerically controlled machine tools or computer-aided design of parts, mangers perceive it as a bold step towards the Fordist ideal of the rationalized factory. . . . But if managers could step back from their work, as only a few of them can do, they would see that the present reorganization reinterprets Fordism as much as it perfects it and, depending on how workers respond to these changes, could perhaps undermine the existing factory hierarchies rather than reinforce them. (1982, p. 209)

It would be mistaken to dismiss such changes totally. Firms are extremely enthusiastic about these kinds of programme, which provide remodelled production and a degree of flexible automation. Indeed, some neo-Fordist approaches are further along the spectrum towards innovative production than others. For example, Berggren (1989) examines the Swedish car maker Volvo and its programme of work design. He traces the progress made in each of Volvo's plants, some of which score quite highly on the extent of integration of work team and production tasks. However, the dominant trend is what Berggren calls 'flexible Taylorism', i.e. a certain level of group working and upskilling but still based on machine-paced assembly. Thus these are 'modified solutions rather than qualitative changes' (p. 193), or types of neo-Fordism. (For a more detailed account, see the Volvo case study in Chapter 9.)

THE FLEXIBLE FIRM

These kinds of flexible methods and technologies came to be regarded by many firms during the 1980s as the only solution to market uncertainty and global competition. Particularly in Britain – where the problems of recession never seem far away – emphasis was on the removal of occupational and skill barriers to the rational use of labour, and replacement of the old demarcated crafts by more integrated working arrangements. These changes highlight two distinct faces of flexibility: *functional* and *numerical*. Functional flexibility is a work process factor that refers to flexibility across different kinds of production technology and to workers' capacity to overlap technical, maintenance and production work. Numerical flexibility is a labour market factor, and refers to employers' capacity to shed or take on the types of labour they require as market changes dictate.

Both forms of flexibility were combined in a new organizational model called *the flexible firm*. Originally developed by Atkinson (1984; 1985), the flexible firm is essentially an attempt to combine the control and efficiency of the factory with the flexibility of out-sourcing. A 'core' of workers who are well rewarded and secure, possess the integrated skills that the firm needs to perform its central tasks; they provide functional flexibility. Numerical flexibility is provided by a 'periphery' of workers in less secure jobs who can be hired and fired easily. These workers perform less important tasks and comprise different types of labour – temporary, part-time, agency employees, subcontractors, self-employed and so on. The flexible firm is therefore adaptable to market expansion and contraction (via numerical flexibility), and to qualitative changes in the demand for new types of product (via functional flexibility). It is a kind of small-scale dual economy, with core workers drawn from the primary labour market and peripheral workers from the secondary market.

With its complex labour structure the flexible form can pursue a strategic approach to labour utilization. Firms that want a stable workforce, with as little labour turnover as possible, can at the same time become less reliant on their workers – for example, by hiving off areas of production to subcontractors, or by mechanizing to eliminate skills. Headcount can be adapted to market changes, but key skills can be retained.

Evaluation of the flexible firm model
Despite apparent benefits, though, many have cast doubt on this model of the firm. To begin with two types of 'flexibility' may actually be hard to contain in any one firm because of the different meanings they have for labour. Functional flexibility needs to be underpinned by extensive skills training and should result in upskilling. But British firms' record in this area is very poor. Britain is virtually alone among advanced nations in leaving training to voluntary forces. Most employers define training as an unwelcome cost, to be cut during recessionary times, rather than an investment. In the 1980s, the

long decline in industrial training reached crisis proportions as firms reduced training budgets and the weakened unions were unable to safeguard apprenticeship schemes. So while there is some evidence of a shift towards the enlargement of job responsibilities and creation of firm-specific skills, the kind of serious investment in training that would be needed to create true multi-skilled workers has been sadly lacking (Lee, 1989).

British firms have tended to be much more interested in numerical flexibility. The broad trend appears to reflect a greater proportion of a secondary-type jobs, with labour increasingly used as a mere commodity. As Child had pessimistically concluded, this may be an attractive scenario for employers and a minority of skilled core workers, but a 'social problem of enormous proportions attends the rest of society' (1984, p. 265). In his own research Atkinson (1988; Atkinson and Meager, 1986) found that many firms were pursuing some version of flexibility, although very few were adopting the full version of the model, and that change overall was relatively limited. Indeed, Wood (1989, p. 7) has queried whether many firms ever pursue these kinds of systemic and coherent strategy. Can firms actually design this kind of complicated core–periphery structure?

Anna Pollert (1988) has confirmed the view that most of these claims are exaggerated. She surveyed a wide range of labour process and labour market practices and points out, for instance, that areas like out-working and temporary work show no signs of increasing; these traditional industrial sectors have always been with us. Part-time work has been a massive sector of employment in Britain, but it is stabilizing now, and in any case reflects the need for reserves of cheap labour rather than for flexibility. Pollert concludes that the flexible firm is something of a myth. The model is really a construct of trends that exist singly but are not actually present together in any one enterprise. The enthusiasm for the model in fact has come mostly from political quarters. During the 1980s the British government became strongly committed to the flexible firm as a new employment policy. It reflected broader interest in curbing trade union power and removing restrictions on the use of labour. From the employers' side, the concept of flexibility also tended to be expressed at the strategic level but, again, not necessarily followed through in practice. The reality, Pollert suggested, is mixed: certain kinds of flexibility have increased but the main feature of recent industrial relations has been the removal of employment rights.

Flexible Specialization

This brings us to the search for more meaningful examples of innovative work patterns. Is there any sign in the industrialized countries of production systems that make a decisive break with Fordism, and go beyond neo-Fordist solutions? Piore and Sabel, in the most influential part of their analysis, coined the term *flexible specialization* to refer to such systems. The flexibly specialized firm is diametrically opposed to Fordism with its intensive, fragmented work systems (Figure 15.1).

Defining this new production regime precisely is a little difficult. It is not a specific technique, such as the assembly line. Piore and Sabel (1984, p. 259) emphasized the link between computer technology and flexibility. They were enthusiastic about the use of programmable machines because such technologies allow production runs to be modified without breaking down the machine sequence, and permit customization at low unit cost; they can also be controlled by workers, thus enhancing skills. However, this is not a 'technical fix' or a determinist argument. Computer equipment could just as easily be used in a rigid, deskilling mode. Production policies aimed at enhancing skills, and the demand for customized goods from changing consumer tastes, are also prerequisites. Additional features stand out in Piore and Sabel's model. The production process itself is reshaped and its components remodelled to provide adaptable responses. The flexible specialized firm utilizes a high-skill labour force. Old craft demarcations have evolved into a multi-faceted skills that support integrated production systems. Worker–management relations are high-trust and the work itself conforms to meaningful job redesign. Others have also adopted this broad definition. Wood, for example, talks of

> the new flexibly specialized firm which can quickly respond to sudden changes in costs, market opportunities and/or new technologies, through adapting flexible, multi-purpose equipment and creating a flexible re-integrated and cooperative workforce free of the shackles of rigid job specifications, narrow job-centred orientations and excessive regulation and control. (1989, p. 11)

How far the flexible specialization model has become a reality is unclear – which is perhaps to be expected if we are in the midst of industrial and social change. Some have suggested that it might best be seen as an *ideal*; Fordism and flexible specialization represent the ends of a continuum, with neo-Fordism as the 'middle path'. The space between the extremes is where we should explore for real-life work systems. This differs from Piore and Sabel's original usage which clearly saw neo-Fordism as reproducing the classic problems of Fordism. Piore and Sabel surveyed some of the major industrial nations and concluded that the innovative path out of crisis remains confined to relatively small sectors within economies still dominated by mass production. Any attempt to visualize an entire economy based on flexibility is 'an exercise in imagination' (p. 258). However, they drew a distinction between one group of countries (Italy, Japan, Germany) where the 'success stories' do at least extend to geographic regions or industrial sectors, and other countries (United States, France) where examples of flexible production are embryonic and 'founded often in opposition to the organizing principles of the national economy' (p. 222).

We can look at some of these countries separately. In Italy the example of the so-called Third Italy was originally picked out by Sabel (1982, p. 220) as a case of 'high-technology cottage industry'. In this area in the north of the country, networks of small firms have successfully developed a range of industries including textiles, ceramics and machinery (Murray, 1985). In Japan the application of NC machinery across small firms in the machine tools industry has also reflected flexible reorganization. By contrast, in the United States there have been only hesitant moves towards flexibility. America, of course, is the home of Fordism and Taylorism, and this legacy has meant that neo-Fordist solutions have dominated. The response of US corporations on the whole has been marked by protectionism and attempts to saturate existing mass markets. As Piore and Sabel argue, America is still trying to make the rest of the world play the game it knows best.

The German case is more interesting. Piore and Sabel acknowledge a much wider movement there toward flexible specialization across major industries like steel, chemicals, machine tools and cars. But they still classify Germany with countries (Italy and Japan) where 'the success stories are not so exceptional'. However, other writers (notably Lane, 1988) claim that Germany is one country where innovative production has been established economy-wide. The German case is thus worth examining in more detail. First, however, we can put together a country-by-country analysis of flexibility trends. Three broad bands of countries can be detected (Figure 15.2):

1. A lowest band in which moves towards flexible specialization are restricted, and may sometimes merely be new forms of work intensification masquerading as 'flexibility'. Piore and Sabel describe France and the USA in these terms, but we could also nominate Britain for this category, where industries like engineering and motor vehicles have a long history of deskilling.

2. A middle band of countries where the success stories are more wide-spread. This includes Japan and Italy, and to these we might add Sweden. As we saw in Chapter 9, the Swedish motor industry, especially projects like Volvo's Uddevalla plant, measure up to the flexibility criterion.
3. In splendid isolation Germany represents the main example where the shift to greater flexibility has really challenged the mass production paradigm.

Exceptional success stories	USA	Saturation of mass markets, protectionism
	France	Bureaucratic, state-supported growth in mass production
	Britain	Skills polarization, low-trust industrial relations/restrictive union practices
Success stories 'not so exceptional'	Italy	'Third Italy': high-technology cottage industries
	Japan	NC equipment in machine tools industry
	Sweden	Volvo, Saab: autonomous work groups
Relatively widespread flexibility	Germany	Steel, chemicals, machine tools, motor vehicles

Figure 15.2 *The spread of flexible methods.*

FLEXIBLE SPECIALIZATION IN GERMANY

The German industrial system, as we have said, may represent more than a short-lived or small-scale triumph over Fordism. Lane (1988) in particular has built on the work over the past two decades of a group of German researchers (notably Kern and Schumann, 1984) who have argued that Germany virtually alone among industrial nations has embraced a new strategy of production. This claim is based on research carried out in industries including chemicals, automobiles, machine tools, food-processing and shipbuilding. These are all large-scale industries, neither 'cottage industries' nor regionally confined. German production patterns consistently reflect product quality and diversity and adaptive methods. Taylorism is replaced by new forms of labour deployment defined by the overlap between specialisms and the retention of skills. Lane points out a number of features of German industrial development that link it to flexible specialization.

1. Surviving craft traditions

Piore and Sabel focused explicitly on craft orientations as the only genuine alternative to mass production (1984, p. 222). The presence of craft skills were a reminder of other possibilities and resisted trends towards total Fordism/Taylorism. Germany has traditionally been a producer of customized goods for export, but in the 1960s it moved towards 'Americanization' and mass production. By the 1970s it had become clear that German industry was losing its competitive edge, and in the 1980s it began to shift back 'ever more deliberately towards flexible production' (Piore and Sabel, 1984, p. 234). Lane confirms this but goes further and argues that Taylorist methods never really took hold in Germany at any period. There has been some imitation of the Fordist model but far less than has happened in, for example, Britain. The craft model has not merely survived; it has adapted and been modified, with skills being constantly updated.

2. Polyvalent skills

A resurgent craft tradition has meant that the manual working class as a whole in Germany still contains a predominance of skilled workers. Even in mass production the growth of these industries has drawn heavily on multi-skilled workers, with a resultant emphasis on group working and labour flexibility. Such 'polyvalent' skills are based on a wide range of task experiences acquired by job rotation during training.

> Polyvalency of skill permits a broad and flexible utilisation of labour across boundaries between production work on the one side and technical and maintenance work on the other. Polyvalency has not, as in the case of British craftsmen, been undermined by the erection of highly formalised barriers between skills. Polyvalency of the German type also furthers co-operation within workgroups across hierarchical divisions and thus provides a natural foundation for the institution of semi-autonomous work groups. German semi-skilled workers' training, although less broad and deep, is nevertheless also systemically oriented towards polyvalency. (Lane, 1988, p. 144)

German industry employs the interesting term *Berufsarbeiter* for multi-skilled workers in mass industries. The word literally means 'professional worker' – which in Anglo-American usage would be self-contradicting. How can you be a professional and a worker when 'worker' carries the meaning of unskilled manual employee? Yet this reveals cultural differences in the basic conception of skill. In Britain we have a narrow *occupational* meaning of skill; there are certain occupations (brain surgeons, engineers) that are defined as skilled and others (assembly-line workers, shop assistants) that are not. If you happen to be a shop assistant, say, you cannot be skilled. In contrast, in the German industrial culture even 'unskilled' workers can be skilled – if they take pride in their work, exercise some discretion, are good at what they do. Thus it is possible to be a skilled unskilled worker – a *Berufsarbeiter*.

Case example: Flexible Skill Strategies

This case example concerns the German and British subsidiaries of a multinational car manufacturer. The company-wide job structure was based on a three-tier system of grades: A, B and C. A-graded jobs were purely for new entrants; B-grade jobs were for workers who had acquired the necessary speed and skills to perform a job on the line; and C-grade jobs were for multi-skilled workers who could perform several different types of assembly work, and tasks like basic maintenance and quality control.

Although this wage/skill structure was identical in both plants, the distribution of skills was very different. In the British plant the vast majority of manual employees were on the B grade and were regarded simply as normal line workers. Workers on the highest grade, the so-called C-men, were in a minority of around 10 per cent and were used as a labour pool. In cases of absenteeism, particularly on difficult or critical jobs, production foremen tended to request a C-man.

In the German plant, however, a far higher proportion of employees, between 60 and 70 per cent, were C-graded. The grading system was seen as kind of career structure for labour. Workers were encouraged to acquire skills and to move through the grades, and job rotation and training were provided to help them do this.

Significant points about this case include the difference in *managerial attitudes*. This was a company with a very strong corporate policy for uniform production operations across all plants, irrespective of national differences. Despite this the German management had secured the resources needed to maintain a high-skill workforce. The British attitude was to use skilled labour only selectively. Also important is the fact that the case is from *mass production*. This was a typical Fordist industry associated with deskilling. But the German management still succeeded in upskilling workers.

---

3. High-quality industries

For the past thirty years the German industrial strategy of producing high-quality goods for export has been based on technical and design excellence, rather than low price. In motor vehicles this is clearly illustrated by firms like BMW, Mercedes, Audi and Volkswagen. German firms are also in the forefront of the machine tool industry, and for many mass-produced consumer goods 'German-made' is

THE SOCIOLOGY OF WORK

synonymous with quality. Industries like these are fertile ground for the survival of craft skills.

Thus in many large German industries work is characterized by upskilling, holistic tasks and group working. Computerized technology in particular has not led to deskilling as it has elsewhere. In the engineering industry, for example, as we saw in the previous chapter, the new technology of CNC machine tools has been integrated with trade skills; by contrast, in Britain CNC appears to have accelerated deskilling trends. Changes like these in Germany are the basis of claims for a fully fledged industrial policy of flexible specialization. How has Germany been able to achieve this? In large part it seems to reflect historic patterns. Germany seems to have got a number of key national policies right. State intervention in getting financial bodies to invest in industry is the opposite of British and American *laissez-faire*. At the same time Germany manages to avoid the pitfalls of the French type of bureaucratic interventionism. The role of the state in Germany has similarities to Japan. But compared with Japan, Germany seems to enjoy an even greater national consensus, particularly the deep-rooted belief in the skills of the ordinary workforce.

Lane (1988) has highlighted other features of German industrial culture which may explain this approach to workplace regulation:

1. A harmonious, 'high-trust' form of industrial relations. The approach of German management of raising all labour to the highest standards assumes that an expensive labour force will pay for itself in terms of commitment and flexibility. There is also more confidence about the balance of control; German managements are not continually seeking tighter workplace regulation, but accept that effort and worker autonomy are compatible.
2. German employers have pursued functional rather than numerical flexibility. There has been little attempt to casualize employment or undermine job security.
3. German employers have managed to maintain a 'virtuous circle' of training and investment. High levels of expenditure on new technology have necessitated investment in training because only skilled and committed workforces are able fully to exploit the technology and justify capital investment.
4. German managers themselves are highly qualified, having a strong predominance of professional engineering skills. When managements are themselves skilled, they are less interested in deskilling others. (This contrasts with a country like Britain, where poor levels of management education have often been suggested as a cause of

348

shopfloor deskilling; in other words, deskilling is a means of control that reflects management's own insecurity and lack of skills.)

Evaluation of the German model
Piore and Sabel (1984), as we have said, concluded that flexible specialization was still not a consistent pattern even in German industry. The main question mark for them was the terms on which labour would be absorbed into the new systems. Similarly, in the first half of the 1980s, German researchers accepted that it was only a minority of workers in the primary industries who were involved in flexibly organized production (Kern and Schumann, 1984; Altmann et al., 1982). But by 1988 Lane was arguing that the flexibility trend had emerged more strongly. Labour market conditions – low levels of unemployment plus large quantities of skilled labour – favoured flexible/responsible patterns. Lane suggested that the most recent evidence points to a strengthening of flexibility trends that the earlier research had picked up.

However, there are some less optimistic factors we can point to, in particular the unification of the two Germanies. The staggering cost of modernizing East German industry may prove to be unaffordable – at least in the context of the stable industrial order and strong social welfare systems that have sustained the flexible forms of work organization. Cheap labour from the East and potential unemployment may undermine these unique labour market conditions and tip the balance in favour of Americanized mass production (Wiedermeyer, 1989). Also the factual evidence still needs verification. As Wood (1989, p. 34) points out, some of the research on which the flexibility claim is based seems to have been conducted fairly loosely, using only simple observation and small-scale interviews. The trend of the 1990s will therefore need to be carefully assessed. Nonetheless, the argument is persuasive that in Germany the progressive restructuring of work along non-Fordist (rather than neo-Fordist) lines does reflect a distinctive new production strategy.

Just-in-time and Japanization

If we turn now to the other wonder economy of the past thirty years, the rise of Japan to the position of a major economic power has long attracted attention. Japanese industries seem to have developed as if the entire country has been on a learning curve. Japan grew through clear-cut stages, first copying western technology and being known for cheap consumer goods of doubtful quality; then Japanese industry gradually overhauled western companies producing for the most sophisticated markets like consumer electronics, cars and engineering machinery. The main motive behind western interest in Japan has undoubtedly been the head-on competition with our own industries. For two decades or more Japanese companies have been capturing markets in the United States and Europe – bringing out new products and models, design improvements and extra features at a cost and frequency that local manufacturers seem unable to match. How do they do it? and Can we learn it too? are questions that are asked repeatedly.

Japanese ascendancy has been attributed in the past to many factors, among them cultural and historic factors. Japan was a feudal society until little more than a hundred years ago, and came very quickly into the industrial era. This was thought to provide tight vertically integrated industrial and financial structures (Sakai, 1990). In particular, the broad cultural factors with which Japanese society seems imbued – the extreme diligence and self-sacrifice of workers (the supposed Japanese of ethic of 'living to work') and the capacity to identify with common goals at all levels of the organization – have been regarded as the bedrock of Japan's phenomenal industrial success.

More recently, though, another explanation has gained ground, namely that Japanese success is in large part due to Japanese management's organization of manufacturing. A new form of work organization has been identified: the system known as *just-in-time*. Just-in-time production has the same basic objective of all post-Fordist systems: to achieve flexibility while retaining the economies of scale of the assembly line. JIT achieves this by ideally producing only the amount at each stage of production necessary to complete the next stage. A simple definition of JIT might be that it is a system for delivering the exact quantity and defect-free quality of parts just in time for each stage of production.

With the focus on systems of manufacture, the desire to emulate Japanese success has taken a new turn. 'Japanization' has come to refer to the transformation of industrial practices, especially in countries like Britain, according to the JIT model. Japanization works on different levels: British firms in increasing numbers are adopting Japanese practices; there are attempts to get British workers to absorb the social attitudes of Japanese workers; Japanese inward investment in this country has provided direct experience of these management techniques; and JIT methods are now regarded as a kind of global best practice in the production engineering professions.

JUST-IN-TIME PRODUCTION

The basic features of JIT can be outlined as follows.

1. *A pull system*. The traditional assembly line operates with each

work station on a fixed schedule, which in effect means pushing work up from back-end work stations. If one stage of assembly fails or slows down, work piles up causing overproduction and storage problems. But JIT systems are more responsive because production is 'pulled' through from the front end. Work at any given stage only goes ahead when some type of signal is received from the stage in front. This is achieved via the so-called *kanban* system of parts control. Kanban principles can be observed in very simple systems of racks for components: when a kanban rack is emptied by the forward worker using the component, this activates production by the rear worker to replenish it.

2. *Total quality management.* A just-in-time system has to be operated with the reciprocal concept of total quality. This means using defect-free supplies of parts and materials – not 99 per cent or even 99.9 per cent but 100 per cent quality. The reason is that when exactly the right amount of parts is being supplied, just in time, any quality defects would immediately halt production. Of course, total quality management is itself a massive cost-saver and the basis of customer satisfaction.

3. *Stockless production.* In assembly-line production, traditional push systems need to be 'buffered' with internal stock zones. On lengthy assembly lines it is impossible to have every section working to the specified schedule. So assemblies are taken off in buffer zones (like being shunted on to a siding) and the stock is used to return the line to the correct schedule. But the buffer stock represents waste; capital is tied up and there are deterioration costs. Reducing buffer stocks ideally to zero is a key objective of JIT.

4. *JIT supply relationships.* Just-in-time principles should also extend upstream to a firm's suppliers. This means smaller, more frequent deliveries, synchronized with the main plant's production. The ideal is line-side deliveries that go straight into production. If JIT methods are used in the supplier plant as well, a complete production–supply chain can be achieved. Indeed, in practice when firms decide to adopt JIT methods one of the first things they look at is relationships with their suppliers. In traditional assembly-line or large-batch manufacture, it is common for the main assembler to require suppliers to compete against each other on price and delivery. But a central principle of JIT is the strong relations that develop between companies and their suppliers. When firms move towards JIT they shift to a smaller number of 'preferred suppliers' which enjoy long-term contracts and a more supportive relation with the main plant.

These production principles result in a number of important advantages. Perhaps the central one is the removal of the safety net that is normally provided by stocks of materials and systems of inspection. If parts are introduced straight into production, any quality faults have an immediate impact. The genuine threat that the process really would grind to a halt puts pressure on all groups (workers, supervisors, suppliers) to operate a total quality regime. Japanese-style production also embraces other methods, like team working. A variety of control tasks are typically assigned to workers, such as inspection, simple maintenance and materials-handling, so that they form self-supervised groups. Long, straight assembly lines undermine JIT principles, so flexible, shorter units are used, or U-shaped lines which encourage communications. Quality circles are typically employed as well. These involve a period of discussion at the end of each workshift to review the day's problems and suggest remedial action.

JUST-IN-TIME PHILOSOPHY

In addition to concrete policies, though, Japanese management thinking is infused with a deeper set of ideals. In many respects the real criticism of western methods that JIT implies lies in its simplicity. JIT philosophy is suspicious of complicated systems of production control, and in some ways is even anti-technology; it is very much a back-to-basics ethos. A main element is that of *kaizen* or continuous improvement. JIT is a multi-sided never-ending programme for cutting out forms of waste. The ethos of production improvement means examining everything that happens as parts move through a production sequence. The aim is to increase the throughput of work, focusing exclusively on operations that add value and eliminating the forms of time-wasting that add cost but not value. This is where worker involvement becomes critical. In the West, the streamlining of production has traditionally been the task of specialist engineers, but the kind of methods improvement programmes that the Japanese have in mind depend on the broad mass of workers bringing forward problems for solution. For instance, Toyota claim that in 1990 over two million improvements were suggested by their employees (an average of thirty-five per employee) of which 97 per cent were adopted. Systems of team working and quality circles support this level of participation. But the key factor is an attitudinal change: rather than ignore problems or feel that little will be done if they are highlighted, workers must feel encouraged to seek out problems.

Somewhat ironically, the Japanese themselves often react with annoyance at the interest shown in JIT, or refuse to accept that it represents some objective new production system. They see the whole idea as an invention of western (largely American) business commentators anxious to place a simple label on the Japanese experience. In this context Zipkin (1991) has distinguished two different versions of JIT: the idealized and the pragmatic. Idealized JIT stems from the worry that the American business community originally felt that Japanese manufacturing excellence was unlearnable because rooted in culture. In response a set of production principles that could be marketed and copied has been defined. By contrast, the pragmatic version of JIT comes from the Japanese pioneers of the system. Instead of seeing JIT as some kind of technical fix, they stress the accumulation of small gains and the long time periods needed to get a JIT system in place.

There is some justification for stressing JIT as a process of incremental improvements. After all, ideas like the advantages of operating with minimum stock, or that quality should be built in rather than inspected out, are hardly new. The difference is that the Japanese appear to have done something about it. Rather than merely exhort workers to 'get it right first time', or run half-hearted 'suggestion schemes', Japanese firms have actually created systems of stockless production and responsible autonomy.

CRITICAL EVALUATION: THE LIMITS OF JUST-IN-TIME

Or have they? There is no doubting that Japanese success has been built at least partly on the country's production strategy. Yet there have been some highly critical evaluations of who has borne the cost. Questions have also been raised about the limits to the application of these methods outside Japan, as well as their actual impact inside the country.

An intensified labour process

Any major production system has complex effects on human factors. Advocates of just-in-time see it as being based on new forms of task variety that enhance the work environment. Some have argued that when workers experience new forms of efficiency and responsibility at first hand, their morale is automatically boosted. This kind of claim, that merely being a part of a progressive new system is its own reward, seems somewhat abstract. But JIT has been placed within the broad movement towards worker involvement. Team working and high-trust industrial relations, the basis of the flexibility of JIT, are also behind theories like Human Relations and sociotechnical systems, and job designs intended to enrich work.

On the other hand, there is mounting criticism about the potential of JIT systems for intensifying work. Some accounts of conditions inside production plants describe an incredibly intense pace of work (Klein, 1989; 1990). Long overtime hours increase the image of workers' lives given over to production. (Excessive overtime tends to be part and parcel of a JIT supply system because workers have to finish each batch, rather than working to the clock.) We saw that Piore and Sabel considered the Japanese machine tool industry as an example of genuine flexibility, but work intensification seems much more the pattern in industries like automobiles and electronics (and their interpretation of the case of machine tools has been disputed – Berggren, 1989, p.172). Others would certainly place Japan on the neo-Fordist side of Piore and Sabel's 'industrial divide'. The products on which Japan's industrial miracle has been based – cars, videos, TVs – are all mass produced, and the quality and specification that make them so competitive come from refinements and extensions to the assembly line. As Wood says, 'nothing in these innovations implies an end to mass production' (1989, p. 33); or again, as Berggren strongly argues, the Japanese are the 'modern masters' of standardization and Taylorism (1989, p.172).

More specifically, the idea that JIT can eliminate 'slack' from the system (idle time, buffer stocks, work-in-progress) and still be human-centred is hotly disputed. In conventional large-batch/line systems, important forms of worker autonomy depend on informal practices of producing for stock (like working 'up the line'). But in a JIT system work is initiated only when there is an immediate production need, so workers have little control over the pace of work. Having to be responsive to kanban discipline thus means even less discretion than in conventional systems. Oliver (1991), for example, has listed a number of ways in which a JIT environment is likely to be more stressed than a buffered one. Stockless production may actually involve increased idle time (because there is no production for stock) and so be objectively less intensive, yet workers may experience increased insecurity and pressure because they lack any control over a body of work to be completed. Workers are more 'hooked up' to the system; the removal of inventory means that work units become highly interdependent, so there is more lateral pressure from other groups and less scope for work group autonomy. In addition, there is nothing in practices like team working and multi-skilling that necessarily enhances work; it depends entirely on how they are applied. Multi-skilling may simply mean an enlargement of responsibilities, while the work group becomes the context for removal of restrictions on the use of labour.

Supplier and labour market relationships
Market-based relations also have implications for the nature of work. A 'close' relationship with a big manufacturer can be a double-edged sword for a supplier. The preferred status relationship is based on the supplier's capacity to provide just-in-time deliveries. But the demand

for zero defects and frequent deliveries may in reality mean inter-
ference with the supplier's business. The motive has often been that
of the main assembler using its monopoly power to squeeze suppliers
for additional burdens of delivery and quality. The application of JIT
methods upstream should in theory remove these causes of friction
between companies and their suppliers. But the supply-chain concept
has proved unrealistic. In reality, suppliers firms often have to expand
their own stock levels and pressurize workers in order to cope with
JIT deliveries. Thus the overall production system may be no more
efficient; the inefficiencies are merely being moved about and the
costs borne by the weaker partner.

In the USA and Europe production trends have favoured integration – that is, for the work done by suppliers to be taken over by
main assemblers, so that a relatively high proportion of value added
comes from the big manufacturing plants. In Japan the balance
between internal and external production is very different. The
country has one of the most strongly developed dual economies of
all industrial nations, and the high rate of out-sourcing reflects the
responsibility borne by networks of suppliers. This can mean savage
downward pressures on labour. Unionization levels and working
conditions in the secondary sector are relatively poor, so costs can
be cut by shifting production there. Critics have argued that this is
a central part of the JIT rationale – to offset tendencies to create
expensive, centralized labour. In this sense, the popular image of
Japanese lifetime employment is partly a myth; it applies to perhaps
20 per cent of Japan's workers employed by large companies. The
other face of Japanese employment is a massive sector of 'sweated'
industries that feed the major companies. For example, Sakai (1990)
points out that in the consumer electronics industry the costs of
constant redesign and product improvement that make Japanese firms
so competitive are borne by anonymous suppliers.

> How extensive is the sub-contracting pyramid? Would you guess a few
> dozen companies? A few hundred? Think again. One electronics company
> I know has well over 6,000 sub-contractors in its industrial group, most
> of them tiny shops that exist just to fill a few little orders for the companies
> above them. Welcome to the real world of Japanese manufacturing.

Sakai likens the relationship between the giant companies and their
suppliers to almost a master–slave relation, with the big firms ruthlessly ordering price cuts from sub contractors whenever their competitive position comes under threat. There is also a dynamic relation
between primary and secondary sectors. Workers in the large companies tend to accept intensified labour because dismissal would mean
moving down into secondary sector jobs.

This market structure has led to doubts about the *transferability* of Japanese methods. Outside Japan industrial dualism is not usually so pronounced. For example, Turnbull (1988) has examined the British West Midlands motor industry and found several cases where supplier firms resisted attempts by motor manufacturers to impose new demands. Workers have also been quick to realize that JIT systems are vulnerable to industrial action. Low stock levels and production integration mean that they can be operated only in the absence of disruption from labour, which gives workers considerable bargaining strength. Turnbull found that firms like Austin Rover were mostly interested in JIT delivery as a way of shifting costs on to suppliers. But he reports a number of cases where companies had to climb down in the face of threatened industrial action after trying to impose wage or price cuts.

Conclusion: post-Fordism and the restructuring of work

Interest in new forms of flexible work organization has revitalized debate about the nature of work. That debate was examined in previous chapters (mainly 9, 10 and 14), and many of the themes have surfaced again. In particular there are implications for the most influential and long-running argument about work: the deskilling debate and critique of Braverman (Chapter 10). Braverman, we recall, put forward the controversial idea that under industrial capitalism work becomes progressively degraded and deskilled, especially as a result of Taylorist work practices. A tide of criticism of the deskilling thesis suggested that this was a one-sided view, though there were also some notable defences of this basically Marxist position. The interest in flexibility confirms much of the criticism, but offers some interesting support for Braverman as well.

The flexibility thesis suggests a broadly favourable view of industrial society, one that clearly challenges any ideas of work degradation. Braverman assumed that deskilling was a specifically *capitalist* trend. Yet the economies in which flexible methods may be emerging are certainly no less capitalist for that. Piore and Sabel saw flexible specialization as a way out of the crisis of Fordism and the alienating conditions of the assembly line. Flexible specialization stresses the potential of new technology to upgrade skills and 'opens up long term prospects for improvement in the condition of working life' (Piore and Sabel, 1984, p. 278). There are echoes, too, of Blauner's old technology trajectory thesis (Chapter 10). We recall that this proposed industrial society would come through an era of degraded labour conditions and generate a progressive and harmonious economic culture. In this sense we might classify Piore and Sabel under a broadly positivist approach, which stresses the spontaneous generation of improved work forms.

Yet flexibility is nothing if not a complex concept. In some perhaps unexpected ways it opens up the debate about the nature of work. For instance, another criticism of Braverman was that he saw in Taylorism the purest expression of capitalist rationality and allowed for no alternatives, nor for the fact that Taylorism itself might eventually be superseded. In contrast, the concern with flexibility implies that Fordism/Taylorism has reached the limits of its technical efficiency. However, this point can easily be turned round. If Japanese-style production is neo-Fordist and is increasingly characterizing our employment landscape, then the broad thrust of the deskilling thesis is confirmed. Piore and Sable themselves, it should be remembered, did not directly challenge the idea of work degradation. They suggested that the breakthrough in flexible methods in countries like Italy, Germany and Japan was where the future lay, but neo-Fordism was no less likely an option. Furthermore, in highlighting Germany as the chief example of flexible specialization, writers such as Lane implicitly accept that countries like Britain and the United States are typified by deskilling.

Perspectives on change

However, the debate has gone far beyond simple ideas of deskilling or upskilling; market and occupational factors are involved, as well as work organization. The global backdrop to these changes is the transition from a period of settled economic relations dominated by a single economy, and based on relatively stable industrial technologies. The changing balance of international power has seen US domination give way to domination of the Big Three. Japan now has overtaken the USA in total investment, and by the end of the century is projected to outstrip the USA in the size of its economy; Germany exports half as much again as either the USA or Japan. Here Lash and Urry (1987) speak of a new era of 'disorganized capitalism' – more competitors, greater market orientation, and industries that restlessly seek an edge through flexibility and the use of microtechnologies.

Amidst such uncertainties the debate over work restructuring is very much alive. Just as in the last chapter we saw that there were enthusiasts for and critics of the new technology, there are also some very different perspectives on flexibility. Philimore (1989) has distinguished three views: optimists, pessimists and sceptics. Optimists stress the new work forms as a way forward for progressive work design and positive industrial relations. Models like the 'Third Italy' or Japanese methods are regarded as potential future prototypes of work (Murray, 1985; Wickens, 1987). Pessimists reject the idea that labour flexibility can benefit workers and employers equally. Under the new 'partnership' between labour and capital, enhanced work and wages exist within a transformed set of exchange relations whereby workers take on responsibility for higher quality and productivity (Holloway, 1987; Gorz, 1990). The sceptics fall into a number of camps. Some argue that it is greatly oversimplified to speak of a single transition from mass production to flexible specialization (Williams *et al.*, 1987), and others that all these methods are open-ended and depend heavily on how they are implemented.

In a sense, of course, we are all sceptics. The lessons of the Braverman debate have been well learned, and few astute observers express unqualified optimism or pessimism but they remain aware of the variations across occupations and sectors. Surveying the research evidence of the recent period, Tony Elger points out that some people are doubtful about whether the flexible methods have actually spread beyond a few enclaves and support a 'not much has changed' view; others suggest that under the impact of new demands for flexibility there has indeed been a radical restructuring of work. Elger himself argues that extreme views are misplaced. It is possible to define dominant patterns in the restructuring of work while still accepting the enormous variations in the impact on work. He discounts the idea that in Britain at least the quest for flexibility has brought change 'in the direction of polyvalent high-trust team-working'. Rather 'the mix tends to remain that of increased flexibility at the margins through job enlargement and intensification, coupled with more concerted management efforts to enhance their control' (1990, p. 91).

Pattern and variety

One of the chief problems of the post-Fordism debate has been agreeing terms. A number of the contributions tend to use the single label 'flexible specialization' to refer to *all* current changes. Just-in-time, the flexible firm, etc. are all regarded as forms of 'FS'. The emphasis then is on studying the new production systems – industry by industry, or even factory by factory – each on its merits (e.g. Philimore, 1989; Wood, 1989; Coombs and Jones, 1988). This follows Piore and Sabel's original understanding, although we should remember that since then the varied experiences of production systems have come into much sharper focus. However, there are problems of definition even here. Reading between the lines, some of those who regard flexibility as a generic model seem to have a specific model in mind. British researchers in particular often see FS as the flexible firm; they project that moves towards flexibility will pose challenges to the trade unions and divide workers within core–periphery structures (Philimore, 1989; Pollert, 1988).

We have taken a rather different line and made strong distinctions between different cases of 'flexibility'. The flexible firm, flexible specialization and JIT were each linked to a national culture. Our approach has its own drawbacks. It might easily underestimate the flexibility movement as a force for change. Also, by lumping together all 'Japanese methods' or all 'German methods', there are obvious dangers of underestimating the differences within countries. On the other hand, there are certain advantages to be gained in making some attempt at comparative distinctions, and in clarifying the differences between the forms of work organization currently on offer.

One important distinction lies in the varying impact that flexible systems have had on management thought and practice. Japanese systems have registered by far the largest impact. Talk of the 'Japanization' of Anglo-American management contrasts rather oddly with a far lower level of interest in German manufacturing methods. The sense in which Japan has taken the West by surprise, and the new phase of Japanese multinational growth, may explain the interest in that country. But why not the 'Germanization' of our industries? Germany is possibly an easier industrial culture for us to understand, and the German economic miracle has been no less impressive. No, the popularity of the Japanese model seems to reflect the close match between Japanese methods and the Taylorized industries of the United States and Britain. The weight of evidence we saw points to JIT being a revitalized Fordist system, and this makes more immediate sense to British and American managers, given the production habits they are used to. The German model, with its emphasis on high-trust industrial relations and upskilling, would be much more difficult to assimilate into our industrial culture.

Further reading

Hyman, R. and W. Streek (eds.) (1988) *New Technology and Industrial Relations*. Oxford: Blackwell.

Kamata, S. (1983) *Japan in the Passing Lane*. London: Allen and Unwin.

Lash, S. and J. Urry (1987) *The End of Organized Capitalism*. Cambridge: Polity Press.

Lawrence, P. (1980) *Managers and Management in West Germany*. London: Croom Helm.

McMillan, C.J. (1989) *The Japanese Industrial System* (2nd edn). Berlin: de Gruyter.

Ohno, T. (1988) *Toyota Production System*. Cambridge, Mass.: Productivity Press.

Oliver, N. and B. Wilkinson (1988) *The Japanization of British Industry*. Oxford: Blackwell.

Pollert, A. (ed.) (1991) *Farewell to Flexibility?* Oxford: Blackwell.

Sorge, A. and M. Warner (1986) *Comparative Factory Organization*. London: Aldershot.

Wood, S. (ed.) (1989) *The Transformation of Work?: Skill, Flexibility and the Labour Process*. London: Unwin Hyman.

Work, Employment and Society (1990) 'The 1980s: a decade of change?' Special issue, May.

Section Four

Organizations

If the issues dealt with in Section Three were mostly concerned with aspects of the division of labour, there is another major dimension along which the structuring of work takes place and that is the division of power and authority. This 'vertical' dimensions embodies the hierarchy of control which forms the basic structure of the modern large-scale organization. A closely related aspect of this has already been discussed in Chapter 10, namely the systematic methods of work organization (like Taylorism) which brought about the rationalization of labour. We considered these as part of the labour process and the employment relationship, but they could equally have been included here, for they hinge on the central theme of the control that managerial groups exercise over subordinate groups of workers.

Historically, these methods belong to that important period in the last quarter of the last century – from about the mid-1870s to 1900 – which saw the emergence of what today we would recognize as the modern industrial economy. In this period industry in America and Europe was transformed. The new work methods emerged against a background of new technologies, like chemicals and steel, together with the new manufacturing and mass production industries. During the 1880s the commercial office and government bureaucracy first appeared. And all these enterprises were being managed on a much larger scale than had hitherto been either necessary or possible. Altogether, an industrial and commercial landscape was taking shape which was quite different from the small-scale capitalism of only twenty or thirty years earlier.

Seen from another perspective, what was happening was the rise of the modern organization. Presthus has summarized this process in America as follows:

Beginning about 1875, social, economic and political trends in the United States prepared the way for the 'organization society', characterized by large-scale bureaucratic institutions in virtually every social area. The

361

master trends included the separation of ownership from management; increasing size and concentration in business; the decline of competition as financial resources required for entry in almost every sector became prohibitive; and the emergence of an employee society (1979, p. 84)

The importance of these changes is easily appreciated. Many of us will spend all or some part of our working lives in large organizations, and we will be their clients and come into other forms of contact on countless other occasions. This should not be exaggerated, because as much as half the total employment is still provided by small firms. Nevertheless, the organizational setting has had a profound effect on the nature of work.

In this final part of the book, we will look first, in Chapter 16, at the sociological study of organizations. This is a subject that in recent years has been radically transformed in its approach. The classical writings have been reappraised and reinterpreted, and a whole new body of theory and research has been developed. Much of this, as we will see, has centered on the model of organizations as control structures.

This will be followed, in Chapter 17, by an account of the managerial approach to organizations – usually referred to as organizational analysis, or simply as organization theory. In contrast with the sociology of organizations, the emphasis here is one the improvement of performance, and on a model of organizations as systems for goal attainment. However, as we will see, organizational analysis is by no means 'managerialist' in the crude sense of being unaware of issues of conflict and control – even if these are not treated in quite the same way or given as much prominence as in sociological accounts.

Chapter 18 looks at a topic that has attracted an enormous amount of attention recently, that of organization culture. The chapter explores the ways in which sociological and managerial interests have shaped the study of culture – one being concerned with expressive and symbolic aspects of organization life, and there other with how culture can be managed in pursuit of organization goals.

Finally, Chapter 19 examines another area of great recent interest which also makes common ground between the sociological and managerial approaches. This is the study of power in organizations. Here, the radical concept of power is applied to relations within groups of managers, and the model of the organization as an arena of bargaining and influence is explored.

16

Structure and Control in Organizations

One of the major developments behind the rise of large-scale organizations has been the so-called division between ownership and control. In small-scale enterprises it is common for legal ownership and management to overlap and be vested in the same person or group. But increasingly, with modern large-scale organizations, day-to-day control is exercised by mangers who are themselves salaried employees, while share ownership has become so diffuse that it would be impossible for all the shareholders actually to run a company. In reality, the issue is rather more complex, and the separation between ownership and control is by no means so clear-cut. Ownership of many of the largest corporations throughout the world can be traced to groups that exercise corporate control, not uncommonly families (for a detailed account, see Hill, 1981, pp. 71–6). However, the point we wish to raise here is that the growth of organizations had led to the rise of a separate and distinct managerial structure.

In this context, Offe (1976) had distinguished what he calls 'task continuous' and 'task discontinuous' forms of organization. The former would include the small owner-managed firm, the craft workshop and the partnership, which are run co-operatively by those who actually perform the work. Planning is simply an outgrowth of the work process itself, and any authority is based on the possession of skills. In contrast to this, task discontinuous organizations are far more typical of modern employment. They have a discrete authority structure, unrelated to those who do the work.

Such changes reflect the growth of *bureaucratic* forms of organizing work. In the early stages of industrialization the need to plan and administer work presented few problems, but once the size and complexity of plants had increase, administration came to be seen as something distinctive. Nowadays in all areas of economic life – in industry, government and both public and private services – there are complex and highly developed administrative structures.

These structures, moreover, are set up as means of pursuing explicit corporate objectives – goals which are not necessarily shared by all of the members. Central processes in organizations therefore involve the *control* of activities. The mechanisms of controlling the behaviour of people in organizations are reflected in the structuring of the rewards and deprivations of work, with increasing pay, discretion and power as one ascends to senior levels, and decreasing amounts in the lower ranks. This encompasses the concern with alienation, discussed in Chapter 10, where the central issue involved workers being denied control over their working lives and the products of their labour. Certainly many of the problems of repetitive dehumanized work, so characteristic of the modern factory or office, have been attributed to the power structure and to systematic control in organizations. However, the sociology of organizations has developed a rather broader view than this. The control of organizational personnel is not seen as being confined to the labour process, nor does it stop short at the factory or office floor. It also applies in varying degrees to the more privileged layers of an organization's employees.

Bureaucracy

The term 'organization' can be thought of in two ways: first in terms of concrete, real-life organizations (factories, offices, etc.); and secondly, in terms of the principle of structuring work on hierarchical basis. Bearing this in mind, we can see that real-life organizations will embrace other principles of 'organizing' work than the purely hierarchical one – there will be a range of occupations, a social division of labour (based on gender, race, age, etc.) and perhaps trade unions. Now the significance of the bureaucracy in this context–in addition, that is, to the fact that bureaucracies are important in themselves for managing modern business – is that in this form of organization the two meanings of the term merge. We can study a real-life organization which approximates very closely to the pure principle of hierarchy.

Indeed, the defining feature of the bureaucracy is that it is solely concerned with the task of administration; it is a purely 'task discontinuous' type of organization. In contrast to other major forms of work, like manual and professional, no concrete task is performed in the bureaucracy. Instead, it carries out the task of maintaining a system of records upon which the direction and control of the work of others is based. Typical employees are clerical officers and secretaries. Indeed, the classic example of bureaucracy is the civil service, although other large white-collar organizations like banks, and building societies and insurance companies also have strong bureaucratic elements.

Modern sociological thought on this subject is traced to Max Weber, whose study of bureaucracy has had an enormous influence both on the theory of organizations and on how we understand the impact of organizations on society at large (Weber, 1970, pp. 196–244, 1964, pp. 330–3). Weber wrote during the years spanning the turn of the century, towards the end of the period when the modern German nation became consolidated. Unlike the pattern of industrialization in Britain, the German industrial economy developed along highly centralized lines, and one aspect of this was the growth of a huge state apparatus. It was experience of seeing this central state machine develop and spread that persuaded Weber of the varied implications of the bureaucratic form of organization.

THE BUREAUCRATIC MODEL

In Weber's (1970) account of bureaucracy the following basic elements were included:

1. *A staff* consisting of a body of employees whose full-time work was to administer the activities of the particular institution. The employee's post carries with it authority over specific areas, but it is a cardinal principle that the incumbent should not overstep the bounds of his or her authority. Such behaviour (for example, the use of formal authority to gain wider influence) might result in various forms of corruption.

2. *A division of labour* which assigns specific tasks to sub-units and individuals. The division of labour in bureaucracies is highly developed: departmental boundaries and individual jobs are closely specified and duties and responsibilities carefully set out.

3. *The hierarchy*, or division of power, involves the ranking of offices to provide clear lines of command. In bureaucracies the hierarchy also is typically very complex, its many levels providing a highly differentiated structure of authority.

4. *Competence* refers to the basis upon which office is held. Factors like luck, favoritism or personal connections should play no part in the position that officials attain; advancement should be decided by expertise and ability alone. Thus organizations have to pay close attention to the process of selection, whereby these qualities can be identified in personnel.

5. *Objectivity* suggests that all dealings within the bureaucracy and with clients should be conducted on the basis of equal treatment according to a procedural routine. The objective conduct of business, free from any personal feelings, is the basis of the reliability of formal administration.

From the point or view of technical efficiency, Weber believed that the above characteristics gave far-reaching advantages, making the bureaucratic form of organization absolutely necessary in a modern economy:

The decisive reason for the advance of bureaucratic organization has always been its purely technical superiority over any other form of organization. The fully developed bureaucratic mechanism compares with other organizations exactly as does the machine with the non-mechanical modes of production.... Today it is primarily the capitalist market economy which demands that the official business of the administration be discharged precisely, unambiguously, continuously and with as much speed as possible. Normally, the very large capitalist enterprises are themselves unequalled models of strict bureaucratic organization. (1964, pp. 214–15)

Two things are apparent from this account. First, any large-scale organization will in some measure have a bureaucratic structure. All have a lateral division of tasks and a vertical division of authority, and embrace principles of objectivity and competence. Yet some of these factors may vary quite considerably across different organizations. Some, for instance, may have a relatively relaxed division of labour, with work being accomplished in diffuse groups and with little attention paid to exact responsibilities. In the bureaucratic model, however, these factors are present in an exaggerated form. The civil service, for example, has an extremely complex hierarchy, in which close attention is given to differentials covering a whole range of fringe benefits, privileges and status symbols.

Secondly, it is obvious that the above factors present too faultless a picture. No real-life bureaucracy meets all of these requirements all of the time. Nor was it Weber's intention to describe actual patterns of behavior. The model that he set out was what he termed an *ideal type*. The word 'ideal' here does not have the evaluative meaning it has in common usage; it refers instead to the pure idea that lay behind the reality. What Weber described was the consistent and logical form of bureaucracy, rather than its day-to-day operations.

Nevertheless, in reality organizations do approximate quite closely to Weber's model. People are mostly appointed on the basis of merit, tasks on the whole are clearly allocated and clients are dealt with impartially. In other ways, the model also represents the *standard* that we expect from organizations. There is normally an outcry if official corruption is uncovered, and we would usually be affronted when dealing with bureaucracies to be treated according to the personal whim of the official. However, although values of objectivity and competence help to guarantee integrity in public life, and we tend to take them for granted, they are at the bottom arbitrary and relative like all social institutions. In the historical past organizations were based on quite different rules, where, for example, it was quite normal for an officer-holder to confer privilege on his relatives or favourites.

ORGANIZATIONAL AUTHORITY AND RATIONALITY

In common with most sociologists, Weber was centrally concerned with the problem of social order. Why should people accept the roles allocated to them by some external power, and why do they obey the directives issued on its behalf? There can be many possible reasons. People may comply simply because they are coerced, or because they perceive some advantages in obeying, they may obey out of sheer habit, or even because they feel affection for the person issuing orders, and so on. However, if the motives people have for accepting rules reflect only factors like expediency or coercion, Weber reasoned, social order would hardly be stable in the long term. At some basic level there must be a feeling of solidarity with rules. This all-important voluntary element is embodied in a special type of social control, namely *authority*.

The crucial feature of all forms of authority as a basis of social control is that the power of senior officials should be accepted by those under control. The latter should believe that it is right and proper for people in senior positions to issue directives and equally justifiable that their orders be complied with. In short, authority should be regarded as a *legitimate* form of social control.

> ... custom and personal advantage, purely affectual or ideal motives, do not, even taken together, form a sufficiently reliable basis for a system of imperative coordination. In addition, there is normally a further element, the belief in legitimacy. No system of authority voluntarily limits itself to the appeal to material or affectual or ideal motives as a basis of guaranteeing its continuance. In addition, such a system attempts to establish and to cultivate the belief in its legitimacy. (Weber, 1964, p.325)

Weber distinguished three types of authority:

1. *Charismatic authority* which is based on the personal qualities, heroic or mystical, of leaders.
2. *Traditional authority*, based on established customs and the right to rule of dominant groups sanctified by such customary beliefs.
3. *Rational authority*, based on the legal occupancy of senior positions by those who exercise authority.

Mouzelis (1975, p. 16), in his thorough account of the Weberian approach to bureaucracy, makes the important point that each of these types of authority gives rise to a different kind of organization. Movements based on charismatic leaders tend to be associated with a temporary and loose type of administrative structure. Traditional

367

authority, vested in the inherited status of a king or lord, gives rise to a more permanent apparatus where officials owe their position to some privilege or contract granted by the superior. Finally, rational authority forms the basis of the modern work organization, and in particular the bureaucracy. Here is the basis of order seems obvious: people conform with the directives of those in senior positions because they are paid to do so and because they may be dismissed if they refuse. A rational calculation on the part of the employee is inherent in this kind of contractual arrangement. But in addition to this Weber was convinced that bureaucracy was of fundamental importance in industrial society because of its distinctively rational structure.

We discussed this briefly in Chapter 10, and pointed out that rationality reflects the application of a formal structure of administration as the means of managing complex tasks. Bureaucracy thus permits the calculation and predictability of future outcomes, together with accountability and close control of activities. Bureaucratic authority has advantages over other types since rational action is in evidence throughout the organization, as well as in the organization's relations to its markets and clients. When people perceive that office-holders are competent, that decisions are taken formally, resources are accounted for, and so forth, this upholds the belief in legitimacy. Such beliefs are further supported by the fact that office-holders themselves are subject to the same impersonal rules. The appeal of rationality therefore remains independent of the personal qualities of leaders and so outlasts individuals. Nor is it based on the forces of tradition and habit which may come to be questioned. For these reasons, rational bureaucratic authority should prove to be by far the most stable form of authority.

Finally, all three authority types are themselves ideal types. Thus in real organizations authority will be a mixture of types, and there will always be traces of motives other than the purely rational. Senior management, for instance, are always very careful about projecting the right image, for they known full well that their personal charisma is important if they wish to command authority. Similarly, all forms of authority depend in part upon force of habit; indeed some organizations can be very traditional and hidebound in this respect. As Weber himself put it, all systems of authority rest on a *belief* held by subordinates, and by virtue of which those exercising authority are accepted willingly. The belief is invariably complex and composed of several elements, including habit and personal charisma (Weber, 1964, p. 382). Nevertheless, in a bureaucratic organization one type should predominate, namely the appeal that rational procedures have for the majority of members of the organization.

Social action in organizations

BUREAUCRATIC DYSFUNCTIONS

A more obvious meaning attached to the idea of bureaucracy, however, presents a major problem with Weber's account, and that is that it has always seemed at odds with common-sense notions. 'Bureaucracy' in every day terms usually means the exact opposite of the highly rational and efficient system that Weber seemed to refer to. The popular view of bureaucracy conjures up an image of unnecessary paperwork, time-consuming procedure, strict adherence to rules and unresponsiveness to clients. In short, administrative procedures often seem to be designed to get in the way of achieving goals, rather than rationally facilitating them. This critical, common-sense view has formed the basis of a lengthy 'debate with Weber' in which a great deal of modern writing and research has been cast. Later writers, particularly in the United States, stress the major 'dysfunctional' features that bureaucracies have. The post-Weberian analysis of bureaucracy, following Merton (1940) and Selznick (1943), has focused on the rigid and impersonal character of bureaucracy, contrasting this with the perfect form of administration that Weber appear to be describing (Table 16.1).

Table 16.1   *Weber and his critics.*

The 'ideal type' model of bureaucracy	High degree of internal efficiency Rational: effective administration means to corporate ends
The 'efficiency' critique of Weber's model	Bureaucracy as 'red tape': irrational Goal displacement: the displacement of corporate ends by administrative means Inflexible: unresponsive to environmental changes and demands
The 'social' critique of Weber's model	Erosion of individual democratic freedoms Depersonalization: the 'bureaucratic personality'

It helps to separate out two different themes in this critique. First there is the suggestion that bureaucracy is actually an *inefficient* form of organization. The question of efficiency is chiefly a managerial concern (one that we deal with in much more detail in the next chapter), but for the moment we can note that the emphasis here is on the inability of bureaucratic organizations to achieve their goals in a flexible way, or to respond to changes in their market environment.

This common-sense view of bureaucracy as 'red tape' mounts an explicit challenge to the Weberian notion of bureaucracy as a highly rational means to an end. The criticism centers on the idea of *goal displacement*. What this refers to is the forms of incapacity that emerge in elaborate bureaucratic structures when officials become preoccupied with the administrative process itself. This can happen as a result of an extreme division of labour that allows the bureaucrat to see only a small part of the operation, and also because people's reputations and careers become bound up with established procedures. In any case, if the smooth running of the bureaucracy becomes the real goal of officials, the stated goals for which the bureaucracy was originally set up tend to slip into the background. This sort of shift, from ends to means, can be a familiar experience of dealing with centralized bureaucracies, where the quality of service appears to have been sacrificed to the goal of easy administration.

Secondly, there is criticism that bureaucracy has major *social* dysfunctions. Included here is Merton's (1940) original idea of the 'bureaucratic personality' as a narrow, one-dimensional kind of individual. This basic problem, that large-scale bureaucratic systems produce 'organization men' who are the harbingers of a new kind of bland, conformist middle class, has been a strong theme in American sociology (e.g. Mills, 1951). In a broader sense this reflects the *depersonalization* of social and economic life. Objectivity was mentioned as a key criterion of rational administration, but objectivity has a negative side. The price that has to be paid is that the quality of human relations, both within the bureaucracy and between the bureaucracy and its clients, becomes transformed into anonymous calculative exchanges.

These socially dysfunctional features have major implications for the erosion of individual freedom. The state bureaucracy is in theory the servant of society, responsible for major forms of welfare provision, like health, education, social security and protection of the environment. Yet the belief that in some quite straightforward way the state distributes the services to which we are entitled can prove to be rather naive. 'The state' as a principle of government may stipulate this, but in reality the relationship of the state to society is mediated by the bureaucratic machine. At times the individual has little chance of redress against officialdom, and for all practical purposes has to accept the treatment he or she is meted out. Cases of 'bureaucratic abuse' give sufficient grounds for believing that the different departments of the modern state are remarkably autonomous, and that they can and often do appropriate wider powers from their official position. A great many officials of the state – the police, social security officers, welfare officials, immigration officials – in reality have wide-ranging forms of discretions over the way laws are interpreted, and consequently have very real power over the members of the public with whom they come into contact.

It now tends to be recognized, however, that these criticisms of the nature of bureaucracy were misjudged as criticisms of Weber. In the first place, it was indeed true that Weber regarded bureaucracies as a highly efficient form of administration. Without efficiency the whole basis of authority in large organizations would have been undermined. And this is certainly at odds with the goal-displacing picture of inflexible, bureaucratic organizations that critics have drawn. Yet, after all, how accurate is their viewpoint? Much of it relies upon appealing to common-sense views, or to anecdotal evidence. By comparison the emphasis on rationality, and the honest fulfillment of contractual obligations, is at least as well founded. If we take a broader comparative viewpoint, compared with organizations in countries where political factors intervene in commercial life far more prominently, the bureaucracies we are familiar with often do seem to be models of efficiency and fair dealing. These positive features therefore form the first impression we receive of bureaucracy, as Weber intended they should.

Secondly, fears about the impact of bureaucracy on society were actually consistent with the viewpoint that Weber held. As we saw in Chapter 10, he was chiefly concerned with much broader issue of *rationalization* as the key historical trend in the development of industrial society. This meant a world dominated by the calculative logic of rational decision-making and the remorseless spread of bureaucratic rationality. It embraced fears of the erosion of individual freedom – and indeed the very efficiency of bureaucracy was what made it a potent threat. Of course, the fear of an overbearing state is as old as the idea of democracy itself, and certainly did not originate with Weber. Yet the idea that bureaucracy poses previously unforeseen problems is no less important today, while the threats that Weber identified when state bureaucracies and business corporations first appeared are perhaps more urgent now.

Therefore, considered as criticisms of Weber these points are some-what irrelevant. The problems of bureaucratic inefficiency and the erosion of democratic freedom were not radical new ideas, even in Weber's time, so he did not develop his 'ideal' model of bureaucracy in a state of ignorance or naivity. As Mouzelis (1975, p. 43) has pointed out, the ideal type concept was not meant to describe a 'typical' or even an 'ideal' form of bureaucracy; it was a logical

371

extension of the underlying principle of rationality. Nonetheless, although it has followed from a rather narrow interpretation of Weber, the detailed study of the 'dysfunctional' side of organizational life has added much to our understanding of how real bureaucracies and other large organizations work, and we can discuss this in more detail now.

THE DYNAMICS OF BUREAUCRACY

If we are to do justice to the full complexity of social action within organizations, it is necessary to see that much more is involved than just conformity to external rules. Formal authority is not merely accepted in some straightforward way by subordinates; those under authority do not necessarily obey automatically. Subordinates may resent the imposition of control and resist in whatever ways are available to them. Also, people in authority usually devote considerable efforts to persuasion aimed at shoring up the image of themselves as legitimate office-holders (much the same as the tactics of 'impression management' that are used by group members, as discussed in Chapter 6). Authority is thus a *dynamic* relationship, and legitimacy can come under threat at any time or ultimately be withdrawn by organization members. In other words, the conflict between bureaucratic control and individual resistance is a major source of instability, and the distinction has to be drawn between official expectations and real activities.

The discrepancy between formal rules and actual behaviour reflects one of the most persistent themes of sociology, that of the individual 'making out' in an established, sometimes coercive social structure, and the tactics developed to cope with externally imposed controls. In his classic study, *Work and Authority in Industry*, Bendix saw in the growth of bureaucratic work structures the increasing estrangement of employees from their work. When they seek to modify external control, in one way or another they overreach the strict limits of their office, and this resistance further prompts the penetration of formal authority.

> The strict separation between office and incumbent, between the position and the employee, is an ideal condition which is rarely achieved, in practice, especially with regard to salaried employees and skilled workers. Incumbents endow their work performance with personal qualities that range from dispensable idosyncrasies to untransferable and often indispensable skills, so that some measure of identification of the employee with his position is unavoidable.... Managers endeavor to minimise or eliminate this 'silent bargaining' (and thereby to maximise the predictable performance of employees) by the strategic use of penalties, incentives and ideological appeals. (1956, pp. 246–7)

These distinctions have often been referred to in terms of the difference between *formal* and *informal* organization. Informal structure is not so readily identifiable as the formal, since it is not officially recognized, yet it is no less important for behaviour. Informal structure includes all of the subtle customs and attitudes, the expectations and unwritten rules that stamp an organization with a specific character. These may involve general patterns of activity – the degree of formality of behaviour, the deference to those in authority that is expected, and the autonomy that people are normally allowed to show in their work. They also include the 'real' distribution of power, i.e. the possibility of particular departments or managers being highly influential while officially they have no more authority than others at their level. What is referred to as 'learning the ropes' by people newly recruited to an organization usually means gaining a working knowledge of this informal structure.

The ways in which informal actions serve to undermine rational authority have long been a favourite topic of sociological research (resistance to the formal constraints of Taylorist methods of work study on the part of work groups is one of the best known examples, as we saw in Chapter 11). However, the interplay between formal and informal spheres is in fact highly complex. In many cases, informal action serves to *support* formal rules – indeed it is often suggested that organizations would cease to operate without this kind of informal co-operation. Employees very often will take responsibility on themselves to see that tasks are completed, rather than merely following procedures, and this may involve short-cutting the formal rules. Furthermore, in even more subtle ways, formal institutions can exploit employees' willingness to take informal action for the benefit of management objectives. These include the formal acceptance, whether grudging or not, of informal practices which have become desirable or indispensable.

Thus patterns of action in organizations are influenced by many different and sometimes conflicting social rules. Informal codes of practice can bind behaviour just as tightly as formal rules, while the occupational values of groups like craftsmen and professionals, as well as trade unions, are no less important. In short, official rules and the formal structure compete with the informal rules of groups enjoying varying degrees of recognition from the organization's hierarchy.

CLASSIC STUDIES OF BUREAUCRACY

In one way or another the classical empirical studies in the neo-Weberian tradition, such as Blau's *Dynamics of Bureaucracy* (1955), Gouldner's *Patterns of Industrial Bureaucracy* (1954) and Crozier's *The*

Bureaucratic Phenomenon (1964), have all emphasized this tension between formal rules and social action. Impersonal rules and social responses are both equally important parts of the total organization.

Thus Gouldner distinguished between the varying content of rules, types of enforcement and the motives which sustained acceptance, as well as the conditions under which the legitimacy of social order might be suspended. Bureaucratic patterns in which conformity had to be strongly enforced were distinguished from the genuine acceptance of authority because interests were widely represented, and these in turn were distinguished from conformity with the form rather than the essence of rules: 'punishment-centred', 'representative' and 'mock' bureaucracies. Similarly, in his study of government recruitment agencies, Blau stressed that competition between employees acted as an important mechanism of control. He too focused on the interplay between formal and informal, seeing in the 'daily operations and interpersonal relationships' the main dynamic of organizational change, namely the continual modification of formal procedures by social practice. Finally, in the rigidly bureaucratic factory that Crozier studied, major problems in an otherwise routine production task were created by machine breakdowns; and this gave maintenance workers who dealt with breakdowns a degree of informal influence, which was reflected in their superior pay and general treatment by management. In this sense, Crozier indicated how an organizational authority structure could in effect become distorted as a result of special powers possessed by particular groups.

While such studies have stressed the *interplay* between formal rules and social action, in the end this is really a matter for interpretation. Others, who are more radically or perhaps pessimistically inclined, have seen things differently. Instead of viewing formal and informal spheres as competing rationalities, they have stressed the extent of formal control. Individuals who come under these controls will invariably put up resistance, but 'making out' in an oppressive bureaucratic environment frequently has a defensive character.

An example of the near-complete negation of individual freedom is offered in Goffman' famous study of mental institutions, *Asylums* (1968). Goffman emphasized that rules, ostensibly for the benefit of inmates, were in fact used coercively in order to make 'care' a relatively easy task for the hospital staff. He showed, for example, how treatment (particularly the issuing of drugs) could be used as punishment rather than cure, and how doctors often withheld treatment until patients had accepted the psychiatric diagnosis of their condition. Furthermore, patients' apparently bizarre behaviour could often be interpreted as attempts to gain a few basic rights (such as a degree of privacy) denied them in the artificial conditions of the asylum. The psychiatric profession usually regarded this as further evidence of the patient's illness. In other words, on the basis of his findings Goffman was arguing that the true purpose of bureaucratic rules lies in the way the majority of organizational members can be controlled for the benefit of the minority in power.

In mental institutions the power of staff over inmates was greatly amplified because these were what Goffman referred to as 'total institutions', where inmates live entirely within the system (another common example of which would be prisons). Total institutions serve as an extreme case of the control that powerful groups exercise over others in organizations. Nevertheless, the issue of control generally lies at the heart of the hierarchial structuring of work.

Control in organizations

The notion of control that prevails in much of the literature on organizations reflects essentially managerial interests. This approach (which we will take up in the next chapter) focuses on the kinds of structure which best allow managers to regulate their subordinates' activities, with improved performance as the end in view. However, a much broader notion of organizational control is one where the whole structure of organizations is viewed as a mechanism for controlling employees' behaviour – and indeed their beliefs and motivations as well. With the emphasis squarely on the constraint and manipulation of members' activity, this represents a radical view of organizations and one which challenges more conventional views of the organization as a system for the attainment of corporate goals. (For accounts of this perspective, see Salaman, 1979, 1981; Clegg and Dunkerley, 1980, Chapter 13; Burrell and Morgan, 1979, Chapter 11; and Storey, 1983, Chapter 7.)

The origins of this more radical approach can partly be found in Marx's critique of capitalism. Focusing on the conflict between labour and capital, Marx viewed administrative control as an active force in the exploitation of labour. As we saw in Chapter 10, the Marxist view of the labour process is that the natural control of work of the craftsman is taken over by the capitalist control, and replaced by an elaborate system of supervision. Thus the co-operation of workers in large enterprises is in no way spontaneous or willing, but rather an enforced integration of effort (Marx, 1974, pp. 313–14).

Marxist writers have held to the idea of organizations as a control *over* productive labour. Baldamus, for example, has defined this as follows:

> ... the orginisation of industry, with all its complexities and diversities, ultimately revolves on a single process: the administrative process through

which the employees' effort is controlled by the employer. This means that the entire system of industrial production will be viewed as a system of administrative controls which regulate quantity, quality and distribution of human effort. (1961, p. 1)

Thus the hierarchy of supervision and management, production planning and work-pacing technology, indeed the whole edifice of organizational authority, is seen as representing an artificial structure which alienates the control of work from workers themselves.

NORMATIVE CONTROL AND MANAGEMENT

However, the concept of organizational control applied *within* the administrative structure has a further important feature. We usually think of managers and other administrative employees as being *in* control rather than *under* control. Yet organizations are highly complex structures, with extended hierarchies of rewards, status and power, as well as differences of occupation and function. With this go varying degrees of *commitment*. Very senior corporate managers receive such rewards of money, prestige and other benefits that they normally identify very closely with organizational goals. However, in the middle and lower ranks commitment is more in doubt. For employees who make up the bulk of administration – the junior managers, supervisors, technical specialists – the rewards fall far short of those going to top management, albeit a wide differential still separates them from the shopfloor. Employees in these positions, therefore, constitute part of the organization's problem of control.

Of course, some of the constraints on workers apply within the administrative structure as well. Managers and professionals may be dismissed if they fail to meet performance standards, and their jobs are subject to many other regulations. But while there is a degree of overlap, the constraints that apply to managers differ in important respects from those on workers. Because workers' effort tends to be controlled by direct and coercive means (like intensive supervision, systems of fines and incentives for output), there is relatively little concern with engaging their loyalty. By contrast, the control exerted over managers is concerned far more centrally with their loyalty and commitment. In their case, rewards are not merely an exchange for effort, as they are with workers, but involve a crucial moral element, so that conformity arises from managers' own internal motivation. The essential *normative* element in organizational control is reflected in the attempt to secure the self-involvement of managerial groups.

This brings us back to the Weberian account of bureaucracy. Weber, as we saw, stressed that control in bureaucratic organizations, although to some extent enforced, is also in a crucial sense accepted. People co-operate in systems of formal authority essentially because of the conviction that a particular form of rationality is operating. This in turn rests on the belief that organizations are governed by formal *rules*. The proper discharge of the duties of office, advancement based on merit, objective notions of competence and so on, all constitute the basis of organizational legitimacy.

The idea of bureaucratic control as 'self-control' has informed much of the sociology of organizations. For example, Fox (1974) has described the organizational hierarchy in terms of two variables: the *discretion* that attaches to managerial jobs in the senior levels, which in turn reflects the fact that managers enjoy varying degrees of *trust* and are held accountable only over the longer term. One of the pioneers of the radical approach to organizational control, Graeme Salaman, has put it this way:

> ... forms of control vary in their effects. Some are highly alienative; others actually encourage normative commitment. The reason for variation in the sorts of organisational control employed for various groups is not only that the sort of work is more or less amenable to this or that form of control. It is also because it would generally be regarded as inapplicable and dangerous to expose senior organisational members in the crucial, decision-making jobs to alienative forms of control, because of the importance of their normative involvement. (1979, p. 129)

Definite features of administrative structures serve to engage managers' commitment. At a fundamental level, because organizations are social systems, a distinctive *culture* develops within them, and like all cultures enforces a degree of conformity. The values and beliefs which make up organizational culture take the form of rules of behaviour, which define informal understandings about how members are expected to act. Secondly, the *division of labour* within management also helps to sustain the central authority. This differs crucially from the division of labour on the shopfloor. As Child (1984, pp. 26–7) has pointed out, workers' jobs tend to be fragmented by Taylorist work practices, giving routine and deskilled operations. But in managerial, technical and professional work, the division of labour is manifest in terms of the *specialization* of tasks. And whereas fragmentation is aimed at removing any discretion or freedom in workers' jobs, with specialization a good deal of discretion is retained. Thus managerial work becomes 'narrow in scope but founded on considerable depth of knowledge'.

As a result, while the division of labour tends to isolate workers, within management the effect is to create departments and units which are interdependent. Within these networks of relationships managers put pressure on one another for greater effort, since they depend upon one another in their jobs. However, the important difference is that here organizational control appears to originate within the management group and does not seem so coercive – although, of course, it ultimately derives from external controls like budgets and output targets. Thus it is common to hear managers complain about such pressure but not to resent it, because 'other people have their jobs to do'.

PROFESSIONALS IN ORGANIZATIONS

With growing technological sophistication and the rise of many science-based industries, people with professional training and skills now form an increasingly important part of organizational work-forces. Groups like engineers, technicians and accountants have become much more numerous and central in industrial and commercial organizations. Although such experts can be included simply as part of management, their role in organizations is in certain ways quite distinctive.

As we saw in Chapter 12, sociologists have come to regard the professions as a kind of occupational control strategy – a means by which groups seek to upgrade the rewards they obtain from employment by gaining recognition as professions and claiming professional status. Occupational groups organize themselves into professions, it is argued, essentially as a way of gaining control over their own market situation and working conditions (Johnson, 1972; Child and Fulk, 1982). What this means, however, is that the *organizational structures of control may be incompatible with the occupational* controls upon which the profession bases itself. Thus within organizations the priorities of cost-cutting and tidy administration might be at odds with a professional orientation to 'best practice' in the performance of work. These problems are often made much worse because experts and specialists often have relatively little influence within management, despite the importance of their skills. In short, the organizational work setting may deny professionals the autonomy they expect and may be experienced as constraining.

Gouldner's (1957) noted distinction between 'cosmopolitans' and 'locals', for example, contrasted professional attachment to wider occupational ideas with the narrower commitment to an organizational career. Similarly, in Burns and Stalker's (1961) classic study of the Scottish electronics industry, the occupational identity of industrial scientists was seen to conflict with many features of their employment context. The scientists became isolated within firms, and found difficulty in fitting into the status conventions. In particular, their identification with technological change perpetually caused them to clash with management orientated to more stable operations.

However, it is important not to overgeneralize the conflict between professional loyalties and organizational employment. It is by no means always true that professionals experience organizations as hostile environments. Indeed, one line of argument has suggested the exact opposite, that professional training and work orientations actually resolve many problems of organizational control. Organizations are willing to confer superior rewards and privileges upon employed professionals in return for their 'responsible' approach to work, while for professionals, applying their technical expertise to the problems the organization sets them means that any conflicts are reduced to minor matters. In this sense, Whalley (1986) has referred to production engineers as 'trusted workers'; their occupational socialization and training make them unlikely to engage in acts of resistance or to use their autonomy against the strategic interests of the organization.

EXPLAINING PROFESSIONAL STATUS

The wide variety of organizational settings that professionals work in has been seen as the key to explaining the differences between occupations that are more or less successful in gaining professional status. Johnson (1972) has referred to three types of occupational control. First, in organizations where professionals predominate (e.g. private practice, universities, research establishments) they usually achieve high levels of status. This 'collegiate' type of occupational control is typical of the senior professions. Secondly, occupations defined by 'corporate patronage' are found within large private corporations, where the employer defines the service he needs, and so shapes the development of the profession over time. Such professions (like accounting, engineering and computing) still enjoy considerable status, although they tend to be 'tied' to a particular employer. Thirdly, 'state mediation' refers to the creation by government bureaucracy of occupations that are only marginally professional. The ethics of such groups (e.g. teachers and social workers) reflect the rules of the employing agency rather than true occupational values, while control of the service provided resides with the state – all of which detract from professionalism.

It seems clear, however, that the nature of the organizational employer does not account for all of the variation in professional status. What does seem to be universally true is that *bureaucratic* work settings impede professional autonomy. Rigid division of labour, insistence on formal authority and a preoccupation with the detail of administration conflict sharply with a professional work ethic (Scott, 1966; Hall, 1968). But it is not obvious that such bureacratic work settings are found only in the state sector, as Johnson seemed to suggest. Many large private corporations are run along strictly bureaucratic lines, while in the public sector there are organizations – hospitals within the National Health Service and universities are two examples that spring to mind – which operate very favourably for the professionals within them.

Within different sectors (private practice, private corporate, public) there may be as much variety in the status enjoyed by professionals as exists between sectors. Particularly in the private corporate sector, where many modern professions and technical occupations are found, studies have revealed that the levels of occupational control that professions enjoy can vary across a wide range. For example, Kraft (1979) has argued that the occupation of computer programmer has become 'industrialized'. In the early years of commercial computing, when programming was an uncertain business, computer staff enjoyed high status. But increasingly the work has become rationalized and higher-level tasks have been hived off to systems analysts. In contrast to this, Watson (1977) gives an account of personnel officers as a profession of improving status. The tasks of labour management that they perform (often taken over at the expense of first-line supervisors) are crucial for profitability, and have brought to the personnel function levels of reward comparable with other corporate professions, like accounting and engineering.

A different approach is taken by Armstrong (1985). Rather than try to predict the success of professions from the functions that they perform in organizations, he stresses *inter-professional competition* as being decisive for the relative standing of occupations. Accounting in particular, he points out, has been remarkably successful in achieving access to senior levels within organizations; and the profession has seen the 'language' of finance adopted as the chief strategy of organizational control in very many firms. Yet other professions that might have been equally successful, most notably engineering, have failed to gain anything like the prominence of accountants in top management. Only dynamic factors can explain these differences: the historic success of particular occupations in mounting collective campaigns to upgrade their status.

ORGANIZATIONAL SELECTION

The above forms of control are to an extent simply part of human interaction in organizations, or in the case of experts are reliant on occupational factors. But there is another means of control, namely organizational selection, which represents a strategy much more consciously and explicity applied. Selection is the process whereby people are initially recruited into an organization, and then continue (as long as their promotion continues) to progress to the inner circles of organizational power. Although there are important technical functions served in choosing people who are competent to perform particular jobs, selection also has a crucial *political* function. The whole of the power structure of organizations rests to a very large extent on the hierarchy as a 'selective mechanism'. For it is vital in ensuring control over personnel that appropriate people are chosen to enter positions of authority. 'Appropriate' here refers to people who will not merely conform, but actively pursue the goals of the organization, however defined. Thus considerable resources are normally devoted to the allocation of posts; and the procedures of selective recruitment and promotion became increasingly elaborate and formalized the further up the hierarchy one goes, comprising interviews and tests as well as criteria such as track record and past experience.

We might also add that selection automatically implies *rejection*. Thus selection is often portrayed as a 'gatekeeping' function, stressing that unsuccessful candidates are kept out, as well as the successful ones being let in. In this context, Blau and Schoenherr (1971) have emphasized that senior management usually have little need to resort to direct, coercive control because they are able to rely on gatekeeping. Selection ensures that potentially critical groups, which may challenge the settled practice, are simply not allowed entry; they remain as outsiders – or they do at least to the extent that selection is effective.

Given the secrecy and confidentiality which surrounds organizational selection, research on the subject is, not surprisingly, rather thin on the ground. However, Salaman and Thompson (1974) have contributed important empirical findings describing the interview procedures used in selecting candidates for officer training in the British army and for selecting management trainees in the Ford Motor Company (see also Salaman, 1979, pp. 187–95). In the army case study, for example, a precisely defined military culture was used as a yardstick for selection. Although the language army selectors used to describe the characteristics they were looking for was apparently rather vague, the selectors themselves knew exactly what they meant. For instance, the capacity in a candidate to remain composed and to present a confident front, even when he had made an obviously incompetent decision, was highly rated, being defined as 'coolness' and 'natural leadership'. The usefulness of such an ability to an organization such as the army, where discipline is of the utmost importance, is readily apparent.

ORGANIZATIONAL CAREERS

From the employee's point of view, the selection process is experienced in terms of his or her progress, or lack of progress, through the hierarchy – that is, in terms of career. Many sociologists have stressed the potency of career as a form of social control (Wilensky, 1968; Sofer, 1970; Presthus, 1979). The prospect of promotion offers huge potential rewards of material gains, prestige and power. Possibly the greatest appeal is that it resolves the contradiction between extrinsic and intrinsic rewards that appears to be the natural lot of manual workers. If manual workers want higher wages, they usually have to forego some other reward; they have to work overtime and so lose leisure, or perhaps take on dangerous work, or unpleasant work, or unsociable hours. With a career, however, increasingly interesting and responsible work is automatically matched by increasing financial rewards.

Career acts as both carrot and stick. If the rewards of promotion motivate management, so too does the fear of failure. Organizations typically are strewn with people who failed to get on, and their fate can be a cruel one in terms of the great psychological pressures that bear upon the unsuccessful. Certainly their presence acts as a constant reminder to the ambitious of the price of being passed over in the promotion race.

Promotion structures therefore engender a particularly intense kind of conformity. Becoming adept at manipulating the organization's belief systems and culture is essential for those with ambition. Learning to interact with colleagues and gaining recognition as an important participant in organizational life are the ingredients of success. The consequences of all this for social control are clear. Such a huge personal investment is involved that a career normally brings about increasing attachment to the organization and its ways of seeing and doing. As Salaman (1979, pp. 140–1) put it: 'When the self is so enmeshed within the organization, the distinction between personal priorities and organizational goals becomes relatively meaningless, and self-control becomes little different from organizational regulation.'

Further reading

Brown, R. (1992) *Understanding Industrial Organizations*. London: Routledge.

Burrell, G. and G. Morgan (1979) *Sociological Paradigms and Organisational Analysis*. London: Heinemann.

Clegg, S. (1990) *Modern Organizations*. London: Sage.

Clegg, S. and D. Dunkerley (1980) *Organization, Class and Control*. London: Routledge and Kegan Paul.

Eldridge, J.E.T. and A.D. Crombie (1974) *A Sociology of Organisations*. London: Allen and Unwin.

Knights, D. and H. Willmott (1986) *Managing the Labour Process.* London: Gower.

McKinlay, J.B. (ed.) (1975) *Processing People: Cases in Organizational Behaviour.* London: Holt, Rinehart and Winston.

Morgan, Gareth (1986) *Images of Organization.* London: Sage.

Morgan, Glenn (1990) *Organizations in Society.* Basingstoke: Macmillan.

Reed, M. (1986) *Redirections in Organisational Analysis.* London: Tavistock.

Reed, M. and M. Hughes (eds.) (1992) *Rethinking Organization.* London: Sage.

Thomson, P. and D. McHugh (1990) *Work Organisations.* Basingstoke: Macmillan.

17

Structure and Performance in Organizations

Although there are different perspectives on organizations, and a proliferation of research and writing on the subject, it is possible to single out two predominant schools of thought. One is concerned with the sociology of organizations, and focuses on what Mouzelis has called 'the organizational problems of society's power structure' (1975, p. 79). This corresponds broadly with the approach of the previous chapter, and owes much to the Weberian analysis of bureaucracy. The second is a managerial tradition deriving from F.W. Taylor's theory of scientific management and his studies of work administration. The concerns here are with the internal efficiency of organizations: the design of structure and the motivation of groups and individuals to perform in line with stated goals. To a large extent these two approaches have been mutually exclusive, not to say antagonistic. Writers interested in the 'problem' of organization tend not to regard organizational efficiency as an issue of first importance, and writers preoccupied with efficiency usually disregard awkward questions about the social and political impact of organizations (though there are notable exceptions in those who have tackled the problem of integrating the two approaches, e.g. Mouzelis, 1975; Perrow, 1980; Albrow, 1980.)

However, we will now turn our attention to the managerial approach. Although in some ways it seems hardly necessary to have to justify this, the concerns of management merit our interest for a number of reasons. Modern large-scale organizations produce the goods and services of our material life, and the problems of providing these benefits efficiently affect all of society. Furthermore, since management has the power to direct activities in organizations, a knowledge of managerial priorities and objectives is necessary for wider understanding of organizational behaviour.

Organizations have many different objectives and engage in a variety of activities, so there is a problem in defining an initial perspective on organization theory and what we expect the theory to cover. The following ideas have been particularly influential.

Organizations as systems

A similarity with living organisms suggests itself, and while there are dangers in taking this analogy too far, it has proved a useful model and one which keeps cropping up in organizational analysis. The parts of an organization – departments, divisions – must integrate their efforts, just as the parts of any living organism are interdependent. Moreover, organizations may be viewed as existing in a competitive environment, as do plants and animals, and they have to adapt to environmental conditions or perhaps find their existence threatened.

Organizations have system boundaries in the sense that they may occupy a definite geographical area, although this is not always the case. Government departments and multinational companies, for example, are dispersed over wide areas. Nonetheless, great care is taken in organizations to ensure that the membership is identified and kept under review. The writers who have developed the systems approach, however, have been at pains to emphasize that organizations should not be viewed merely as closed systems; to do this is to adopt a very static picture of how they operate (Elliott, 1980). Organizations have suppliers and clients; and there are wider social and economic forces that affect them, such as the labour market, the community, government legislation and, of course, other organizations. Thus, organizations are open systems, and transactions across the organizational boundary take place continuously, so much so that it can be difficult in practice to define exactly where an organization stops and its environment begins.

Structure and performance

It follows from the systems approach that organizations have a structure – an established set of relationships, with the emphasis on ordered and regularly occurring activities. Because tasks in organizations are almost always interdependent, it is essential that personnel act in a calculable and predictable manner. Hence performance and structure are inextricably linked. And, of course, the desire to improve performance is the underlying reason for studying the management process in organizations. This aim does not refer to the effectiveness of actual decisions taken in given circumstances (which is the central problem of business policy), but rather to the attempt to identify those structures of behaviour which contribute to the achievement of organizational goals.

Reference here is mainly to the *formal* structure of organizations – that is, the official hierarchy of positions, the division of labour and specified operating procedures. This is not to ignore the informal side of organizational activity. We focused on this in the previous chapter,

385

and indeed, as we shall see, organizational analysis has increasingly taken serious notice of factors which lie outside the structure of formal authority. However, as Child (1984) has pointed out, only the formal structure is subject to control and planning by management, thus it remains the fundamental concern of organization theory. In practical terms, the design of an effective structure must reflect the objectives of the organization and the context in which it operates. Good management also means anticipating the circumstances which make structural development and adaptation necessary.

Goals and the problem of reification

The formal nature of organization structure reflects the fact of goals having been identified and the criteria of achievement specified. Indeed, organizations are set up and designed explicitly as means of achieving certain goals. While some goals refer to broad aims, such as efficiency or the pursuit of profit, these afford little insight into the operations of a specific enterprise, and so more detailed goals are normally of interest.

For example, the management of a retail chain specializing in cut-price furniture might well decide that the goal of quality is not its first priority. They may be content to put up with a certain proportion of customer complaints for a given volume of business. On the other hand, a high-class interior designer would be far more likely to regard quality as a goal that could not be compromised, and might regard a single dissatisfied customer as a threat to future business. Thus, while both firms have the same overall goal of selling furniture for profit, the more detailed breakdown of goals tells us much more about the different ways in which the two businesses will be run.

An important problem relating to the use of goal analysis is that of *reification*. This refers to the tendency of attributing human motives to social institutions, in this case of thinking about organizations as if *they* were pursuing the goals in question. Of course only the personnel of organizations can pursue goals. Still, it is all too easy to refer to organizations as the active party – to speak of organizations controlling their personnel, adapting to their environments and so on. The danger in viewing the organization as a purposeful entity is that one ends up with a highly abstract and artificial analysis. The people making decisions and the motives behind their actions tend to be overlooked. There is also the danger of unwittingly shielding the actions and motives of senior management from criticism by implying that it was 'the organization' that was responsible for particular decisions. Thus when analysing organization goals, one must be clear that one is referring to the objectives officially sanctioned in the organization, and not to the goals that organizations pursue.

Organizational analysis

Having discussed these introductory points, we can proceed to examine some of the ways in which the structure of organizations contributes to the achievement of the goals set by management.

There are several distinct but related aspects of organization structure. At its most basic level, formal structure refers to the physical shape of the organization – the distribution of jobs and lines of command – often set out in an organization chart, if the firm in question has one. At a more analytic level we can distinguish two main components of the management structure:

1. The division of task or function – the division between groups, departments, specialisms and organizational divisions.
2. The division of power and authority – the division between superordinate and subordinate which forms the organizational hierarchy.

This gives the familiar picture of organizations as pyramidal structures of laterally connected departments and hierarchical levels. Thus, for example, Salaman (1979, p. 61) has defined structure as 'the way in which work is organised and control exercised', a definition in which we can see the twofold emphasis on relationships of communication and authority.

As well as these basic relationships, formal structure is identified with the major areas of managerial responsibility. John Child (1984, Chapter 1) has set out in some detail the requirements for the formulation and successful implementation of managerial plans. They include an established procedure for decision-making, with arrangements for the collection of information, the notification of decisions to groups and individuals, and a schedule for meetings. Another important managerial task is the control and co-ordination of activities. Here, operational procedures have to be set down in advance in order to specify areas of accountability and standards of performance; there must be a monitoring system to feed back information on performance to the right authority centres, and arrangements to correct operational activity in the light of any shortcomings. Thus the success and viability of an enterprise depend upon creating the most effective structure of administration, given the circumstances in which the organization is operating – one which distributes the necessary tasks, delegates required authority and controls the outcomes of actions.

THE CLASSICAL SCHOOL

The established theory generally regarded as the starting point of organizational analysis is, as we have said, Taylor's scientific management. This was an approach which gave a decidedly formalistic slant to early theory. Taylor had developed a 'science' of the control of manual work that employers had applied to great advantage; and the first writers on organizations, the so-called classical school, set themselves the task of developing along similar lines a formal theory of administration. Many of them were or had been managers themselves, and they emphasized such practical aspects of administration as the importance of strict specialization in management, and the exercise of strong leadership with clear lines of authority. Henri Fayol, a French engineer, is regarded as the founder of the classical school, and other prominent writers included Gulick and Urwick, Mary Parker Follet, and Mooney and Reiley. (For discussion of the classical school, see March and Simon, 1958, Chapter 2; Pugh, et al., 1984; Mouzelis, 1975, Chapter 4; Clegg and Dunkerley, 1980, pp. 99–106.)

By modern standards their work was probably not very impressive. Their emphasis on the correct 'principles of management' had a slightly archaic flavour, like the search for some magic formula. Concepts were not clearly specified, nor were their claims based on any empirical research. Perhaps their major shortcoming was a failure to take human factors into account (in this they were the true heirs of Taylor) so that an appropriately designed structure was supposed to eliminate all further problems of control and integration. This is something that certainly cannot be assumed away; indeed the central concern of modern organization theory has been precisely those behavioural factors ignored by the classical writers. Nonetheless, the classical school did tackle some of the basic problems of organization design. It cleared a space for organization analysis to develop, and their concerns with formal structure and the functions of management remain valid today.

THE CONTINGENCY APPROACH

After the initial impact of the classical school, interest in organizations shifted to psychological and group aspects (dealt with under the Human Relations school in Chapter 7) and little concern with structure was shown until as late as the 1950s. Then a new line of thought emerged which took a fresh look at structure and at the original focus on the principles of efficient administration. This was the so-called contingency theory. As with many important insights, the idea behind the theory was quite simple, namely that organization structure should be regarded as a contingent variable. In other words, the search of the classical theorists for universal principles of administration was held to be misguided; managers face circumstances which vary, and they must choose whatever structural arrangements are most appropriate in the prevailing context. The proper role of organization theory, therefore, is not to seek any 'one best way' to manage, but to provide insight and guidance for managers to help them formulate responses in the complex situations of organizational decision-making.

The general model implicit in contingency theory assumes that, for an organization to be effective, there must be an appropriate 'fit' between structure and context. Such a model can be set out as follows.

$$\text{CONTEXTUAL FACTORS} \longrightarrow \text{ORGANIZATION STRUCTURE} \longrightarrow \text{PERFORMANCE}$$

Thus structure is essentially seen as an *intervening variable*, which modifies the effect of contingent factors upon performance, given the context in which the organization operates. Structure is also essentially *adaptive* since it may need to be changed if the context is dynamic and makes demands that alter over time. (For discussion of contingency theory, see Burrell and Morgan, 1979, pp. 164–81; Child, 1984, pp. 217–25.)

Contextual factors embrace all of the given elements which serve to constrain managerial decision-making, so the context may vary over time and from firm to firm in an almost endless variety of ways. However, it has proved possible to isolate some of the most important contextual variables. These include chiefly the type of *technology* an organization uses and the kind of *environment* in which it operates.

Technology

As well as the hardware used in production, the term 'technology' is used to refer to production methods and work organization. Thus technology has become a sort of shorthand term for the general task structure of an organization. A mass production technology, for example, involves large numbers of semi-skilled operatives, and hence the task of labour management and supervision becomes critical. Conversely, science-based technologies generate tasks involving professional and technical skills, and employees with these sorts of ability tend to be self-regulating in their work. Craft technologies are similar in this respect. Thus different production technologies give rise to different systems of tasks, which in turn affect structure.

The best-known research on the technology–structure relationship is Joan Woodward's (1965) study of manufacturing firms in south-east Essex. Woodward obtained measures (some of them admittedly rather simple and crude) of three organizational variables: first, the commercial success of firms; secondly, their production technology (which she classified in three types: technologies that produce single units or small batches, mass production, and process production technologies); and thirdly, certain dimensions of structure (e.g. the number of levels in the hierarchy, the labour intensity and the first line spans of control). These, we can see, cover the three variables in the contingency model above.

Woodward arrived at two major findings. (1) There was a link between structure and technology in that firms in the same technical category (say, all of the unit production firms) tended to have similar organization structures. (2) She then discovered that all three variables – technology, structure and performance – were related. She found that successful firms in each technical category had structural characteristics near the average for the category as a whole, while the firms with below average success fell in the extremes of the range of structural variables.

This seemed to imply that a given technology 'demands' a particular structure, and firms that obey this 'technological imperative' reap the rewards in terms of organizational efficiency and business success. Moreover, the relationship was clearly a contingent rather than an unvarying one. Thus, for example, in successful mass production firms tasks tended to be clearly defined and the structure bureaucratic. By contrast, in continuous-process firms the technology was often advanced and science-based; firms employed a high proportion of professional and technical staff who required more flexible working arrangements, hence a bureaucratic structure was too rigid and tended to be associated with commercial failure.

Environment

The environment with which an organization engages (like its technology) is chiefly defined by the decision to enter a particular product market. But once that initial choice has been made, the environmental pressures it creates – pressures from competitors, from technical change, etc. – become part of the given context of decision-making. The general effect of environment on an organization is determined by the level of *uncertainty* it generates, i.e. whether the environment is stable or the source of rapid and unpredictable change. The more uncertain and complex an organization's environment, the more internally differentiated that organization will tend to become because it will need to develop new functions to cope with environmental problems.

As an example of this link between environment and structure, we can consider the uncertainty created by raw material inputs to an organization. If inputs could always be precisely relied upon, the organization would need no separate purchasing and stock control functions. But this is rarely the case. In practice, organizations have to secure their supplies, monitor quality and suitability, and create buffer stocks to enable flows to be regulated. In this way a need is created for specialized functions to manage the interface with the environment.

Burns and Stalker's study *The Management of Innovation* (1961) was an early and very influential piece of research which focused on the organization–environment relationship These researchers studied the Scottish electronics industry, which underwent rapid expansion in the post-war period under the impact of advances like television and the transistor. With rapid technical change and fierce competition, the firms upon which Burns and Stalker based their research existed in an extremely turbulent, uncertain environment. The researchers sought an explanation of survival and success in such an environment, and they found it in a particular kind of organization structure.

They distinguished two structural types, which they termed 'mechanistic' and 'organic' (1961, pp 119–25). The mechanistic structure was highly bureaucratic, with a strict division of authority and preoccupation with matters of internal efficiency. By contrast, organic structures were flexible and informal, with a good deal of sharing of responsibility, and lower-ranked staff had considerable influence delegated to them. Of crucial importance was the fact that the organic structure retained a strong sense of direction and commitment which embraced all the personnel.

> The distinctive feature of the organic system is the pervasiveness of the working organization as an institution. In concrete terms, this makes itself felt in a preparedness to combine with others in serving the general aims of the concern .... The individual's job ceases to be self-contained; the only way in which 'his' job can be done is by his participating continually with others in the solution of problems which are real to the firm. (1961, p. 125)

The organic structure was thus able to adapt to uncertain environments. Indeed, the research showed that firms that survived and prospered in the electronics industry at that time were the ones with organic structures. The firms which floundered (as many did) tended to be the ones with mechanistic structures, their problems arising from their inability to respond to new and unforeseen circumstances.

Once again, however, this was a contingent relationship. Burns and Stalker wished to avoid any suggestion that organic structures are always superior – indeed they can be very expensive in terms of the managerial time taken up in integrating activities. In an environment where there is little need for adaptability the mechanistic structure comes into its own.

CRITICISMS OF CONTINGENCY THEORY AND MANAGERIAL CHOICE

Organizational analysis subsequently moved away from the consensus of opinion which made contingency theory the main school of thought in the 1960s and early 1970s, and we should now consider some of the criticisms that have been levelled at it.

First, contingency theory suggested an unrealistic and over-simplified model of managerial activity. For although the theory stressed that there is no *one* best way to manage, it did assume that there was *a* best way given a limited number of contextual conditions. The reality, critics have pointed out, is far more complex than this. Managers are required to formulate policy and strategy in far more varied circumstances than ever contingency theory acknowledged, and in fact there is little convincing evidence that structural designs can be made to 'fit' the context of operations. Secondly, the simple *causal* link between structure and performance has also been challenged. Contingency theory proposed that an appropriate structure gives rise to high performance, but all the empirical research showed (or indeed ever could show) was a *correlation* between structure and performance. The direction of causation was assumed. Critics have therefore suggested that in some cases causality may run the other way. In other words, a more realistic and dynamic argument may be that it is the initial performance of organizations which determines the kinds of structure they are able to adopt (Child, 1984, pp. 225–30).

A good illustration of this was provided by a company in which one of the authors of this book conducted some research This was a highly successful manufacturer of surgical equipment, which had adopted a fully integrated management structure. While it was possible that the structure had led to their success, it seemed equally likely that the reverse had happened, that once the company had achieved a dominant market position it often had the resources to develop its matrix structure. This involved a considerable managerial overhead (there was a network of interdepartmental teams permanently established to deal with many specific projects and problems of long-range planning), and it seemed rather unlikely that any company that had been performing badly would have been able to sustain this level of expenditure as a precondition of success.

A third criticism is that contingency theory plays down the importance of *power*, both the power of strategically placed managers and the power of the organization itself. In this context, Child (1972) has referred to the 'strategic choice' exercised by managers as the 'critical variable in organization theory'. Corporate groups with effective power in organizations have a great deal of discretion; their decisions are not predetermined by context and structure, nor are they without the power to enforce choices which suit their purposes irrespective of constraints placed upon them. Wood (1979) has similarly argued that management policy and the development of the organization's human resources are critical factors, and that firms have the capacity to organize themselves from within, rather than being forced to adapt to technical and market contexts. It would be naive not to recognize that organizations often exercise considerable control over their environments. Large-scale organizations dispose of enormous advertising revenues to stimulate markets, they can exert influence via political lobbying, and much modern technology comes under their control. Indeed, organizations with monopolistic powers over markets and potential competitors are readily able to sustain a poor level of performance, or an inappropriate structure, if they wish to do so for whatever reasons.

However, while the force of these criticisms has to be accepted, certain points in defence of contingency theory can be put forward. The model linking context, structure and performance perhaps inevitably involved simplification, but researchers like Woodward and Burns were well aware of this, and in their detailed accounts made a good deal of perceptive comment on the complexity of these relationships. For example, Woodward has frequently been criticized for an order of 'technological determinism' in her work, for suggesting that technology determines organization structure and that human choice plays no significant role. Such criticism is to an extent valid, since she did argue that technology seemed to have an effect on structure and performance of which managers were unaware. However, Woodward also stressed that technology acts only as a *constraint* on behaviour, and that within certain limits conscious choices are exercised.

Thus the contingency theorists' notion of decision-making as an activity partially constrained by structure, but displaying choice and variability, does not seem unreasonable. As Wood has suggested, it may be the popularizers of contingency theory who, with 'their limited reading of the work in which they propose to be rooted', are responsible for any oversimplification, rather than the writers who conducted the classic studies (1979, p. 353). Certainly these writers' empirical research took our understanding of organization and management a stage further, and their contributions remain extremely important.

Managerial problems and responses

Clearly, however, the criticisms that have been made of contingency theory have changed our notions of how managers go about their work. In reality decision-making involves multiple and often conflicting goals, and hence implies the search for workable compromises rather than permanent solutions.

For instance, the choice between rationalized versus flexible structures, which Burns and Stalker investigated, presents itself at many different levels in the organization. Thus the advantages of tight control of costs and labour in a rigidly designed system may be decisive in certain circumstances, but it may be necessary to switch to a more flexible, albeit less efficient system, which can absorb the uncertainties of production and supply, if circumstances change. Moreover, even these choices rarely present themselves as simple alternatives. Managers may have to combine different elements of each approach, and they may need to make constant adjustments if the operation or market context changes. Therefore, rather than try to specify appropriate structural designs or the functional areas of responsibility, modern theory seeks to define the basic problems that managers face, and how in successful firms they go about resolving them. Invariably such central problems present themselves as actual dilemmas which entail the perpetual juggling of different demands.

CONTROL AND INTEGRATION

Child (1984) has drawn attention to two fundamental managerial tasks, which reflect the basic structures of authority and the division of labour: these are the twin problems of *control* and *integration*.

1. Control refers to the problem of regulating the activities of subordinates. We have spoken about the control of organizational work at length in previous chapters, but the control mechanisms typically used by management include standardized operating procedures, job specifications, the monitoring of performance, and the assigning of specific responsibilities. The problem involved here is part of the wider issue of choosing between bureaucratic structures and more flexible relationships. The essential point is that mechanisms for keeping tight control can be self-defeating. The experience of being closely supervised may demoralize people; it may make them surrender initiative and lose interest in their jobs. On top of problems of motivation, centralized control may cause related problems of inflexibility. Organizations remain responsive to change in part because of power being delegated to those with operational roles. Specialists keeping abreast of innovations in their field, middle managers aware of the state of markets and able to act on their know-

ledge – these strengths keep an organization adaptive. Too rigid a control structure tends to withdraw decision-making capacity from those close to the boundary with the environment.

Strategies of control aim to resolve this dilemma by attempting to satisfy the conditions both of the centralization of control and its decentralization. They do this essentially by centralizing and decentralizing different kinds of power: major policy decisions are centralized, while operational responsibility is delegated. Thus, the typical structure of multinational and other large divisionalized companies will embrace a corporate headquarters with authority over things like product development, forward planning and major new investment, while the divisions and individual plants remain profit centres and hence responsible for operational efficiency.

This overall strategy is sustained by corporate management keeping a tight hold of the purse strings. The capital budget will be controlled from the corporate centre, and since important policy decisions always involve capital expenditure, this will effectively keep policy centralized. The plants and divisions are free to run their operations efficiently, but only within an established budget outside which their powers are strictly limited. Thus, within certain limits, this arrangement achieves the best of both worlds: central control over policy and organizational development, and an operational management able to take on-the-spot decisions.

2. Turning to integration, within any large organization there are enormous problems ensuring that information reaches people in time and in sufficient detail to enable them to co-ordinate their activities. However, to develop a structure so that people *can* integrate their efforts is one thing, but whether they *will* integrate even with an efficient structure may be quite another matter. In other words, on top of the purely technical problems of the dissemination of information there are often behavioural difficulties of achieving integration. Moreover, separating the two aspects is really to oversimplify, for managers' willingness to co-operate has to be assumed in any formal system of communication.

A major cause of conflict in organizations, and lack of integration, involves the communications problems that arise out of the division of labour. Differences in outlook, occupational values and style of behaviour can become entrenched in organizations; and they can cause serious problems of co-operation. This diversity within management is encompassed by a general concept: *differentiation*. The term was defined in a well-known early empirical study by Lawrence and Lorsch as 'the difference in cognitive and emotional orientation among managers in different functional departments' (1967, p. 11). These researchers found evidence of a general model linking differentiation and integration. They suggested that, other things being equal, there would be an inverse relationship between the two variables: the higher the differentiation, the lower the integration (or the higher the conflict), and vice versa.

Differentiation covers many aspects of behaviour. One very common source of conflict, which we discussed in the previous chapter, involves the difference between managers having a professional approach to their work and those with a bureaucratic orientation. Another important relationship, which is related to conflicting professional and bureaucratic orientations, is that between line and staff management. Line managers, within the central chain of command, and managers of staff or service departments typically experience problems with which they have to come to terms if the relationship between them is not to break down. Services which are centralized for economy and control become a scarce resource. Thus service managers find themselves under constant pressure for quicker and more comprehensive service, while line managers are often forced to compete for services in order to meet their own targets.

Lawrence and Lorsch themselves focused on major types of intergroup relations in organizations which give rise to recurring problems of integration. They looked at the relationships between production, sales, and research and development departments, and revealed typical patterns of conflict. For example, production managers favoured stable output and low product variation, as these helped them to meet production targets and stay within budget, while managers in sales desired the exact opposite. Rapid delivery and a high degree of variation helped salespeople to meet customer requirements. Similar problems arose between production and R&D: development engineers became preoccupied with the technical problems of product design and were oriented towards long-range planning; production managers, on the other hand, wanted engineers to be available to solve immediate practical problems. Differences along these and other dimensions caused managers to fail to communicate properly and to be unable to understand one another's problems.

THE RESOLUTION OF CONFLICT

The distinction we have made between control and integration, although quite helpful in understanding managerial activity, can be rather artificial. In practice managers do not always simply issue orders and then leave subordinates to take care of lateral integration (although subordinates are usually more responsible for this). Managerial actions have a more *systematic* character, which includes both order-giving and the necessary co-ordination. Nonetheless, if such systems are to be viable, the conflicts that can arise when orders are issued, or when attempts are made to integrate activities, must somehow be dealt with.

The obvious answer to the problem of excessive levels of conflict – given the above model showing that differentiation leads to conflict – would seem to lie in only having homogeneous bodies of managers. However, the solution is unfortunately not that simple. Organizations often require a wide range of specialist skills, as well as needing to allocate tasks to well-defined sub-units, both of which lead to high levels of differentiation. A contradiction therefore arises: for high performance, high levels of differentiation are required, but these lead to conflict, which in turn has a deleterious effect on performance. What this means in practice is that conflict can never be wholly eliminated, and hence the resolution of conflict remains a central problem of management.

One of the most common management practices aimed at resolving conflict is the *mediation* of relationships of potentially high conflict. Here intermediate departments or channels of communication intervene between the two groups concerned in effect preventing them from coming into direct contact. For example, the relationships between production departments in mass assembly plants contain a major source of conflict in the problems that departments create for one another. Such departments are highly interdependent, since the product passes between them, and if the work of one department is not to specification it means that another department will be unable to do its work. In such cases, when problems of integration arise, production management in one department first approach some intermediate department (quality control or production engineering often fulfil this role) who then investigate the problem with production management in the department concerned. Thus potential confrontation may be avoided.

In fact there are many variants of structure and managerial practice designed to resolve the conflict that would otherwise be generated in organizations. In their research, Lawrence and Lorsch found that the most successful organizations had managed to achieve high levels of integration together with high levels of differentiation (i.e. at variance with the general rule) by means of effective mechanisms for continually resolving conflict as it arose. They report several such mechanisms, including special integrating groups, but also appropriate forms of motivation, influence and interpersonal style among integrating managers, which enabled them to understand and accommodate the points of view of other groups (1967, p. 80). Similarly, Child (1984, pp. 127–32) set out a number of different methods of integration. These ranged from simply making an individual manager responsible for liaison with another department, to highly elaborate matrix structures comprised of intersecting project teams. The point stressed in both these accounts is that particular organizations have levels of 'required integration' matching the context in which they operate. And the more powerful integrating mechanisms (and hence the more costly in terms of managerial overheads) are appropriate only where an organization faces an extremely demanding task (highly uncertain environment, complex technical problems, competitive markets), otherwise the less sophisticated alternative methods are preferred.

Further reading

Child, J. (1984) *Organization* (2nd ed.). London: Harper and Row.

Dawson, S. (1992) *Analysing Organisations* (2nd ed). Basingstoke: Macmillan.

Donaldson, L. (1985) *In Defence of Organization Theory.* Cambridge: Cambridge University Press.

March, J.G. and H.A. Simon (1958) *Organizations.* New York: Wiley.

Perrow, C. (1970) *Organizational Analysis.* London: Tavistock.

Perrow, C. (1979) *Complex Organizations: A Critical Essay.* Glenview, Ill.: Scott, Foresman.

Pugh, D. (ed.) (1984) *Organization Theory* (2nd edn). Harmondsworth: Penguin.

Rose, M. (1975) *Industrial Behaviour: Research and Control* (2nd ed). London: Penguin.

18

Organizational Culture

The focus on structure in the previous two chapters had the virtue of highlighting the patterns of behaviour that are observable and repeated in organizations. But the structural approach can overlook some important aspects of organizational reality. The qualitative aspect of organizations, what an organization is 'really like', is often poorly captured by structure (particularly formal structure). However, a concept that does try to encapsulate the whole reality is that of *culture*.

Originally an anthropological term, culture refers to the underlying values, beliefs and codes of practice that makes a community what it is. The customs of a society, the self-images of its members, the things that make it different from other societies, are its culture. There are objective factors at work here, in the sense that social beliefs constrain behaviour, but culture is also powerfully *subjective*. It reflects the meanings and understandings that we typically attribute to situations, the solutions that we apply to common problems. Being a 'member of society' means that we have acquired core values through the process of growing up and being socialized. Large swathes of our culture are taken for granted – we are more or less unconscious of the huge fund of meanings and ideas that we hold in common with others. But these social bonds and common knowledge remain integral to our identity and sense of personal cohesion.

The idea of a common culture suggests possible problems about whether *organizations* can be considered as having cultures. Organizations are only one constituent element of society. People enter them from the surrounding community and bring their culture with them. We already have a good many examples of this kind of broader work culture. What were referred to in Chapter 12 as 'orientations to work' are attitudes that can be understood only by reference to workers' social background. Similarly, in Chapter 9, Rice's classic (1958) study of job redesign in an Indian textile mill showed how workers' responses towards new forms of responsibility very much reflected the work attitudes traditional in the country. And studies of comparative management have shown that managerial practices and values can be very different in different countries. We saw in Chapter 15 that much of the success of countries like Germany and Japan has been attributed to industrial cultures that foster high levels of performance.

Factors like these would tend to cut across anything that might exist in an organization. Nonetheless, it is still possible to think of organizations as having cultures of their own. Organizations possess the paradoxical quality of being both 'part of' and 'apart from' society. They are embedded in a wider social context, but they are also communities in their own right with distinctive rules and values. They can thus be thought of as 'culture producing phenomena' (Smircich, 1983).

In this chapter we look first at the importance of the business context. An emphasis on values and beliefs might appear to be of mainly sociological interest, yet corporate culture has become one of the great management buzz words. Thus it is necessary to establish what the material gains are perceived to be. What does culture contribute to the bottom line? Secondly, culture is clearly a complex concept, and one we will need to explore in some detail. It refers to the totality of knowledge in an organization or society. But if almost anything is part of culture, the concept runs the risk of becoming vague, a dumping ground of unexplained factors in organizations. So does the concept mean everything and nothing, or can it be defined in more precise ways? Culture is basically substantive; it reflects the beliefs and techniques that characterize *specific* organizations. We therefore need to distinguish the ways in which beliefs are unique to each organization, as well as between different cultural types. Thirdly, we need to review the strengths and weaknesses of the cultural metaphor – in particular the tensions that exist between the idea that beliefs and meanings can be 'managed', and that of culture as a unique set of attributes.

Organizational culture and strategic management

In certain respects culture has long been on the agenda of management theorists. Influential writers like Chester Barnard in the 1930s and 1940s, and Peter Drucker from the 1950s to the present, emphasized the centrality of *values* in the management of enterprises. Management for them always meant more than mere decision-making and the planning of procedures. Management meant corporate leadership, which in turn implied motivating people and providing a vision of where the enterprise is going.

The Hewlett-Packard Way
Values
Trust and respect for individuals
A high level of achievement and contribution
Conducting business with uncompromising integrity
Achieving common objectives through teamwork
Encouraging flexibility and innovation

Objectives
Profit
Customer respect and loyalty
Participating in relevant fields of interest
Growth
Helping our people share in company success
Management that fosters initiative and creativity
Corporate citizenship and responsibility

Strategies and practices
Management by wandering around
Management by objectives
Open-door policy
Total quality control

Not really until the 1980s, however, has culture *explicitly* been identified as the 'something extra' on top of planning and administration. The limitations of conventional ideas of planned change, based on things like organizational design and effective personnel selection techniques, are now being recognized. What is the point in trying to change the staff if new people merely absorb the existing custom and practice? Design and structure are important but organizations can be successful in spite of poor structures, or fail even when correctly designed. Instead of changing structures, real change must mean changing the corporate ethos, the images and values that inform action; and this new way of understanding the life of organizations must be brought into the management process. In this context a number of companies – Hewlett-Packard, Johnson and Johnson, IBM and the like – have long been known for their explicit avowal of corporate values (the table above shows an abbreviated version of the Hewlett-Packard 'way'). More recently others have followed suit and have produced mission statements which combine prescriptions for action with company goals, but which are heavily imbued with culture and values.

CULTURE AND ORGANISATIONAL CHANGE

As a result of the interest in corporate culture, the belief has become firmly established that *culture fosters success*. Here, Deal and Kennedy (1982) have argued that culture was the single most important factor accounting for success or failure. Their survey of US corporations found that the firms which were perceived to 'believe in something' or to 'stand for something' were both the strong culture companies and the high performers. The researchers identified four key dimensions of culture.

1. *Values:* the beliefs that lie at the heart of the corporate culture. These should be strongly held and openly supported, because identification with other things (the union, colleagues, instrumental goals) can mean weak or fragmented culture.
2. *Heroes:* the people who embody values. Organizational heroes are the actors who carry culture; by providing role models they assist in getting values widely accepted and adopted.
3. *Rites and rituals:* routines of interaction that have strong symbolic qualities. Whether mundane or elaborate, rites and rituals demonstrate to individuals the expectations that the organization has of them.
4. *The culture network:* the informal communications system or 'hidden hierarchy of power' in the organization. People must be adept at manipulating this if they are to be effective at all.

Culture and corporate excellence: Peters
A recent management writer who trades heavily on culture is Tom Peters. In a popular and highly influential book that Peters co-authored, *In Search of Excellence* (Peters and Waterman, 1982), a model is developed of what it takes to achieve corporate 'excellence'. The famous eight prescriptions were distilled out of research with a cross-section of US companies deemed to have that magic quality.

Bias for action
Closeness to the customer
Autonomy and entrepreneurship
Productivity through people
Hands on, value driven
Stick to the knitting
Simple form, lean staff
Simultaneous loose–tight properties

The possession of a unique set of cultural attributes lies behind many of these factors (1982, p. 26). For example, sticking to the knitting means staying close to the core business; we can see that the opposite policy of growth by acquiring unrelated enterprises is likely to dilute corporate culture. Similarly, autonomy is closely related to culture insofar as the freedom to act on one's own initiative is what commits people to central goals. More generally, it is culture which prevents the eight prescriptions from becoming mere platitudes. Everyone knows that 'the customer comes first' or that 'people are our greatest asset', but successful companies make these clichés a reality; they create *specific* customer- and people-orientated climates.

Peters and Waterman also suggest an interesting psychological theory of the link between organizational culture and business performance. Culture can be looked on as a reward of work. We sacrifice much to organizations, and culture is a form of return on effort. Culture provides ordinary people in humdrum jobs with a sense of the significance of their work. People need to find meaning in their lives; culture provides meaning and hence reinforces motivation and morale. It is this that accounts for the 'unusual effort on the part of ordinary employees' (1982, p. xvii) that is the hallmark of corporate excellence.

In his later book, *Thriving on Chaos* (1987), Peters had to deal with the somewhat uncomfortable fact that several of the companies declared 'excellent' in 1982 were experiencing serious difficulties by the late 1980s; some had even gone out of business. His response was to emphasize the market uncertainty of the new economic order. He concedes that he underestimated the seriousness of US economic decline and the threat of competitors (particularly Japan). In this 'world turned upside down' his earlier concept of excellence had proved too static; there are no safe companies. Instead the only prescription is for ceaseless innovation. Interestingly, too, this approach provides a critique of the old systems theories of organization, or contingency theory as presented in Chapter 17. There we noted that in certain contingencies of market stability, bureaucratic companies could be the most effective. Peters disagrees; the idea that there are companies that have little need for flexibility no longer applies. Innovation is paramount. 'The old saw, if it ain't broke, don't fix it, needs revision. I propose: fix it anyway' (1987, p. 3).

Culture and innovation: Kanter
Another of the gurus of modern management, Rosabeth Moss Kanter, has likewise focused on the pressing need for innovation. In *When Giants Learn to Dance* (1989) she refers to the growing intensity of global competition as 'the corporate Olympics' – the fact that now there are more competitors than ever, more industrializing nations. The model she develops of 'post-entrepreneurialism' centers on the need for large corporations to retain the flexibility and dynamism of the entrepreneurial roots (teaching the giants to dance). Her earlier book, *The Change Masters* (1984), had also dealt with the cultural

403

changes needed to make large firms innovative, in particular the *implementation* of change and the complex organizational (cultural) processes that go with this. She notes, for example, the paradox implicit in linking culture with change. On the surface, culture has essentially traditional and stable qualities. So how can you have a 'culture of change'? Yet this is precisely what the innovative organization needs.

> To manage change as a normal way of life requires that people find their stability and security not in specific organizational arrangements but in the culture and direction of the organization. It requires that they feel integrated with the whole rather than identified with the particular territory of the moment. (1984) (p. 133)

Kanter is more concerned than most writers with the problematic aspects of culture. Whereas writers like Peters and Deal and Kennedy dismiss alternative values as 'weak cultures', Kanter takes full account of these complexities. She describes a number of cultural types as polar opposites. Some companies have a 'culture of inferiority': a tendency to doubt their own ability, to feel that they need to recruit managerial talent from other firms, and to rely on outsiders (e.g. consultants) to create innovation. Contrasted to these are companies with a 'culture of success', reflected in pride in the company, can-do attitudes and a confidence in developing their own managerial talent (1984, p. 92). Another interesting set of cultural types are what she calls cultures of 'age versus youth' (p. 349). Companies in established industrial sectors seem to be more prone to leaving their heads in the sand, seeing little need for change and believing that problems will resolve themselves without being squarely confronted (culture of age). In contrast, newer high-tech industries tend to empower innovators and make it easier for people to question existing patterns (culture of youth). Being a 'young' company has built-in advantages, insofar as innovation and enterprise become the norm for the whole sector.

Politico-cultural mechanisms of change: Pettigrew
To understand organizations in this complex way is to accept that the means of 'managing culture' have to be subtle and indirect. In particular, cultural change has to be achieved through the medium of *power*. Perhaps the most influential writer identified with this approach over the past two decades has been Andrew Pettigrew. In this major study of Imperial Chemical Industries, for example, Pettigrew looks at the relations between the political process and corporate culture (1985, Chapters 10 and 11).

In the period up to 1980 ICI had a 'segmentalist' culture, reflecting the weakness of the corporate centre. The company tradition was for a kind of comfortable continuity in which chairmen served for only a short period, often at the end of their careers, which effectively ruled out any radical changes. Real power lay with the divisions and divisional managing directors. They ran their operations as independent fiefdoms, so that strategic action was next to impossible. Instead there was an obsession with short-termism and financial targets. However, between 1980 and 1982 ICI faced a profits crisis which paved the way for changes at the top, particularly the appointment of John Harvey-Jones as chairman. But the changes that Harvey-Jones implemented did not begin then and there; the real change process had a much longer history. Pettigrew charts the emergence of a managerial group led by Harvey-Jones that became identified with change. In the decade leading up to the crisis they developed a perception of the inadequacies of ICI's corporate culture and a vision of a more strategic culture. They were able to communicate this vision through a network of contacts and loyalties. Thus Pettigrew identified the problems of getting the need for change accepted, and the fact that change happens only when powerful interest groups line up behind it. These developments in social perceptions precede any planning or action on change (1985, p. 434).

Pettigrew also stressed the necessity of this kind of deep cultural shift if change is to be *stabilized* (1985, p. 434). One of the least acknowledged problems of change is that of the situation lapsing once initial 'changes' have occurred. Because change is often linked to strong personalities, the situation can easily revert back when the initiators move on. Thus if innovations are to be reinforced, they have to be embedded in the historic practices of the organization.

THE MANAGEMENT OF CHANGE

The above analysis suggests that cultures are resistant to many forms of attempted change, but they can also be amazingly dynamic. In the right circumstances, 'tradition' can be adaptive and self-modifying. Indeed, if real change is to occur in organizations – rather than cosmetic or short-lived change – it has to happen at the cultural level. Given the past failures of management theory, corporate culture therefore has many powerful attractions as a lever for change; the problem is how to get a hand on the lever. The above analysis suggests some pointers.

First, the case has been argued that cultures can be *explicitly created*. Understanding culture and being able to modify it are crucial both to market success for the company and to career success for the individual. You have to work with the culture – or be very much aware of what it takes to change an existing culture. In this sense, successful companies are not shy about promoting their heroes and symbols. Writers like Peters and Deal and Kennedy also dispel any ideas about culture being 'soft'. Strong-culture companies do not generate cosy sets of values that make people committed by making them more content. Such companies are not particularly tolerant of those who reject core values. A strong culture creates powerful behavioural expectations and constraints, more so than any formal structure of procedures and rules.

Second, all of the main management writers are clear that the ability in companies to be culturally innovative is strongly related to *leadership*. Top management must take responsibility for building strong cultures that fit market needs. Deal and Kennedy, for example, supplemented their survey of senior management with biographical material on business leaders, and found that people who pioneer successful companies rarely operate on a narrow economic or administrative front. Rather, they are obsessed with developing values and acting as role models. Similarly, as Peters became aware of the turbulent markets that companies have to survive in, he refined his original eight prescriptions. These became a simplified four-part model centered on *customers*, *innovation* and *people*, all linked via *leadership*. Peters, and other writers too, are strongly drawn to the concept of 'transformational leadership' (see Chapter 8 above). This stresses that the role of leader extends beyond that of the rational analyst. Leaders construct the social reality of the organization for members; they shape values and attend to the drama and vision of the organization. As Peters notes, the leader is 'orchestrator and labeller: taking what can be gotten in the way of action and shaping it – generally after the fact – into lasting commitment to a new strategic direction. In short, he makes meanings' (1982, p. 75). Pettigrew likewise stresses that leadership means using power in a positive way to manage the process of cultural change – or, in his celebrated phrase, politics becomes the 'management of meaning' (1985, p. 44).

A third point is that culture is frequently counterposed to *formal rationality*. As Kanter notes, organizations need to be 'conscious of themselves as a culture, not just as a technical system' (1984, pp. 133–4). In this sense culture helps to resolve the dilemma of bureaucracy: the fact that formal procedures are necessary for business integrity and planning (Weber was right on this point), but they also stifle autonomy and innovation. Peters especially is highly critical of the 'rationalists' who for so long have dominated management theory. Americans are among the worst offenders here. American managers and management writers are strongly inclined towards complicated systems and technical fixes (reflected in systems like Taylorism). But culture can hold bureaucracy at bay. The stronger the corporate culture, the less need there is for detailed procedures and rules, because culture itself guides employee action. Thus firms are able to have proper administrative back-up and engage in formal planning without these activities becoming ends in themselves.

OTHER CULTURES

As already suggested, the reasons for urgency in the current debate on organization culture reflect to a great extent the new global competition. The period from the mid-1970s has been one of growing uncertainty for firms, with the appearance of new competitor nations, new technologies and new types of consumer demand. In response to a changing environment and business crises, adaptable cultures that are responsive to strategic pressure and corporate guidance have become vital.

According to Morgan (1986, p. 111) a central factor in all this has been the ascent to economic power of Japan. The very differences that are perceived between Japanese culture and ours have highlighted culture as a factor in managerial success. But also the *nature* of Japanese organizational culture, Morgan suggests, focuses on the whole organization, the cultivation of harmonious relations at all levels in the organization, the merging of individual with common goals, and a reliance on worker responsibility. All this contrasts with our own cultural biases. The Anglo-American obsession with bureaucratic systems betrays a tendency to break down processes in mechanical fashion and to seek 'efficiencies in the elements of management'. Under the western (especially American) ethic of competitive individualism, the key metaphor is the game: the obsession with excellence, the need to distinguish winners from losers. Anglo-American production culture is anti-person in other fundamental ways; the ideas of making work systems 'idiot proof' and reducing labour content are endemic to western production values.

This argument may have been oversimplified, however. As was pointed out in Chapter 15, it was the belief that cultural factors lay at the root of Japanese success that caused western industrialists to despair of ever being able to learn from Japan. In contrast, the later focus on more 'copyable' production principles (the just-in-time system) was what really sparked off interest in Japanese methods. Also, the view of Japanese industrial culture as being rooted in moral qualities of sacrifice may be somewhat idealized. In many ways, Japanese society is just as competitive and individualistic as our own. As we also saw in Chapter 15, an alternative view of the Japanese principles of duty and obligation is that these are the means by which large enterprises exploit smaller ones. And an alternative view of the

Japanese production ethos is that they are the 'modern masters' of Taylorism.

The most influential American management writers have always been resistant to the 'learn from Japan' movement. Peters, for example, argued that there is no need to look elsewhere for models of corporate excellence; the best American businesses provide these. The problem is that they have been paid insufficient attention (1982, p. xxii). Later, in *Thriving on Chaos* (1987), he takes the American decline much more seriously. He bemoans the 1980s as a decade of corporate 'madness' characterized by merger mania, asset-stripping and financial corruption. Moreover, the habits of production that the USA persists in (giantism, anti-labourism) continue to put it at a disadvantage with Japan. Despite this analysis, however, Peters still sticks with his original formula: he looks to home-grown exemplars of success, implicitly rejecting arguments about Japan's superior management culture. Similarly, Kanter (1989) was also concerned with the rejuvenation of corporate America, and her models were all local ones. She believed that she saw the beginnings of a tide of change sweeping through American big business, and a number of 'post-entrepreneurial prototypes' exclusively in US firms.

There is no need to delay over this debate. A belief in the importance of a unifying culture, among certain sections of the business community, may well have arisen in the way that Morgan describes. Not only Japan, but also other success economies like Germany and the Pacific rim countries are seen as having cultures that emphasize open communications and the ability to absorb delegated power. It is how these organization cultures are perceived in the minds of managements that is the crucial issue.

Exploring organizational culture

Attempts to define organizational culture have adopted a number of different approaches. Some focus on its *manifestations* – the heroes and villains, rites and rituals, myths and legends that populate organizations. Others emphasize the stocks of collective *knowledge* that members hold. These make up the institutional memory of the organization and make action possible. Culture is also *socially constructed*; it reflects meanings that are constituted in interaction and that form commonly accepted 'definitions of the situation'. Rather than try to cover all this ground in a single statement, however, a better understanding might be gained by sifting out some of the basic attributes to the concept.

CULTURE IS SYMBOLIC

We have all had the experience of being asked what the organization we work in is 'really like'. We might attempt to respond in general terms, but if that fails (which it usually does) we start telling stories – we describe a particular person, or recount an anecdote that we feel is somehow typical of the organization. In this sense the stories and legends, which all organizations have, seem to say something deeper; they are the representations of culture.

A symbol 'stands for' something more than itself. The symbol can be many things – an event, an object, a person – but the essential point is that a symbol is invested with meaning by us, and expresses forms of understanding derived from our past collective experiences. The sociological view of culture is that organizations exist in the minds of their members. How members define reality is just as important for outcomes as concrete techniques and procedures. Kanter, for example, points out that organizations frequently 'talk up' the emphasis on change. In defining as 'changes' events which may not have been particularly innovative, new definitions of the situation are being created: 'Organizational change consists in part of a series of emerging constructions of reality, including revision of the past, to correspond to the requisites of new players and new demands' (1984, p. 287).

In terms of understanding what is going on in organizations, the simple point is that appearances can be deceptive. Situations that seem to have a straightforward function often have a deeper meaning. A good example of this kind of symbolism is afforded by *organizational meetings*. Much decision-making in companies is conducted within managerial cliques, while at formal meetings (where decision-making is supposed to occur) other things may be happening. Meetings may be chances for the rising stars to shine, or for the boss to convey what great people he thinks his staff are. Indeed, given that meetings are the main public arena in organizations, they may in a paradoxical sense be too important for routine business discussions. They are where key cultural processes are acted out. Carnall (1990) refers to an extreme and pathological example of this in an insurance company. The company had been formed by a merger several years earlier, but the staff from the original two firms had never overcome their antagonisms. As a result the culture of the company reflected a kind of false consensus: people were afraid to confront tough issues, fearing that deeper conflict might break out. Corporate meetings were highly ritualized affairs in which progress reports would receive praise and support from senior management. The meetings were used not for discussion or decision-making, but for a much more critical purpose, to try to preserve the precarious company unity.

It is not entirely clear why symbolic communication is so necessary. Why describe one thing in terms of another rather than directly? Why resort to fables and anecdotes? What is clear is that symbolism plays a major part in daily communication, much more than we usually realize. Symbols are about the *dramatization* of messages and this can be vital for an organization's operation.

Stories

The point is well illustrated if we see the communication system of organizations as an unfolding story line. More than any other event, stories show how culture acts as a 'sense-making device'. The collective experiences of people are almost always ambivalent and open to different interpretations. But in a story they are assembled together in a way that rationalizes complex events. There is always a 'line' or a 'point' to a story. Stories are used to manage uncertainty and enable collective action to occur. Indeed, without this dramatizing aspect, organizations could be paralysed by uncertainty. As Boje (1991) points out: 'when a decision is at hand, the old stories are recounted and compared to unfolding story lines to keep the organization from repeating historically bad choices and to invite the repetition of past successes'. Stories are a way of rehearsing complex situations that enable us to check our own understanding with others. Group interests may be embodied in stories, which serve the ideological purpose of advancing those interests and may be used by groups to initiate change. Boje also points out that we should not see stories as static things, wheeled out to prove a point. The enactment or *performance* of the story is the crucial thing: different versions of stories are told in different situations, different actors will have rights over different parts of the story, and getting the story woven into the culture is itself part of the organizational power game. (See also Martin and Meyerson, 1988; McConkie and Boss, 1986; Mitroff and Kilmann, 1975; Wilkins, 1984.)

The US Trip

This is a case example of an organizational story. The background was the purchase of a computer package by a large financial services organization. The company had identified the only package that was really suitable, but there were other potential problems. The supplier of the package was a computer agency that the company had used before and of which it had had a disastrous experience. Not to put too fine a point on it, the agency had made a complete mess of an important project a couple of years earlier. The company was nervous about employing them again because the agency would be doing the conversion programming to integrate the package into the mainframe systems, as well as undertaking future maintenance.

At this point 'the US trip' took place. The parent of the computer agency was an American firm, and because the package was not widely used in Britain a fact-finding trip to the United States had been arranged. The British team held talks there with the agency's top management and visited several user firms that had the package in operation. On returning they pronounced themselves more than satisfied. They stressed that they were initially wary about the cost involved, and about whether an 'expensive foreign junket' could be justified. But the trip had been worthwhile and one they would repeat in similar circumstances. All their fears about purchasing the package had been removed.

It seemed clear, however, that the US trip had developed a kind of ritual significance. It had taken place at a time of uncertainty in an important investment decision. Later, whenever doubts about the purchase were raised, or when managers were being asked to account for their decision, they would say, 'Ah, but there was the US trip', and this single reference stood for a whole bundle of initiatives and effort that went into testing the suitability of the package. It also seems clear that certain aspects of the US trip had been dramatized. This is not to say that any crude lies were told, simply that events had been 'worked over' with benefit of hindsight. The trip had become a story that was retold in order to make sense of an equivocal situation.

Managers made great play of their initial concern about the expense involved, yet it seems unlikely that *at the time* they went about stressing what all this was going to cost and whether it would be of any benefit. Also, the great success claimed for the trip may have been overplayed. In the retelling this was dramatically compared with concerns about the trip's cost; the story line was: 'At first I was doubtful, then I was converted.' Managers actually used the term, 'conversion', as if to suggest a religious experience.

In fact, it was not at all obvious why the trip should have been so reassuring. The computer package itself was not the real problem; all parties agreed that it was the best available. It was the supplying agency that caused the worries. The package was to be converted and maintained by the American parent's British operation. The crucial issue, the professionalism of the staff in Britain, could not have been resolved in the United States.

Thus it seems clear that 'the US trip' was referred to partly in a symbolic way to legitimize a somewhat risky course of action. In the event the gamble paid off; the British staff turned out to be highly professional, and they completed the project on time and to everyone's satisfaction.

CULTURE IS UNIFYING

Secondly, culture refers to processes that bind the organization together. In this sense, cultural processes stand opposed to the many forms of conflict that occur in organizations. Although conflict is certainly an ever-present reality, culture represents an equally real and valid alternative face of the organization. Culture then is consensual not conflictual. The idea of corporate culture reinforces the unifying strengths of central goals and creates a sense of common responsibility – which is why it has assumed such an important place in management thinking.

Here we can refer to one of the foremost British management writers, Tom Burns. Burns's early work had stressed organizations as 'plural social systems' that encompassed political as well as rational action (Burns, 1969). But he later turned to the *interaction* of plural systems, 'the working organisation with the political system, the career system and so forth' (1977, p. xi). In his masterly study of the BBC, Burns (1977) anticipated the current interest in organizational culture by several years. Plural systems were integrated at the level of culture, and constituted 'a way of defining the "rules of the game" according to which the internal and external business of the Corporation and all the manifold social intercourse to which this business gives rise should be conducted' (p. xiii).

Burns's famous concept of 'organic' structure (see Chapter 17) was also underpinned by culture. The organic concept stresses the importance of flexible matrix structures, something it shares with quite a few other influential management theories. But though he is usually represented in this way, Burns was trying to convey more than just a non-bureaucratic or flexible approach. Organic structures reflect internalized goals and a deeply held sense of common purpose. This applies especially to workers, and groups like technical specialists, that develop objectives that are often seen as opposing central interests and goals. In an organic enterprise all groups retain a sense of central purpose. This produces an adaptive organization because it enables conventional work habits and authority structures to be modified according to changing demands.

Another important linkage is to organizational *rationality*. This was referred to earlier in the chapter in terms of 'formal rationality': that whole web of procedures, systems and controls designed to make organizational performance predictable and accountable. Yet a more common-sense version of rationality can be related to culture. What people usually mean by 'rational behaviour' is simply the ability of organizational members to work together. If we think of people being able to tackle problems in a reasoned manner, without politicking and without being drawn into hidden agendas, this is what we instinctively think of as acting rationally. The unifying force of beliefs and values held in common lies at the heart of such rational action. Certainly, when managements are advocating strong corporate cultures, this type of exchange is what they have in mind.

412

Case example: Organic culture

This apparently trivial case example occurred on a research visit to the Scottish subsidiary of an American electronics multinational.

On first contact the plant's chief executive and the researcher met in the reception area. During this conversation the CE called across to the receptionist to ask for some coffee to be brought. She replied that she had such-and-such a report to finish typing and asked if he could get the coffee himself. The CE said, yes, that report needed to go out quickly, and off he went to get the coffee.

During this brief exchange a total reversal of authority (not to mention gender) roles had taken place. Formal authority had been upended; the boss was acting on the subordinate's initiative. This was not a unique event, nor perhaps should we read too much into it. However, mundane events can often be seen as microcosms of a wider reality. The obvious explanation was that both knew the report was more important than the coffee. But in how many companies would the receptionist have simply 'done her job' and fetched the coffee? And in how many companies would the CE have felt his authority under threat if he had performed the menial task? Perhaps a deeper reality was that the CE and the receptionist had an ever-present sense of company needs, and this shared knowledge enabled them to navigate a potentially difficult situation.

CULTURE IS HOLISTIC

Culture refers to the *essence*, the *reality* of an organization – what it is like to work there, how people deal with each other, what behaviours are expected. Before the culture concept was widely employed, the term organizational 'climate' was often used; this was vaguer but also referred to the experience of being part of an organization.

One important way in which the holistic character of the organization is expresses is through *rules*. By these, social scientists do not usually mean formally stated and recorded rules (though these can be included); they mean the unspoken, taken-for-granted rules that regulate social conduct. Indeed, the question of what an organization is really like is often followed up with enquiries about the 'rules of the game' or 'learning the ropes'. Because organizations are competitive places, one absolutely vital rule-set for members is that which defines good performance. This is manifest in career rewards like promotions and pay rises. But 'getting on' involves a much wider and more subtle array: being included in discussions, consulted, given good assignments. Making it in an organization means learning to navigate in the subtle and dangerous currents that bring these rewards. And the rules of the game can be very different. In one organization

413

success might come from bureaucratic abilities, while in another inputs into some productive enterprise might be the key to success.

This latter type of 'rational' rule is interestingly reflected in Michael Lewis's *Liar's Poker* (1989). An insider account of the 1980s investment banking boom, this book shows the dealing rooms of New York and London as an obsessive and enclosed world, a world of 'hysterical greed and ambition'. The culture of bond-dealing is full of symbols – legends grew up around the main players, epithets were attached to them, they took on heroic or villainous qualities. (Indeed, many of the heroes were also villains – by 1991 the firm that Lewis worked for, Saloman Brothers, had been cited for massive fraud.) The key ritual of Liar's Poker, versions of which are played in most Wall Street firms, is based on players each holding a dollar bill and bidding on combinations of the serial numbers. The game was a potent symbol of the real game: making money.

> When you managed a firm, well, sure, you received your quota of envy, fear and admiration. But for all the wrong reasons. You did not make the money for Saloman. You did not take risk. You were hostage to your producers. They took risk. They proved their superiority every day by handling risk better than the rest of the risk-taking world.... And if you wanted to show off, Liar's Poker was the only way to go. The game had a powerful meaning for traders. They believed that it had a lot in common with bond trading. It tested a trader's character. It honed a trader's instincts. A good player made a good trader, and vice-versa. We all understood it. (1989, p. 17)

As we see, in one sense the game *became* the reality: it prevented the skills of the real producers from being submerged by management. Success at Liar's Poker was a flag of status that top management craved as well. Lewis recounts a Saloman Brothers legend in which a senior trader, the 'king of the players', faced down the company chairman in a million-dollar hand of the game. Hence his book is also a kind of homage to the skills of the bond traders. In the final analysis, the rules of success reflected the only thing that mattered – the profit that traders showed on their accounts.

We can see that all of the above elements – culture as symbolic, unifying and holistic – are interlocking. The symbolic nature of culture is unifying. Symbols by definition are based on shared meanings (we would not understand them as symbols otherwise); and since organizational culture is built out of symbolic events it expresses the values and beliefs that members hold in common. Likewise, symbolic/unifying events express the holism of the organization. These processes work through many levels of reality. Culture is rooted deep in unconscious sources, but is also represented in superficial practices and behavioural codes. Indeed, in one way culture has to be mundane as it is reproduced in daily interaction. Because organizations *are* social organisms (not mechanisms) the whole is present in the parts and symbolic events become microcosms of the whole – which is why we often learn what organizations are 'really like' from trivial-sounding incidents.

CLASSIFYING CULTURES?

An initial way of elaborating and exploring the cultures of different organizations is to classify them into types. For example, we saw the polar-opposite types that Kanter developed above, and there have been a number of other such frameworks. One very influential classification scheme, developed by Charles Handy (1986), distinguishes three types of culture stabilized in large enterprises.

1. *Role culture.* This is very similar to the classic Weberian bureaucracy, or to Burns's idea of the mechanistic organization (described in Chapters 16 and 17). Role cultures are highly formalized, they abound with regulations and paperwork, and relations between members are dominated by authority and the hierarchy. A strict division of labour fragments works so that people tend to be reluctant to take on wider responsibilities. Instead, they become obsessed with fulfilling narrow job definitions. Likewise, formal structures of communication tend to restrict information flow rather than maximizing communication links. Such cultures have the strong disadvantage of being resistant to change, and like many bureaucracies have the tendency to lose sight of their basic objectives and to become preoccupied with day-to-day administration. On the other hand, the tight control of resources is easier under these kinds of culture; indeed, it is what they are intended for.

2. *Task culture.* This is the opposite of the role culture, and similar to Burns's organic type of organization. Task cultures preserve a strong sense of the basic mission of the organization. They tend to be designed along product-based lines, with the various divisions and groups in the organization devoted to forms of tangible output. Team working is the basis on which jobs are organized; project teams draw on the specialisms needed for task performance, breaking down rigid structures of hierarchy and function. Members' loyalties tend to be oriented towards the work rather than towards formal rules. Obvious advantages of the task culture are that it fosters creativity and is readily adaptable to high-quality services and products. The other side of the coin is that such cultures can be expensive to operate. The control of overheads and the centralization of resources tends to be difficult.

415

3. *Power culture.* This occurs in organizations with a single power source, which may be an individual or a corporate group. All policy and strategic decisions are centralized, so that a power culture reflects the web of influence that emanates from the figurehead personality or clique. The key power-holders rule through their control of rewards (appointments, promotions, etc.); subordinates defer to power-holders and attempt to anticipate their wishes and attract their attention. Power-holders themselves often adopt ideosyncratic styles of management; things get done by the boss letting subordinates 'into his thinking'. Power structures have the advantage that plans can be formulated and decisions taken swiftly with a single control centre, and the leadership can provide inspiration to sustain a strong culture. On the other hand, if such organizations go wrong, they can go very badly wrong because they depend on the skills and integrity of individuals. Also, a company with a power culture may suffer a crisis of succession when the leadership retires or moves on. This is because central power is jealously guarded and little provision is made for a new generation to take over.

Handy points out in addition that these cultural types are usually tied to particular kinds of organization structure and design. The role culture tends to be linked to the typical pyramid-shaped bureaucratic structure, with formal divisions between functional groups and hierarchical levels. The task structure is associated with flexible matrix structures of management. These contain strong lateral as well as vertical linkages, and groups with overlapping membership. And, finally, the power culture maps on to a web-like communications structure, with the dominant group at the centre and lines of authority radiating out to functional groups and personnel.

The limits of classification
Classifications like Handy's can be very useful in analysing real-life organizations; they show us what to look for and highlight key features of the culture. This is especially true if we can find organizations which fit very closely the role, task and power culture types. What is more likely is that cultures will be a complex mix of types, although even then it may still be possible to see in the organizational culture some of the key dimensions of the classification. For example, the culture of the Wall Street investment banks that Lewis described in *Liar's Poker* could be seen as a mix of two of Handy's types – there was certainly a strong strain of the power culture in a firm like Saloman Brothers, but Lewis (a bond salesman himself) described the traders and salesmen as being basically good at their jobs, so an element of task culture was present as well. The ICI culture (the one that John Harvey-Jones was intent on changing) was also a mix of

types. In the lack of strategic direction one might detect a role culture, and the divisions may have been run as power cultures, while power was notably absent form the corporate centre.

Nevertheless, attempts to classify organizational cultures have their limitations. Once a category system is imposed, the diversity of types is constrained and this tends to defeat the purpose of cultural analysis. For example, Handy's different cultural types seem to add very little to the account that was provided by *structure*. The idea of a power culture does have some very interesting aspects and dimensions; but it is hard to see that role and task cultures add much more than, for example, Burns was able to do with his concepts of mechanistic and organic structures. On the other hand, the cultural types that Kanter (1984) developed seem less open to this criticism – probably because they did not imply a fixed classification scheme. Inferiority versus success, age versus youth and so on represented an open-ended set of types that could go on being elaborated.

Culture refers to the unique constellation of beliefs and norms found in each organization, while the categories of a classification scheme are a set of descriptive stereotypes; in themselves they provide little basis for linking different themes and variables. Nor are they particularly sensitive to the symbolic and interpretive aspects of culture. Better approaches focus on actual organizations, attempt to explain how particular cultures arise and are sustained, and link culture to other central organizational processes like power, leadership and the rewards system.

Evaluating concepts of culture

There can be little doubt that cultural analysis has opened up new ways of both understanding and managing organizations. Our understanding of organizations has often been blinkered by the tendency to see our own lives, in the modern science-dominated world, as reasoned and logical, not acted out in dramas, myths and legends. These we associate with ancient history or distant societies. But, of course, people in all societies think of their own behaviour as 'normal' and find it difficult to see the 'magical' elements in daily life. This is doubly true of organizations where conventional theory has long emphasized *rationality*. The primacy of the belief in formal structures and procedures has meant that subjective and symbolic dimensions have tended to be ignored or pushed to the periphery.

Yet cultural analysis brings to centre stage a rich vein of behaviours, and stands on its head much of the conventional wisdom about organizations. Stories, legends and rituals are not insignificant; nor are they 'not supposed' to be there. They are key elements of organizational functioning, and in some cases may actually serve more important objectives than formal decision-making. The cultural emphasis teaches us to think more broadly about organizations. The old rule of contingency theory, that 'there is no one best way to manage', receives a new lease of life from a cultural perspective. Looking at organizations, we find an astonishing variety of value and belief systems, many of which appear to 'work' quite well for the given organization.

Culture also represents one of the few concepts that has had a genuine impact on management thinking. After the many past failures and false dawns of management theory, people at the highest levels in corporations appear satisfied that culture provides at least a partial answer to the perennial question of what accounts for business success. Indeed, it is mistaken to imagine that business has simply borrowed or taken over culture from the social sciences. To a large extent the interest in values and symbolism has developed along its own path in the business world. In taking these concepts over, corporations and management writers have refashioned them. Explicit statements of corporate missions show how companies are reinventing themselves out of the need to compete at new levels.

Conflicting views of culture
However, we need to consider in more depth the different ways in which 'culture' has been used in organization study – in particular the difference between the concern to explain and describe cultural processes, and the managerial interest in relating culture to organizational performance. For example, Wilson and Rosenfeld (1990, p. 233) distinguish two schools of thought on culture, which they call the analytical and the applicable. The analytical school stresses the context and history of the organization and the way that culture acts as a socializing force, controlling the behaviour of members. This approach is concerned with all levels of the organization and with group and informal processes. The applicable school, on the other hand, views culture in terms of commitment to central goals and as a means of managing successful organizational change.

Smircich (1983) also distinguishes a managerial from an analytic approach. The former she criticizes as being a version of systems theory, which views strong internal cultures as means of adapting the organization to external market uncertainties. She argues that treating culture in this way, as a strategy for change, simply means that it will go the way of other failed concepts.

The notion of 'corporate culture' runs the risk of being as disappointing a managerial tool as the more technical and quantitative tools that were faddish in the 1970s. Those of a skeptical nature may also question the extent to which the term corporate culture refers to anything more than an ideology cultivated by management for the purpose of control and legitimation of activity.

In contrast to this, she favours deeper sociological and psychological approaches. Here culture is viewed as a network of interpretations and meanings; organizations are perceived as social constructions, not planned around formal goals, but constituted in interaction around symbols and other expressive representations. Crude functionalism – the view that 'strong cultures' lead to business success – likewise is replaced by a view of culture as a sense-making device, or as a set of practices and understandings for dealing with problems faced in common. For Smircich culture becomes a 'root metaphor'. Organizations are seen not as 'like' cultures or as 'having' a culture, but as *being* cultures. Culture is not an attribute; culture is what an organization *is*: 'organizations are expressive forms, manifestations of human consciousness'.

Corporate culture or corporate image?
These perspectives are not just different ways of looking at the same thing. They are contrasting and conflicting viewpoints. Much of what is rather loosely called 'corporate culture' is really a kind of image of the organization which top management would like to project. This is reflected in the research methods often adopted in this area. Frequently, these consist merely of trawling senior management opinion in a sample of organizations, while explicitly excluding any systematic data from other employees (e.g. Deal and Kennedy, 1982; Child and Smith, 1987). The dangers of an élitist version of culture creeping in are very evident here. And the contrast to the original, anthropological idea of culture, as the gradual emergence of social beliefs and practices in a community of people, could not be greater.

The image of the organization differs according to where you view it from. Many of the 'mission statements' coming out of corporations reflect the official version of culture, which may or may not be the same as the real culture. In this sense, several writers have highlighted the negative faces of culture – the power vacuum at the centre of ICI that Pettigrew revealed, the culture of age and inferiority from Kanter, and the culture of the false consensual style from Carnall. These are certainly not images fashioned by companies to promote themselves, and we might be more inclined to believe them for that reason. Even in companies with a strong ethos of caring for people, the social distance between senior management and shopfloor reality can be very wide. Down among the workforce a culture of employee welfare (team working, productivity through people) may be diluted to a vague feeling of the company as a 'good employer'.

Crucially, the idea of a single corporate culture ignores the *diversity* of groups and interests within the boundaries of the organization. A number of accounts have been at pains to stress organizational culture not as a monolithic concept, but as encompassing the idea of multiple cultures. Organizations are made up of different occupations and professions, different social classes and sexes, and are perhaps spread over different geographical areas. All these can form the basis of distinctive sub-cultures and counter-cultures that compete to define the reality of the organization.

This kind of challenge from below was well illustrated in a giant pharmaceuticals company. Its corporate creed was expressed as a series of statements that started with the ethical (duty to customers, the environment) and proceeded lastly to the economic (profit). The standing joke among employees was that if you wanted to know the company's real creed, simply reverse the order.

Managing culture?
The central problem, then, is whether organizational cultures are indeed 'manageable'. Cultures are hardly planned or predictable; they are the natural products of social interaction, and evolve and emerge over time, the residue of countless events and actions. So is it valid to allow such a notion of culture to give way to a version of managed consensus?

Some management writers certainly provide more sociologically informed accounts of culture. Pettigrew, for example, believes that cultures can be shaped to suit strategic ends, but he is not referring to any kind of corporate brainwashing. What he has in mind is the capacity of organizations to transform themselves from within. He seeks to develop comprehensive models of organizational change that show cultures adapting and being enacted at the level of key symbols by powerful organizational members. Such accounts centre on how shared beliefs interact with the political process, and with new forms of leadership that provide a 'transforming vision'. Morgan (1986) is another writer not averse in principle to tackling managerial problems, but who stresses that this must be combined with a full awareness of the subtleties of culture. Morgan warns against 'management theorists scurrying to find ways of managing culture' (p. 138) and advocates the building up of a sense of commitment among enterprise members, and via that the desired corporate ethos.

Managers can influence the evolution of culture by being aware of the symbolic consequences of their actions and by attempting to foster desired values, but they can never control culture in the sense that many management writers advocate.... An understanding of organizations as cultures opens our eyes to many crucial insights that elude other metaphors, but it is unlikely that these insights will provide the easy recipe for solving managerial problems that many hope for. (p. 139)

Even accepting these strictures, however, there still exists a tension between the practical goals of management and those of the social scientist trying to understand organizational life. Martin (1985), for example, distinguishes a pragmatic and a purist approach. Some pragmatists are crudely prescriptive, others more subtle, but in the end they see culture as the key to employee commitment and believe that it must be managed. Purists, on the other hand, regard culture as unmanageable by definition; they are sceptical about claims of fundamental cultural changes being managed. Culture is a way of endowing experience with meaning, and any ideas of managing it are both naive and unethical.

Certainly for managers there are strong reasons for wanting to simplify cultural processes. Values of progress and innovation represent the high ground of corporate achievement, and managers not unnaturally want to stake out a claim in this area. There are strong reasons for wanting to identify with programmes of cultural innovation, and this may mean 'objectifying' the recipes for change. To be fair, the more astute management writers are in no way guilty of crudely simplifying culture. But even here there can be tendencies to confuse culture with the images of themselves that corporations seek to promote, or to overemphasize the manipulation of the symbolic elements of organization life. For instance, Kanter at one stage is pondering the huge workloads that seem to accompany the new management and production systems, and concludes rather conveniently that people actually welcome a culture of pressure and overload; it is the 'lure of work' (1989, p. 271) that fuels the post-entrepreneurial society. Similarly, Pettigrew's famous phrase, the management of meaning, strikes a slightly chilling Orwellian note – how would you like to have your meanings managed?

More generally, the *consensual* nature of culture implies that conflict between interest groups, or forms of resistance from below, can be overlooked or played down. Writers like Pettigrew, Kanter and Morgan, who have taken the cultural perspective a large step forward, have tried to combine the emphasis on shared meanings with precisely such issues, namely those of power processes in organizations. Power, though, is an issue in its own right, and it is to this that we turn in the final chapter.

421

Further reading

Administrative Science Quarterly, Special Issue: 'Organization Culture', 28, 3, September 1983.

Frost, P.J., L.F. Moore, M.R. Louis, C.C. Lundberg and J. Martin (eds.) (1985) *Organizational Culture*. Beverly Hills: Sage.

Frost, P.J., L.F. Moore, M. Reis, C.C. Lundberg and J. Martin (eds.) (1991) *Reframing Organizational Culture*. Newbury Park, Calif.: Sage.

Hassard J. and D. Pym (eds.) (1990) *The Theory and Philosophy of Organizations*. London: Routledge.

Journal of Management Studies, Special Issue: 'Organizational Culture and Control', G. Hofstede (ed.), 23, 3, May 1986.

Pettigrew, A.M. (1979) 'On studying organizational cultures', *Administrative Science Quarterly*, 24, 4, 570–81.

Pettigrew, A.M. (1985) 'Culture and politics in strategic decision making and change', in J.M. Pennings (ed.) *Strategic Decision Making in Complex Organizations*. San Francisco: Jossey Bass.

Sackman, S.A. (1991) *Cultural Knowledge in Organizations*. Newbury Park, Calif.: Sage.

Reed, M. and M. Hughes (eds.) (1992) *Rethinking Organization*. London: Sage.

19

Power and Organizations

As we saw in Chapter 18, the interest in the organizational culture in many ways represented a challenge to managerialist or systems theories that view organizations as sites of rational decision-making and the attainment of business goals. Over the past decade or so another aspect of organizational theory has also been inspired by dissatisfaction with conventional approaches. This is the concern with organizational power.

The study of power in organizations can present problems. Power, as we will see, is a rather slippery concept, difficult to pin down and define. Power is also one of the major concerns of social theorists, and organizational power (which does have its own distinctive forms) inevitably gets mixed up with the forms of power that occur in wider society. And, as well as understanding the actual arguments, there can be problems in appreciating what point there is in discussing managerial activity in these terms. Managerial work is typically thought of in terms of decisions made on the basis of training and experience (the rationalist view). Within organizations 'politics' is often regarded with great distaste, as the main barrier to getting on with the job. Thus an approach which takes this activity from the margins and places it at the focus of attention – which seems to see organizational activity as nothing other than politics – might seem perverse and hard to accept.

Bacharach and Lawler (1980, p. 1) lead us into the topic of power by suggesting that it occupies the middle ground between two major schools of thought – the contrasting schools of managerial/systems theory and conflict or radical theory. From our discussion in previous chapters this view may seem rather oversimplified. For their part, as we saw in Chapter 17, the managerialists were never quite so naive as to believe that organizations are purely rational and consensual entities. Even the early theorists had a practitioner's eye for problems of workers' resistance, and certainly more recent theory has been able to incorporate issues of conflict within management. Conversely, as seen in Chapter 16, the radical approach obviously does not imagine that conflict in organizations boils over into class struggle; nor does it ignore the fact that organizational life is partly about co-operation. Even Marxist theory is quite clear about the two sides of capitalist enterprise: production happens at the same time as economic exploitation. However, the approach taken by Bacharach and Lawler is at least helpful in setting out the scene. It is useful to look at power as a concept which retains aspects of both the managerialist and radical approaches – power as a radical idea but applied in the context of managerial decision-making. In this sense Bacharach and Lawler suggest a view of organizations as 'politically negotiated orders'.

> Adopting this view, we can observe organizational actors in their daily transactions, perpetually bargaining, repeatedly forming and reforming coalitions, and constantly availing themselves of influence and tactics ... politics in organizations involve the tactical use of power to retain or obtain control of real or symbolic resources. In describing the processes of organizations as political acts, we are not making a moral judgement; we are simply making an observation about a process. (Bacharach and Lawler, 1980, pp. 1–2)

This view of power as *strategic* and *processual* reflects the widespread interest in the topic. Given such a background, a number of fairly straightforward reasons for wanting to study organizational power suggest themselves.

Power is interesting
At the risk of seeming trite, the role of power in human affairs has always been intrinsically interesting. To watch a power struggle develop between protagonists can be a fascinating experience. Power-play focuses on the *differences* between individuals and groups, the variety of goals and interests. The power game is also by definition open-ended. Part of its fascination is that we can never be entirely sure about the outcome. No protagonist ever entered the arena in the certainty of losing; nor is there any position so superior that it might not be overturned by subtle tactics.

Power is positive
Though 'politicking' in organizations may be resented, power is also about the creative actions of people and the possibilities for organizational change. Anyone who knows organizations knows that little happens unless some powerful group is behind a particular course of action, and that political manoeuvring is always needed to get change under way. The power perspective thus reinforces the importance of managerial skills. It paints a dramatic and perhaps

even flattering picture of managers as power-brokers and wheeler-dealers. The Machiavellian image means that power (like culture) is an academic concept of great interest to management audiences.

Power is realistic
Power is about how organizations 'really' operate. Often when some course of action is being publicly announced or explained, the impression is given that the decision was consensual, or that the organization had somehow 'arrived at' the most sensible course of action. But in reality we frequently suspect that the 'explanation' is at least partly justification – that a power-process was involved behind the scenes and that the 'decision' was in fact the outcome of a struggle. Decision-making is thus never purely rational or consensual; power is often the underlying reality.

Finally in these introductory remarks we need to explore some further points about the links between power, rationality and conflict.

The behavioural limits on rationality
The rationalist approach quite deliberately restricts itself to the formally sanctioned aspects of behaviour in organizations, since its aim is the effective control of organizational tasks. While this approach does take account of some aspects of conflict and power, the extent to which it can do this will always be limited. Thus, in spite of undoubted progress and refinements in organization theory since the days of the classical writers, some of the processes underlying real organizational activity are bound to be overlooked, or at least explained inadequately.

To begin with, any focus on organizations as structures for achieving goals runs the risk of becoming too prescriptive. Too great an emphasis on goal achievement, and obsession with efficiency and effectiveness, can mean that we are not explaining how organizations really operate. So while decision-making has often been thought of as a rational process, in reality managers do not act jointly to resolve problems in a purely unproblematic way – decision-making is also a *human* process constrained by the limits on people's abilities.

Writers on organization and management have for long been aware of the deficiencies of human rationality. For instance, March and Simon (1958, pp. 137–71) used the term 'bounded rationality' to point out that decision-making is only rational up to a certain point. Managerial action is rarely optimal in the sense of the best solution being sought and found. In practice, a *satisfactory* solution, one that will cope with the problem in hand, is the most common outcome. The reason, quite simply, is that decision-making and

425

problem-solving between managers involves the expenditure of a good deal of time and effort. In this sense, decision-making is frequently described as a *search process*. Defining alternative courses of action, and testing their relative efficiency, happens only to a limited extent because once a satisfactory solution has been found the search tends to stop.

Conflict and power

As well as the simple fact of human abilities being limited, any preoccupation with formal management tasks, like planning and control, also risks neglecting factors outside the structure of formal authority. The behavioural limits on decision-making corrected this bias to some extent. But the processes of conflict and power in organizations are also important in shaping managerial activity. We saw in Chapter 17 that formal organization structures invariably contain the means for resolving conflict. However, to represent conflict merely as something that has to be resolved is to fail to explain it in its own right.

In this sense, organizations may be thought of as compromising a dual reality. On one level there is a set of relationships which represent the organization as an *operating system* – these would include the actions of managers in problem-solving, as well as the view of organizations as systems for rational goal attainment. But there is also a parallel system based on the internal *struggle for power*. Much informal managerial activity – the deals and favours that are inevitably a part of real life in organizations – would be included here, as would be the pursuit of self-interest and the defence of departmental interests against other conflicting groups. In this vein, Burns (1969) has referred to organizations as 'plural social systems'.

> Business enterprises are cooperative instrumental systems assembled out of the usable attributes of people. They are also places in which people compete for advancement. Thus, members of a business concern are at one and the same time cooperators in a common enterprise and rivals for the material and tangible rewards of successful competition with each other. The hierarchical order of rank and power, realized in the organization chart, which prevails in all organizations is both a control system and a career ladder. (p. 232)

The fact that the political side of organizations has been largely ignored until quite recently, plus the suggestion that power in organizations can actually be the decisive factor in decision-making, has meant that organizational politics is increasingly regarded as a key explanation of managerial behaviour.

The concept of power

The concept of power has always proved difficult to define, even though a common-sense grasp of the term seems easy enough. This is partly because the activity being described is itself dynamic and complex. For example, suppose someone has been influenced to follow a course of action against their original inclination. Has power been exercised over them? The answer might be yes, if their compliance was obtained with the use of threats, but no, if the advantages of a particular course of action of which they were unaware had simply been pointed out to them. However, if they were persuaded by force of argument, then it might be quite difficult to determine whether or not power had been used. It would depend upon exactly how aggressively the case was put: whether threats were implied or whether the case was merely stated enthusiastically.

The complex nature of these types of behaviour is reflected in the number of terms similar to power, such as authority, control and influence, which are often used interchangeably in normal conversation. In social science analysis, however, one would want to know how precisely they differ from the notion of power. Do the different terms refer to types of power, or are they quite separate forms of behaviour?

The framework for the sociology of power, originally set out by Weber, also stressed the ambiguous nature of the concept. For Weber power represented the *potential* to act in certain ways. Weber was interested in the way power could most often be effective when used as a threat rather than actually being exercised. Thus he spoke of the probability or chance of groups or individuals prevailing over others: 'We understand by "power" the chance of a man or a number of men to realize their own will in a communal action even against the resistance of others who are participating in the action' (Weber, 1970, p. 180). We can also see that Weber's definition stressed power as a *collective* phenomenon. This use of the term is certainly appropriate within organizations, where groups of one kind or another – teams, departments, divisions – typically exercise power as the product of collective and social relationships. Even where power appears to be exercised by an individual, its true basis often lies in some group or other collectivity. The power of managers, for example, represents a mandate from the legal owners of the firm and is exercised on their behalf.

LUKES AND THE THREE FACES OF POWER

Since the pioneering work of Weber, a number of writers have developed different viewpoints on the operation of social power. One

427

of the most widely influential models is that of Steven Lukes (1974). Lukes offers not so much a theory of power, or a distinctive approach in its own right, as a framework within which other major approaches can be located, and which makes sense of them in relation to each other. He builds a dimension of 'radicalness' into his account, arguing that three major perspectives – or, as he puts it, 'faces of power' – can be regarded as giving understandings that get increasingly closer to the real roots of power in society.

The first face of power, perhaps the simplest, rests on an account of actual power behaviour. In an early attempt the political scientist Robert Dahl (1957) argued that a common-sense definition along the following lines was a useful starting point: 'A has power over B to the extent that he can get B to do something that B would otherwise not do.' This raised the issue of *resistance* on the part of B, because his wishes are being overridden, and hence of *conflict* between A and B. Certainly for Dahl, and many others, the acid test of a power relationship was the existence of this observable, behavioural conflict as evidence of a clash of interests between persons or groups.

In addition, though, in order to arrive at the root causes of power we need to take account of behaviour that, in a sense, does not take place. According to Bacharach and Baratz (1962), this 'other face of power' reflects the ability of powerful groups to prevent various options or choices from even being considered. The original view expressed by Dahl – that power is reflected in the actions of the powerful – looked only at actual decisions and the groups which prevailed over them, so that even those who are overruled will still take part in the decision-making process. But what of the groups which are never admitted to the decision arena in the first place? Bacharach and Baratz argued that real power in this sense is exercised by suppressing their preferences. Thus, power in the form of 'non-decision-making' does not necessarily involve resistance or overt conflict at all. Indeed, the fact that those under power are never permitted to resist, or to engage in conflict, is a measure of the degree of power exercised over them.

Lukes then took the argument even further, saying that we need a fully radical view of power. This would include power that is exercised by preventing people from forming conscious preferences or choices. Such a type of power might apply, for example, to the way in which the social horizons of many working-class people are narrowed and constrained by education and upbringing. They perceive that certain ambitions and aspirations are simply 'not for them' – which means that they may never challenge the economic position of the middle and upper classes. This formed the basis of Luke's 'three-dimensional view of power'. The first dimension was the most obvious one, power observable in the clash of interests between decision-makers (as stressed by Dahl). The second referred to the interests of certain groups being excluded from a particular bargaining arena (as in Bacharach and Baratz). The third, or radical, dimension referred to certain groups under power never being able consciously to formulate their real interests.

FOUCAULT AND DISCIPLINARY POWER

The view of power that results from an analysis like Luke's is essentially structural. His 'radical face' of power reflects a dominant set of interests or ideology that is somehow imposed on the majority. For the French social scientist, Michel Foucault, the weakness of structural approaches is that they fail to distinguish the realities of power, and have yet to catch up with the changed nature of power in 'post-modern' society. The approach developed by Foucault has stressed a *disciplinary* notion of power. This is a distinctive and unusual theory, but it is currently very influential and worth some attention.

Foucault begins by identifying older, archaic forms of power, which he calls *sovereign power*. In traditional society this emanated from the monarch, but the main point is that sovereign power is institutional in nature; it stands outside those under power and is imposed as a kind of superstructure. In *Discipline and Punish* (1979), Foucault develops this theme in a historical analysis of criminality. It may seem curious to take 'deviant' behaviour as a starting point, but the punishment of crime is seen as a generalizable 'political tactic'. Up to the eighteenth century, punishment involved strong elements of torture and public spectacle; the stocks, the chain gang and the public exhibition of prisoners were normal. The point about such punishments, Foucault argues, is that they were symptoms of a particular kind of power. A policy of terror and atrocity against the wrongdoer represented the sovereign exacting vengeance and was designed to make people aware of that power. The purpose was to deter by enveloping the populace in the horror of punishment.

Foucault goes into considerable detail on this point (including grisly descriptions of public executions) in order to demonstrate the total contrast with modern forms of power. During the eighteenth century and by the beginning of the nineteenth, 'the great spectacle of physical punishment disappeared' and was replaced by imprisonment. Large-scale projects of prison building were accompanied by pro-grammes of rehabilitation. This, says Foucault, was the beginning of the disciplinary age. Whereas sovereign power was external, brutal and dramatic, disciplinary power is mundane and based on the surveillance of behaviour. In one sense this idea is not new. It was certainly part of the Weberian tradition to emphasize indirect and 'rational' forms of control. Weber was concerned with the 'iron cage of bureaucracy', and with modern systems of calculation that submerged all natural and localized human relations. Similarly, Weberian writers like Blau and Shoenherr (1971) stressed the 'insidious' nature of bureaucratic power (see Chapters 10 and 16). But with Foucault we see a much broader development of these ideas, and disciplinary power is identified as the basis of modern forms of stratification.

> The movement from one project to the other, from a schema of exceptional discipline to one of a generalized surveillance, rests on a historical transformation: the gradual extension of the mechanisms of discipline throughout the 17th and 18th centuries, their spread through the whole social body, the formation of what might be called in general the disciplinary society. (1979, p. 209)

Under Foucault's conception of power there is no centre, no superstructure, no imposition from above. Instead power is *systematic* in the precise sense of being integral to all social relationships. Disciplinary power is insinuated in daily routines, it involves the 'meticulous observation' of action and the 'penetration of regulation into even the smallest details of everyday life'. The principles of disciplinary power are those of the enclosure of personnel on functioning sites (factories, hospitals, prisons), the partitioning of behaviour and the control of activity with systems such as timetables. These power relations can be elaborated in many locations; Foucault talks of the 'swarming of the disciplines' and suggests that disciplinary power may be 'unlocked' within any enclosed arena of activity. The full range of modern organizations contain many differences of appearance, but they share the same underlying programmes of power and a common parent in the prison: 'prisons resemble factories, schools, barracks, hospitals, which all resemble prisons'. Other instruments of disciplinary power that Foucault was interested in include procedures like the examination, the investigation and systematic training. These constrain human motivation into 'collectively useful aptitudes' through the organization of occupations and professions (also aptly called disciplines).

They contribute to what Foucault called the *normalizing judgement*. The process of normalization is 'one of the great instruments of power' in modern society; it involves the establishment of limits of accepted behaviour, standards to be achieved. Those who comply may be rewarded, but anyone falling outside the routines is automatically defined as deviant. These techniques of control, if in the form of distributions of attainment, will by their very nature exclude some participants. The ones who are bottom of the list, or in the last quartile, are defined as the unpromotable, the ignorant, the incapable.

The panoptic schema

Foucault conjures one particularly compelling image of disciplinary power: the *Panopticon* of the English social reformer, Jeremy Bentham. This was an architectural design the principle of which was a circular building with an observation tower at the centre. The outer perimeter was divided into cells with windows facing out for light, and inward so that each space could be constantly observed. Bentham devised the Panopticon as the basis of prison design, and although largely forgotten today the idea had a considerable impact on the great nineteenth-century projects of penal reform. Foucault was struck by the sheer economy of the Panopticon, the way in which 'just a gaze' could hold sway over a mass of individuals. It represented a 'technology of power designed to solve the problems of surveillance' (1980, p. 147).

> ... the major effect of the Panopticon is to induce in the inmate a state of conscious and permanent visibility that ensures the automatic functioning of power. So to arrange things that the surveillance is permanent in its effects, even if it is discontinuous in its action; that the perfection of power should tend to render its actual exercise unnecessary; that this architectural apparatus should be a machine for creating and sustaining a power relation independent of the person who exercises it; in short that the inmates should be caught up in a power situation of which they themselves are the bearers. (1979, p. 201)

Of course, Bentham's design was impractical – a fixed observatory could hardly accommodate the divisions of labour and communications networks found in modern organizations – and Foucault was well aware of this. He notes, for example, the 'disciplinary gaze needs relays' (1979, p.173), and that the pyramidal structure of organizations is really a kind of modern Panopticon, with successive levels supervising each other. But he saw the Panopticon as a kind of image or metaphor of disciplinary power.

Power/knowledge

A key aspect of the panoptic image is the *visibility* of the prisoner. The basic function of a centre of observation, Foucault suggests, is fulfilled by modern institutions like the training of professional and educational institutions.

This idea has been translated into organizational terms in studies of the accounting function. Accounting has become the universal language of business, and accountancy an extremely influential corporate profession. The reason that accountants are so central to managerial power, it is argued, is that they make the implicit visible. The potential for activities in organizations to be concealed is enormous. How do managers know that the operations they are supposed to be supervising are working to plan? Accounting provides the techniques for achieving this. Accountants are able to evaluate inputs and outputs and aggregate complex activities into money flows, and so enable management to evaluate business performance. In this vein Miller and O'Leary (1987) have stressed that accountants assist in the social construction of the 'governable person'. In industry the production of disciplined work forces has usually been attributed to groups like supervisors and production engineers; but accountants too produce standards of effort and in this way contribute to normalized assessments that are the basis of rational power.

Foucault was interested in the role of 'experts' of all kinds. Experts themselves have gone through lengthy training which reproduces in them aspects of disciplinary power; they then become active agents who produce normalized judgments of others. As Burrell points out; 'Today, a "normalizing" function is performed by a whole series of subsidiary authorities who swarm around the "disciplines". For example, educationists, psychiatrists, psychological experts, members of the prison service and magistrates all form parallel judgments of the "cases" coming before them' (1988, p. 227). However, there is more to this than just the monitoring of activity. Foucault employed the term *power/knowledge*. Note, it is not power *and* knowledge, in the sense that we would all recognise of 'knowledge giving power'. For Foucault the relationship between knowledge and power was more intimate and dynamic; experts actually create the categories with which they establish factual knowledge.

Of central importance here is the idea of 'discourse'. This refers to the specific languages of occupations and professions – the sales talk, the technical jargon and so on. Professional discourses are an independent source of power, such that experts 'through their talk' can define situations and create key areas of knowledge. Thus if the psychiatrist diagnoses a person (as schizophrenic, say), the attachment of the label will empower psychiatric professionals with control over the patient as regards incarceration and treatment. But the central item of knowledge (the patient is schizophrenic) and the category itself (schizophrenia) were created by the discourse of the profession in the first place.

Parallel power
As well as arguing that modern organizations are all 'alike' in sharing an underlying power dynamic, Foucault also argued for the

'difference' and distinctive origins of organizations. Burrell (1988, p. 227) points out that Foucault was concerned not with generalized power but with parallel centres developed around specific social problems. Foucault's historic research into areas like medicine, psychiatry and criminology showed at what point the spark of disciplinary power jumped from one area to another.

Moreover, penal organizations themselves had antecedents, and in tracing these Foucault uncovered an entirely new set of historic connections. They derive from the social responses to disease. The reaction to the leper in early medieval times was one of exclusion; the later reaction to the plague involved detailed regulations for the containment of the disease in any village it had struck, very much akin to disciplinary power.

> This enclosed segmented space, observed at every point, in which the individuals are inserted in a fixed place, in which the slightest movements are supervised, in which all events are recorded, in which an uninterrupted work of writing links the centre and periphery, in which power is exercised without division, according to a continuous hierarchical figure, in which each individual is located, examined and distributed among the living beings, the sick and the dead – all this constitutes a compact model of the disciplinary mechanism. (1979, p. 197)

These two 'projects' – 'the leper and his separation; the plague and its segmentations' – Foucault suggests were merged in the great 'carceral' institutions of the nineteenth century – the prisons, approved schools, asylums and workhouses. The new distributions of power for 'correcting the abnormal' then became the model for the divisions of labour in productive organizations. In particular, the problem that industrial capitalism poses is that of the use of mass labour. Owners effectively have to entrust their wealth (technology, materials, etc.) to workers; hence, Foucault points out, the strong emphasis in early capitalism on morality – strict timekeeping, abstinence, a fair day's work – and the creation of crime and criminals as separate categories. This contrasted with the 'amiable tolerance' of crime that characterized earlier centuries (1980, p. 41).

In a sense this represents a similar approach to Weber's. Weber saw the modern organization as deriving from a particular type of social control, the bureaucracy, and traced its historic antecedents. (He was much interested in the ancient Chinese civil service, military organization and church as precursors of bureaucracy.) With Foucault the parallel issue was the control of deviancy. He noticed the rise of the incarceral institutions of the eighteenth and nineteenth centuries, and in writing their history indicated some of the origins of modern organizations.

Debating Foucault

The above analysis clearly departs from many conventional views of power, and in recent years a good deal of criticism has been levelled at it (Fine, 1979; Gane, 1986; Hoy 1986). There is in Foucault's theory no central motivation to power by some identifiable body – a ruling class or dominant interest. Instead, power becomes a web of social relations, a set of strategies, 'a mechanism that no one owns' (1980, p. 156). Such an analysis often appears descriptive and lacking in satisfying causal explanations. For example, there seems to be no explanation of the transition to a disciplinary mode; we are told simply that society lost its taste for physical punishment some time around the turn of the nineteenth century (Foucault, 1979, p. 14). Likewise Foucault's method of spotting analogies and similarities between very different organizational form – the containment of the plague, prisons, factories – may seem rather far-fetched. However, there is little point in regarding these criticisms of Foucault. We simply have to accept him on his own terms. Foucault belonged to a stream of thinkers (allied to Weber and the phenomenologists) for whom no ultimate 'causality' exists. Models of cause and effect may be appropriate for the natural sciences, but not for the social world. Instead, we look for symbolic connection and collectively defined 'problems' to which society seeks 'solutions'. This is the message behind Foucault's search for historic antecedents and exotic organizational forms: there are no mechanical causes, only circular processes of response that go back indefinitely. Nor does it do any harm to stand the accepted wisdom on its head from time to time, which Foucault certainly does. Rather than always regarding economic institutions as self-sufficient, his focus shifts to 'deviant' models of power. Bringing the periphery to the centre in this way frees up the analyst and greatly enriches understanding.

A more damaging critique of Foucault centres on his *pessimism*, which in social science inevitably tends to be linked with determinism. The paradox with Foucault is that, while his analysis is supposed to oppose structural solutions, his use of incarceration as a motif for human existence is gloomy and deterministic in the extreme. As even his supporters argue, his theory is about 'a global unity of domination' (Burrell, 1988, p. 227). The central issue with Foucault is not economic exploitation but the domination of behaviour. Exploitation for profit is at least human and understandable by comparison. But there is something chilling about the 'mechanism that no one owns'.

A related criticism has been based on Goffman's (1968) concept of 'total institutions'. Goffman, we may recall from Chapter 16, gave an account of asylums and the psychiatric profession which in many ways agreed with the Foucauldian emphasis on control of inmate behaviour. However, the crucial difference was that Goffman classed asylums as total institutions – organizations in which inmates spend their time entirely within the system. The inference is that total institutions cannot simply be extrapolated to the majority of organizations (like work organizations) in which members spend only a portion of their time. The power of staff over the lives of the inmates in total institutions does resemble disciplinary power, but such extremes of control do not apply across the board.

Foucault's supporters have replied to this criticism by reference to the 'society of organizations' idea. This Weberian notion stresses that bureaucratic organizations have so grown that they now influence all areas of our lives. The fact that different organizations enclose different areas is irrelevant. As Burrell puts it: 'the real point is that we are encarcerated within an organizational world ... whilst we may not live in total institutions, the institutional organization of our lives is total' (1988, p. 232). Again, the critics of Foucault respond that this is hardly convincing, and have reaffirmed the pluralist position. Here they bracket Foucault with Weber, of whom a long-standing criticism was that he exaggerated the potency of bureaucracy. They reject over-rationalization, and insist that the informal cultures and centres of resistance possessed by organizations prevent them from being disciplined in the way that Foucault suggests (Giddens, 1984; Morgan, 1990, p. 94).

Foucault himself denied the charge of pessimism. He accepted that his analysis implied that one can never 'step outside' disciplinary power; but it does not follow that domination is inevitable. 'To say that one can never be "outside" power does not mean that one is trapped and condemned to defeat no matter what' (1980, p. 141). Power relations do not take the sole form of constraints and punishments. The passivity of those under power is not assumed; indeed power encourages the emergence of counter-strategies to cope with it. Disciplinary power does not always take a 'negative' form; power is frequently the force behind organizational changes, and resistance is also part of the power relation. Resistance often *assists* the rule of disciplinary power, more so than passive acceptance. (In the case of psychiatry, for example, resistance in the form of patients denying that they are ill, or refusing medication, is often taken as a symptom of the complaint.)

Whatever one makes of the positions in this debate, we would argue that there remain unresolved tensions in Foucault's thinking on power. Foucault (like Weber) had strong liberal and humanist instincts, but was deeply worried by insidious forms of control and what he saw as unstoppable trends towards a 'Big Brother' scenario in modern society. This meant that he was at once too optimistic

435

and too pessimistic. He was too optimistic in assuming that sovereign-type power has been superseded by the 'gentle way to punishment'. Plenty of brutal regimes survive around the world and, more mundanely, external forms of power based on factors like property and gender still determine social stratification. He was too pessimistic in assuming that disciplinary power penetrates all social relations.

What Foucault gives us, however, is a new language of power, one that captures the subtle and internalized constraints produced in modern bureaucratic situations. How many of us have felt these sorts of pressure on realizing that our department's performance is worse than others', or when waiting for the results of an exam? The complex and 'literary' method employed by Foucault succeeds where structural theories of power might obscure these intricacies. Furthermore, his emphasis on power strategies leads directly to more conventional accounts of *organizational* power that have focused on managerial decision-making and interaction.

ORGANIZATIONAL POWER

The above approaches and definitions should help in understanding the terms related to power, and in particular in focusing on the specific forms of power that are of interest in organizations. If we consider the amount of resistance offered by those under power, and also the strength of the sanctions brought to bear by those in power, then the different types of power can be seen to fall within a continuum. This represents the extent of conflict between the interests

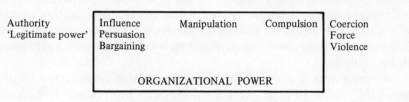

Figure 19.1 *Types of power.*

of the 'in-power' group and the 'under-power' group (Fig. 19.1). As the figure shows, power covers a very broad range of behaviours, from almost pure agreement to the resort to violence. The topic of this chapter, organizational power, clearly applies to a much narrower band of activities. Forms of violent coercion would need to be left out when speaking of power in organizations – or at least power in the kinds of commercial and public sector organization we are most familiar with.

In addition, the concept of authority overlaps with that of power, and the two terms can be quite ambiguously related. As we saw in Chapter 16, Weber regarded authority, in the sense of power accepted as legitimate by the under-group, as being of vital importance for maintaining social order; and within organizations authority remains the basis of formal control. Yet if authority were *purely* consensual, it is doubtful whether we would speak of power bring exercised. However, authority is nearly always backed up by sanctions, so the resort to power remains a choice for the group in authority. Thus the other dimensions of power, discussed by Bachrach and Baratz and by Lukes, can be placed in the same category as authority – even though these authors make the point that the agreement of the under-group is hardly freely given.

Levels of power
One of the present authors (Fincham, 1992) has suggested another way of looking at the kinds of power found in organizations, namely the different 'levels' on which power is constituted. Three main levels of analysis are distinguished: processual, institutional and organizational. The first, processual power, focuses on the 'micropolitics' of organizational life, and stresses power as negotiation and bargaining. The level of analysis is that of the 'lateral' relations between managerial interest groups, and the basis of explanation is *strategic*. Power is a dynamic phenomenon originating 'in the process' of daily interaction. The 'enactment' of rules is stressed. In other words, the emphasis is not on concrete power resources that people possess, but on how these resources are employed in the power game. It cannot be assumed, for instance, that people in power can simply 'give orders'; in reality they may use their position but only backed up by strategic action. A true processual analysis should also be longitudinal, studying power processes as they emerge over time. Research that does this (e.g. Pettigrew, 1973, 1985) is able to show how power positions reflect rich patterns of past alliances between groups.

At the other extreme, the institutional perspective sees managerial power resting on external social and economic structures, so that power is explained as being *mandated* to the organization. Here, for example, Willmott (1987) has stressed that wider economic struc-

tures – class, ownership, the state – create beliefs about the inevitability of managerial authority. In this sense, managers can draw
on a set of institutionally produced rules when they seek to exercise
power, such as cultural beliefs about the 'right to manage'. Another
institutional factor that has attracted recent attention is that of *gender*.
In the past a 'desexualized' model of the organization has often been
assumed, because the rationalist view has tended to be accepted.
Rational principles of control, even if oppressive, were regarded as
being even-handed. However, many are now insisting that bureaucratic procedures are actually deeply imbued with sex-biased values,
and that formal rationality itself is part of the ideological construct
of 'maleness'. It is suggested that there are strong links between the
formalist treatment of issues like promotion, and practices that favour
the advancement of men (Hearn *et al.*, 1989). Similarly, the attitudes
of organizational 'gatekeepers' – those who control access to training
and entry into jobs, like personnel officers – have been identified as
crucial factors in discrimination (Crompton and Jones, 1984).

These two levels of analysis – process and institution – have
produced a dualist view of power. We saw a similar contrast in
Foucault's link between disciplinary and traditional power. Others
have linked action and structure, i.e. whether we take a view of
social life constructed by individual agents, or one that depicts people
as the objects of external constraints (Giddens, 1984). Reflected in
these dichotomies is the deepest dilemma in social science, that of the
relationship between the individual and the social; and corresponding
problems are created for explaining power in these terms.

By themselves the processual and institutional views can appear
unsatisfactory. The processual approach often seems to overstate the
importance of power-play and to produce an exaggerated sense of
choice. The institutional approach, on the other hand, can appear to
be too fixed and deterministic; if power rests on structures external
to the organization, deviance from those structures or forms of
resistance become difficult to account for. What is obviously needed
is a framework that brings the two together, and indeed this has
been argued for in a number of debates (Reed, 1985). But attempts
at a 'unified' account have also run into difficulties. The processual
and institutional views tend to be incompatible: any stress on the
spontaneous qualities of action finds it hard to take account of
wider constraints, while the emphasis on structural factors has little
sympathy for the detail of human strategies and motives. Various
ways out of the 'structure and action' dilemma have been proposed.
Hales (1988) argues that we need a level of analysis 'between
something as specific as individual action and something as broad as
capitalist production relations'. Fincham (1992) suggests that this

intermediate level is in fact the organization, and that paradoxically, in focusing on process and institution, studies of organizational power have actually neglected the organization.

This level of analysis stresses the organization's own power system, and the *hierarchy* as a means of reproducing power. A number of types of hierarchical relationship are pertinent here. For example, organizations are frequently observed to have *dominant beliefs*, the values and knowledge that set the 'rules of the game' and shape organizational priorities and solutions. These may reflect the interests of a ruling function (marketing or accounting, say) or dominant beliefs articulated around the interests of strategic groups, the senior managerial coalitions that hold real power. Furthermore, organizational *selection* is crucial as an instrument by which such strategic groups perpetuate themselves. Those in authority select others who will sustain the existing power structure. Some writers have doubted that selection can be effective as a power mechanism because of the impossibility of defining 'managerial qualities' (Armstrong, 1989). However, the lack of 'objective' criteria does not make selection ineffective. Selection rules are necessarily ambiguous and intangible; the point is that those with the power to choose know what *they* mean, even if the criteria are vague.

The organizational level, then, represents a kind of third way, between the strategic and the structural; and the three levels of analysis suggest how organizational hierarchies transmit power between institutional interests and the rules and resources governing action. In the final sections of the chapter, however, we need to return to one particular level: the processual. By far the strongest interest has been shown in this aspect, and in a sense 'organizational power' has come to mean the lateral relations within management and the specific power strategies that are used. Nor is the reason hard to find: the processual perspective has effectively opposed static systems models and emphasized power as a mobilizing force in organizational change.

The organization as a political system

The concern with power in organizations includes, first and foremost, an emphasis on *process* rather than structure. Although hierarchical position is one important power resource, it is not accepted that real power necessarily mirrors the formal hierarchy. Furthermore, managerial decision-making is seen as a *political* activity. People never suspend the pursuit of individual interests, nor cease to identify with the sectional loyalties which support them. So there are practical reasons for studying these political processes, since anyone who is to prosper, or even survive, in organizations must be able to bargain effectively for a share of resources. In short, they need to be equipped to play the game of organizational politics.

Thus, while power can be seen in terms of power *over* subordinates, the emphasis here is on the *use* of power and the range of tactics that people employ. This does not always mean the pursuit of career and self-interest. There is also a vitally important sense in which this power struggle and the broader attainment of organizational goals actually overlap and mutually support each other. It reflects management's responsibility for organizational development, and for designing an organization structure which is competent to meet a changing environment. Given the tendency of all institutions to resist change and settle into a routine, decision-makers in the real world often have their hands full merely getting organizations started towards change. Yet organizations must be made to adapt if they are to survive and prosper. It is only be deploying power that managers can intervene in the change process and guide their organizations along desired paths. First, though, we need to know something of the power resources that different groups are able to draw upon and about the organizational arena in which power is exercised.

POWER RESOURCES

The social psychologists French and Raven, in a now-classic study (1959), developed a scheme of five categories of power, which reflected the different bases or resources that power holders rely upon. They identified reward, coercive, legitimate, referent and expert power.

Reward power depends upon the ability of the power-wielder to confer valued material rewards, such as promotions or increases in pay or responsibility. *Coercive power* is the reverse side of this coin, in the sense that those who have the power to reward usually also have the power to punish. Thus coercive power might refer to the ability to demote or to withhold other rewards. In both cases, it is the desire for valued rewards or the fear of having them withheld that ensures the obedience of those under power. *Legitimate power* is identical with authority, and depends upon the belief of individuals in the right of senior people to hold their positions, and their consequent willingness to accept the power-holder. *Referent power* is based on the 'charisma' of the power-holder. Here the person under power desires to identify with these personal qualities, and gains satisfaction from being an accepted follower. Lastly, *expert power* rests on the skills or expertise of the person holding power. Unlike the others, this type of power is usually highly specific and limited to the particular area in which the expert is trained and qualified.

There are, however, certain defects in the French and Raven

scheme. Their reward and coercive forms of power are not in fact power resources in themselves – they merely describe the actions of people who have other power resources. So, for example, senior managers with formal positions in the organizational hierarchy (legitimate power) can confer or withhold promotions. In addition, their legitimate and referent forms of power are taken directly from Weber's typology of authority, although without the addition of his third type, namely traditional authority (see Chapter 16). Still, French and Raven's approach does serve to emphasize the fact that within organizations people can call upon a range of different bases of power and influence.

Although hierarchical rank – legitimate power – is obviously a crucial power resource, when we consider power as a political process the focus of interest shifts to the resources that people can mobilize irrespective of their official positions. Here expertise, or French and Raven's expert power, represents an important power resource. Professionals, technical experts and tradespeople, who are employed in organizations for their specific skills, derive power from the fact that the organization depends upon that skilled work being performed. The 'expert power' of the professional or the tradesperson very frequently comes into conflict with formal authority. In the long run this is a struggle for control in which experts are unlikely to prevail. The organization is still the employer and retains the ultimate power to hire and fire. Experts are also self-defeating in certain respects – it is often part of the expert's job to streamline and automate operations, and thereby to eliminate the need for his or her own skill. However, while there is innovation and growth in an organization expert power is enhanced, and in these kinds of circumstance experts can be highly influential, albeit in an informal way.

An attempt to explain power in more universal terms involves the twin concepts of *uncertainty* and *dependency* – ideas which have been developed most fully by Hickson *et al.* (1971) in their 'strategic contingencies' theory of power. Uncertainty for an organization stems from its system of operations (the technology and work organization) and from the environment. Reducing the uncertainty of operations is vital for management, and groups of employees who 'cope with uncertainty' gain influence and power. The more strategic the form of uncertainty for a particular organization, the more powerful will the group which controls it become. Therefore organizations become heavily dependent on the groups which cope with central areas of uncertainty. For example, Crozier (1964) has shown how skilled workers were able to exploit a source of residual uncertainty in an otherwise routine production system. Machine breakdowns were the only major contingency that disrupted operations. The organization was thus dependent on the maintenance crews which dealt with breakdowns, which enabled these workers to enhance their status and rewards.

Another important study using this approach is Pettigrew's *The Politics of Organizational Decision-Making* (1973). This was based on an expanding computer system in a retailing organization, and examined the impact of this huge new resource on organizational politics. The first computer was installed in the 1950s, when commercial data-processing was a very uncertain business. Skills of a high order were involved, and the company itself was anxious to get the system working due to a rapid expansion in their volume of business. All these factors made the organization heavily dependent on the group of programmers in charge of the installation, and this was reflected in the programmers' total control of computer operations – a clear example of expert power. However, the programmers simply did not fit into the organization. It was traditional and bureaucratic, while the programmers were university graduates who behaved and dressed casually, and who worked outside normal hours setting up the installation. They came to regard the firm's employees as dull and authoritarian, while the employees regarded the programmers as arrogant and immature. The very powerful antipathy between the two groups put paid to the programmers ever becoming an integral part of the organization; and senior management in particular greatly resented having to rely upon the programmers' skills. Pettigrew charts the struggle that ensued as management tried to undermine the programmers' control of technical information – by, for example, breaking up the programming function and hiving off parts of it to other staff. For their part, the programmers sought to protect their power base by mystifying their skills and withholding information. In this way, this professional group challenged formal authority essentially by seeking to retain the dependence of the organization upon their expertise.

DECISION-MAKING AS A POLITICAL PROCESS

Having examined the bases of power in organizations, we can now turn to look at the organizational setting in which the political process takes place. It is important to bear in mind here, as we stressed earlier, that management is not the harmonious group it is often made out to be. Persistent conflict exists within management which is manifest in a variety of ways: in the manipulation of information, in hostility and lack of trust in intergroup relations, and in unwillingness to co-operate with colleagues. While it is possible for conflict to escalate to the point where it becomes highly destructive of organizational effort, where groups isolate themselves and become suspicious and hostile, even in the normal process of reaching joint decisions conflict and co-operation occur together. Therefore if joint decisions are to be arrived at, and conflict continually resolved, a negotiation or bargaining model of organizational interaction is implied.

Several studies have explored the notion of organizational decision-making as a process of negotiation (Bacharach and Lawler, 1980; Pfeffer, 1981). They stress that decisions are not simply 'made' or 'taken' but rather they *emerge* from interaction. Rules and relationships within organizations are outcomes of negotiation, constantly created and recreated; they are never merely part of an established structure. Conflict plays a central role in this, because it is conflicts of interest which cause people to use their power resources to bargain for outcomes favourable to themselves. Yet conflict does not merely occur at random. It can also be a direct result of the formal structure of organizations. As we saw above, specialization and departmentalization within management create sub-units with discrete tasks and goals, and they also develop their own distinctive commitments and outlooks. While this differentiation is necessary for organizational performance, nevertheless the goal conflict it gives rise to creates the motives behind conflict.

The early writers of the classical school thought that goals were normally integrated. Under their model, the overall goal of the organization, being itself highly complex, is supposedly broken down into various sub-goals and allocated to specific units via the division of labour. The organization structure formally unites these sub-goals and hence the overall goal is achieved. We can see that this model must to an extent be true, otherwise little would ever get done in organizations. The goal of one department has to be formulated in accordance with the needs of other departments with which it interacts. But equally clearly the view of organizations as structures for the rational pursuit of goals is much too simplistic. Goals may in fact be poorly defined and provide an inadequate guide to behaviour; the real goals that actors pursue may be subtly different (or indeed very different) from stated goals; personal goals (the pursuit of promotion, power, income, security) may clash with official goals; and goals may change over time, or the original goals may be displaced by other real goals.

Similarly, if we look only at the *power resources* that actors possess, to some extent we receive a static picture of the negotiation process, as if actors merely command influence in some fixed proportion of their expert power or position power. In reality, organizational politics is more dynamic and new sources of power can be generated actually in the process of negotiation itself. French and Raven were aware of this. They noted that there was also a 'subjective' side to power – people may not actually possess certain power resources, but as long as they can persuade others that they do, they can still gain the substance of power. Implied here is a *tactical* conception of decision-making, in which power-seekers can amplify (or reduce if they choose the wrong tactics) the power resources at their disposal.

For example, probably the most basic power tactic is the *control of information*. Information flows to high-ranking organizational members as part of the normal process of decision-making, and the possession of important information naturally reinforces their formal power. But lower-ranking members can also mobilize this particular resource to their advantage. They can exploit the fact that they are directly involved with the work process to gain control of strategic information. Withholding information, releasing information at the moment likely to cause maximum embarrassment to your opponent, and even distorting information are all very common tactics in the power game.

Morgan (1986. p. 159) provides an extensive account of the range of tactics that people employ in pursuit of individual and sectional interests. He identifies, for example, *persuasion* as a form of influence in which people try to amplify their power by convincing others that they possess power resources that they do not; a form of bluff, in other words. There is also *controlling the agenda*. This can be regarded as a version of Lukes's second face of power; it involves setting the terms of debate and preventing issues getting into the bargaining arena. Tactical power has also become the subject of a highly refined theory, which has been reviewed in detail by Bacharach and Lawler (1980). We have no space to go fully into their survey here, although we will indicate some of its main points.

Coalitions and interest groups

One common power tactic involves the formation of *sponsor–protégé relationships*. These are informal alliances between a senior and junior manager in which the protégé may assist the more senior person in some specialist area: he or she may perform various detailed work (e.g. write reports, speeches) and may provide the senior manager with intelligence reports. In return the sponsor will guide the career of the protégé. Sponsors often have clusters of protégés; and when the sponsor moves up or out, to a better job, he or she may move the whole team too. In this way corporate management is frequently made up of interlocking cliques of senior people and their followers.

But perhaps the most important power tactic is *coalition formation* (indeed, sponsor-protégé relationships are a special kind of coalition). Coalition formation represents the essence of political action, since it holds out the possibility of groups actually creating power for themselves. When interest groups face powerful opposition, a viable course of action is for them to join forces with other similar groups. A coalition, then, is *an informal relationship between two or more interest groups for the purpose of increasing their joint power in relation to some other group or groups.*

The obvious reason why groups should form coalitions is the gains they expect to make. But this does not take us very far. The more important question concerns the conditions under which groups might expect to gain little or much from forming a coalition. At least three factors can be distinguished here.

1. The most important objective condition is usually the *relative power* of the interest groups involved, for this decides whether a winning coalition can be formed. Thus, if two weaker groups have sufficient power together to override a third group with which they are in conflict, then other things being equal it is likely they will form the coalition. On the other hand, if their joint power is still insufficient to prevail against the third group, they may well decide that the coalition is not worth forming.

2. Managerial *differentiation* also plays a part. Interest groups in which the members are very different from each other, and have conflicting priorities, are usually capable of forming only unstable coalitions. So even if an issue does arise over which such groups might usefully pool resources, they may find day-to-day co-operation so difficult that they have to pursue their interests separately.

3. In certain ways the *issue at stake* can itself become a condition of formation. First, if it is a specific issue, resolved once and for all at a given time, then the most unlikely groups may be tempted into a temporary coalition because they know there will be no lasting commitment. Secondly, a highly important issue – one in which the potential gains are large, or where the very survival of the groups is at stake – may also force into a coalition groups that would otherwise never contemplate joint action.

The circumstances in which groups might expect to gain more from going it alone'are readily identified as the reverse of those that produce coalitions. Thus if an interest group is especially powerful, it will not need to engage in a coalition. Similarly, if it is highly differentiated from other organizational groups, its members may decide that they share no interest with other groups. In such circumstances the costs of coalition formation – the most obvious one being that any spoils have to be shared – are liable to outweigh the benefits. Moreover, benefits can be transformed into costs: interacting with colleagues, which is a rewarding experience among people of like mind, can itself become a burden if they share little in common.

Perhaps the most widespread example of organizational staff likely to rely upon interest-group tactics is *professionals*. Employed professionals (engineers, technical specialists, etc.) very often have a degree of expert power, perhaps conferred by control of strategic technology. They are likely to be differentiated from other organizational members in terms of occupational values, and their technical qualifications may also make them mobile and independent of the organization to a certain extent. Thus they are quite likely to pursue their interests via their profession rather than the organization.

The interest-group tactic represents true political behaviour only where it is actively chosen, or where it is used as an occupational strategy. However, in organizational terms it may often amount to opting out of the political game. The programmers in Pettigrew's (1973) case study, discussed above, seemed to present a good example of this. They clearly did see the organization in terms of the technical problems it provided rather than as secure employment. In the long term they seemed to be storing up trouble for themselves by choosing to defend an isolated position and not seeking wider organizational influence. On the other hand, of course, one might regard a defensive tactic as the only sensible course given their extreme social distance from other groups in the organization. In any case, the programmers managed to preserve some of their status, and their skills gave them the option of seeking other employment.

Human rationality in decision-making
While these structural factors influence coalition formation, they are not the whole story. In practice, losing coalitions form quite frequently, for, as we have stressed, decision-making is a human and political process, and factors other than the purely rational calculation of costs and benefits enter into it.

To begin with, coalition formation is an *indeterminate* process, one in which there is always uncertainty as to the outcome. This is so for several reasons. People's information is never perfect, nor their judgments completely objective. Thus when we speak of the gains and losses involved in a coalition, the unspoken qualifier is that these are always people's *expectations* of gains and losses. In addition, important elements in the political process are non-comparable. One can never say exactly how much power a potential ally or adversary has, and thus one can never be entirely sure in advance whether the combination of these powers would produce a winning coalition.

More important, though, is the *tactical* nature of the organizational power game. Leadership, the deployment of resources and the formation of intelligent alliances are all going to be decisive. These are open-ended factors, which involve initiative and which take shape only as part of the political process. It follows that it is possible only with hindsight to say that so-and-so would inevitably win, or could never have won. At the time of conflict, each participant had the opportunity of winning; otherwise, of course, no certain loser would ever enter the political arena. Indeed, the essence of political action lies in the ability to convert an apparently weak position into a winning one via the intelligent use of tactics.

Another reason why losing coalitions may be formed stems from the subtle and dynamic nature of political processes. Gains other than purely material ones may be had from coalition membership. Being part of such power cliques, playing the game of organizational politics, is far more rewarding than being left on the sidelines. Moreover, material gains may eventually be forthcoming, since a losing coalition today may be the basis of a winning coalition in the future. Thus, people often judge this kind of group experience as being useful as well as enjoyable. They are right to do so, because coalitions are an integral part of organizational life, and to be an active participant in these crucial processes is to be pursuing one's career in the long term.

Conclusion

The study of negotiation and power, then, has some very positive things to recommend it: the stress on 'real' organizational activity is refreshing when compared with the overly formal and prescriptive approach of the managerial theorists, while the ability to manipulate power is vital for organizational as well as managerial development. The mere fact that this side of the management role has been played down until quite recently encourages an interest in power – any new approach which promises to take our understanding forward is naturally welcome. Certainly the idea that power and negotiation are the 'name of the game' in organizations and remain the decisive factor in decision-making is very persuasive. However, in concluding we should consider the claims of a broader range of theories.

Perhaps the main weakness of the power in organizations approach lies in the 'bargaining' emphasis. This reflects Dahl's early behavioural view of power and tends to assume a real power arena and power interactions that are 'happening'. We saw that the thrust of Lukes's critique of this view was a concern with the 'hidden' dimensions of power. To really understand power, the groups that are excluded and the interests that never have the opportunity to form have to be taken into account. Of course, the radical view has its own problems in revealing that which is hidden. How do you know whether interest groups exist if they have been excluded, or worse not even constituted?

447

You are on very shaky ground when telling people what their 'real interests' are. Yet the need for some notion of the concealed aspects of power comes through strongly from a number of quarters. Weber's view of power contained two such paradoxes – power as a potential for action rather than action itself; and the idea that power is strongest where it does not have to be wielded, or where the threat of power is the central resource. These more complex views have had an effect. We saw that a number of writers mentioned exclusionary tactics in their accounts of organizational power. The notion of management decision-making as a political process is broader than that of 'bargaining'.

Reviewing the different approaches to power reveals some strong lines of convergence. A common theme was the distinction between power generated in action and power devolved from wider structures. The 'two views' of power are long established. Thus Clegg (1989, p. 5) has indicated some much older lines of thinking on power: the Machiavellian and Hobbesian views. From the former we inherit a view of power as partial strategies appropriate in particular spheres. Machiavelli was preoccupied with tactical concerns and the attainment of power. Hobbes, by contrast, stressed the power of an established authority over a set of subjects. This is the source of Foucault's idea of sovereign power, and the basis of modern structural perspectives. The point can be expressed more simply in the distinction between 'power for' and 'power over' – the former stresses the use of power to generate change, while the latter emphasizes the established power of particular groups. Several of the above theories argued along these lines. Processual and institutional types reflect this power duality; and we can see that the distinction in Lukes between the first and third 'faces' of power (the behavioural and the radical), and Foucault's disciplinary power versus sovereign power, have similarities.

This said, we should not try to convince ourselves that all views can be reconciled. For example, the more structured view of power seems to relate Weberian authority and Foucault's type of sovereign power. But Weber's notion of authority was built on the rational acceptance of legitimate position, which is worlds away from the kind of state-inspired terror that backed Foucault's sovereign power. Likewise, Foucault's disciplinary power has some similarities with processual power, namely that both are created within human interaction; but unlike processual power, disciplinary power contains strong elements of domination.

The search for a resolution between these different approaches is almost bound to be misleading. Different forms of power arising from different resources and bases co-exist within organizations. Moreover, as well as the reality differing, our views of reality differ. The above are not competing theories that give either 'true' or 'false' explanations of events. Rather they are *perspectives* – ways of seeing organizational activity and emphasizing some aspect of it. Ultimately the existence of so many different approaches reflects the complexity of behaviour and our inability to ascribe a single 'reality' to organizations. To seek to encapsulate them within one theory is asking rather a lot; different observers will have their own preferred perspective, and the uses to which theory is put will differ across a wide spectrum.

Further reading

Clegg, S. R. (1989) *Frameworks of Power*. London: Sage.

Clegg, S. R. (1990) *Modern Organizations*. London: Sage.

Dawson, S. (1992) 'Power and conflict', Chapter 7 in *Analysing Organisations (2nd edn)*. Basingstoke: Macmillan.

Lee, R. and P. Lawrence (1986) *Organizational Behaviour: Politics at Work*. London: Hutchinson.

Lukes, S. (ed.) (1986) *Power*. Oxford: Blackwell.

Mintzberg, H. (1983) *Power in and Around Organizations*. Englewood Cliffs, N. J.: Prentice-Hall.

Morgan, G. (1986) 'Organizations as political systems', Chapter 6 in *Images of Organization*. London: Sage.

Pfeffer, J. (1981) *Power in Organizations*. Marshfield, Mass.: Pitman.

Reed, M. and J. Hughes (eds.) (1992) *Rethinking Organization*. London: Sage.

References

Abercrombie, N. and J. Urry (1983) *Capital, Labour and the Middle Classes.* London: Allen and Unwin.

Adams, J.S. (1965) 'Inequity in social exchange', in L. Berkowitz (ed.) *Advances in Experimental Social Psychology*, vol. 2. New York: Academic Press.

Adams, J.S. and P.R. Jacobsen (1964) 'Effects of wage inequities on work quality', *J. of Abnormal and Social Psychology*, 69, 19–25.

Adams-Webber, J. (1981) 'Empirical developments in personal construct theory', in H. Bonarius, R. Holland and S. Rosenberg (eds.) *Personal Construct Psychology.* London: Macmillan.

Alban-Metcalfe, B. (1984) 'Microskills of leadership: a detailed analysis of the behavior of managers in the appraisal interview', in J.G. Hunt, D.M. Hosking, C.A. Schriesheim and R. Stewart (eds.) *Leaders and Managers.* New York: Pergamon.

Albrow, M. (1980) 'The dialectic of science and values in the study of organizations', in G. Salaman and K. Thompson (eds.) op. cit.

Alderfer, C.P. (1972) *Existence, Relatedness and Growth.* New York: Free Press.

Allen, V.L. (1975) *Social Analysis.* London: Longman.

Allen, V. and D.A. Wilder (1979) 'Group categorization and attribution of belief similarity', *Small Group Behaviour*, 110, 73–80.

Altmann, N., Binkelmann, P., Dull, K. and Stuck, H. (1982) *Grenzen neuer Arbeitzformen.* Frankfurt: Campus.

Argyle, M. (1983) *The Psychology of Interpersonal Behaviour* (4th ed.) Harmondsworth: Penguin.

Argyle, M. and H. Cook (1976) *Gaze and Mutual Gaze.* Cambridge: Cambridge University Press.

Argyle, M., A. Furnham, and J.A. Graham (1981) *Social Situations.* Cambridge: Cambridge University Press.

Armstrong, P. (1985) 'Changing management control strategies: the role of competition between accountancy and other organisational professions', *Accounting, Organizations and Society*, 10, 124–48.

Armstrong, P. (1989) 'Management, labour process and agency', *Work, Employment and Society*, 3, 3, 307–22.

Arsenault, A. and S. Dolan (1983) 'The role of personality, occupation and organization in understanding the relationship between job stress, performance and absenteeism', *J. of Occupational Psychology*, 56, 227–40.

Atkinson, J. (1984) 'Manpower strategies for flexible organizations', *Personnel Management*, August.

Atkinson, J. (1985) 'Flexibility: planning for an uncertain future', *Manpower Policy and Practice*, 1, Summer, 26–9.

Atkinson, J. (1988) 'Recent changes in the internal labour market structure in the UK', in W. Buitelaar (ed.) *Technology and Work*. Aldershot: Avebury.

Atkinson, J. and N. Meager (1986) 'Is "flexibility" just a flash in the pan?', *Personnel Management*, September.

Attwood, M. and F. Hatton (1983) ' "Getting on": Gender differences in career development: a case study in the hairdressing industry', in E. Gamarnikow, D. Morgan, J. Purvis and D. Taylorson (eds.) *Gender, Class and Work*. London: Heinemann.

Bacharach, S.B. and E.J. Lawler (1980) *Power and Politics in Organizations*. London: Jossey-Bass.

Bachrach, P. and M.S. Baratz (1962) 'The two faces of power', *American Political Science Rev.*, 56, 947–52.

Bainbridge, L. (1978) 'The process controller', in W.T. Singleton (ed.) *The Analysis of Practical Skills*. Lancaster: MTP Press.

Baldamus, W. (1961) *Efficiency and Effort*. London: Tavistock.

Baldry, C. and A. Connolly. (1986) 'Drawing the line: computer-aided design and the organization of the drawing office', *New Technology, Work and Employment*, 1, 1, 59–66.

Bales, R.F. and P.E. Slater (1955) 'Role differentiation in small decision-making groups', in T. Parsons *et al.* (eds.) *Family, Socialization and Interaction Processes*. New York: Free Press.

Bamforth, K. (1965) 'T-group methods within a company', in G. Whitaker (ed.) *ATM Occasional Papers*. Oxford: Blackwell.

Banks, M.H., P.R. Jackson, E.M. Stafford and P.B. Warr (1982) *The Job Components Inventory Mark 2*. Sheffield: Manpower Services Commission Training Studies.

Barker, C. (1983) 'The psychotherapist', in W.T. Singleton (ed.) *Social Skills*. Lancaster: MTP Press.

Barker, J. and H. Downing (1980) 'Word processing and the transformation of the patriarchal relations of control in the office', *Capital and Class*, 10, 64–99.

Barrett, P. and P. Kline (1980) 'Personality factors in the EPQ', *Personality and Individual Differences*, 1, 317–23.

Bass, B.M. (1981) *Stodgill's Handbook of Leadership*. New York: Free Press.

Bass, B.M. and E.R. Valenzi (1974) 'Contingent aspects of effective management styles', in J.G. Hunt and L.L. Larson (eds.) *Contingency Approaches to Leadership*. Carbondale: Southern Illinois University Press.

Bass, B.M., P.C. Burger, R. Doktor and G.V. Barrett (1979) *Assessment of Managers: An International Comparison*. New York: Free Press.

Bass, B.M., E.R. Valenzi, D.C. Furnow and R.J. Solomon (1975) 'Management styles associated with organizational task, personal and interpersonal contingencies', *J. of Applied Psychology*, 60, 720–29.

Belbin, R.M. (1981) *Management Teams: Why they Succeed or Fail.* London: Heinemenn.

Bell, D. (1948) ' "Screening" leaders in a democracy', *Commentary*, 5, 368–75.

Bell, R.C. and H.R. Weaver (1987) 'The dimensionality and scaling of job satisfaction: an internal validation of the Worker Opinion Survey', *J. of Occupational Psychology*, 60, 147–55.

Bendix, R. (1956) *Work and Authority in Industry.* New York: Wiley.

Berggren, C. (1989) 'New production concepts in final assembly: the Swedish experience', in S. Wood (ed.) op. cit.

Berry-Lound, D. (1990) 'Towards the family-friendly firm', *Employment Gazette*, February, 85–91.

Beynon, H. (1984) *Working for Ford* (2nd ed.) Harmondsworth: Penguin.

Beynon, H. and Blackburn, R. (1972) *Perceptions of Work.* Cambridge: Cambridge University Press.

Billings, A.G. and R.M. Moos (1981) 'The role of coping responses in attenuating the impact of stressful life events', *J. of Behavioural Medicine*, 4, 139–57.

Blackburn, R.M. and M. Mann (1979) *The Working Class in the Labour Market.* London: Macmillan.

Blackler, F.H.M. and C.A. Brown (1978) *Job Design and Management Control.* Farnborough: Saxon House.

Blackler, F.H.M. and C.A. Brown (1980) 'Job redesign and social change: case studies at Volvo', in K.D. Duncan, M.M. Gruneberg and D. Wallis (eds.) op. cit.

Blau, P.M. (1955) *The Dynamics of Bureaucracy.* Chicago: University of Chicago Press.

Blau, P.M. and Schoenherr, R.A. (1971) *The Structure of Organizations.* New York: Basic Books.

Blauner, R. (1964) *Alienation and Freedom.* Chicago: University of Chicago Press.

Blinkhorn, S. and C. Johnson (1990) 'The insignificance of personality testing', *Nature*, 348, 671–2.

Boje, D.M. (1991) 'The story-telling organization: story performance in an office supply firm', *Administrative Science Quarterly*, 36, 1, 106–26.

Bradley, H. (1989) *Men's Work, Women's Work.* Cambridge: Polity Press.

Braun, E. and S. MacDonald (1978) *Revolution in Miniature.* Cambridge: Cambridge University Press.

Braverman, H. (1974) *Labor and Monopoly Capital: The Degradation of Work in the Twentieth Century.* New York: Monthly Review Press.

Bray, D.W., Campbell, R.J. and Grant, D.C. (1974) *Formative Years in Business: A Long-Term AT&T Study of Managerial Lives.* New York: Wiley.

Brenner, M. (1982) 'Actors powers', in M. von Cranach and R. Harré (eds.) *The Analysis of Action.* Cambridge: Cambridge University Press.

Brett, J.M. (1980) 'The effect of job transfer in employees and their families', In C.L. Cooper and R. Payne (eds.) op. cit.

British Psychological Society (1981) 'Principles governing the employment of psychological tests', *Bull. of the British Psychological Society*, 34, 317–18.

British Psychological Society (1989) *Psychological Testing: Guidance for the User*. Leicester: British Psychological Society.

Brown, D. and M.J. Harrison (1980) 'The demand for relevance and the role of sociology in busies studies degrees', *J. of Further and Higher Education*, 4, 54–61.

Brown, G.W. and T. Harris (1978) *Social Origins of Depression: A Study of Psychiatric Disorder in Women*. London: Tavistock.

Brown, R. (1984) 'Women as employees: social consciousness and collective action', in J. Siltanen and M. Stanworth (eds.) op. cit.

Bruning, N.S. and D.R. Frew (1987) 'Effects of exercise relation and management skills training in physiological stress exercises: a field experiment', *J. of Applied Psychology*, 72, 515–21.

Buchanan, D.A. and D. Boddy (1983) *Organizations in the Computer Age*. Aldershot: Gower.

Burnes, B. (1988) 'New technology and job design: the case of CNC'. *New Technology, Work and Employment*, 3, 2, 100–11.

Burns, J.M. (1978) *Leadership*. New York: Harper and Row.

Burns, T. (1969) 'On the plurality of social systems', in T. Burns (ed.) *Industrial Man*. Harmondsworth: Penguin.

Burns, T. (1977) *The BBC: Public Institution and Private World*. London: Macmillan.

Burns, T. and G.M. Stalker (1961) *The Management of Innovation*. London: Tavistock.

Burnstein, E. (1983) 'Persuasion as argument processing', in I.M. Brandstatter, J.H. Davis and G. Stocker-Kreichgauer (eds.) *Group Decision Processes*. London: Academic Press.

Burrell, G. (1988) 'Modernism, post-modernism and organizational analysis 2: the contribution of Michel Foucault, *Organization Studies*, 9, 2, 221–35.

Burrell, G. and G. Morgan. (1979) *Sociological Paradigms and Organisational Analysis*. London: Heinemann.

Byrne, D.G. and M.I. Rheinhart (1989) ' Work characteristics, occupational achievement and the Type A behavior pattern', *J. of Occupational Psychology*, 62, 123–34.

Cameron, R. and D. Meichenbaum (1982) 'The nature of effective coping and the treatment of stress related problems: a cognitive–behavioural perspective', in L. Goldberger and S. Breznitz (eds.) *Handbook of Stress: Theoretical and Clinical Aspects*. London: Macmillan.

Campbell, A and M. Warner (1987) 'New technology, innovation and training', *New Technology, Work and Employment*, 2, 2, 86–99.

Cantor, N. and J.F. Kihlstrom (1987) *Personality and Social Intelligence*. Englewood Cliffs, NJ: Prentice Hall.

Caplan, R.D., S. Cobb, J.R.P. French, R. van Harrison and S.R. Pinneau (1975) *Job Demands and Worker Health*, pp. 75–160. U.S. Department of Health, Education and Welfare/NIOSH.

Carchedi, G. (1977) *On the Economic Identification of Social Classes*. London: Routledge Direct Editions.

Carey, A. (1967) 'The Hawthorne studies: a radical criticism', *American Sociological Rev.*, 32, 403–16.

Carnall, C.A. (1990) *Managing Change in Organizations*. Hemel Hempstead: Prentice Hall.

Carrell, M.R. and J.E. Dittrich (1978) 'Equity theory: the recent literature, methodological considerations and new directions', *Academy of Management Rev.*, 3, 202–10.

Carrère, S., G.W.M. Evans, N. Palsane and M. Rivas (1991) 'Job strain and occupational stress among urban public transport operators', *J. of Occupational Psychology*, 64, 305–16.

Carruthers, M. (1980) 'Hazardous occupations and the heart', in C.L. Cooper and R. Payne (eds.) op. cit.

Cartwright, D. and A. Zander (1968) (eds.) *Group Dynamics: Research and Theory* (3rd ed.) New York: Harper and Row.

Carver, C.S. and D.C. Glass (1978) 'Coronary-prone behaviour patterns and interpersonal aggression', *J. of Personality and Social Psychology*, 36, 361–6.

Cassidy, T. and R. Lynn (1989) 'A multifactorial approach to achievement motivation; the development of a comprehensive measure', *J. of Occupational Psychology*, 62, 301–12.

Cathcart, E.P. (1928) *The Human Factor in Industry*. Oxford: Oxford University Press.

Cattell, R.B. (1967) *The Scientific Analysis of Personality*. Harmondsworth: Penguin.

Charlesworth, E.A. and R.G. Nathan (1986) *Stress Management*. London: Souvenir Press.

Chesney, M.A. and R. Rosenman (1980) 'Type A behaviour in the work setting', in C.L. Cooper and R. Payne (eds.) op. cit.

Child, J. (1972) 'Organizational structure, environment and performance: the role of strategic choice', *Sociology*, 6, 1–22.

Child, J. (1984) *Organization* (2nd ed.) London: Harper and Row.

Child, J. and J. Fulk (1982) 'Maintenance of occupational control: the case of professions', *Work and Occupations*, 9, 155–92.

Child, J. and C. Smith (1987) 'The context and process of organizational transformation – Cadbury Limited in its sector', *Journal of Management Studies*, 24, 6, 565–93.

Child, J., R. Loveridge, J. Harvey and A. Spencer (1984) 'Microelectronics and the quality of employment in services', in P. Marstrand (ed.) *New Technology and the Future of Work and Skills*. London: Frances Pinter.

Chinoy, E. (1955) *Automobile Workers and the American Dream*. New York: Doubleday.

Cialdini, R.B. (1988) *Influence: Science and Practice*. Glenview, Ill.: Scott, Foresman, Little, Brown.

Claridge, G.S. (1970) *Drugs and Human Behaviour*. London: Allen Lane.

Clarke, D.D. (1983) *Language and Action: A Structural Model of Behaviour*. Oxford: Pergamon Press.

Clarke, T. (1990) 'Automation and craftwork'. Paper presented to ISA World Congress, Madrid, July.

Clegg, C. and M.J. Fitter (1978) 'Management information systems: the Achilles Heel of job redesign', *Personnel Rev.*, 7, 5–11.

Clegg, S. (1989) *Frameworks of Power*. London: Sage.

Clegg, S. and D. Dunkerley (1980) *Organization, Class and Control*. London: Routledge and Kegan Paul.

Cliff, T. (1970) *The Employers' Offensive*, London: Pluto Press.

Cockburn, C. (1983) *Brothers: Male Dominance and Technological Change*. London: Pluto Press.

Cockburn, C. (1985) *Machinery of Dominance: Women, Men and Technical Know-how*. London: Pluto Press.

Cockburn, C. (1988) 'The gendering of jobs: workplace relations and the reproduction of sex segregation', in S. Walby (ed.) op. cit.

Conger, J.A. (1989) *The Charismatic Leader: Behind the Mystique of Exceptional Leadership*. San Fransisco: Jossey Bass.

Cooley, M. (1987) ' Human centered systems: an urgent problem for systems designers', *AI and Society*, 1, 1, 40.

Coombs, R. and B. Jones (1988) ' Alternative successors to Fordism'. UMIST and Bath University (mimeo).

Cooper, C.L. (1975) 'How psychologically dangerous are T-groups and encounter groups?', *Human Relations*, 28, 249–60.

Cooper, C.L. and A. Melhuish (1980) 'Occupational stress and the manager', *J. of Occupational Medicine*, 22, 588–92.

Cooper, C.L. and R. Payne (eds.) (1980) *Current Concerns in Occupational Stress*. Chichester: Wiley.

Cowling, A. G., M.J.K. Stanworth, R.D. Bennet, J. Curran and P. Lyons (1988) *Behavioural Sciences for Mangers*. (2nd edn). Oxford. Blackwell.

Cox, T. (1980) 'Repetitive work', in C.L. Cooper and R. Payne (eds.) op. cit.

Craig, C., E. Garnsey and J. Rubery (1983) 'Women's pay in informal payment systems', *Employment Gazette*, April. (London: Department of Employment.)

Crompton, R. and G. Jones (1984) *White Collar Proletariat: Deskilling and Gender in Clerical Work*. London: Macmillan.

Crompton, R. and S. Reid (1982) 'The deskilling of clerical work', in S. Wood (ed.) op. cit.

Cross, J.A. (1989) 'The Worker Opinion Survey: a measure of shop floor satisfaction', *J. of Occupational Psychology*, 47, 193–208.

Crossman, E.R.F.W. and J.E. Cooke (1962) 'Manual control of slow response systems', in E. Edwards and F.P. Lees (eds.) *The Human Operator in Process Control*. London: Taylor and Francis.

Crowder, N.A. (1960) 'Automatic tutoring by intrinsic programming', in A.A. Lunsdaine and R. Glaser (eds.) *Teaching Machines and Programmed Learning*. Washington: NEA.

Crozier, M. (1964) *The Bureaucratic Phenomenon*. London: Tavistock.

Currie, W. (1989) *Managerial Strategy for New Technology*. Aldershot: Averbury.

Dahl, R.A. (1957) 'The concept of power', *Behavioral Science*, 2, 201–5.

Dahrendorf, R. (1959) *Class and Class Conflict in Industrial Society*. London: Routledge and Kegan Paul.

Daley, M.R. (1979) 'Burnout: smouldering problems in protective services', *Social Work*, 24, 375–9.

Deal, T. and A. Kennedy (1982) *Corporate Cultures*. Reading, Mass.: Addison-Wesley.

Deem, R. (1981) 'The teaching of industrial sociology in higher education: an exploratory analysis', *Sociological Rev.*, 29, 237–51.

de Waele, J.P. and R. Harŕe (1976) *Personality*. Oxford: Blackwell.

Dewe, P. (1991) 'Primary appraisal, secondary appraisal and coping: their role in stressful work encounters', *J. of Occupational Psychology*, 64, 331–51.

Dewe, P. and D.E. Guest (1990) 'Methods of coping with stress at work: a conceptual analysis and empirical study of measurements issues', *J. of Organizational Behaviour*, 11, 135–50.

Dex, S. (1985) *The Sexual Division of Work*. Brighton: Harvester Wheatsheaf.

Dobb, M. (1963) *Studies in the Development of Capitalism*. London: Routledge and Kegan Paul.

Dornstein, M (1989) 'The fairness of judgements of received pay and their determinants', *J of Occupational Psychology*, 62, 287–99.

Downs, S. and P. Perry (1982) 'How do I learn?', *J. of European Industrial Training*, 6, 27–32.

Downs, S. and P. Perry (1984) *Developing Skilled Learners: Learning to Learn in the Youth Training Scheme*. Sheffield: Manpower Services Commission, R & D Publication No. 22.

Downs, S. and P. Perry (1986) 'Can trainers learn to take a back seat?', *Personnel Management*, March.

Drakely, R.J., P. Herriot and A. Jones (1988) 'Biographical data, training success and turnover', *J. of Occupational Psychology*, 61, 145–52.

Drazen, M., J.S. Nevid, N. Pace and R.M. O'Brien. (1982) 'Worksite-based behavioural treatment of mild hypertension', *J. Occupational Medicine*, 24, 511–14.

Duck, S.W. (1973) *Personal Relationships and Personal Constructs: A Study of Friendship Formation*. Chichester: Wiley.

Duncan, K.D., M.M. Gruneberg and D. Wallis (eds.) (1980) *Changes in Working Life*. Chichester: Wiley.

Duranti, A. and Ochs, E. (1979) 'Left-dislocation in Italian conversation', in T. Givon (ed.) *Syntax and Semantics*, vol. 12: *Discourse and Syntax*. New York: Academic Press.

Durbeck, D.C., F. Heinzelmann, J. Schacter, W.I. Haskell, G.H. Payne, R.T. Moxley, M. Nemeroff, D.D. Limoncelli, L.B. Arnoldi and S.M. Fox (1972) 'The National Aeronautics and Space Administration: U.S. Public Health Service Health Evaluation and Enhancement Programme', *American J. of Cardiology*, 30, 784–90.

Durcan, J., W.E.J. McCarthy and G.P. Redham (1983) *Strikes in Post-War Britain*. London: Allen and Unwin.

Edwardes, M. (1984) *Back from the Brink*. London: Pan.

Edwards, P.K. (1979) ' "The awful truth about strikes in our factories": a case study in the production of news', *Industrial Relations J.*, 10, 7–11.

Edwards, P.K. (1990) 'Understanding conflict in the labour process: the logic and autonomy of struggle', in D. Knights and H. Willmott (eds.) op.cit.

Edwards, R., M. Reich and D.M. Gordon (eds.) (1975) *Labor Market Segmentation.* Lexington, Mass.: D.C. Heath.

Eldridge, J.E.T. (1968) *Industrial Disputes.* London: Routledge and Kegan Paul.

Elger, T. (1990) 'Technical innovation and work reorganization in British manufacturing in the 1980s: continuity, intensification or transformation?', *Work, Employment and Society*, May, 67–101.

Elliott, D. (1980) 'The organization as a system', in G. Salaman and K. Thompson (eds.) op. cit.

Ellis, V. (1988) 'Current trade union attempts to remove occupational segregation in the employment of women', in S. Walby (ed.) op. cit.

Entwistle, N.J. and J.D. Wilson (1977) *Degrees of Excellence: The Academic Achievement Game.* London: Hodder and Stoughton.

Equal Employment Opportunity Coordinating Council (EEOCC) (1978) *Uniform Guidelines on Employee Selection Procedures.* Federal Register, 38290–38315.

Esland, G. (1980) 'Professions and professionalism', in G. Esland and G. Salaman (eds.) *The Politics of Work and Occupations.* Milton Keynes: Open University Press.

Evans, M.G. (1970) 'The effects of supervisory behavior on the path–goal relationship', *Organizational Behavior and Human Performance*, 5, 277–98.

Evans, M.G. (1973) 'The moderating effect of internal versus external control on the relationship between various aspects of job satisfaction', *Studies in Personnel Psychology*, 5, 37–46.

Evans, M.G., M.M. Kiggundu and R.J. House (1979) 'A partial test and extensions of the job characteristics model of motivation', *Organizational Behavior and Human Performance*, 24, 354–81.

Evison, R. and R. Horobin (1983) *How to Change Yourself and Your World.* Sheffield: Co-counselling Phoenix.

Eysenck, H.J. (1953) *Uses and Abuses of Psychology.* Harmondsworth: Penguin.

Eysenck, H.J. (1985) *Decline and Fall of the Freudian Empire.* Harmondsworth: Viking.

Eysenck, H.J. and S.B.G. Eysenck (1976) *Psychotism as a Dimension of Personality.* London: Hodder and Stoughton.

Exley, M. (1977) 'A job satisfaction study in H.M. Customs and Excise: a participative approach to research management and a contingency approach to research design', *Personnel Rev.*, 6, 12–20.

Fazio, R.H., L.M. Cooper, K. Dayson and M. Johnson (1981) 'Control and the coronary-prone behaviour pattern: responses to multiple situation demands', *Personality and Social Psychology Bull.*, 7, 97–102.

Feldberg, R. and E.N. Glenn (1979) 'Male and female: job versus gender models in the sociology of work', *Social Problems*, 26, 5, 524–38. Reprinted in J. Siltanen and M. Stanworth (eds) (1984) op. cit.

Feltham, R. (1988) 'Validity of a police assessment center: a 1–19 year follow up', *J. of Occupational Psychology*, 61, 129–44.

Ferguson, D.A. (1973) 'Comparative study of occupational stress', *Ergonomics*, 16, 649–64.

Ferster, C.B. and B.F. Skinner (1957) *Schedules of Reinforcement*. New York: Appleton.

Fiedler, F.E. (1967) *A Theory of Leadership Effectiveness*. New York: MacGraw-Hill.

Fiedler, F.E. (1970) 'Leadership experience and leader performance – another hypothesis shot to hell', *Organizational Behavior and Human Performance*, 5, 1–14.

Fiedler, F.E. (1982) 'Are leaders an intelligent form of life? A long neglected question of leadership theory', *Abstracts*, 20th International Congress of Applied Psychology, 113.

Fiedler, F.E. and M.E. Chemars (1984) *Improving Leadership Effectiveness: The Leader Match Concept*. Chichester: Wiley.

Fiedler, F.E. and A.F. Leister (1977a) 'Intelligence and group performance: a multiple screen model', *Organizational Behavior and Human Performance*, 20, 1–11.

Fiedler, F.E. and A.F. Leister (1977b) 'Leader intelligence and task performance: a test of a multiple screen model', *Organizational Behavior and Human Performance*, 20, 11–14.

Fiedler, F.E. and L. Mahar (1979) 'The effectiveness of contingency model training: validation of leader match', *Personnel Psychology*, 32, 45–62.

Fiedler, F.E., P.M. Bons and L. Hastings (1975) 'The utilization of leadership resources', in W.T. Singleton and P. Spurgeon (eds.) *Measurement of Human Resources*. London: Taylor and Francis.

Field, R.H.G. (1979) 'A critique of the Vroom–Yetton contingency model of leadership behaviour', *Academic Management Rev.*, 4, 249–57.

Fincham, R. (1982) 'The diffusion of new technology: a study of Edinburgh firms'. Paper presented to BSA (Scotland) conference on Technological Change and Unemployment, University of Strathclyde, 13 November.

Fincham, R. (1989) 'Natural workgroups and the process of job design', *Employee Relations*, 11, 6, 17–22.

Fincham, R. (1992) 'Perspectives on power: processual institutional and "internal" forms of organizational power', *Journal of Management Studies*, 29, 6.

Fine, B. (1979) 'Struggles against discipline', *Capital and Class*, 9, 75–96.

Fleishman, E.A. and E.F. Harris (1962) 'Patterns of leadership behavior related to employee grievances and turnover', *Personnel Psychology*, 15, 43–56.

Fleishman, E.A., E.F. Harris and H.E. Burtt (1955) *Leadership and Supervision in Industry*. Columbus: Ohio State University, Bureau of Educational Research.

Fletcher, C. (1991) 'Candidates' reactions to assessment centers and their outcomes', *J. of Occupational Psychology*, 64, 117–27.

Fodor, E.M. and T. Smith (1982) 'The power motive as an influence on group decision making', *J. of Personality and Social Psychology*, 42, 178–85.

Fogarty, M., I. Allen and P. Walters (1981) *Women in Top Jobs 1968–1979*. London: Heinemann.

Folkman, S. and R.S. Lazarus (1980) 'An analysis of coping in a middle-aged community sample', *J. of Health and Social Behaviour*, 21, 219–39.

Forester, T. (1987) *High-Tech Society: the Story of the Information Technology Revolution*. Oxford: Blackwell.

Forester, T. (ed.) (1985) The Information Technology Revolution. Oxford: Blackwell.

Foucault, M. (1979) *Discipline and Punish: The Birth of the Prison*. London: Penguin.

Foucault, M. (1980) *Power/knowledge: Selected Interviews and Other Writings 1972–1977*. Hemel Hempstead: Harvester Wheatsheaf.

Fox, A. (1974) *Beyond Contract*. London: Faber and Faber.

Fox, A. (1977) 'The myths of pluralism and a radical alternative', in T. Clarke and L. Clements (eds.) *Trade Unions Under Capitalism*. London: Fontana.

French, J.R.P. and B. Raven (1959) 'The bases of social power', in D. Cartwright (ed.) *Studies in Social Power*. Ann Arbor, Mich.: Institute for Social Research.

Frese, M. (1982) 'Occupational socialization and psychological development: an underemphasized research perspective in industrial psychology', *J. of Occupational Psychology*, 55, 209–24.

Freshwater, D.L. (1982) *Basic Skills Analysis*. Sheffield: Manpower Services Commission.

Freud, S. (1939) *Moses and Monotheism*. Standard Edition, 23.

Freudenberger, H.J. (1974) 'Staff burn out', *J. of Social Issues*, 30, 159–65.

Freidman, A.L. with D.S. Cornford (1989) *Computer Systems Development*. Chichester: Wiley.

Freidman, A.L. (1990) 'Managerial strategies, activities techniques and technologies: towards a complex theory of the labour process', in D. Knights and H. Willmott (eds.) op. cit.

Friedman, M. and R.H. Rosenman (1974) *Type A Behaviour and Your Heart*. New York: Knopf.

Gallie, D. (1978) *In Search of the New Working Class*. London: Cambridge University Press.

Game, A. and R. Pringle (1983) *Gender at Work*. Sydney: Allen and Unwin.

Gane, M. (ed.) (1986) *Towards a Critique of Foucault*. London: Routledge and Kegan Paul.

Ganster, D.C., B.T. Mayers, W.E. Sime and G.D. Tharp (1982) 'Managing occupational stress: a field experiment', *J. of Applied Psych.*, 67, 533–42.

Garden, A.M. (1989) 'Burnout: the effect of psychological type on research findings', *J. of Occupational Psychology*, 62, 223–34.

Gershuny, J. and I. Miles (1983) *The New Service Economy*. London: Frances Pinter.

Ghiselli, E.E. (1963) 'Intelligence and managerial success', *Psychological Reports*, 12, 898.

Gibson, J.J. (1968) *The Senses Considered as Perceptual Systems*. Boston: Houghton Mifflin.

Giddens, A. (1984) *The Constitution of Society*. Cambridge: Polity Press.

Glass, D.C. (1977) *Behavior Patterns, Stress and Coronary Disease*. Hillsdale, NJ: Lawrence Erlbaum.

Goethals, G.R. and J.M. Darley (1977) 'Social comparison theory: an attributional approach', in J.M. Suls and R.L. Miller (eds.) *Social Comparison Perspectives*. Washington, DC: Hemisphere.

Goffman, E. (1968) *Asylums*. Harmondsworth: Penguin.

Goffman, E. (1971) *The Presentation of Self in Everyday Life*. Harmondsworth: Penguin.

Goldthorpe, J.H., D. Lockwood, F. Bechofer and J. Platt (1968) *The Affluent Worker: Industrial Attitudes and Behaviour*. Cambridge: Cambridge University Press.

Goode, W.J. (1957) 'Community within a community: the professions', *American Sociological Rev.*, 22, 194–200.

Goodfellow, M.M. (1983) 'The schoolteacher', in W.T. Singleton (ed.) *Social Skills*. Lancaster: MTP Press.

Goodrich, C.L. (1975) *The Frontier of Control*. London: Pluto Press.

Gorz, A (1990) 'The new agenda', *New Left Review*, 184, Nov–Dec.

Gospel, H. (1983) 'The development of management organization in industrial relations: a historical perspective', in K. Thurley and S. Wood (eds.) *Industrial Relations and Management Strategy*. Cambridge: Cambridge University Press.

Gouldner, A.W. (1954) *Patterns of Industrial Bureaucracy*. Glencoe, Ill.: Free Press.

Gouldner, A.W. (1955) *Wildcat Strike*. London: Routledge and Kegan Paul.

Gouldner, A.W. (1957) 'Cosmopolitans and locals', *Administrative Science Quarterly*, 2, 281–306.

Gowler, D. and K. Legge (1982) 'The integration of disciplinary perspectives in problem-oriented organizational research', in N. Nicholson and T.D. Wall (eds.) *The Theory and Practice of Organizational Psychology*. London: Academic Press.

Greene, C.N. (1975) 'The reciprocal nature of influence between leader and subordinate', *J. of Applied Psychology*, 60, 187–93.

Greene, C.N. (1979) 'Questions of causation in the path goal theory of leadership', *Academic Management J.*, 22, 22–41.

Grice, H.P. (1975) 'Logic and conversation', in P. Cole and J.L. Morgan (eds.) *Syntax and Semantics*, vol. 3: Speech Acts. London and New York: Academic Press.

Guest, D., R. Williams and P. Dewe (1980) 'Workers' perceptions of changes affecting the quality of working life', in K.D. Duncan, M.M. Gruneberg and D. Wallis (eds.) op. cit.

Guilford, J.P. (1967) *The Nature of Human Intelligence*. New York: McGraw-Hill.

Guilford, J.P. (1982) 'Cognitive psychology's ambiguities: some suggested remedies', *Psychological Rev.*, 89, 48–59.

Guirdham, M. (1990) *Interpersonal Skills at Work*. London: Prentice-Hall.

Guzzo, R., R.D. Jette and R.A. Katzell (1985) 'The effects of psychologically based intervention programs on worker productivity: a meta analysis', *Personnel Psychology*, 38, 275–91.

Gyllenhammar, P.G. (1977) 'How Volvo adapts work to people', *Harvard Business Rev.*, 55, 102–13.

Hackett, R.D., P. Bycio and R.M. Guion (1989) 'An idiographic–longitudinal analysis of absenteeism among hospital nurses', *Academy of Management Journal*, 32, 2.

Hackman, J.R. (1978) 'The design of work in the 1980s', *Organizational Dynamics*, Summer, 3–17.

Hackman, J.R. (1980) 'Changing views of motivation in work groups', in K.D. Duncan, M.M. Gruneberg and D. Wallis (eds.) op. cit.

Hackman, J.R. and G.R. Oldham (1975) 'Development of the job diagnostic survey', *J. of Applied Psychology*, 60, 159–70.

Hackman J.R. and G.R. Oldham (1976) 'Motivation through the design of work: test of a theory', *Organizational Behavior and Human Performance*, 16, 250–79.

Hakim, C. (1980) 'Census reports as documentary evidence: the Census Commentaries 1801–1951' *Sociological Rev.*, 28, 551–80.

Hales, C. (1988) 'Management processes, management divisions of labour and managerial work: towards a synthesis'. Paper presented to 6th Aston/UMIST Labour Process Conference, Aston University, Birmingham.

Hall, J. (1971) 'Decisions decisions', *Psychology Today*, June.

Hall, R.H. (1968) 'Professionalisation and bureaucratisation', *American Sociological Rev.*, 33, 92–104.

Halpin, A.W. and B.J. Winer (1957) 'A factoral study of the leader and behavior descriptions', in R.M. Stogdill and A.E. Coons (eds.) *Leader Behavior: Its Description and Measurement*. Columbus: Ohio State University, Bureau of Business Research.

Halsey, A.H., Heath, A.F. and Ridge, J.M. (1980) *Origins and Destinations: Family, Class and Education in Modern Britain*. Oxford: Clarendon Press.

Handy, C.B. (1986) *Understanding Organizations* (2nd edn). Harmondsworth: Penguin.

Harré, R. (1979) *Social Being: A Theory for Social Psychology*. Oxford: Blackwell.

Harrell, T.W. and M.S. Harrel (1945) 'Army classification test scores for civilian occupations', *Educational and Psychological Measurement*, 5, 229–39.

Harri-Augustein, S. and L. Thomas (1991) *Learning Conversations*. London: Routledge.

Harrison, R.V. (1976) 'Job stress as person–environment misfit'. Paper presented to annual meeting of the American Psychological Association, Washington, DC.

Harvey, R.J. (1991) *The Common Metric Questionnaire*. London: The Psychological Corporation.

Hearn, J., D.L. Sheppard, P. Tancred-Sherriff and G. Burrell (eds.) (1989) *The Sexuality of Organisation*. London: Sage.

Heinzelmann, F (1975) 'Psycho-social implications of physical activity', in

Employee Physical Fitness in Canada. Ottawa: National Health and Welfare, Information Canada.

Hemphill, J.K. (1950) 'Leader behavior description'. Columbus: Ohio State University, Personnel Research Board (mimeo).

Hendry, C. (1990) 'New technology, new careers: the impact of flexible specialisation on skills and jobs', *New Technology, Work and Employment,* 5, 1, 31–43.

Herzberg, F., B. Mausner and B.B. Snydeman (1959) *The Motivation to Work.* New York: Wiley.

Hickson, D.J., C.R. Hinings, C.A. Lee, R.E. Schneck and J.M. Pennings (1971) 'A strategic contingencies theory of intraorganizational power', *Administrative Science Quarterly,* 16, 216–29.

Hill, G.W. (1982) 'Group versus individual performance: are N + 1 heads better than one?', *Psychological Bull.,* 91, 517–39.

Hill, S. (1976) 'The new industrial relations?' *British J. of Industrial Relations,* 14, 214–19.

Hill, S. (1981) *Competition and Control at Work.* London: Heinemann.

Hofstede, G. (1978) 'Value systems in forty countries'. Proceedings of the 4th International Congress of the International Association for Cross-Cultural Psychology.

Hollander, E.P. (1958) 'Conformity, status and idiosyncrasy credit', *Psychological Rev.,* 65, 117–27.

Hollander, E.P. (1961) 'Emergent leadership and social influence', in L. Petrullo and B.M. Bass (eds.) *Leadership and Interpersonal Behavior.* New York: Holt, Rinehart and Winston.

Hollander, E.P. (1978) *Leadership Dynamics: A Practical Guide to Effective Relationships.* New York: Free Press.

Holloway, J. (1987) 'The red rose of Nissan', *Capital and Class,* 32, 142–64

Holroyd, K.A. and R.S. Lazarus (1983) 'Stress, coping and somatic adaptation', in L. Goldberger and S. Breznitz (eds.) *Handbook of Stress: Theoretical and Clinical Aspects.* London: Macmillan.

Horner, M. (1972) 'Toward an understanding of achievement-related conflicts in women', *J. of Social Issues,* 15, 157–75.

House, R.J. (1971) 'A path goal theory of leader effectiveness', *Administrative Science Quarterly,* 16, 321–38.

Hoy, D.C. (1986) *Foucault: A Critical Reader.* Oxford: Blackwell.

Hughes, E. (1975) 'Professions', in G. Esland, G. Salaman and M. Speakman (eds.) *People and Work.* Edinburgh: Holmes-McDougall and Open University Press.

Hunt, P. (1980) *Gender and Class Consciousness.* London: Macmillan.

Hyman, R. (1983) 'White-collar workers and theories of class', in R. Hyman and R. Price (eds.) *The New Working Class? White-Collar Workers and their Organizations.* London: Macmillan.

Hyman, R. (1989) *Strikes* (4th ed.) Basingstoke: Macmillan.

Ivancevich, K.M. (1978) 'The performance to satisfaction relationship: a causal analysis of stimulating and non-stimulating jobs', *Organizational Behavior and Human Performance,* 22, 350–65.

Jacobs, T.O. and E. Jaques (1990) 'Military executive leadership', in K.E.

Clark and M.B. Clark (eds.) *Measures of Leadership*. West Orange, NJ: Leadership Library of America.

Jaques, E. (1989) *Requisite Organisation*. Arlington, Va: Casson Hall.

Jamous, H. and B. Peloille (1970) 'Professions or self-perpetuating systems?', in J.A. Jackson (ed.) *Professions and Professionalization*. London: Cambridge University Press.

Janis, I.L. (1972) *Victims of Groupthink*. Boston: Houghton Mifflin.

Janis, I.L. (1982) 'Decision making under stress', in L. Goldberger and S. Breznitz (eds.) *Handbook of Stress: Theoretical and Clinical Aspects*. London: Macmillan.

Jemmot, J.B., J. Borysenko, M. Borysenko, D.C. McClelland, R. Chapman, D. Meyer and H. Benson (1983) 'Academic stress, power motivation and decrease in secretion rate of salivary secretory immuno globulin A', *The Lancet*, 8339, 1400–2.

Jessup, G. (1991) *Outcomes: NVQs and the Emerging Model of Education and Training*. London: Falmer Press.

Johnson, C.E., R. Woods and S.F. Blinkhorn (1988) 'Spuriouser and spuriouser: the use of ipsative personality tests', *J. of Occupational Psychology*, 61, 153–62.

Johnson, T. (1972) *Professions and Power*. London: Macmillan.

Jones, E.E. and H.B. Gerard (1967) *Foundations of Social Psychology*. New York: Wiley.

Jones. R. (1988) 'Work and flexible automation in Britain: a review of developments and possibilities', *New Technology, Work and Employment*, 2, 4, 451–86.

Kanter, R.M. (1984) *The Change Masters*. London: Allen and Unwin.

Kanter, R.M. (1989) *When Giants Learn to Dance: Mastering the Challenges of Strategy, Management and Careers in the 1990s*. London: Simon and Schuster.

Kaplinsky, R. (1982) *Computer-aided Design: Electronics, Comparative Advantage and Development*. London: Frances Pinter.

Karson, S. and J.W. O'Dell (1976) *Clinical Use of the 16PF*. Champaign, Ill.: Institute for Personality and Ability Testing.

Kasl, S.V. (1980) 'The impact of retirement', in C.L Cooper and R. Payne (eds.) op. cit.

Katz, R. and G. Farris (1976) 'Does performance affect LPC?' Boston: Massachusetts Institute of Technology (mimeo).

Kelloway, E.K. and J. Barling (1991) 'Job characteristics, role stress and mental health', *J. of Occupational Psychology*, 64, 291–304

Kelly, G.A. (1955) *The Psychology of Personal Constructs*. New York: Norton.

Kelly, J.E. (1980) 'The costs of job design: a preliminary anaylsis', *Industrial Relations Journal*, 11, 3, 22–34.

Kelly, J.E. (1982) *Scientific Management, Job Redesign and Work Performance*. London: Academic Press.

Kelly, J.E. (1985) 'Management redesign of work', in D. Knights, H. Willmott and D. Collinson (eds.) *Job Redesign*. Aldershot: Gower.

Kelly, J.E. and C.W. Clegg (1982) *Autonomy and Control at the Workplace*. London: Croom Helm.

Kemp, N.J., C.W. Clegg and T.D. Wal (1980) 'Job redesign: content, process and outcomes', *Employee Relations*, 2, 5–14.

Kemp, N.J., T.D. Wall, C.W. Clegg and J.L. Cordery (1983) 'Autonomous work groups in a greenfield site: a comparative study', *J. of Occupational Psychology*, 56, 271–88.

Kern, H. and M. Schumann (1984) *Das Ende der Arbeitsteilung*. Munich: Verlag C.H. Beck.

Kets de Vries, M.F.R. (1989) *Prisoners of Leadership*. Chichester: Wiley.

Kimmons, G. and J.H. Greenhaus (1976) 'Relationship between locus of control and reactions of employees to work characteristics', *Psychological Reports*, 39, 815–20.

Klein, J.A. (1989) 'The human costs of manufacturing reform', *Harvard Business Review*, 67, 2, 60–6.

Klein, J.A (1990) 'A re-examination of autonomy in the light of new manufacturing practices', *Human Relations*, 43.

Klein, L. (1981) 'Trebor factory, Colchester, Essex: appraisal', *Architects' Journal*, June.

Kline, P. (1980) 'Burt's false results and modern psychometrics: a comparison', *Supp. to the Bull. of the British Psychological Society*, 33, 20–3.

Kline, P. (1983) *Personality: Measurement and Theory*. London: Hutchinson.

Kline, P. (1986) *A Handbook of Test Construction*. London: Methuen.

Knights, D. and A. Sturdy (1990) 'New technology and the intensification of production in insurance and clerical work', in S. Yearly (ed.) *Deciphering Science and Technology*. London: Macmillan.

Knights, D. and H. Willmott (eds.) (1990) *Labour Process Theory*. Basingstoke: Macmillan.

Knights, D., H. Willmott and D. Collinson (eds.) (1985) *Job Redesign*. Aldershot: Gower.

Korda, M. (1976) *Power in the Office*. London: Weidenfeld and Nicolson.

Kotter, J.P. (1990) *A Force for Change: How Leadership Differs from Management*. New York: Free Press.

Kraft, P. (1979) 'The industrialization of computer programming: from programming to "software production" ', in A. Zimbalist (ed.) op. cit.

Lamm, H. and D.G. Myers (1978) 'Group-induced polarization of attitudes and behavior', in L. Berkowitz (ed.) *Advances in Experimental Social Psychology*, vol. 2. New York: Academic Press.

Landy, F. (1982) 'Models of man: assumptions of theorists', in N. Nicholson and T.D. Wall (eds.) *The Theory and Practice of Organizational Psychology*. London: Academic Press.

Lane, C. (1988) 'Industrial change in Europe: the pursuit of flexible specialisation in Britain and West Germany', *Work, Employment and Society*, 2, 2, 141–68.

Lane, T. and K. Roberts (1971) *Strike at Pilkingtons*. London: Fontana.

Lash, S. and J. Urry (1987) *The End of Organized Capitalism*. Cambridge: Polity Press.

Latham, G.P. and J.J. Blades (1975) 'The practical significance of Locke's theory of goal setting', *J. of Applied Psychology*, 60, 122–4.

Latham, G.P., L.M. Saari, E.D. Pursell and M.A. Campion (1980) 'The situational interview', *J. of Applied Psychology*, 65, 422–7.

Lawrence, P.R. and Lorsch, J. (1967) *Organization and Environment*. Cambridge, Mass.: Harvard University Press.

Lazarus, R.S., Cohen,J.B., Folkman, S., Kanner, A. and Schaefer, C. (1980) 'Psychological stress and adaption: some unresolved issues', in H. Selye (ed.) *Selye's Guide to Stress Research*, vol. 1. New York: Van Nostrand.

Lee, D. (1989) 'The transformation of training and the transformation of work in Britain', in S. Wood (ed.) op. cit.

Lee, D. and H. Newby (1983) *The Problem of Sociology*. London: Hutchinson.

Lee, G. (1991) 'The challenge of CAD/CAM: some experiences of British and Canadian engineering companies', *New Technology, Work and Employment*, 6, 2, 100–11.

Levidow, L. and B. Young (eds.) (1981) *Science, Technology and the Labour Process*, vol. 1. London: CSE Books.

Levidow, L. and B. Young (eds.) (1985) *Science, Technology and the Labour Process*, vol. 2. London : Free Association Books.

Lewis, M. (1989) *Liar's Poker*. London: Hodder and Stoughton.

Lewis, S. and C.L. Cooper (1983) 'The stress of combining occupational and parental roles: a review of the literature', *Bull. of the British Psychological Society*, 36, 337–40.

Liff, S. (1990) 'Clerical workers and information technology: gender relations and occupational change', *New Technology, Work and Employment*, 5, 1, 44–55.

Likert, R. (1961) *New Patterns of Management*. New York: McGraw-Hill.

Likert, R. (1977a) 'Management styles: the human component', *Management Rev.*, 66, 23–8, 43–5.

Likert, R. (1977b) 'Past and future perspectives on System 4', Proceedings of the Academy of Management.

Lindblom, C. (1959) 'The Science of muddling through', *Public Administration Rev.*, 19, 79–88.

Littler, C.R. (1982) 'Deskilling and changing structures of control', in S. Wood (ed.) op. cit.

Littler, C.R. (1990) 'The labour process debate: a theoretical review 1974–1988', in D. Knights and H. Willmott (eds.) op. cit.

Littler, C.R. and G. Salaman (1982) 'Bravermania and beyond: recent theories of the labour process', *Sociology*, 16, 251–69.

Locke, E.A. (1968) 'Toward a theory of tasks motivation and incentives', *Organizational Behavior and Human Performance*, 3, 157–89.

Locke, E.A. (1976) 'The nature and causes of job satisfaction', in M.D. Dunnette (ed.) *Handbook of Industrial and Organizational Psychology*. Chicago: Rand McNally.

Lockwood, D. (1958) *The Blackcoated Worker*. London: Allen and Unwin.

Loher, B.T., R.A. Noe, N.L. Moeller and M.P. Fitzgerald (1985) 'A meta-analysis of the relation of job characteristics to job satisfaction', *J. of Applied Psychology*, 70, 280–9.

Loveridge, R.J. (1983) 'The professional negotiator: roles, resources and the run of the cards', in W.T. singleton (ed.) *Social Skills*. Lancaster: MTP Press.

Löwstedt, J. (1988) 'Prejudices and wishful thinking about computer-aided design', *New Technology, Work and Employment*, 3, 1, 30–7.

Lukes, S. (1974) *Power: A Radical View*. London: Macmillan.

Lupton, T. (1963) *On the Shop Floor*. Oxford: Pergamon Press.

Lupton, T. and I. Tanner (1980) 'Work design in Europe', in R.D. Duncan, M.M. Gruneberg and D. Wallis (eds.)op. cit.

Luthans, F. and R. Kreitner (1975) *Organizational Behavior Modification*. Glenview, I11.: Scott, Foresman.

Luthans, F. and M. Martinko (1987) 'Behavioural approaches to organizations', in C.L. Cooper and I.T. Robertson (eds.) *International Review of Industrial and Organizational Psychology*. Chichester: Wiley.

Luthans, F., R. Paul and D. Baker (1981) 'An experimental analysis of the impact of a contingent reinforcement intervention on salespersons' performance behaviors', *J. of Applied Psychology*, 66, 314–23.

MacInnes, J. (1983) 'The labour process debate and the commodity status of labour: some problems'. Paper presented to 1st Aston/UMIST Labour Process Conference.

MacKay, C. and C.L. Cooper (1987) 'Occupational stress and health: some current issues', in C.L. Cooper and I.T. Robertson (eds.) *International Review of Industrial and Organizational Psychology*. Chichester: Wiley.

Maher, J.P. (1976) 'Situational determinants of leadership behaviour in task oriented small groups', *Dissertation Abstr. International*, 37, 693–4.

Manwaring, T. and S. Wood (1985) 'The ghost in the labour process', in D. Knights, H. Willmott and D. Collinson (eds.) op. cit.

March, J.G. and H.A. Simon (1958) *Organizations*. New York: Wiley.

Marglin, S.A. (1974) 'What do bosses do? The origins and functions of hierarchy in capitalist production', *Rev. of Radical Political Economics*, 6, 33–60. Reprinted in A. Gorz (ed.) *The Division of Labour*. Hassocks, Sussex: Harvester Press, 1976.

Marsh, P. (1982) 'Rules in the organization of action', in M. von Cranach and R. Harré (eds.) *The Analysis of Action*. Cambridge: Cambridge University Press.

Martin, J. (1985) 'Can organizational culture be managed?' in P.J. Frost, L.F. Moore, M.R. Louis, C.C. Lundberg and J. Martin (eds.) *Organizational Culture*. Beverley Hills: Sage.

Martin, J. and D. Meyerson (1988) 'Organizational cultures and the denial, channeling and acknowledgement of ambiguity', in L.R. Pondy, R. Boland and H. Thomas (eds.) *Managing Ambiguity and Change*. New York: Wiley.

Martin, J. and C. Roberts (1983) *Women and Employment: A Lifetime Perspective*. London: HMSO Books.

Martin, R. (1981) *New Technology and Industrial Relations in Fleet Street*. Oxford: Oxford University Press.

Martin, R. and J. Wallace (1986) *Working Women in Recession: Employment, Redundacy and Unemployment*. Oxford: Oxford University Press.

Martindale, D. (1977) 'Sweaty palms in the control tower', *Psychology Today*, October.

Marx, K. (1973) *Grundrisse*. Harmondsworth: Penguin.

Marx, K. (1974) *Capital*, Vol. 1. London: Lawrence and Wishart.

Marx, K. (1975) *Early Writings*. Translated by R. Livingstone and G. Benton. Harmondsworth: Penguin.

Maslow, A.H. (1954) *Motivation and Personality*. New York: Harper.

Matsui, T., M. Kagawa, J. Nagamatsu and Y. Ohtsuku (1977) 'Validity of expectancy theory as a within-person behavioural choice model for sales activity', *J. of Applied Psychology*, 62, 764–7.

Mayo, E. (1943) 'Forward', in F.J. Roethlisberger and W. J. Dickson, op. cit.

McCall, G.I. and I.L. Simmons (1966) *Identities and Interaction*. New York: Free Press.

McClelland, D. (1961) *The Achieving Society*. Princeton: Van Nostrand.

McClelland, D. and R.E. Boyatzis (1982) 'Leadership motive pattern and long-term success in management', *J. of Applied Psychology*, 67, 737–43.

McClelland, D. and D.H. Burnham (1976) 'Power is the great motivator', *Harvard Business Rev.*, 54, 100–10.

McConkie, M.L. and W.R. Boss (1986) 'Organizational stories: one means of moving the informal organization during change efforts', *Public Administration Quarterly*, 10, 2, 189–205.

McCormick, E.J., P.R. Jeanneret and R.C. Mecham (1969) *The Development and Background of PAQ*. Report No. 5, Occupational Research Center, West Lafayette, In.: Purdue University.

McCrae, R.R. and P.T. Costa (1987) 'Validation of the five-factor model of personality across instruments and observers', *J. of Personality and Social Psychology*, 52, 81–90.

McGregor, D. (1960) *The Human Side of Enterprise*. New York: McGraw-Hill.

McHenry, R. (1981) 'The selection interview', in M. Argyle (ed.) *Social Skills and Work*. London: Methuen.

McLoughlin, I. (1989) 'CAD–The Taylorisation of drawing office work', *New Technology, Work and Employment*, 4, 1, 27–39.

Meindl, J.R. (1990) 'On leadership: an alternative to conventional wisdom", in B.M. Staw and L.L. Cummings (eds.) *Research in Organizational Behaviour 12*. Greenwich, Conn: JAI Press.

Merton, R.K. (1940) 'bureaucratic structure and personality', *Social Forces*, 18, 560–8.

Mettlin, C. (1976) 'Occupational careers and the prevention of coronary-prone behaviour' *Social Science and Medicine*, 10, 367–72.

Michaels, C. E. and P.E. Spector (1982) 'Causes of employee turnover: a test of the Mobley, Griffeth, Hand and Meglino model', *J. of Applied Psychology*, 67, 53–9.

Michener, H.A. and E.J. Lawler (1975) 'Endorsement of formal leaders: an integrative model', *J. of Personality and Social Psychology*, 31, 216–23.

Mikes, P.S. and C.L. Hulin (1968) 'Use of importance as a weighting component of job satisfaction', *J. of Applied Psychology*, 52, 394–8.

Miles, R.M. (1980) 'Organization boundary roles', in C.L. Cooper and R. Payne (eds.) op. cit.

Miller, E.J. (1975) 'Sociotechnical systems in weaving 1953–70: a follow-up study', *Human relations*, 28, 349–86.

Miller, G.A. (1956) 'The magical number seven, plus or minus two: some limits on our capacity for processing information', *Psychological Rev.*, 63, 81–97.

Miller, N. and M.B. Brewer (1984) 'The social psychology of desegregation: an introduction', in N. Miller and M.B. Brewer (eds.) *Groups in Contact.* London: Academic Press.

Miller, P. and T. O'Leary (1987) 'Accounting and the construction of the governable person', *Accounting, Organization and Society*, 12, 3, 235–65.

Millon, T. (1990) *Towards a New Personology.* Chichester: Wiley.

Mills, C.W. (1951) *White Collar.* New York: Oxford University Press.

Miner, J.B. (1980) *Theories of Organizational Behavior.* Hinsdale, Ill.: Dryden Press.

Mitchell, T.R., C.M. Smyser and S.E. Weed (1975) 'Locus of control: supervision and work satisfaction', *Academy of Management J.*, 18, 623–31.

Mitroff, I.I. and R.H. Kilmann (1975) 'Stories managers tell: a new tool for organizational problem-solving', *Management Review*, 64, 7, 18–28.

Mobley, W.H. (1977) 'Intermediate linkages in the relationship between job satisfaction and employee turnover', *J. of Applied Psychology*, 62, 237–40.

Mobley, W.H., S.O. Horner and A.T. Hollingsworth (1978) 'The evaluation of precursors of hospital employee turnover', *J. of Applied Psychology*, 63, 408–14.

Moorhouse, P. (1981) 'Production management', in W.T. Singleton (ed.) *Management Skills.* Lancaster: MTP Press.

Moorhouse, P. (1983) ' The industrial sales team', in W.T. Singleton (ed.) *Social Skills.* Lancaster: MTP Press.

Moos, R.H. and A.G. Billings (1982) 'Conceptualizing and measuring coping resources and process', in L. Goldbserger and S. Breznitz (eds.) *Handbook of Stress: Theoretical and Clinical Aspects.* London: Macmillan.

Morgan, Gareth (1986) *Images of Organization.* Beverley Hills: Sage.

Morgan, Glenn (1990) *Organizations in Society.* Basingstoke: Macmillan.

Moscovi, S. and G. Paicheler (1978) 'Social comparisons and social recognition: two complementary processes of identification', in H. Tajfel (ed.) *Differentiation betweeen Social Groups: Studies in the Social Psychology of Intergroup Relations*, European Monographs in Social Psychology, 14. London: Academic Press.

Mouzelis, N. (1975) *Organization and Bureaucracy.* London: Routledge and Kegan Paul.

Muchinsky, P.M. (1977) 'A comparison of within- and across-subjects analyses of the expectancy-valence model for predicting effort', *Academy of Management J.*, 20, 154–8.

Mumford, E. (1976) 'A strategy for the redesign of work', *Personnel Rev.*, 5, 33–9.

Murphy, L.R. (1984) 'Occupational stress management: a review and appraisal', *J. of Occupational Psychology*, 57, 1–15.

Murray, R. (1985) 'Bennetton Britain: the new economic order', *Marxism Today*, November, 28–32.

Myers, C.S. (1924) *Industrial Psychology in Great Britain.* London: Cape.

Nash, A.N., J.P. Muczyk and F.L. Vettori (1971) 'The relative practical effectiveness of programmed instruction', *Personnel Psychology*, 24, 397–418.

National Institute for Occupational Safety and Health (1987) *Stress Management in Work Settings*. Cincinatti: NIOSH.

NCVQ (1990) 'Core skills in NVQs: response to the Secretary of State', July, NCVQ.

Neimeyer, G.J. and J.E. Hudson (1985) 'Couple's constructs: personal systems in marital satisfaction', in D. Bannister (ed.) *Issues and Approaches in Personal Construct Theory*. London: Academic Press.

Nemeroff, W.F. and J. Cosentino (1979) 'Utilizing feedback and goal setting to increase performance appraisal interviewer skills of managers', *Academy of Management J.*, 22, 566–76

Neu, D. (1991) 'Trust impression management and the public accounting profession', *Critical Perspectives on Accounting*, 2, 295–313.

Newman, J.D. and T. Boehr (1979) 'Personal and organizational strategies for handling job stress: a review of research and opinion', *Personnel Psychology*, 32, 1–43.

NFER-Nelson (1985) *Graduate and Managerial Assessment Tests*. Windsor: NFER-Nelson.

Nichols, T. and H. Beynon (1977) *Living with Capitalism*. London: Routledge and Kegan Paul.

Noble, D. (1978) 'Social choice in machine tool design', *Politics and Society*, 8, 313–47.

Nord, W. (1969) 'Beyond the teaching machine: the neglected area of operant conditioning in the theory and practice of management', *Organizational Behavior and Human Performance*, 4, 375–401.

Norman, W.T. (1963) 'Toward an adequate taxonomy of personality attributes', *J. of Abnormal and Social Psychology*, 66, 574–83.

Ochs, E. (1983) 'Planned and unplanned discourse', in E. Ochs and B.B. Schieffelin (eds.) *Acquiring Conversational Competence*. London: Routledge and Kegan Paul.

Ochs, E. and B.B. Schieffelin (1983) 'Topic as a discourse notion: a study of topic in the conversations of children and adults', in E. Ochs and B.B. Schieffelin (eds.) ibid.

Offe, C. (1976) *Industry and Inequality*. London: Edward Arnold.

Oliver, N. (1991) 'The dynamics of just-in-time', *New Technology, Work and Employment*, 6, 1, 19–27.

Orpen, C. (1978) 'Work and non-work satisfaction: a causal-correlational analysis', *J. of Applied Psychology*, 63, 530–2.

Park, B. and M. Rothbart (1982) 'Perception of out-group homogeneity and levels of social categorization: memory for the subordinate attributes of in-group and out-group members', *J. of Personality and Social Psychology*, 42, 1051–68.

Parry, N. and J. Parry (1976) *The Rise of the Medical Profession*. London: Croom Helm.

Paul, R.J. and Y.M. Ebadi (1989) 'Leadership decision making in a service organization: a field test of the Vroom–Yetton model', *J. of Occupational Psychology*, 62, 201–11.

Perrow, C. (1980) 'Zoo story or life in the organizational sandpit', in G. Salaman and K. Thompson (eds.) op. cit.

Peters, T. (1987) *Thriving on Chaos*. London: Macmillan.

Peters, T. and R.H. Waterman (1982) *In Search of Excellence*. New York: Harper and Row.

Pettigrew. A. (1973) *The Politics of Organizational Decision-Making*. London: Tavistock.

Pettigrew, A. (1985) *the Awakening Giant*. Oxford: Blackwell.

Pfeffer, J. (1981) *Power in Organizations*. Marshfield, Mass.: Pitman.

Philimore, J. (1989) 'Flexible specialisation, work organisation and skills', *New Technology, Work and Employment*, 4, 2, 79–91.

Piore, M.J. and Sabel, C.F. (1984) *The Second Industrial Divide*. New York: Basic Books.

Pollert, A. (1981) *Girls, Wives, Factory Lives*. London: Macmillan.

Pollert, A. (1988) 'The "flexible firm": fixation or fact?', *Work, Employment and Society*, 2, 3, 281–316.

Poppleton, S.E. (1981) 'The social skills of selling', in M. Argyle (ed.) *Social Skills and Work*. London: Methuen.

Porter, L.W. (1962) 'Job attitudes in management: 1. Perceived deficiencies in need fulfillment as a function of job level', *J. of Applied Psychology*, 46, 375–84.

Porter, L.W. and E.E. Lawler (1968) *Managerial Attitudes and Performance*. Homewood, Ill.: Dorsey Press.

Potter, R.M.C. (1983) 'The statesman', in W.T. Singleton (ed.) *Social skills*. Lancaster: MTP Press.

Presthus, R. (1979) *The Organizational Society*. London: Macmillan.

Price, K.H. and H. Garland (1981) 'Compliance with a leader's suggestions as a function of perceived leader/member competence and potential reciprocity', *J. of Applied Psychology*, 66, 329–36.

Pritchard, R.D. and M.S. Sanders (1973) 'The influence of valence, instrumentality, and expectancy on effort and performance', *J. of Applied Psychology*, 57, 55–60.

Psychological Corporation, The (1990) *The Watson Glaser Critical Thinking Appraisal*. London: The Psychological Corporation.

Psychological Corporation, The (1993) *The Millon Personality Style Inventory*. London: Harcourt Brace Jovanovich.

Pugh, D.S., D.J. Hickson and C.R. Hinings (1984) *Writers on Organizations*. Harmondsworth: Penguin.

Purcell, K. (1979) 'Militancy and acquiescence among women workers', in S. Burman (ed.) *Fit Work for Women*. London: Croom Helm. Reprinted in J. Siltanen and M. Stanworth (eds.) op. cit.

Quick, J.C., D.L. Nelson, and J.D. Quick (1990) *Stress and Challenge at the Top: The Paradox of the Successful Executive*. Chichester: Wiley.

Ramsay, H. (1985) 'What is participation for?: a critical evaluation of labour process analysis of job reform', in D. Knights, H. Willmott and D. Collinson (eds.) op. cit.

Randall, G.A. (1981) 'Management education and training', in W.T. Singleton (ed.) *Management Skills*. Lancaster: MTP Press.

Reason, J. (1987) 'The Chernobyl errors', *Bull. of the Psychological Society*, 40, 201–6.

Reed, M. (1985) *Redirections in Organizational Analysis*. London: Tavistock.

Rhodes, P.S. (1983) 'The prediction of success in business studies students', *Business Education*, 4, 31–5.

Richbell, S. (1976) 'Participation and perceptions of control', *Personnel Rev.*, 5, 13–9.

Rice, A.K. (1958) *Productivity and Social Organisation*. London: Tavistock

Rice, B. (1982) 'The Hawthorne defect: persistence of a flawed theory', *Psychology Today*, February.

Robey, D. (1977) 'Computers and management structure', *Human Relations*, 30, 963–76.

Rodger, A. (1952) *The Seven Point Plan*. Windsor: MIIP/NFER-Nelson.

Roethlisberger, F.J. and W.J. Dickson (1943) *Management and the Worker*. Cambridge, Mass.: Harvard University Press.

Rolfe, H. (1990) 'In the name of progress?: skill and attitudes towards technological change', *New Technology, Work and Employment*, 5, 2, 107–21.

Rose, M. (1975) *Industrial Behaviour: Theoretical Developments since Taylor*. London: Allen Lane.

Rose, R.M., C.D. Jenkins and M.W. Hurst (1978) 'Air traffic controller health change study: a prospective investigation of physical, psychological and work related changes', Galveston: University of Texas (mimeo).

Rosen, B. and T.H. Jerdee (1977) 'Influence of subordinate characteristics on trust and use of participative decision strategies in a management simulation', *J. of Applied Psychology*, 62, 628–31.

Rosenman, R.H., R.J. Brand, D. Jenkins, M. Friedman, R. Straus and M. Wurm (1975) 'Coronary heart disease in the western collaborative group study', *J. of the American Medical Association*, 233, 872–7.

Ross, L. and R.E. Nisbett (eds.) (1991) *The Person and the Situation*. London: McGraw-Hill.

Ross, L. and C. Stillinger (1991) 'Barriers to conflict resolution', in L. Ross and R.E. Nisbett (eds.) ibid.

Rotter, J.B. (1966) *Generalized Expectancies for Internal versus External Control of Reinforcement*. Psychological Monographs: 80.

Roy, D. (1952) 'Quota restrictions and goldbricking in a machine shop', *American J. of Sociology*, 57, 427–42.

Roy, D. (1954) 'Efficiency and the "fix": informal inter-group relations in a piecework machine shop', *American J. of Sociology*, 60, 255–66.

Rubery, J. (1980) 'Structured labour markets, worker organization and low pay', in A. Amsden (ed.) *The Economics of Women and Work*. Harmondsworth: Penguin.

Rust, J., P. Sinclair and S. Barrow (1992) 'The RPQ: validation of the five-factor model in the workplace', *Proceedings of the Occupational Psychology Conference*. Leicester: British Psychological Society.

Sabel, C.F. (1982) *Work and Politics*. Cambridge: Cambridge University Press.

Sacks, H., E. Schegloff and G. Jefferson (1974) 'A simplest systematics for the organization of turn-taking for conversation', *Languages*, 50, 696–735.

Sakai, K. (1990) 'The feudal world of Japanese manufacturing', *Harvard Business Review*, Nov.–Dec., 38–49.

Salaman, G. (1979) *Work Organisations: Resistance and Control*. London: Longman.

Salaman, G. (1981) *Class and the Corporation*. London: Fontana.

Salaman, G. and K. Thompson (1974) Media Booklets 1 and 2. *People and Organisations* DT352. Milton Keynes: Open University Press.

Salaman, G. and K. Thompson (eds.) (1980) *Control and Ideology in Organizations*. Milton Keynes: Open University Press.

Sashkin, S. and M.G. Sashkin (1991) 'Leadership and culture-building in schools: quantitive and qualitative understandings', in J.G. Hunt (ed.) *Leadership*. London: Sage.

Saville and Holsworth (1980) *Verbal Critical Reasoning (VA 3)*. London: Saville and Holsworth Ltd.

Saville, P. and E. Wilson (1991) 'The reliability and validity of normative and ipsative approaches in the measurement of personality', *J. of Occupational Psychology*, 64, 219–38.

Schaffer, R.H. (1953) *Job Satisfaction as Related to Need Satisfaction in Work* Psychological Monographs: 67.

Schein, E.H. (1988) *Organizational Psychology*. (3rd edn). London: Prentice Hall.

Schieffelin, B.B. (1983) 'Talking like birds: sound play in a cultural perspective', in E. Ochs and B.B. Schieffelin (eds.) *Acquiring Conversational Competence*. London: Routledge and Kegan Paul.

Schneider, J. and E.A. Locke (1971) 'A Critique of Herzbserg's incident classification system and a suggested revision', *Organizational Behavior and Human Performance*, 6, 441–57.

Schriesheim, C.A. and D. Hosking (1978) 'Review essay of F.E. Fiedler, M.M. Chemers, and L. Mahar: "Improving Leadership effectiveness: The Leader Match concept"', *Administrative Science Quarterly*, 23, 496–505.

Schriesheim, C.A., R.J. House and S. Kerr (1976) 'Leader initiating structure: a reconciliation of discrepant research results and some empirical tests', *Organizational Behavior and Human Performance*, 15, 297–321.

Schriesheim, C.A. and C.J. Murphy (1976) 'Relationships between leader behavior and subordinate satisfaction and performance: a test of some situational moderators', *J. of Applied Psychology*, 61, 634–41.

Schriesheim, C.A. and A.S. de Nisi (1981) 'Task dimensions as moderators of the effects of instrumental leadership: a two-sample replicated test of Path–Goal leadership theory', *J. of Applied Psychology*, 66, 589–97.

Science Research Associates (1989) *Manual for the Leadership Questionnaire*. Henley: Science Research Associates.

Scott, R. (1966) 'Professionals in bureaucracies: areas of conflict', in H.M. Vollmer and D.M. Mills (eds.) *Professionalization*. Englewood Cliffs, NJ: Prentice-Hall.

Sear, Baroness (1985) 'There is much to be done', *Training and Development*, January.

Seligman, M.E.P. (1975) *Helplessness: On Depression, Development and Death.* San Francisco: Freeman.

Selye, H. (1936) 'A syndrome produced by diverse nocuous ages', *Nature,* 138, 32.

Selye, H. (1975) 'Stress', in *Employee Physical fitness in Canada.* Ottawa: National Health and Welfare, Information Canada.

Selye, H. (1983) 'History and present status of the stress concept', in L. Goldberger and S. Breznitz (eds.) *Handbook of Stress: Theoretical and Clinical Aspects.* London: Macmillan.

Selznick, P. (1943) 'An approach to a theory of bureaucracy', *American Sociological Rev.,* 8, 47–54.

Senker, P. and P. Simmonds (1991) 'Changing technology and design work in the British engineering industry 1981–88', *New Technology, Work and Employment,* 6, 2, 91–9.

Shaiken, H., S. Hertzenberg and S. Kuhn (1986) 'The work process under more flexible production', *Industrial Relations,* 25, 2, 167–83.

Shamir, B., R.J. House and M. Arthur (1990) 'The transformational effects of charismatic leadership: a motivational theory', in J.G. Hunt (ed.) *Leadership.* London: Sage.

Shearman, C. and G. Burrell (1988) 'New technology based firms and new industries: employment implications', *New Technology, Work and Employment,* 3, 2, 87–99.

Sherif, M. and C.W. Sherif (1982) 'Production of intergroup conflict and its resolution: robbers' cave experiment', in J.W. Reich (ed.) *Experimenting in Society: Issues and Examples in Applied Social Psychology.* Glenview, Ill.: Scott, Foresman.

Sherif, M., O.J. Harvey, B. White, W.R. Hood and C.W. Sherif (1961) *Intergroup Conflict and Cooperation: The Robbers' Cave Experiment.* Norman: University of Oklahoma Press.

Siltanen, J. and M. Stanworth (eds.) (1984) *Women and the Public Sphere.* London: Hutchinson.

Simpson, D.H. (1981) *Commercialization of the Regional Press.* Aldershot: Gower.

Singleton, W.T. (1978) 'Final discussion', in W.T. Singleton (ed.) *The Analysis of Practical Skills.* Lancaster: MTP Press.

Singleton, W.T. (1983) 'Final discussion', in W.T. Singleton (ed.) *Social Skills.* Lancaster: MTP Press.

Skinner, B.F. (1954) 'The science of learning and the art of teaching', *Harvard Educational Rev.,* 24, 86–97.

Skinner, B.F. (1971) *Beyond Freedom and Dignity.* Harmondsworth: Penguin.

Slocum, J.W. and H.P. Sims (1980) 'A typology for integrating technology, organisation and job redesign', *Human Relations,* 33, 193–212.

Smircich, L. (1983) 'Concepts of culture and organizational analysis', *Administrative Science Quarterly,* 28, 3, 339–58.

Smith, A. (1982) *The Wealth of Nations.* Harmondsworth: Penguin.

Smith, F.J. (1977) 'Work attitudes as predictors of attendance on a specific day', *J. of Applied Psychology,* 62, 16–19.

Smith, M. (1991) 'Selection in organisations' in M. Smith (ed.) *Analysing Organisational Behaviour*. Basingstoke: Macmillan.

Smith, M., M. Gregg and R. Andrews (1989) *New Horizons in Selection and Assessment*. London: Pitman.

Smith, P.B. and M.P. Peterson (1988) *Leadership, Organisations and Culture*. London: Sage.

Sofer, C. (1979) *Men in Mid-Career*. Cambridge: Cambridge University Press.

Sorge, A., M. Hartmann, M. Warner and I. Nicholas (1982) 'Technology, organization and manpower: applications of CNC manufacturing in Great Britain and West Germany', in N. Bjorn-Anderson, M. Earl, O. Holst and E. Mumford (eds.) *Information Society: For Richer For Poorer*. Amsterdam: North Holland.

Sorrentino, R.M. and R.G. Boutillier (1975) 'The effect of quantity and quality of verbal interaction on ratings of leadership ability', *J. of Experimental and Social Psychology*, 11, 403–11.

Sparrow, J. (1989) 'The utility of PAQ in relating job behaviours to traits', *J. of Occupational Psychology*, 62, 151–62.

Spearman, C. (1904) 'General intelligence objectively determined and measured', *American J. of Psychology*, 14, 201–93.

Spearman, C. (1927) *The Abilities of Man*. New York: Macmillan.

Steers, R.M. and S.R. Rhodes (1978) 'Major influences on employee attendance: a process model', *J. of Applied Psychology*, 63, 391–407.

Stephenson, G.M. (1981) 'Inter-group bargaining and negotiation', in J.C. Turner and H. Giles (eds.) *Intergroup Behaviour*. Oxford: Blackwell.

Sternberg, R.J. (1985) *Beyond IQ: A Triarchic Theory of Human Intelligence*. Cambridge: Cambridge University Press.

Sterns, L., R.A. Alexander, B.V. Barett and F.M. Dambrot (1983) 'The relationship of extraversion and neuroticism with job preferences and job satisfaction for clerical employees', *J. of Occupational Psychology*, 56, 145–53.

Stewart, A., K. Prandy and R.M. Blackburn (1980) *Social Stratification and Occupations*. London: Macmillan.

Stillinger, C., M. Epelbaum, D. Kelter and L. Ross (1990) 'The reactive devaluation barrier to conflict resolution', in L. Ross and R.E Nisbett (eds.) *The Person and the Situation*. London: McGraw-Hill.

Stogdill, R.M. (1948) 'Personal factors associated with leadership: a survey of the literature', *J. of Psychology*, 25, 35–71.

Stogdill, R.M. (1974) *Handbook of Leadership: A Survey of Theory and Research*. New York: Free Press.

Storey, J. (1983) *Managerial Prerogative and the Question of Control*. London: Routledge and Kegan Paul.

Storey, J. (1986) 'The phoney war? New office technology: organization and control', in D. Knights and H. Willmott (eds.) *Managing the Labour Process*. London: Gower.

Strube, M.J. and J.E. Garcia (1981) 'A meta-analytic investigation of Fiedler's contingency model of leadership effectiveness', *Psychological Bull.*, 90, 307–21.

Summers, T.P. and W.H. Hendrix (1991) 'Modelling the role of pay equity perceptions: a field study', *J. of Occupational Psychology*, 64, 145–57.

Synder, M. (1979) 'Self-monitoring processes' in L. Berkowitz (ed.) *Advances in Experimental Social Psychology*. London: Academic Press.

Tajfel, H. (1978) 'Social categorization, social identity and social comparison', in H. Tajfel (ed.) *Differentiation between Social Groups*. London: Academic Press.

Tajfel, H. (1981) 'Social stereotypes and social groups', in J.C. Turner and H. Giles (eds.) *Intergroup Behaviour*. Oxford: Blackwell.

Taylor, L. and P. Walton (1971) 'Industrial sabotage: motive and meanings', in S. Cohen (ed) *Images of Deviance*. Harmondsworth: Penguin.

Taylor, R. (1980) *The Fifth Estate*. London: Pan.

Taylor, S.M. and J.A. Sniezek (1984) 'The college recruitment interview: topical content and applicant reactions', *J. of Occupational Psychology*, 57, 157–68.

Thompson, P. (1989) *The Nature of Work* (2nd ed). London: Macmillan.

Thompson, P. (1990) 'Crawling from the wreckage: the labour process and the politics of production', in D.Knights and H. Willmott (eds.) op.cit.

Thompson, V. (1961) *Modern Organization*. New York: Knopf.

Thurstone, L.L. (1938) *Primary Mental Abilities*. Chicago: University of Chicago Press.

Trist, E.L. and K.W. Bamforth (1951) 'Some social and psychological consequences of the longwall method of coal-getting', *Human Relations*, 1, 3–38.

Turnbull, P. (1988) 'The limits to Japanisation: "just-in-time"' labour relations and the UK automotive industry', *New Technology, Work and Employment*, 3, 1, 7–20.

Turner, J.C. (1982) 'Towards a cognitive redefinition of the social group', in H. Tajfel (ed.) *Social Identity and Intergroup Relations*. Cambridge: Cambridge University Press.

Turner, J.C. and H. Giles (eds.) (1981) *Intergroup Behaviour*. Oxford: Blackwell.

Vernon, P.E. (1971) *The Structure of Human Abilities*. London: Methuen.

Vroom, V.H. (1964) *Work and Motivation*. New York: Wiley.

Vroom, V.H. (1976) 'Leadership', in M.D. Dunnette (ed.) *Handbook of Industrial and Organizational Psychology*. Chicago: Rand McNally.

Vroom, V.H. (1984) 'Leadership and decision-making', in Osaka University 50th Anniversary International Symposium on Democratization and Leadership in Industrial Organization. Osaka: Faculty of Human Sciences, Osaka University, Japan.

Vroom, V.H. and A.G. Jago (1978) 'On the validity of the Vroom–Yetton model', *J. of Applied Psychology*, 63, 151–62.

Vroom, V.H. and P.W. Yetton (1973) *Leadership and Decision-Making*. Pittsburgh: University of Pittsburgh Press.

Wagner, U. and P. Schönbach (1984) 'Links between educational status and prejudice: ethnic attitudes in West Germany', in N. Miller and M.B. Brewer (eds.) *Groups in Contact*. London: Academic Press.

Wahba, M.A. and C.B. Bridwell (1976) 'Maslow reconsidered: a review of research on the need hierarchy theory', *Organizational Behavior and Human Performance*, 15, 212–40.

Wainright, H. (1984) 'Women and the division of labour', in P. Abrams and R. Brown (eds.) *UK Society*. London: Weidenfield and Nicolson.

Walby, S. (1988) *Gender Segregation at Work*. Milton Keynes: Open University Press.

Wall, T. (1980) 'Group work redesign in context: a two-phase model', in K.D. Duncan, M.M. Gruneberg and D. Wallis (eds.) op. cit.

Wall, T. and J.L. Cordery (1982) *Work Design and Supervisory Practice*. Social and Applied Psychology Unit, Memo 470, University of Sheffield.

Wallis, D. and D. Cope (1980) 'Pay-off conditions for organizational change in the hospital service', in K.D. Duncan, M.M. Gruneberg and D. Wallis (eds.) op. cit.

Wanous, J.P. (1974) 'A causal-correlational analysis of the job satisfaction and performance relationship', *J. of Applied Psychology*, 59, 139–44.

Wanous, J.P. and A. Zwany (1977) 'A cross-sectional test of need hierarchy theory', *Organizational Behavior and Human Performance*, 18, 78–97.

Watson, O.M. (1970) *Proxemic Behavior: A Cross-Cultural Study*. The Hague: Mouton.

Watson, T.J. (1977) *The Personnel Managers*. London: Routledge and Kegan Paul.

Weaver, C.N. (1980) 'Job satisfaction in the United States in the 1970s', *J. of Applied Psychology*, 65, 364–7.

Weber, M. (1964) *The Theory of Social and Economic Organization*. New York: Free Press.

Weber, M. (1970) From Max Weber: *Essays in Sociology*. Translated by H.H. Gerth and C.W. Mills. London: Routlege and Kegan Paul.

Webster, J. (1990) *Office Automation: The Labour Process and Women's Work in Britain*. Hemel Hempstead: Harvester Wheatsheaf.

Wedderburn, D. and R. Crompton (1972) *Workers' Attitudes and Technology*. Cambridge: Cambridge University Press.

Welford, A.T. (1973) 'Stress and Performance', *Ergonomics*, 16, 567–80.

West, J. (1982) 'New technology and women's office work', in J. West (ed.) *Work, Women and the Labour Market*. London: Routledge and Kegan Paul.

West, J. (1990) 'Gender in the labour process', in D. Knights and H. Willmott (eds.) op. cit.

West, M.A. and J.L. Farr (1990) *Innovation and Creativity at Work*. Chichester: Wiley.

West, M.A. and R. Rushton (1989) 'Mismatches in the work-role transition', *J. of Occupational Psychology*, 62, 271–86.

West, M.A., N. Nichoson and A. Rees (1987) 'Transitions into newly created jobs', *J. of Occupational Psychology*, 60, 97–113.

Whalley, P. (1986) *The Social Production of Technical Work*. London: Macmillan.

Wickens, P. (1987) *The Road to Nissan*. London: Macmillan.

Wiedermeyer, M. (1989) 'New technology in West Germany: the employment debate', *New Technology, Work and Employment*, 4, 1, 56–65.

Wilensky, H.L. (1968) 'Careers, life-styles and social integration', in B. Glaser (ed.) *Organizational Careers*. Chicago: Aldine.

Wilkins, A. (1984) 'The creation of company cultures: the role of stories in human resource systems', *Human Resource Management*, 23, 1, 41–60.

Williams, K., T. Cutler, J. Williams and C. Haslam (1987) 'The end of mass production', *Economy and Society*, 16, 3, 405–39.

Williams, V. (1984) 'Employment implications of new technology', *Employment Gazette*, April. (London: Department of Employment).

Willmott, H. (1987) 'Studying managerial work: a critique and a proposal', *J. of Management Studies*, 24, 3, 249–70.

Wilson, D.C. and R.H. Rosenfeld (1990) *Managing Organizations*. Maidenhead: McGraw-Hill.

Winter, D.G. (1978) *Navy Leadership and Management Competencies: Convergence among Test, Interviews and Performance Ratings*. Boston: McBer.

Wood, S. (1979) 'A reappraisal of the contingency approach to organization', *J. of Management Studies*, 16, 334–54.

Wood, S. (ed.) (1982) *The Degradation of Work?* London: Hutchinson.

Wood, S. (ed.) (1989) *The Transformation of Work?* London: Unwin Hyman.

Wood, S. (1989) 'The transformation of work?', introduction in S. Wood (ed.) ibid.

Woodruffe, C. (1990) *Assessment Centres*. Wimbledon: Institute of Personnel Management.

Woodward, J. (1965) *Industrial Organization: Theory and Practice*. London: Oxford University Press.

Wright, P.M., P.A. Lichenfells and E.D.Pursell (1989) 'The structured interview: additional studies and a meta-analysis', *J. of Occupational Psychology*, 62, 191–9.

Yuki, G.A. (1987) 'Development of new measures of managerial behaviour: preliminary report on validation of the MPS'. Paper presented at the Easter Academy of Management meeting, Boston.

Yuki, G.A. (1989) *Leadership in Organisations* (2nd edn.). Englewood Cliffs: Prentice Hall.

Zimbalist, A. (1979) *Case Studies on the Labor Process*. London: Monthly Review Press.

Zimbardo, P.G., C. Harey, W.C. Banks and D. Jaffe (1973) 'The mind is a formidable jailer: a Pirandellian prison', *New York Times Magazine*, 8 April, 38–60.

Zipkin, P.H. (1991) 'Does manufacturing need a JIT revolution?', *Harvard Business Review*, Jan.–Feb., 40–50.

Author Index

481

Subject Index